Communications in Computer and Information Science 1659

More information about this series at https://link.springer.com/bookseries/7899

Miguel Félix Mata-Rivera ·
Roberto Zagal-Flores ·
Cristian Barria-Huidobro (Eds.)

Telematics and Computing

11th International Congress, WITCOM 2022
Cancún, México, November 7–11, 2022
Proceedings

Springer

Editors
Miguel Félix Mata-Rivera
Instituto Politécnico Nacional
Mexico, Mexico

Roberto Zagal-Flores
Instituto Politécnico Nacional
Mexico, Mexico

Cristian Barria-Huidobro
Universidad Mayor
Santiago, Chile

ISSN 1865-0929 ISSN 1865-0937 (electronic)
Communications in Computer and Information Science
ISBN 978-3-031-18081-1 ISBN 978-3-031-18082-8 (eBook)
https://doi.org/10.1007/978-3-031-18082-8

This Springer imprint is published by the registered company Springer Nature Switzerland AG
The registered company address is: Gewerbestrasse 11, 6330 Cham, Switzerland

Preface

The hybrid format is a new modality in many conferences around the world, and the 11th International Congress of Telematics and Computing (WITCOM 2022) was no exception. This volume shows some of the advances in various fields of knowledge, such as artificial intelligence techniques, data science, blockchain, environment monitoring, cybersecurity, education, and software for communications protocols, with applications to different areas of study.

The WITCOM conference, in its eleventh edition and for first time in a hybrid format, attracted numerous students, researchers, and entrepreneurs to share experiences and knowledge; the return to in-person activities combined with virtual activities represented an interesting challenge. These proceedings contain selected research papers, where submissions went through a peer-review process. We received 73 research papers; three members of the Program Committee reviewed each submission, and 30 were accepted (an acceptance rate of 40%).

The conference program featured a broad set of session topics that extend beyond the documents contained in these proceedings. Materials for all sessions are available on the conference website at www.witcom.upiita.ipn.mx and www.witcom.org.mx.

All the tracks and workshops at WITCOM 2022 contributed to make a well-rounded program. We want to thank God and all those who contributed to this effort, especially ANTACOM A.C. and UPIITA-IPN which supported the event. Of course, thanks also go to UDI-UPIITA, including all managers, staff, and administrators, the Geospatial Intelligence and Mobile Computing Laboratory, authors of submitted papers, session presenters, coordinators, and members of the Program Committee. Without your help and collaboration, the event could not be successful.

November 2022

Miguel Félix Mata-Rivera
Roberto Zagal-Flores
Cristian Barria-Huidobro

Preface

[illegible] format is [illegible] the 11th International [illegible] and Computing (WiCON 2022) [illegible] adopted. The volume shows [illegible] the advances in [illegible] field of knowledge [illegible] [illegible] wireless [illegible] software for [illegible] to difficult [illegible].

The WiCON [illegible] numerous [illegible] knowledge [illegible] these proceedings [illegible] research papers [illegible] submissions [illegible] review process. We received [illegible] research papers [illegible] of the Program Committee reviewed each submission, and 30 were accepted, [illegible] acceptance rate of [illegible].

The [illegible] a broad [illegible] topics [illegible] the [illegible] proceedings [illegible] are available [illegible].

All [illegible] WiCON 2022 [illegible] [illegible] especially [illegible] EAI [illegible] thanks also [illegible] the [illegible] [illegible] Without your help [illegible] successful.

November 2022 [illegible]
[illegible]
[illegible]

Organization

Organizing Committee

General Chair

Miguel Félix Mata-Rivera	UPIITA-IPN, México

General Co-chair

Roberto Zagal-Flores	ESCOM-IPN, México

Cybersecurity Track Chair

Cristian Barria Huidobro	Universidad Mayor, Chile

Local Manager

Jairo Zagal-Flores	UnADM, México

Applied Maths Chair

Christian Carlos Delgado Elizondo	UNAM FES Acatlan, México

Staff Chair

Sergio Quiroz Almaraz	UNAM FES Acatlan, México

Program Committee

Christophe Claramunt	Naval Academy Research Institute, France
Cristian Barria Huidobro	Universidad Mayor, Chile
Lorena Galeazzi	Universidad Mayor, Chile
Claudio Casasolo	Universidad Mayor, Chile
Alejandra Acuña Villalobos	Universidad Mayor, Chile
Clara Burbano	Unicomfacauca, Colombia
Gerardo Rubino	Inria, France
Cesar Viho	IRISA, France
Jose-Ernesto Gomez-Balderas	GIPSA, Université Grenoble Alpes, France
Kenn Arizabal	Delft University of Technology, The Netherlands
Mario Aldape Perez	CIDETEC-IPN, México

Anzueto Rios Alvaro	UPIITA-IPN, México
Ludovic Moncla	INSA Lyon, France
Jose Lopez	Hochschule Furtwangen University, Germany
Shoko Wakamiya	Kyoto Sangyo University, Japan
Patrick Laube	Zurich University of Applied Sciences, Switzerland
Sergio Ilarri	University of Zaragoza, Spain
Sisi Zlatanova	TU Delft, The Netherlands
Stephan Winter	University of Melbourne, Australia
Stephen Hirtle	University of Pittsburgh, USA
Steve Liang	University of Calgary, Canada
Tao Cheng	University College London, UK
Willington Siabato	Universidad Nacional de Colombia, Colombia
Xiang Li	East Normal China University, China
Andrea Ballatore	King's College London, UK
Carlos Di Bella	INTA, Argentina
Haosheng Huang	Ghent University, Belgium
Luis Manuel Vilches	CIC-IPN, México
Victor Barrera Figueroa	UPIITA-IPN, México
Blanca Tovar Corona	UPIITA-IPN, México
Thomaz Eduardo Figueiredo Oliveira	CINVESTAV-IPN, México
Homero Toral-Cruz	UQROO, México
Giovanni Guzman Lugo	CIC-IPN, México
Cristian Delgado	UNAM, México
Alma Lopez Blanco	UNAM, México
Mario H. Ramírez Díaz	CICATA-IPN, México
Mario Eduardo Rivero Ángeles	CIC-IPN, México
Izlian Orea	UPIITA-IPN, México
Ingrid Torres	UNAM, México
Javier Rosas	UNAM, México
Julio César Ramirez Pacheco	Universidad del Caribe, México
Fabian Castillo Peña	Universidad Libre, Cali, Colombia
Ana Herrera	UAQ, México
Adriana Davila	UNAM, México
Hugo Jimenez	UAQ, México
José-Antonio León-Borges	UQROO, México
Francisco Quintal	Universidad Tecnológica de Cancún, México
Néstor Darío Duque Méndez	Universidad Nacional de Colombia, Colombia
Diego Muñoz	Universidad Mayor, Chile
David Cordero	Universidad Mayor, Chile
Jacobo Gonzalez-Leon	UPIITA-IPN, México

Saul Ortega	Universidad Mayor, Chile
Robinson Osses	Universidad Mayor, Chile
Raul Garcia-Segura	UQROO, México
Daniel Soto	Universidad Mayor, Chile
Nayeli Joaquinita Melendez Acosta	Universidad Veracruzana, México

Sponsors

ANTACOM A.C.
UPIITA-IPN

Collaborators

UNAM FES Acatlan
Alldatum Systems
CISCO Systems

Contents

Data Obfuscation in Network Coding to Mitigate the Effects of Pollution Attacks

Raúl Antonio Ortega-Vallejo and Francisco de Asís López-Fuentes(✉)

Department of Information Technology, Universidad Autónoma Metropolitana - Cuajimalpa, Av. Vasco de Quiroga 4871, Cuajimalpa, 05348 México City, México
raulantonio@protonmail.com, flopez@cua.uam.mx

Abstract. Network coding is a technique mainly used to maximize the throughput, minimize the delay, or optimize the reliability in the communication networks. However, network coding presents vulnerabilities problems in security terms and is susceptible to security attacks. We analyze impact of a security attack called pollution attack in traditional network coding based on butterfly scheme and propose a solution to deal with this problem. Cryptographic algorithms can protect the information into the data stream combined with network coding, but the processing cost could be high. Our solution considers a hybrid protocol which combines AES algorithm with obfuscation techniques. Our results show that our protocol has a better performance than fully encryption in term of processing time.

Keywords: Security · Network coding · Networking · Information theory

1 Introduction

According to the Cisco report [18], there are 5.3 billion users connected to the Internet. The consumption of data has increased, as has the demand for network infrastructures with higher performance (speed, throughput) [18]. In recent years, network coding has been studied as a technique from information theory to optimize the transmission of messages in communication networks [1]. Network Coding is done in the intermediate nodes which relay received messages toward somewhere destiny but adding other function about the simple forwarding of data [1]. Several benefits in the communication networks related to network coding has been related in the literature (e.g.: maximize the throughput, minimize the delay, optimize the reliability) [19].

For understand the essence of network coding, let us consider a network for a multicast scenario where the intermediate nodes compute algebraic operations on the packets received from the sources. This allows create packets with combined data, this means that a codified packet content more information than non-codified packet. The authors in [1, 2] use a butterfly topology to expose the communication procedure between nodes using network coding.

In Fig. 1a is shown a simple forwarding sending with multicast environment. The main source node *S* is sending the packets *a* and *b*, to nodes N1 and N2, which just are forwarding the streams *a* and *b* to node N3. The node N3 is a relay node and decides

M. F. Mata-Rivera et al. (Eds.): WITCOM 2022, CCIS 1659, pp. 1–17, 2022.
https://doi.org/10.1007/978-3-031-18082-8_1

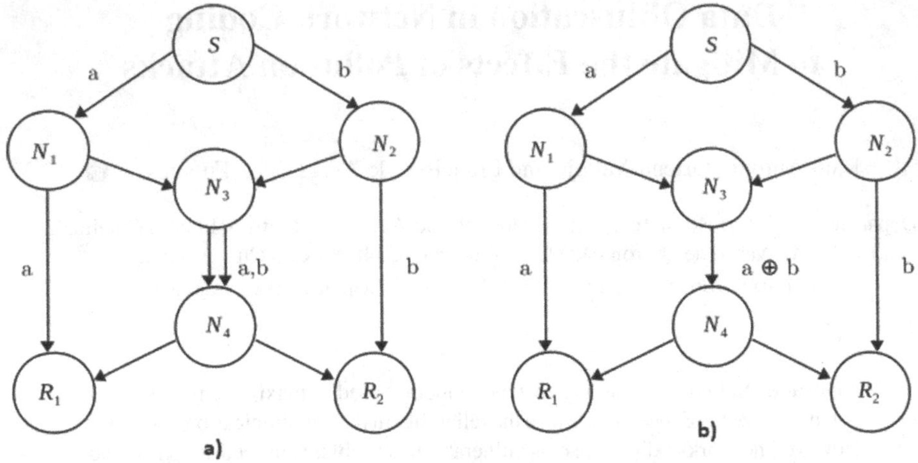

Fig. 1. Butterfly topologies: a) simple forwarding, b) network coding [1].

when forwarding the packet, *a* or *b* but not both to the same time, because it is not possible [2]. The arrows between the nodes N3 and N4, reveal the times required to complete the forwarding of packets (2 per unit of time) [1, 2]. On the other hand, in Fig. 1b the multicast with network coding improves the times to relaying the packets, because only takes 1 (per unit of time) for N3 to send a codified packet to N4 [1, 2].

In the traditional network coding, the intermediate node (N3 for this case, Fig. 1) computes an xor (⊗) from packets received [1]. In this case, in Fig. 1b, the packets *a* and *b* are combined as ($a \otimes b$) during the encoding process done by node N3, which sends the result to N4. This node is forwarding ($a \otimes b$) to the receivers (R1 and R2). The sink node R1, recovers both packets *a* and ($a \otimes b$), while the sink node R2 recuperates *b* and ($a \otimes b$). After that, using the decoding process, the receivers can know the sense of ($a \otimes b$) for each one. For example, the node R1 has the packet *a* from N1, computing in sequence another binary operation, $a \otimes (a \otimes b)$ gets the packet *b*. The similar way is for R2, which recovers the packet *a*, using $b \otimes (a \otimes b)$. This means that each sink node, cans recover the packets *a* and *b* to the same time (1 per unit of time) and the limit capacity of each communication channel is not exceeded [1–3].

With the advantage times, the paradigm network coding proves a better throughput compared to a simple forwarding method [2–4]. The investigation in [2], denotes that the latency problems could be reduced. A use case of network coding is when the file to be transmitted can be separated in multiple files. For example, if the topology network is required for steaming media like video and audio N1 could be the video source and N2 the audio source, harnessing the distribution of the butterfly topology. The authors in [4], introduce a framework to optimize a variant of this paradigm, such that approach is on CPU processing devices (nodes) to allow network members use light algorithms by encoding and decoding processes. In [5] is shown another application related to multimedia storage using peer to peer networks with network coding. The authors compared the typical server to client distribution centralized against decentralized scheme using codification.

However, this paradigm is susceptible to security attacks [6, 7], because it has not focused on security for interception attacks [6]. In this paper, we study the vulnerability consequence of the pollution attack in the traditional network coding scheme. Our motivation is based on investigations which ensure possible damage in the communication networks when a pollution attack occurs [6]. There are different network coding schemes [2, 3], in this work, we have chosen the traditional network coding to know how the sending times can be optimized.

The rest of this paper has been organized as follows. Pollution attack in traditional network coding is explained in Sect. 2. Related work is introduced in Sect. 3. We explain the steps used in our methodology in Sect. 4, where also are explained how the obfuscation techniques and network coding are implemented an integrated to mitigate a pollution attack. Then, evaluation of our proposal and its obtained results are discussed in Sect. 5. Finally, conclusions and future work are presented in Sect. 6.

2 Background

A pollution attack is when an attacker or process does a channel interception and sends its own stream instead of a legitimate flow [22, 23]. The buffer of attacker could contend rubbish data [6, 7] and the receiver could read the corrupt packets. For example, in Fig. 2 if an attacker intercepts the interaction of N2 and N3, the attacker does a stream to the node N3 instead of N2 flow, the node N3 could be an *xor* with rubbish data and a legitimate packet (*a* or *b*). A corrupted packet is the result of this, furthermore other nodes could expand the attack to the rest of the network. Figure 2 shows how N4 forwarding the corrupt packet, in consequence the sink nodes (R1 and R2) cannot recovery *a* or *b*.

The real damage impact of pollution attack is depending of the objective of the attacker, for example if the attack pretends generate a *DOS* (*Denial of Service*) from a pollution attack, perhaps the node N3 is the possible candidate to attack first. In this work, we simulated attacks at various points if the network using the traditional codification (XOR). This allows analyze the possibilities for the attacker and evaluates the damage on the network. As result, we propose a protocol which uses a cryptography algorithm and obfuscation techniques.

In computational context "obfuscation" refers to produce non-understandable text for humans [14]. The mean intention is hide information or procedures at the code of program or hide some strings from one text [14]. Obfuscation make a program more difficult to understand because its structure is changed, while the original functionalities is preserved [24]. Sometimes obfuscation activities are used for the cybercrime [12]. This is possible, because if a computational forensic scientific want to use a special software to investigate a suspicious code, maybe the software cannot recognize anything from the file. Furthermore, the forensics could be confused with the obfuscated code. However, we believe obfuscation can be used for positive activities such as protect valuable information [12, 13]. Our objective in this work is to develop a protocol which allows to mitigate the damage produced by pollution attacks. Our proposed protocol tries the attackers desist to steal the information from the packets.

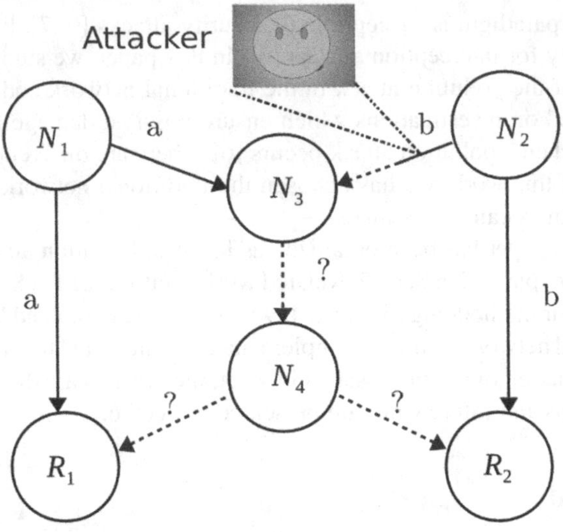

Fig. 2. A pollution attack example between N2 and N3 nodes.

3 Related Work

Recently security for network coding has generated great interest for the researchers [6, 8–10]. The adversary model in [6], explains about several ways network coding can be attacked. We found interesting works about it, with proposals, models and techniques using cryptography. There are contributions centered in cryptographic methods as the *KEPTE* model [8]. This model has a key distribution scheme for encrypt and decrypt the vectors. In this model there is a *KDC (key distribution center)*. For example, with this proposal, we have two special vectors as a public key and as a private key. For that reason, the nodes must interact with the KDC and request these keys to protect the flows. Unfortunately, this asymmetric model only has one generation of keys for encrypt and decrypt the source vectors [8]. In [9] authors explain the possible vulnerabilities that this model has. To integrate a key distribution with network coding is complicated. However, author in [9] proposes a dynamic generation of secret keys to complement the KEPTE approach.

Another model is *SPOC* (safe practical of network coding) [10], where the authors use end-to-end encryption for the data on network coding. The algorithm AES (Advanced encryption standard) is used for making it. One interest of using AES in SPOC, is because this scheme requires an encryption mechanism with ciphertext size equal to that of the plaintext. This means that the intermediate nodes can operates on the locked coefficients without the need for the decryption keys [10].

The authors in [20] present a scheme for detect suspicious activities or attacks using network coding. The idea is to has a SDN (centralized software defined controller), which seem a special tunnel for classify packets [20]. On the other hand, the SDN takes the byzantine problem [6]. Where the node, makes reports about the packet, but maybe this will produce more connections than we need. Anyway, the focus in [20] was on mobile technologies.

In the obfuscation context, the authors propose in [11] to use obfuscation for network coding. This model called *CNC* (*Conceal network coding*), does obfuscation using bitwise movements during the codifying process [11]. Other proposal for obfuscate data for this paradigm is [16], where exists an interesting comparison between typical and homomorphic encryption algorithms. Where the homomorphic strategy is more expensive for the nodes. The authors use *SRC* (*Secret random checksum*) for each node that receives a packet. This allows to the receivers know which packet was corrupted, furthermore is possible to discard it. Also, in this approach an attacker cannot recover the file completely if the vector file was obfuscated [16]. For example, if an attacker intercepts a fragment from the original file, means the attacker only got a file portion which could be an was obfuscated part and it is not enough to recovery the entire file. Considering this characteristic, our investigation tries to develop a strategy to confuse the attacker to intercept the obfuscated packets during a pollution attacks instead of the legitimate packets.

4 Methodology

Contrasting with the CNC proposal [11], our obfuscation protocol is used in the sources and receivers. Therefore, we do not append more processing work to the intermediate nodes. Furthermore, these nodes should not know the content of the packets, only parameters as the information of its destiny. In this way, we avoid possible user privacy affectation in the intermediate nodes. The source nodes have the task of protect the flows before to send it, while the sink nodes know the mechanism for recovery the information from the packets. Thus, in the intermediate nodes only network coding operations are implemented. To create the butterfly topology (see Fig. 1a), we classified the groups for each node. In this case, we have the *source nodes* (N1 and N2), the *intermediate nodes* (N3 and N4) and *sinks nodes* (R1 and R2), such that we have 6 nodes. We decided to employ our lab simulated occupying the same machine for set up the network. It was possible with Linux containers, where everyone represented a node. This allows to prepare a specific network configuration for some nodes. For example, the IP address and port number. In next step, we set up the specifications about the files related to their size and type. Because on an Ethernet real scenario there are few limitations to transfer files, we do not specific in our program any file type to be transmitted on the Ethernet network. However, in our experiments we have used text, images, binaries, and pdf files. The source nodes do a vector representation using a serialization process. The network can operate in three modes. 1. Using simple codification. 2. Encrypting the source vectors. 3. Using our proposed protocol. When the network uses the first mode, a file is serialized, and the vector without protection is transmitted over the network. In the second mode, a file is serialized, and the vector is encrypted using AES algorithm (with 192-bit keys). For example, if file A is serialized and encrypted, such that | A | is equal to | AES (A) |. This is the encrypted vector that would be sent, merged, and retrieved. The sinks nodes known the secret key to decrypt it. On the other hand, the third mode use the obfuscated technique with network coding. In this mode the obfuscation procedure is done in the source nodes. Figure 3 shows the output final vector to transmit with the treated packet using our proposed protocol.

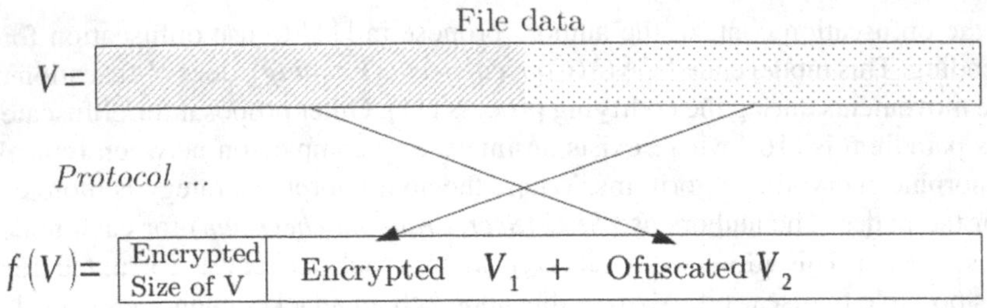

Fig. 3. Final vector as output of our proposed protocol.

In Fig. 3, V represents the vector which is serialized by the protocol. V is split in two sub-vectors (V1 and V2), such that |V| = |V1| + |V2|. The sub-vector V2, is obfuscated using arithmetic operations. For example, V2 contains the string "ABC", in binary the value is "01000001 01000010 01000011". Thus, we can turn it to "CBA", so the binary file is "01000011 01000011 01000001". Applying some changes, we have "1011110 10111101 10111100", that is the result of interchange the 1 and 0. This produces the ascii value "^½¼", which is very different to "ABC". This allows to generate operations which can be included in our protocol, so that we can know the changes that were made to the values of V2. Once the operations with V2 are finished, we can concatenate V1 and V2 to form an obfuscated vector, which may be more difficult to be interpreted by an attacker. Figure 3 shows the result using the third mode (vector obfuscation). The operator '+' represents a concatenation on the final vector (buffer). The "Encrypted size" label indicates the size of the obfuscated vector. This information helps to the receiver nodes know the dimension of the vector. We assume that the source nodes and the sink nodes know the secret key and length for crypt and decrypt vectors (AES of 192-bit). Note that the encryption algorithm is used AES192(|V|/2) times, this mean its cost was reduced to the half of the vector. We believe that it is not necessary to encrypt the entire vector to protect the information of the nodes.

Once the source nodes have processed the vector under our protocol, to recover an encoded vector must be done the reverse process. For example, we know that the vector is composed of two sub-vectors, then we must swap the positions of the data blocks. Thus, if in Fig. 3, the sub-vector V2 is placed at the beginning, it must swap its position with V1. In other words, the vector must be rotated. After that, we need to interpret the sub-vectors, because one has been encrypted (V1) and the other has been obfuscated (V2).

Our methodology has the following steps:

a) First, we implemented the traditional network coding scheme. The network should support any extension of file. However, we use images files as input vectors.
b) Then, we simulated different attacks to study the impact in all nodes included the sinks nodes. This is important because we can know where an attack causes the most damage, if our intention is avoiding that damage be expanded. Our study with different cases of pollution attacks and its methodology were presented in [21].

c) We use a protocol based on the AES algorithm, but it is not used to encrypt all data. The length of key for AES is 192-bit, and both sinks nodes as sources nodes know the key to decrypt the encrypted vector.
d) After that, the AES algorithm is used to protect against the interception attacks, because it could limit the chance for the attacker.

Finally, we compare the overall transmission times using only traditional network coding with network coding using AES (192-bit) and with our protocol (AES of 192-bit + Obfuscation).

5 Evaluation and Results

In this project, we develop our prototype using the C language of programing, and the GPG-Libcrypt library for the cryptography algorithms. Our experiments were done in a computer powered by a 2.16 Ghz Intel Celeron processor and 8GB of RAM. We use Linux as our operating system. Initially, we tested our prototype with text files as input vectors for check communication between the nodes. However, our network coding prototype supports any extension of file. Through Linux containers we can specify the network options for each node of the butterfly network. Table 1 describes the necessary configurations for each node.

Table 1. Network configuration nodes.

Node sets	Description	IP Address
N1, N2	Sources	172.18.0.2-3
N3, N4	Intermediate/Relays	172.18.0.4-5
R1, R2	Sinks	172.18.0.7-8

Our evaluation is divided in two parts. In the first part, we evaluate de network coding performance and the impact of pollution attack in the network coding operation. In the second part, we evaluate the network coding performance using two different security strategies.

To evaluate the first part, we tested a traditional network coding based on the butterfly scheme. The sources N1 and N2 distributes two different image files called "photo1.jpg" and "photo2.jpg". Figure 4 shows the activities monitor running in node N1, where a JPG file named "photo1.jpg" is processed. In this example, the file name is the same as the name of the image inside the file system of container where node N1 is hosted. This node is configured with the IP address 172.18.0.2, processes the file and serializes it to be transmitted to nodes N3 and R1.

In Fig. 4, we can see that our program takes the time of each file processing procedure and the time of interaction with the nodes. This information allows to feed a log file, with the activities of source node N1. All nodes of our network record their binnacle in a log file. These log files contain data such as time and connections between the nodes on the network. With these records, we can identify possible time variations during the communication between the nodes. Figure 5 shows a scenario similarly to previously described, but for source node N2.

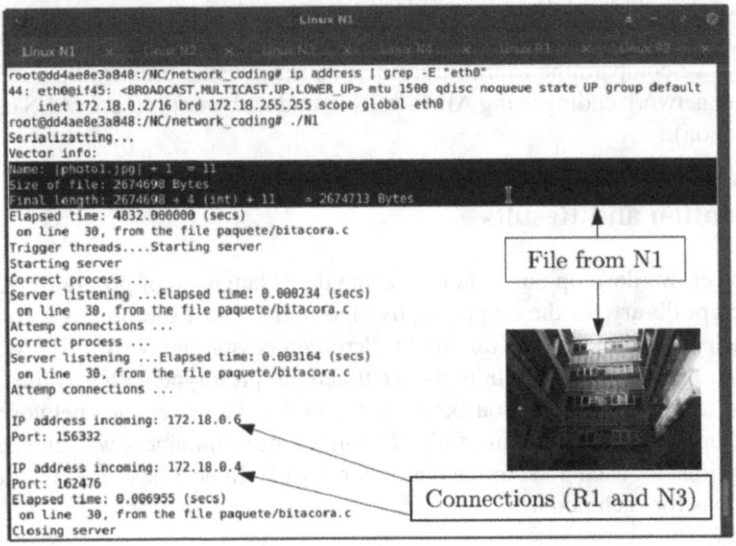

Fig. 4. Monitor of N1 sending the file “photo1.jpg”.

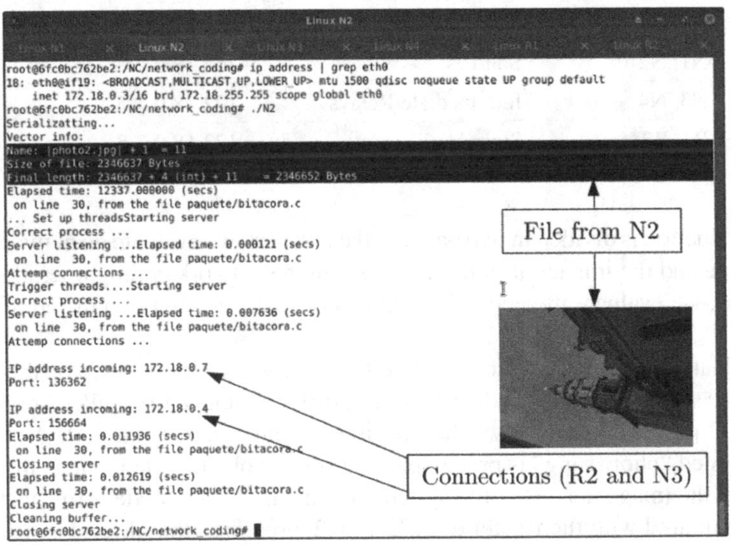

Fig. 5. Monitor of N2 sending the file “photo2.jpg”.

Figure 6 shows the monitor for node N3, which is the intermediate node responsible to apply network coding in both encrypted vectors received from source nodes N1 and

N2. It is important to note that both vectors must have equal length to be encoded. Then, the encoded packets are sent to node N4. If the received vectors in the node N3 are of different size network coding is not done, and node N3 simply forwards the incoming packets to node N4.

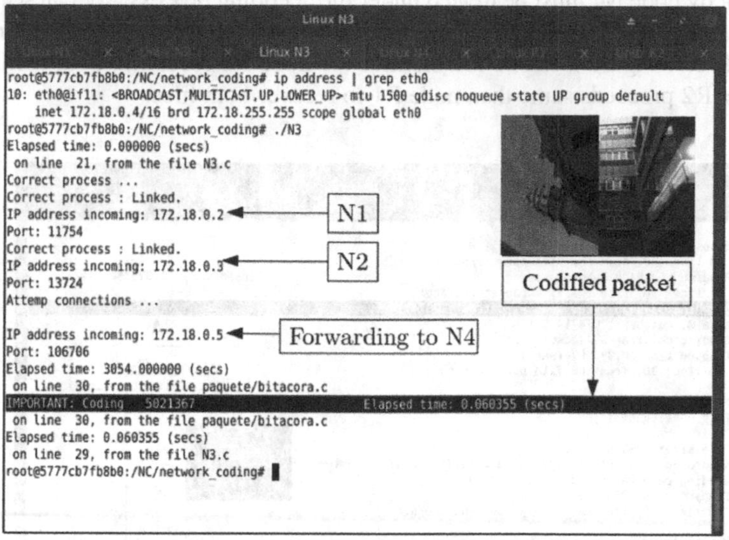

Fig. 6. Monitor for node N3 coding the packets from N1 and N2.

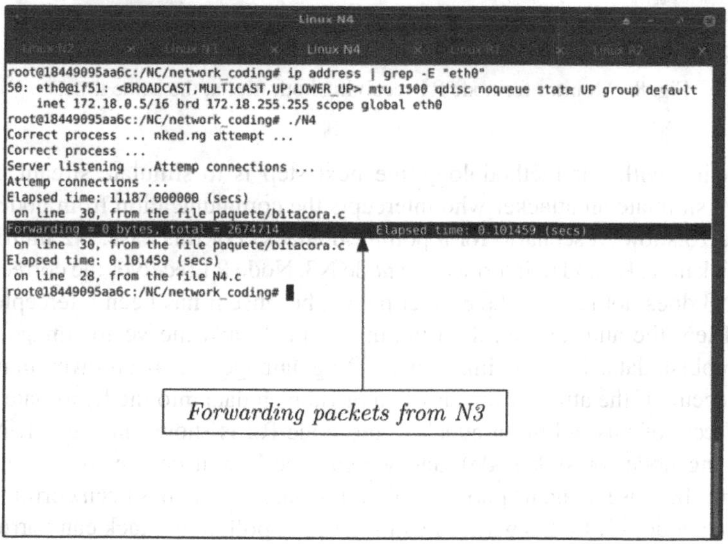

Fig. 7. Monitor for node N4 forwarding the flows received from node N3.

On the other hand, Fig. 7 shows the processing performed by node N4, which has the IP address "172.18.0.5" and receives the flow from node N3. Consequently, node N4 broadcasts the encoded packets to the sink nodes, in this case to the nodes R1 and R2.

The receiving node R1 receives the files "photo1.jpg" and "photo2.jpg" at the same time. We can see this scenario in Fig. 8. It is necessary to specify that the encoded packet sent by node N4 must be treated under the decoding process. We can see that our program retrieves the original file name and it is recorded in the registers within the log file in node R1. Figure 9 shows the monitor for node R2 receiving both files at same time. Node R2 proceeds same than node R1 to recover both files.

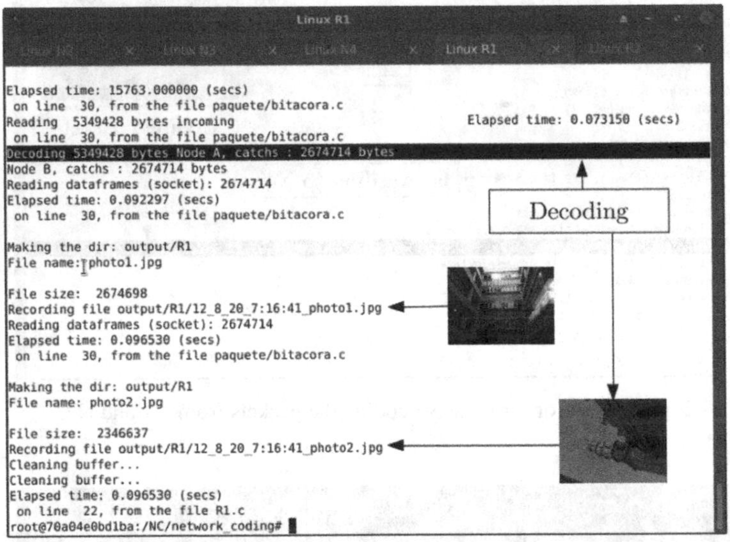

Fig. 8. Monitor for node R1 receiving both files at the same time.

Continuing with our methodology, the next step is to simulate stream pollution attacks. We simulate an attacker who intercepts the communication from node N2 and N3. Figure 10 shows a scenario for a pollution attack. For this case, N2 multicasts an image to sink node R1 and to intermediate node N3. Node R1 receives the correct packet, but node N3 does not receive the correct packet because it has been intercepted by an attacker. Then, the attacker can do a pollution attack, and the vector image presents errors or rubbish data. Thus, an image presenting damages has been saved in node N3. This case occurs if the attacker injects extra or rubbish data into the legitimate buffer.

The effects of this pollution attack in the node R2 is shown in Fig. 11. Node R2 is a receiving node (or sink node), and we can see how it can recovery only image "photo1.jpg" because imagen "photo2.jpg" sent from node N2 has been corrupted in the intermediate node N3. In this way, we can see how a pollution attack can corrupt a file.

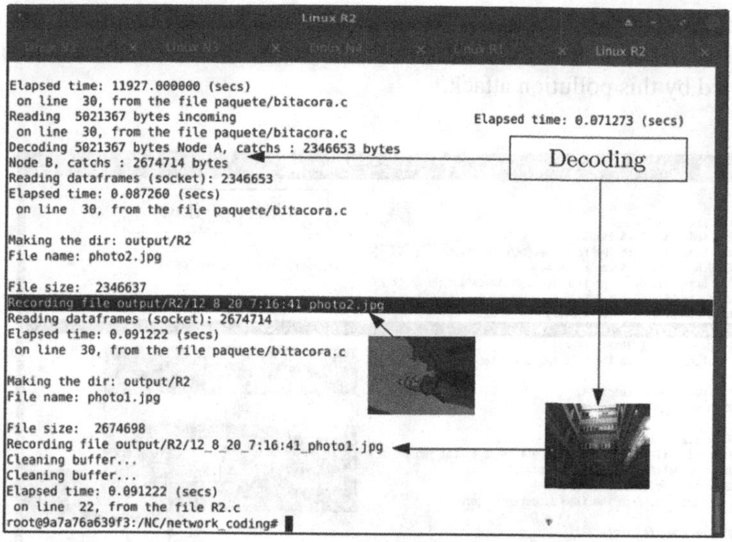

Fig. 9. Monitor for node R2 receiving both files at the same time.

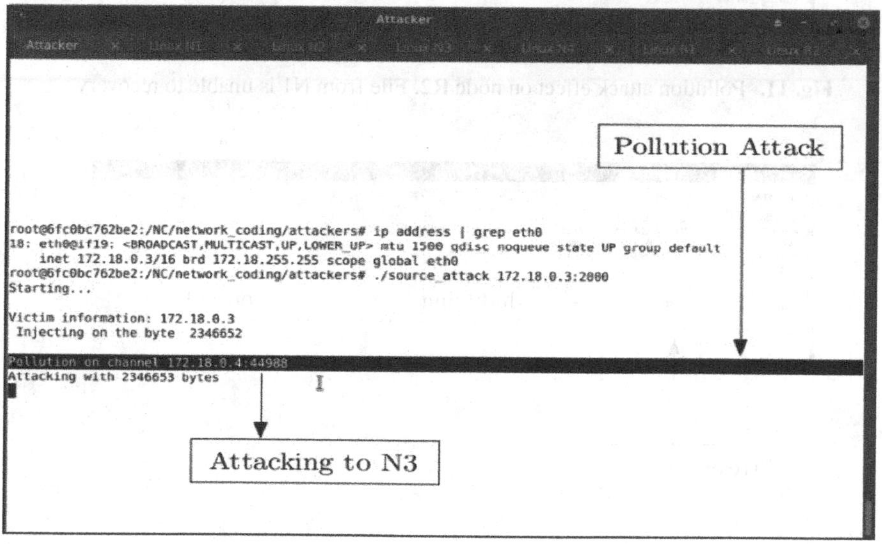

Fig. 10. An attacker intercepts the message between source node N2 and intermediate node N3, and a pollution attack can be done.

Another possible case is when the image could not be recovery in its totality (incomplete imagen). For example, we simulate an intercepted communication between the source node N1 and the sink node R1. This case is shown in Fig. 12. The attacker alters the file "photo1.jpg" sent to node R1 from node N1. Therefore, the file "photo2.jpg" sent from source node N2 is unrecoverable because the file "photo1.jpg" is corrupted, and it cannot be used to decode the file "photo2.jpg" using network coding in this scheme. Figure 13 shows both files received in the sink node R1. We can see how both files have been affected by this pollution attack.

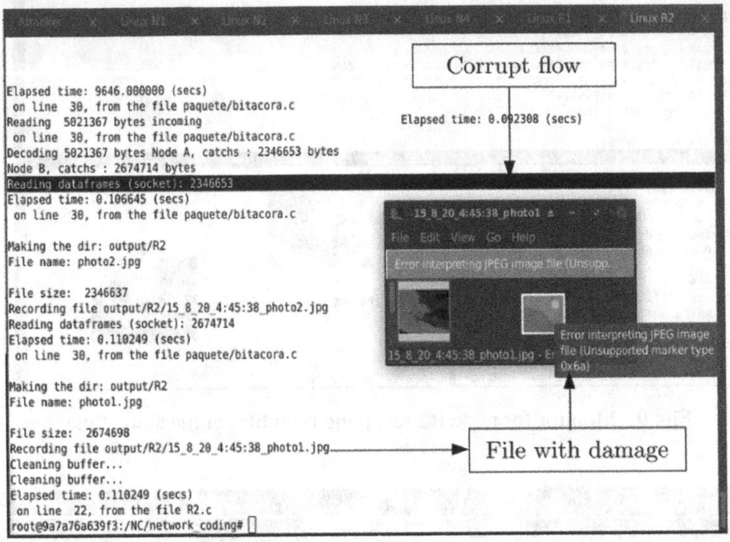

Fig. 11. Pollution attack effect on node R2. File from N1 is unable to recovery.

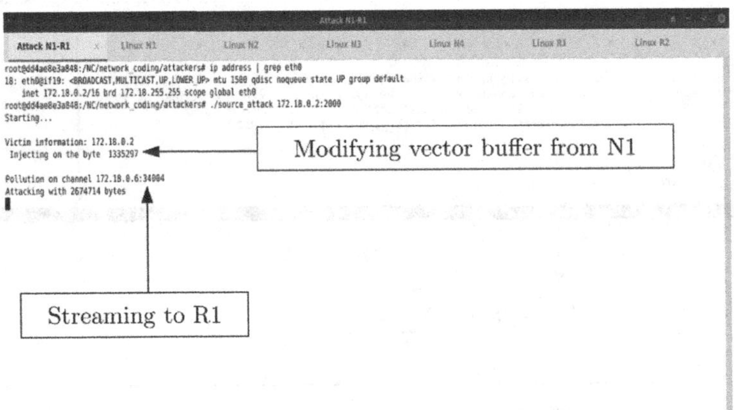

Fig. 12. A pollution attack is produced in the link between source node N1 and sink node R1.

We have done several experiments simulating other pollution attacks in different nodes or links of our butterfly network. In Table 2 we have summarized these potential pollution attacks and indicated how a specific encoded file is affected by a pollution attack.

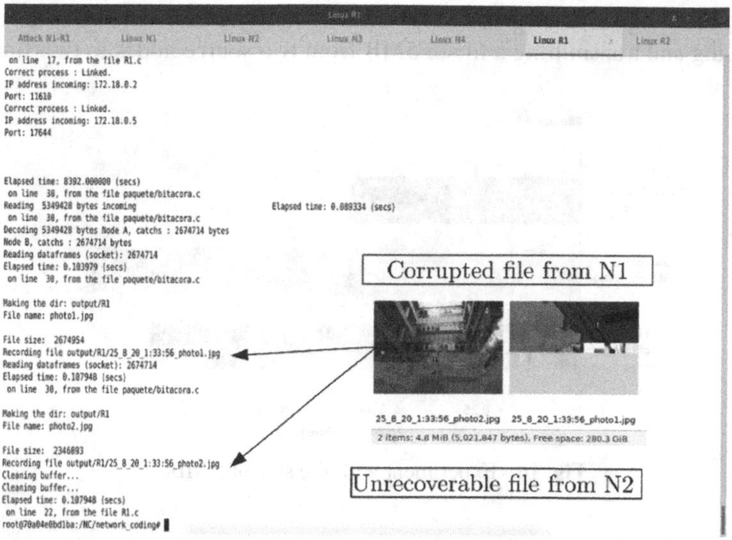

Fig. 13. Affected files in sink node R1.

For example, if the attack is done in the link between source node N1 and sink node R1, only this receiver is affected with a corrupt packet. Other case is when the attacker intercepts all communication of source node N2 such that both sinks nodes receive incomplete packets from the sources. The worst case is when the packets in the intermediate node N3 is intercepted and the attacker cans control all communications with this node. This case produces a very negative impact on the network because each codified packet by node N3 is a corrupted packet. This case is shown in Table 2 too.

Table 2. Impact under pollution attack according to node interaction.

Intercepted	Sink R1	Sink R2
Link N1 to R1	Complete file	Corrupt file
Node N2	Incomplete file	Incomplete file
Node N3	Corrupt file	Corrupt file

The second part of our evaluation is developed once we know the negative impact of the pollution attacks can have on traditional network coding (butterfly scheme). Now, we need to consider different security strategies to mitigate the pollution attack impact. In the first strategy the source vectors are fully encrypted. Here, source and sink nodes know the secret key to encrypt and to decrypt the data. This strategy implies a higher cost of computing power, which we try to reduce in our second strategy that uses our protocol based on the obfuscation techniques that we have explained in Sect. 4.

The results from both strategies are compared with the results obtained using network coding only. Figure 14 shows results from our experiments in term of average time required by the computational processing for each strategy. Results in Fig. 14 are obtained by processing and transmitting a file of 5MB from two source nodes to two sink nodes.

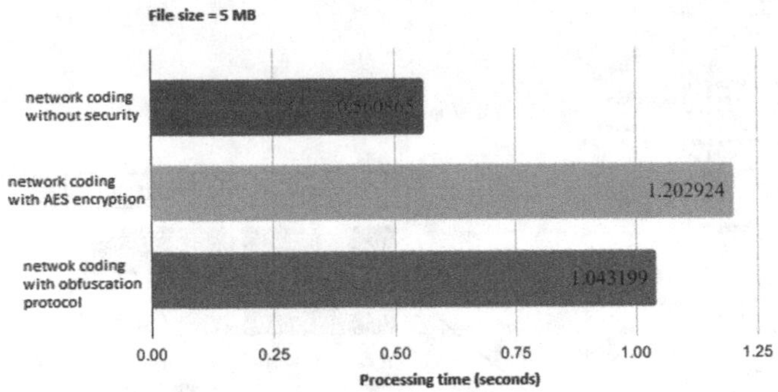

Fig. 14. Experiment with file size of 5 MB.

The elapsed time considers encryption time of original file in the source nodes, obfuscate time (it only apply in the second strategy), network coding time in the intermediate node, decoded and decryption time in the sink nodes, and the transmission time in all nodes. In Fig. 14 we can see how results using our obfuscation protocol has a less processing time compared with fully encryption strategy in around 0.159725 s. Processing time using our obfuscation protocol is 86% greater than processing time using traditional network coding without data protection, but processing time using our protocol is 13.3% less than network coding using fully encryption.

To experiment our protocol with files of different sizes, we have tested used files of 15 MB and 30 MB. Results for processing and transmitting the file of 15 MB using the three strategies (network coding without security, network coding with our obfuscation protocol and network coding with fully encryption) are shown in Fig. 15.

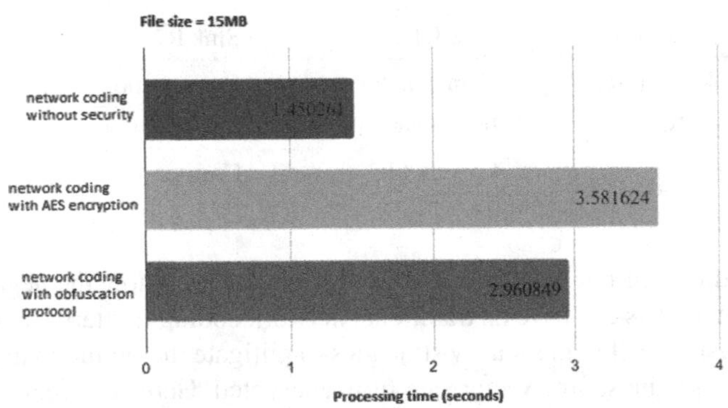

Fig. 15. Experiment with file size of 15 MB.

Experiments with a file of 30 MB are shown in Fig. 16. We can see in both figures that the difference between the use of fully encryption and our proposed protocol is more remarkable. For example, processing time using our protocol is less 17.3% than fully encryption for the file of 15 MB, while for the file of 30 MB this processing time is reduced in around 21.6%. Therefore, we see how fully encrypting the files is more expensive than using our obfuscation protocol. Finally, a general comparison is shown in Fig. 17. Here we can note how the difference in processing times between full encryption and our protocol increase as the processed files are larger.

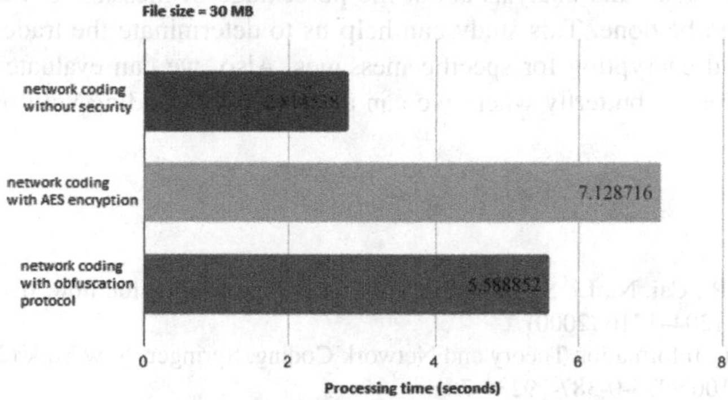

Fig. 16. Experiment with file size of 30 MB.

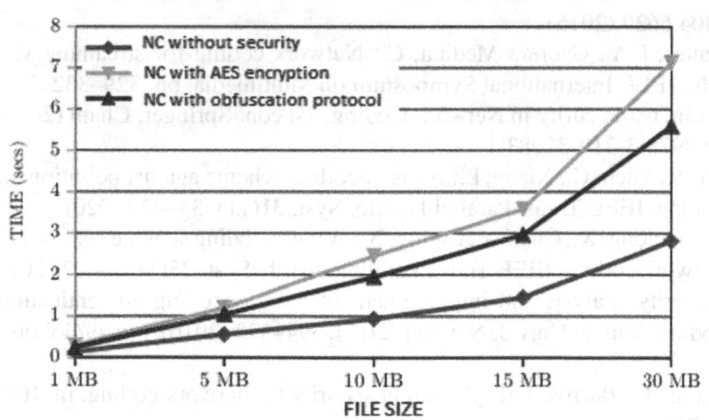

Fig. 17. Comparison of different file sizes from nodes N1 and N2.

6 Conclusions

Network coding has become an effective solution to increase throughput in the communication systems during last years. However, this technique is susceptible to attacks which can influence in the loss of data, and cause damage to the integrity of a communication system. In this paper we have shown how networking schemes based on network coding can be affected by pollution attacks. Data can be protected using some cryptography techniques. However, cryptography algorithms can have high processing costs.

Our protocol presented in this work integrates obfuscation techniques and cryptographic algorithms that allow files to be obfuscated before applying network encryption to them. Our results show that obfuscation combined with partial cryptography can be an efficient alternative solution to do secure network coding in communication networks because the processing times are more reduced respect to fully encryption. We believe that our proposal to face the pollution attacks in network coding open the doors to different possible solutions in the cybersecurity context. Our work can be extended in different directions. For example, a study and analysis about the percentage of message to be obfuscated o encrypted can be done. This study can help us to determinate the tradeoff between obfuscation and encryption for specific messages. Also, we can evaluate networking schemes different to butterfly where we can apply network coding with our proposed protocol.

References

1. Ahlswede, R., Cai, N., Li. S.-Y., Yeung, R.W.: Network information flow. IEEE Trans. Inf. Theory **46**, 1204–1216 (2000)
2. Yeung, R.H.: Information Theory and Network Coding. Springer, New York (2008). https://doi.org/10.1007/978-0-387-79234-7
3. Ho, T., Lun, D.: Network Coding: An Introduction. Cambridge University Press, Cambridge (2008)
4. Lucani, D., et al.: Fulcrum network codes: a code for fluid allocation of complexity. CoRR, vol. abs/1404.6620 (2015)
5. Lopez-Fuentes, F.A., Cabrera Medina, C.: Network coding for streaming video over P2P networks. In: IEEE International Symposium on Multimedia, pp. 329–332 (2013)
6. Zhang, P., Lin, C.: Security in Network Coding, 1st edn. Springer, Cham (2016). https://doi.org/10.1007/978-3-319-31083-1
7. Wu, X., Xu, Y., Yuen, C., Xiang, L.: A tag encoding scheme against pollution attack to linear network coding. IEEE Trans. Parallel Distrib. Syst. **31**(11), 33–42 (2020)
8. Xiaohu, W., Yinlong, X., Chau, Y., Liping, X.: A tag encoding scheme against pollution attack to linear network coding. IEEE Trans. Parallel Distrib. Syst. **25**(1), 33–42 (2014)
9. Liu, G.: Security analysis and improvement of a tag encoding authentication scheme for network coding. Wuhan Univ. J. Nat. Sci. **21**(5), 394–398 (2016). https://doi.org/10.1007/s11859-016-1186-1
10. Vilela, J, Lima, L., Barros, J.: Lightweight security for network coding. In: IEEE ICC 2008, pp. 1750–1754 (2008)
11. Hessler, A., Kakumaru, T., Perrey, H., Westhoff, D.: Data obfuscation with network coding". Comput. Commun. **35**(1), 48–61 (2012)
12. Alazab, M., Venkatraman, S., Watters, P., Alazab, M., Alazab, A.: Cybercrime: the case of obfuscated malware. In: Georgiadis, C.K., Jahankhani, H., Pimenidis, E., Bashroush, R., Al-Nemrat, A. (eds.) ICGS3 2011. LNICST, vol. 99, pp. 204–211. Springer, Heidelberg (2012). https://doi.org/10.1007/978-3-642-33448-1_28
13. Bakken, D.E., Rarameswaran, R., Blough, D.M., Franz, A.A., Palmer, T.J.: Data obfuscation: anonymity and desensitization of usable data sets. IEEE Secur. Priv. **2**(6), 34–41 (2004)
14. Dalai, A.K., Das, S.S., Jena, S.K.: A code obfuscation technique to prevent reverse engineering. In: International Conference on Wireless Communications, Signal Processing and Networking, pp. 828–832 (2017)
15. Lin, D., Hamdi, M., Muppala, J.: Distributed packet buffers for high-bandwidth switches and routers. IEEE Trans. Parallel Distrib. Syst. **23**(7), 1178–1192 (2012)

16. Cascella, R.G., Caoy, Z., Gerlay, M., Crispo, B., Battiti, R.: Weak data secrecy via obfuscation in network coding based content distribution. In: 1st IFIP Wireless Days, pp. 1–5 (2008)
17. Liu, Q., Zhang, W., Ding, S., Li, H., Wang, Y.: Novel secure group data exchange protocol in smart home with physical layer network coding. Sensors **20**, 1138, pp. 1–17 (2020)
18. CISCO, Cisco Annual Internet Report, 2018–2023 white paper. https://www.cisco.com/c/en/us/solutions/executive-perspectives/annual-internet-report/infographic-c82-741491.html
19. Fragouli, C.: Network coding: beyond throughput benefits. Proc. IEEE **99**(3), 461–471 (2011)
20. Adat, V., Parsamehr, R., Politis, I., Tselios, C., Kotsopoulos, S.: Malicious user identification scheme for network coding enabled small cell environment. In: IEEE International Conference on Communications (ICC 2020), Dublin, Ireland, pp. 1–6 (2020)
21. Ortega-Vallejo, R.A., de Asís López Fuentes, F.: Vulnerability of network coding under pollution attacks. In: Vasant, P., Litvinchev, I., Marmolejo-Saucedo, J.A., Rodriguez-Aguilar, R., Martinez-Rios, F. (eds.) Data Analysis and Optimization for Engineering and Computing Problems. EAISICC, pp. 243–253. Springer, Cham (2020). https://doi.org/10.1007/978-3-030-48149-0_18
22. Fiandrotti, A., Gaeta, R., Grangetto, M.: Simple countermeasures to mitigate the effect of pollution attack in network coding-based peer-to-peer live streaming. IEEE Trans. Multimedia **17**(4), 562–573 (2015)
23. Liang, J., Kumar, J., Xi, Y., Ross, K.W.: Pollution in P2P file sharing systems. In: IEEE INFOCOM 2005, vol. 2, pp. 1174–1185 (2005)
24. Behera, C.K., Bhaskari, D.L.: Different obfuscation techniques for code protection. Procedia Comput. Sci. **70**, 757–763 (2015)

Adaptive Based Frequency Domain Filter for Periodic Noise Reduction in Images Acquired by Projection Fringes

O. A. Espinosa-Bernal(✉), J. C. Pedraza-Ortega, M. A. Aceves-Fernández, V. M. Martínez-Suárez, and S. Tovar-Arriaga

Faculty of Engineering, Autonomous University of Queretaro, Cerro de las campanas s/n, Queretaro, Mexico
oespinosa07@alumnos.uaq.mx, {marco.aceves,saul.tovar}@uaq.mx

Abstract. An application of interest of images 2D is to obtain the shape of 3D objects by fringe projection. However, such images contain periodic or quasi/periodic noise produced during the generation of the images and interference during the transmission of digital images. The application of an adaptive filter based in the frequency domain with a smoothing filter based in the spatial domain reduced the noise from corrupted digital images acquired by projection fringes. This paper presents an algorithm that determines the frequencies corrupted and replaces them with the mean of its neighbors in the frequency domain, then, a smooth filter is applied to the image in the spatial domain. With the implementation of the proposed algorithm, it was possible to reduce the mean square error (MSE) in the 3D reconstruction. Finally, a 3D reconstruction can be built based on phase-shifting techniques. The implementation and experimental results show high-precision 3D information.

Keywords: Quasi/periodic noise · Periodic noise · Fourier transform · Adaptive filtering · Adaptive threshold filtering · Noise attenuation

1 Introduction

The reduction of periodic or quasi/periodic noise present in images arose since images could be obtained in digital ways. However, it was not until the sources that produced such contamination were analyzed, as well as the way in which they are presented digitally, that work began on a way to eliminate the contamination present in corrupted images.

There are different types of noise present in digital images. For example, in the spatial domain of the image, the periodic or quasi/periodic noise can appear as fringes on the image, while in the spatial domain, this same periodic noise stands out on the frequencies that form the uncorrupted image in a star shape, as Fig. 1 shows.

M. F. Mata-Rivera et al. (Eds.): WITCOM 2022, CCIS 1659, pp. 18–32, 2022.
https://doi.org/10.1007/978-3-031-18082-8_2

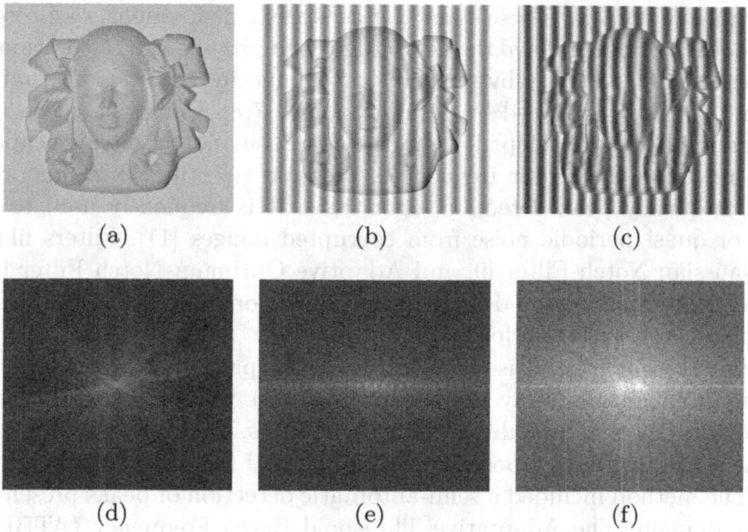

Fig. 1. a) Image not corrupted in the spatial domain, b) Image corrupted with periodic noise in the spatial domain, c) Image corrupted with quasi/periodic noise in the spatial domain, d) Image not corrupted in the frequency domain, e) Image corrupted with noise periodic in the frequency domain, f) Image corrupted with quasi/periodic noise in the frequency domain.

Early research to develop filters in the spatial domain of images to reduce periodic or quasi/periodic noise managed to attenuate them in the images is shown in Fig. 1. However, it was found that these filters failed, since the noise present in the images affected the entire image, the noise reduction was not complete or image information was lost [2]. The components that make up the periodic or quasi/periodic noise in the spatial domain are generally mixed with the image information, which makes them almost impossible to detect for their correct attenuation or correction. Applying Smooth Morphology Filter (SMF) replaces the pixels in an image by the average of soft erosion and dilation outputs [3]. OSMF (Optimized Smooth Morphology Filter) is a variant of SMF that uses a particle swarm optimizer to optimize SMF, however, the restored images are highly distorted and blurry so it was ineffective in reducing images with a high degree of periodic noise or quasi/periodic [4].

Further investigations to try to reduce periodic or quasi/periodic noise resulted in dealing with corrupted images in the frequency domain [5]. Due to the fact that when applying a Fourier transform to the corrupted image, the periodic or quasi/periodic noise appears as repetitive patterns, the frequencies of these types of noise are concentrated as conjugate peaks located at different frequencies depending on the frequency of the sinusoidal functions [6]. As the positions of the frequencies correspond to those produced by the periodic or quasi/periodic types of noise, they are easily detected from the other frequencies in the frequency domain. These stand out as star-shaped regions, so filters based on the frequency domain have the advantage of improving the restoration of the image corrupted in this way by replacing or eliminating said regions that would correspond to those produced by periodic noises [7,8]. Filters based on the frequency domain were developed, thus the Gaussian notch filter is capable of not only rejecting the center frequencies but also rejecting its neighbors, thus applying frequency peak detection algorithms, it is frequently used to reduce periodic or quasi/periodic noise from corrupted images [11]. Filters like Windowed Gaussian Notch Filter [9] and Adaptive Optimum Notch Filter [10] are capable of restoring corrupted images, but their non-adaptive nature to detect noisy regions limits their performance.

Because the periodic noise pattern was also present in x-ray microscopy (Scanning Transmission X-ray Microscopy(STXM)), producing significant errors in both quantitative and qualitative image analysis, Wei et al. (2011) [13], proposed the introduction of a post-processing method for noise filtering in STXM images. The method included a semi-automatic detection of peaks present in the frequency domain. The Adaptative Threshold Based Frequency (ATBF) filter to reduce periodic noise from corrupted images is an algorithm that adaptively determines the threshold function for the identification of noisy regions, replacing the pixels in the noisy regions by applying a minimum filter using its neighbors to determine the new frequency value and thus reduce the noise quasi/periodic present in the images [14].

Spatial smoothing filters are used to blur digital images but also to reduce the noise present in digital images. Noise present in images can be reduced by applying a linear filter to corrupted images. An image that has a spatial smoothing filter applied to it simply applies an average of the neighboring pixels [11]. Other techniques applied to the spatial domain of corrupted images include algorithms that remove texture from the corrupted image, because it contains repetitive components of high-frequency periodic noise [24–26]. Recent techniques make use of convolutional neural networks after demonstrating that are capable of classifying [19] and recognizing images [16,17], they have also demonstrated their potential in low-level vision and image processing tasks. Such tasks as image super-resolution [20], demosaicking, denoising [21] and image restoration [22] are constantly evolving applications. Thus denoising convolutional neural network (DnCNN) removes Gaussian white noise of different levels using residual learning noise removal strategies cleaning the images within the hidden layers of the DnCNN model [18]. Multiresolution Convolutional Neural Network uses a fully convolutional network to automatically remove periodic or quasi/periodic noise patterns from photos and digital images [12].

This paper presents a novel algorithm to attenuate the noise on images corrupted by quasi/periodic noise obtained by fringe projection. The filter incorporates an algorithm for noise detection and replaces the corrupted frequencies components of the quasi/periodic noise with the minimum of uncorrupted frequencies of its pixels neighbors and a smoothing filter that operates in the spatial domain of the image. The scope of the research will not make use of convolutional neural networks. The algorithm will only use conventional techniques for quasi/periodic noise removal. The paper has four section. Sect. 1. Introduction, The proposed algorithm is explained in Sect. 2. The experiments and results are explained in Sect. 3 and finally, the conclusions are discussed in Sect. 4.

2 Proposed Algorithm

The proposed algorithm is a variant of ATBF [14] that convert the image corrupted with periodic noise to the frequency domain by applying forward origin shifting and Fourier transform, to apply noise reduction by identifying the contaminated regions and reducing them by replacing their pixels with the average value of their neighbors. Since the algorithm processes the image in the frequency domain, highlighting corrupt frequencies in the image, the corresponding pixels are replaced by the average of their neighboring pixels. This process is used to determine the corrupted pixels of images with quasi/periodic noise and attenuate said noise. However, the corrupt frequencies present in the images obtained by fringe projection are mostly far from the center where the most important frequencies are concentrated. So the processing of the pixels starts from the extremes of the image (upper and lower) and converges in the center, to first process the corrupted frequencies far from the center and placing a mask in the center to later recover the original frequencies of the image. image. . image in that region. Doing a convolution to the image in the frequency domain with a Laplacian kernel, Fig. 3, L, the corrupted frequencies of the corrupted images with quasi/periodic noise are highlighted, in addition, the image L is used, to replace those pixels with corrupted frequencies and provide the final image restored with this part of the proposed algorithm.

Considering A as an image corrupted by quasi/periodic noise with size $m \times n$, then the origin shifted Fourier transformed image, F of the same size is determined by

$$F(u,v) = \frac{1}{MN} \sum_{x=0}^{M-1} \sum_{y=0}^{N-1} (-1)^{x+y} A(x,y) e^{-j2\pi(\frac{ux}{M}+\frac{vx}{N})}. \quad (1)$$

where $j^2 = -1$ and $(-1)^{x+y}$ denotes the origin shifting operation [11]. Since images are corrupted by periodic/quasi-periodic noises, the corrupted frequencies form regions that stand out when the image is transformed to the frequency domain forming star-shaped regions [14], as Fig. 2 shows. Once the image is transformed to the frequency domain, the detection and correction of the corrupted regions begin for the restoration of the corrupted image.

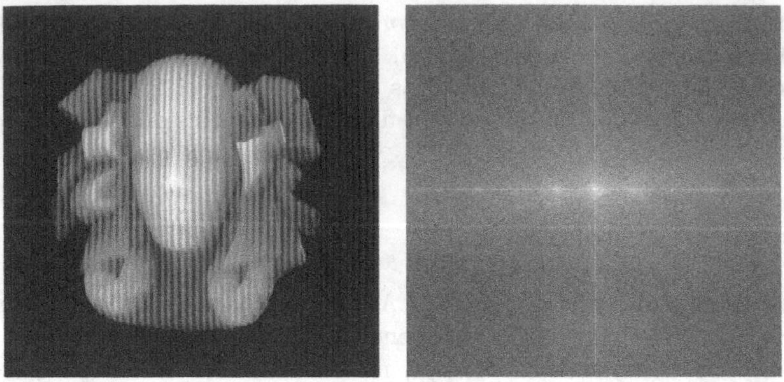

(a) (b)

Fig. 2. a) Image with periodic noise in the spatial domain. b) Image with periodic noise. It can be seen how the regions where it is affected by the star-shaped periodic noise stand out.

2.1 The Pre-processing Stage

After the image F is converted to the frequency domain, convolution is performed with a 5 × 5 Laplacian kernel, L, to highlight the noisy regions from the background. The Laplacian kernel is shown in Fig. 3. The convolution operation of the image in the frequency domain is performed mathematically at position (u,v) by

$$L(u,v) = \sum_{ker=-2}^{2} \sum_{ker=-2}^{2} F(u+k, v+l) \times K(3+k, 3+l). \tag{2}$$

-1	-1	-1	-1	-1
-1	-1	-1	-1	-1
-1	-1	24	-1	-1
-1	-1	-1	-1	-1
-1	-1	-1	-1	-1

Fig. 3. 5 × 5 Laplacian kernel [11]

The Laplacian convolved image, L is processed to isolate noisy areas and normalized, so a linear contrast stretching is applied to it by stretching the intensity of the image values to fill the entire dynamic range. The operation is defined by

$$Xnew = \frac{Xinput - Xmin}{Xmax - Xmin} \times 255. \tag{3}$$

Pixels of L with lower values are set to 0 while the high values are assigned to 255. All other values are reassigned following Fig. 3. This final preprocessed frequency domain image is denoted by E, and an example of the same is shown in Fig. 4.

Fig. 4. Contrast-adjusted image to highlight noisy regions.

2.2 Adaptive Peak Detection and Filtering Stage

The adaptive threshold-based noise identification process starts from the top and bottom of the normalized frequency image and traverses the image row by row until they meet in the center of the image to effectively identify the noise frequencies. The algorithm is explained through the following steps.

Step 1: An image of the same size as the normalized image E is created to obtain windows that allow obtaining the mean and maximum of pixel and its neighbors and identifying noisy regions. Initial threshold images $T1 = E$ and $T2 = E$, and a restored frequency domain image $F_th = F$ are fitted. The algorithm starts from the top and the bottom of the image at positions $(m = 1, n = 1)$ and $(m = m, n = 1)$ until converging at the center of the image at position $(m/2, n = n)$. A mask $maskF$ is also created over the image F forming an ellipse of 35 pixels from the center of the image. This region concentrates most of the information of the original image, so it is important that it is not affected.

Step 2: For each pixel at position (row, col) the following steps are executed:

Step 2.1: To adaptively determine the threshold for identifying noisy positions of E, the algorithm finds the $Mean$ of the neighbors of the pixel at position $Mean(T1(row-1 : row+1, col-1 : col+1).*(row-1 : row+1, col-1 : col+1))$ and the $Maximum$ of the threshold values at position $Maximum(T1(row - 1 : row + 1, col - 1 : col + 1). * (row - 1 : row + 1, col - 1 : col + 1))$.

By analyzing $Mean$ and $Maximum$, the following is concluded:

Case 1: If $Maximum$ corresponds to an uncorrupted frequency and its value is less than $Mean$, then $Maximum$ is the better choice for being the threshold value since it has the least frequency.

Case 2: If $Maximum$ corresponds to an uncorrupted frequency and its value is higher than $Mean$, then $Maximum$ is the better choice for the threshold value.

Case 3: If $Maximum$ corresponds to a corrupted frequency value, then $Mean$ is the better choice for threshold value since $Maximum$ obviously is a very high value.

To facilitate the selection, a multiplicative parameter alpha is included to decide the purity state of frequency value at position (row, col) as $T2 = \alpha \times Minimum(m1, m2)$. α is a multiplicative parameter that is used to ensure that the surface generated by T is always on top of the uncorrupted version of E.

Step 2.2: If the value of the pixel at position (row, col) of the image E is greater than the value obtained with the multiplicative parameter α, it is determined that the frequency value at that position is corrupted and is replaced by the value $Minimum$ of its neighbors at position $F\_th(row, col) = min(min(F\_th(row - 2 : row + 2, col - 2 : col + 2)))$. Otherwise, the value at that position is preserved as it is in the original $F\_th(row, col)$ image.

Step 3: Once all the pixels in the row are processed, it moves on to the next row and the process of step 2 begins.

Step 4: If the center of the image $(ay/2)$ is reached on both the top and the bottom sides, the algorithm stops.

Step 5: When the algorithm stops, the mask $maskF$ is added with the restored frequency domain image.

The image showing the identified noisy regions of E that need to be restored is shown in Fig. 5.

Fig. 5. Image with corrupted regions identified in the frequency domain.

Step 6: A smoothing filter is applied to the restored image after being converted to the spatial domain to improve the attenuation of noisy regions. The kernel used for this operation is shown in Fig. 6.

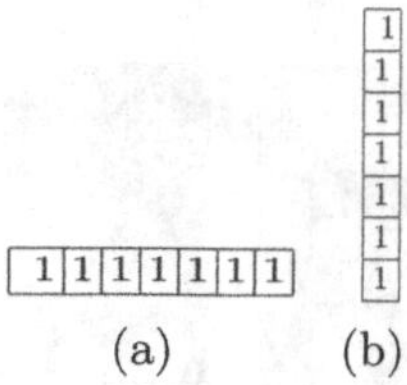

Fig. 6. a) 1 × 7 horizontal kernel. b) 1 × 7 vertical kernel [11].

When the restoration process concludes in the frequency domain, the restored image is transformed back to the spatial domain by applying an inverse Fourier transform. Then, to achieve better noise attenuation, a smoothing filter is applied in the spatial domain with the kernel shown in Fig. 6. The final restored image shows a better attenuation of periodic noise compared to the original image, as Fig. 7 shows.

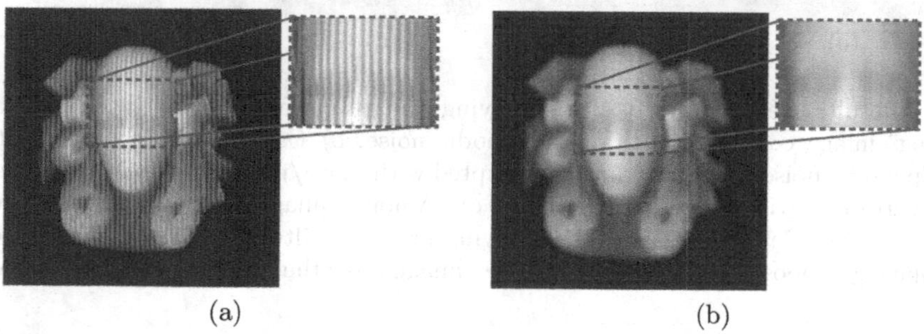

Fig. 7. a) Image corrupted before quasi/periodic noise filtering. b) Image corrupted after quasi/periodic noise filtering.

3 Experiments and Results

The performance of the algorithm is compared with ATBF [14], Cross Filter [15], and Smoothing Filter [11]. The experiments and tests were carried out in Matlab R2020b on Microsoft Windows 10 platform with an i7-10750H processor at 2.60hz speed and an NVIDIA GeForce RTX 3060 Laptop GPU. The tests were performed on a set of 15 synthetically and non-synthetically created corrupted images from which Claw (540 × 539), Among (540 × 539), Cat (540 × 539), and Turtle (540 × 539) were taken for analysis in this paper. The comparison was made with IMMSE (Image Media Square Error), PSNR (Peak Signal-to-Noise Ratio), SSIM (Structural Similarity Index) [23], and MSE (Profile) using image profiles as shown in Tables 1, 2, 3 and 4. The results of the performance for such images are shown in Fig. 8.

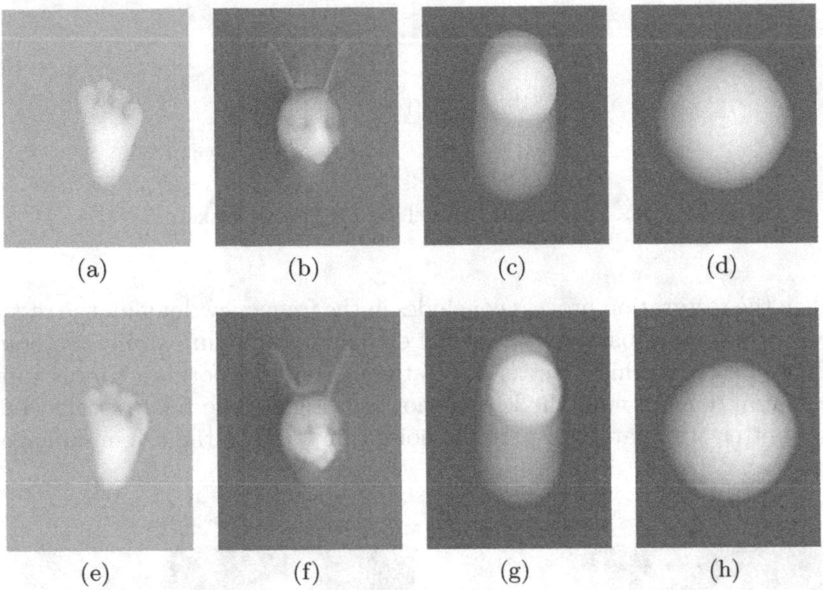

Fig. 8. Results were obtained after applying the proposed filtering algorithm. a) "Among" image corrupted with quasi/periodic noise, b) "Cat" image corrupted with quasi/periodic noise, c) "Claw" image corrupted with quasi/periodic noise, d) "Turtle" image corrupted with quasi/periodic noise, e) "Among" image after applying the proposed filter, f) "Cat" image after the applying proposed filter, g) "Claw" image after the applying proposed filter, and h) "Turtle" image after the applying proposed filter.

Taking the "Claw" image for a more detailed observation with each filter used for comparison, the performance of the algorithm can be observed. A visual analysis clearly shows how the quasi/periodic noise is blurred from the synthetically corrupted image as shown in Fig. 9 where the original synthetically corrupted "Claw" image 9a is shown, in 9b the output of the corrupted image is shown after applying the ATBF filter, in 9c the output of the corrupted image is shown after applying the cross filter, in 9d shows the output of the corrected image after applying the smoothing filter, and in 9e the proposed filter.

Table 1. Metrics are produced by different filters applied to the "Claw" image.

Filters	PSNR	IMMSE	SSIM	MSE (Profile)
Proposed Filter	**26.9915**	**0.0020**	**0.9774**	**0.0110**
ATBF	27.1032	0.0019	0.9749	0.0112
Cross Filter	27.0722	0.0020	0.9747	0.0113
Smoothing Filter	26.9086	0.0020	0.9772	0.0114

Table 2. Metrics are produced by different filters applied to "Among" image.

Filters	PSNR	IMMSE	SSIM	MSE (Profile)
Proposed Filter	**20.0729**	**0.0098**	**0.9626**	**0.0037**
ATBF	20.1021	0.0098	0.9571	0.0038
Cross Filter	20.0741	0.0098	0.9525	0.0040
Smoothing Filter	20.0845	0.0098	0.9633	0.0039

Table 3. Metrics are produced by different filters applied to "Cat" image.

Filters	PSNR	IMMSE	SSIM	MSE (Profile)
Proposed Filter	**21.5975**	**0.0069**	**0.9453**	**0.0082**
ATBF	21.5982	0.0069	0.9433	0.0086
Cross Filter	21.5907	0.0069	0.9435	0.0085
Smoothing Filter	21.5908	0.0069	0.9455	0.0084

Table 4. Metrics are produced by different filters applied to "Turtle" image.

Filters	PSNR	IMMSE	SSIM	MSE (Profile)
Proposed Filter	**22.6388**	**0.0054**	**0.9481**	**0.0148**
ATBF	22.6400	0.0054	0.9411	0.0150
Cross Filter	22.6345	0.0055	0.9342	0.0148
Smoothing Filter	22.6341	0.0055	0.9487	0.0151

Although the values of the metrics obtained by the proposed PSNR and IMMSE algorithm may be slightly lower than the other algorithms used for comparison, it is observed, however, that it stands out in the SSIM and MSE (profile), these being indicative of visual quantification, which is desired to be larger, since it means that the image obtained is similar to the ground truth. A profile analysis of the Claw image with attenuated quasi/periodic noise is also performed with the proposed filter to measure the mean square error and is compared with the outputs of the filters used for comparison as shown in Fig. 10. It is also compared with the ground-truth profile and the unfiltered corrupted image Claw. High values of PSNR and SSIM show that an algorithm

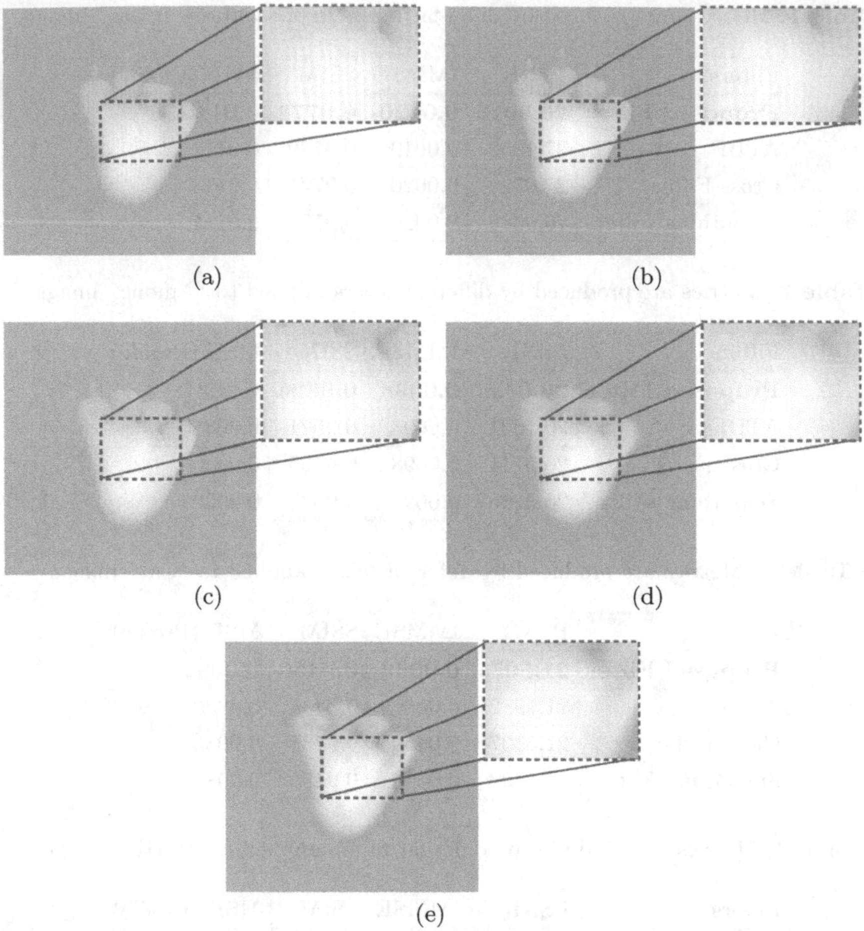

Fig. 9. a) Synthetic image corrupted with quasi-periodic noise filtering. b) Synthetic image corrupted with quasi-periodic noise after applying ATBF filter, c) Cross Filter, e) Smooth Filter and e) The proposed filter.

provides good results. However, since the objective of this paper is to provide an algorithm that significantly reduces the quasi/periodic noise of images obtained by fringe projection to obtain 3D information about objects, it is verified that the outputs of the different filters applied to compete with the proposed algorithm outperform slightly the proposed algorithm. But a visual analysis reveals that there are regions where the quasi/periodic noise that it is intended to eliminate is still perceptible. This is demonstrated when performing a 3D reconstruction with the outputs of the used filters and comparing them with the proposed filter and the ground truth.

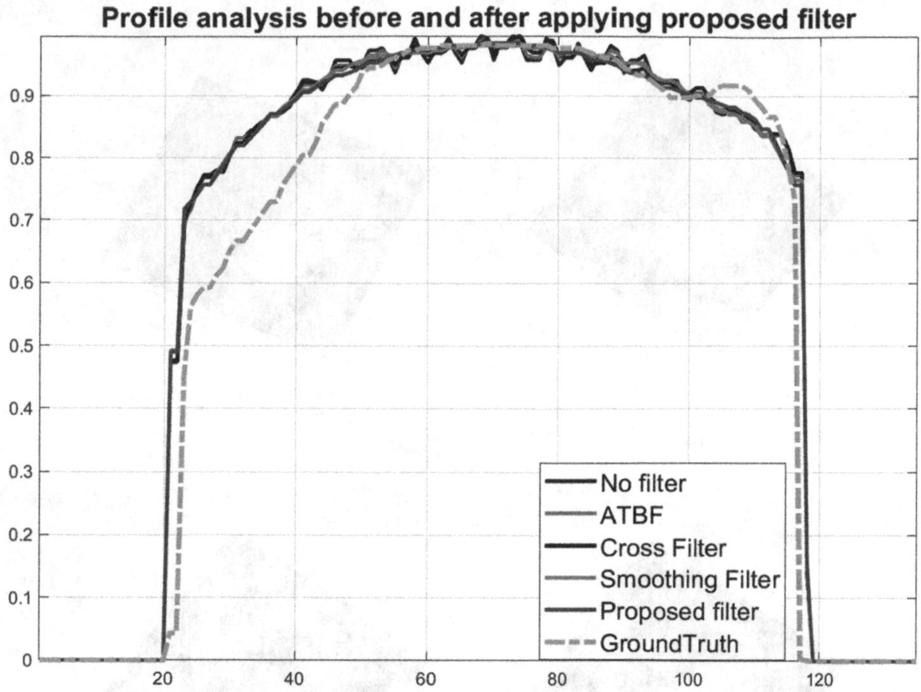

Fig. 10. Proposed algorithm profile analysis and comparison algorithms.

When a profile of the filtered image is analyzed with the filters used and the proposed filter, the performance of the proposed algorithm stands out from the others and it is observed how the mean square error decreases, with which a better 3D information of the objects is obtained. An analysis of the 3D reconstructions with the image shown in Fig. 11 allows us to visually appreciate the performance of the proposed filter and the filters used for comparison, and it is observed how the reconstruction provided by the output of the proposed filter shows a smoother and more precise texture.

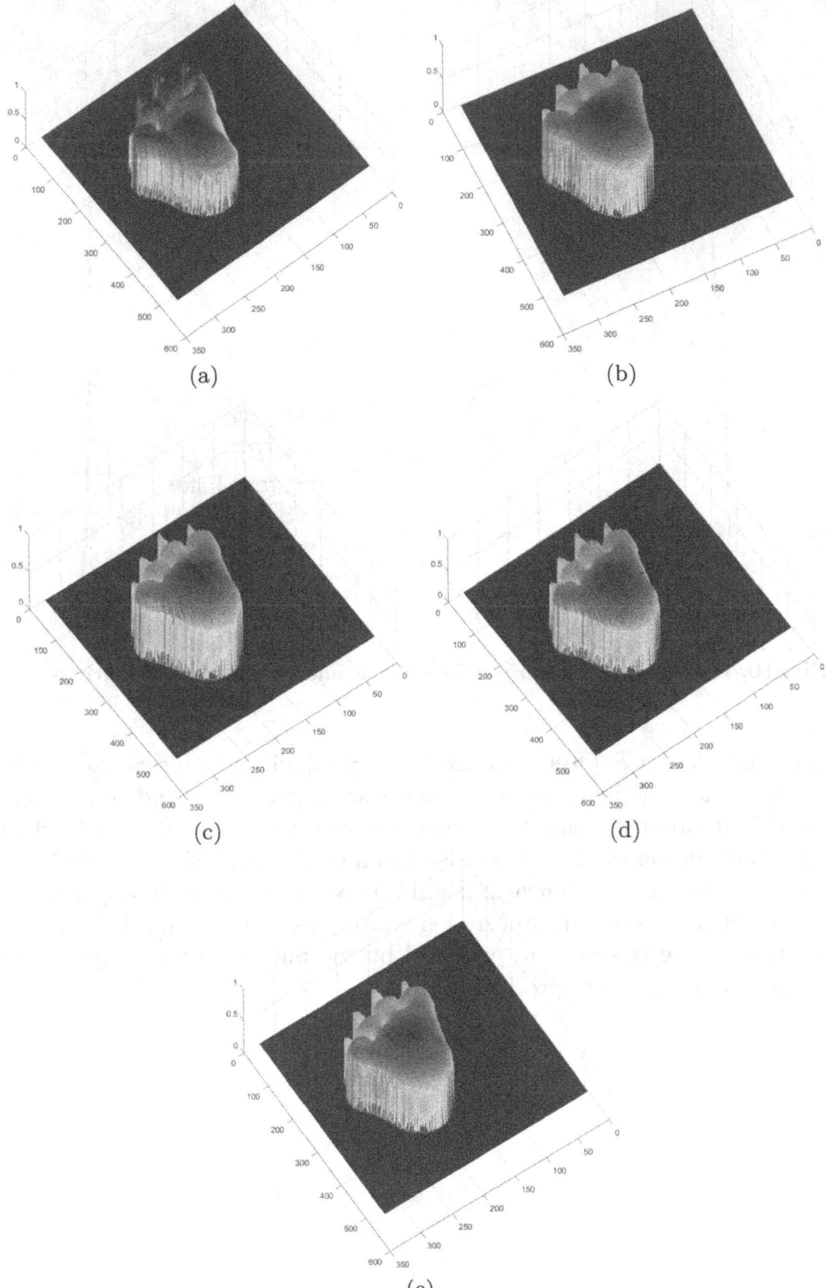

Fig. 11. a) Object reconstructed in 3D from a synthetic ground-truth image, b) With noise quasi/periodic attenuated by a smooth filter, c) Cross filter, d) ATBF filter and e) Proposed filter

4 Conclusions and Future Work

The article presented a filter based on the frequency domain and also a filter based on the spatial domain in order to reduce the periodic or quasi/periodic noise that occurs in images obtained by fringe projection. The proposed algorithm determines the corrupted frequencies in the frequency domain of an image with quasi/periodic noise and replaces the corrupted pixels with the mean of their neighboring pixels, then a smoothing filter is applied in the spatial frequency domain to attenuate the noise present. The tests carried out with synthetic and non-synthetic images showed that the algorithm is capable of reducing the noise present in the images. Although the quantitative results do not show a significant improvement, the qualitative results are better since they show high precision in 3D information.

In future work, we hope to make use of convolutional neural networks to improve the results obtained and automate the task of filtering corrupted images with quasi/periodic noise.

Acknowledgments. This work was supported in part by the Consejo Nacional de Ciencia y Tecnoloía (CONACyT), México, in the Postgraduate Faculty of Engineering by the Autonomous University of Queretaro, under Grant CVU 1099050 and CVU 1099400.

References

1. Feuerstein, D., Parker, K.H., Boutelle, M.G.: Practical methods for noise removal: applications to spikes, nonstationary quasi-periodic noise, and baseline drift. Anal. Chem. **81**(12), 4987–4994 (2009)
2. Fehrenbach, J., Weiss, P., Lorenzo, C.: Variational algorithms to remove stationary noise: applications to microscopy imaging. IEEE Trans. Image Process. **21**(10), 4420–4430 (2012)
3. Ji, Z., Ming, Z., Li, Q., Wu, Q.: Reducing periodic noise using soft morphology filter. J. Electron. **21**(2), 159–162 (2004)
4. Ji, T.Y., Lu, Z., Wu, Q.H.: Optimal soft morphological filter for periodic noise removal using a particle swarm optimiser with passive congregation. Signal Process. **87**(11), 2799–2809 (2007)
5. Rai, A.: An empirical study of periodic noise filtering in Fourier domain: an introduction to novel autonomous periodic noise removal algorithms. In: LAP Lambert Academic Publishing (2013)
6. Srinivasan, R., Cannon, M., White, J.: Landsat data destriping using power spectral filtering. Opt. Eng. **27**(11), 939–943 (1988)
7. Lebrun, M., Colom, M., Buades, A., Morel, J.M.: Secrets of image denoising cuisine. Acta Numer. **21**, 475–576 (2012)
8. Milanfar, P.: A tour of modern image filtering: new insights and methods, both practical and theoretical. IEEE Signal Process. Mag. **30**(1), 106–128 (2012)
9. Aizenberg, I., Butakoff, C.: A windowed Gaussian notch filter for quasi-periodic noise removal. Image Vis. Comput. **26**(10), 1347–1353 (2008)
10. Moallem, P., Masoumzadeh, M., Habibi, M.: A novel adaptive Gaussian restoration filter for reducing periodic noises in digital image. SIViP **9**(5), 1179–1191 (2015)

11. Gonzalez, C.R., Richard, E.: Digital image processing, 4th edn. Pearson Education, New Jersey (2008)
12. Sun, Y., Yu, Y., Wang, W.: Moire Photo Restoration Using Multiresolution Convolutional Neural Networks. IEEE Trans. Image Process. **27**(8), 4160–4172, (2018). https://doi.org/10.1109/TIP.2018.2834737
13. Wei, Z., Wang, J., Nichol, H., Wiebe, S., Chapman, D.: A median gaussian filtering framework for Moire patterns noise removal from X-ray microscopy image (2011). https://doi.org/10.1016/j.micron.2011.07.009
14. Varghese J.: Adaptive threshold based frequency domain filter for periodic noise reduction. AEU - Int. J. Electron Commun. **70**(12), 1692–1701 (2016). https://doi.org/10.1016/j.aeue.2016.10.008
15. Alvarado Escoto, L.A., Ortega, J.C.P., Ramos Arreguin, J.M., Gorrostieta Hurtado, E., Tovar Arriaga, S.: The effect of bilateral filtering in 3D reconstruction using PSP. In: Mata-Rivera, M.F., Zagal-Flores, R., Barria-Huidobro, C. (eds.) WITCOM 2020. CCIS, vol. 1280, pp. 268–280. Springer, Cham (2020). https://doi.org/10.1007/978-3-030-62554-2_20
16. Simonyan, K., Zisserman, A.: Very deep convolutional networks for large-scale image recognition. arXiv preprint arXiv:1409.1556 (2014)
17. Szegedy, C., et al.: Going deeper with convolutions. In: Proceedings of the IEEE Conference on Computer Vision and Pattern Recognition, pp. 1–9 (2015)
18. Zhang, K., Zuo, W., Chen, Y., Meng, D., Zhang, L.: Beyond a gaussian denoiser: residual learning of deep CNN for image denoising. IEEE Trans. Image Process. **26**(7), 3142–3155 (2017)
19. Krizhevsky, A., Sutskever, I., Hinton, G.E.: ImageNet classification with deep convolutional neural networks. In: Advances in Neural Information Processing Systems 25 (2012)
20. Dong, C., Loy, C.C., He, K., Tang, X.: Learning a deep convolutional network for image super-resolution. In: Fleet, D., Pajdla, T., Schiele, B., Tuytelaars, T. (eds.) ECCV 2014. LNCS, vol. 8692, pp. 184–199. Springer, Cham (2014). https://doi.org/10.1007/978-3-319-10593-2_13
21. Gharbi, M., Chaurasia, G., Paris, S., Durand, F.: Deep joint demosaicking and denoising. ACM Trans. Graph. (ToG) **35**(6), 1–12 (2016)
22. Zhang, K., Zuo, W., Gu, S., Zhang, L.: Learning deep CNN denoiser prior for image restoration. In: Proceedings of the IEEE Conference on Computer Vision and Pattern Recognition, pp. 3929–3938 (2017)
23. Wang, Z., Bovik, A.C., Sheikh, H.R., Simoncelli, E.P.: Image quality assessment: from error visibility to structural similarity. IEEE Trans. Image Process. **13**(4), 600–612 (2004)
24. Karacan, L., Erdem, E., Erdem, A.: Structure-preserving image smoothing via region covariances. ACM Trans. Graph. (TOG) **32**(6), 1–11 (2013)
25. Ono, S., Miyata, T., Yamada, I.: Cartoon-texture image decomposition using blockwise low-rank texture characterization. IEEE Trans. Image Process. **23**(3), 1128–1142 (2014)
26. Ok, J., Youn, S., Seo, G., Choi, E., Baek, Y., Lee, C.: Paper check image quality enhancement with Moire reduction. Multimedia Tools Appl. **76**(20), 21423–21450 (2017)

A Study on the Behavior of Different Low-Cost Particle Counter Sensors for PM-10 and PM-2.5 Suspended Air Particles

Raúl Emiliano Gómez Trejo[1], Bernardo Buitrón Rossainz[2], Jorge Alfredo García Torres[1], and Antonio Hernández Zavala[1(✉)]

[1] Instituto Politécnico Nacional, CICATA-IPN Unidad Querétaro, 76146 Querétaro, Mexico
jgarciat2002@alumno.ipn.mx, anhernandezz@ipn.mx

[2] Vórtice IT Clúster Querétaro, El Marqués, 76267 Querétaro, Mexico
direccion@vorticeit.mx

Abstract. Particulate matter refers to suspended particles in the air that was responsible for 1.2 million deaths in the world in 2012, raising this number to 10 million by 2021. For this reason, air quality becomes a major interest area for governments in developed and undeveloped countries due to its high mortality rate. The air quality in the majority of cities around the world is getting worst given the exponential growth of population and their necessities. Some studies show the relation of high concentrations of PM to many negative effects on human health regarding respiratory diseases. There is a worldwide increase in the usage of low-cost sensor technology for the construction of portable air pollution measuring stations to support the official stations. In this paper, we present a study to analyze the performance of three commercial particle counter sensors with similar characteristics. The experiment required a system in which the sensors are simultaneously measured and the data is sent to a visualization interface for IoT. Both measurements PM-2.5 and PM-10 are statistically analyzed to prove the trend and show the behavior in particular locations in Queretaro City. For comparing the sensor measurements obtained, a commercial particle counter instrument was employed as a reference. The sensors presented a similar behavior for which it becomes necessary to realize some comparisons. The worst performance is by the Plantower PMS3003S sensor, which has the lower determination coefficient and the higher Root Mean Squared Error values. In contrast, the best performance is by the Sensirion SPS030 sensor.

Keywords: Air pollution · Air quality sensing · Data acquisition · Internet of Things · Low-cost sensors · Particulate matter

1 Particulate Matter in Air Pollution

According to data from the World Health Organization [1], 3 million deaths were caused by ambient air pollution (AAP) in 2012. By 2019, there were 4.5M deaths only outdoors and a total of 6.67M in the world [2]. These numbers raised in 2020 to 8M deaths

M. F. Mata-Rivera et al. (Eds.): WITCOM 2022, CCIS 1659, pp. 33–50, 2022.
https://doi.org/10.1007/978-3-031-18082-8_3

worldwide according to the World Health Organization. Where 4.2M corresponds to outdoor exposure and 3.8M to indoor exposure, remarking that 91% of people in the world live where the air quality exceeds the established limits [3]. Those numbers are low according to the 8.8M estimated by the European Heart Journal in the same year [4]. There were 800k deaths only in Europe [5]. By 2021, Bloomberg estimated that 10 million people would die because of air pollution [6].

This is the reason that air quality becomes a major interest area for governments in both developed and undeveloped countries due to its high mortality rate. The air quality in the majority of cities around the world is deteriorating as the amount of traffic, overpopulation, destruction of forests, and unregulated industrial activities are increasing given the insatiable human appetite for consumption.

Among the different pollutants, particulate matter (PM) refers to suspended particles in the air, which are divided into two main categories: coarse particles, which are larger than 2.5 μm in diameter (PM-10), and fine particles, which are smaller than 2.5 μm (PM-2.5). Particulate matter originates from natural or anthropogenic sources [7]. Natural sources are wildfires, dust storms, or gaseous sulfur from volcanoes. By anthropogenic sources, we understand artificial sources like coal combustion for energy generation, as well as industrial activities, the huge number of cars circulating at the same time, and livestock farming among others.

It is important to notice the close relationship between the size of particulate matter and its potential harm to human health [8–10]. Some studies show the relation of high concentrations of PM to many negative effects on human health regarding respiratory diseases like deterioration of lung function, worsening of asthma symptoms, allergic reactions, and airway obstruction [9]. One easy way to improve air quality is to reduce traffic and industrial activities [11], but it is not an easy job to identify the sources given that urban physiography is very diverse.

Today, there is a wealth of air quality information available on websites and apps. The data for such portals originates from different monitoring stations, mainly government-owned. The most common instruments used to monitor particulate matter are ß-ray attenuation (BAMs) and tapered element-oscillating microbalances (TEOMs). Such instruments are capable of obtaining hourly and daily readings, in an accurate way. However, for a massive application where many monitoring stations are required in order to generate hyperlocal monitoring to identify the sources such instruments are not suitable because of their high cost.

For that reason, there is a large number of on-the-shelf small devices capable of measuring the particulate matter concentration at different prices according to the application necessities. These devices are based on the laser scattered light measuring principle in which the particles are transported inward with the help of a low-power fan. Another important factor to consider is the low-power consumption since most of them require a 5 V power supply with an active current of around 100–200 mA. Nonetheless, optical sensors have to be calibrated with a reference instrument under the final conditions such as weather, temperature, location, and season of the year [12–14].

In this paper, we present a study to analyze the performance of three commercial particle counter sensors with similar characteristics. The experiment required setting up a system in which the three particle counter sensors are measured simultaneously, and the data is sent to an internet visualization interface for IoT. Both measurements PM-2.5 and PM-10 are analyzed statistically in order to prove the trend and show the behavior in particular locations in Queretaro City. In order to compare the sensor measurements obtained, a HoldPeak HP-5800D Particle counter instrument was employed.

2 Current Usage of Low-Cost Sensors for Air Quality Measurement Support

There is a worldwide increase in the usage of low-cost sensor technology for the construction of portable air pollution measuring stations to support the official stations. It shall be taken into account that a single low-cost sensor should not be deployed individually, therefore, collocating multiple sensors in a single station provide data redundancy in order to facilitate outliers or error detection in measurements, ensuring full data coverage [17]. However, low-cost particle matter sensors should not be used for government regulatory applications. So, it is reasonable to use them in an informative way to present a non-official value for the particle mass concentrations in the air throughout the day, in order to let the final user, know the ongoing air quality [19].

According to different studies [12, 15, 18], there is a better correlation between the sensors and the reference instruments in relation to the measurements of PM-2.5 as opposed to PM-10. Furthermore, an edge computing and IoT architecture system can be deployed, as recommended in [21]. Their system consists of three layers: the sensing layer consists of acquiring the data provided by the sensors. The edge-computing layer consists of gathering the data and sending it to the application layer. The application layer, which is the channel where the final user will be able to receive the data in real-time, can be either a database for storing the information or a data scientist that will analyze the information.

The trend of the output from SDS011 and PMS3003S sensors have a high linear relationship when compared with a TEOM according to different studies presented in [14–16]. Remarking that these sensors were precise in terms of reproducibility between the same units indicates that those two sensors are suitable when for dense monitoring networks. Another study [16], demonstrated that SDS011 sensors present a high linearity response against official reference instruments in concentrations of PM-2.5, also demonstrating that high relative humidity (RH $>$ 80%) negatively affected the measurements. Low-cost sensors demonstrated that they are useful for the assessment of short-term changes in the air [15].

In cities where connectivity is a problem, Steven J. states that air quality monitoring is possible using the LoRaWAN technology [20]. Remarking that coverage is not an obstacle since it is capable of receiving and transmitting data in an entire city, considering that the messages using that infrastructure were received at distances over 12 km. However, many different things should be considered such as current environmental conditions or in the case of LoRaWAN the Spreading Factor, since different values represent better or worse reliable received or sent data.

There is a recent interest in using low-cost sensors for air quality monitoring as presented in the paper [22] they made a sampling by using low-cost technology at an urban district of Germany with samples in September and march, observing that there are seasonal variances, increasing the measures during spring. In the work [23], they analyzed the performance of 30 community-maintained, indoor and outdoor low-cost sensors at a California university campus. They found highly temporal correlation and spatially homogeneous measures. Finally, in the work [24], they realized a one-year study in Malawi, with low-cost sensors. They found that this period did not affect the sensor performance, but relativity humidity does. So is a variable that affects the measurements.

2.1 The Optical Particle Counter Detection Principle

Optical particle counters are the most used sensing technologies for PM2.5 and 10 at low volume. Their main advantages are their ability to sample particles in real time, they don't require preparation of the sample before its collection, the detection limits are wide for large particles, and their size is optimal for portable instruments. In the study of [25] the optical scattered counters presented the best accuracy. Besides their low cost, so they were found to be the optimal for our application. The enhancements for scattered light-based sensors, are focused on enhancing the measurements by changing the position of lenses and detectors as in [26].

All the sensors utilized in this experiment work using the laser light scattering principle from Fig. 1. It consists of the following: first, a fan is responsible for allowing the samples to enter the measuring chamber through a cavity. Second, since the particulate matter passes through the laser beam, it will scatter the light proportionately to their quantity. Third, a photodetector will measure the amount of light received which is reflected by the particles, hence the remainder of the total amount transferred. Fourth, a microprocessor converts the light measurements to particulate matter concentration, measured in micrograms per cubic meter, utilizing a process called "Lorenz-Mie Theory" [27].

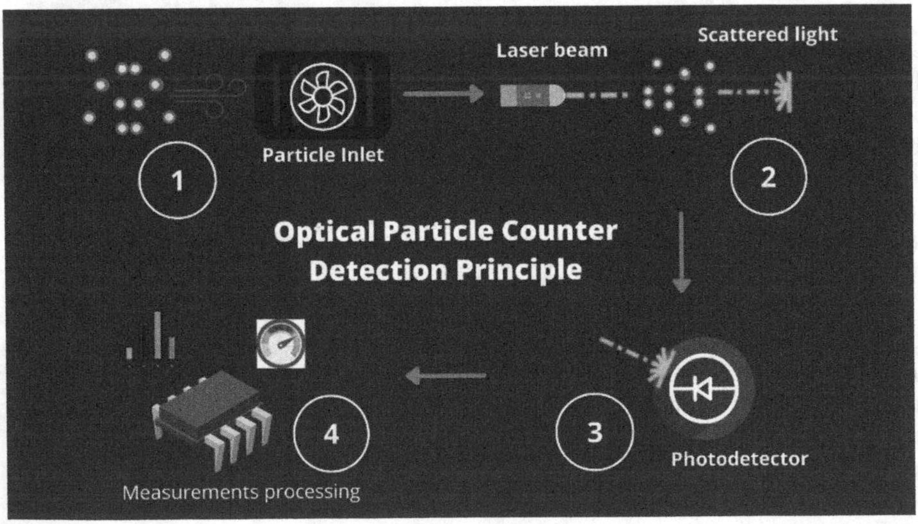

Fig. 1. Light scattering principle.

2.2 Low-Cost Sensors for PM-10 and PM-2.5 Particulate Matter

The particle counter sensors used in this experiment are the Plantower PMS3003S, Nova SDS011, and Sensirion SPS030. These sensors come in compact sizes, are lightweight, have low power consumption and provide PM-2.5 and PM-10 measures. Such sensors are propitious to be deployed in the outdoor environment in terms of their size, cost, and ease of use. Their main operating characteristics are summarized in Table 1. It is possible to identify that all the sensors use a similar power source (5v), serial communication (UART), and measuring range (0–1000 µg/m^3).

Table 1. Main characteristics of the particulate matter sensors employed

	PMS3003S	SPS030	SDS011
Protocol	UART 9600	UART 115200 I2C standard	UART 9600
Error	±10%@100~500µ g/m³ ±10µ g/m³ @ 0~100 µg/m³	PM1 & PM2.5 → 0 a 100 µg/m³ = ±10 µg/m³ PM4 & PM10 → 0 a 100 µg/m³= ±25 µg/m³	Max 15% & ±10µg/m³
Measuring range	0~1000 µg/m³	0 - 1000 µg/m³	0-999.9 µg/m³
Power consumption	5V - 100 mA active state 200 µA en Standby	5V - Max 80 mA max 50 µA Sleep Mode	5V - 70 mA < 4 mA
Response time	Simple response 1s Total response 10s	1 ± 0.4 s	1s
Lifetime	> 3 years till failure	10 years – 24 hrs operation	>8000 hrs
Particle sizes	PM1.0, PM2.5 & PM10	PM1.0, PM2.5, PM4 & PM10	PM2.5 y PM10
Working temperature	-10 ºC to 60 ºC	-10 ºC to 60 ºC	-10 ºC to 50 ºC

3 The PM-10 and PM-2.5 Data Acquisition System

The developed data acquisition system for PM-2.5 and PM-10 particulate matter is comprised of a Plantower PMS3003S sensor, a Nova SDS011 sensor, and a Sensirion SPS030 sensor. The block diagram for the whole system is presented in Fig. 2. Each sensor must be read by an ESP32 data acquisition board, for which it was necessary to include a 74151 multiplexor for measuring each sensor at different times using the same serial port available in the board providing shared time to each sensor. A measure is comprised of the PM-2.5 and PM-10 values for each sensor, so we have six samples and the time and date for that sample. Once a measure is complete, it is sent through the internet to the host computer in which we collect the samples and store them in column format for further processing and analysis.

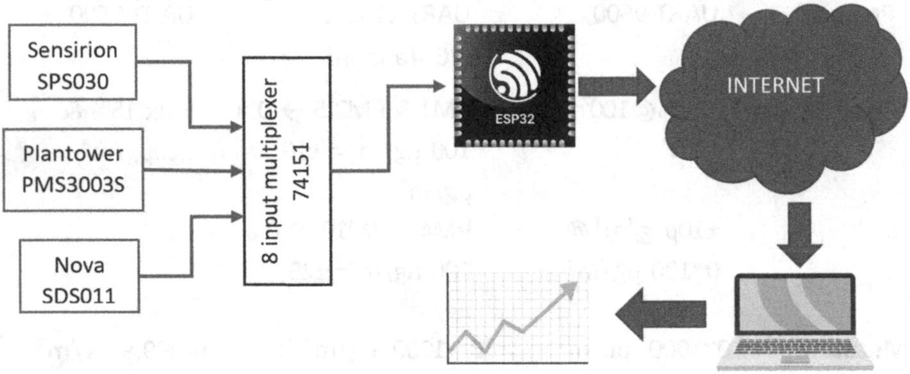

Fig. 2. Block diagram of the data acquisition system.

3.1 Data Transmission

The ESP32 board is memory limited for storing all the measures since it has 448 KB of ROM and 520 KB RAM which is not capable of storing data without an external module. For this reason, it was necessary to transmit all the data through the internet to a desktop computer for data storage and further analysis. The ESP32 board is equipped with a Wi-Fi 802.11 b/g/n peripheral that allows the application to be connected to a wide physical area and the internet through a Wi-Fi router. The data is transmitted via the Message Queuing Telemetry Transport protocol MQTT to a specific and secure server, known as the broker. In order to request the transmission of the data through that server, a user and password are required since security is a priority for the application. Right after publishing data to a specific topic on the server, a client on a remote site is subscribed to the specific topics in order to retrieve the full dataset.

3.2 Data Storage

In an effort to analyze the whole dataset, it is required to be capable of downloading the full spectrum of data at any given moment. To do so, every time the data acquisition board gets data from each sensor, the data is transmitted via MQTT to two different destinies. The first one is the proprietary database for the purpose of storing the data in a secure way; its development is by using SQL Server 2019 developer edition. The second one is for testing the data storage and processing in the cloud using the Thingspeak server.

4 The PM-2.5 and PM-10 Measuring Experiment

In order to test our instrument, we realized two data acquisition experiments at different locations. During those periods, PM-2.5 and PM-10 measurements were taken, using the three different low-cost particulate matter sensors in one single station.

4.1 First Experiment: Free Run Sampling

The first experiment was during 5 weeks in San Pedrito los Arcos, Querétaro, México. This location was selected since we required to continuously measuring while physically supervising the functioning of the equipment and there, we had those facilities. From May 30 to July 2 obtaining 29161 samples per sensor in free-run mode. Given that during some periods, some glitches were detected as noise, and it must be cleaned. Therefore, data cleaning techniques were applied with a focus on presenting more reliable data for PM-2.5 particles as shown in Fig. 3, where there is still a noisy signal, but it is much more representative. As result, we conserved 27610 useful samples to perform the analysis.

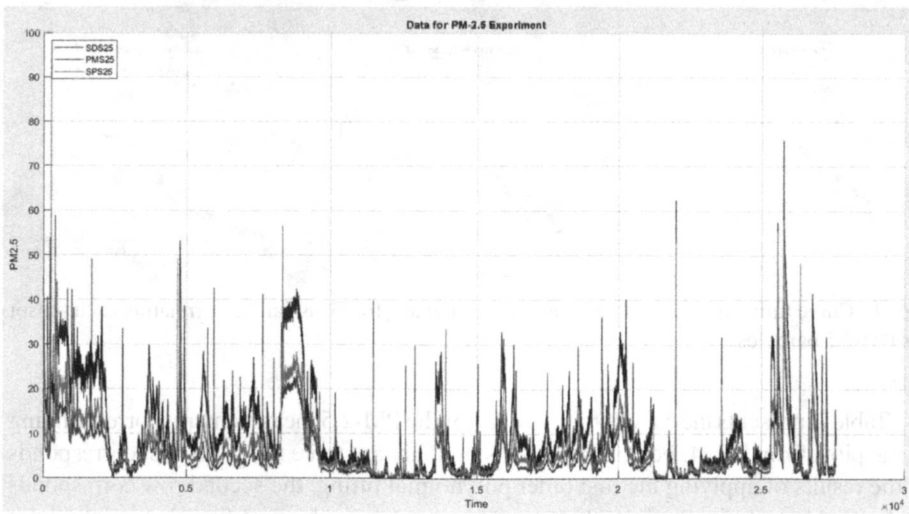

Fig. 3. Results of PM-2.5 measurements from the three sensors in the period from May 30 to July 2, 2021.

Curve fitting analysis was also realized for comparing the sensors with each other as presented in Fig. 4. The first row corresponds to the first order polynomial fit that uses Eq. (1) for the approximation. The measurements are from PM-2.5 particles, the plot from the left corresponds to the PMS3003S and SDS011 relation, the plot in the center corresponds to the SDS011 and SPS030 relation and the plot on the right corresponds to the PMS3003S and SPS030 relation. The second row corresponds to the Gaussian fit that uses Eq. (2) for the approximation. The measurements are for PM-2.5 particles, the plot from the left corresponds to the PMS3003S and SDS011 relation, the plot in the center corresponds to the SDS011 and SPS030 relation and the plot in the right corresponds to the PMS3003S and SPS030 relation.

$$f(x) = a_1 x + b_1 \tag{1}$$

$$f(x) = a_1 e^{-\left(\frac{x-b_1}{c_1}\right)^2} \tag{2}$$

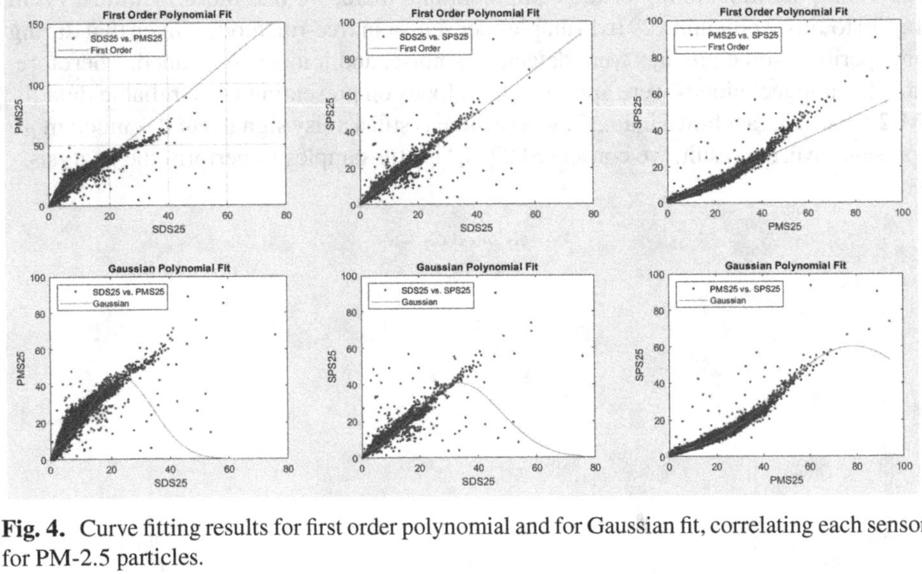

Fig. 4. Curve fitting results for first order polynomial and for Gaussian fit, correlating each sensor for PM-2.5 particles.

Table 2, presents the curve fitting results for the PM-2.5 measurements corresponding to the plots from Fig. 4. For each comparison, there are three rows, the first corresponds to the results of applying the first order polynomial fitting, the second row corresponds to the Gaussian fitting and the third row corresponds to the best-fit polynomial whose order is indicated. The column order is as follows: type of fit; the sum of squared errors; the coefficient of determination; the degrees of freedom of the error; the root mean squared error (RMSE); and the a_1, b_1, and c_1 coefficients for the corresponding fit. Notice that those coefficients are not shown for the best fit polynomial given that is a variable number.

Table 2. Curve fitting results for the PM-2.5 measurements (first experiment).

Fit	SSE	R^2	DFE	RMSE	a_1	b_1	c_1
SDS2.5 vs PMS 2.5							
First order polynomial	2.674e+05	0.9025	27607	3.112	1.942	1.893	—
Gauss	4.264e+05	0.8446	27606	3.93	45	23.39	15.43
Best polynomial fit: 4th order	1.241e+05	0.9548	27604	2.12	—	—	—
SPS25 vs PMS 2.5							
First order polynomial	1.531e+05	0.9442	27607	2.355	1.59	0.4691	—
Gauss	3.274e+05	0.8807	27606	3.444	50.88	32.98	20.73
Best polynomial fit: 3rd order	6.178e+04	0.9775	27605	1.496	—	—	—
SDS2.5 vs SPS25							
First order polynomial	6.522e+04	0.9364	20607	1.537	1.209	0.9511	—
Gauss	1.318e+05	0.8714	27606	2.185	40.76	33.36	20.68
Best polynomial fit: 3rd order	5.843e+04	0.943	27605	1.455	—	—	—

For the case of PM-10 suspended particles, there are also 27610 useful samples to perform the analysis after data cleaning as presented in Fig. 5.

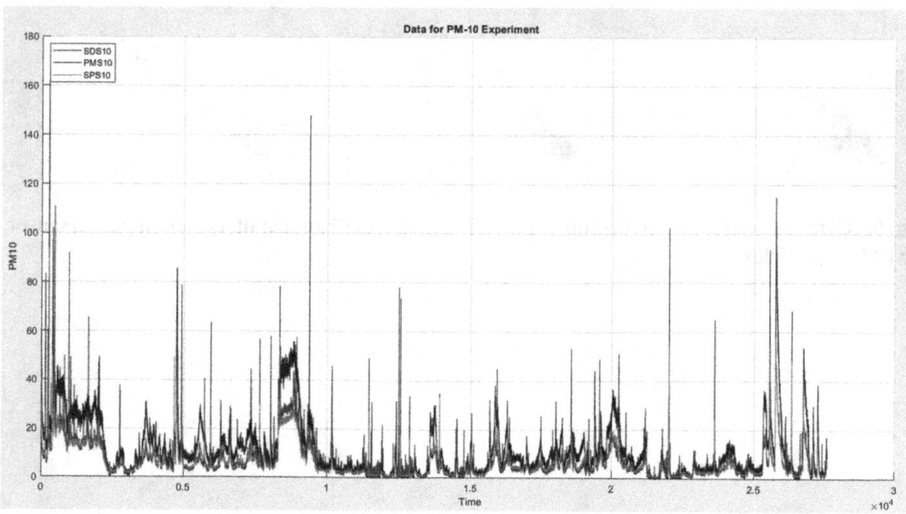

Fig. 5. Results of PM-10 measurements from the three sensors in the period from May 30 to July 2, 2021.

Curve fitting analysis was also realized for comparing the sensors with each other as presented in Fig. 6. The first row corresponds to the first order polynomial fit that uses Eq. (1) for the approximation. The measurements are from PM-10 particles, the plot on the left corresponds to the PMS3003S and SDS011 relation. The plot in the center corresponds to the SDS011 and SPS030 relation and the plot in the right corresponds to the PMS3003S and SPS030 relation. The second row corresponds to the Gaussian fit that uses Eq. (2) for the approximation. The measurements are for PM-10 particles, the plot from the left corresponds to the PMS3003S and SDS011 relation, the plot in the center corresponds to the SDS011 and SPS030 relation and the plot in the right corresponds to the PMS3003S and SPS030 relation.

Table 3, presents the curve fitting results for the PM-10 measurements corresponding to the plots from Fig. 6. For each comparison, there are three rows, the first corresponds to the results of applying the first order polynomial fitting, the second row corresponds to the Gaussian fitting and the third row corresponds to the best-fit polynomial whose order is indicated. The column order is as follows: type of fit; the sum of squared errors; the coefficient of determination; the degrees of freedom of the error; the root mean squared error; and the a_1, b_1, and c_1 coefficients for the corresponding fit. Notice that those coefficients are not shown for the best fit polynomial given that is a variable number.

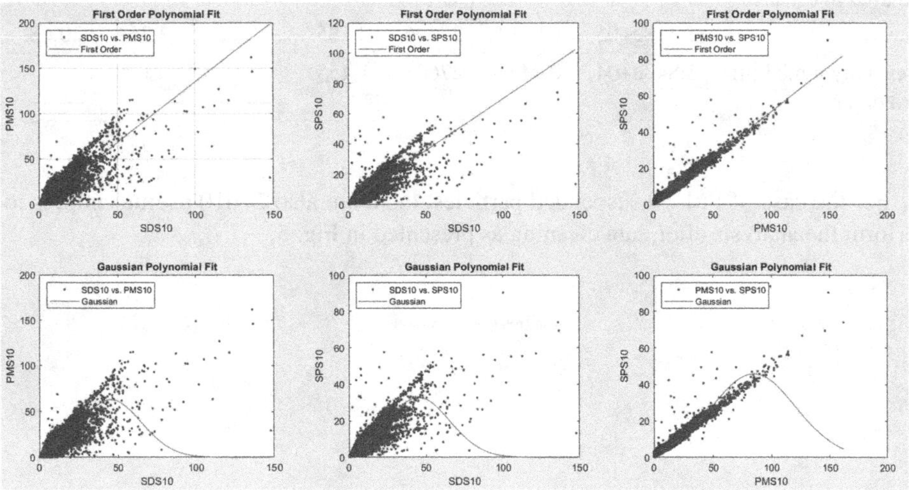

Fig. 6. Curve fitting results for first order polynomial and for Gaussian fit, correlating each sensor for PM-10 particles.

Table 3. Curve fitting results for the PM-10 measurements (first experiment).

Fit	SSE	R^2	DFE	RMSE	a_1	b_1	c_1
SDS10 vs. PMS10							
First order polynomial	9.252e+05	0.7668	27607	5.789	1.33	1.608	—
Gauss	1.167e+06	0.7058	27606	6.502	63.02	45.08	28.27
Best polynomial fit: 3rd order	7.925e+05	0.8002	27605	5.358	—	—	—
SPS10 vs. PMS10							
First order polynomial	1.198e+05	0.9698	27607	2.083	1.933	−0.7194	—
Gauss	4.284e+05	0.892	27606	3.939	86.13	43.04	25.2
Best polynomial fit: 2nd order	2.083	0.9711	27606	2.038	—	—	—
SDS10 vs. SPS10							
First order polynomial	2.304e+05	0.7762	27607	2.889	0.6818	1.251	—
Gauss	2.821e+05	0.7259	27606	3.197	32.73	45.15	28.82
Best polynomial fit: 3rd order	1.954e+05	0.8102	27605	2.66	—	—	—

4.2 Second Experiment: Comparison with a Reference Instrument

The second experiment was conducted during 4 days at Vortice iTech Park El Marques, Querétaro. The measurement period was from July 7 to July 10, 2021. For the sake of clarity, each sample was taken manually every 15 min for 6 h a day and saved in CSV format for further analysis. Figure 7 presents the measures for the PM-2.5 particulate matter with 57 samples. In this case, we used as a reference instrument a HoldPeak HP-5800D particle counter for comparing the sensor outputs.

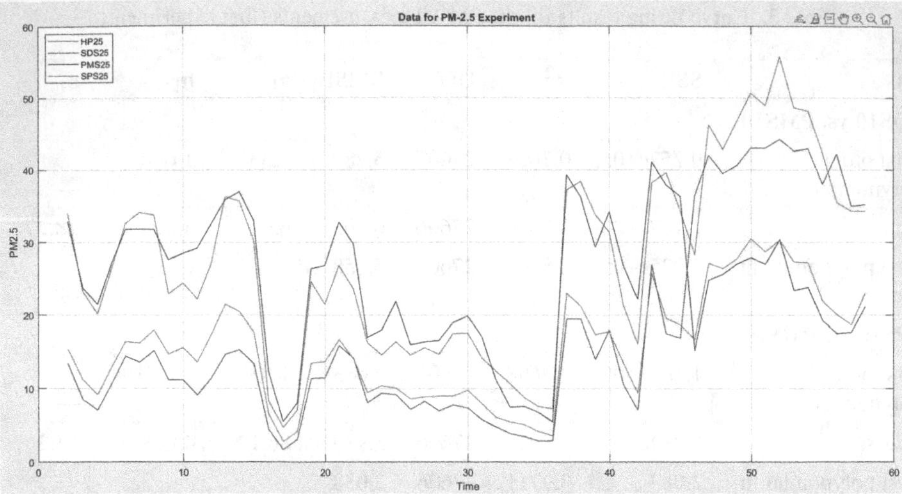

Fig. 7. Results of PM-2.5 measurements from the three sensors and the reference instrument in the period of July 7 to 10 2021.

Curve fitting analysis was realized for comparing the sensors with each other as presented in Fig. 8. The first row corresponds to the first-order polynomial fit that uses Eq. (1) for the approximation. The measurements are from PM-2.5 particles, the plot from the left corresponds to the HP-5800D and SDS011 relation, the plot in the center corresponds to the HP-5800D and PMS3003S relation and the plot on the right corresponds to the HP-5800D and SPS030 relation. The second row corresponds to the Gaussian fit that uses Eq. (2) for the approximation. The measurements are for PM-10 particles, the plot from the left corresponds to the HP-5800D and SDS011 relation, the

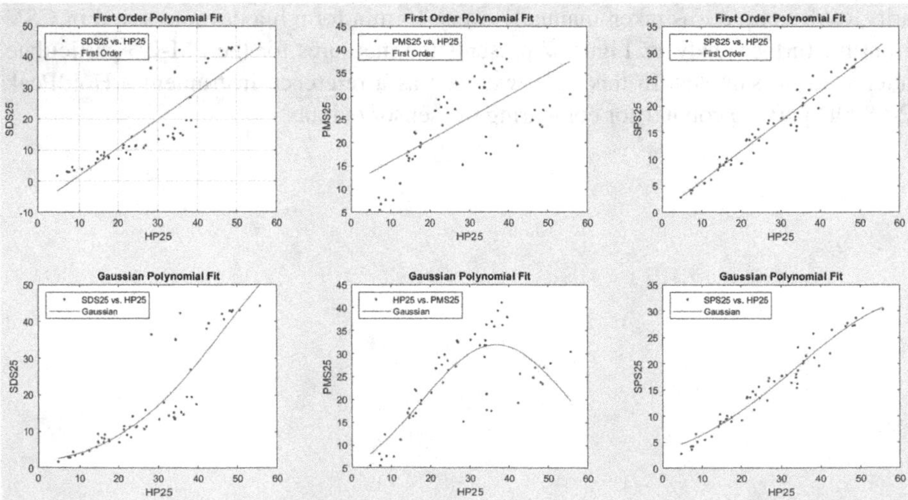

Fig. 8. Pairwise plots between PM sensors and reference instrument (HP-5800D) in the first case providing the linear equation.

plot in the center corresponds to the HP-5800D and PMS3003S relation and the plot on the right corresponds to the HP-5800D and SPS030 relation.

Table 4, presents the curve fitting results for the PM-2.5 measurements corresponding to the plots from Fig. 7. For each comparison, there are three rows, the first corresponds to the results of applying the first order polynomial fitting, the second row corresponds to the Gaussian fitting and the third row corresponds to the best-fit polynomial whose order is indicated. The column order is as follows: type of fit; the sum of squared errors; the coefficient of determination; the degrees of freedom of the error; the root mean squared error; and the a_1, b_1, and c_1 coefficients for the corresponding fit. Notice that those coefficients are not shown for the best fit polynomial given that is a variable number.

Table 4. Curve fitting results for the PM-2.5 measurements (second experiment).

Fit	SSE	R^2	DFE	RMSE	a_1	b_1	c_1
HP2.5 vs SDS2.5							
First order polynomial	2457	0.7595	55	6.683	0.9062	−7.37	—
Gauss	2037	0.8006	54	6.142	63.33	74.8	39.26
Best polynomial fit: 4th order	1974	0.8068	52	6.161	—	—	—
HP2.5 vs PMS 2.5							
First order polynomial	2676	0.4407	55	6.976	0.4724	11.11	
Gauss	1563	0.6733	54	5.381	31.93	36.75	27.32
Best polynomial fit: 4th order	1355	0.7169	52	5.104	—	—	—
HP2.5 vs SPS25							
First order polynomial	137.3	0.9563	55	1.58	0.564	0.2009	—
Gauss	151	0.9519	54	1.672	31.92	64.37	42.96
Best polynomial fit: 5th order	129.9	0.9587	51	1.596	—	—	—

Figure 9 presents the measures for the PM-10 particulate matter with 57 samples. In this case, we also used as a reference instrument the HoldPeak HP-5800D particle counter for comparing the sensor outputs.

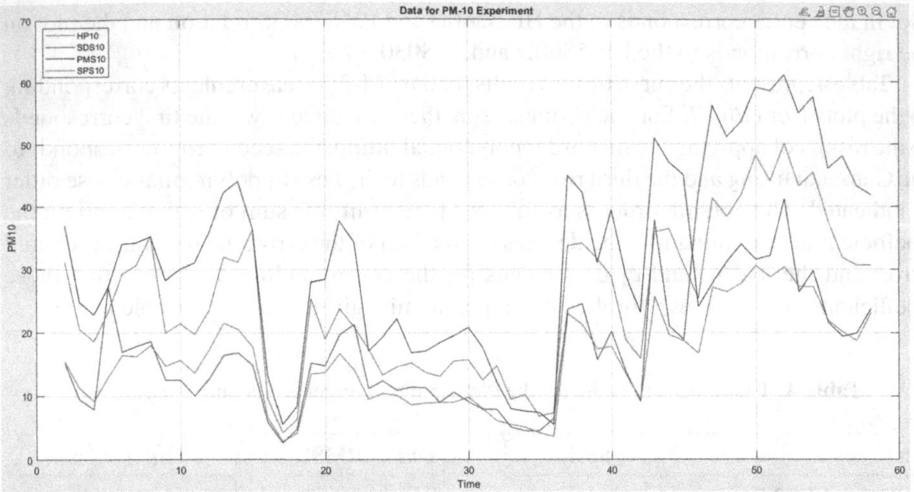

Fig. 9. Results of PM-10 measurements from the three sensors and the reference instrument in the period of 7 July to 10 July 2021.

The curve fitting analysis for this case is presented in Fig. 10. The first row corresponds to the first order polynomial fit that uses Eq. (1) for the approximation. The measurements are from PM-10 particles, the plot on left corresponds to the HP-5800D and SDS011 relation, the plot in the center corresponds to the HP-5800D and PMS3003S relation and the plot on the right corresponds to the HP-5800D and SPS030 relation. The second row corresponds to the Gaussian fit that uses Eq. (2) for the approximation. The measurements are for PM-10 particles, the plot from the left corresponds to the HP-5800D and SDS011 relation, the plot in the center corresponds to the HP-5800D and PMS3003S relation and the plot on the right corresponds to the HP-5800D and SPS030 relation.

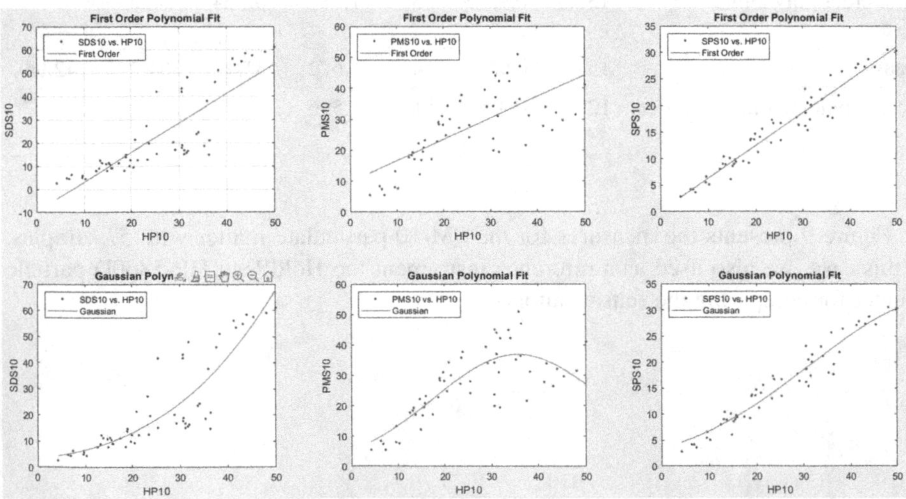

Fig. 10. Pairwise plots between PM-10 sensors and reference instrument (HP-5800D) in the second case providing the linear equation.

Table 5, presents the curve fitting results for the PM-10 measurements corresponding to the plots from Fig. 10. For each comparison, there are three rows, the first corresponds to the results of applying the first order polynomial fitting, the second row corresponds to the Gaussian fitting and the third row corresponds to the best-fit polynomial whose order is indicated. The column order is as follows: type of fit; the sum of squared errors; the coefficient of determination; the degrees of freedom of the error; the root mean squared error; and the a_1, b_1, and c_1 coefficients for the corresponding fit. Notice that those coefficients are not shown for the best fit polynomial given that is a variable number.

Table 5. Curve fitting results for the PM-10 measurements (second experiment).

Fit	SSE	R^2	DFE	RMSE	a_1	b_1	c_1
HP10 vs SDS10							
First order polynomial	4901	0.7149	55	9.44	1.264	−9.5	—
Gauss	3913	0.7724	54	8.513	274.8	113.7	53.86
Best polynomial fit: 5th order	3612	0.7899	51	8.416	—	—	—
HP10 vs. PMS10							
First order polynomial	3474	0.5122	55	7.948	0.6885	9.733	—
Gauss	2435	0.6581	53	6.715	36.86	35.68	25.64
Best polynomial fit: 5th order	2121	0.7023	51	6.448	—	—	—
HP10 vs. SPS10							
First order polynomial	204.7	0.9349	55	1.929	0.6181	0.08227	—
Gauss	225.7	0.9282	54	2.044	32.03	59.44	39.73
Best polynomial fit: 5th order	195	0.938	51	1.955	—	—	—

5 Discussion

It is notorious, from Tables 2, 3, 4, 5 that the first order polynomial provides better curve fitting than the Gaussian approximation this is due to the distribution of the samples, as seen in Figs. 4, 6, 8, and 10. The coefficient of determination R2 is a valuable help for deciding the best performance that must deliver a value close to one. We also presented in the mentioned tables, the best fit with a polynomial. In these cases, the higher order of the polynomial provides a higher value for the coefficient of determination meaning that it fits better with the data. We made different tests in order to find the best values with a minimal change, for that reason we did not select a higher order polynomial given that the variation was very low, so we kept the lowest order with the better fitting.

In the free run sampling experiment, we obtained 27610 samples of PM-10 and PM-2.5 for the three sensors. We analyzed the fitting results for PM-2.5 particles from Table 2 and found that the lowest values for the coefficient of determination correspond to the SDS011 and PMS3003S sensors in comparison with 0.8446 for the Gaussian fitting. The best fit is for the SPS030 and PMS3003S sensors with a 0.9775 R2 value and an RMSE of 1.49 for a third-order polynomial. For the case of PM-10 particles from Table 3 is possible to identify the worst approximation that is also for the SDS011 and PMS3003S sensors with an R2 value of 0.7058 for the Gaussian fitting. The best fit for PM-10 Particles is for the PMS3003S and SPS030 sensors reaching a 0.9711 value for a second-order polynomial with an RMSE of 2.038.

In the second experiment, we aimed to obtain a comparison with a commercial measuring instrument, in this case, the HoldPeak HP-5800D. In this experiment, the sampling was taken every 15 min for the three sensors and the reference instrument obtaining 57 samples. Is notorious from Table 3 that the worst fit for PM-2.5 particulate matter is given by the PMS3003S sensor for the three approximations obtaining a 0.4407 value for R2 with a 6.976 RMSE value. The best fit for this case is for the SPS030 sensor that has a 0.9587 R2 value for a fifth-order polynomial with an RMSE of 1.596. For the case of PM-10 particles from Table 5, the worst fit is also for the PMS3003S sensor presenting a 0.5122 R2 value for the first order polynomial with an RMSE of 7.948. The best fit for PM-10 particles is for the SPS030 sensor with a fifth-order polynomial that has a 0.938 R2 value and 1.929 RMSE value.

For selecting the most appropriate sensor according to the reference instrument, the linear equation's slope has the major weight since it indicates the actual value in increasing the rate of change of one sensor and the reference instrument. A value close to one is ideal, for the reason that it implies that there is not either an overestimation or underestimation of particulate matter concentration.

6 Conclusions

A data cleaning procedure should be performed prior to data analysis for getting rid of outliers since there is where most unreliable data take place. The noise could be due to incorrect measurements, electromagnetic interference, or internal errors in the sensor. After cleaning the data, we can have reliable information for processing.

From Fig. 3 and Fig. 5 for the first experiment and Fig. 7 and 9 for the second experiment, we can observe a similar tendency for each sensor against each other. For that reason, it was necessary to perform a statistical analysis. As result, we observed that the worst performance with respect to the reference instrument is presented by the Plantower PMS3003S sensor, which has lower determination coefficient R2 values (0.4407) and a higher RMSE (7.948). In contrast, the best performance is given by the Sensirion SPS030 sensor with a 0.9587 R2 value and 1.596 RMSE, concluding that it is an option for implementing low-cost air particle measurements.

Acknowledgment. The authors would like to thank the Instituto Politécnico Nacional, and CONACYT for their financial support to realize this work. We would also thank to Vórtice IT Cluster for their facilities.

Disclosure Statement. The authors claim that there is no conflict of interest derived from this work.

References

1. World Health Organization: Ambient Air Pollution: A Global Assessment of Exposure and Burden of Disease. Switzerland, Geneva (2016)
2. Ritchie, H., Roser, M.: Outdoor Air Pollution. https://ourworldindata.org/outdoor-air-pollution. Accessed 30 Mar 2022
3. World Health Organization: Air Pollution. https://www.who.int/health-topics/air-pollution#tab=tab_1. Accessed 30 Mar 2022
4. Fresneda, C.: La contaminación contribuye a una de cada cinco muertes. https://www.elmundo.es/ciencia-y-salud/medio-ambiente/2021/02/09/6022421c21efa06b6c8b45ca.html. Accessed 30 Mar 2022
5. European Society of Cardiology: Air pollution causes 800,000 extra deaths a year in Europe and 8.8 million worldwide. https://www.escardio.org/The-ESC/Press-Office/Press-releases/Air-pollution-causes-800-000-extra-deaths-a-year-in-Europe-and-8-8-million-worldwide. Accessed 30 Mar 2022
6. Cowen, T.: Air pollution kills far more people than COVID ever will. https://www.bloomberg.com/opinion/articles/2021-03-10/air-pollution-kills-far-more-people-than-covid-ever-will. Accessed 30 Mar 2022
7. Kim, K.H., Kabir, E., Kabir, S.: A review on the human health impact of airborne particulate matter. Environ. Int. **74**, 136–143 (2015)
8. Anderson, J.O., Thundiyil, J.G., Stolbach, A.: Clearing the air: a review of the effects of particulate matter air pollution on human health. J. Med. Toxicol. **8**(2), 166–175 (2012)
9. Liu, H.Y., Dunea, D., Iordache, S., Pohoata, A.: A review of airborne particulate matter effects on young children's respiratory symptoms and diseases. Atmosphere **9**(4), 150 (2018)
10. Lelieveld, J., Evans, J.S., Fnais, M., Giannadaki, D., Pozzer, A.: The contribution of outdoor air pollution sources to premature mortality on a global scale. Nature **525**, 367–371 (2015)
11. Karagulian, F., et al.: Contributions to cities' ambient particulate matter (PM): a systematic review of local source contributions at global level. Atmos. Environ. **120**, 475–483 (2015)
12. Brattich, E., et al.: How to get the best from low-cost particulate matter sensors: guidelines and practical recommendations. Sensors **20**(11), 3073 (2020)
13. Holstius, D.M., Pillarisetti, A., Smith, K.R., Seto, E.: Field calibrations of a low-cost aerosol sensor at a regulatory monitoring site in California. Atmos. Meas. Tech. **7**(4), 1121–1131 (2014)
14. Badura, M., Batog, P., Drzeniecka-Osiadacz, A., Modzel, P.: Evaluation of low-cost sensors for ambient PM2.5 monitoring. J. Sens., 5096540 (2018)
15. Mukherjee, A., Stanton, L.G., Graham, A.R., Roberts, P.T.: Assessing the utility of low-cost particulate matter sensors over a 12-week period in the Guyama Valley of California. Sensors **17**(8), 1805 (2017)
16. Zikova, N., Masiol, M., Chalupa, D., Rich, D., Ferro, A., Hopke, P.: Estimating hourly concentrations of PM2.5 across a metropolitan area using low-cost particle monitors. Sensors **17**(8), 1922 (2017)

17. Bulot, F.M.J., et al.: Long-term field comparison of multiple low-cost particulate matter sensors in an outdoor urban environment. Sci. Rep. **9**, 7497 (2019)
18. Tagle, M., et al.: Field performance of a low-cost sensor in the monitoring of particulate matter in Santiago, Chile. Environ. Monit. Assess. **192**, 171 (2020)
19. Jayaratne, R., Liu, X., Thai, P., Dunbabin, M., Morawska, L.: The influence of humidity on the performance of a low-cost air particle mass sensor and the effect of atmospheric fog. Atmos. Meas. Techn. **11**(8), 4883–4890 (2018)
20. Idrees, Z., Zou, Z., Zheng, L.: Edge computing based IoT architecture for low cost air pollution monitoring systems: a comprehensive system analysis, design considerations & development. Sensors **18**(9), 3021 (2018)
21. Johnston, S.J., et al.: City scale particulate matter monitoring using LoRaWAN based air quality IoT devices. Sensors **19**(1), 209 (2019)
22. Harr, L., Sinsel, T., Simon, H., Esper, J.: Seasonal changes in urban PM2.5 hotspots and sources from low-cost sensors. Atmosphere **13**, 694 (2022)
23. Connolly, R.E., et al.: Long-term evaluation of a low-cost air sensor network for monitoring indoor and outdoor air quality at the community scale. Sci. Total Environ. **807**(2), 150797 (2022)
24. Bittner, A.S., Cross, E.S., Hagan, D.H., Malings, C., Lipsky, E., Grieshop, A.P.: Performance characterization of low-cost air quality sensors for off-grid deployment in rural Malawi. Atmos. Meas. Technol. **15**, 3353–3376 (2022)
25. Amaral, S.S., De Carvalho, J.A., Costa, M.A.M., Pinheiro, C.: An overview of particulate matter measurement instruments. Atmosphere **6**(9), 1327–1345 (2015)
26. Hales, B.S., Jones, M.R., Lewis, R.S.: Effects of optical configuration on the accuracy and response of low-cost optical particle counters. Int. J. Thermophys. **43**(6), 1–21 (2022). https://doi.org/10.1007/s10765-022-03001-4
27. Gouesbet, G., Gréhan, G.: Generalized lorenz-mie theory in the strict sense, and other GLMTs. In: Gouesbet, G., Gréhan, G. (eds.) Generalized Lorenz-Mie Theories, pp. 37–88. Springer, Heidelberg (2011). https://doi.org/10.1007/978-3-642-17194-9_3

Computational Simulation Applied to Microstrip Patch Antenna Design for the Ground Penetrating Radar Technology

Salvador Ricardo Meneses González(✉) and Rita Trinidad Rodríguez Márquez

Escuela Superior de Ingeniería Mecánica y Eléctrica, Unidad Zacatenco, Instituto Politécnico Nacional, Cd. de México, Mexico
rmenesesg@ipn.mx

Abstract. Ground Penetrating Radar is a geophysical non-destructive method whose primary purpose is locate all kind of submerged or buried objects, pipelines, cables, clandestine graves, archaeological remain, etc., to that end, the GPR device emits a radioelectric signal pulse and the reflected signal gives specific data about abnormal areas, measuring changes and contrasts in the signal, in this sense, an antenna which satisfies gain, bandwidth, impedance, and low cost is demanded in order to collect vast amounts of data about the subsurface. This work proposes a 1 GHz bow tie microstrip patch antenna for GPR devices application.

Keywords: Ground penetrating radar · Microstrip antenna · S_{11} parameter · Radiation pattern · 1 GHz band

1 Introduction

When the antennas transmit the electromagnetic waves, pulse passes through the ground and subsurface objects and is then distorted by dielectric and conductive properties, the reflected pulse travels back to the receiving antenna and displays images and graphs about the subsurface [1–3]. Ground-penetrating radar typically use signal frequencies ranging in the microwave band. Higher frequencies in this band are used to provide much better resolution, but they don't penetrate deeply, on the other hand, when it is not necessary much greater depth, the frequency band used is ranging between 12 MHz to 500 MHz [4].

Ground penetrating radar system operating principle consists of the following: In the stage of transmission a phase modulator modulates the radio frequency signal which is transmitted by the antenna to the ground and the signal reflected by the target is collected by the receiving antenna, this one is combined in a mixer with the original radio frequency signal to produce a resultant signal which is demodulated to produce a series of direct current voltage signal. The envelope forms a cosine wave shaped plot, which is processed by a Fast Fourier Transform into frequency domain data [5]. The position of a preponderant frequency is indicative of distance to the target and magnitude is indicative of the nature of the target.

M. F. Mata-Rivera et al. (Eds.): WITCOM 2022, CCIS 1659, pp. 51–59, 2022.
https://doi.org/10.1007/978-3-031-18082-8_4

The penetrating depth depends to a large extent on the geometry of the ground subsurface, the relative permittivity and electrical conductivity values due to GPR is based on the reflected wave magnitude and some materials show increased attenuation. Figure 1 shows geometry of a possible subsurface model, first layer asphalt or grass, approximately 30 cm, to locate rebar mapping, second layer in the same way asphalt or it can be soil, conduit detection, 45 cm, and located at a higher depth, using frequency bands, 1 GHz and 400 MHz, to locate clandestine graves or archaeological pieces such as stelae, pottery and glyphs.

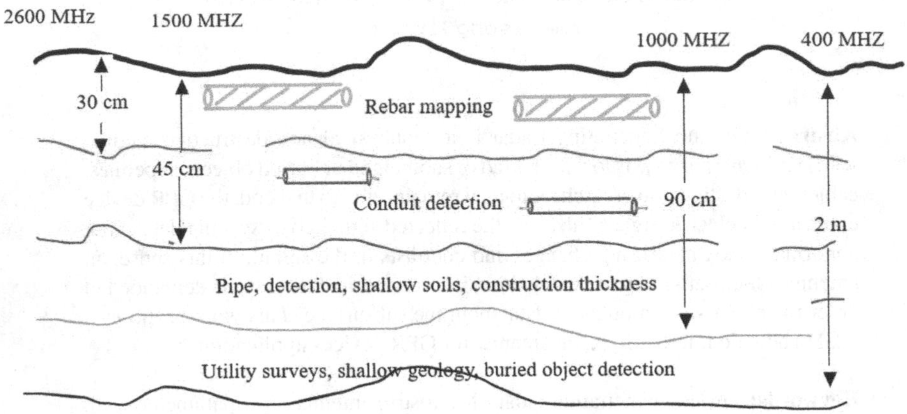

Fig. 1. Ground subsurface layers.

Table 1 shows typical penetration depths achieved by different frequencies and applications.

The antenna it is an part important of the system, several different antenna designs have been considered, for instance, [4] proposes the use of spiral antennas for a GPR for antipersonnel landmines operate in a UWB domain from 400 MHz up to 5 GHz, [6] develops a cavity-backed logarithmic spiral antenna for detection of anti-personnel land mines operates covers from 0.5 to 1.6 GHz, [7] a UWB antenna for subsurface searching, [8] makes a selection of the antennas for a ground penetrating radar for landmine detection and [9] proposes a Vivaldi antenna and [10] develops a bow tie antenna, etc.

Table 1. GPR applications.

Frequency band (MHz)	Penetration depth (m)	Application
2600	0.3	Rebar mapping
1500	0.45	Conduit detection

(continued)

Table 1. *(continued)*

Frequency band (MHz)	Penetration depth (m)	Application
1000	0.9	Pipe, detection, shallow soils, construction thickness
400	2	Utility surveys, shallow geology, buried object detection

In this way, in this work, we propose a small bow tie patch antenna operating in 1 GHz microwave band, to balance resolution with penetration, reducing the size antenna, increasing bandwidth, directivity and improve the quality detection of the monitor/control equipment, and it will allow a better performance of the GPR device.

The paper is organized as follows: Sect. 2 describes a brief bow tie antenna basis, Sect. 3, the design, and simulation antenna, concluding the presently work with conclusions and references.

2 Antenna Design

The antennas suitable for applications in GPR systems due to its distinct radiation characteristics are air coupling antennas, for instance, horn, Vivaldi [11] and tapered slot antennas and the dielectric coupling type antennas, which the radiated electromagnetic energy penetrating into the ground is highly dependent of the antenna height above the surface, for instance, bow tie [12, 13] and spiral antenna. In this way, the bow tie antenna is of a particular interest to design due to it is noted for being a compact antenna with good impedance matching characteristics, small size, wide bandwidth ad low cost.

Bow tie antenna operation is based on the Rumsey's principle, which states that infinite-length antennas completely defined by angles present wavelength-independent capabilities [14], this principle holds when the antenna dimensions are large compared to the wavelength, in this way, the electric current flowing through the antenna, vanish before reaching the radiators' ends, thereby avoiding any length-dependent mode, in such a way that, if the flare angle of the bow is 90°, ensures frequency-independent properties to the input impedance.

2.1 Antenna Structure Design

The proposed bow tie antenna design is based on two triangular elements joined together at one of the vertices, forming a dipole, embedded on a patch which is seen as a bow tie like structure, as shown in Fig. 2.

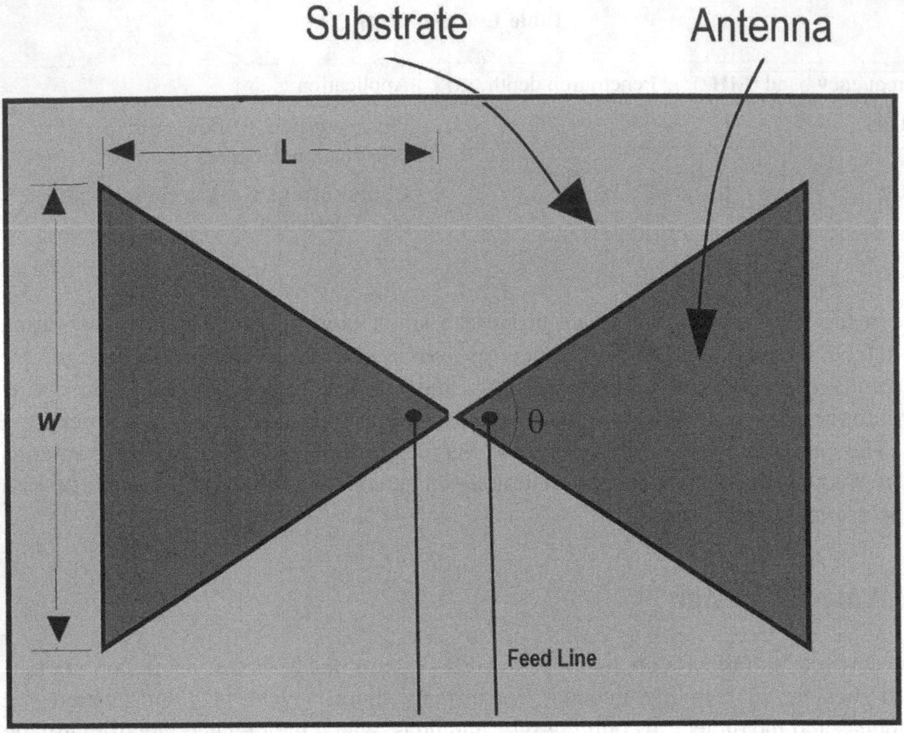

Fig. 2. Bow tie antenna structure.

Considering the epoxy FR-4 as the substrate to serve as ground plane, which relative permittivity, $\varepsilon_r = 4.4$, tangential loss, tan $\delta = 0.02$ and thickness substrate, $h = 3$ mm, $h < \lambda_0$ and the resonance frequency as central frequency at 1 GHz, it is possible to calculate the antenna dimensions applying the following [15–17]:

$$w = \frac{1.33\lambda_0}{\sqrt{\varepsilon_r}} \quad (1)$$

where:

w, width substrate.
ε_r, relative permittivity.
λ_0 resonance frequency wavelength.

The half-length of the bow tie dipole, L, is approximately equal to $\lambda_0/2$, modified by the factor $1/\sqrt{\varepsilon_{r_{eff}}}$, that is:

$$L = \frac{\lambda_0}{2}\frac{1}{\sqrt{\varepsilon_{r_{eff}}}} \quad (2)$$

being:

$$\varepsilon_{r_{eff}} = \frac{\varepsilon_r + 1}{2} + \frac{\varepsilon_r - 1}{2}\left[1 + \frac{1}{\sqrt{1 + 12\frac{h}{w}}}\right] \quad (3)$$

where:

h, thickness substrate.
$\varepsilon_{r_{eff}}$, effective dielectric constant.

The resonance frequency is basically determined by the bow tie length, while the bandwidth is affected by the opening angle θ; the feeding line length, λ/4, enables the match impedance antenna with SMA connector. Designed antenna dimensions are shown in Table 2.

Table 2. Designed antenna dimensions.

Frequency (GHz)	Wavelength (cm)	Entire length, 2L (cm)	Width w (cm)
1	30	12	19

3 Antenna Simulation

FEKO, a simulation technology software [18] has been used to simulate the designed antenna, it is an electromagnetic simulation software tool, based on state-of-the-art computational electromagnetics (CEM) techniques, it is a numerical method in computational electromagnetics, in this case the method of moments (MoM) has been applied. Figure 3 shows the simulated antenna structure.

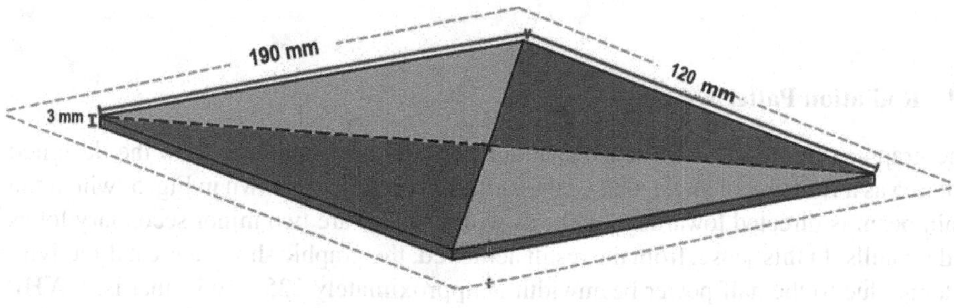

Fig. 3. Simulated antenna structure.

On the other hand, S-parameters describe the input-output relationship between ports (or terminals) in an electrical system, in such a way that to evaluate the antenna performance, the S_{11} parameter known as the reflection coefficient or return loss, expressed in dB, gives us the ratio of the reflected energy and transmitted energy, if the value is quantity is less than or equal to – 10 dB, within a designated frequency range, it means that 90% of the energy is radiated and the 10% of the energy is reflected. Figure 4 shows the simulation result, Magnitude vs. Frequency graphic, parameter S_{11}.

From the Fig. 4, it is possible observe that resonance frequency is equal to 1 GHz and the bandwidth 100 MHz, limited by 950 MHz as lower frequency and 1050 MHz as upper frequency.

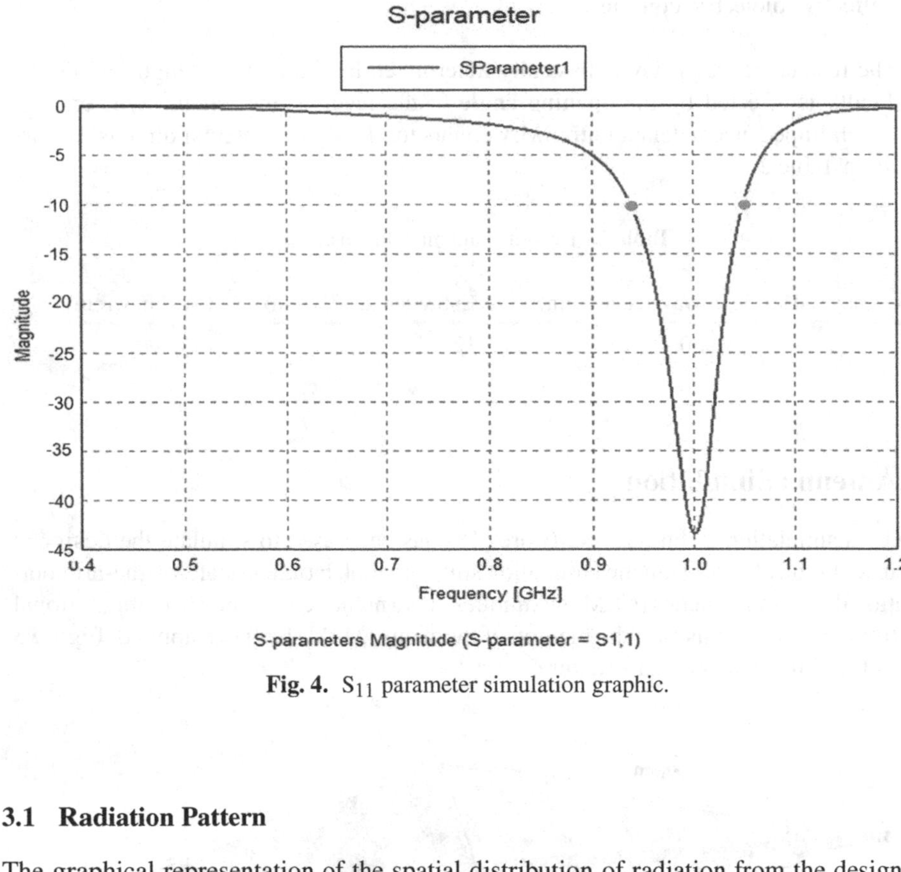

Fig. 4. S_{11} parameter simulation graphic.

3.1 Radiation Pattern

The graphical representation of the spatial distribution of radiation from the designed antenna as a function of angle, that is, the radiation pattern, is shown in Fig. 5, which the main beam is directed towards to 200°, as well as there are two minor secondary lobes and no nulls. In this sense, from the result achieved, the graphic shows a great directivity antenna due to the half power beamwidth is approximately 225°–165°, that is, BWHP ≈ 60°, in such a way that the radiated energy by the antenna, the main beam, should be directed towards the ground.

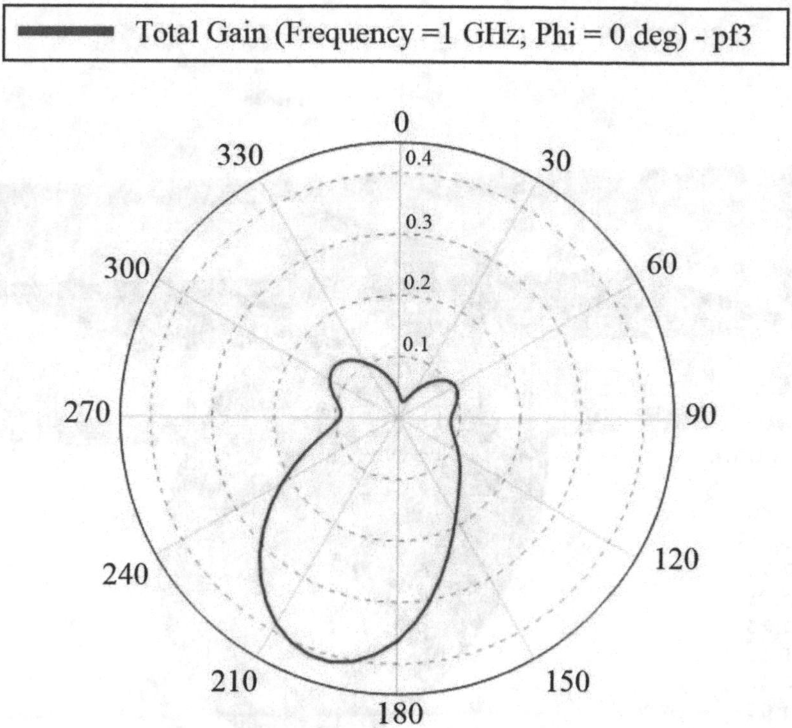

Fig. 5. Radiation pattern.

This kind of radiation pattern is an asset, due to the GPR device can cover selected areas, thanks to the directivity of the antenna. Figure 6 shows the 3-D radiation pattern, which is the result of the combination of radiation pattern vertical plane, E-Plane, |E| vs. θ, whose geometry is round, and the radiation pattern horizontal plane |E| vs. ϕ (depicted in Fig. 5).

On the other hand, detect and discover objects is dependent of the characteristics of the material, the penetration depth parameter, that is, the depth at which the intensity of the radiation inside the material, part of the electromagnetic radiation incident on the surface of a material is absorbed and it may be not reflected, making difficult the GPR device operation, in such a way that the antenna efficiency improves this natural situation.

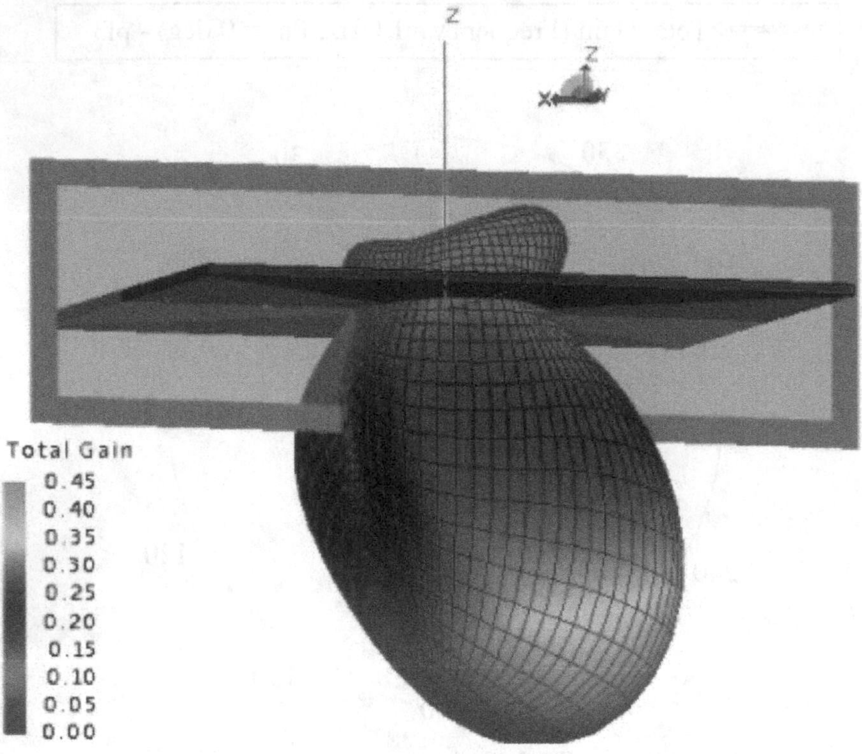

Fig. 6. 3-D radiation pattern.

4 Future Work

The scope of this work was limited to design and simulation due to the health emergency, in such a way that the experimental laboratories were not completely available. As soon as possible the designed antenna will be under test.

5 Conclusions

A bow tie microstrip patch antenna for Ground Penetration Radar application is simulated and designed to operate at 1GHz resonance frequency. Based on the obtained results, parameters as resonance frequency, bandwidth and radiation pattern, the designed antenna particularly suitable for use in GPR devices, as well as it meets with small size requirement, flexible, cheap, and easily constructed.

It is a high-directivity antennas due to beam width is narrow, the backward energy is minimum, small secondary lobes, no nulls and the radiated energy is focused towards to a particular area, making the detection process most efficient.

Semi null ubicated at 0° and 70° are present, so, these positions should be not focused towards the area under test.

In relation to other microstrip antennas as simple dipoles, folded dipoles, the designed antenna provides a much better gain a significant efficiency improvement, functionality and flexibility, therefore, it is recommended to be applied to GPR device.

References

1. Benedetto, A., Pajewski, L.: Civil engineering applications of ground penetrating radar. Springer, Cham (2015). https://doi.org/10.1007/978-3-319-04813-0
2. Annan, A.: Ground penetrating radar principles, procedures and applications, p. 3. Sensor and Software Inc. (2003)
3. Kadaba, K.: Penetration of 0.1 GHz to 1.5 GHz electromagnetic waves into the earth surface for remote sensing applications. In: Proceedings of the IEEE Southeast-con. Region 3 Conference, pp. 48–50 (1976)
4. Genderen, P., Nicolaescu, I., Zijderveld, J.: Some experience with the use of spiral antennas for a GPR for landmine detection. In: International Conference on Radar, Adelaide, SA, Australia, 3–5 September 2003
5. Zeng, X., McMechan, G.A., Cai, J., Chen, H.W.: Comparison of ray and Fourier methods for modelling monostatic ground-penetrating radar profiles. Geophysics **60**, 1727–1734 (1995)
6. Kazemi, R.: Development of a logarithmic spiral antenna in UWB GPR for humanitarian demining. Electromagnetics **38**(6), 366–379 (2018)
7. Nicolaescu, I., Buzincu, L., Anton, L.: UWB antenna for a radar sensor. In: 2020 13th International Conference on Communications (COMM)
8. Van Genderen, P., Zijderveld, J.H.: Selection of the antennas for a ground penetrating radar for landmine detection. In: German Intitute of Navigation (ed.) German Radar Symposium, GRS 2002, pp. 345–349. German Institute of Navigation (2002)
9. Zhou, B., Cui, T.J.: Directivity enhancement to Vivaldi antennas using compactly anisotropic zero-index metamaterials. IEEE Antennas Wirel. Propag. Lett. **10**, 326–329 (2011)
10. Ajith, K., Bhattacharya, A.: Improved ultra-wide bandwidth bow-tie antenna with metamaterial lens for GPR applications. In: Proceedings of the 15th International Conference on Ground Penetrating Radar (GPR), pp. 739–744 (2014)
11. Dong, Y., Choi, J., Itoh, T.: Vivaldi antenna with pattern diversity for 0.7 to 2.7 GHz cellular band applications. IEEE Antennas Wirel. Propag. Lett., **17**(2), 247–250 (2018)
12. Liu, S., et al.: Cavity-backed bow-tie antenna with dielectric loading for ground-penetrating radar application. IET Microw. Antennas Propag. **14**(2), 153–157 (2020)
13. Kiminami, K., Hirata, A., Shiozawa, T.: Double-sided printed bow-tie antenna for UWB communications. IEEE Antennas Wirel. Propag. Lett. **3**, 152–153 (2004)
14. Rumsey, V.H.: Frequency Independent Antennas. Academic Press, New York (1966)
15. Guo, Ch., Liu, R.: The study of wideband bowtie antenna for ITDAMS. In: 4th International Conference on Microwave and Millimeter Wave Technology Proceedings (2004)
16. Jawad, A.: Ultra-wideband antenna design for GPR applications: a review. (IJACSA) Int. J. Adv. Comput. Sci. Appl. 393 (2017). University Tun Hussein Onn Malaysia
17. Chen, G., Liu, R.: A 900 MHz shielded bow-tie antenna system for ground penetrating radar. In: Proceedings of the XIII International Conference on Ground Penetrating Radar, Lecce, pp. 1–6 (2010)
18. Feko suite 7.0 software simulation

Monitoring and Prediction of Drinking Water Consumption

Rigoberto Escobar-Jiménez[1], Fernando Salvide-Hernández[1], Raúl López-Muñoz[2], René Tolentino-Eslava[1], and Mario Cesar Maya-Rodriguez[1(✉)]

[1] Instituto Politécnico Nacional, Escuela Superior de Ingeniería Mecánica y Eléctrica, Unidad Zacatenco, Av. Luis Enrique Erro S/N, Unidad Profesional Adolfo López Mateos, Zacatenco, Alcaldía Gustavo A. Madero, 07738 Mexico City, Mexico
{rtolentino,mmayar}@ipn.mx

[2] Instituto Politécnico Nacional, Centro de Innovación y Desarrollo Tecnológico en Cómputo, Av. Juan de Dios Bátiz S/N, Nueva Industrial Vallejo, Alcaldía Gustavo A. Madero, 07700 Mexico City, Mexico
rlopezm1209@alumno.ipn.mx

Abstract. In this work, a methodology to determine the amount of drinking water consumption in real time with open-source hardware and software is proposed as an alternative, more efficient way to the current approaches by adding consumption forecasts to better manage water usage. Two prototypes were constructed to generate consumption data, each one consisting of a water storage tank, a centrifugal pump, and a pipeline to simulate a typical household water measurement arrangement, where a flow sensor is installed and connected to a data acquisition board with internet connectivity. The pump was activated as the water was being requested, and the data are acquired and sent periodically to a record in the cloud. Additionally, a predictive model was designed in the cloud to predict the next month's consumption, the chosen approach is a Neural Network (NN), this was selected after comparing it with the performance of lineal regressive models, e.g., for prototype 1 the NNs Mean Squared Error (MSE) is 10 987.77 against an Autoregressive (AR) - Moving Average (MA) model $ARMA(1,1)$ with $MSE = 20\ 734.26$, and for prototype 2 the NNs MSE is 5 753.16 against a Seasonal ARMA model $SARMA(7,7)_7$ with $MSE = 37\ 603.51$. All the data are synchronized with a mobile app where the interface allows one to search the data in cost or volume in liters for a specific day or the whole month, as well as the graphs of the predictions.

Keywords: IoT at home · Monitoring · Prediction · Neural networks

1 Introduction

In the present time, water conservation represents a critical social topic, since the closeness with "Day Zero", when free water usage will no longer be available, is undeniable, which is why the efforts to better take care of it must be prioritized.

M. F. Mata-Rivera et al. (Eds.): WITCOM 2022, CCIS 1659, pp. 60–75, 2022.
https://doi.org/10.1007/978-3-031-18082-8_5

Relatable works on this topic are: in [18] the authors focus on the selection of low-cost hardware and software to monitor the water consumption in residences, they interconnect each residence via radiofrequency modules to a base station and then store the data in the cloud.

On the other side, in [15] an Internet of Things (IoT) approach of alerting the inhabitants from a certain location of a possible flood by continuously reading the water level with an ultrasonic sensor is shown.

In [5] a wide range of IoT applications in the water distribution network and pumping equipment, such as water pressure, temperature, quality, and other measurements that help in the optimization of the water distribution system is presented.

A comparison of 8 protocols used in IoT is given in [1], the intention, rather than putting one protocol over another, is to let the reader know by different criteria, which one is best suited to their application.

Water quality monitoring projects which apply a Wireless Sensor Network (WSN) employing nodes that can detect physicochemical parameters such as pH, conductivity, turbidity, and chlorine are presented in [16].

In [6] a system for the real-time smart monitoring of pH, temperature, conductivity, flow, and oxidation-reduction potential (ORP) parameters in water is developed. This enables water quality alerts to take action on time.

A project regarding water consumption monitoring, daily forecasting with Support Vector Machines (SVM), and leakage detection with an IoT system for the control of water usage is presented in [10].

To study the impact of replacing toilets in buildings on the amount of water used, a system for monitoring water consumption with Statistical Control Charts (SCC) is shown in [9].

The focus of this work is improving the way household water consumption monitoring and measurement is achieved, by implementing the concept of IoT, which aims the interconnection of real-world objects with the Internet, interchanging, adding up, and processing information regarding the physical environment to provide value-added services to end-users [3].

This work contributes with a methodology that does not require many modifications to the pipeline arrangement. The benefit is for both, the administrators of the service, as they save time and human resources by replacing the traditional in-person readings of the consumption, and the final user, who has practically real-time information of their usage.

Moreover, a time series analysis using lineal regressive models and an Artificial Neural Network (ANN) as predictive models were designed. The first ones are models built using regression analysis, which is a collection of methods for the study of relationships between the variables and estimation and prediction of values of one variable using the values of other variables incorporated in a joint time series. The ANNs are an approach that reduces computational efforts and their learning and predicting capabilities do not require previous knowledge of the observations' internal relations [14].

The time series were constructed with the data gathered in the cloud by two prototypes simulating the water consumption pattern. The final information can be easily accessed by the user through a mobile phone app just by signing in with their defined credentials. In the app, one can find different user-friendly sections showing graphs for longer periods or punctual data for a specific date in volume or monetary units.

2 Prototype Design

The prototype was designed similarly to the typical arrangement used for the measurement of household water consumption according to [7], in Fig. 1 the design is displayed. It consists of a tank of 19.69 in × 12.99 in × 11.81 in dimensions with a capacity of 50 liters, filled with 25 liters of water, equipped with a centrifugal pump (a 12 V, 13.3 L/min, 5 m max head, 1/2 in threaded connections pump) in charge of recirculating it through a 1/2 in, CPVC pipeline. The flow sensor is installed horizontally in the pipeline with its corresponding free 5 in at its input and 4 in at its output (10 and 8 diameters, respectively), before it there is a check valve and after it a 2 in upward deviation, located to reduce the error, keeping the horizontal section where the sensor is always filled with water. A ball valve at the end of the arrangement is installed to regulate the flow if needed. Two prototypes were built.

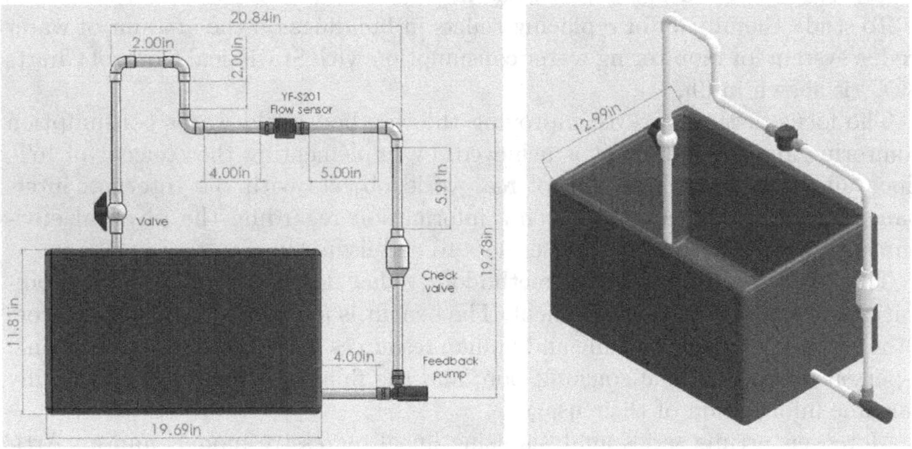

(a) Front view. (b) Isometric.

Fig. 1. Prototype design.

3 Methodology

The proposed procedure is to first measure the input water flow to the household pipeline and integrate it through time to obtain the volume, then send and store the data in the cloud, and finally analyze the acquired data with cloud computing tools (Fig. 2).

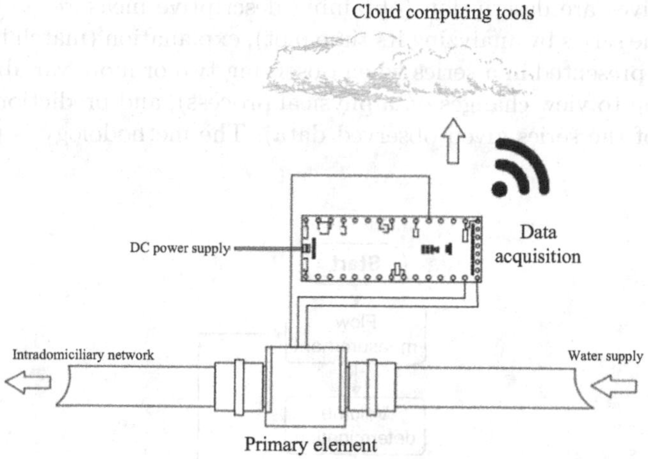

Fig. 2. Procedure pictorial sketch.

The selected primary element is the YF-S201 flow sensor, which is based on the turbine working principle since it has a rotatory element that maintains a direct relationship between the revolutions and the volume or flow passing through [12]. This sensor also works with the Hall effect, which according to [17] means that a potential difference occurs at the ends of a conductor, a current passes through, and it is exposed to a perpendicular magnetic field. In the sensor this happens when it rotates and a magnet in one of the blades activates the Hall effect every revolution generating a pulse signal at the sensor's output terminal, this signal is then converted into flow by the Eq. (1) found in [13], that is done by a data acquisition board:

$$Q\left[\frac{Liters}{second}\right] = \frac{Pulses}{7.5} \times \frac{1}{60}. \tag{1}$$

An Arduino Nano 33 IoT was selected for the data acquisition and connectivity with the cloud, it is a comprehensive solution for many IoT projects. Its main processor is the 32 bits SAMD21 Arm® Cortex®-M0 board, the WiFi and Bluetooth® connection is done with the NINA-W10 u-blox, and the communication is ensured through the Microchip® ECC608 crypto chip [2].

For the cloud provider, the integration of a couple of Google services was proposed, so the storage of the data is achieved in Google Drive with a structured Google Sheets file, the data can then be accessed by Google Colab, which allows to code a Notebook instance with Python to analyze the data as a time series.

Colab is optimal for automatic learning applications, it does not require the development of a server, and provides free access to CPU, GPU, and TPU [11].

A time series is a collection of data observed sequentially through time [4], they are implemented in different fields, from economics to engineering. Some of their objectives are description (obtaining descriptive measures of the main properties of the series by analyzing its time plot), explanation (match the effects and variations presented in a series when observing two or more variables), control (take action to view changes on a physical process), and prediction (predict future values of the series given observed data). The methodology is presented in Fig. 3.

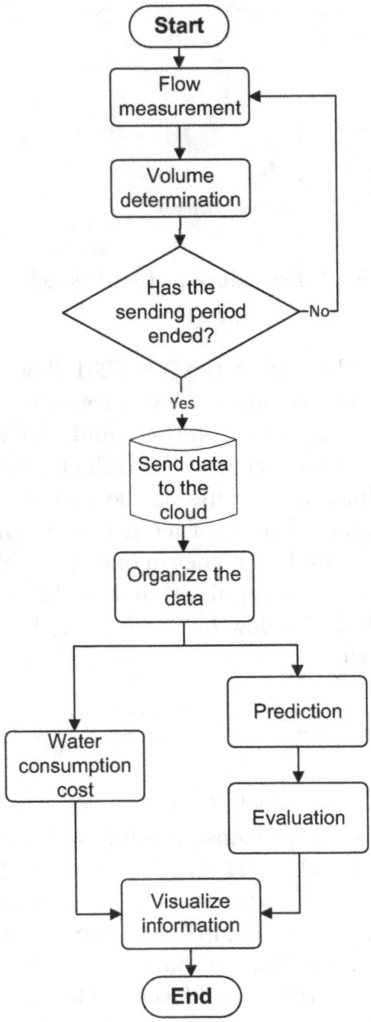

Fig. 3. Methodology to determine water consumption.

4 Data Acquisition

The Arduino Nano 33 IoT was programmed to keep track of the sensor every second (sample time), measuring the water flow in L/s, and converting it to volume by calculating its integral with the discrete rectangular approximation (Eq. (2)). That is done for periods of 1 h when the Arduino sends the total volume consumed in that period to a record in a Google Drive Sheets file. In that file, the data are automatically organized by a script in different sheets corresponding to hours, days, months, and years:

$$V = \int Q(t) \approx T \sum_{k} Q(k), \tag{2}$$

where V is the volume in liters, $Q(t)$ is the continuous-time flow in L/s, T is the sample time in seconds, and $Q(k)$ is the discrete-time flow in L/s.

Both prototypes were operated for 3 months (from May 1 to July 31, 2021, i.e., 92 values) simulating different water consumption dynamics. Previewing the design of a predictive model, the gathered data are separated into two sets, one for the training of the model (first two months, i.e., 61 values) and the other for its validation (the last month, i.e., 31 values).

The daily data collected with the first prototype is shown in Fig. 4.

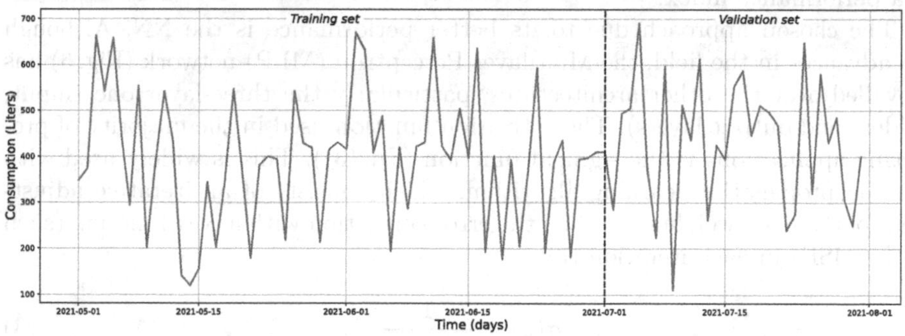

Fig. 4. Water consumption record (prototype 1).

In the case of the second prototype, the collected data are presented in Fig. 5.

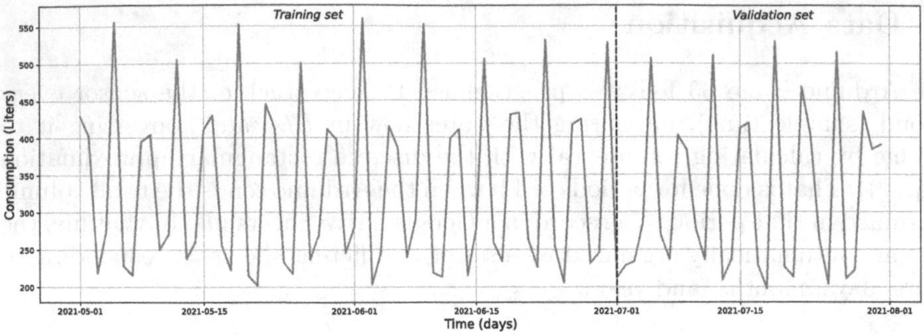

Fig. 5. Water consumption record (prototype 2).

5 Predictive Model Design

The most popular linear regressive models are the Autoregressive (AR) model, the Moving Average (MA) model, and the combination of both (ARMA). There are two ways to propose the hyperparameters of these models, they are the Box-Jenkins procedure which requires analyzing the time series properties (described in detail in [8]), and the Grid Search algorithm, which is an iterative trial and error of the hyperparameters and choosing the most appropriate ones according to a performance index.

The chosen approach due to its better performance is the NN. Although the advances in the field, the Multilayer Perceptron (MLP) network (Fig. 6) has prevailed over the other architectures, particularly the three-layer one (input, hidden, and output layers). The activation function used in the majority of predicting applications is the sigmoid function (Eq. (3)). This is widely used with the backpropagation learning algorithm, which consists of an iterative adjustment of the net's weights based on the error correction with a cost function (such as the MSE) in each iteration [14].

$$\sigma(z) = \frac{1}{1 + e^{-z}} \tag{3}$$

The algorithm first does a forward step from inputs to outputs, mathematically defined by:

$$y = \sigma\left(\sum w_h \sigma\left(\sum w_i^T x\right)\right), \tag{4}$$

where x are the inputs, w_i are the weights between the input and hidden layers, w_h are the weights between the hidden and output layers, and y are the outputs.

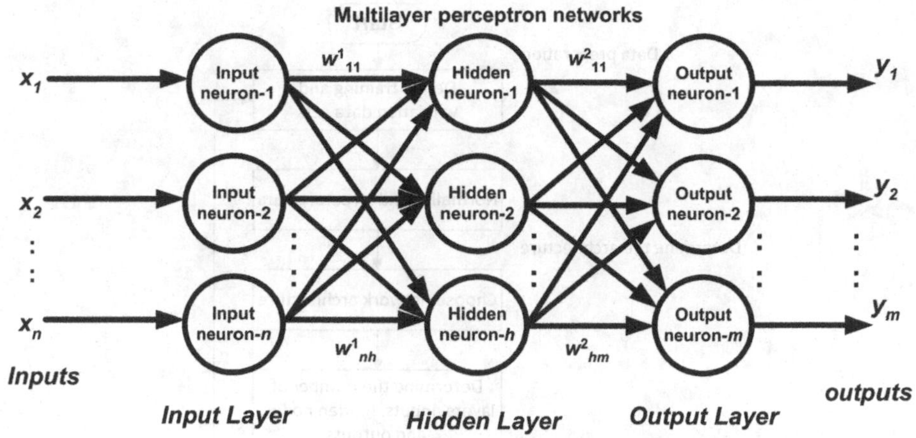

Fig. 6. Multilayer perceptron general architecture [14].

The updating of the weights with the backpropagation is described by:

$$w(k+1) = w(k) + \eta \frac{\partial S(k)}{\partial w(k)}, \tag{5}$$

where $w(k+1)$ is the updated weight, $w(k)$ is the current weight, η is the learning rate, and $S(k)$ is the cost function.

A general methodology to predict time series with neural networks is broken down in Fig. 7.

The programming of the NN was done from scratch with Python programming language in the corresponding Colab Notebook instance defined for each prototype. The data are imported to the Notebook directly from the Sheets file as *dataframe* type by using the Google authentication library (google-auth), then it is conveniently converted to a *numpy* array as well as separating it into the training and validation sets. The following functions were created to accomplish the NN's algorithm: *forward*, in charge of obtaining the outputs of the network by mathematically calculating Eq. 4, *backwardO* function that updates the weights (same that are initialized with random values between −1 and 1) according to the backpropagation algorithm, and *target*, which iterates through the 61 days of the training array in order to update the target of the network.

The hyperparameters required for the neural network are the number of inputs, predictions, outputs, hidden layer nodes, epochs, and learning rate, and since the goal is to predict the daily water consumption of the following month taking as inputs the previous month, therefore the number of inputs corresponds to the days of the last month in the training set, which is June with 30 days, whereas the number of predictions is the same as outputs and corresponds to 31, the days of July (validation set).

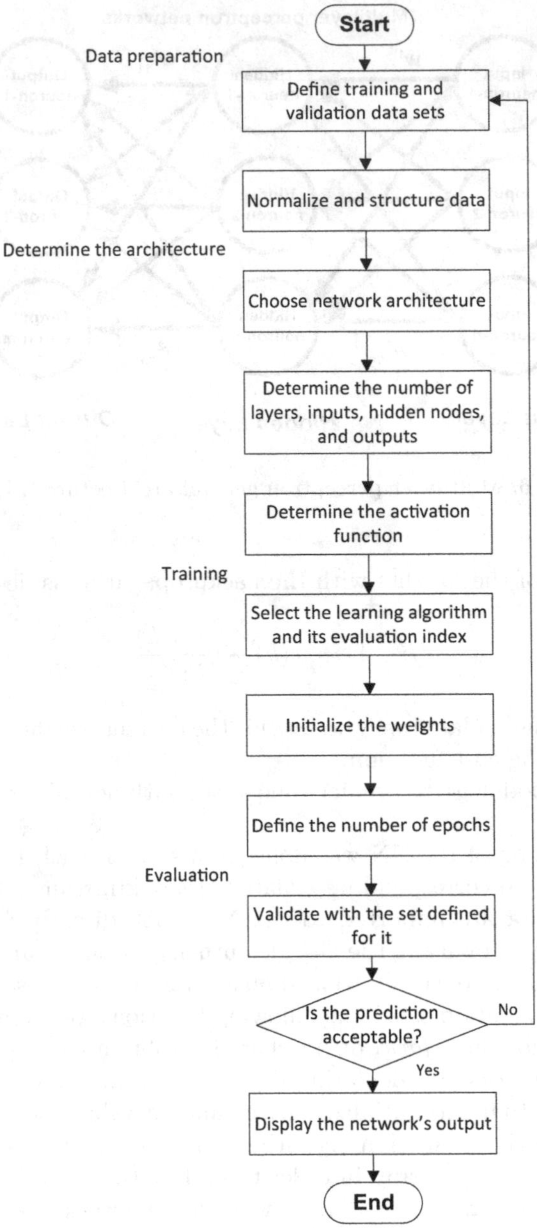

Fig. 7. Process for the prediction of time series with neural networks.

5.1 Prototype 1

The rest of the hyperparameters to be determined are proposed heuristically and chosen once the training graph looks similar to the training data, afterward comparing as well the validation data with the network's output and trying to get a decent mean squared error. After that process is done, the hyperparameters for prototype 1 are defined (Table 1).

Table 1. Hyperparameters for prototype 1's neural network.

Hyperparameter	Value
Inputs:	30
Nodes in hidden layer:	50
Predictions:	31
Outputs:	31
Learning rate:	0.3
Epochs:	100

The training graph (Fig. 8) shows the last 30 values from the training set (i.e., the daily consumption in June) since the network is being trained to predict 31 days with 61 values that the training set has. The two variables shown are the target (the real collected data) and the network output, from it one can see that the network output is, in fact, trying to follow the real data dynamics and it is proven by the fact that the Mean Error is $ME = -0.0639$ L and the Mean Squared Error is $MSE = 3\ 120.96$.

On the other hand, the evaluation of the prediction is done by comparing the validation data to the network prediction (Fig. 9), in this case, the network does show a similar dynamic, although not as in the training, this is due to the inherent properties of this time series, which does not present any pattern nor expected behavior. Nevertheless, the ME presented is only 9.61 L. Furthermore, in Table 2 the $MSEs$ of the lineal regressive models adapted to forecast this data compared with the one of the NN are shown. The NN remarkably outperforms its opponents.

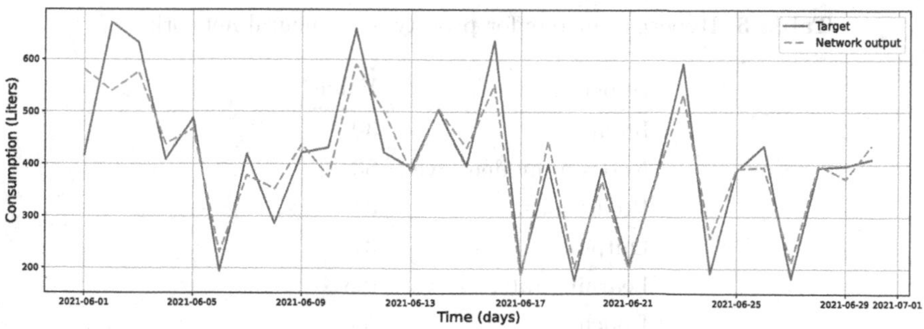

Fig. 8. NN training graph (prototype 1).

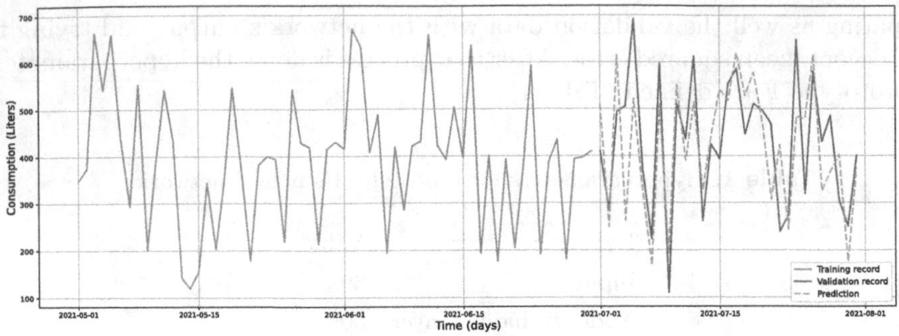

Fig. 9. NN prediction (prototype 1).

Table 2. MSEs of the lineal regressive models and the NN (prototype 1).

Model	MSE
$AR(10)$	28 611.32
$ARMA(1,1)$	20 734.26
NN	10 987.77

Important values to note are the three largest errors, they correspond to the pairs (04/07/2021, 242.06 L), (05/07/2021, 170.45 L), and (22/07/2021, −183.92 L), whereas the smallest errors are (14/07/2021, −15.8 L), (19/07/2021, 25.95 L), and (31/07/2021, 25.25 L).

5.2 Prototype 2

In the same way as for prototype 1, the hyperparameters for prototype 2 were proposed (Table 3), obtaining the training and validation graphs in Figs. 10 and 11, respectively, both show an even better visual approximation with the real data than the first prototype.

Table 3. Hyperparameters for prototype 2's neural network.

Hyperparameter	Value
Inputs:	30
Nodes in hidden layer:	63
Predictions:	31
Outputs:	31
Learning rate:	0.5
Epochs:	50

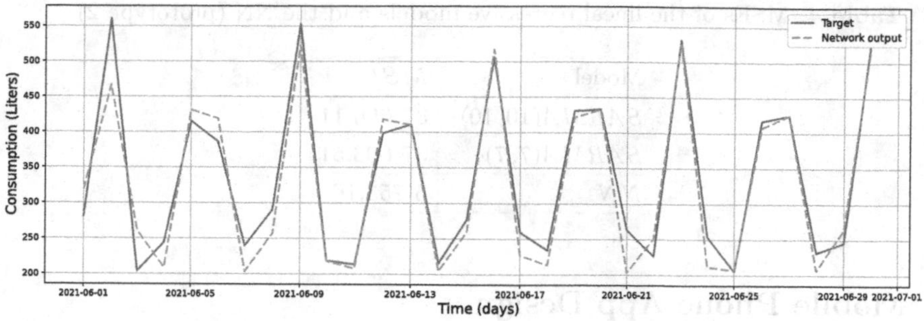

Fig. 10. NN training graph (prototype 2).

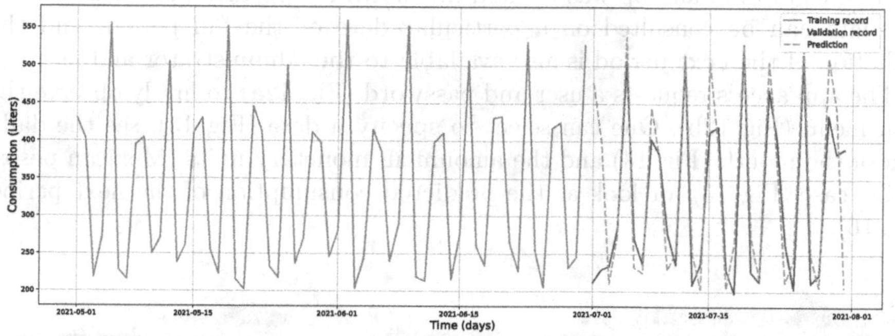

Fig. 11. NN prediction (prototype 2).

It is important to note that this time series has a property that in time series analysis is known as seasonality, a repetitive pattern every fixed period, in this case, every 7 days (i.e., weekly), however on 03/07/2022 that pattern was altered being shifted. Since that date is part of the data intended for the validation, that change was not considered in the training, which could have been part of the reason for the not most optimal performance of the model. The training yielded the errors $ME = 8.496$ L and $MSE = 958.64$, while the validation, even with the shifted seasonality gives $ME = -17.65$ L, and the MSE overpasses by far the ones from the lineal regressive models (Table 4).

The greatest deviations are only on 01/07/2022, 2/07/2022, and 31/07/2022, corresponding to errors of −265.51 L, −171.6 L, and 184.9 L, meanwhile, practically negligible errors were found on 12/07/2022, 19/07/2022, and 21/07/2022, with only $-3.54\ L$, $0.51\ L$, and $-4.1\ L$, respectively.

Table 4. MSEs of the lineal regressive models and the NN (prototype 2).

Model	MSE
$SARMA(10, 10)_7$	37 650.11
$SARMA(7, 7)_7$	37 603.51
NN	5 753.16

6 Mobile Phone App Design

So that the final user is able to have a practical way of viewing their household water consumption an app was created in the MIT App Inventor environment. The data can be consulted on a particular date or the full period, and the prediction of the next period is also available to the administrator and user.

The app access requests a user and password (Fig. 12a) to firstly observe the main menu (Fig. 12b). One can select to specify a date (Fig. 13), see the daily data of the month (Fig. 14) and the amount in monetary units (Mexican pesos, in this case, Fig. 15); or look at the predicted consumption of the next period (Fig. 16).

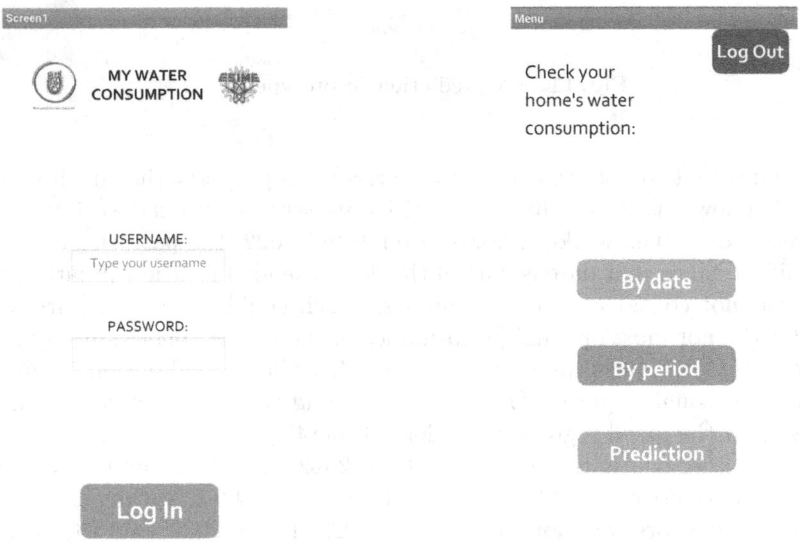

(a) Access screen. (b) Main menu.

Fig. 12. App's initial screens.

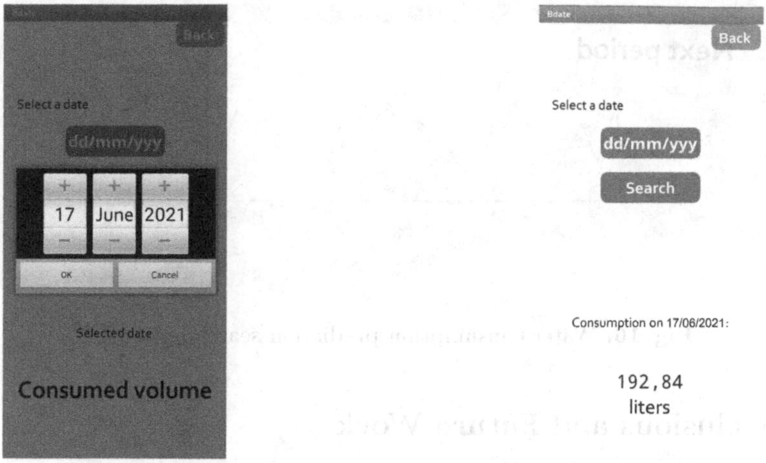

(a) Date selection. (b) Search result.

Fig. 13. Water consumption search by date option.

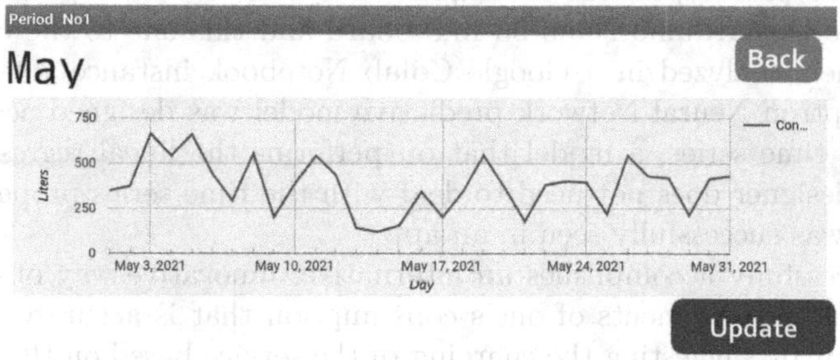

Fig. 14. Water consumption search by period option.

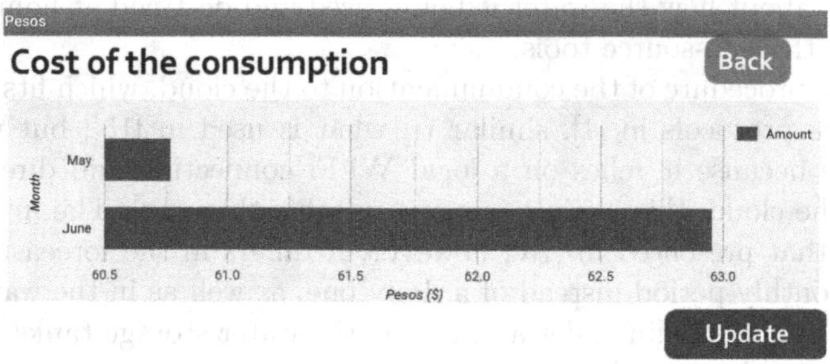

Fig. 15. Water consumption cost.

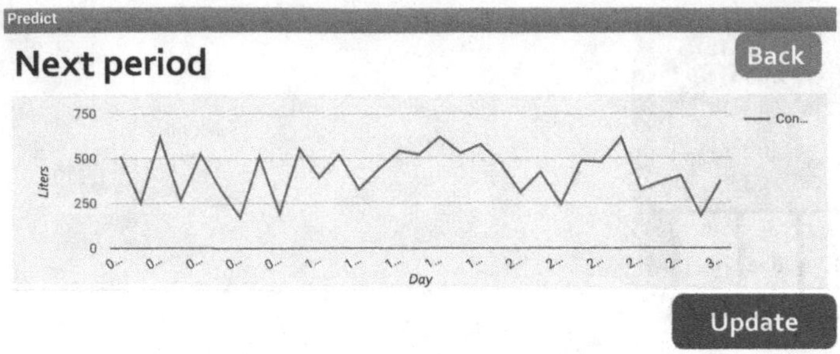

Fig. 16. Water consumption prediction search option.

7 Conclusions and Future Work

The monitoring of the water consumption as well as the record of it in the cloud for its analysis and visualization is achieved by the approach developed in this work. The automatic collection of the water consumption patterns simulated by each of the prototypes was accomplished by interconnecting the YF-S201 flow sensor to the Arduino Nano 33 IoT board and this one to the cloud. The data were then analyzed in a Google Colab Notebook instance where a Multilayer Perceptron Neural Network predictive model was designed according to the gathered time series, a model that outperforms the lineal regressive models and the designer does not need to deal with the time series properties. The information was successfully seen in an app.

This successfully accomplishes an alternative, innovative way of doing and presenting the measurements of one's consumption that is accurate, semiautomatic, and fair by suggesting the charging of the service based on the consumed volume. Moreover, the user is aware of both past and future data since a record and forecast with the NN are presented in the app, which is valuable to take consciousness about how the water is being used and destined at home. All this is achieved with open-source tools.

Due to the procedure of the communication to the cloud, which fits the short-range network protocols in [1], similar to what is used in [15], but with more independence because it relies on a local Wi-Fi connection and directly sends the data to the cloud, this project is more suitable than [18]. The intent of this is similar to that presented in [10], however, it differs in the forecast approach by using a monthly period instead of a daily one, as well as in the way the data are collected at the pipeline inlet and not at the water storage tanks. Since this is continuous monitoring, the impact of changes such as the toilet replacement example in [9] on consumption can also be detected.

In future work, the approach can generally become more robust and independent of some of the tools used until now, for example, by developing a server to host a private database as well as transfer the app to another environment, although maintaining the open-source scheme. The NN can additionally be adapted to online training. It is important to note that the behavior of the prediction model will improve as more data are collected, allowing it to get better and longer-period forecasts. This work can be integrated into projects such as [5,6,16] on a smaller scale for water applications at home.

References

1. Al-Sarawi, S., Anbar, M., Alieyan, K., Alzubaidi, M.: Internet of things (IoT) communication protocols: review. In: 2017 8th International Conference on Information Technology (ICIT) (2017)
2. Arduino: Arduino nano 33 iot (2021). https://docs.arduino.cc/hardware/nano-33-iot
3. Barrio Andrés, M.: Internet de las Cosas. Reus (2018)
4. Chatfield, C., Xing, H.: The Analysis of Time Series, chap. 1. CRC Press (2019)
5. Chirilă, A.I., Deaconu, I.D., Năvrăpescu, V., Ghiţă, C., Smeu, G.A.: Internet of things applications in water pumping stations and distribution networks. 2020 International Symposium on Fundamentals of Electrical Engineering (2020). https://doi.org/10.1109/ISFEE51261.2020.9756161
6. Cloete, N.A., Malekian, R., Nair, L.: Design of smart sensors for real-time water quality monitoring. IEEE Access **4**, 3975–3990 (2016). https://doi.org/10.1109/ACCESS.2016.2592958
7. Comisión Nacional del Agua: Manual de Agua Potable, Alcantarillado y Saneamiento - Diseño de Redes de Distribución de Agua Potable. CONAGUA (2019)
8. De la Fuente Fernández, S.: Series temporales: Modelo ARIMA. Universidad Autónoma de Madrid (2012)
9. Freitas, L.L.G., Kalbusch, A., Henning, E., Walter, O.M.F.C.: Using statistical control charts to monitor building water consumption: a case study on the replacement of toilets. Water **13**(18) (2021). https://doi.org/10.3390/w13182474
10. Gautam, J., Chakrabarti, A., Agarwal, S., Singh, A., Gupta, S., Singh, J.: Monitoring and forecasting water consumption and detecting leakage using an IoT system. Water Supply **20**(3), 1103–1113 (2020). https://doi.org/10.2166/ws.2020.035
11. Google Colab: Welcome to colaboratory (2022). http://www.colab.research.google.com/?utm_source=scs-index&hl=en
12. Méndez, M.: Tubería a presión en los sistemas de abastecimiento de agua, chap. 5.4. Publicaciones UCAB (2007)
13. Naylamp Mechatronics: Sensores de flujo (2020). http://www.naylampmechatronics.com/sensores-liquido/108-sensor-de-flujo-de-agua-12-yf-s201.html
14. Palit, A.K., Popovic, D.: Computational Intelligence in Time Series Forecasting, chap. 3. Springer (2005)
15. Perumal, T., Nasir Sulaiman, M., Leong, C.Y.: Internet of things (iot) enabled water monitoring system. In: 2015 IEEE 4th Global Conference on Consumer Electronics (GCCE) (2015)
16. Pule, M., Yahya, A., Chuma, J.: Wireless sensor networks: A survey on monitoring water quality. J. Appl. Res. Technol. **15**(6) (2019). https://doi.org/10.1016/j.jart.2017.07.004
17. Pállas, R.: Sensores y acondicionadores de señal, p. 224. Boixareu Editores, 7 edn. (2003)
18. Rodrigues Alves, A.J., Tiago Manera, L., Veloso Campos, M.: Low-cost wireless sensor network applied to real-time monitoring and control of water consumption in residences. SciELO (2019). https://doi.org/10.4136/ambi-agua.2407

Visualization of the Regular Mobility of Trips Between Bike Stations in the ECOBICI System

Gilberto Martínez[1(✉)], Samuel Benitez[2], and Adolfo Guzmán[1]

[1] Centro de Investigación en Computación (CIC), Avenida Juan de Dios Bátiz S/N, 07738 Mexico City, Mexico
{lluna,aguzman}@cic.ipn.mx

[2] Instituto Politécnico Nacional (IPN), Avenida Juan de Dios Bátiz S/N, 07738 Mexico City, Mexico
sbenitezm1701@alumno.ipn.mx

Abstract. It is important to know the mobility in terms of the origin and destination of trips made by users of station-based bike-sharing systems (BSS), such as the ECOBICI system in Mexico City. The importance lies in the fact that it can help to understand the problem of lack of bikes and saturation of stations and therefore could partially help to solve this balancing problem (moving bikes to where they are needed).

Mobility patterns are discovered in this paper using one and two-variable graphs (histograms, scatter plots, and box plots), tools used in the early stages of Data Science to describe a complex phenomenon in a simple but effective way. With the help of these graphs, temporal, and geographic patterns of urban bike mobility in Mexico City are described.

This paper describes the following patterns: a) neighborhoods of origin and destination of bike trips; b) recurrent patterns on weekdays and weekends; c) patterns in different schedules; d) patterns between neighborhoods and e) neighborhoods where most of the trips are made locally.

Neighborhoods with similar mobility have been identified, having a proportion of recurring trips at defined schedules throughout the day, with one or more increases in the demand for bikes. However, neighborhoods with abnormal mobility have also been found with a single schedule in which demand increases, as well as some relationships between some neighborhoods that regularly share trips. This is an example of the application of Data Science using data visualization tools applied to urban mobility and bike-sharing systems.

Keywords: Bike-sharing system · Urban mobility · Data science · Exploratory analysis · Data visualization · Geographic patterns

1 Introduction

1.1 Bike-Sharing System

A bike-sharing system (BSS) is an urban mobility solution that temporarily makes a limited number of bikes available to users. They are part of a sustainable transport

M. F. Mata-Rivera et al. (Eds.): WITCOM 2022, CCIS 1659, pp. 76–99, 2022.
https://doi.org/10.1007/978-3-031-18082-8_6

approach by governments and urban planning agencies to stimulate sustainable mobility, reduce traffic congestion, reduce car use, improve air quality, improve connectivity, and promote a healthy lifestyle [1].

They are usually based on the principle of station management, places where bikes can be picked up so that they can later be left at the same station or at any other station throughout the city where they are located.

1.2 ECOBICI

ECOBICI is the public BSS of Mexico City that has integrated the bike as an essential part of mobility, aimed at the inhabitants of the city, its surroundings, and tourists [2].

It allows registered users to take a bike from any bike station and return it to the nearest one to their destination in unlimited 45-min rides. Those who want to access the ECOBICI system can pay a subscription for one year, one week, three days, or even one day.

According to its official web page [2, 3], in 2022 this system currently has more than 374,000 registered users and the service is active around 55 neighborhoods of Mexico City in an area of 38 km^2.

ECOBICI has been in operation since 2010 and thanks to the great acceptance of this system and a continuous increase in demand, after 8 years, in 2018 bike stations increased to 480 with more than 6,800 bikes available throughout a limited area of the city.

Public Data. ECOBICI makes all its historical data since 2010 available to the public on its official web page [4]. The trip data is stored and published monthly, that is, it is possible to obtain the trips for each year and each month up to the current year since at the end of a month a new CSV file is added with the registered trips.

Each of these CSV files has the following data and format:

- *Genero_Usuario*: Female or male (F, M)
- *Edad_Usuario*: Age of the user who made the trip
- *Bici*: ID of the bicycle used in the trip
- *Ciclo_Estacion_Retiro*: ID of the bike station in which the trip began
- *Fecha_Retiro*: Date on which the trip began in dd/mm/yyyy format
- *Hora_Retiro*: Time the trip started in hh:mm:ss format
- *Ciclo_Estacion_Arribo*: ID of the bike station where the trip ended
- *Fecha_Arribo*: Date on which the trip ended in dd/mm/yyyy format
- *Hora_Arribo*: Time the trip ended in hh:mm:ss format

Similarly, it is possible to obtain the information of each bike station: name, location (neighborhood and district), and coordinates. This information is obtained directly from the ECOBICI public API on the same web page.

2 Literature Review

In this section, we first review recent studies on BSS and some of their most common challenges. The planning process of these systems commonly involves strategic, tactical, and operational activities and decisions that require constant research, evaluation, and the use of multiple tools to facilitate all the possible adjustments and improvements they may need during their design or management.

In [14] are described and summarized some of the BSS planning problems, including bicycle station design, inventory management, static or dynamic bicycle relocation or rebalancing, static or dynamic demand management, etc. This work also describes and compiles the research that currently makes up the state of the art and the solutions proposed to face the abovementioned problems in the BSS in multiple cities around the world.

The bicycle rebalancing problem consists of the strategic positioning of bikes to cover the expected demand throughout the day, preventing a station from running out of bikes or being full for a very long time. If all the stations of a BSS are balanced, then the system is balanced, and the overall demand will be covered. This is a problem since the imbalance ultimately results in a decrease in users' satisfaction and, therefore, in the system usage. A BSS must be able to offer one bike for each user who requires it in the place and time they need it.

However, this problem is complex and strongly depends on the type of BSS (station-based or free-floating), the type of rebalancing: during the night when the system is closed or the usage is negligible (static balancing) or during the day when the status of the system changes rapidly (dynamic balancing), and the transportation method used to redistribute the bikes, among other variables.

In the literature, there are approaches such as those discussed in [16] and [19], works that aim to implement and develop algorithms capable of repositioning bikes with the lowest possible cost or with the best available route according to the availability and demand of the systems, respectively.

These two works focus on station-based BSS, such as ECOBICI, and static bicycle rebalancing. Other investigations analyze free-floating BSS or dynamic balancing, although the latter become even more complicated due to the freedom that users have to leave bikes in non-predefined stations and the complexity of predicting demand at different times of the day. For this reason, generating tools that allow visualizing the demand in the different areas of a city becomes a necessity and a fundamental aid for the definition of strategies to solve this balancing problem.

On the other hand, inventory management is another very common problem in BSSs that is directly related to rebalancing. It consists of adjusting the network of bike stations and the inventory of resources in each station with the appropriate number of bikes and parking docks to minimize the events of a shortage and improve service quality. Although this problem also involves the detection and prevention of broken bikes, as well as their replacement or repair.

For this problem, in [17] a simulation-optimization heuristic is proposed to optimize the bike inventory in ECOBICI BSS for both static and dynamic rebalancing operations. In that work, different algorithms are used for static inventory optimization, as well as a heuristic for dynamic optimization that places and removes bikes during the day to reduce shortage and saturation events.

They presented an interesting solution with favorable results for both problems, although they only use data from ECOBICI between June and August 2017, historically the year with the highest number of trips. However, mobility can change significantly from one year to another and even in different months of the same year due to other factors, such as vacations or school periods. Therefore, it is extremely important to keep track of patterns and variations in demand, in conjunction with the management of stations and parking docks.

Other works focus directly on demand prediction, for example, the proposed in [15]. Statistical models are used to try to predict the number of trips that a pair of stations will have in a specific hour, as well as the duration of the trip. Other variables that influence this prediction are also studied, such as the weather, effects of the bike stations that are close to different points of interest, etc.

Finally, there are other works with the objective of not only predicting demand but also generating visualization tools that allow them to do so dynamically and interactively. These tools can be very useful for system operators, such is the case of the work presented in [18]. In this work, a visualization tool capable of predicting the demand concerning the beginning and end of the trips in each station during the day was developed.

This tool is based on different machine learning regression algorithms that were tested in a BSS in Greece to identify the correlation that exists between the number of trips and other characteristics of the system such as the location and space of a station, the season of the year, the weather and different times of the day. It is also an interesting approach since it shows the possible bike demand that the BSS will have according to different internal and external factors of the system itself at different time intervals during the day.

The approach proposed in this paper consists of a similar approach, analyzing the patterns at the neighborhood level through the creation of visualizations and thereby facilitating the detection of the bike demand throughout the day between weekdays and weekends. The main objective is not to develop a specific model or algorithm to solve the problems described above but to generate visualization tools that are useful to study these problems in a much more comprehensive way and support operational decisions. This will result in the generation of hypotheses and will serve as a basis for future work that focuses on predicting the number of trips per station and day and thereby facilitating the static and dynamic bike rebalancing in the different neighborhoods of the ECOBICI BSS.

Some of the existing data analysis and visualization systems that integrate the open data provided by ECOBICI are listed below (See Fig. 1).

2.1 PLANBIKE [5]

It is an open data analysis system of ECOBICI available and for public use to be a reliable source of statistics and support information for user decision-making. It has different visualizations of trips as origin or destination on mobility patterns at the neighborhood level, districts, or even at the bike station level, on weekdays or weekends. It was developed and managed by the Data Science and Software Technology Laboratory (LCDyTS), of CIC - IPN.

2.2 System of Historical Analysis of Individual Mobility (SAHMI) [6]

SAHMI is a system for analyzing and visualizing historical data published by ECOBICI to reveal historical patterns and trends of trips made by users to generate knowledge of the use of bikes and the advancement of the service over the years.

It has visualizations referring to the number of annual and monthly trips, the comparison of the number of trips by gender or age of the users, and the registration or elimination of bike stations and bikes, among others.

Like PLANBIKE, it was developed and is currently managed by the CIC's LCDyTS.

2.3 Bike Share Map

It is a real-time system focused on visualizing the different bike-sharing systems in the world and some of their general statistics, including ECOBICI [7]. In this, it is possible to obtain the geographical position of each bike station, as well as the number of bikes available and a general description of the different systems: the operator, station-based or free-floating systems, the type of bicycles, the technology used, etc.

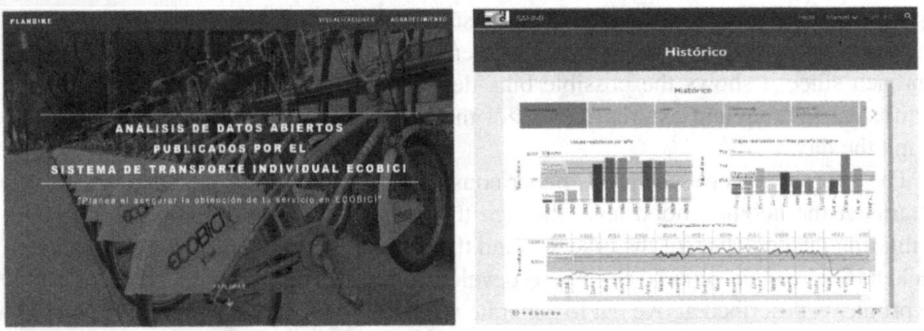

a) PLANBIKE (CIC-IPN) b) SAHMI (CIC-IPN)

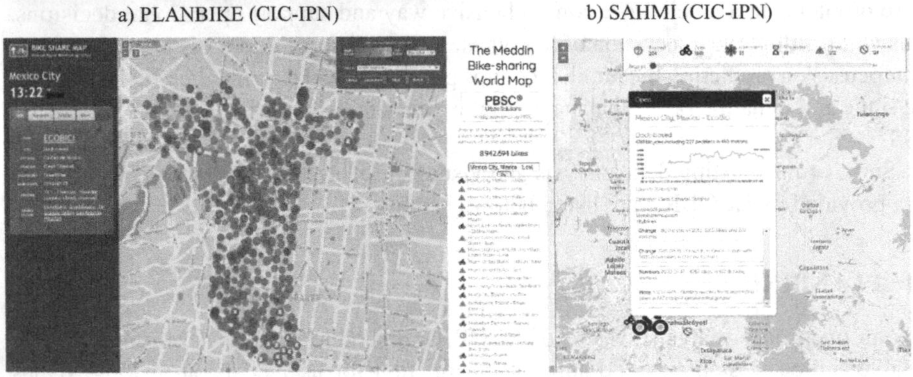

c) Bike Share Map d) The Meddin Bike-sharing World Map

Fig. 1. Software with analytical information from ECOBICI

2.4 The Meddin Bike-Sharing World Map

Similarly, The Meddin Bike-Sharing World Map has a map of all the bike-sharing systems in the world but also provides a directory of information on the general growth of each of these [8, 9].

This system focuses on the general view of the growth of the bike-sharing system industry. Recently, in October 2021, a report was released as a result of the constant analysis of these systems and the changes that were experienced in the COVID-19 pandemic [10].

3 Methodology

3.1 Mobility Patterns and Visualizations

This paper aims to study the different mobility patterns of users' trips in the multiple neighborhoods in which the service is currently active.

To achieve this, Tableau will be used, a tool for data analysis and visualization [11], in addition to two of the systems related to ECOBICI data managed by the LCDyTS of CIC: PLANBIKE and SAHMI.

These last two represent works to publicly provide a way to analyze ECOBICI data simply and practically, generating statistics of interest to any user of the system. PLANBIKE focuses on the analysis of the patterns in the different levels of the data, while SAHMI only focuses on the historical analysis and the progress of the system over the years, for this reason, the visualizations presented throughout this work will be later added to a future extended version of PLANBIKE.

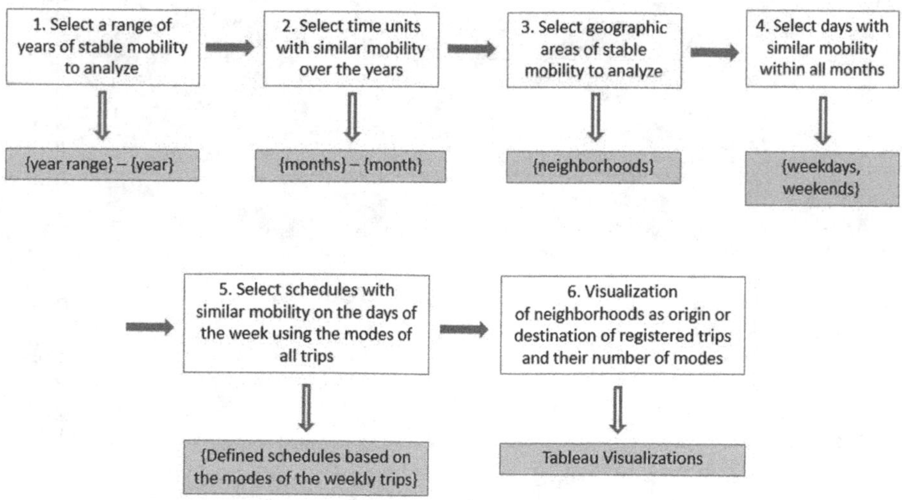

Fig. 2. Methodology for the analysis of the mobility of ECOBICI trips

3.2 Analysis Plan

The analysis follows the steps shown in Fig. 2, which are discussed in more detail throughout the following sections. These steps will be illustrated with data from the year 2019 since it represents the last year with bike mobility without variations in bike stations, the number of bikes, and phenomena that alter mobility, concerning previous years, but also to subsequent years, since in the latter there was a decrease in the number of trips, a direct effect of the COVID-19 pandemic (See Fig. 4).

4 Mobility Analysis Between Neighborhoods

Select a Range of Years for Analysis. Figure 3 supports the fact of selecting the year 2019 since it did not present too much fluctuation with the number of bike stations added or disabled, the number of these remained relatively constant, oscillating in the 480 stations that were mentioned previously and in a very similar way the number of available bikes circulating in the system.

Select Time Units with Similar Mobility. In this case, the analysis will be focused on the number of trips per unit of time, the month, since holidays, school activities, workdays, and mobility between weekdays and weekends depend on the month to be analyzed and not on a certain week or another unit of time.

March is taken as a reference since it represents one of the months with the highest frequency of registered trips in several of the 12 years of service in which ECOBICI

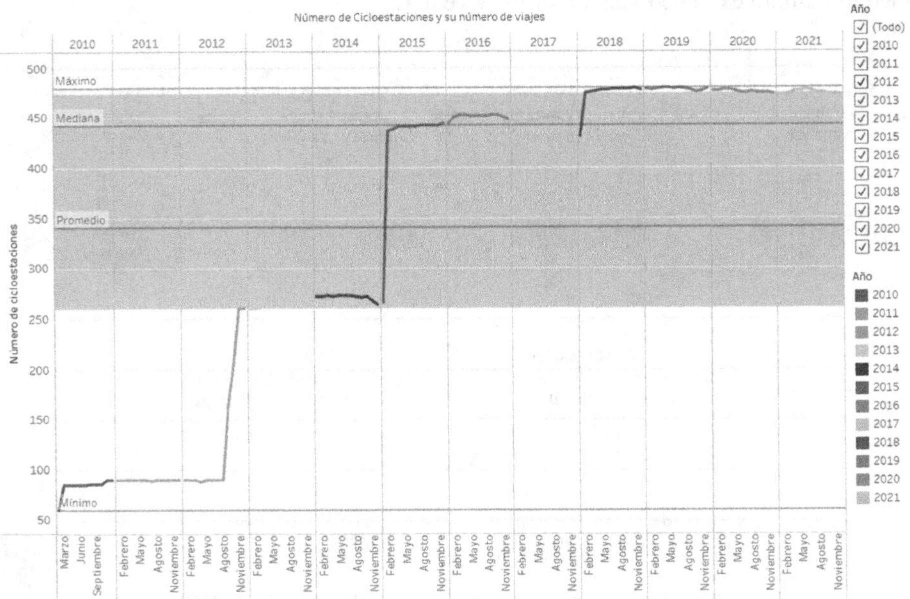

Fig. 3. SAHMI: historical graph of the number of bike stations over the years. Since 2019, no stations have been added or removed, they have only had maintenance.

has been active. In the case of the year 2019 (see Fig. 4), this month had over 750,000 bicycle trips.

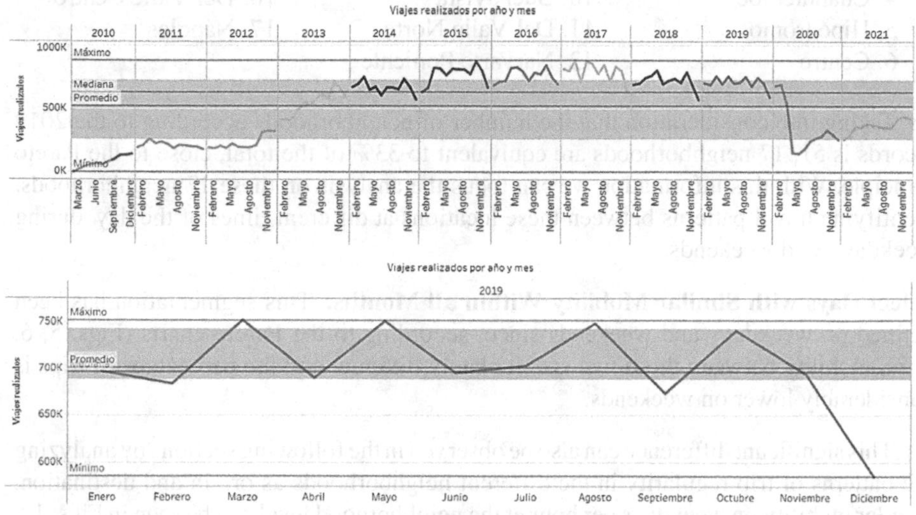

Fig. 4. SAHMI: graph of annual travel history, focused on the year 2019. Among the months with greater mobility can be observed: March, May, August, and October.

Select Geographic Areas to Analyze. The geographical areas to be analyzed are the neighborhoods since they represent the objective of this study, in addition to the fact that mobility patterns can be generalized on a larger scale by focusing on different city areas and not only bike stations.

4.1 Neighborhoods with the Highest Number of Trips

The analysis starts with the hypothesis of the Pareto principle (80/20 rule) [12], which describes that 80% of all the effects of a statistical phenomenon result from 20% of all its causes, that is, that we can obtain a smaller subset with which a maximum effect is obtained. In this case, the effect is represented as the number of monthly trips and the causes as the neighborhoods.

The first thing is to identify which neighborhoods are those that gather 80% of monthly trips, from Monday to Friday or on weekends. We can easily know this by observing the Pareto charts in the neighborhoods as the origin and destination of trips. From the Figs. 5, 6, 7, 8 there are approximately 17 neighborhoods that contribute 80% of the trips in a month like March:

1. Roma Norte
2. Juárez
3. Polanco
4. Cuauhtémoc
5. Hipódromo
6. Centro
7. Roma Sur
8. San Rafael
9. Condesa
10. Buenavista
11. Del Valle Norte
12. Narvarte Poniente
13. Escandón
14. Del Valle Sur
15. Anzures
16. Del Valle Centro
17. Nápoles

Taking into consideration that the number of neighborhoods according to the 2019 records is 51, 17 neighborhoods are equivalent to 33% of the total, close to the Pareto principle. With this information we can focus the analysis on these 17 neighborhoods, identifying travel patterns between these locations at different times of the day, during weekdays, and weekends.

Select Days with Similar Mobility Within all Months. This segmentation has been defined on weekdays and weekends since, according to the Pareto charts (Figs. 5, 6, 7, 8), mobility between those two is completely different and the percentage of trips is considerably lower on weekends.

This significant difference can also be observed in the following sections by analyzing the patterns of trip regularity in the different neighborhoods as origin and destination. Similar mobility on weekdays per hour at the neighborhood level can be seen in Figs. 12, 14, and 15, while mobility on weekends per hour is exemplified in Fig. 13.

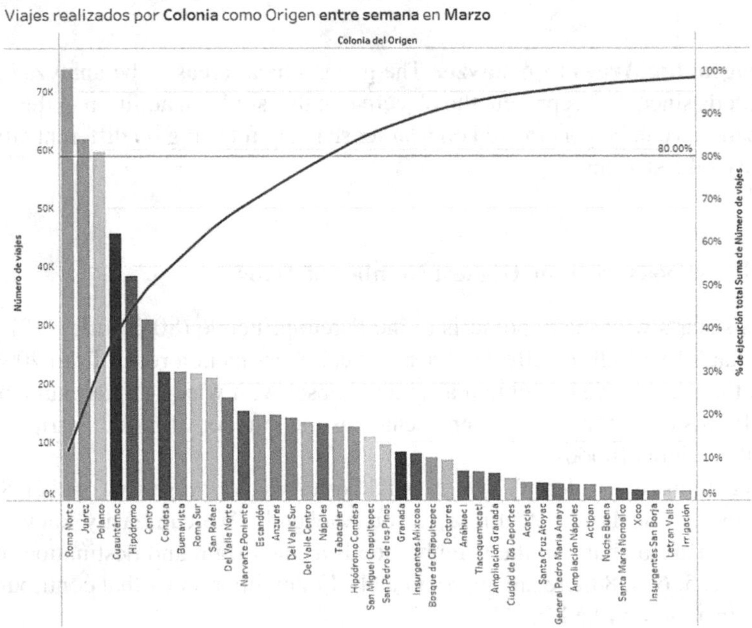

Fig. 5. PLANBIKE II: pareto chart of trips by origin neighborhood on weekdays in March. 17 neighborhoods make up 80% of the trips in a similar order to those listed above.

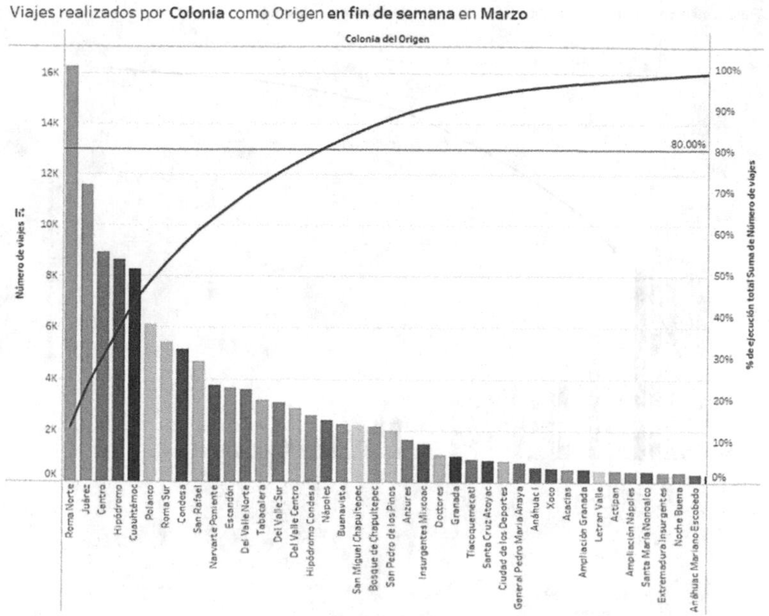

Fig. 6. PLANBIKE II: pareto chart of trips by origin neighborhood on weekends in March. The number of trips is significantly reduced compared to Fig. 5; however, the same neighborhoods are maintained, except for Tabacalera and Hipódromo Condesa.

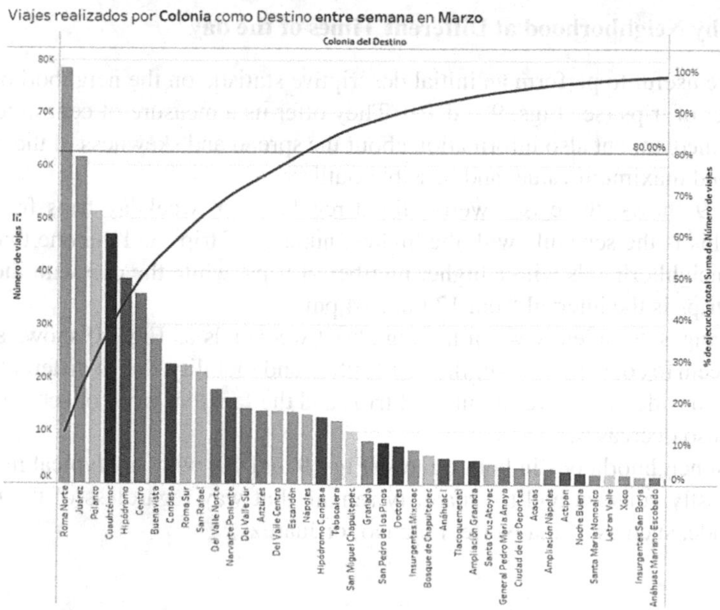

Fig. 7. PLANBIKE II: pareto chart of trips by destination neighborhood on weekdays in March. As in Fig. 5, the same neighborhoods are observed in a different order since this time they are taken as the destination of the trips.

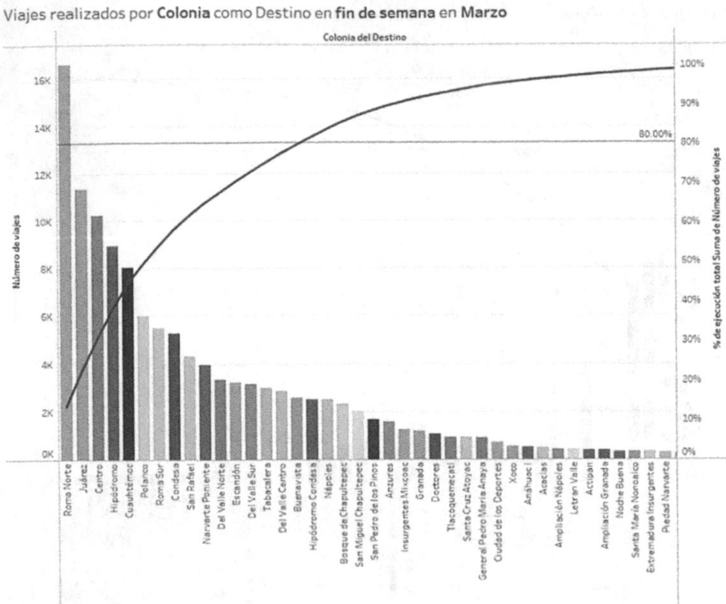

Fig. 8. PLANBIKE II: pareto chart of trips by destination neighborhood on weekends in March. Contrary to what is shown in Fig. 7, trips have again reduced significantly and presented a similar distribution to the neighborhoods in Fig. 6.

4.2 Trips by Neighborhood at Different Times of the day

Boxplots are useful to perform an initial descriptive statistic on the neighborhoods and their number of trips (see Figs. 9 and 10). They offer us a measure of central tendency such as the median, but also information about the spread and skewness of the data, the minimum and maximum value, and possible outliers.

As Fig. 9 shows, there is a well-defined regularity of weekday trips from 4 pm onwards. This is the schedule with the highest number of trips and the one that shows the outlier neighborhoods with a higher number of trips, while the one with the fewest number of trips is the interval from 12 pm to 4 pm.

This changes completely when talking about weekends as Fig. 10 shows since all schedules seem to converge to a similar distribution and mobility, due to different factors, such as the considerably lower number of trips and the fact that work or school activity in the city also decreases.

The first neighborhoods in both figures (Figs. 9 and 10) with an atypical number of trips are mostly constant and the majority remain that way regardless of the time the trips are made, such as Roma Norte, Polanco, or Juárez.

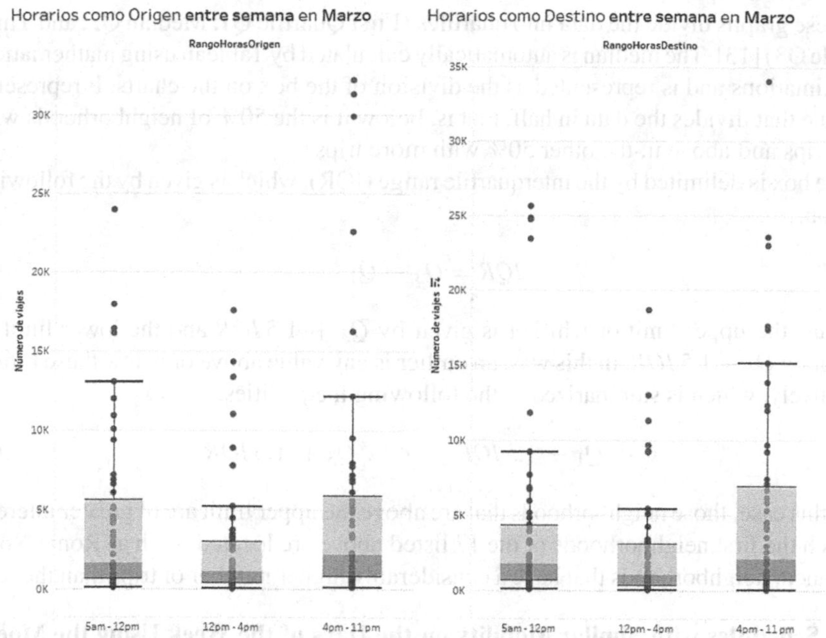

Fig. 9. Distribution of trips at different schedules in neighborhoods as the origin (left) and destination (right) during weekdays.

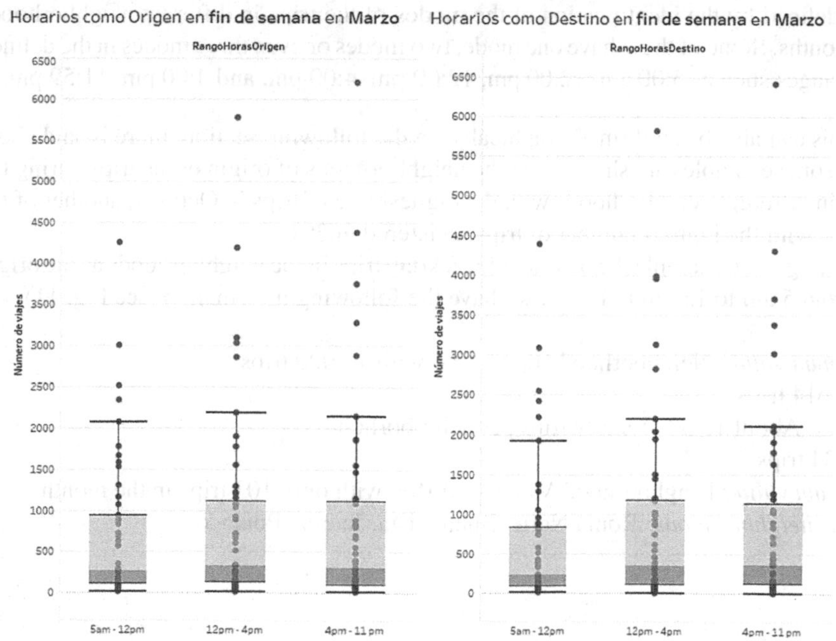

Fig. 10. Distribution of trips at different schedules in neighborhoods as the origin (left) and destination (right) during weekends. A more balanced distribution is observed.

These graphs divide the data into quartiles (First Quartile Q1, Median Q2, and Third Quartile Q3) [13]. The median is automatically calculated by Tableau using mathematical approximations and is represented as the division of the box on the charts. It represents the value that divides the data in half, that is, below it is the 50% of neighborhoods with fewer trips and above it, the other 50% with more trips.

The box is delimited by the interquartile range (IQR), which is given by the following equation.

$$IQR = Q_3 - Q_1 \tag{1}$$

Thus, the upper limit or whisker is given by $Q_3 + 1.5\,IQR$ and the lower limit or whisker by $Q_1 - 1.5\,IQR$. In this way, an outlier is any value above or below these limits, respectively, which is summarized in the following inequalities.

$$x < Q_1 - 1.5\,IQR \qquad x > Q_3 + 1.5\,IQR \tag{2}$$

In this case, those neighborhoods that are above the upper limit are of greater interest, in which the first neighborhoods of the 17 listed above are located, such as Roma Norte or Polanco, neighborhoods that have a considerably higher number of trips than the rest.

Select Schedules with Similar Mobility on the Days of the Week Using the Modes of All Trips. It is important to mention that the ECOBICI BSS is active every day from 5:00 am to 12:30 am, however, the trips made at midnight are minimal and in some of the graphs, it has been decided to omit them. In Figs. 9 and 10, the ranges of the schedules were defined by the identification of the modes of the trips in different neighborhoods and months. Some of these have one mode, two modes or even three modes in the defined time ranges such as 5:00 am–12:00 pm, 12:00 pm–4:00 pm, and 4:00 pm–11:59 pm.

This can also be confirmed graphically. In the following section, more is said about it and some examples are shown with the neighborhoods of origin of the trips during the week in different neighborhoods with the highest rate of trips in October, another of the months with the highest number of trips registered in 2019.

Taking as an example the boxplot of weekday trips in the neighborhoods as the origin and from 5 am to 12 pm in Fig. 9, we have the following information (see Fig. 11):

Maximum value: Neighborhood Hipódromo with 13,000 trips
Q3: 5,614 trips
Median: About 1,700 monthly trips per neighborhood
Q1: 634 trips
Minimum value: Neighborhood Molino del Rey with only 103 trips in the month
Outlier neighborhoods: Roma Norte, Buenavista, Juárez, Polanco.

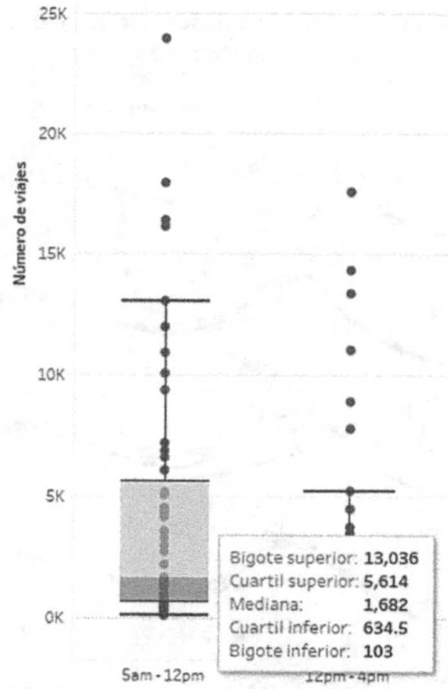

Fig. 11. Five-number summary of trips from the origin neighborhoods between the hours of 5 am to 12 pm. There is a positively skewed distribution, many of the neighborhoods do not represent a large contribution to the total number of trips.

4.3 Mobility Patterns Between Neighborhoods

Visualization of Neighborhoods as Origin or Destination of Registered Trips and Their Number of Modes. Using other PLANBIKE visualizations (see Figs. 12, 13, 14, 15), we can verify the patterns of the trips in the schedules that were previously defined. Below are some examples of the neighborhoods as the origin of trips in October, each of the colored lines represents a day of the week from Monday to Friday or Saturday and Sunday in the case of Fig. 13.

In the neighborhood Roma Norte (see Fig. 12), which represented the neighborhood with the most annual trips in 2019, the three travel modes are presented, with different slopes throughout the day due to the continuous demand for bikes. This behavior is completely different when talking about trips on weekends as shown in Fig. 13. Other neighborhoods with this behavior are also: Hipódromo, and Centro, among others (visualizations are omitted to avoid over-exemplifying the same pattern).

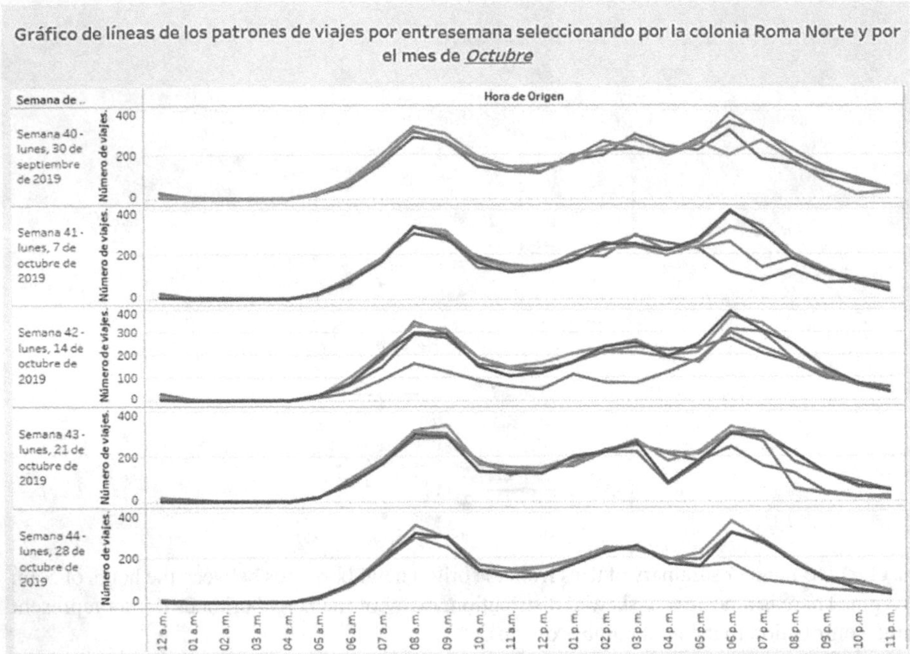

Fig. 12. PLANBIKE: distribution of weekdays (one color per day) trips throughout the day in Roma Norte in October. Trips are constantly made in the 3 schedules of the day.

On the other hand, one of the most atypical cases is found in the Buenavista neighborhood as shown in Fig. 14, one of the neighborhoods that only has a single mode in its trips as origin, this is immediately notorious and shows us an interesting pattern to follow. Other neighborhoods that have a similar behavior are Narvarte Poniente and Tabacalera, although not with the same high percentage of trips at the same range of hours.

Finally, there are also cases such as the Del Valle Norte neighborhood shown in Fig. 15, with two modes, in this case, one in the morning and the other in the evening. Other neighborhoods with this behavior are: Juárez and Polanco.

These weekly patterns and bike demand are repeated in the different neighborhoods with the highest number of trips, so it is worth studying which neighborhoods have similar behaviors and thereby identify more detailed mobility patterns.

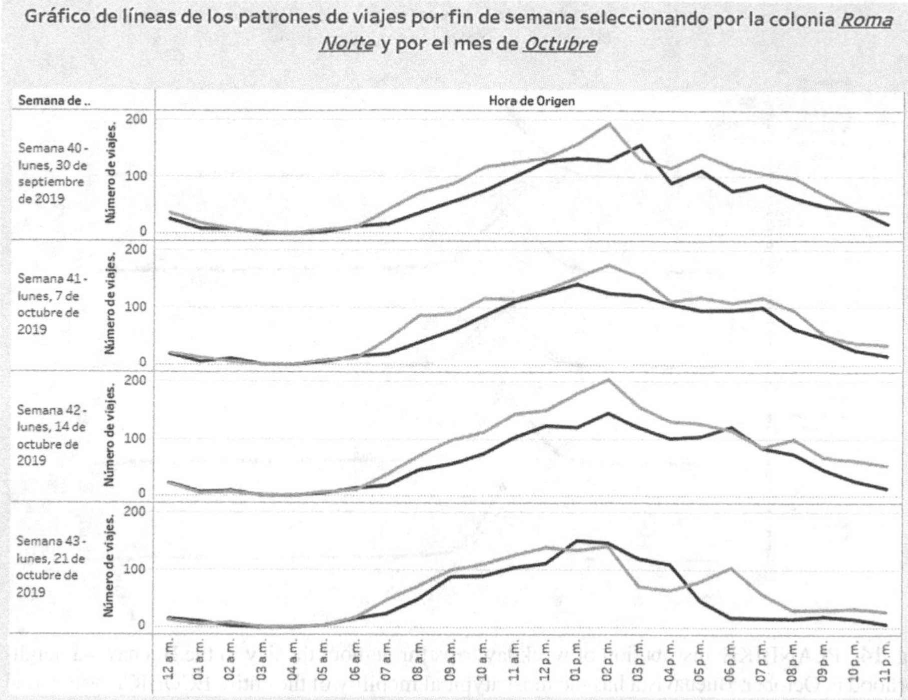

Fig. 13. PLANBIKE: distribution of weekend (Saturday as yellow and Sunday as green) trips throughout the day in Roma Norte in October. There is no defined distribution of trips in any of the schedules, trips are made arbitrarily throughout the day. (Color figure online)

In Figs. 16 and 17 are shown the distribution of trips by neighborhood at the defined schedules, either in neighborhoods as origin or destination of the trips. In general, as already mentioned, the busiest time, both in the hours of origin and in those of destination, is from 4 pm to 11 pm in most of the neighborhoods during the week, although not in all of them.

Trips on weekends show a much more balanced distribution between the different schedules, however, the number of trips is significantly reduced (approximately one trip on the weekend is equivalent to 5 trips on weekdays).

In the same Figs. 16 and 17, we also observe some interesting patterns, such as, for example, in Juárez, most of the cyclists leave around 4 pm to 11 pm, however, the majority arrive in this neighborhood in the morning from 5 am to 12 pm. This behavior is also found in other neighborhoods such as Polanco or Cuauhtémoc. (See Figs. 16 and 17).

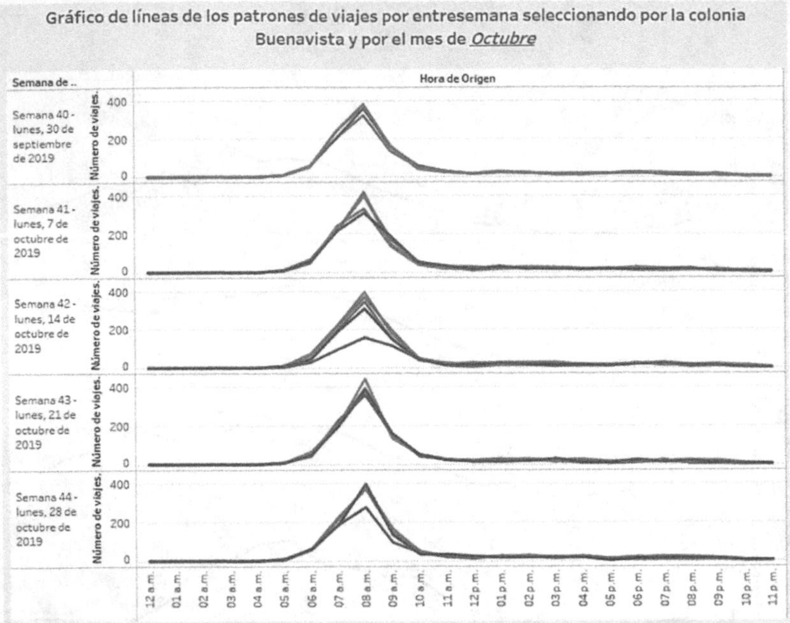

Fig. 14. PLANBIKE: distribution of weekday trips throughout the day in the Buenavista neighborhood in October. Buenavista has the most atypical mobility of the entire ECOBICI system due to the extremely high demand for bikes in the morning and a poorly demand for the rest of the day.

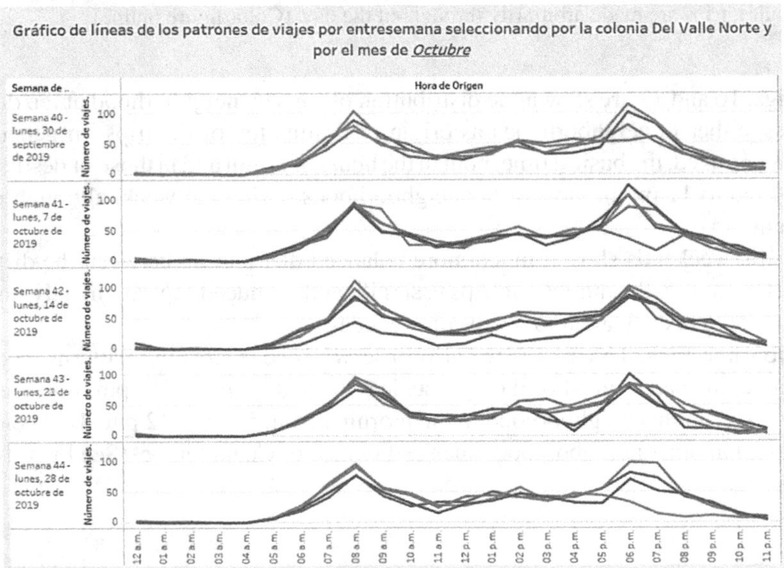

Fig. 15. PLANBIKE: distribution of weekday trips throughout the day in the Del Valle Norte neighborhood in October. This is an example of a neighborhood with two modes in its trips during the day. (Color figure online)

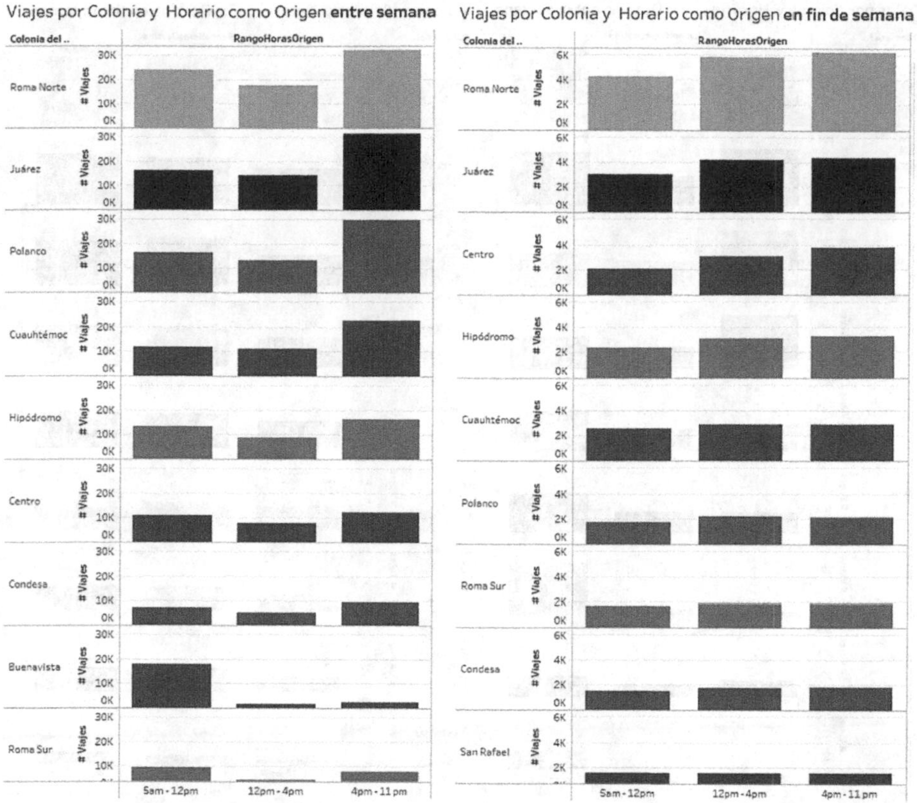

Fig. 16. PLANBIKE II: distribution of trips by schedule and by neighborhood as origin in March. Each color represents one neighborhood and its trips during the defined schedules on weekdays (left) and weekends (right). The departure times of the users in every neighborhood.

Another example is the Buenavista neighborhood, 80% of the people who start a trip in this neighborhood leave between 5 am and 12 pm (see Fig. 16), as shown in Fig. 14. However, this pattern also seems to be related to trips made to this neighborhood as the destination where 80% of the people who return to this neighborhood do so between the hours of 4 pm and 11 pm (see Fig. 17), therefore it is a very contrasting behavior in comparison with other neighborhoods in the system.

No other neighborhood has such remarkable behavior, we could say that this neighborhood is probably a critical point for the beginning of the trips and the end of them, possibly due to its geographical location. It represents the neighborhood that is further north of the region delimited by the ECOBICI system and that has one of the most used bike stations in the entire system, 271 on Carlos J. Meneses street with almost 90,000 annual trips in 2019. (See Fig. 18).

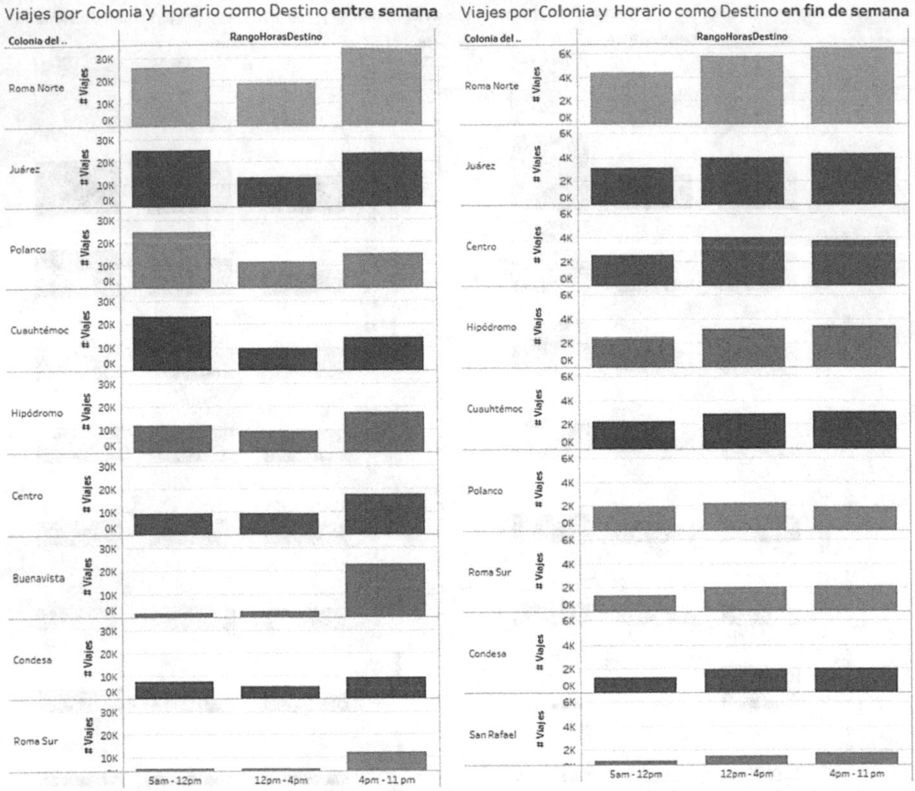

Fig. 17. PLANBIKE II: distribution of trips by schedule and by neighborhood as the destination in March. The arrival times of the users in every neighborhood.

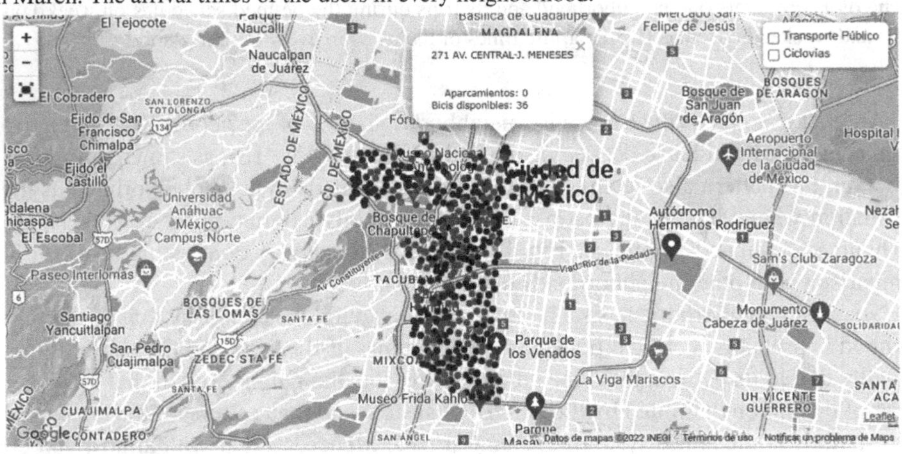

Fig. 18. ECOBICI bike stations map: bike station 271 was the most used in the system in 2019. Each point represents a bike station and the color the status of it. Green: 5 or more bicycles in the station, Yellow: less than 5 bicycles, Red: no bicycles available, and Grey: out of service.

5 Results: Important Observations Derived from the Visualizations

With all the above information, it is possible to analyze the mobility between each of the neighborhoods and how they share trips to identify where people go and what time they do it. Figures 19 and 20 show the top 8 neighborhoods with most trips as origin and destination in March, as well as the neighborhoods from which they come or to which they go, respectively, to show a general overview of mobility between neighborhoods and how some of them have strong relationships.

5.1 Local Mobility Patterns

It is evident that, in most cases, the trips can take place within the same neighborhood, that is, the origin and destination of a trip take place in the same neighborhood since they represent very short trips (see Figs. 19 and 20). This behavior can be associated with the terms known as the first or last mile of mobility as they represent trips that serve as a connection with other public transport such as the subway or Mexico City's Metrobús or that are part of a person's global mobility. It is a behavior in which users decide to use the bikes in the last or first stage of their trips.

The neighborhood that meets these characteristics and represents the one with the most local trips is Polanco ■(see Figs. 19 and 20) since it does not show much mobility to other neighborhoods and a very high percentage of the trips start and end in this same neighborhood. This may be due to different factors, such as the fact that it is a neighborhood on the edge of the western zone of ECOBICI or that due to its high concentration of economic and business activity, most of the trips are for very short journeys in time and distance, possibly from people on their way to work or even tourists.

Other examples of this behavior are observed in Roma Norte ■and Centro ■, although in a much smaller proportion than in Polanco. (See Figs. 19 and 20).

5.2 Neighborhood-to-Neighborhood Mobility Patterns

Even though many neighborhoods have a large number of trips made locally, others have great mobility between different neighborhoods. Juárez ■, for example, has a strong relationship between Cuauhtémoc ■and Buenavista ■. It receives trips in the morning from these two (see Fig. 20) and in the evening from Juárez, there also seems to be a return to these two neighborhoods (see Fig. 19).

Another example is Hipódromo ■, which constantly shares trips with the Roma Norte, both as the origin and as the destination. (See Figs. 19 and 20).

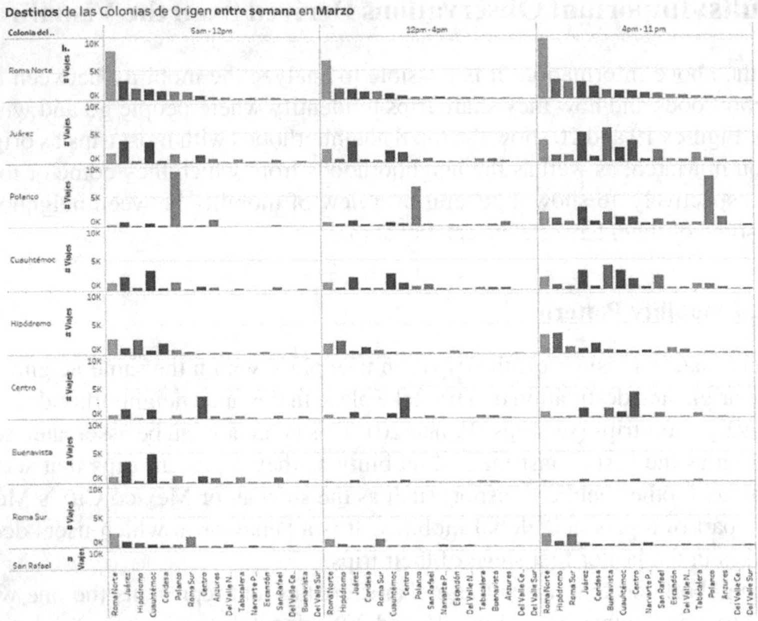

Fig. 19. PLANBIKE II: destinations of the origin neighborhoods of the trips during weekdays in March. Patterns are observed throughout the day between the top origin neighborhoods. Each color represents one neighborhood.

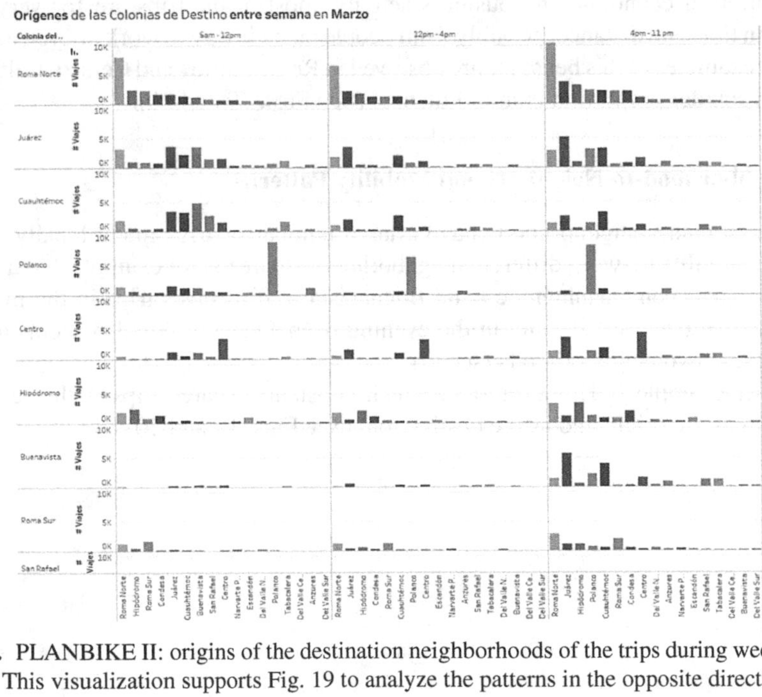

Fig. 20. PLANBIKE II: origins of the destination neighborhoods of the trips during weekdays in March. This visualization supports Fig. 19 to analyze the patterns in the opposite direction.

The pair of visualizations in Fig. 19 and 20 are very useful since they show us in more detail how mobility occurs between different areas of Mexico City's BSS, behaviors that could well be directly related to socioeconomic factors to discover even more descriptive and interesting patterns.

In this way, thanks to the use of a data visualization tool such as Tableau, ECOBICI's data analysis systems developed and maintained by the CIC's LCDyTS, and the exploratory analysis of public data it has been possible to fulfill the initial objective of this work, identifying and describing different patterns that make it possible to publicize mobility between neighborhoods within the ECOBICI system graphically and simply.

It has been possible to describe in a general way the mobility between bike stations in the different time ranges on weekdays and weekend days, identifying neighborhoods with a similar activity or others with totally abnormal behaviors that are worth continuing to explore in future work.

On the other hand, the visualizations presented here will be later added to the PLANBIKE system or a later version of it, so that they can be used publicly in the same way that the other visualizations have already been added to continue increasing the robustness and operation of the ECOBICI data analysis tools, encouraging different users to carry out their exploratory analysis dynamically and reliably.

6 Conclusions

A BSS not only provides a healthy and environmentally friendly alternative for individual mobility in the world's largest cities but also helps to relieve saturation from other transportation methods, such as buses or subways, and reduces car traffic. However, to promote bike usage for personal transportation, the operators of BSS must ensure that users' satisfaction is achieved. Therefore, demand management, bike rebalancing, and inventory management are particularly important to achieve this goal to improve service quality.

The developed visualization tools empower the management of ECOBICI BSS enabling accurate, data-driven decisions to optimize the system's operation and it can provide very useful insight for the development of mobility strategies. The bidirectional analysis of monthly trips (neighborhoods as origin or destination of the trips) makes it easy to analyze the demand for bicycles but also for parking docks at different times of the day, that is, it is possible to show which neighborhoods will possibly need bikes at a specific time and the same for parking docks to avoid shortage events.

Because of this, generating more diverse visualizations results in the identification of more and different mobility patterns, it becomes a much more interactive and enriching process for users. This is exactly the objective that PLANBIKE and SAHMI systems achieved, the inspiration for the creation of the visualizations presented in this paper, and that allowed us to exemplify in more detail the mobility patterns in a year with a great number of bike trips before the COVID-19 pandemic.

Due to the aforementioned, it is expected that this work can be used as a descriptive example of what is possible to analyze in an urban individual mobility system such as ECOBICI and use that information to improve the design, quality, and use of these systems focused on the shared use of bicycles.

No doubt analyzing a system with these characteristics has endless approaches and possible applications. The approach presented was exclusively for a particular year and analysis between neighborhoods, however, it is possible to scale this research and identify patterns on a larger scale (by districts, by year, by geographical areas, etc.), with the help of different data mining and machine learning tools to identify relationships in the data in a much more dynamic and automated way with different levels of data granularity or with other additional data features, such as the age of the users, the weather or any other external factor to identify more complex patterns.

References

1. Castellanos, S., De la Lanza, I., Lleras, N.: Guía para la Estructuración de Sistemas de Bicicletas Compartidas. In: Mecanismos y Redes de Transferencia de Tecnologías de Cambio Climático en Latinoamérica y el Caribe (LAC), pp. 17–20. Inter-American Development Bank (2019)
2. ECOBICI, What's ECOBICI? https://www.ecobici.cdmx.gob.mx/en/service-information/what%20is%20ecobici. Accessed 12 June 2022
3. ECOBICI. ECOBICI Statistics. https://www.ecobici.cdmx.gob.mx/en/stats. Accessed 14 June 2022
4. ECOBICI, Open Data. https://www.ecobici.cdmx.gob.mx/en/informacion-del-servicio/open-data. Accessed 12 June 2022
5. PLANBIKE. http://148.204.66.79/neoecobiciweb. Accessed 12 June 2022
6. Sistema de Análisis Histórico de Movilidad Individual (SAHMI). https://sites.google.com/view/sahmi/inicio. Accessed 12 June 2022
7. Bike Share Map: Mexico City. https://bikesharemap.com/mexicocity/#/13.220450784310541/-99.204/19.4008/. Accessed 14 June 2022
8. The Meddin Bike-sharing World Map: Mexico City. https://bikesharingworldmap.com/#/mexicocity_dezba. Accessed 14 June 2022
9. PBSC Urban Solutions, The Meddin Bike-Sharing World Map. https://www.pbsc.com/blog/2021/10/the-meddin-bike-sharing-world-map. Accessed 14 June 2022
10. The Meddin Bike-sharing World Map Mid-2021 Report PBSC Urban Solutions. https://bikesharingworldmap.com/reports/bswm_mid2021report.pdf. Accessed 14 June 2022
11. Tableau, Why choose Tableau? https://www.tableau.com/why-tableau. Accessed 14 June 2022
12. Tanabe, K.: Pareto's 80/20 rule and the Gaussian distribution. Phys. A: Stat. Mech. Appl. **510**, 635–640 (2018)
13. Han, J., Kamber, M., Pei, J.: Data Mining: Concepts and Techniques, 3rd edn., pp. 48–50. Morgan Kaufmann, Waltham (2012)
14. Shui, C., Szeto, W.: A review of bicycle-sharing service planning problems. Transp. Res. Part C Emerg. Technol. **117**, 1–3 (2020)
15. Lucas, V., Andrade, A.: Predicting hourly origin-destination demand in bike sharing systems using hurdle models: lisbon case study. Case Stud. Transp. Policy **9**, 1836–1848 (2021)
16. Dell'Amico, M., Iori, M., Novellani, S., Subramanian, A.: The bike-sharing rebalancing problem with stochastic demands. Transp. Res. Part B Methodol. **118**, 362–380 (2018)
17. Gómez, H., López, R., Ramirez-Nafarrate, A.: A simulation-optimization study of the inventory of a bike-sharing system: the case of Mexico City Ecobici's system. Case Stud. Transp. Policy **9**, 1059–1072 (2021)

18. Boufidis, N., Nikiforiadis, A., Chrysostomou, K., Aifadopoulou, G.: Development of a station-level demand prediction and visualization tool to support bike-sharing systems' opera-tors. In: Codina, E., Soriguera, F., (eds.) EURO Working Group on Transportation Meeting, EWGT 2019, vol. 47. Elsevier (2020)
19. Zhang, D., Xu, W., Li, S.: An adaptive tabu search algorithm embedded with iterated local search and route elimination for the bike repositioning and recycling problem. Comput. Oper. Res. **123**, 105035 (2020)

An Entropy-Based Computational Classifier for Positive and Negative Emotions in Voice Signals

A. D. Herrera-Ortiz[1], G. A. Yáñez-Casas[2,4], J. J. Hernández-Gómez[2,4](✉), M. G. Orozco-del-Castillo[3,4], M. F. Mata-Rivera[1], and R. de la Rosa-Rábago[2]

[1] Unidad Profesional Interdisciplinaria en Ingeniería y Tecnologías Avanzadas, Sección de Estudios de Posgrado e Investigación, Instituto Politécnico Nacional, Mexico City, Mexico

[2] Centro de Desarrollo Aeroespacial, Instituto Politécnico Nacional, Mexico City, Mexico

jjhernandezgo@ipn.mx

[3] Departamento de Sistemas y Computación, Tecnológico Nacional de México/IT de Mérida, Mérida, Yucatán, Mexico

[4] AAAI Student Chapter at Yucatán, México (AAAIMX), Association for the Advancement of Artificial Intelligence, Mexico City, Mexico

Abstract. The detection, classification and analysis of emotions has been an intense research area in the last years. Most of the techniques applied for emotion recognition are those comprised by Artificial Intelligence, such as neural networks, machine learning and deep learning, which are focused on the training and learning of models. In this work, we propose a rather different approach to the problem of detection and classification of emotion within voice speech, regarding sound files as information sources in the context of Shannon's information theory. By computing the entropy content of each audio, we find that emotion in speech can be classified into two subsets: positive and negative. To be able to perform the entropy computation, we first compute the Fourier transform to digital audio recordings, bearing in mind that the voice signal has a bandwidth 100 Hz and 4 kHz. The discrete Fourier spectrum is then used to set the alphabet and then the occurrence probabilities of each symbol (frequency) is used to compute the entropy for non-hysterical information sources. A dataset consisting of 1,440 voice audios performed by professional voice actors was analysed through this methodology, showing that in most cases, this simple approach is capable of performing the positive/negative emotion classification.

Keywords: Emotion analysis · Pattern recognition · Computational entropy · Information theory · Information source · Fourier transform · Frequency alphabet · Voice signals · Sound · Speech

M. F. Mata-Rivera et al. (Eds.): WITCOM 2022, CCIS 1659, pp. 100–121, 2022.
https://doi.org/10.1007/978-3-031-18082-8_7

1 Introduction

The identification, classification and analysis of emotions is a fertile, active and open research area within the pattern recognition field. Historically, the widest source of information to perform emotion detection has been text. However, a remarkable surge in the availability of text sources for sentiment analysis arrived in the last two decades with the massive spreading of Internet [1]. Moreover, the arisal of web-based social networks, particularly designed for the social interaction, eased their usage for the sharing of sentiments, generating massive amounts of information to be mined for the comprehension of human psyche [1,2]. Traditionally, as emotions detection and classification has been performed (mostly on text sources) with different techniques of Artificial Intelligence (AI), sentiment analysis is commonly regarded as an area of this same field [3].

Furthermore, the rise of social networks also allowed people to find new ways of expressing their emotions, with the use of content like emoticons, pictures as memes, audio and video [1,4], showing the necessity of generating methods to expand the sentiment analysis to this novel sources of information. Accordingly, much research has been performed in the field of emotion analysis within social networks content, which is mostly based on the analysis of text/comments with AI techniques [5–11]. Several applications in this field are healthcare [12,13], social behavioural assessment [14,15], touristic perception [16], identification of trends in conflicting versus non-conflicting regions [17], evaluation of influence propagation models on social networks [18], emotions identification in text/emoticons/emojis [19], among many others. A review on textual emotion analysis can be found in [20].

With respect to images, the analysis has been focused on facial emotion recognition mainly through the combination of AI and techniques of digital image processing [21]. In [22] a 2D canonical correlation was implemented, [23] combines the distance in facial landmarks along with a genetic algorithm, [24] used a deep learning approach to identify the motions of painters with their artwork, [25] used the maximum likelihood distributions to detect neutral, fear, pain, pleasure and laugh expressions in video stills, [26] uses a multimodal Graph Convolutional Network to perform a conjoint analysis of aesthetic and emotion feelings within images, [27] uses improved local binary pattern and wavelet transforms to assess the learning states and emotions of students in online learning, [28] uses principal component analysis and deep learning methods to identify emotion in children with autism spectrum disorder, [29] used facial thermal images, deep reinforcement learning and IoT robotic devices to assess attention-deficit hyperactivity disorder in children, while [30] fuzzifies emotion categories in images to assess them through a deep metric learning. A recent review on the techniques for emotion detection in facial images is reported in [31].

However, a much lesser studied area within emotion recognition is the emotion analysis within audio sources, specifically in voice/speech. The first attempts were based on the classification of emotions by parameters of the audio signal; for instance, for english and malayan voices and for six emotions, the average pitch, the pitch range and jitter were assessed for signals of both male and female voices, finding that the language does not affect the emotional speech [32], while [33] applied data mining algorithms to prosody parameters extracted from non-professional voice actors. Also, [34] extracted 65 acoustic parameters to assess anger, contempt, fear, happiness, interest, lust, neutral, pride, relief, sadness, and shame emotional stages in over 100 professional actors from five English-speaking countries. Later, medical technology was applied using functional magnetic resonance images to measure the brain activity while the patient was giving a speech which in turn was recorded and computer-processed [35]. More algorithmical approaches were developed later, such as fuzzy logic reasoners [36,37], discriminant analysis focused on nursing experience [38], the use of statistical similarity measurements to categorise sentiments in acted, natural and induced speeches [39,40], the use of subjective psychological criteria to improve voice database design, parametrisation and classification schemes [41], among others. Machine learning approaches have also been developed, as the recognition of positive, neutral and negative emotions on spontaneous speech in children with autism spectrum disorders through support vector machines [42], the application of the k-nearest neighbour method to signal parameters as pitch, temporal and duration on theatrical plays for identification of happy, angry, fear, and neutral emotions [43], the simultaneous use of ant colony optimisation and k-nearest neighbour algorithms to improve the efficiency of speech emotion recognition, focusing only on the spectral roll-off, spectral centroid, spectral flux, log energy, and formats at few chosen frequency sub-bands [44], as well as the real time analysis of TV debates' speech through a deep learning approach in the parameter space [45]. In the field of neural networks, a neurolinguistic processing model based on neural networks to conjointly analyse voice through the acoustic parameters of tone, pitch, rate, intensity, meaning, etc., along with text analysis based on linguistic features was developed by [46], while [47] proposes the use of a multi-layer perceptron neural network to classify emotions by the Mel frequency Cepstral Coefficient, its scaled spectrogram frequency, chroma and tonnetz parameters. Moreover, some studies suggest that, when available, the conjoint analysis of voice and facial expressions could lead to a better performance on emotion classification than the two techniques used separately [48].

As can be observed, there exist two main approaches to the problem of emotion analysis in voice/speech records, which can be used together: the direct analysis of parameters derived from the sound signal, and the use of AI techniques at many levels to build recognition and classification schemes. The main drawback of the systems based on AI methods is that they are subject to a training process that might be prone to bias and that highly depends on the training dataset, which might be inappropriately split [49]; moreover, the presence of hidden variables as well as mistaking the real objective are common drawbacks in the field [49,50]. Collateral drawbacks are likely the large amount of time and computer resources required to train the AI-based systems. In [51] and [52] the subject of how to build representative AI models in general is explored.

In this work, we deviate from the traditional approaches to the problem of emotion analysis in order to explore a novel approach that regards the voice/speech recording as an information source in the framework of Shannon's information theory [53]. In particular, we compute the information entropy of a voice/speech signal in order to classify emotion into two categories, positive and negative emotions, by generating an alphabet consisting on the frequency content of a human-audible sub-band. Although Shannon entropy has been previously used to perform pattern recognition in sound, it has been applied mainly to the heart sounds classification [54,55]. The outcome shows that this approach is suitable for a very fast automatic classification of positive and negative emotions, which lacks of a training phase by its own nature. This work is organised as follows: in Sect. 2 we show the theoretical required background as well as the dataset under use, while in Sect. 3 we show the followed procedure along with the obtained results. Finally, in Sects. 4 and 5 we pose some final remarks as well as future possible paths to extend the presented work.

2 Materials and Methods

2.1 Frequency Domain Analysis

Since the inception of the analysis in the frequency domain by Joseph Fourier in 1882 [56], Fourier series for periodic waveforms and Fourier transform for non-periodic ones have been cornerstones of modern mathematical and numerical analysis. Fourier transforms place time series in the frequency domain, so they are able to provide their frequency content. Moreover, both continuous and discrete waveforms are likely to be analysed through Fourier analysis. In this work, we focus on discrete time series because most of audio sources available nowadays are binary files stored, processed and transmitted in digital computers. Let $x(n)$ be a discrete time series of finite energy, its Fourier transform is given by

$$X(w) = \sum_{n=-\infty}^{\infty} x(n)e^{-jwn}, \tag{1}$$

where $X(w)$ represents the frequency spectrum of $x(n)$ [57]. Such frequency content allows to classify the signal according to its power/energy density spectra, which are quantitatively expressed as the bandwidth. Fourier transform has been successfully applied for more than a century, in virtually any field of knowledge as it can be imagined for signal analysis, such as in medicine [58–61], spectroscopy/spectromety [60–69], laser-material interaction [70], image processing [59,71–73], big data [74], micro-electro-mechanical systems (MEMS) devices [75], food technology [73,76,77], aerosol characterisation and assessment [78], vibrations analysis [79], chromatic dispersion in optical fiber communications [80], analysis of biological systems [81], characterisation in geological sciences [82], data compression [83], catalyst surface analysis [84], profilometry [85], among several others.

Frequency domain analysis can be applied to any signal from which information is to be extracted. In the case of the voice signal herein studied, the bandwidth is limited to a frequency range 100 Hz and 4 kHz.

2.2 Shannon's Entropy Computation

The fundamental problem of communications, i.e. to carry entirely a message from one point to another, was first posed mathematically in [53]. Within his theory, messages are considered discrete in the sense that they might be represented by a number of symbols, regardless of the continuous or discrete nature of the information source, because any continuous source should be eventually discretised in order to be further transmitted. The selected set of symbols to represent certain message is called the alphabet, so that an infinite number of messages could be coded by such alphabet, regardless of its finitude.

In this sense, different messages coded in the same alphabet use different symbols, so the probability of appearance of each could vary from each one to the other. Therefore, the discrete source of information could be considered as a stochastic process, and conversely, any stochastic process that produces a discrete sequence of symbols selected from a finite set will be a discrete source [53]. An example of this is the digital voice signal.

For a discrete source of information in which the probabilities of occurrence of events are known, there is a measure of how much choice is involved in selecting the event or how uncertain we are about its outcome. According to theorem 2 of [53], there should be a function H that satisfies the properties of being continuous on the probabilities of the events (p_i), of being a monotonically increasing function of n and as well as being additive. The logarithmic function meets such requirements, and it is optimal for considering the influence of the statistics of very large messages in particular, as the occurrence of the symbols tends to be very large. In particular, base 2 logarithms are singularly adequate to measure the information, choice and uncertainty content of digital (binary) coded messages. Such a function then takes the form

$$H = -K \sum_{i=1}^{n} p_i log(p_i), \tag{2}$$

where the positive constant K sets a measurement unit and n is the number of symbols in the selected alphabet. H is the so called information (or Shannon's) entropy for a set of probabilities $p_1, \ldots, p_n$. It must be noted that the validity of Eq. 2 relies in the fact that each symbol within the alphabet is equiprobable, i.e. for information sources that do not possess hysteresis processes. For alphabets with symbols that are not equally probable, Eq. 2 is modified, yielding the conditional entropy.

Beyond the direct applications of information entropy in the field of communications systems, it has been also used for assessment and classification purposes. For instance, [86] evaluates non-uniform distribution of assembly features in precision instruments, [87] applies it to multi-attribute utility analysis, [88] uses a generalised maximum entropy principle to identify graphical ARMA models, [89] studies critical characteristics of self-organised behaviour of concrete under uniaxial compression, [90] explores interactive attribute reduction for unlabelled mixed data, [91] improves neighbourhood entropies for uncertainty analysis and intelligent processing, [92] proposes an inaccuracy fuzzy entropy measure for a pair of probability distribution and discuss its relationship with mean codeword length, [93] develops proofs for quantum error-correction codes, [94] performs attribute reduction for unlabelled data through an entropy based missclassification cost function, [95] applies the cross entropy of mass function in similarity measure, [96] detects stress-induced sleep alteration in electroencephalographic records, [97] uses entropy and symmetry arguments to assess the self-replication problem in robotics and artificial life, [98] applies it to the quantisation of local observations for distributed detection, etc.

Although the information entropy has been largely applied to typical text sources, the question of how to apply it to digital sound sources could entail certain difficulties, as the definition of an adequate alphabet in order to perform the information measurement. In this work, we first implement a fast Fourier transform algorithm to a frequency band of digital voice audios in order to set a frequency alphabet. The symbols of such alphabet are finite as the sound files are sampled to the same bitrate.

2.3 Voice Signals Dataset

The dataset used in this work was obtained from the Ryerson Audio-Visual Database of Emotional Speech and Song (RAVDESS) [99], and it consists of 1,440 audio-only WAV files, performed of 24 professional voice actors (12 women, 12 men), who vocalise English matching statements with a neutral American accent.

Each actor performs calm, happy, sad, angry, fearful, surprised, disgusted, and neutral expressions. Each expression is performed at two levels of emotional intensities: normal and loud. Each actor vocalised two different statements: 1 stands for "Kids are talking by the door" and 2 for "Dogs are sitting by the door". Finally, each vocalisation was recorded twice which is stated as 1st or 2nd repetition. Each audio is approximately 3 s long. Table 1 shows the classification of the voice dataset, in which it can be observed that such emotions have been separated into two subsets of positive and negative emotions.

Table 1. Number of files within the voice dataset, distributed by emotions, which are separated in positive and negative emotions subsets.

		Emotions																Total
		Positive						Negative								Neutral		
		Happy		*Surprised*		*Calm*		*Sad*		*Fearful*		*Disgusted*		*Angry*				
Message		1	2	1	2	1	2	1	2	1	2	1	2	1	2	1	2	
Loud	1st	24	24	24	24	24	24	24	24	24	24	24	24	24	24	-	-	336
	2nd	24	24	24	24	24	24	24	24	24	24	24	24	24	24	-	-	336
Normal	1st	24	24	24	24	24	24	24	24	24	24	24	24	24	24	24	24	384
	2nd	24	24	24	24	24	24	24	24	24	24	24	24	24	24	24	24	384
Total		96	96	96	96	96	96	96	96	96	96	96	96	96	96	48	48	1440
		192		192		192		192		192		192		192		96		

3 Development and Results

The methods in the aforementioned section were implemented with the Python programming language. First, the librosa library, which is focused on the processing of audio and music signals [100], was implemented to obtain the sampled data of the audio at a sampling bitrate of 22,050 Hz. In order to obtain the frequency spectrum, the Fast Fourier Transform (FFT) algorithm was used to perform the discrete fourier transform. FFT was implemented through the SciPy library, a collection of mathematical algorithms and functions built on top of the NumPy extension to Python, adding significant enhancement by providing high-level commands and classes for manipulating and displaying data [101]. SciPy is a system prototyping and data processing environment that rivals systems like MATLAB, IDL, Octave, R-Lab, and SciLab [101].

As the audios were all sampled to a bitrate of $br = 22,050$ Hz, if their duration is of t s, then the number of time samples they possess is just $br \cdot t$, which conform a $br \cdot t$-sized vector. Then, the scipy.fft.rfft function is used to compute the 1D discrete Fourier transform (DFT) of n points of such real-valued vector [102].

In order to compute the value of entropy of each voice source with the described alphabet, the probability of each symbol (frequency values available in the Fourier spectra) is computed and then the entropy through Eq. (2) is finally calculated, as each frequency does not depend on the occurrence of another, i.e. the sound information source can be regarded as non-hysterical.

3.1 Entropy Analysis

After the processing of the data set (Table 1), the entropy outcome of each audio was analysed for the following emotions: calm, happy, sad, angry, afraid, surprised and disgusted. As neutral expression does not express any emotion intentionally, it was discarded from the analysis. Due to the length of the dataset, here we only show some representative graphics of the obtained results. We also display the average results in what follows.

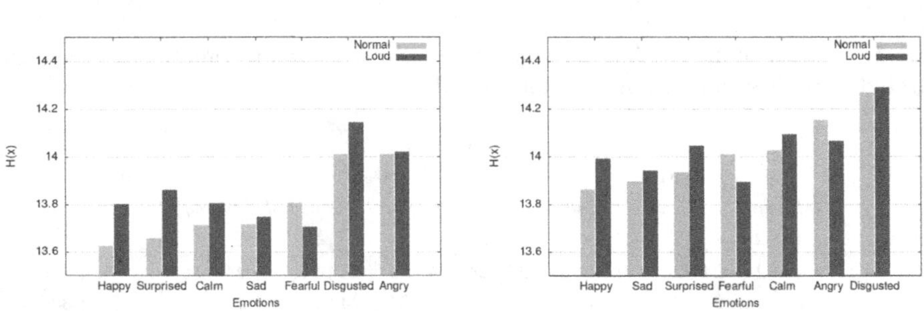

(a) Message 1 on 2nd repetition. (b) Message 2 on 1st repetition.

Fig. 1. Comparison of the average entropy for all actors on each emotion.

The first analysis is over the average of the entropy of all the actors comparing the loud against the normal emotional intensities. Results can be observed for both messages in Fig. 1, where the results are presented in ascending order with respect to normal emotional intensity values of entropy.

Table 2 shows in detail the average values of the entropy obtained from all of the 24 actors, including the cases of Fig. 1, classified according to intensity (loud and normal). The values are in ascending order in accordance with normal intensity. The values obtained in each repetition (1st and 2nd) of the messages are shown separately.

Table 2. Average entropy of all actors comparing intensity.

Message 1			Message 2		
Emotion	Normal	Loud	Emotion	Normal	Loud
		1st Repetition			
Happy	13.62937	13.78712	*Happy*	13.86193	13.99179
Surprise	13.67065	13.93201	*Sad*	13.89544	13.94124
Sad	13.72977	13.65707	*Surprise*	13.93365	14.04495
Calm	13.74445	13.91538	*Fear*	14.00737	13.89378
Fear	13.78522	13.72170	*Calm*	14.02606	14.09250
Angry	13.99452	14.01461	*Angry*	14.15280	14.06335
Disgusted	14.04117	14.18401	*Disgusted*	14.26644	14.28761
		2nd Repetition			
Happy	13.62500	13.80204	*Surprise*	13.87808	14.07231
Surprise	13.65754	13.85815	*Happy*	13.91507	13.94989
Calm	13.71306	13.80327	*Sad*	13.96764	13.93037
Sad	13.71528	13.74593	*Fear*	13.99382	13.84644
Fear	13.80536	13.70516	*Calm*	14.03019	14.12940
Disgusted	14.00738	14.14444	*Angry*	14.19368	14.12245
Angry	14.00800	14.01744	*Disgusted*	14.22615	14.33484

In order to explore the entropic content of the audios by gender, we compared the loud and normal intensities for both gender, whose graphics are in ascending order with respect to normal intensity, here shown in Figs. 2a and 2b for men and Figs. 2c and 2d for women.

Table 3a shows in detail the average values of the entropy obtained from the 12 male interpreters, as well as in Table 3b for women, which include the cases shown in Fig. 2. Both tables classify the entropy values according to intensity (normal and loud) in ascending order with respect to normal intensity, featuring separately the values of the 1st and 2nd repetitions of the messages.

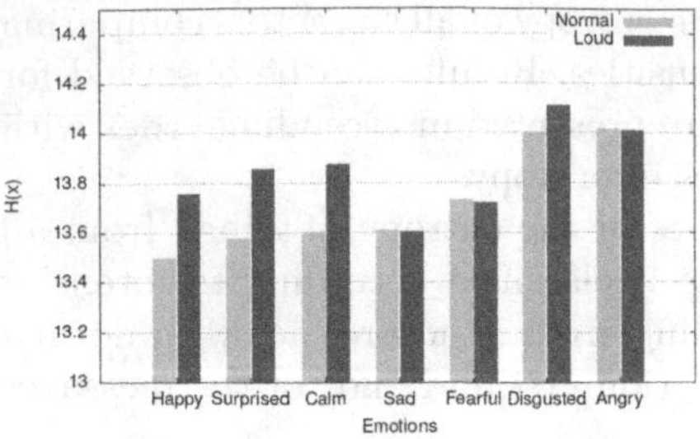

(a) Men's message 1 on 1st repetition.

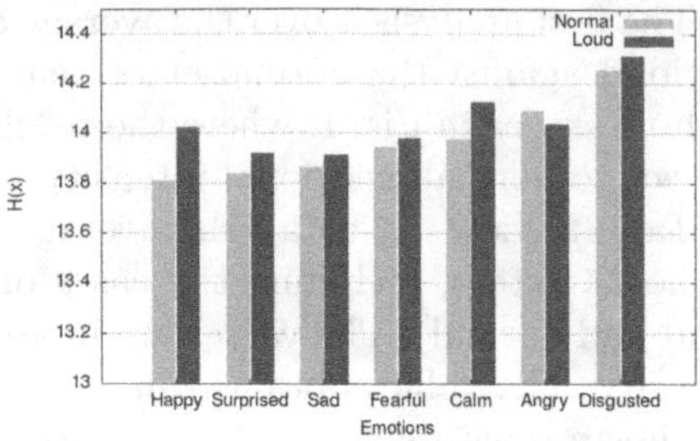

(b) Men's message 2 on 1st repetition.

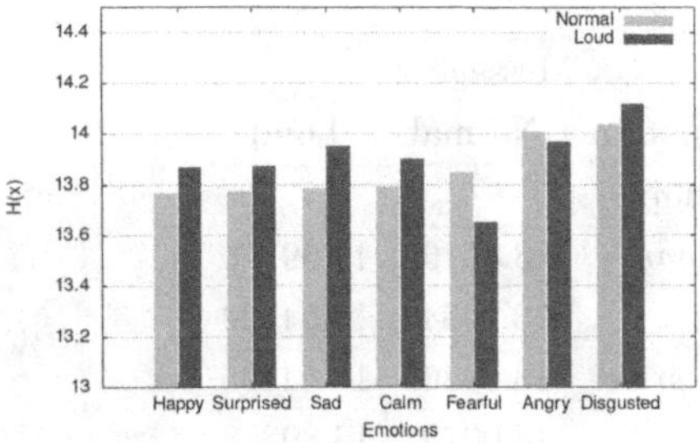

(c) Women's message 1 on 2nd repetition.

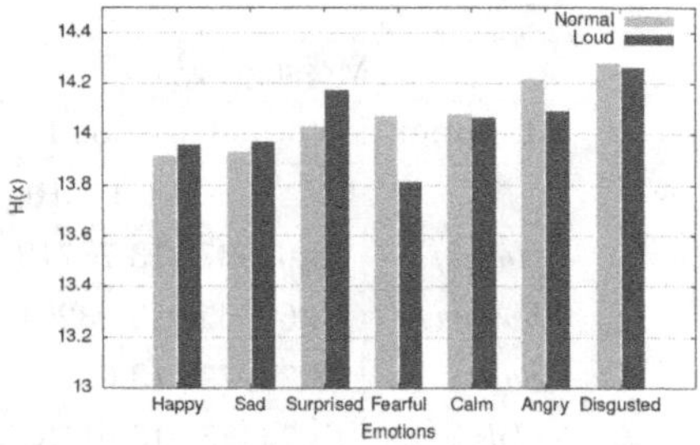

(d) Women's message 2 on 1st repetition.

Fig. 2. Normal vs loud intensity for both gender interpreters.

Table 3. Average entropy for both genders and messages, comparing intensity.

(a) Male interpreters					
Message 1			Message 2		
Emotion	Normal	Loud	Emotion	Normal	Loud
1st Repetition					
Happy	13.49931	13.75591	*Happy*	13.80846	14.02408
Surprised	13.57929	13.85501	*Surprised*	13.83677	13.91841
Calm	13.60234	13.87002	*Sad*	13.86316	13.91226
Sad	13.60938	13.60310	*Fearful*	13.94512	13.97890
Fearful	13.73046	13.72030	*Calm*	13.97587	14.12232
Disgusted	14.00011	14.11143	*Angry*	14.09121	14.03747
Angry	14.01447	14.00702	*Disgusted*	14.25447	14.31288
2nd Repetition					
Happy	13.48353	13.73792	*Surprised*	13.79324	13.97323
Surprised	13.54198	13.84495	*Happy*	13.86438	13.93191
Calm	13.63455	13.70720	*Fearful*	13.90677	13.91836
Sad	13.64754	13.54204	*Sad*	13.94234	13.83481
Fearful	13.76416	13.75924	*Calm*	13.96887	14.02359
Disgusted	13.97689	14.17172	*Disgusted*	14.14322	14.39701
Angry	14.00588	14.06509	*Angry*	14.15684	14.10251

(*continued*)

Table 3. (*continued*)

(b) Female interpreters					
Message 1			Message 2		
Emotion	Normal	Loud	Emotion	Normal	Loud
1st Repetition					
Happy	13.75942	13.81833	*Happy*	13.91540	13.95950
Surprised	13.76201	14.00901	*Sad*	13.92772	13.97022
Fearful	13.83999	13.72310	*Surprised*	14.03053	14.17150
Sad	13.85016	13.71104	*Fearful*	14.06962	13.80866
Calm	13.88657	13.96074	*Calm*	14.07626	14.06269
Angry	13.97456	14.02220	*Angry*	14.21440	14.08923
Disgusted	14.08223	14.25659	*Disgusted*	14.27841	14.26233
2nd Repetition					
Happy	13.76648	13.86615	*Surprised*	13.96292	14.17139
Surprised	13.77310	13.87135	*Happy*	13.96576	13.96787
Sad	13.78301	13.94982	*Sad*	13.99293	14.02593
Calm	13.79157	13.89934	*Fearful*	14.08087	13.77452
Fearful	13.84656	13.65107	*Calm*	14.09151	14.23521
Angry	14.01012	13.96978	*Angry*	14.23052	14.14239
Disgusted	14.03787	14.11715	*Disgusted*	14.30908	14.27268

In what follows, we present the results of the average entropy for message 1 against message 2, for the same motional intensity. The general results for the 24 actors are observed in Fig. 3, where each plot is ordered in ascending order with respect to message 1.

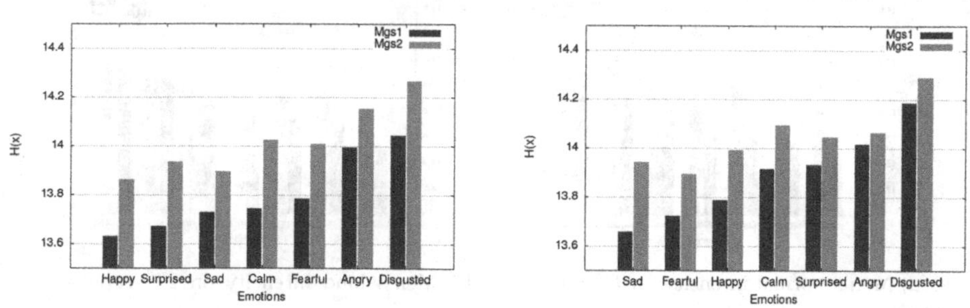

(a) Normal intensity.

(b) Loud intensity.

Fig. 3. Message 1 vs 2 on 1st repetition.

Likewise, Table 4 shows all the average values of the entropy obtained from the 24 actors, including the cases shown in Fig. 3, classified in accordance to the type of message (1 or 2). The values are presented in ascending order with respect to the normal intensity. The values obtained in each repetition (1st and 2nd) of the messages are clearly separated.

Table 4. Average entropy of all actors comparing type of message.

	Normal			Loud	
Emotion	Mgs 2	Mgs 1	Emotion	Mgs 2	Mgs 1
		1st Repetition			
Happy	13.86193	13.62937	*Sad*	13.94124	13.65707
Surprise	13.93365	13.67065	*Fear*	13.89378	13.72170
Sad	13.89544	13.72977	*Happy*	13.99179	13.78712
Calm	14.02606	13.74445	*Calm*	14.09250	13.91538
Fear	14.00737	13.78522	*Surprise*	14.04495	13.93201
Angry	14.15280	13.99452	*Angry*	14.06335	14.01461
Disgusted	14.26644	14.04117	*Disgusted*	14.28761	14.18401
		2nd Repetition			
Happy	13.91507	13.62500	*Fear*	13.84644	13.70516
Surprise	13.87808	13.65754	*Sad*	13.93037	13.74593
Calm	14.03019	13.71306	*Happy*	13.94989	13.80204
Sad	13.96764	13.71528	*Calm*	14.12940	13.80327
Fear	13.99382	13.80536	*Surprise*	14.07231	13.85815
Disgusted	14.22615	14.00738	*Angry*	14.12245	14.01744
Angry	14.19368	14.00800	*Disgusted*	14.33484	14.14444

Moreover, the average entropy comparison between messages 1 and 2 (with the same emotional intensity) is then shown for men in Figs. 4a and 4b and in Figs. 4c and 4d for women. Each graph is ordered in ascending order with respect to message 1.

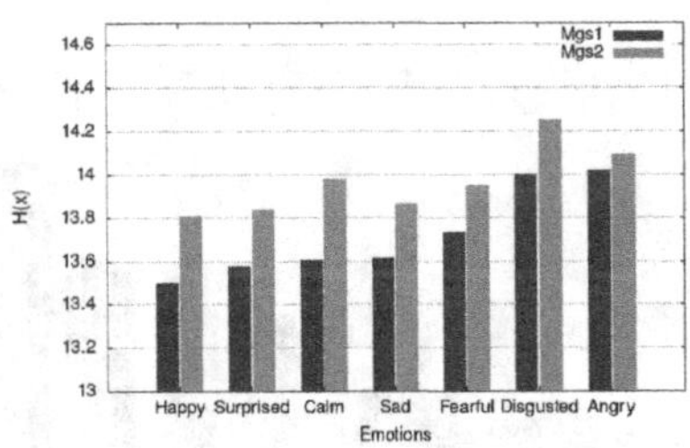

(a) Men's normal intensity on 1st repetition.

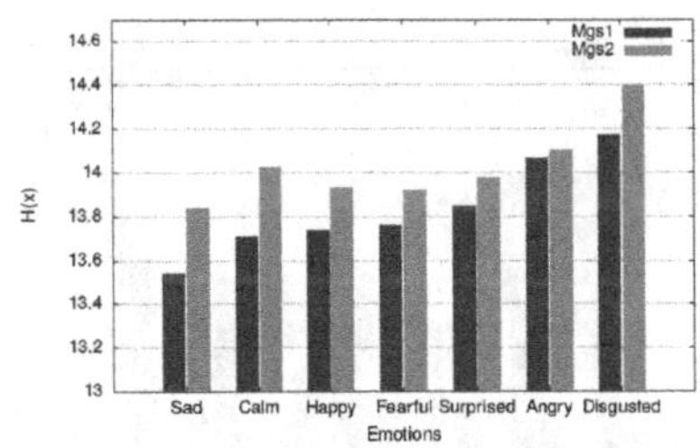

(b) Men's loud intensity on 2nd repetition.

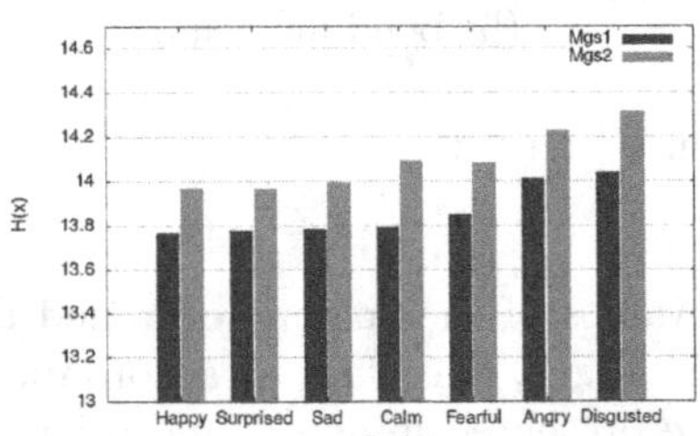

(c) Women's normal intensity on 2nd repetition.

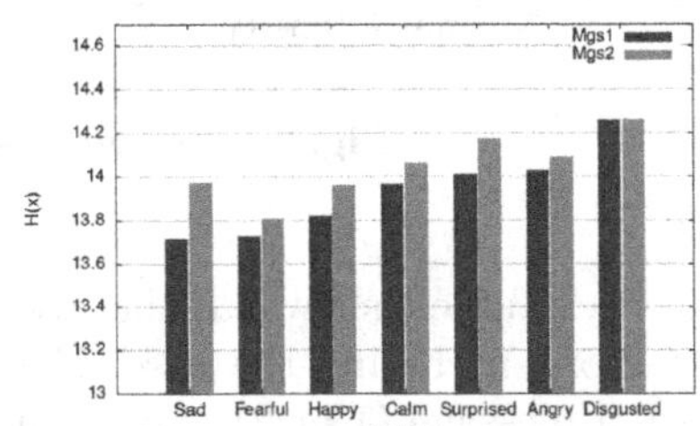

(d) Women's loud intensity on 1st repetition.

Fig. 4. Message 1 vs 2 with the same intensity for both gender interpreters.

Table 5a shows in detail the average values of the entropy obtained from the 12 male interpreters, classified according to the message 1 or 2. The values are in ascending order with respect to the normal intensity. The values obtained in each repetition (1st and 2nd) of the messages were separated. The exact same setup for the average values of the entropy obtained from the 12 female interpreters can be observed in Table 5b. The cases shown in Fig. 4 are also include here.

Table 5. Average entropy for both gender actors comparing type of message.

	Normal			Loud	
Emotion	Mgs 2	Mgs 1	Emotion	Mgs 2	Mgs 1
(a) Male interpreters					
1st Repetition					
Happy	13.97587	13.49931	*Sad*	14.02408	13.60310
Surprise	13.86316	13.57929	*Fear*	14.03747	13.72030
Calm	13.80846	13.60234	*Happy*	14.12232	13.75591
Sad	13.94512	13.60938	*Surprise*	13.97890	13.85501
Fear	14.25447	13.73046	*Calm*	14.31288	13.87002
Disgusted	13.81052	14.00011	*Angry*	13.91841	14.00702
Angry	13.83677	14.01447	*Disgusted*	13.91226	14.11143
2nd Repetition					
Happy	13.94234	13.48353	*Sad*	13.83481	13.54204
Surprise	13.96887	13.54198	*Calm*	14.02359	13.70720
Calm	14.15684	13.63455	*Happy*	13.93191	13.73792
Sad	13.86438	13.64754	*Fear*	13.91836	13.75924
Fear	13.79324	13.76416	*Surprise*	13.97323	13.84495
Disgusted	13.90677	13.97689	*Angry*	14.10251	14.06509
Angry	14.14322	14.00588	*Disgusted*	14.39701	14.17172
(b) Female interpreters					
1st Repetition					
Happy	14.07626	13.75942	*Sad*	14.17150	13.71104
Surprise	13.91540	13.76201	*Fear*	13.80866	13.72310
Fear	14.03053	13.83999	*Happy*	14.26233	13.81833
Sad	14.21440	13.85016	*Calm*	14.08923	13.96074
Calm	13.88075	13.88657	*Surprise*	13.97022	14.00901
Angry	14.06962	13.97456	*Angry*	14.06269	14.02220
Disgusted	13.92772	14.08223	*Disgusted*	13.95950	14.25659
2nd Repetition					
Happy	14.08087	13.76648	*Fear*	14.23521	13.65107
Surprise	13.99293	13.77310	*Happy*	14.14239	13.86615
Sad	14.09151	13.78301	*Surprise*	13.96787	13.87135
Calm	13.96576	13.79157	*Calm*	14.27268	13.89934
Fear	14.23052	13.84656	*Sad*	14.02593	13.94982
Angry	13.88605	14.01012	*Angry*	13.77452	13.96978
Disgusted	14.30908	14.03787	*Disgusted*	14.17139	14.11715

4 Discussion and Conclusions

In this work, a different approach to the analysis of emotion was proposed, since instead of applying the widely common methods of AI, a classification of emotions into positive and negative categories within speech sources is proposed through a tool of the theory of the information: the frequency-based Shannon's entropy. In order to compute information entropy, an alphabet based on the frequency symbols generated by the decomposition of original audio time series through the FFT algorithm is generated. Then, the probability of appearance of each frequency symbol is obtained from the Fourier spectrum so to finally compute the non-hysterical Shannon's entropy (see Eq. (2)).

As already mentioned in Sect. 1, the typical sources of information in which entropy calculation is performed are texts where the average entropy value ranges between 3 and 4. However, as it was observed in the average values herein provided, they range between 13 and 15. This is clearly due to the nature of the alphabet developed here. Given that in the texts, alphabets are composed of a number of symbols of the order of tens, they yield small values of entropy. However, in the frequency domain, sound signals generate much larger alphabets, yielding average entropies for a voice signal that are considerably higher than that of a text. It is also clear that if richer sound sources would be analysed through this method, as music files and not only speech, they would certainly yield larger values of entropy. It must be considered that a value of about 14 is much greater than the typical values of text entropy of 3–4, given the logarithmic function that characterises the computation of entropy.

As it can be observed through Sect. 3, a general tendency of positive emotions (happy, surprise and calm) to have lower values of entropy than the negative emotions (sad, fear, disgust and anger) is present. Thus, large values of entropy generally characterise negative emotions while lower values are typical of positive emotions, allowing to perform a pre-classification of emotions into these two categories, without the necessity of going to a training phase as in general machine learning algorithms.

Table 6. Average entropy classified by positive and negative emotion according to intensity.

Case Study	Positive Emotion		Negative Emotion	
	Normal	Loud	Normal	Loud
All actors	13.80708	13.94823	13.98687	13.97565
Men	13.71571	13.89704	13.94074	13.96713
Women	13.89846	13.99942	14.03300	13.98416

In order to better grasp the main result, in Table 6 we feature the average entropy values according to the (normal and loud) intensities, by considering both the positive and negative categories of emotions covered by this work.

Such values are presented for all of the actors, as well as separated by gender. It can be clearly observed that for the normal intensity, for the three averages (for all actors, for men and for women), positive emotions yield smaller values of entropy than those given by the negative emotions.

It is important to remember that for an information source within the context of Shannon's theory of information, symbols with lower probabilities to occur, are the ones that represent more information, since the number of symbols required to represent a certain message is less. If the symbols are more equiprobable for a message, the entropic content will be small. In other words, when there are symbols that occur infrequently, the entropic content would be higher. Also, the longitude of the message plays an important role since for short messages, the entropy will vary compared to a long ones, where the entropy will tend to stabilise [103]. In this sense, it can be clearly observed from Table 6 that the entropy values for the same intensity, comparing men against women, turn out larger for women, in both positive and negative emotions (normal intensity). This fact is consistent with the previous observation, because women in general excite a narrower frequency bandwidth, thus making more unfrequently symbols available, yielding to larger values of entropy.

The same pattern from the normal intensity is observed for the loud intensity for the average of all actors as well as for the average of men (see Table 6). It should be noted that for the loud intensities, the gap between the positive and negative emotions is smaller than for the normal intensity of the message. This is clearly because at a loud intensity, the amplitude of the time series is larger, thus in general increasing the probabilities of occurrence of each symbol. The particular case of female interpreters in which the loud intensity has a lower value for the negative emotion than for the positive emotion is likely because when women shout, they narrow their voices' frequency bandwidth, thus yielding less symbols with larger probabilities. This is not the case of male interpreters, that when they shout, tend to excite a larger portion of the spectrum, yielding lower values of entropy.

On the other side, Table 7 also shows the average values of entropy for the positive and negative categories of emotions, but according to the type of message. It could be noted that the general results are coherent because in general, message 2 has larger values of entropy than message 1. This could be explained subjectively because people could tend to be more expressive with his emotions when talking about animals (dogs, in the case of message 2) than when talking about kids (message 1). Moreover, the high values of entropy for message 2 could be due to the fact that naturally, persons are more susceptible to get negative emotions to animals. These facts could have influenced the actors when vocalising message 2 with respect to message 1. Moreover, Table 7 confirms that for all the cases (all of the actors, the men and the women), the entropy values of positive emotions are lower than the values of entropy for negative emotions, regardless of the analysed message, confirming the results shown in Table 6.

Table 7. Average entropy classified by positive and negative emotion according to message.

Case Study	Positive Emotion		Negative Emotion	
	Message 1	Message 2	Message 1	Message 2
All actors	13.76150	13.99381	13.89231	14.07021
Men	13.67599	13.93675	13.85805	14.04983
Women	13.84700	14.05087	13.92657	14.09059

Various sound classification applications using AI techniques are based on the implementation of neural network variants, such as Deep Neural Network (DNN) [104], Convolutional Neural Networks (CNN) [105,106], Recurrent Neural Networks (RNN) [107], among others. Although the use of AI techniques allows predicting the behaviour of the data from an exhaustive training of the chosen algorithm, fixed parameters such as entropy always allows an analysis without estimates or predictions. Thus, entropy values gives a clear idea of the behaviour of the signal from itself, yielding a more reliable and direct result [108].

Although not directly related to information classification, entropy calculation is useful in the context of communication systems, as it represents a measure of the amount of information that can be transmitted. Parameters such as channel capacity, joint entropy, data transmission rate, error symbol count, among others, use entropy to be determined [53]. These parameters become important when the information already classified or processed needs to be transmitted. Various applications such as those exposed in [109] and [110] combine the classification of information with its use in communication systems, especially those that require direct interaction with humans. Despite Shannon's entropy has been previously used to perform pattern recognition in sound, it has been mainly applied to the heart sounds classification [54,55], and not in the context herein studied.

As final remarks, in this work we find Shannon's information to be a reliable tool that is able to perform a very quick classification of emotions into positive and negative categories. The computation of entropy based on the Fourier frequency spectrum also allows to categorise a message considering the amplitude of the original time series (if it is vocalised in normal or loud manner) as well as into male and female broadcaster. However, as previously mentioned through this section, further experiments with larger speech datasets should be performed in order to find stabilised entropy values to pose limiting quantitative criteria. In this way, for its simplicity and quickness, this novel approach could also serve as a pre-classification system for emotions in order to prepare training datasets for more complex machine learning algorithms to perform finer classifications of sentiments.

5 Future Work

This research can be extended in the following pathways:

- To expand this analysis to longer voice records as complete speeches.
- To expand this proposal to perform emotion analyses in analogical voice signals.
- To extend this analysis to assess the entropic content of voice audios in languages different than English.
- To explore the entropic content of other sound sources as music.
- To complement this approach with further tools of information theory [53] and signal analysis techniques, in order to be able to perform a finer emotion classification.

Acknowledgements. This work was supported by projects SIP 20220907, 20222032, 20220378 and EDI grant, by Instituto Politécnico Nacional/Secretaría de Investigación y Posgrado, as well as by projects 13933.22-P and 14601.22-P from Tecnológico Nacional de México/IT de Mérida.

References

1. Nandwani, P., Verma, R.: A review on sentiment analysis and emotion detection from text. Social Network Analysis and Mining **11**(1), 1–19 (2021). https://doi.org/10.1007/s13278-021-00776-6
2. Li, H.H., Cheng, M.S., Hsu, P.Y., Ko, Y., Luo, Z.: Exploring Chinese dynamic sentiment/emotion analysis with text Mining–Taiwanese popular movie reviews comment as a case. In: B. R., P., Thenkanidiyoor, V., Prasath, R., Vanga, O. (eds) Mining Intelligence and Knowledge Exploration, MIKE 2019. LNCS, vol. 11987. Springer, Cham (2020). https://doi.org/10.1007/978-3-030-66187-8_9
3. Tyagi, E., Sharma, A.: An intelligent framework for sentiment analysis of text and emotions - a review. In: 2017 International Conference on Energy, Communication, Data Analytics and Soft Computing (ICECDS), pp. 3297–3302 (2018)
4. Fulse, S., Sugandhi, R., Mahajan, A.: A survey on multimodal sentiment analysis. Int. J. Eng. Res. Technol. **3**(11), 1233–1238 (2014)
5. Wu, D., Zhang, J., Zhao, Q.: A text emotion analysis method using the dual-channel convolution neural network in social networks. Math. Probl. Eng. **2020**, 1–10 (2020)
6. Lu, X., Zhang, H.: An emotion analysis method using multi-channel convolution neural network in social networks. Comput. Model. Eng. Sci. **125**(1), 281–297 (2020)
7. Chawla, S., Mehrotra, M.: A comprehensive science mapping analysis of textual emotion mining in online social networks. Int. J. Adv. Comput. Sci. Appl. **11**(5), 218–229 (2020)
8. Wickramaarachchi, W., Kariapper, R.: An approach to get overall emotion from comment text towards a certain image uploaded to social network using latent semantic analysis. In: 2017 2nd International Conference on Image, Vision and Computing (ICIVC), pp. 788–792 (2017)

9. Jamaluddin, M., Abidin, S., Omar, N.: Classification and quantification of user's emotion on Malay language in social network sites using latent semantic analysis. In: 2016 IEEE Conference on Open Systems (ICOS), pp. 65–70 (2017)
10. Iglesias, C., Sáinchez-Rada, J., Vulcu, G., Buitelaar, P.: Linked data models for sentiment and emotion analysis in social networks. Elsevier (2017)
11. Colnerič, N., Demšar, J.: Emotion recognition on twitter: comparative study and training a unison model. IEEE Trans. Affect. Comput. **11**(3), 433–446 (2018)
12. Li, T.S., Gau, S.F., Chou, T.L.: Exploring social emotion processing in autism: evaluating the reading the mind in the eyes test using network analysis. BMC Psychiatry **22**(1), 161 (2022)
13. Jiang, S.Y., et al.: Network analysis of executive function, emotion, and social anhedonia. PsyCh J. **11**(2), 232–234 (2022)
14. Yu, J.: Research on key technologies of analysis of user emotion fluctuation characteristics in wireless network based on social information processing. In: Liu, S., Ma, X. (eds.) ADHIP 2021. LNICST, vol. 416, pp. 142–154. Springer, Cham (2022). https://doi.org/10.1007/978-3-030-94551-0_12
15. Han, Z.M., Huang, C.Q., Yu, J.H., Tsai, C.C.: Identifying patterns of epistemic emotions with respect to interactions in massive online open courses using deep learning and social network analysis. Comput. Hum. Behav. **122**, 106843 (2021)
16. Chen, X., Li, J., Han, W., Liu, S.: Urban tourism destination image perception based on LDA integrating social network and emotion analysis: the example of Wuhan. Sustainability (Switzerland) **14**(1), 12 (2022)
17. Wani, M., Agarwal, N., Jabin, S., Hussain, S.: User emotion analysis in conflicting versus non-conflicting regions using online social networks. Telematics Inform. **35**(8), 2326–2336 (2018)
18. Liu, X., Sun, G., Liu, H., Jian, J.: Social network influence propagation model based on emotion analysis. In: 2018 14th International Conference on Semantics, Knowledge and Grids (SKG), pp. 108–114 (2018)
19. Egorova, E., Tsarev, D., Surikov, A.: Emotion analysis based on incremental online learning in social networks. In: 2021 IEEE 15th International Conference on Application of Information and Communication Technologies (AICT) (2021)
20. Peng, S., et al.: A survey on deep learning for textual emotion analysis in social networks. Digit. Commun. Netw. (2021)
21. Gonzalez, R., Woods, R.: Digital Image Processing. Pearson (2018)
22. Ullah, Z., Qi, L., Binu, D., Rajakumar, B., Mohammed Ismail, B.: 2-D canonical correlation analysis based image super-resolution scheme for facial emotion recognition. Multimedia Tools Appl. **81**(10), 13911–13934 (2022)
23. Bae, J., Kim, M., Lim, J.: Emotion detection and analysis from facial image using distance between coordinates feature. In: 2021 International Conference on Information and Communication Technology Convergence (ICTC), vol. 2021, pp. 494–497 (2021)
24. Zhang, J., Duan, Y., Gu, X.: Research on emotion analysis of Chinese literati painting images based on deep learning. Front. Psychol. **12**, 723325 (2021)
25. Prossinger, H., Hladky, T., Binter, J., Boschetti, S., Riha, D.: Visual analysis of emotions using AI image-processing software: possible male/female differences between the emotion pairs "neutral"-"fear" and "pleasure"-"pain". In: The 14th PErvasive Technologies Related to Assistive Environments Conference, pp. 342–346 (2021)
26. Miao, H., Zhang, Y., Wang, D., Feng, S.: Multi-output learning based on multimodal GCN and co-attention for image aesthetics and emotion analysis. Mathematics **9**(12), 1437 (2021)

27. Wang, S.: Online learning behavior analysis based on image emotion recognition. Traitement du Sign. **38**(3), 865–873 (2021)
28. Sushma, S., Bobby, T., Malathi, S.: Emotion analysis using signal and image processing approach by implementing deep neural network. Biomed. Sci. Instrum. **57**(2), 313–321 (2021)
29. Lai, Y., Chang, Y., Tsai, C., Lin, C., Chen, M.: Data fusion analysis for attention-deficit hyperactivity disorder emotion recognition with thermal image and internet of things devices. Softw. Pract. Experience **51**(3), 595–606 (2021)
30. Peng, G., Zhang, H., Xu, D.: Image emotion analysis based on the distance relation of emotion categories via deep metric learning. In: Magnenat-Thalmann, N., et al. (eds.) CGI 2021. LNCS, vol. 13002, pp. 535–547. Springer, Cham (2021). https://doi.org/10.1007/978-3-030-89029-2_41
31. Rai Jain, P., Quadri, S., Lalit, M.: Recent trends in artificial intelligence for emotion detection using facial image analysis. In: 2021 Thirteenth International Conference on Contemporary Computing (IC3-2021), pp. 18–36 (2021)
32. Razak, A., Abidin, M., Komiya, R.: Emotion pitch variation analysis in Malay and English voice samples. In: 9th Asia-Pacific Conference on Communications (IEEE Cat. No. 03EX732), vol. 1, pp. 108–112 (2003)
33. Garcia, S., Moreno, J., Fanals, L.: Emotion recognition based on parameterized voice signal analysis [reconocimiento de emociones basado en el anáilisis de la señal de voz parametrizada]. In: Actas da 1a Conferência Ibérica de Sistemas e Tecnologias de Informação, Ofir, Portugal, 21 a 23 de Junho de 2006, vol. 2, pp. 837–854 (2006)
34. Iraki, F., et al.: The expression and recognition of emotions in the voice across five nations: a lens model analysis based on acoustic features. J. Person. Soc. Psychol. **111**(5), 686–705 (2016)
35. Mitsuyoshi, S., et al.: Emotion voice analysis system connected to the human brain. In: 2007 International Conference on Natural Language Processing and Knowledge Engineering, pp. 476–484 (2007)
36. Farooque, M., Munoz-Hernandez, S.: Easy fuzzy tool for emotion recognition: prototype from voice speech analysis. In: IJCCI, pp. 85–88 (2009)
37. Chaturvedi, I., Satapathy, R., Cavallari, S., Cambria, E.: Fuzzy commonsense reasoning for multimodal sentiment analysis. Pattern Recogn. Lett. **125**, 264–270 (2019)
38. Gao, Y., Ohno, Y., Qian, F., Hu, Z., Wang, Z.: The discriminant analysis of the voice expression of emotion - focus on the nursing experience - focus o. In: 2013 35th Annual International Conference of the IEEE Engineering in Medicine and Biology Society (EMBC), pp. 1262–1265 (2013)
39. Manasa, C., Dheeraj, D., Deepth, V.: Statistical analysis of voice based emotion recognition using similarity measures. In: 2019 1st International Conference on Advanced Technologies in Intelligent Control, Environment, Computing & Communication Engineering (ICATIECE), pp. 46–50 (2019)
40. Busso, C., Lee, S., Narayanan, S.: Analysis of emotionally salient aspects of fundamental frequency for emotion detection. IEEE Trans. Audio Speech Lang. Process. **17**(4), 582–596 (2009)
41. Hekiert, D., Igras-Cybulska, M.: Capturing emotions in voice: a comparative analysis of methodologies in psychology and digital signal processing. Ann. Psychol. **22**(1), 15–34 (2019)

42. Ringeval, F., et al.: Automatic analysis of typical and atypical encoding of spontaneous emotion in the voice of children. In: Proceedings INTERSPEECH 2016, 17th Annual Conference of the International Speech Communication Association (ISCA), 08–12 September 2016, pp. 1210–1214 (2016)
43. Iliev, A., Stanchev, P.: Smart multifunctional digital content ecosystem using emotion analysis of voice. In: Proceedings of the 18th International Conference on Computer Systems and Technologies, vol. Part F132086, pp. 58–64 (2017)
44. Panigrahi, S., Palo, H.: Analysis and recognition of emotions from voice samples using ant colony optimization algorithm. Lect. Notes Electr. Eng. **814**, 219–231 (2022)
45. Develasco, M., Justo, R., Zorrilla, A., Inés Torres, M.: Automatic analysis of emotions from the voices/speech in Spanish tv debates. Acta Polytech. Hung. **19**(5), 149–171 (2022)
46. Koren, L., Stipancic, T.: Multimodal emotion analysis based on acoustic and linguistic features of the voice. In: Meiselwitz, G. (ed.) HCII 2021. LNCS, vol. 12774, pp. 301–311. Springer, Cham (2021). https://doi.org/10.1007/978-3-030-77626-8_20
47. Sukumaran, P., Govardhanan, K.: Towards voice based prediction and analysis of emotions in ASD children. J. Intell. Fuzzy Syst. **41**(5), 5317–5326 (2021)
48. Chengeta, K.: Comparative analysis of emotion detection from facial expressions and voice using local binary patterns and Markov models: computer vision and facial recognition. In: Proceedings of the 2nd International Conference on Vision, Image and Signal Processing (2018)
49. Riley, P.: Three pitfalls to avoid in machine learning. Nature **572**, 27–29 (2019)
50. Eyben, F., et al.: The Geneva minimalistic acoustic parameter set (GeMAPS) for voice research and affective computing. IEEE Trans. Affect. Comput. **7**(2), 190–202 (2015)
51. Wujek, B., Hall, P., Günes, F.: Best practices for machine learning applications. SAS Institute Inc (2016)
52. Biderman, S., Scheirer, W.J.: Pitfalls in machine learning research: reexamining the development cycle (2020). arXiv:2011.02832
53. Shannon, C.E.: A mathematical theory of communication. Bell Syst. Tech. J. **27**(3), 379–423 (1948)
54. Moukadem, A., Dieterlen, A., Brandt, C.: Shannon entropy based on the s-transform spectrogram applied on the classification of heart sounds. In: 2013 IEEE International Conference on Acoustics, Speech and Signal Processing, pp. 704–708 (2013)
55. Wang, X.P., Liu, C.C., Li, Y.Y., Sun, C.R.: Heart sound segmentation algorithm based on high-order Shannon entropy. Jilin Daxue Xuebao (Gongxueban) J. Jilin Univ. (Eng. Technol. Ed.) **40**(5), 1433–1437 (2010)
56. Fourier, J.B.J., Darboux, G., et al.: Théorie analytique de la chaleur, vol. 504. Didot Paris (1822)
57. Proakis, Jonh G., D.G.M.: Tratamiento Digital de Señales. Prentice Hall, Madrid (2007)
58. Fadlelmoula, A., Pinho, D., Carvalho, V., Catarino, S., Minas, G.: Fourier transform infrared (FTIR) spectroscopy to analyse human blood over the last 20 years: a review towards lab-on-a-chip devices. Micromachines **13**(2), 187 (2022)
59. Gómez-Echavarría, A., Ugarte, J., Tobón, C.: The fractional Fourier transform as a biomedical signal and image processing tool: a review. Biocybernetics Biomed. Eng. **40**(3), 1081–1093 (2020)

60. Shakya, B., Shrestha, P., Teppo, H.R., Rieppo, L.: The use of Fourier transform infrared (FTIR) spectroscopy in skin cancer research: a systematic review. Appl. Spectrosc. Rev. **56**(5), 1–33 (2020)
61. Su, K.Y., Lee, W.L.: Fourier transform infrared spectroscopy as a cancer screening and diagnostic tool: a review and prospects. Cancers **12**(1), 115 (2020)
62. Hertzog, J., Mase, C., Hubert-Roux, M., Afonso, C., Giusti, P., Barrére-Mangote, C.: Characterization of heavy products from lignocellulosic biomass pyrolysis by chromatography and Fourier transform mass spectrometry: a review. Energy Fuels **35**(22), 17979–18007 (2021)
63. Giechaskiel, B., Clairotte, M.: Fourier transform infrared (FTIR) spectroscopy for measurements of vehicle exhaust emissions: a review. Appl. Sci. (Switzerland) **11**(16), 7416 (2021)
64. Bahureksa, W., et al.: Soil organic matter characterization by Fourier transform ion cyclotron resonance mass spectrometry (FTICR MS): a critical review of sample preparation, analysis, and data interpretation. Environ. Sci. Technol. **55**(14), 9637–9656 (2021)
65. Zhang, X., et al.: Application of Fourier transform ion cyclotron resonance mass spectrometry in deciphering molecular composition of soil organic matter: a review. Sci. Total Environ. **756**, 144140 (2021)
66. He, Z., Liu, Y.: Fourier transform infrared spectroscopic analysis in applied cotton fiber and cottonseed research: a review. J. Cotton Sci. **25**(2), 167–183 (2021)
67. Chirman, D., Pleshko, N.: Characterization of bacterial biofilm infections with Fourier transform infrared spectroscopy: a review. Appl. Spectrosc. Rev. **56**(8–10), 673–701 (2021)
68. Veerasingam, S., et al.: Contributions of Fourier transform infrared spectroscopy in microplastic pollution research: a review. Crit. Rev. Environ. Sci. Technol. **51**(22), 2681–2743 (2021)
69. Hirschmugl, C., Gough, K.: Fourier transform infrared spectrochemical imaging: Review of design and applications with a focal plane array and multiple beam synchrotron radiation source. Appl. Spectrosc. **66**(5), 475–491 (2012)
70. Oane, M., Mahmood, M., Popescu, A.: A state-of-the-art review on integral transform technique in laser-material interaction: Fourier and non-Fourier heat equations. Materials **14**(16), 4733 (2021)
71. John, A., Khanna, K., Prasad, R., Pillai, L.: A review on application of Fourier transform in image restoration. In: 2020 Fourth International Conference on I-SMAC (IoT in Social, Mobile, Analytics and Cloud)(I-SMAC), pp. 389–397 (2020)
72. Ghani, H., Malek, M., Azmi, M., Muril, M., Azizan, A.: A review on sparse fast Fourier transform applications in image processing. Int. J. Electr. Comput. Eng. **10**(2), 1346–1351 (2020)
73. Su, W.H., Sun, D.W.: Fourier transform infrared and Raman and hyperspectral imaging techniques for quality determinations of powdery foods: a review. Compr. Rev. Food Sci. Food Saf. **17**(1), 104–122 (2018)
74. Pralle, R., White, H.: Symposium review: big data, big predictions: utilizing milk Fourier-transform infrared and genomics to improve hyperketonemia management. J. Dairy Sci. **103**(4), 3867–3873 (2020)
75. Chai, J., et al.: Review of mems based Fourier transform spectrometers. Micromachines **11**(2), 1–28 (2020)
76. Valand, R., Tanna, S., Lawson, G., Bengtström, L.: A review of Fourier transform infrared (FTIR) spectroscopy used in food adulteration and authenticity investigations. Food Addit. Contam. Part A Chem. Anal. Control Exposure Risk Assess. **37**(1), 19–38 (2020)

77. Bureau, S., Cozzolino, D., Clark, C.: Contributions of Fourier-transform mid infrared (FT-MIR) spectroscopy to the study of fruit and vegetables: a review. Postharvest Biol. Technol. **148**, 1–14 (2019)
78. Takahama, S., et al.: Atmospheric particulate matter characterization by Fourier transform infrared spectroscopy: a review of statistical calibration strategies for carbonaceous aerosol quantification in us measurement networks. Atmos. Meas. Tech. **12**(1), 525–567 (2019)
79. Lin, H.C., Ye, Y.C.: Reviews of bearing vibration measurement using fast Fourier transform and enhanced fast Fourier transform algorithms. Adv. Mech. Eng. **11**(1), 168781401881675 (2019)
80. Ravisankar, M., Sreenivas, A.: A review on estimation of chromatic dispersion using fractional Fourier transform in optical fiber communication. In: 2018 International Conference on Smart Systems and Inventive Technology (ICSSIT), pp. 223–228 (2018)
81. Calabró, E., Magazú, S.: A review of advances in the analysis of biological systems by means of fourier transform infrared (FTIR) spectroscopy. In: Moore, E. (ed.) Fourier Transform Infrared Spectroscopy (FTIR): Methods, Analysis and Research Insights, pp. 1–32. Nova Science Publishers Inc (2016)
82. Chen, Y., Zou, C., Mastalerz, M., Hu, S., Gasaway, C., Tao, X.: Applications of micro-Fourier transform infrared spectroscopy (FTIR) in the geological sciences-a review. Int. J. Mole. Sci. **16**(12), 30223–30250 (2015)
83. Kaushik, C., Gautam, T., Elamaran, V.: A tutorial review on discrete Fourier transform with data compression application. In: 2014 International Conference on Green Computing Communication and Electrical Engineering (ICGCCEE) (2014)
84. Hauchecorne, B., Lenaerts, S.: Unravelling the mysteries of gas phase photocatalytic reaction pathways by studying the catalyst surface: a literature review of different Fourier transform infrared spectroscopic reaction cells used in the field. J. Photochem. Photobiol. C Photochem. Rev. **14**(1), 72–85 (2013)
85. Zappa, E., Busca, G.: Static and dynamic features of Fourier transform profilometry: a review. Opt. Lasers Eng. **50**(8), 1140–1151 (2012)
86. Xiong, J., Zhang, Z., Chen, X.: Multidimensional entropy evaluation of non-uniform distribution of assembly features in precision instruments. Precision Eng. **77**, 1–15 (2022)
87. Sütçü, M.: Disutility entropy in multi-attribute utility analysis. Comput. Ind. Eng. **169**, 108189 (2022)
88. You, J., Yu, C., Sun, J., Chen, J.: Generalized maximum entropy based identification of graphical arma models. Automatica **141**, 110319 (2022)
89. Wang, Y., Wang, Z., Chen, L., Gu, J.: Experimental study on critical characteristics of self-organized behavior of concrete under uniaxial compression based on AE characteristic parameters information entropy. J. Mater. Civil Eng. 34(7) (2022)
90. Yuan, Z., Chen, H., Li, T.: Exploring interactive attribute reduction via fuzzy complementary entropy for unlabeled mixed data. Pattern Recognit. **127**, 108651 (2022)
91. Zhang, X., Zhou, Y., Tang, X., Fan, Y.: Three-way improved neighborhood entropies based on three-level granular structures. Int. J. Mach. Learn. Cybernetics **13**(7), 1861–1890 (2022)
92. Kadian, R., Kumar, S.: New fuzzy mean codeword length and similarity measure. Granular Comput. **7**(3), 461–478 (2022)

93. Grassl, M., Huber, F., Winter, A.: Entropic proofs of singleton bounds for quantum error-correcting codes. IEEE Trans. Inform. Theo. **68**(6), 3942–3950 (2022)
94. Dai, J., Liu, Q.: Semi-supervised attribute reduction for interval data based on misclassification cost. Int. J. Mach. Learn. Cybernetics **13**(6), 1739–1750 (2022)
95. Gao, X., Pan, L., Deng, Y.: Cross entropy of mass function and its application in similarity measure. Appl. Intell. **52**(8), 8337–8350 (2022)
96. Lo, Y., Hsiao, Y.T., Chang, F.C.: Use electroencephalogram entropy as an indicator to detect stress-induced sleep alteration. Appl. Sci. (Switzerland) **12**(10), 4812 (2022)
97. Chirikjian, G.: Entropy, symmetry, and the difficulty of self-replication. Artif. Life Robot. **27**(2), 181–195 (2022)
98. Wahdan, M., Altłnkaya, M.: Maximum average entropy-based quantization of local observations for distributed detection. Digit. Sign. Process. A Rev. J. **123**, 103427 (2022)
99. Livingstone, S.R., Russo, F.A.: The Ryerson audio-visual database of emotional speech and song (RAVDESS): a dynamic, multimodal set of facial and vocal expressions in north American English. PloS one **13**(5), e0196391 (2018)
100. McFee, B., et al.: librosa: Audio and music signal analysis in python. In: Proceedings of the 14th python in science conference, vol. 8, pp. 18–25. Citeseer (2015)
101. The SciPy community: Scipy (2022) Accessed 10 April 2022
102. The SciPy community: Scipyfft (2022) Accessed 10 April 2022
103. Cover, T., Thomas, J.: Elements of Information Theory. Wiley (2012)
104. Veena, S., Aravindhar, D.J.: Sound classification system using deep neural networks for hearing impaired people. Wireless Pers. Commun. **126**, 385–399 (2022). https://doi.org/10.1007/s11277-022-09750-7
105. Khamparia, A., Gupta, D., Nguyen, N.G., Khanna, A., Pandey, B., Tiwari, P.: Sound classification using convolutional neural network and tensor deep stacking network. IEEE Access **7**, 7717–7727 (2019)
106. Kwon, S.: A cnn-assisted enhanced audio signal processing for speech emotion recognition. Sensors **20**(1), 183 (2019)
107. Xia, X., Pan, J., Wang, Y.: Audio sound determination using feature space attention based convolution recurrent neural network. In: ICASSP 2020–2020 IEEE International Conference on Acoustics, Speech and Signal Processing (ICASSP), pp. 3382–3386 (2020)
108. Shannon, C.E.: Prediction and entropy of printed english. Bell Syst. Tech. J. **30**(1), 50–64 (1951)
109. Chamishka, S., et al.: A voice-based real-time emotion detection technique using recurrent neural network empowered feature modelling. Multimed. Tools Appl. 1–22 (2022). https://doi.org/10.1007/s11042-022-13363-4
110. Lee, M.C., Yeh, S.C., Chang, J.W., Chen, Z.Y.: Research on Chinese speech emotion recognition based on deep neural network and acoustic features. Sensors **22**(13), 4744 (2022)

Environment Emulation in 3D Graphics Software for Fringe Projection Profilometry

V. M. Martínez-Suárez[1(✉)], J. C. Pedraza-Ortega[1], S. Salazar-Colores[2], O. A. Espinosa-Bernal[1], and J. M. Ramos-Arreguin[1]

[1] Facultad de Ingeniería, Cerro de las campanas s/n, Universidad Autónoma de Querétaro, Querétaro, Mexico
vicmanuel.mtz.s@gmail.com

[2] Centro de Investigaciones en Óptica, 37150 León, Guanajuato, Mexico
sebastian.salazar@cio.mx

Abstract. The lack of a public data set for specific applications has been a problem for the development of deep learning techniques in recent years. There is limited information for non-contact optical measurement applications such as fringe projection profilometry. The complexity and cost of generating a large amount of data to train the models to present two problems: time and personnel required aren't easy or possible for most developers. Taking advantage of the advanced technology of current graphic simulators, we have generated an emulated environment for the projection of fringes that allows us to simulate projections on objects and perform phase changes according to N-Step. Briefly explaining the unwrapping algorithm and the pre-configuration of the software simulation environment, we determine the most important factors that could affect the quality of our data for the application of the different phase unwrapping techniques. Performing a qualitative evaluation of the reconstructions of the virtual objects by projecting the fringes to obtain the synthetic images throughout the work, we analyze the most important factors to develop a database with the best quality and similarity to the process carried out in the real world to obtain this data.

Keywords: Emulate · Models · Dataset · Synthetic images · Fringe projection · Wrapped · Unwrapped · 3D reconstruction

1 Introduction

1.1 Optical Metrology Methods

Optical metrology methods generate images, such as the generation of projected fringe patterns for processing. Therefore, the image becomes essential for the reconstruction of the object to be measured. In most interferometric methods, the image is formed by the superposition of the reference projections and the

M. F. Mata-Rivera et al. (Eds.): WITCOM 2022, CCIS 1659, pp. 122–138, 2022.
https://doi.org/10.1007/978-3-031-18082-8_8

object to be measured, which results in the fringe patterns of the object being modulated by a harmonic function, resulting in light and dark contrasts [10].

Among the best-known methods of optical measurement are Classical interferometry [4], Photoelasticity [1], Geometric moiré [16], Holographic interferometry [6], Digital holography [3], Electronic speckle pattern interferometry [9], Electronic speckle shearing interferometry [7], Digital image correction [11] and Fringe projection profilometry [5,8,12,13]. Existing variety for the measurement of fringe patterns, the study will focus on Deflectometry or better known as Fringe projection.

Deflectometry hasn't been left behind, and the main area has been the development of Phase Shifting Profilometry (PSP) or also known as Fringe Projection Profilometry (FPP). PSP is a configuration made up of different types of optical hardware, but it is more specialized in data collection and analysis that can be applied for a variety of measurement situations that require precision.

Carrying out the reconstruction of the object from the images with projected fringes has represented a challenge due to the difficulties that the method presents, having among its advantages are high precision, simple installation of the hardware and flexibility of implementation obtaining excellent quality in the reconstruction of objects complex. However, the conventional phase unwrapping method is generally unable to robustly unwrap the phase, without the need for complementary algorithms, being more complicated in dense fringes, so increasing the frequency is crucial for accuracy, but requires a complex calibration of the phase parameters [26], projected fringes, and external factors such as the environment, light, the angle of the cameras, as well as the noise that could be generated by the exposure time of the projection for fast captures and to have the minimum variation in the movement of the object that although they are static, these variations are still present it is.

In this article, the Temporal Phase Unwrapping (TPU) method will be used specifically in order to simplify the study to obtain the three-dimensional shape of the object, although it can be scaled for the application of two or more cameras. A simulated environment will be developed for the acquisition of images with free software such as Blender and we will configure the physical conditions of the projection of fringes where we will experiment with the positions of the cameras, the light of the projection, and the rendering configurations that will allow us to obtain the best quality of the images generated with a completely controlled environment.

1.2 Problems with Optical Measurement Systems

One of the things that most of the methods mentioned above have in common is the projection of a beam of light and the capture of the patterns generated in the object by the reflection of the light employing a sensor or a camera. Most of the time, obtaining the indicated equipment to carry out the optical measurement with any of these techniques is not simple and it is not until practice that we realize different factors that were not considered at the beginning, which requires changing some equipment with Other features [29]. It is also the case that mounting the basic system like the one shown in Fig. 1, does not turn out to be as easy or fast, where it is required to make adjustments between the camera and the projector, to vary the intensity of the wave generated for the projected pattern, change the frequency of the generated wave among others. Having an environment that emulates the physical system is useful both to generate large databases at a precise and affordable time and to carry out adjustment tests in a controlled environment practically and simply.

Throughout the work, the results obtained from the environment that emulates a PSP system for a 3-Step will be shown, in which it is possible to change its characteristics to adapt to different methods such as Digital image correction or techniques derived from the fringe projection profilometry as Stereo phase unwrapping. Thus explaining the methodology to be able to generate a said environment that can be adapted to specific applications.

1.3 Deep Learning Implementation

The most significant changes in the different types of instrumentation during the last 40 years have been the integration of technologies such as computers in the measurement, and in the last decade, more techniques implemented due to computational power [21,22].

Deep Learning (DL) techniques have allowed us to solve problems from a digital processing perspective, leaving aside the hardware limitations for optical methods.

Inspired by the recent successes of Deep Learning for phase analysis, it has proven to be a tool capable of getting the wrapped phase and performing phase unwrapping in a comprehensive framework [14,30].

One of the challenges and difficulties of implementing machine learning and deep learning techniques is having an extensive set of training data, and the limited public databases make it necessary to develop tools that allow emulating their development [20], since doing so can be expensive due to the time, personnel and materials necessary for its development [15].

This proposed approach with these techniques represents a significant step forward in high-speed, accurate, motion-artifact-free absolute 3D shape measurement for complicated single-pattern fringe objects, so it is essential to have access to our data, which fits more to the applications we are developing [14]. It is well known that the limitations in artificial intelligence are the limited data that is publicly accessible, which limits convolutional neural networks (CNN) to learn from the few databases that have been developed and released to the public, and not the possible variants that may exist when performing a measurement with different parameters.

2 Principle of Fringe Projection Profilometry and Phase Unwrapping

As shown in Fig. 1, a basic system consists of a camera and a projector. The N-step phase shift algorithm is a method known for its insensitivity to ambient light and surface reflectivity [19]. A series of phase-shifted patterns are projected with a phase change and the minimum number of images is at least two, among them, are the 3-Step, 4-Step, 8-Step, and 12-Step among others, the last being the more recommendable to acquire the Background intensity. The fringe patterns captured by camera 1 for N-Step can be expressed as:

$$I_{cn}(u^c, v^c) = A_c(u^c, v^c) + B_c(u^c, v^c)\cos(\phi_c(u^c, v^c) + 2\pi n/N) \tag{1}$$

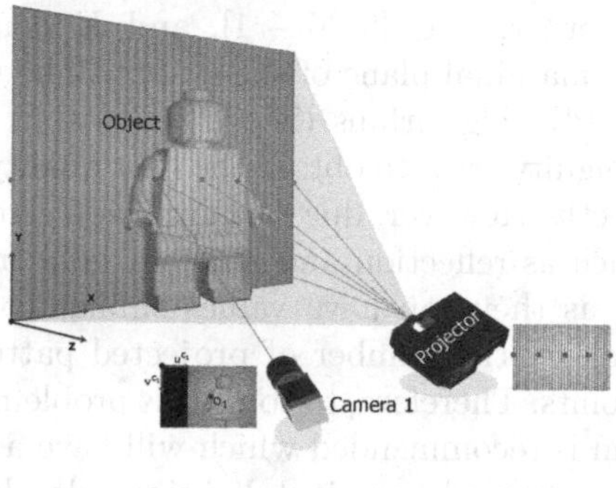

Fig. 1. The basic principle of a PSP system.

where I_{cn} represents the captured image $(n+1)th$, $n \in [0, 2]$, (u, v) are the pixel coordinates of the image and c corresponding chamber ($1[L]$ to N-chambers), A is the mean intensity, B denotes the amplitude, ϕ is the phase, and $2\pi n/N$ is the phase change that we will implement for our work. With the orthogonality of the trigonometric functions, the (average) Background intensity can be obtained as:

$$A_c(u^c, v^c) = \tfrac{1}{N} \textstyle\sum_{n=0}^{N-1} I_{cn}(u^c, v^c) \tag{2}$$

The emulator will allow us to work under the premise that both ambient light and reflectivity will remain constant once the environment is rendered, the three standard phase shift fringe patterns with a shift of $2\pi/3$ are captured for camera 1, where (u^c, v^c) is omitted for convenience:

$$\begin{aligned} I_{L0} &= A_L + B_L\cos(\phi_L), \\ I_{L1} &= A_L + B_L\cos(\phi_L + 2\pi/3), \\ I_{L2} &= A_L + B_L\cos(\phi_L + 4\pi/3). \end{aligned} \tag{3}$$

With the PSP algorithm, the wrapped phase ϕ for N-Step [10] can be obtained with the least square method by:

$$\phi_L = arctan\frac{\sum_{n=0}^{N-1} I_{cn}\, sin(2\pi n/N)}{\sum_{n=0}^{N-1} I_{cn}\, cos(2\pi n/N)} \tag{4}$$

If it is possible to know the phase ϕ_L, the 3D position can be calculated using the calibration parameters between the camera and the projector [25]. Thus, the wrapped phase ϕ_L can be calculated as follows [17]:

$$\phi_L = arctan\frac{\sqrt{3}(I_{L1}-I_{L2})}{2(I_{L0}-I_{L1}-I_{L2})} \tag{5}$$

The absolute Φ_L and wrapped ϕ_L phases satisfy the following relation:

$$\Phi_L = \phi_L + 2k\pi \tag{6}$$

where k is the period order, $k \in [0, K-1]$, and K denotes the number of projected fringes on the marginal plane of the system. The marginal order k can be obtained by several PSP algorithms (See [21–23]) that have the purpose of reducing the phase ambiguity error to obtain the best quality in the order map to unwrap the phase correctly. However, due to calibration errors between elements and external factors such as reflection and ambient light interference, some 2D data may be incorrect as they can have values similar to the matching point O_c. In addition, the greater the number of projected patterns, the greater the possibilities for these points. Therefore, to solve this problem, the application of a multi-step PS algorithm is recommended which will have a higher measurement accuracy and robustness towards ambient lighting, also high-frequency fringe patterns are not recommended as they are susceptible to aliasing problems [14].

3 Methods and Materials

The implementation of the emulated environment was developed in Blender (https://www.blender.org/), which is free software for any purpose, including commercial or educational purposes. It is a 3D creation suite that allows us to model, assemble, animate, simulate, render, compose and follow movement among other options. In recent years Blender has proven to be an excellent choice for developers even for highly regarded animation and game development companies. Therefore, its accessibility, flexibility, and ease of use provide us with an excellent development tool for these emulated environments that can generate synthetic images for our databases.

For the extraction and generation of 3D figures, We used figures developed by other professionals were used, which were obtained from pages such as *TurboSquid* (https://www.turbosquid.com/). TurboSquid models are used by developers and professionals all over the world. This is intended to save users the time of developing large and complex 3D models and instead allow them to spend their time on other areas of their production process.

The development simulation environment for the Blender emulated environment was implemented on an NVIDIA GeForce RTX 2060, 8 GB of RAM, and i5-CPU 2.4 Ghz.

4 Generation of Emulated Environment

The scene collection that allows us to use Blender is made up of cameras, 3D objects, and lights. We developed the development environment emulating a fringe projection profilometry system, which consists of a projector that is represented by a lamp with the configuration described below, and a camera with a focal length of 28 mm with a lens type 'Perspective' by the camera configuration, as shown in Fig. 2 the optical path of phase measuring profilometry, where P is the center of the projection of the projector, $C1$ is the camera imaging center, D is an arbitrary point on the tested object and effective projection area of 15.4 mm represented by l_0. In our experiment, the distance d between the camera and the projector is 3 mm, and the reference plane is placed in front of the project at about 15 mm represented by l. The environment emulates es development by Blender ver 3.1.0.

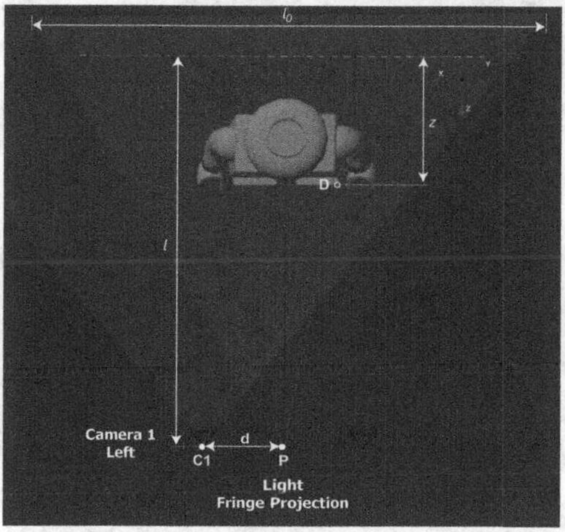

Fig. 2. Optical path of phase measuring profilometry in the enviroment emulate.

The tree of nodes creates generated a projection plane, shown in Fig. 3, followed by a block with the name CLIP where it established a limitation of the projection of the lamps to a specific area. Below the previous block, we have a SINE block, this is the one that generates the projection of the fringe, and it is here where we can modify the phase-shifting according to the N-Step that we are implementing.

The virtual objects that were used can be found in the reference of the site we use or use existing 3D models with extension .obj. They can also be obtained from existing databases [20] such as ModelNet, ShapeNet, ABC, Thingi10K, etc. A varied selection of simple objects to the most complex ones was made in order to observe the behavior of the fringes projected on these objects, as shown in Fig. 4.

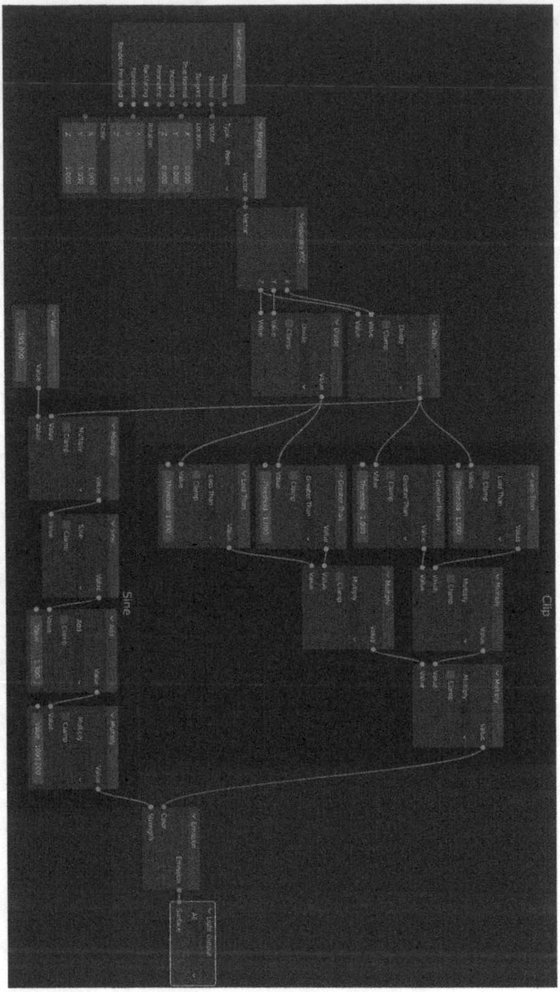

Fig. 3. The main compositing node tree of this Blender system.

The captured images are 640×480 pixels to generate images with good resolution, although fact that Blender allows us to generate up to 4k resolution, this is not recommended given that these types of images are very heavy when training deep networks which complicate the training of our models if we do not have the appropriate hardware. A low resolution can cause a loss in the quality of the fringes which will be studied in the section on experiments.

The generation of each rendered image takes an average of 2.8 s at the chosen resolution but can vary by object type and light settings. For a 4k resolution, the rendering can take up to 60 s, which for the generation of large databases can be slow given the number of images that are generated according to the unwrapping step that we are performing. As shown in Fig. 5, the resolution of

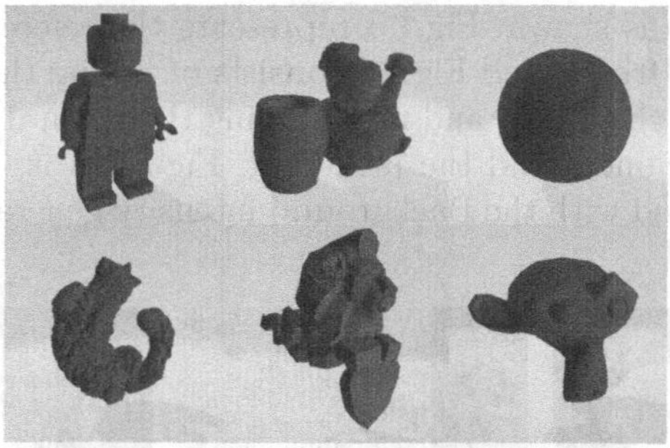

Fig. 4. Models from TurboSquid.

the rendering can affect the quality of the projection of the fringes, which can represent a loss of information in the phase and a low quality in the unwrapped phase. The number of fringes projected on the plane is 32.

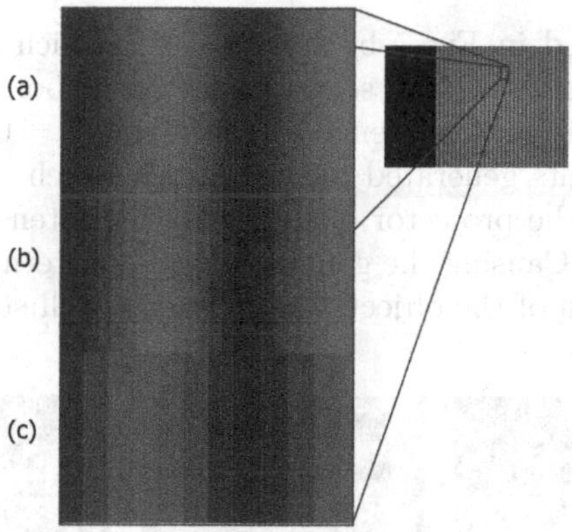

Fig. 5. Fringes projection rendered to different image formats. (a) It is generated with a 4k resolution (3840×2160 resolution) (b) it represents the resolution used VGA-SD (640×480 resolution), and (c) of a smaller CIF format (360×240 resolution).

Better quality is obtained in the Background with a greater number of images with fringes and thus avoid the moire noise that is generated, it is recommendable to apply a 12-Step method, in which a better reconstruction of the object is also obtained when the unwrapping phase [18].

5 Experiments

In our work, for each 3D scene of the object, we require three images with fringes shifted $2\pi/3$ to do the calculations. In addition to each scene, we worked with only one perspective as shown: Fig. 6b represents the reference plane with the respective projection fringe, and Fig. 6c consists of taking the scene considering the background with the object and maintaining the natural shadows generated by the angle of the camera and the projector. Figure 6a is an image generated which will be compared with the Background intensity generated by formula (2).

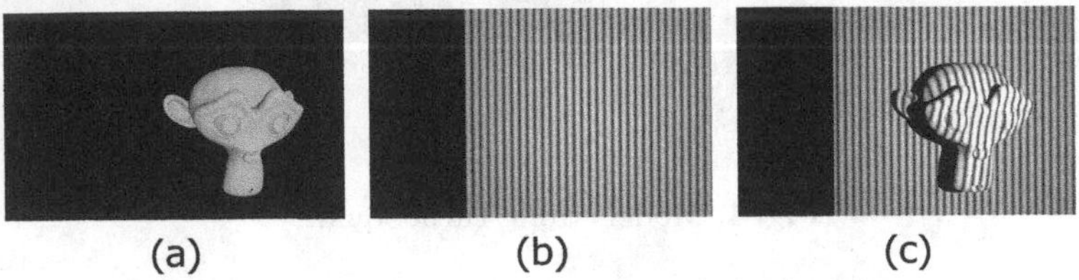

Fig. 6. Examples of the types of capture according to the simulated scenario (a) Background intensity (b) Full shot considering the background with the object (c) Full shot with background and subject considering shadows (d) Shot omitting the background projecting only the subject

The images obtained in Fig. 7 by formula (2), which calculates the Background intensity. A point can be seen in the zoom box which indicates the distance z at which it is with reference to the plane ($z = 0$). With this, we can determine that the lights generated by the lamps which emulate the projects, the closer they are to the projector, the greater the intensity of light they will generate in the region. Causing the generation of a pattern of fringes which, the greater the illumination of the object, the greater it will stand out.

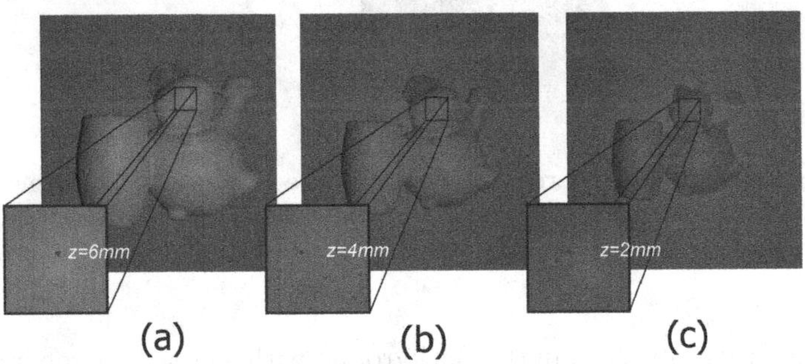

Fig. 7. Background Intensity indicating the highest points with reference to the plane. (a) Represents the object closest to the camera with a separation of $z = 6$ mm from the plane (b) a separation of $z = 4$ mm (c) with a separation of $z = 2$ mm.

If it is necessary to modify this parameter, it is advisable to modify the value in the node tree rather than modify the power of the lamp, since a higher lighting power will make the pattern stand out more and in the 3D reconstruction of the object, a wavy relief will be generated.

5.1 Wrapped Phase with Synthetic Images

In the previous section, we commented on the rendering resolution, as shown in Fig. 5, for a large number of projected fringes we can lose quality due to pixels and generate an aliasing effect. However, for our study, it is important to determine the most optimal quality for the final reconstruction of the object, where not too much ambiguity is generated between the phases, but it doesn't requiring a very high resolution that in the future complicates the training of our models and has the end that reduces the resolution of each image.

As shown in Fig. 8, we have the enveloped phases obtained with Eq. 5, we can appreciate in greater detail what a low resolution generates when we calculate the enveloped phase. Figure 8a shows a better uniformity in the contour of the object. However, this resolution will be very heavy for the calculation of the enveloped phase. In the case of Fig. 8c, the generalization of the pixels will cause a high probability of generating an ambiguity in the jump of the phase. It is determined in this way and based on similar databases [14] to use a VGA resolution as standard.

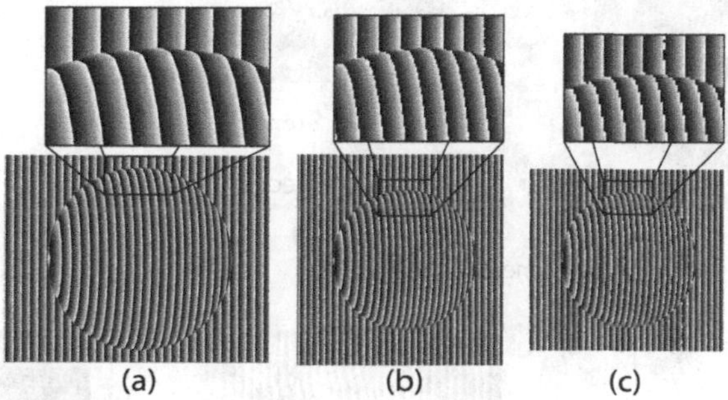

Fig. 8. Wrapped phases obtained with images rendered in (a) 4k (3840×2160pixels) (b) VGA-SD (640×480pixels) and (c) CIF formats (380×210pixels)

5.2 3D Reconstruction Process with Synthetic Images

The phase unwrapping method usually requires several images with projected fringes offset according to the N-Step that is used. However, the complicated auxiliary algorithms require the projection of dense and high-frequency fringes to successfully unwrap the phase. The Flowchart of Fig. 9 shows in a general way the basic procedure to obtain the development of the wrapped phase generated by the emulated images in the graphic environment.

We will briefly discuss the process for obtaining the 3D Object Reconstruction.

Step 1: In order to generate the pattern of offset fringes, it is necessary to vary the value of the $sin(x + \delta)$ signal from the 'Sine' box of the node tree in Fig. 3. For our case, the generated offset was $\delta = 0, 2\pi/3$ and $4\pi/3$, so that the lamp emulates the displacement of the fringes.

Step 2: We will proceed to capture each projection of the Lamp with the camera which we will obtain by the formula (3).
Step 3: Once you capture the images with the formula (5), We will calculate what we know as the Wrapped Phase which is between $-\pi$ and π.
Step 4: To achieve a development of the wrapped phase there are several methods to successfully obtain the absolute phase, in our work the TPU Algorithm was implemented, which is not fast but obtains a robust Phase Unwrapping.
Step 5: Finally, once the Absolute Phase is obtained with the object, it is required to obtain the Absolute Phase of the reference plane (following the same procedure mentioned above) in order to obtain the data of the 3D object.

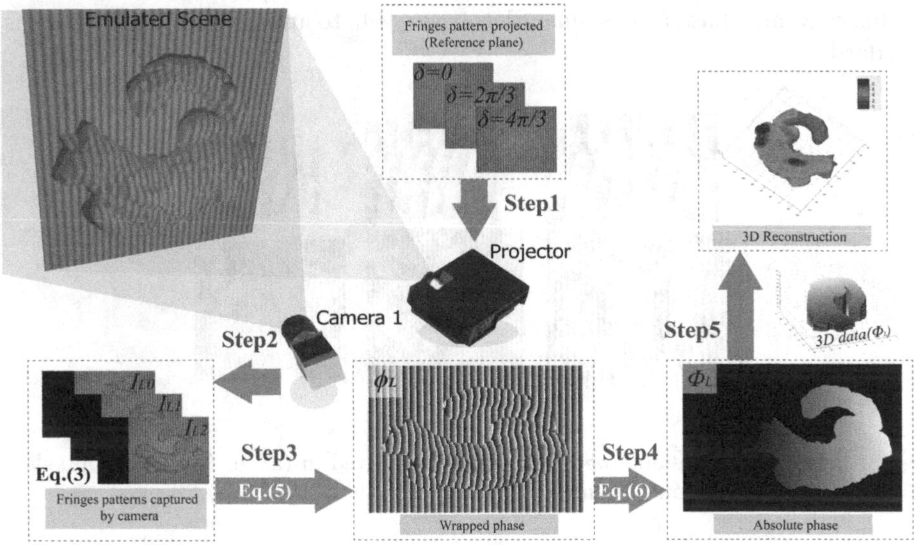

Fig. 9. Flowchart of Phase Shifting algorithm 3-Step.

6 Results and Discussion

To corroborate the effectiveness of the previously proposed approach configurations, which consisted of a camera (640 × 480 pixels) and a projector emulated by several lamps. 32-period PS fringe patterns are implemented in our experiment. The effective size of the projection is 15.4 × 15.4 mm. We evaluate the qualitative results of the angle configuration between the camera and the projector, and the evaluation of obtaining a reference image that can serve as the Ground-Truth.

6.1 Qualitative Evaluation of Angle Between Camera and Projector

For more complex figures in their shape, we will analyze two perspectives with the camera, the projection light will continue to be kept in the center and the camera will take two positions in the simulation environment. For Fig. 10, the camera position is 3 mm at an angle of 0° concerning the projector, keeping both at a distance of 15 mm from the plane and a focal length of 28 mm. For Fig. 11 we change the perspective to cause what generates a very large angle between the camera and the projector, the configuration modified the position of the camera which is now at 7 mm with an angle of 12° with respect and a 27 mm focal length to capture the entire projection frame [24].

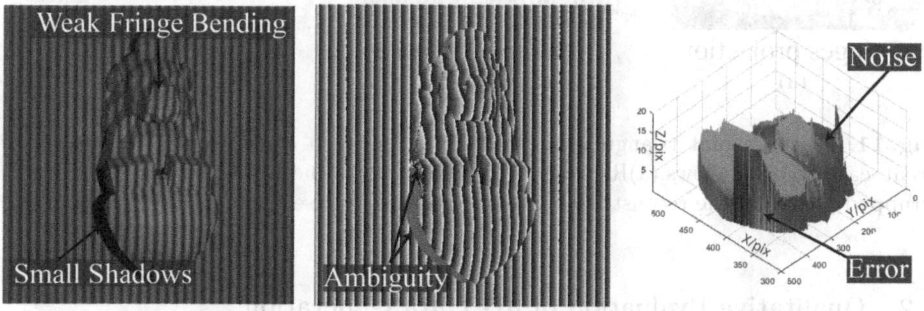

Fringes projection (a) | Wrapped phase (b) | 3D Data (c)

Fig. 10. Feature point triangulation without angle between camera and projector. (a)Represents the capture of the projected fringes (b) the wrapped phase (c) the reconstruction of the absolute phase.

As shown in Fig. 10, for an angle of 0 between the camera and the projector, when projecting the fringes, the natural shadows by the light are formed in the 3D models, which is convenient to simulate the real world and replicate an environment. similar to the typical problems of this method. It should be noted that the small-angle as mentioned will generate small shadows and certain characteristics will be seen as a weak fringe bending in the model. This will cause that when calculating the wrapped phase we will obtain certain ambiguities in the phase generated by the discontinuities of the fringes and when performing the reconstruction of the object we will have errors and some noise due to the type of triangulation between a point, camera, and projector.

However, as the angle between the camera and projector increases, it will generate large shadows and strong fringe bending, as well as a more pronounced plane deformation as shown in Fig. 11a, therefore more ambiguities will be generated in the enveloped phase (Fig. 11b). and which can be eliminated with more advanced techniques leaving large holes as they are lost data. For an angle between 10 and 15, it is convenient to obtain a more natural smoothing in the

3D reconstruction, however, as we noted in Fig. 11c that the 3D Data presenting greater ambiguities can generate errors during the unwrapping phase.

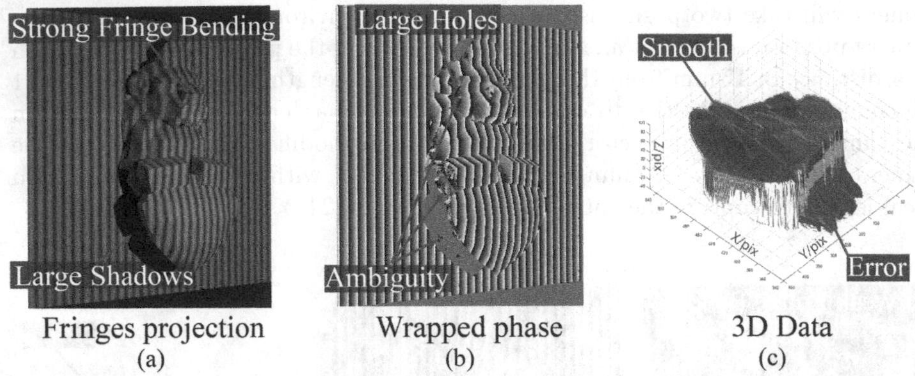

Fig. 11. Feature point triangulation with angle between camera and projector and great casting of shadows.(a)Represents the capture of the projected fringes (b) the wrapped phase (c) the reconstruction of the absolute phase.

6.2 Qualitative Evaluation of 3D Data Generation

A proposal is presented with which it intends is to generate a Ground-Truth with the simulated environment, it was projected on two spheres shown in Fig. 12a, having the 3D reconstruction (Fig. 12b) and our image obtained of the emulator to obtain the Ground-Truth (Fig. 12c). Evaluating the comparisons between the two results, we note the similarity in the results obtained for the shape of the spheres both from the synthetic Ground-Truth and from the reconstruction of the spheres with synthetic images, the graph of Fig. 12d represents the cut in a central point of the spheres concerning Y.

In the reconstructions of the objects that were made, it was observed that the technique that we applied in the configuration of the Blender parameters when complex objects were used as shown in object 13, or with non-uniform shapes as in Fig. 13a the generation of the Ground-Truth (13b), we did not get the correct reconstruction of the object as we did in Fig. 13c. And it is in the graph of Fig. 13d, where we appreciate that the light saturation of the Ground-Truth established the colors in a grayscale within a range, which varied between objects. And the biggest difference between the objects is found in the contour boundaries which vary more in the 3D object compared to the generated Ground-Truth, shown in Fig. 13e.

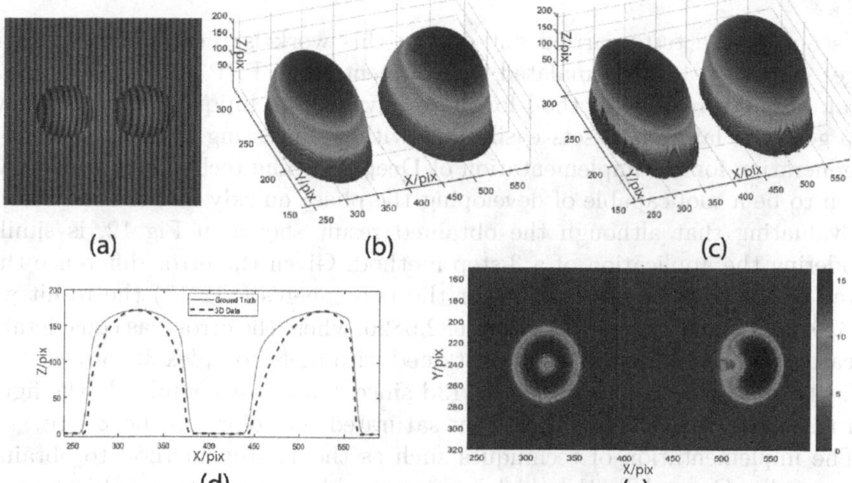

Fig. 12. Results for the evaluation of the generation of Ground-Truth using the emulator with a simple 3D object. Carrying out the reconstruction of the Object (a), to obtain the 3D Data (b) and the Ground-Truth (c), with a cut in its center (d) and obtaining the error difference (e) between the two reconstructions.

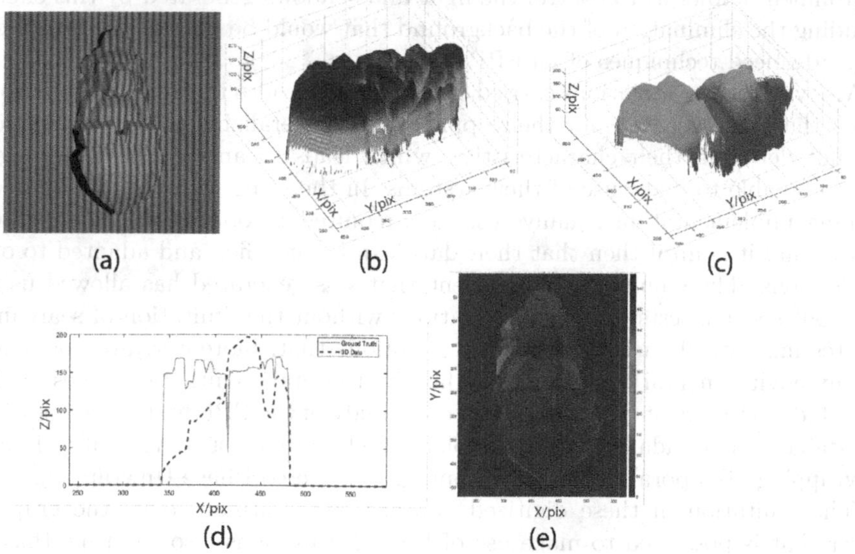

Fig. 13. Results for the evaluation of the generation of Ground-Truth using the emulator with a complex 3D object. Carrying out the reconstruction of the Object (a), to obtain the 3D Data (b) and the Ground-Truth (c), with a cut at the tip of the lion's nose (d) and obtaining the error difference (e) between the two reconstructions.

7 Conclusions

The scope of the tests carried out during this work is the evaluation of the images generated by the emulated environment of an FPP system with which we can obtain a reliable method for more advanced techniques and that allows us to generate large data sets easily and without investing many. resources in the generation for the implementation of Deep Learning techniques, which have proven to be a tool capable of developing the phase quickly and robustly [23].

Evaluating that although the obtained result shown in Fig. 12, is similar considering the application of a 3-step method. Given the error difference that existed in the MSE metric where for the two spheres (Fig. 12) the result was 72.1329 and for the Lion (Fig. 13) was 682.6826, where the error was considerably increased and observing the results obtained with more complex 3D objects such as Fig 13 and this can be seen in Fig. 13d since it was lost completely the figure with respect to the Ground-Truth that saturated the colors on the Z-axis.

The implementation of techniques such as the 12-step method to obtain a higher quality Ground Truth, which is more reliable to generate the object reconstruction for our training models [27].

Despite the limitation of not being able to obtain the 3D data of the reconstruction to use it as Ground Truth, the emulated environment complies with the characteristics of an FPP system, shown in Fig [10,11], where the characteristic effects of the projection of fringes and the relationship with the angle of the capture of the image are still maintained. It is also interesting that the Blender environment allows us to control the light and shadows generated by this effect, including the elimination of the background that would be used in the future for more advanced techniques of an FPP system.

Many of the investigations carried out do not delve into the emulated environments that they generate for their applications, generalizing their construction and not detailing their characteristics, which leads to an extensive investigation to be able to make use of their systems. In the same way, concerning deep learning implementations, many tests are required to obtain the results they present and it is until then that their data can be modified and adapted to our applications. The emulated environment that was generated has allowed us to carry out specific tests in our investigations without the limitation of searching and testing with data from other investigations that, moreover, are not made for any environmental condition. The facility to obtain synthetic images of the emulated environment has allowed a deeper study of the PPF and the generation of databases more adapted to the implemented methods such as Spatial Phase Unwrapping, Temporal Phase Unwrapping, and Stereo Phase Unwrapping.

The limitation in these digitized systems will continue to be the graphic power that is possessed to make use of the software, it is also the time that is required for the generation of the database will depend on the graphic card that you have and as it happens in the FPP physical systems generate complementary algorithms to obtain the different projections of the patterns automatically.

Acknowledgments. This work was supported in part by the Consejo Nacional de Ciencia y Tecnología (CONACyT), México, in the Postgraduate Faculty of Engineering by the Universidad Autónoma de Querétaro, under Grant CVU 1099400 and CVU 1099050.

References

1. Aben H., Guillemet C.: Integrated photoelasticity. In: Photoelasticity of Glass, pp. 86–101 (1993)
2. Bioucas-Dias, J.M., Valadão, G.: Phase unwrapping via graph cuts. IEEE Trans. Image Process. **16**(3), 698–709 (2007). https://doi.org/10.1109/tip.2006.888351
3. Cuche, E., Bevilacqua, F., Depeursinge, C.: Digital holography for quantitative phase-contrast imaging. Opt. Lett. **24**, 291–293 (1999)
4. Creath, K.: Phase-measurement interferometry techniques. Prog. Opt. **26**, 349–393 (1988)
5. Geng, J.: Structured-light 3D surface imaging: a tutorial. Adv. Opt. Photonics **3**, 128–160 (2011)
6. Gabor, D.: A new microscopic principle. Nature **161**, 777–778 (1948)
7. Hung, Y.: Shearography: a new optical method for strain measurement and non-destructive testing. Opt. Eng. **21**, 213391 (1982)
8. López-Torres, C.V., Salazar, C.S., Kells, K., Pedraza-Ortega, J.C., Ramos-Arreguin, J.M.: Improving 3D reconstruction accuracy in wavelet transform profilometry by reducing shadow effects. IET Image Process. **14**(2), 310–317 (2020)
9. Lokberg, O.J.: Electronic speckle pattern interferometry. In: Soares, O.D.D. (eds) Optical Metrology. NATO ASI Series, vol. 131. Springer, Dordrecht (1987). https://doi.org/10.1007/978-94-009-3609-6_36
10. Schreiber, H., Bruning, J.H.: Phase shifting interferometry. pp. 547–666 (2007). https://doi.org/10.1002/9780470135976.ch14
11. Pan, B., et al.: Two-dimensional digital image correlation for in-plane displacement and strain measurement: a review. Meas. Sci. Technol. **20**, 062001 (2009)
12. Pedraza-Ortega, J.C., et al.: A 3D sensor based on a profilometrical approach. Sensors **9**(12), 10326–10340 (2009)
13. Pedraza Ortega, J.C., et al.: Image processing for 3D reconstruction using a modified Fourier transform profilometry method. In: Gelbukh, A., Kuri Morales, Á.F. (eds.) MICAI 2007. LNCS (LNAI), vol. 4827, pp. 705–712. Springer, Heidelberg (2007). https://doi.org/10.1007/978-3-540-76631-5_67
14. Qian, J., Feng, S., Tao, T., Hu, Y., Li, Y., Chen, Q., et al.: Deep-learning-enabled geometric constraints and phase unwrapping for single-shot absolute 3D shape measurement. APL Photonics **5**, 046105 (2020). https://doi.org/10.1063/5.0003217
15. Ribbens, B., Jacobs, V., Vanlanduit, S., Buytaert, J.: Projection Moiré profilometry simulation software for algorithm validation and setup optimalisation, pp. 87–96 (2013)
16. Sciammarella, C.A.: The moiré method–a review. Exp. Mech. **22**, 418–433 (1982). https://doi.org/10.1007/BF02326823
17. Srinivasan, V., Liu, H.C., Halioua, M.: Automated phase-measuring profilometry of 3-D diffuse objects. Appl. Opt. **23**, 3105–3108 (1984)
18. Shijie, F., Qian, C., Guohua, G., Tianyang, T., Liang, Z., Yan, H., et al.: Fringe pattern analysis using deep learning. Adv. Photonics **1**, 1 (2019). https://doi.org/10.1117/1.AP.1.2.025001

19. Tianyang, T., Qian, C., Shijie, F., Yan, H., Jian, D., Chao, Z.: High-precision real-time 3D shape measurement using a bi-frequency scheme and multi-view system. Appl. Opt. **56**, 3646–3653 (2017)
20. Wang, F., Wang, C., Guan, Q.: Single-shot fringe projection profilometry based on deep learning and computer graphics. Opt. Express **29**, 8024–8040 (2021)
21. Zuo, C., Lei, H., Minliang, Z., Qian, C., Anand, A.: Temporal phase unwrapping algorithms for fringe projection profilometry: a comparative review. Optics Lasers Eng. **85**, 84–103 (2016). https://doi.org/10.1016/j.optlaseng.2016.04.022
22. Zuo, C., Feng, S., Huang, L., Tao, T., Yin, W., Chen, Q.: Phase shifting algorithms for fringe projection profilometry: a review. Optics Lasers Eng. **109**, 23–59 (2018). https://doi.org/10.1016/j.optlaseng.2018.04.019
23. Zuo, C., Qian, J., Feng, S., et al.: Deep learning in optical metrology: a review. Light Sci. Appl. **11**, 39 (2022). https://doi.org/10.1038/s41377-022-00714-x
24. Zhang, S.: High-speed 3D Imaging with Digital Fringe Projection Techniques. CRC Press, Taylor and Francis Group LLC, London, UK (2016)
25. Zhang, S., Huang, P.S.: Novel method for structured light system calibration. Opt. Eng. **45**, 083601 (2006)
26. Zhang, M., Chen, Q., Tao, T., Feng, S., Hu, Y., Li, H., et al.: Robust and efficient multi-frequency temporal phase unwrapping: optimal fringe frequency and pattern sequence selection. Opt. Express **25**, 20381–20400 (2017)
27. Qian, J., Feng, S., Li, Y., Tao, T., Han, J., Chen, Q., et al.: Single-shot absolute 3D shape measurement with deep-learning-based color fringe projection profilometry. Opt. Lett. **45**, 1842–1845 (2020)
28. Qian, J., Feng, S., Tao, T., Hu, Y., Liu, K., Wu, S., et al.: High-resolution real-time 360 3D model reconstruction of a handheld object with fringe projection profilometry. Opt. Lett. **44**, 5751–5754 (2019)
29. García-Isáis, C.A., Noé Alcalá, O.: One shot profilometry using a composite fringe pattern. Optics Lasers Eng. **53**, 25–30 (2014). https://doi.org/10.1016/j.optlaseng.2013.08.006
30. Nguyen, H., Wang, Y., Wang, Z.: Single-shot 3D shape reconstruction using structured light and deep convolutional neural networks. Sensors **20**, 3718 (2020). https://doi.org/10.3390/s20133718

Web Platform for the Analysis of Physical and Mental Health Data of Students

C. I. Moo-Barrera[1,2], M. G. Orozco-del-Castillo[1,2], M. R. Moreno-Sabido[1(✉)], N. L. Cuevas-Cuevas[1], and C. Bermejo-Sabbagh[1]

[1] Departamento de Sistemas y Computación, Tecnológico Nacional de México/IT de Mérida, Mérida, Yucatán, México
mario.ms@merida.tecnm.mx

[2] AAAI Student Chapter at Yucatán, México (AAAIMX), Association for the Advancement of Artificial Intelligence, Mérida, Yucatán, México

Abstract. The development of systems that help automate and manage people's lives at different levels is what has driven the enormous growth that humanity has had. On the other hand, the COVID-19 pandemic has meant an unprecedented event that has marked a before and after for the entire world. As a result of this, companies and institutions implemented various technological tools to have a greater capacity to respond to the challenges generated by this and other similar potential diseases, however, the development of these technological tools is not always clear and accessible, particularly to small companies and to academic institutions. This paper describes the development of a web tool for the analysis of physical and mental health data of students using a COVID-19 screening tool, commonly used psychological questionnaires and inventories which help diagnose symptoms of mental illnesses, and a microblogging tool for further natural language processing. The results and conclusions reached at the end of this work are also presented.

Keywords: Web development · Health care · Data analytics · Unified modeling language · SCRUM methodology

1 Introduction

The world is facing one of the most important global challenges since the Second World War: the disease COVID-19 provoked by the coronavirus SARS-CoV-2. The pandemic derived from it has generated a crisis in all aspects of people's lives [1] and was declared a public health emergency by the World Health Organization (WHO) [2], an unprecedented multimodal crisis (health, labor, economic, and social) that has a particular impact on developing countries. Among the preventive measures to avoid contracting the virus are social distancing and confinement, which have negative consequences because they produce a great impact on society and personal interactions [3].

The effects of the pandemic have been well documented. For instance, in [4] an increase in negative emotions (anxiety, depression, and anger) and a decrease in positive

M. F. Mata-Rivera et al. (Eds.): WITCOM 2022, CCIS 1659, pp. 139–156, 2022.
https://doi.org/10.1007/978-3-031-18082-8_9

emotions (happiness and satisfaction) derived from the pandemic are mentioned. This generated erratic behavior among people, which is a common phenomenon. In addition to the negative impact on personal interactions, the quarantine also increased the possibility of psychological and mental problems. In the absence of interpersonal communication, depressive and anxiety disorders are more likely to occur or worsen [5, 6].

There are several mental health issues that have emerged during the pandemic, and they represent one of the most far-reaching consequences. In the context of the COVID-19 pandemic, people with high levels of anxiety are likely to interpret harmless bodily sensations as evidence that they are infected [7], which increases even more their anxiety, and influences their ability to make rational decisions and their behavior. This causes maladaptive behaviors, such as frequent visits to health centers to rule out the disease, excessive hand washing, social withdrawal, and anxiety about shopping [7]. A study conducted in the early phase of the pandemic on 1,210 people found that 13.8% had mild depressive symptoms, 12.2% moderate symptoms, and 4.3% severe symptoms. Higher levels of depression were seen in men, in people with no education, in people with physical complaints (similar to those reported in COVID-19) (chills, myalgia, dizziness, runny nose, and sore throat), and in people who did not trust the ability of doctors to diagnose the disease [8]. Similarly, lower levels of depression were reported in people who learned about the increase in recovered patients and in people who followed public health recommendations [8]. Another study of 52,730 people during the early phase of the pandemic found that 35% of participants experienced psychological stress, with higher levels in women [9], in people between the ages of 18 and 30, and over 60 [9]. The higher scores in the 18–30 age group could be because they use social networks as their main means of information, which can easily trigger stress. On the other hand, given that the highest mortality rate from COVID-19 occurs in older adults, it is not surprising that they are more likely to suffer from stress [9]. This pandemic is also having a psychological impact on undergraduate students. In [10], 7,143 medical students were studied during the initial phase of the pandemic and found that 0.9% of them showed severe anxiety symptoms, 2.7% moderate, and 21.3% mild. In addition, living in an urban area, having family economic stability, and living with parents were protective factors against anxiety [10]. However, having an acquaintance diagnosed with COVID-19 worsens anxiety levels [10]. The presence of symptoms due to post-traumatic stress disorder (PTSD) was described in [11], where a prevalence of 7% was found in the areas of China most affected by the pandemic, which exceeds that reported in other epidemics and suggests that the disease had a greater stressful impact on the general population.

Due to the above, it is important that educational institutions develop work environments that allow timely identification of these problems. Currently, it is a fact that hundreds of educational institutions use management systems that speed up student learning but omit diagnostic tools and real-time collaborative interactions in which students participate. Technologies such as social networks, microblogging, multimedia, etc., could improve the deficiencies that the students present [12].

Web platforms have commonly been used to automate and simplify scientific and research-related processes [13], while making possible the collaboration with other users on the internet [13], particularly exploiting the principle of "availability anywhere, at any time" using web browsers [14], providing multiple users on-demand access across multiple devices and operating systems using an internet connection [14]. These platforms also help to assist the visual interpretation and classification of data and have shown to be very effective in the construction of datasets [15]. Web platforms have successfully been used as research support tools in areas such as chemistry [13], mining [14], remote sensing [15], etc.

In this paper we describe the development of a web platform aimed at the undergraduate student community of Tecnológico Nacional de México (TecNM)/Instituto Tecnológico de Mérida (ITM) that involves physical health diagnostic tools (focused on COVID-19 screening) and mental health commonly used in psychology (questionnaires and psychological inventories), along with a module that enables microblogging, a service widely used by young people, which can also be used for diagnostic purposes through natural language processing techniques. The integral development of this platform is described using the SCRUM software development methodology.

2 Theoretical Framework

2.1 Psychological Questionnaires and Inventories

Psychological questionnaires, particularly those self-reported, are usually comprised by a set of questions formulated with the desire to obtain information from the person to whom it is applied. On the other hand, psychological inventories are a list of traits, attitudes, preferences, interests, abilities, actions, words, among other things, used to evaluate characteristics of a person; these inventories may have various focuses or specializations (e.g., depression, anxiety). Some of the most common depression inventories are listed as follows:

- **Beck Depression Inventory II.** The Beck Depression Inventory (BDI) is a self-administered assessment tool created by psychiatrist Aaron Beck; it consists of 21 items or multiple-choice questions, which rate the severity of 21 symptoms of depression that have been observed, relate the answers and their score to the estimated level of depression in that range; it tends to be a questionnaire that can be completed in less than 10 min [16].
- **Center for Epidemiologic Studies Depression Scale.** The Center for Epidemiologic Studies Depression Scale (CESD) is a measure published by Lenore Radloff in 1977; it consists of 20 items which are scored by the frequency of times a person has experienced symptoms associated with depression in the previous week [17].
- **Carroll Rating Scale for Depression.** The Carroll Rating Scale for Depression (CRSD) is a self-assessment instrument to detect signs of depression developed in the 1970s. It consists of evaluating patients for somatic and behavioral manifestations [18].
- **Patient Health Questionnaire.** The Patient Health Questionnaire (PHQ-9) is an instrument that allows the detection of mild, moderate. or severe depressive symptoms. The results of this questionnaire help detect the presence and severity of depression if it is detected. It consists of 9 items, based on diagnostic criteria for depression through questions about what the patient has experienced in the last two weeks [19].

2.2 Microblogging

Today, distributed environments are of paramount importance for information technologies. Computer applications are constantly evolving, so it is now more common to find easy-to-use, intuitive applications that allow collaboration at highly affordable costs, which could even be free [12]. In relation to education, there is still a large gap in this type of platform for students, so institutions are continually looking to somehow create better Learning Management Systems to enrich student performance; for this, they have dedicated much effort to the study of these platforms, however, they fail to reconcile important factors such as education, support, and interaction between teachers and students, or simply between the student body itself [12].

Microblogging has recently generated a lot of interest in research topics. However, previously little was known about how people used these tools in their daily lives. It is estimated that by the year 2008, only in the United States of America, 11% of the population had published something on a microblogging site, and by the following year, around August 2009, there were already more than 32 million of people on Twitter [20]. These studies revealed that these tools were useful for sharing information, keeping up to date with topics of interest, having direct communication with other people, among other purposes [20]. Currently, microblogging is a form of communication through which users describe their current status in posts with brief content that can be distributed through different media (instant messaging, cell phones, email or web platforms). People use microblogging to share their daily activities or even to search for information [21]. The latter is related to the fact that microblogging is increasingly considered as a means of communication on emergency issues due to its increasing speed and accessibility to the multiplatform, so it could be a place in which information can be collected during some critical event [22].

3 Methodology

For the development of the web platform for the analysis of physical and mental health data of students, the agile development methodology SCRUM [23] was used. Being an agile development methodology, it is based on the idea of closing short development cycles; such cycles are commonly called "Iterations", but in SCRUM they are known as "Sprints" [23]. In Fig. 1 the iterative cycle of SCRUM is shown. The Product Owner identifies and writes the User Stories, which are added to the Product Backlog. Subsequently, the Product Owner determines the priorities of the User Stories and orders the Product Backlog according to the established priorities. The SCRUM Team carries out the Sprint Planning to establish the User Histories that will be considered during the Sprint. This will make up the Sprint Backlog; the User Histories are then broken down into tasks by the development team. The Sprint can be 1, 2, 3 or 4 weeks. The SCRUM Team conducts the Daily SCRUM, which is a daily meeting of approximately 15 min. As a result of the Sprint, a potentially deliverable product is obtained that is part of a demo during the Sprint Review. The cycle ends with the Sprint Retrospective, which is a meeting that takes place at the end of each Sprint [24].

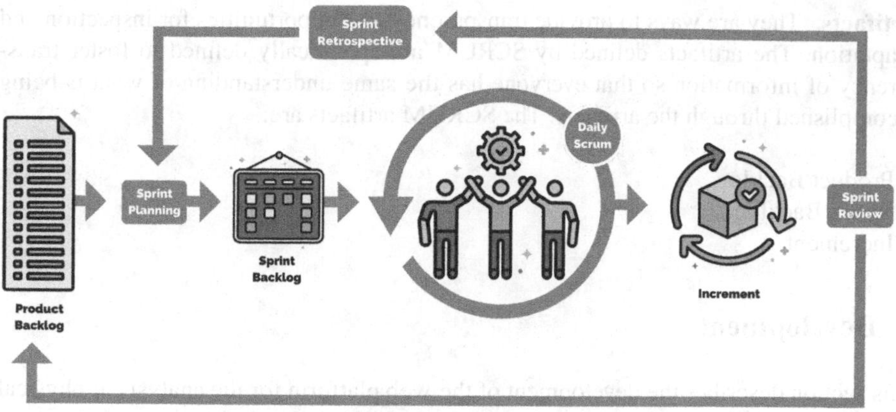

Fig. 1. The Product Owner identifies and writes the User Stories, which are added to the Product Backlog. Subsequently, the Product Owner determines the priorities of the User Stories and orders the Product Backlog. The SCRUM Team carries out the Sprint Planning which will make up the Sprint Backlog; the User Histories are broken down into tasks. The SCRUM Team conducts the Daily SCRUM, and a potentially deliverable product is obtained during the Sprint Review. The cycle ends with the Sprint Retrospective, a meeting that takes place at the end of each Sprint. Adapted from [24].

3.1 Elements of SCRUM

The elements of SCRUM [24] are described as follows:

Roles. They are each of the people or teams that are involved in the process and application of the methodology. The roles make sure that the SCRUM philosophy is carried out in the best way. The roles covered by SCRUM are:

- Product Owner
- Scrum Master
- Team

Events. They are used to minimize the need for undefined meetings and establish a cadence that allows the team to foster communication and collaboration, reducing time in extensive meetings as well as reducing restrictive and predictive processes. All events have a time box or TimeBox. Once a Sprint is started, it has a fixed duration and cannot be shortened or lengthened. The following events can end as long as the purpose of the event is achieved, but within the time box and ensuring the promotion of transparency. The SCRUM events are:

- Sprint
- Sprint Planning
- Daily SCRUM
- Sprint Review
- Sprint Retrospective

Artifacts. They are ways to provide transparency and opportunities for inspection and adaptation. The artifacts defined by SCRUM are specifically defined to foster transparency of information so that everyone has the same understanding of what is being accomplished through the artifacts. The SCRUM artifacts are:

- Product Backlog
- Sprint Backlog
- Increment

4 Development

This section describes the development of the web platform for the analysis of physical and mental health data of students, for which the following technologies were used:

- Python: programming language used for the BackEnd in conjunction with Django; it was also used for data analysis and visualization.
- Vue.js: used for modular development of the FrontEnd, for students and administrative staff.
- PostgreSQL: relational database used for information storage.
- Django: framework for the realization of the Application Programming Interface (API) that performs the necessary services for the correct functioning of the platform.

4.1 Architecture

The platform architecture contains various internal features that work together. Figure 2 shows the technologies used for the FrontEnd of the microblogging and questionnaire platform, with the usual and classic languages of web development, such as CSS, HTML, and JS, along with the Vue.js framework and the Buefy library, which together with the components for the user interfaces became responsive (suitable for any device) with a selection of colors and a pleasant and intuitive distribution for the students and the administrative staff that will use the platform. In Fig. 2, the tools in which the BackEnd is developed are also shown. These allow the FrontEnd to have the ability to interact with the database and the actions through APIs using the Django framework for the development of models, logic, and CRUDs (Create, Read, Update, and Delete). Finally, the database used in the project is shown, PostgreSQL. This database provided facilities for interaction and adaptation with the Django framework.

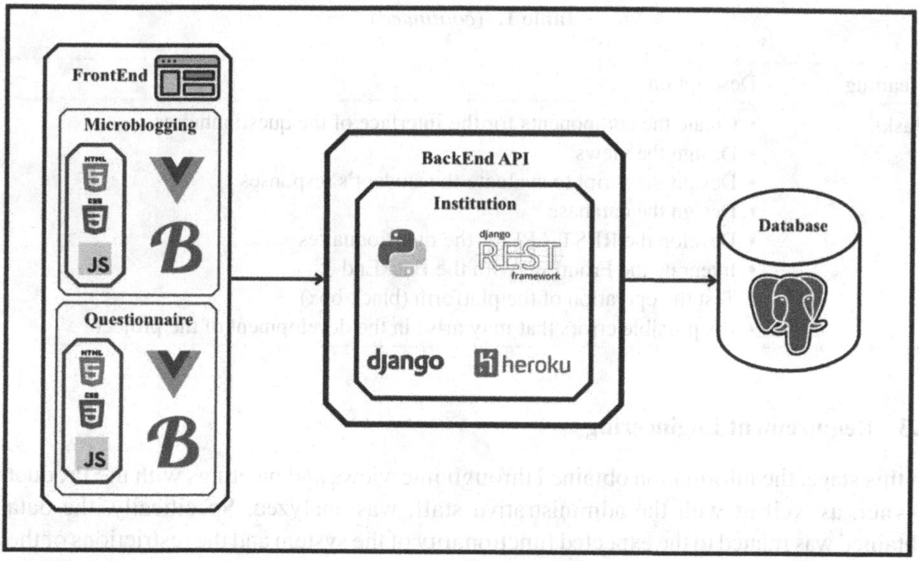

Fig. 2. Architecture that illustrates the services and technologies contained in the platform. On the left side you can see the technologies that were used for the FrontEnd of microblogging and the questionnaires. In the central part, the different Backend APIs to which the platform is linked, as well as the technologies used for development, are represented. These APIs are the ones that connect to the database (represented on the right).

4.2 Sprint Planning

In the Sprint Planning, the tasks to be developed were listed, as well as the start date, the end date, and the progress reviews of the development of the platform. Table 1 shows the Sprint Planning in detail.

Table 1. Sprint Planning that describes the tasks to be carried out, as well as the progress reviews, start date and end date.

Heading	Description
Start date	February 23, 2021
End date	June 23, 2021
Progress review	Progress reviews will be carried out monthly. The review dates will be as follows: • March 15, 2021 • April 15, 2021 • May 15, 2021 • June 22, 2021

(continued)

Table 1. (*continued*)

Heading	Description
Tasks	• Create the components for the interface of the questionnaires • Design the views • Design the script to evaluate the student's responses • Design the database • Develop the REST API for the questionnaires • Integrate the FrontEnd with the BackEnd • Test the operation of the platform (black box) • Fix possible errors that may arise in the development of the project

4.3 Requirement Engineering

In this stage, the information obtained through interviews and meetings with the Product Owner, as well as with the administrative staff, was analyzed. Specifically, the data obtained was related to the expected functionality of the system and the restrictions of the development. The result of such an analysis is presented in a list of system requirements presented below.

Functional Requirements. They are those actions that the system was expected to be able to do. Below are some of the functional requirements that were identified for the development of the platform:

- FR01: Students and administrators must be able to log in to the platform.
- FR02: Students must be able to answer the questionnaire.
- FR03: The platform must generate a dynamic acknowledgment (it must change as the student's responses fall within a predetermined range).
- FR04: The student must be able to download the acknowledgment from the platform.
- FR05: The platform must send the acknowledgment by email to the student.
- FR06: The platform must generate a history of the times the student has answered the questionnaire.
- FR07: The administrator must be able to download a CSV file with the answers of the students to the questionnaires.
- FR08: The administrator must be able to manage the questionnaires (add, modify, delete and consult).

Non-functional Requirements. They represent quality characteristics in the performance of the system to be developed. These requirements were used to detail development constraints. Below are some of the non-functional requirements that were identified:

1. The platform must be able to update the data simultaneously, without affecting the response time of the system.
2. The confidentiality of the student's responses must be guaranteed, as well as their integrity.

3. The interfaces must be friendly and minimally invasive for the user so that their responses are not affected.
4. The platform must be available 24 h a day.
5. The student will only be able to answer the questionnaire once a day.

Use Case Diagram. As part of the platform development process, it was necessary to make use case diagrams to graphically capture the functionalities that the actors could perform on the platform.

In Fig. 3 the diagram of general use cases of the platform is presented.

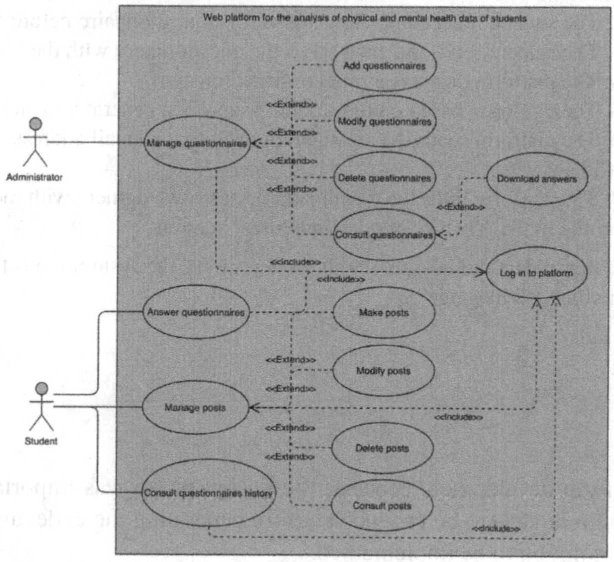

Fig. 3. Diagram of use cases that illustrates the actors of the web platform, as well as the main processes that they can carry out, particularly "Manage questionnaires", "Answer questionnaires", "Manage posts", and "Consult questionnaires history".

Use Case Descriptions. The descriptions of the use cases were made with the purpose of textually describing the ways that the actors could work with the platform. Table 2 shows an example of the use case description for the "Answer questionnaires" process by the "Administrator" actor.

Table 2. Description of the use case to answer a questionnaire by the student.

Heading	Description
Use case	Answer questionnaires
Actor	Student

(*continued*)

Table 2. (*continued*)

Heading	Description
Summary	The student selects the questionnaire to answer, records their answers and saves it
Preconditions	• The student must be logged in to the system • The student must not have answered another questionnaire during the day • There must be at least one active questionnaire to be answered
Main flow	1. The student must access the questionnaire through the main page of the platform 2. The student must completely answer the questionnaire before sending it 3. The student sends the answers to the questionnaire with the "Send" button 4. The platform displays a sent confirmation alert 5. The platform, based on the student's answers, generates an acknowledgment 6. The platform sends the acknowledgment to the email address of the student who answered 7. The platform links the downloadable acknowledgment with the student's profile in the "History of questionnaires" section
Exceptions	If the student did not answer all the questions, the system sends them a notification message
Priority	High

4.4 Design

During the platform development process, the design phase was important because it allowed the system models to be produced before generating the code, and in this way, characterize the solution to be implemented.

As part of the platform design, class diagrams and activity diagrams were mainly made. Below are some examples of the diagrams that were made.

Class Diagrams. The class diagrams were fundamental for the correct understanding of what would have to be encoded. These diagrams allowed describing the classes that made up the model of the web platform. Figure 4 shows the class diagram for the questionnaire module. As can be observed, it is made up of seven classes, each one with its respective attributes and methods (except for the community class, which is only made up of attributes). It is important to note that the diagram does not show the classes of services or utilities that were used for the development.

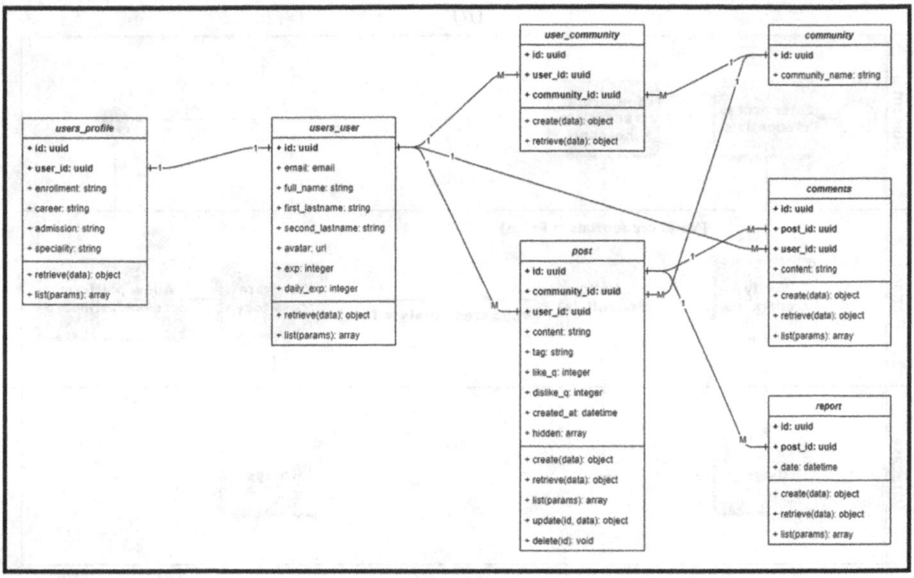

Fig. 4. Class diagram for the questionnaire module which illustrates the developed classes (along with their attributes and methods), as well as the relationships between them.

Activity Diagrams. Activity diagrams helped visualize what was happening within the use cases at a more detailed level, showing the flow of activities through the web platform. These diagrams allowed to illustrate the flow of work from the start point to the end point, detailing many of the decision paths that exist in the progress of events contained in the activity. Figure 5(a) shows the activity diagram for the "Log in to platform" process, and Fig. 5(b) for the "Make posts" process. The diagrams show the interaction of the actor (in this case the student) with the platform to carry out some of the activities that are represented in the use cases of Fig. 3. For the "Log in to platform" process, the student enters their access credentials, the system validates them, and if they are correct, access is allowed; otherwise, they are denied access to the platform. For the "Make posts" process, the student makes the post, but before it is displayed on the platform, the content is validated to see if it is appropriate. If everything is correct with validation, the post is created; otherwise, the student is informed.

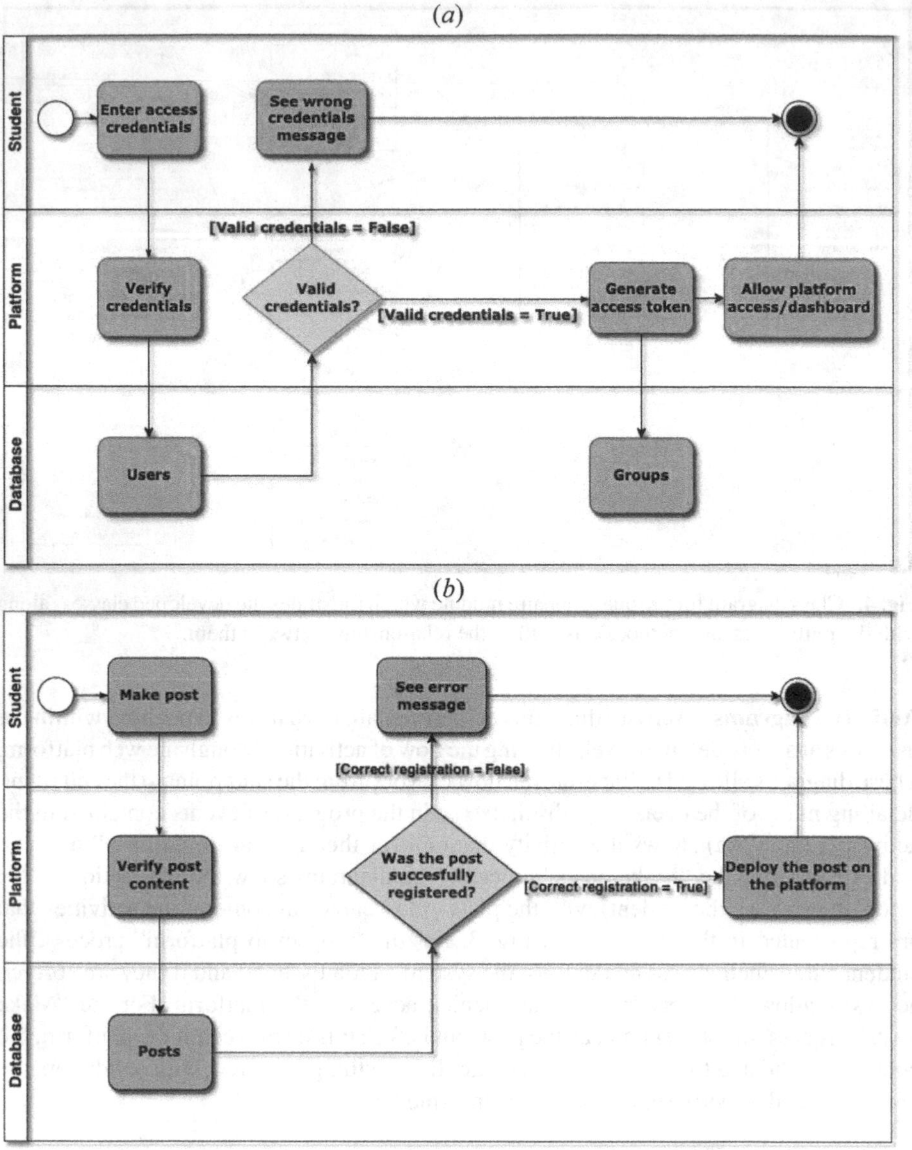

Fig. 5. Activity diagrams for the student (*a*) to log in to the platform and (*b*) to make a post on the platform.

5 Results

5.1 Coding

During this stage, the concepts developed in earlier stages were coded and converted into source code. We here discuss some of the modules developed for the platform. The "COVID-19 Screening Tool", also known as the "SARS-CoV-2 Questionnaire", aims to detect symptoms of this disease among students. It consists of 16 multiple choice questions which were determined by the medical personnel of the TecNM/ITM. As part of these user tools, the "Health and Wellness questionnaire" was also developed. This questionnaire addresses different aspects of physical and mental health in the students. The questionnaire consists of four sections with 279 total items extracted from the BDI, CESD, CRSD, PHQ-9, the Rosenberg self-esteem scale, and other commonly used

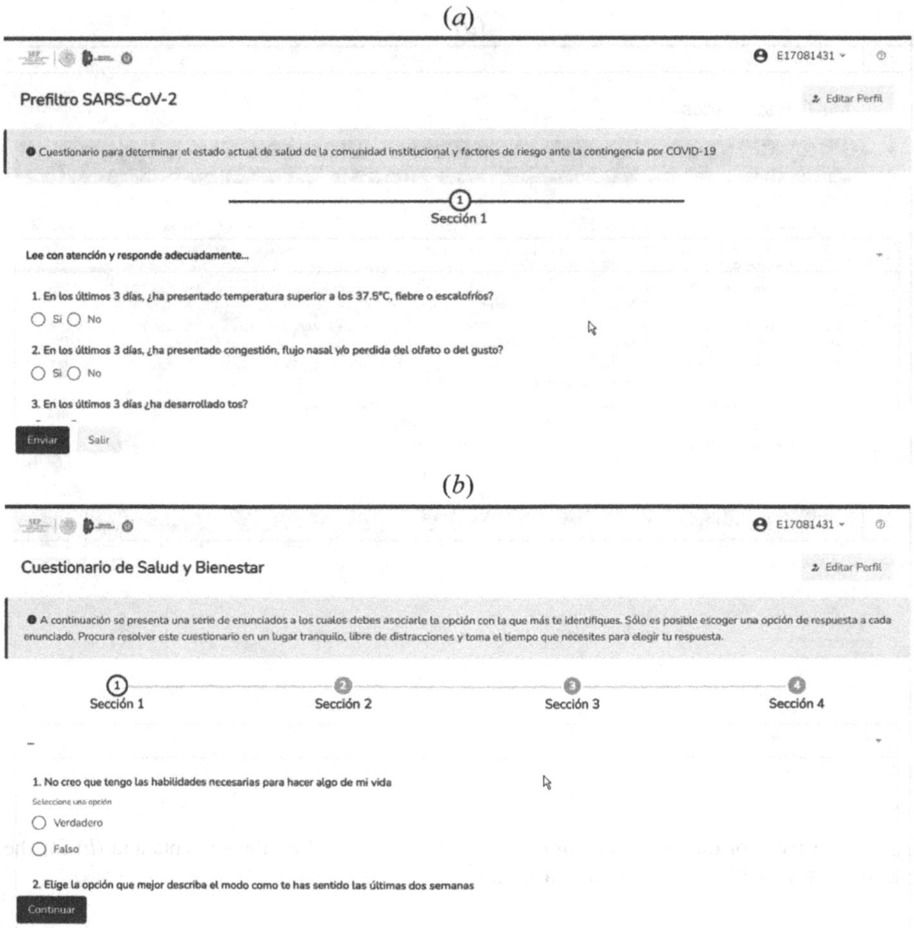

Fig. 6. User interfaces of the (*a*) COVID-19 screening tool and (*b*) the Health and Wellness Questionnaire.

psychology inventories and questionnaires. The interfaces of the COVID-19 Screening Tool and the Health and Wellness Questionnaire are shown in Fig. 6(a) and Fig. 6(b), respectively.

When a student answers a questionnaire, he must enter the corresponding panel to see which ones are active at that moment, select the one they want, answer all the questions, and send the answers. Once the answers have been saved, the system displays the questionnaire in the "My questionnaires" section, where all the questionnaires that have been answered by the student are found. Similarly, a CSV File Download Interface was also developed. This module is for the exclusive use of the system administrator. It allows to download a file in CSV format which contains the data of the students' posts, as well as the questionnaires answers. These data are used to perform sentiment analysis based on the language used by the student. The interfaces of the history of questionnaires and for downloading a CSV file are shown in Fig. 7(a) and Fig. 7(b), respectively.

(*a*)

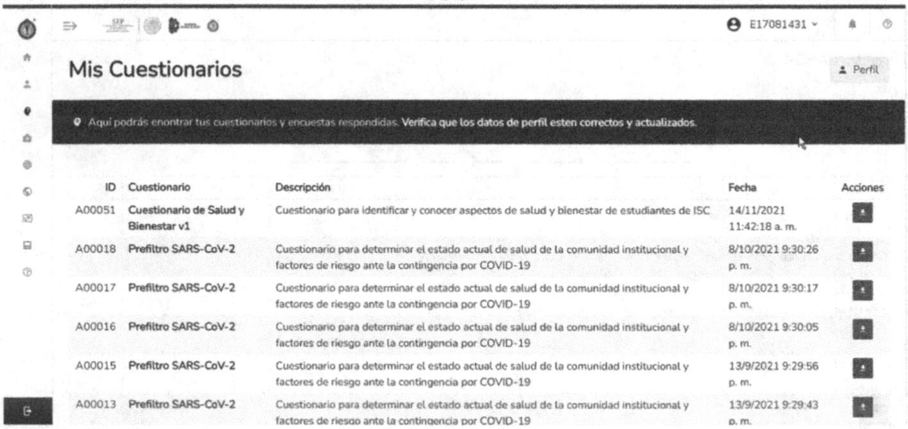

(*b*)

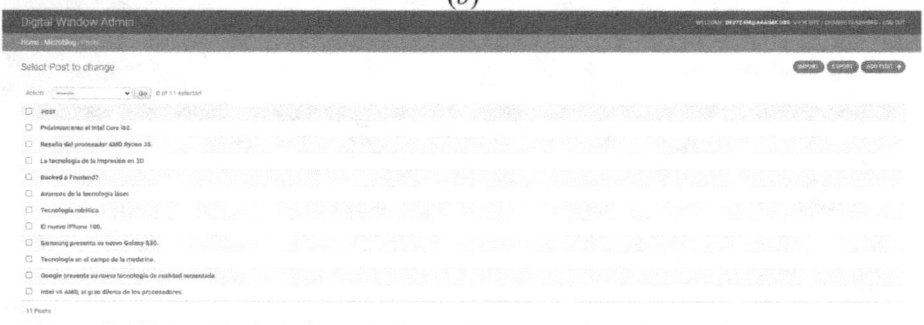

Fig. 7. Interfaces of the (*a*) history of questionnaires answered by the students and (*b*) for the download of the CSV files by the administrator

5.2 Tests

In this phase, performance tests were carried out on the system before its launch. A very common type of tests in the SCRUM methodology are black box tests. For this project they were used to verify the correct functioning of the platform. Table 3 shows an example of the black box tests that were performed.

The complete development of the web platform for the analysis of physical and mental health data of students covered four Sprints, however, in this work only the documentation related to the first Sprint is presented.

Table 3. Black box test to evaluate the correct functioning to answer the Health and Well-being questionnaire by the student.

Heading	Description
Purpose	For the student to answer the Health and Wellness Questionnaire
Prerequisites	• The student must be logged in to the system • The student must not have answered another questionnaire during the day • The questionnaire must be active to be answered
Input data	Questionnaire answers
Steps	1. The student answers the questions in the questionnaire 2. The student sends their answers to the platform 3. The platform saves the data of your answers 4. The platform analyzes the responses to generate the acknowledgment 5. The platform links the acknowledgment generated with the user's profile
Expected result	The platform displays a successful delivery notification
Obtained result	The student's responses were successfully saved, and the acknowledgment was generated
Test result	Satisfying

5.3 Final Modules

The modules were deployed to students of the TecNM/ITM from August 2021 to date. The information collected from the COVID-19 Screening Tool allowed the access of students to the institution during the fall semester. The Health and Wellness Questionnaire allowed us to monitor symptoms associated with mental illnesses and to timely assist and properly channel students to receive psychological assistance. Data obtained from the microblogging application as CSV files was used to feed a natural language processing sentiment analysis tool, whose description is out of the scope of this work.

6 Conclusions and Future Work

6.1 Conclusions

The COVID-19 pandemic has encouraged institutions to develop tools for the analysis of data on the physical and mental health of students. This article presented the development of a platform that serves this purpose, which was developed using the SCRUM agile development methodology. Using this methodology, a web platform for the implementation of questionnaires (COVID-19 Screening Tool and a Health and Wellness Questionnaire based on psychological inventories and questionnaires) and a microblogging module was developed.

The platform described in this work is used to timely detect symptoms associated with different mental health illnesses (depression, anxiety, etc.) and to generate a dataset of responses for subsequent textual analysis to further enhance the detection of the aforementioned illnesses. This analysis can be carried out through the sentiment analysis of the information from the CSV files [25].

On the other hand, the COVID-19 Screening Tool is used to evaluate possible symptoms among students and determine their severity to avoid potential and substantial infections. This tool allowed the efficient access to the TecNM/ITM during the 2022 fall semester, serving over 500 students.

The SCRUM agile development methodology was perfectly adapted to the development team, allowing updates to be released, and measuring the development speed of the team based on the score of the user stories. Likewise, the use of technologies was very convenient for development, since they streamlined the process and the reuse of components, which is an important factor in the development of this type of system.

6.2 Future Work

The development of the web platform for the analysis of physical and mental health data of students described in this article represents a great advance for future projects, such as integrating text analytics techniques, or any other text processing technique in search for patterns or signs of depression in student responses. Future work is planned in terms of upgrading the platform to track peripherals (e.g., mouse, keyboard) to recognize patterns possibly associated with mental illnesses. As well, the platform is expected to allow the recording of audio files of the speech of the students to further analyze the linguistic and the acoustic characteristics of such information.

Acknowledgements. This work was carried out with the support of project 13933.22-P "Diagnóstico preliminar y predicción oportuna de trastornos psicológicos en estudiantes del Instituto Tecnológico de Mérida mediante técnicas de inteligencia artificial" and Project 14601.22-P "Desarrollo de un sistema de refinamiento de cuestionarios psicológicos utilizando técnicas de reducción de dimensionalidad" of the Tecnológico Nacional de México/IT de Mérida.

References

1. Zhu, N., Zhang, D., Wang, W., Li, X., Yang, B., Song, J., et al.: A novel coronavirus from patients with pneumonia in China, 2019. N. Engl. J. Med. **382**, 727–733 (2020)
2. World Health Organization: Coronavirus disease (COVID-19) pandemic. Geneva: WHO (2020). www.htps://who.int/emergencies/diseases/novel-coronavirus-2019
3. Duan, L., Zhu, G.: Psychological interventions for people affected by the COVID-19 epidemic. Lancet Psychiatry **7**, 300–302 (2020). https://doi.org/10.1016/S2215-0366(20)30073-0

4. Ho, C.S., Chee, C.Y., Ho, R.C.: Mental health strategies to combat the psychological impact of COVID-19 beyond paranoia and panic. Ann. Acad. Med. Singapore **49**(1), 1–3 (2020)
5. Xiao, C.: A novel approach of consultation on 2019 novel coronavirus (COVID-19)-related psychological and mental problems: structured letter therapy. Psychiatry Investig. **17**(2), 175–6 (2020). https://doi.org/10.30773/pi.2020.0047
6. Zandifar, A., Badrfam, R.: Iranian mental health during the COVID-19 epidemic. Asian J. Psychiatr. **51**, 101990 (2020). https://doi.org/10.1016/j.ajp.2020.101990
7. Asmundson, G.J.G., Taylor, S.: How health anxiety influences responses to viral outbreaks like COVID-19: what all decision-makers, health authorities, and health care professionals need to know. J. Anxiety Disord. **71**, 102211 (2020). https://doi.org/10.1016/j.janxdis.2020.102211
8. Wang, C., et al.: Immediate psychological responses and associated factors during the initial stage of the 2019 coronavirus disease (COVID-19) epidemic among the general population in China. Int. J. Environ. Res. Public Health **17**(5) (2020). https://doi.org/10.3390/ijerph17051729
9. Qiu, J., Shen, B., Zhao, M., Wang, Z., Xie, B., Xu, Y.: A nationwide survey of psychological distress among Chinese people in the COVID-19 epidemic: implications and policy recommendations. Gen. Psychiatr. **33**(2), e100213 (2020). https://doi.org/10.1136/gpsych-2020-100213
10. Cao, W., Fang, Z., Hou, G., Han, M., Xu, X., Dong, J., et al.: The psychological impact of the COVID-19 epidemic on college students in China. Psychiat. Res. **287**, 112934 (2020). https://doi.org/10.1016/j.psychres.2020.112934.doi:10.1016/j.psychres.2020.112934
11. Liu, N., Zhang, F., Wei, C., Jia, Y., Shang, Z., Sun, L., et al.: Prevalence and predictors of PTSS during COVID-19 outbreak in China hardest-hit areas: gender differences matter. Psychiat. Res. **287**, 112921 (2020). https://doi.org/10.1016/j.psychres.2020.112921
12. Pita Garrido, J.: Plataforma para el apoyo al aprendizaje de manera colaborativa en ambientes distribuidos: aula social – UDLAP. Tesis profesional, Universidad de las Américas Puebla (2012). http://catarina.udlap.mx/u_dl_a/tales/documentos/lst/pita_g_jm/. Accessed 24 June 2021
13. Sushko, I., et al.: Online chemical modeling environment (OCHEM): web platform for data storage, model development and publishing of chemical information. J. Comput. Aided. Mol. Des. **25**(6), 533–554 (2011). https://doi.org/10.1007/s10822-011-9440-2
14. Newman, C., Agioutantis, Z., Schaefer, N.: Development of a web-platform for mining applications. Int. J. Min. Sci. Technol. **28**(1), 95–99 (2018). https://doi.org/10.1016/j.ijmst.2017.11.016
15. Adami, M., Mello, M.P., Aguiar, D.A., Rudorff, B.F.T., De Souza, A.F.: A web platform development to perform thematic accuracy assessment of sugarcane mapping in South-Central Brazil. Remote Sens. **4**(10), 3201–3214 (2012). https://doi.org/10.3390/rs4103201
16. Cummins, N., Scherer, S., Krajewski, J., Schnieder, S., Epps, J., Quatieri, T.F.: A review of depression and suicide risk assessment using speech analysis. Speech Commun. **71**, 10–49 (2015). https://doi.org/10.1016/j.specom.2015.03.004
17. Center for Epidemiological Studies-Depression: American Psychological Association (2011). https://www.apa.org/pi/about/publications/caregivers/practice-settings/assessment/tools/depression-scale. Accessed 23 June 2021
18. Carroll, B.J., Feinberg, M., Smouse, P.E., Rawson, S.G., Greden, J.F.: The Carroll rating scale for depression. I. Development, reliability and validation. Br. J. Psychiatry **138**(3), 194–200 (1981). https://doi.org/10.1192/bjp.138.3.194
19. Baader, T., et al.: Validación y utilidad de la encuesta PHQ-9 (Patient Health Questionnaire) en el diagnóstico de depresión en pacientes usuarios de atención primaria en Chile. Rev. Chil. Neuropsiquiatr. **9**(1), 10–22 (2012). http://www.scielo.cl/scielo.php?script=sci_arttext&pid=S0717-92272012000100002&lng=en&nrm=iso&tlng=en. Accessed 23 June 2021

20. Ehrlich, K., Shami, N.S.: Microblogging inside and outside the workplace. In: ICWSM 2010 - Proceedings 4th International AAAI Conference on Weblogs and Social Media, pp. 42–49 (2010)
21. Java, A., Song, X., Finin, T., Tseng, B.: Why we Twitter: an analysis of a microblogging community. In: Zhang, H., et al. (eds.) SNAKDD/WebKDD -2007. LNCS (LNAI), vol. 5439, pp. 118–138. Springer, Heidelberg (2009). https://doi.org/10.1007/978-3-642-00528-2_7
22. Vieweg, S., Hughes, A.L., Starbird, K., Palen, L.: Microblogging during two natural hazards events: what Twitter may contribute to situational awareness. In: Proceedings of the Conference on Human Factors in Computing Systems, vol. 2, pp. 1079–1088 (2010). https://doi.org/10.1145/1753326.1753486
23. Trigas Gallego, M., Domingo Troncho, A.C.: Gestión de Proyectos Informáticos. Metodología Scrum., Openaccess.Uoc.Edu, p. 56 (2012). http://www.quimbiotec.gob.ve/sistem/auditoria/pdf/ciudadano/mtrigasTFC0612memoria.pdf. http://openaccess.uoc.edu/webapps/o2/bitstream/10609/17885/1/mtrigasTFC0612memoria.pdf
24. The Scrum Framework Poster: Scrum.org (2021). https://www.scrum.org/resources/scrum-framework-poster
25. Kolasani, S.V., Assaf, R.: Predicting stock movement using sentiment analysis of Twitter feed with neural networks. J. Data Anal. Inf. Process. **8**(4), 309–319 (2020)

Identification of SARS-CoV-2 Pneumonia in Chest X-ray Images Using Convolutional Neural Networks

Paola I. Delena-García[1], José D. Torres-Rodríguez[1], Blanca Tovar-Corona[2](✉), Álvaro Anzueto-Ríos[1], Nadia L. Fragoso-Olvera[3], Alberto Flores-Patricio[3], and Victor M. Camarillo-Nava[4]

[1] Bionics Engineering Academy, Instituto Politécnico Nacional, Unidad Profesional Interdisciplinaria en Ingeniería y Tecnologías Avanzadas (UPIITA), Mexico City, Mexico
aanzuetor@ipn.mx

[2] SEPI UPIITA, Instituto Politécnico Nacional, Mexico City, Mexico
bltovar@ipn.mx

[3] Instituto Mexicano del Seguro Social (IMSS), Hospital General de Zona No. 24 "Insurgentes", Mexico City, Mexico

[4] IMSS, Órgano de Operación Administrativa Desconcentrada en el DF Norte, Mexico City, Mexico

Abstract. In 2019, COVID-19 disease emerged in Wuhan, China, leading to a pandemic that saturated health systems, raising the need to develop effective diagnostic methods. This work presents an approach based on artificial intelligence applied to X-ray images obtained from Mexican patients, provided by Hospital General de Zona No. 24. A dataset of 612 images with 2 classes: COVID and HEALTHY, were labelled by a radiologist and also verified with positive RT-PCR test. The first class contains X-ray images of patients with pneumonia due to SARS-CoV-2 and the second contains patients without diseases affecting the lung parenchyma. The proposed work aims to classify COVID-19 pneumonia using convolutional neural networks to provide the physician with a suggestive diagnosis. Images were automatically trimmed and then transfer learning was applied to VGG-16 and ResNet-50 models, which were trained and tested using the generated dataset, both achieving an accuracy, recall, specificity and F1-score of over 98%.

Keywords: COVID-19 · Pneumonia · Convolutional neural networks · Chest X-ray · Artificial Intelligence

1 Introduction

In December 2019, an unusual outbreak of viral pneumonia took place in Wuhan, China. The outbreak was caused by a new strain of coronavirus that was

M. F. Mata-Rivera et al. (Eds.): WITCOM 2022, CCIS 1659, pp. 157–172, 2022.
https://doi.org/10.1007/978-3-031-18082-8_10

named as Severe Acute Respiratory Syndrome Coronavirus 2 (SARS-CoV-2) by the International Committee on Taxonomy of Viruses, the disease was named COVID-19 by the World Health Organization (WHO) [1]. The disease spread rapidly to other countries because of its high transmissibility; resulting in a global health emergency and millions of deaths, mainly due to complications caused by infection [2].

Symptoms caused by the infection include respiratory distress, fever, cough, fatigue, pneumonia and muscle pain. However, due to multiple variants of the virus, different symptoms and severity have been reported. For example, the main symptoms of the Omicron variant include runny nose, headache, fatigue, sneezing and sore throat [3]. The severity of the symptoms may also depend on the patient's health status, age or comorbidities [2].

In order to treat the disease and prevent the spread of the virus, an early diagnosis is essential, therefore different diagnostic methods have emerged. The most widely known and used are diagnostic tests based on the detection of viral RNA. Mainly two types of tests are used, the reverse transcription-polymerase chain reaction (RT-PCR) test and the antigen test, both involve the analysis of a sample collected through oropharyngeal or nasopharyngeal swabs [4].

It is also possible to provide a diagnosis based on the interpretation of chest imaging studies, where the involvement in the lungs could be observed, as many histopathological changes resulting from infection mainly occur in this area [2,4].

Imaging studies used for detection of the disease include radiography (X-Ray imaging), computed tomography (CT) and ultrasound, being radiography the most common technique. These methods have the advantage of providing information about disease progression and lung parenchymal damage, however they require analysis by an expert radiologist [4]. In many cases, different methods are used together to provide an accurate diagnosis.

Radiographies are performed by directing a beam of X-rays (0.01 to 10 nm) over the anatomical area of interest, resulting in a grey-scale image, where the density of a tissue is proportional to the absorption of the beam and thus to the brightness of that tissue in the image [5]. Variations in the shades of grey may indicate lung parenchymal abnormalities or lesions associated with the presence of a disease.

As the respiratory system is the first to be affected by COVID-19, patterns related to pneumonia caused by the presence of the disease have been identified. They are visible through X-ray, making them a feasible method for investigating suspected cases of COVID-19, although X-rays diagnostic yield is limited in early stages of the disease [6,7]. The most frequent radiological findings are: consolidation (59%), ground glass opacity (41%), distributed bilaterally (63%), basally (63%) and peripherally (51%) [8]. Infrequent radiological findings include pleural effusion (6%) and pneumothorax (1%) [9].

As mentioned previously, a qualified healthcare professional is required to analyse X-ray to provide an accurate interpretation. However, for radiographies to be useful for diagnosis, they require an appropriate radiological technique, based on the parameters described in the Table 1.

Table 1. Parameters of an appropriate radiological technique.

Patient positioning	Rotation		Should be no or minimal rotation. The distances between the medial ends of the clavicles and the spinous apophysis of the nearest vertebra should be equidistant
	Lung volume		Patient in maximum inspiration, allowing visualization of 8 to 10 posterior ribs
	X-ray emitter positioning	AP	Patient in a standing or supine position at a distance of 1 m from the X-ray source
		PA	Patient in a standing position at a distance of 1.8 m from the X-ray source
X-ray technique	Penetration		The lower thoracic vertebrae should be clearly visible behind the cardiac silhouette and a well-defined range of grey, black and white should be clearly visible

An alternative that could aid in the diagnosis of COVID-19 is the use of artificial intelligence, and numerous proposals have emerged for the analysis and interpretation of imaging studies, based on convolutional neural networks (CNN), that perform the task of classifying chest X-ray (CXR) or CT scans for the detection of COVID-19 [10,11]. This classification is usually between COVID-19 and Non-COVID, but 3 or more classes can be considered, separating COVID-19 from other respiratory and non respiratory pathologies. It is also possible to include classes of diseases such as bacterial and viral pneumonia or tuberculosis [4].

In literature the use of pre-entrained convolutional networks is found, such as CheXNet, Inceptionv3, VGG-19, VGG-16, ResNet-50, ResNet-18, to mention a few [14]. In addition, some authors have proposed new architectures for the purpose of COVID-19 classification [15].

The following paper proposes using a transfer learning technique applied on two CNN models (VGG-16 and ResNet-50) trained and tested for a binary classification task (COVID-19 vs. Healthy) on CXR images using a dataset of Mexican patients generated by the authors. The following section outlines some of the works related to the proposal.

The following paper proposes using a transfer learning technique applied on two CNN models (VGG-16 and ResNet-50) trained and tested for a binary classification task (COVID-19 vs. Healthy) on CXR images using a dataset of Mexican patients generated by the authors, obtaining an accuracy of 98% detecting COVID-19 cases. The following section outlines some of the works related to the proposal.

2 Related Works

Due to the need of fast diagnosis methods for COVID-19 during the pandemic, medical imaging, such as chest x-rays (CXR), have been used to develop deep learning techniques to identify SARS-CoV-2 pneumonia.

Convolutional Neural Networks (CNN) have been reported for CXR classification, especially, to detect probable COVID-19 cases. To achive this task, several proposals have emerged, one of these is to use pre-trained CNN by applying transfer learning. For instance, Chowdhury et al. [14] compared eight different pre-trained CNN models like: MobileNetv2, SqueezeNet, ResNet18, ResNet101, DenseNet201, CheXNet, Inceptionv3 and VGG19. Getting more than 99% acuracy for a binary classification (Healthy vs. COVID-19), and greater than 95% for a multiclass classification (COVID-19 vs. Healthy vs. Viral pneumonia) with all the networks tested. They stand out CheXNet network with a global acurracy of 96.61% for multiclass case. Another work related was done by Zebin et al. [16] who used VGG-16, ResNet-50 and EfficientNetB0 networks obtaining an accuracy of 90%, 94.3% and 96.8% respectively. The authors preserved the synaptic weights of ImageNet training and modified each network's top layer to adapt them for a multiclass classification (COVID-19 vs. Healthy vs. Viral pneumonia). By doing this procedure, the previous learning of the network is used to solve new tasks.

Futhermore, pre-trained networks and the combination of these looking for improving performance have also been reported. Tiwari et al. [17] report a CNN model they called Visual Geometry group capsule network (VGG-CapsNet), which concatenate VGG-16 and CapsNet networks to get more detailed information about the CXR. The proposed model uses VGG-16 to compute the initial feature maps and then enter them into the CapsNet network, which is responsible for the classification. Authors report 97% and 92% accuracy for a binary (COVID-19 vs. non-COVID-19) and multi-class (COVID-19 vs. normal vs. non-COVID-19) classification, respectively. Another proposal found in the literature is the one made by Gianchandani et al. [18]. They assemble VGG-16 and DenseNet201 networks in parallel by connecting them with a concatenator layer and then using 2 fully connected layers of 64 units, followed by a dense layer with softmax to perform classification. This proposal obtained an 99.21% accuracy for a multi-class classification (COVID vs. normal vs. pneumonia).

Finally, Wang et al. [19] introduced a new open-source network and dataset called COVID-Net and COVIDx, respectively. COVID-Net network was designed via a human-machine collaborative design strategy. It makes extensive use of light residual projection-expansion-projection-extension (PEPX) pattern module, designed by the authors. They report a recall of 93.33% for a multi-class classification (Normal vs COVID vs Non-COVID).

Just as the works mentioned above, the Classification task of CXR using CNN for COVID-19 pneumonia detection has been explored, to the knowledge of the authors, this is the first proposal trained and tested with data from Mexican patients. The following section describes in detail the methodology used.

3 Materials and Methods

3.1 Dataset

A dataset of CXR images was generated to develop this work. Data were provided by Hospital General de Zona (HGZ) No. 24 "Insurgentes" belonging to the Instituto Mexicano del Seguro Social (IMSS), with the approval of the local IMSS ethics committee, registration number **R-2021–3404-066**.

The dataset generated contains 612 CXR images in Antero-posterior (AP) and Postero-anterior (PA) projections. Where 300 samples belongs to COVID-19 patients and the rest belongs to patients without diseases affecting the lung parenchyma. The labelling of the obtained images was carried out under the supervision of a radiologist from HGZ No.24. See Fig. 1, which shows examples of images obtained.

Images of COVID-19 patients were labelled as "COVID"; on the other side, patients without a probable lung disease got the "Healthy" label. In order to consider COVID-19 positive patient, the patient's medical record, the radiologist's interpretation and the result of the RT-PCR test were considered.

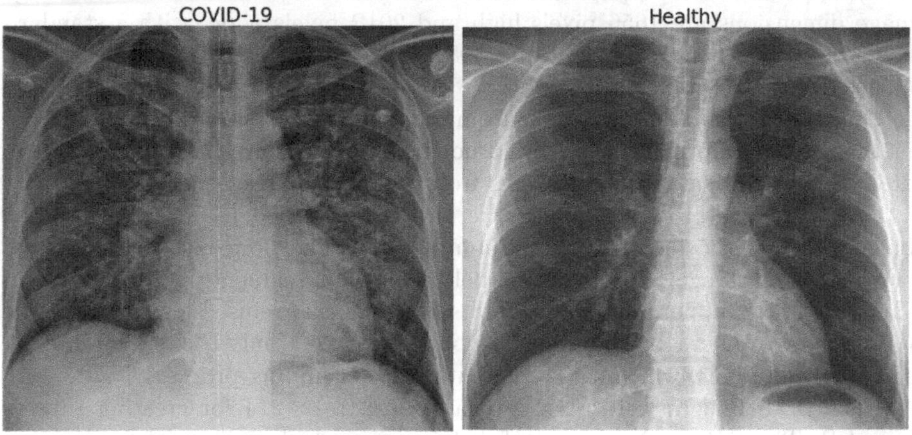

Fig. 1. Examples of images from generated dataset. Left: COVID-19 CXR, Right: Healthy CXR.

Data were obtained from two different periods, COVID class are conformed by CXR images taken during the period from June 1st to June 16th 2020 and, images for Healthy class were selected from July 1st to July 26th 2018. All images were selected using the criteria of the Table 2.

Due to the low sensibility of CXR during the initial phases of COVID-19 infection, data from 2020 and 2019 have not considered to conform “Healthy” class to eliminate the likelihood of considering patients with early-stage COVID-19 as “Healthy” cases [22]. Since the data obtained belong to different periods, the images come from 3 different x-ray machines. Therefore, a processing stage is proposed in order to the CNNs learn only from the area of interest (lung parenchyma and rib cage area) regardless of the equipment with which the X-ray was taken.

Table 2. Inclusion, exclusion and elimination criteria.

Inclusion criteria	Exclusion criteria	Elimination criteria
Antero-posterior (AP) or postero-anterior (PA) CXR that comply the radiological technique described in the Table. 1	Digital X-ray that do not correspond to the thorax, e.g. abdominal X-ray	Left lateral or Right lateral CXR projections

Data Processing. Images were obtained in png format with different resolutions, depending on the equipment with which the X-ray was taken. The average image dimensions are 1656 pixels high and 2012 pixels wide, with a standard deviation of 400 pixels in height and 398 pixels width. See Fig. 2, which shows images size distribution.

Once data was acquired, an automatic trimming was applied on CXRs, removing extra information which did not belong to the area of interest. Therefore, CNN can learn only the features from the target area.

The trimming process is automatic and is performed using a mask of the lungs to define the limits of the trimming area. The lung mask is generated for each X-ray image by a U-Net model trained for segmenting the lung area. Then, the lower, upper, and lateral limits of the mask are used for trimming the original image. As a result, an image is obtained where only the area of interest is visible. See Fig. 3, which shows the automatic trimming process.

Finally, all images were resized to a size of 224×224 for creating subsets A and B. The Subset **A** consists of 484 images, which were used for training and validation, being divided into 80% for training and 20 % for validation, and Subset **B** contains 128 images for testing, these images were not used during the training of the CNNs. In Table 3 is shown subsets distribution.

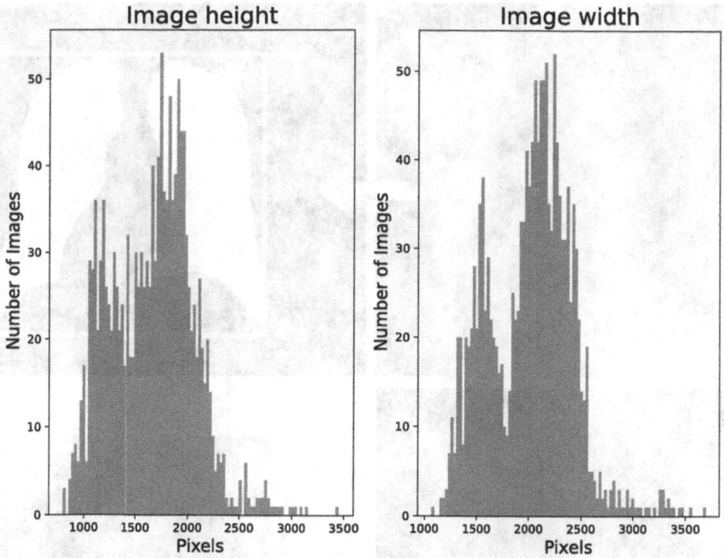

Fig. 2. Width and height distribution.

Table 3. Percentages.

Subset	% Total	Images	Usage	%	Images
A	80.66%	484	Training	80%	387
			Validation	20%	97
B	19.33%	128	Testing		

3.2 Convolutional Neural Network

VGG and ResNet networks are generally used in the literature for COVID-19 classification task of CXR, for the development of the present work VGG-16 and ResNet-50 networks were selected [18].

Visual Geometry Group (VGG-16). CNN known like **VGG-16** was designed by Simonyan and Zisserman [20]. This network consists of 13 convolutions layers using 3×3 kernels followed by max-polling layers with 2×2 kernels and 3 fully connected layers to make the classification. Simonyan et.al, achieved 92.7% of accuracy on ImageNet large scale visual recognition challenge (ILSVRC), placing in the top-5 of the challenge. In literature several authors have reported a higher accuracy than 95% for COVID-19 classification using VGG-16 network [23]. See Fig. 4, in which VGG-16 architecture is shown.

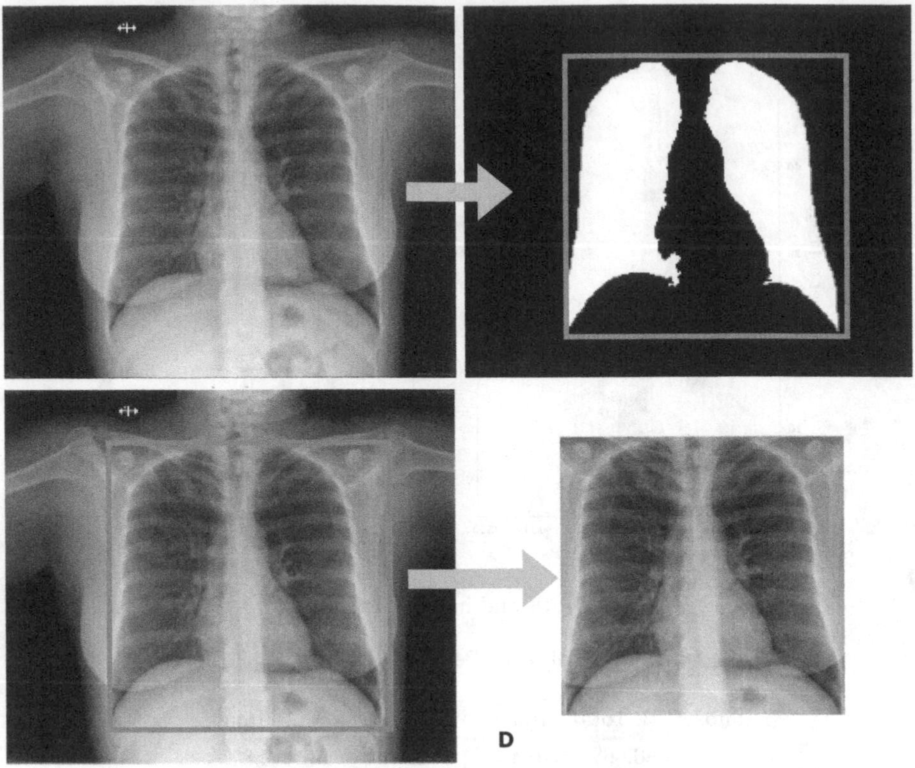

Fig. 3. Automatic trimming process.

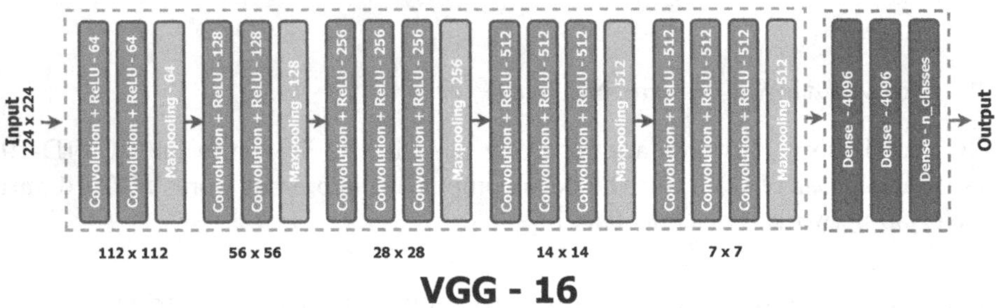

Fig. 4. VGG-16 Block diagram, based on [21].

Residual Networks (ResNet-50). Residual networks were introduced by He and Zhang to solve the degradation problem and the gradient explosion that occurs when training a deep neural network model.They carried out tests with 18, 34, 50, 101 and 152 layers evaluating with ImageNet dataset, achieving an error of 3.57%. This result won first place in the classification task of the ILSVRC of 2015 [24].

Some authors reported an accuracy better than 97% for COVID-19 detection using the ResNet-50 network [23]. See Fig. 5, in which ResNet-50 arquitecture is shown.

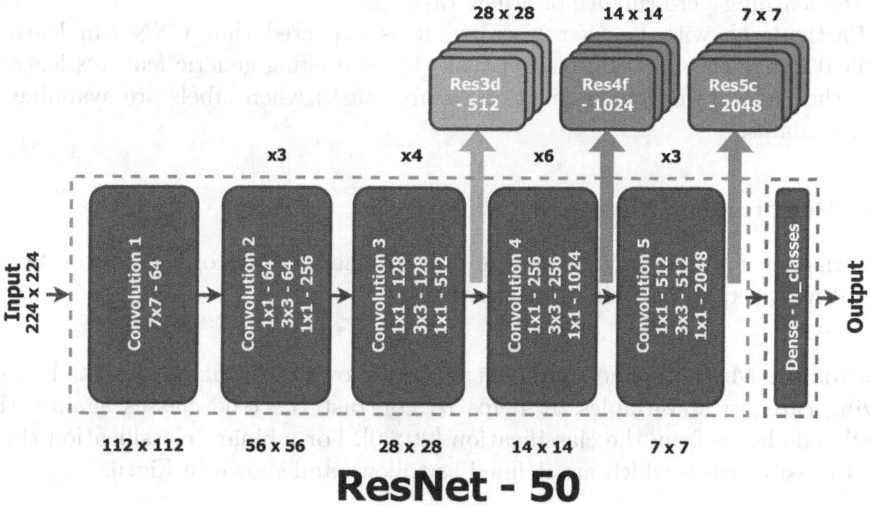

Fig. 5. ResNet-50 block diagram, based on [25]

Following the approach in recent works for COVID-19 detection. It is proposed to use the VGG-16 and ResNet-50 architectures, both networks were implemented using the Keras Python library. Transfer learning technique was used, modifying the top layers of each network to fit a binary classification and preserving the synaptic weights of the training with the ImageNet dataset. Google Colaboratory platform was used to develop this work since it allows training models using a Graphics Processing Unit (GPU). Training parameters are shown in Table 4.

Table 4. Hyperparameters.

	Neural network model	
	VGG-16	ResNet-50
Batch size	4	4
Epochs	50	80
Input image size	224 × 224	224 × 224
Optimizer	Adam	Adam
Learning rate	0.001	0.001
Pre-training dataset	ImageNet	ImageNet

3.3 Transfer Learning

Formally defined by Pan and Yang, transfer learning derives from cognitive research that assumes that knowledge is transferred across related tasks, improving the learning performance of a new task. [26].

Particularly, with transfer learning, it is expected that CNN can learn a medical image classification (target task) by leveraging generic features learned from the natural image classification (source task) when labels are available in both domains.

3.4 Performance Metrics

Performance metrics provide information on the learning of the convolutional neural network, representing it numerically.

Confusion Matrix. The confusion matrix shows the ranking obtained when having categorical variables. It helps to contrast the true classes against the predicted classes from the classification [29,30]. For a binary classification there are 4 possible cases which are defined as follows and shown in Fig. 6.

- **True Positive:** The true value is positive and the prediction was positive. Includes sick cases correctly classified as sick cases.
- **True Negative:** The true value is negative and the prediction was negative. Includes healthy cases correctly classified as healthy cases.
- **False Negative:** The true value is positive, and the prediction was negative. Includes "COVID" cases classified as "Healthy" cases.
- **False Positive:** The true value is negative, and the prediction was positive. Includes "Healthy" cases classified as "COVID" cases.

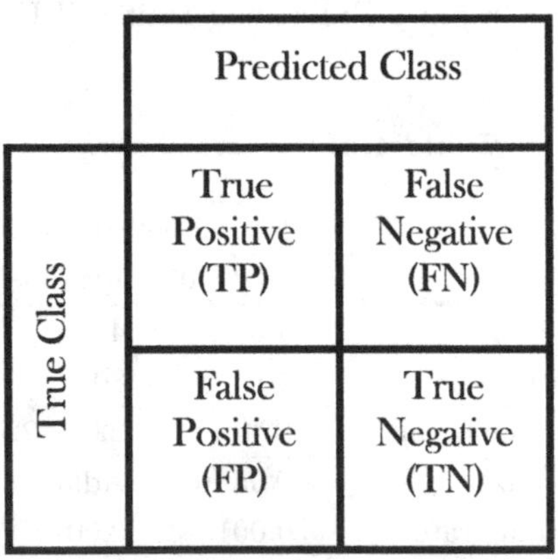

Predicted Class
True Class
True Positive (TP)
False Negative (FN)
False Positive (FP)
True Negative (TN)

Fig. 6. Confusion matrix

In the literature, accuracy is frequently used to show the efficiency of the network in classifying, but other metrics may be useful. In this case, recall is a useful metric to know the results of a diagnostic test. It indicates the percentage of sick patients that were correctly classified and highlights the importance of obtaining true positives, which is relevant when providing information for disease diagnosis. For this work, CNNs will be evaluated under the metrics: Accuracy, Precision, Sensitivity, Specificity and F1 Score. They are defined in Eqs. (1), (2), (3), (4) and (5), respectively [27,28,30].

$$Accuracy = \frac{TP + TN}{TP + FP + TN + FN} * 100 \tag{1}$$

$$Precision = \frac{TP}{TP + FP} * 100 \tag{2}$$

$$Recall = \frac{TP}{TP + FN} * 100 \tag{3}$$

$$Specificity = \frac{TN}{TN + FP} * 100 \tag{4}$$

$$F1Score = 2 * \frac{Precision * Recall}{Precision + Recall} \tag{5}$$

4 Results

To evaluate the proposed models, a classification test was performed using the images from subset B shown in Table 3, these images had not been used in CNNs training. Both proposed models achieve an accuracy of over 98% during the training and validation stages, reaching this value after epoch 30. Even though both models showed similar performance, ResNet-50 required 30 additional epochs. See Fig. 7, with shows the accuracy performance of the models during training.

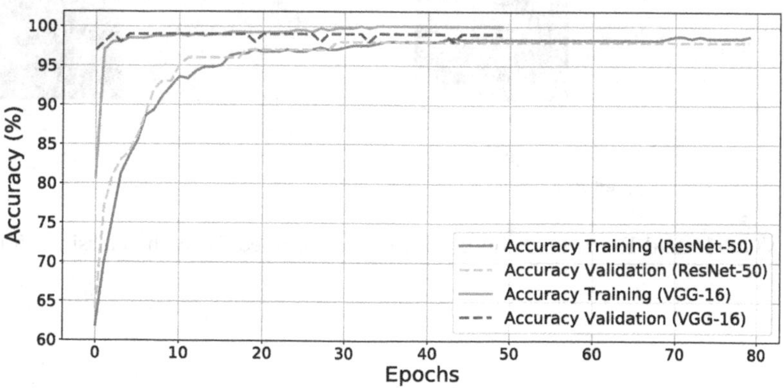

Fig. 7. Comparison of accuracy performance during training.

On the other hand, the loss value decreases consistently for both models. Training and validation loss values approach zero by tracing similar decreasing curves, ending the training with a loss value lower than 0.07, this behaviour indicates the appropriate learning of the model. Loss validation curve denotes the absence of overfitting, because it does not increase while the loss curve for training decrease and its behaviour is similar to loss training curve. See Fig. 8, with shows the loss performance of the models during training.

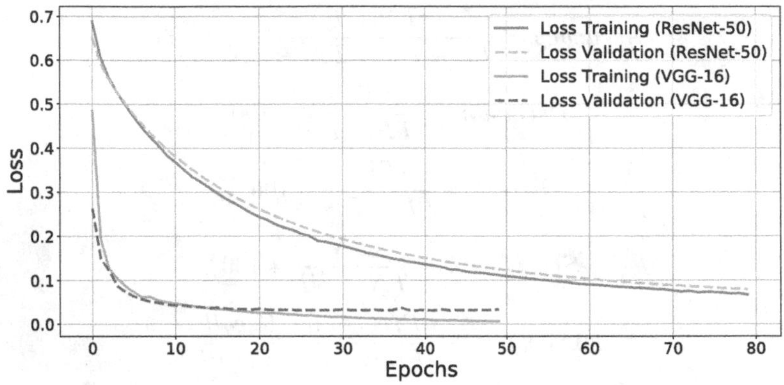

Fig. 8. Comparison of loss performance during training.

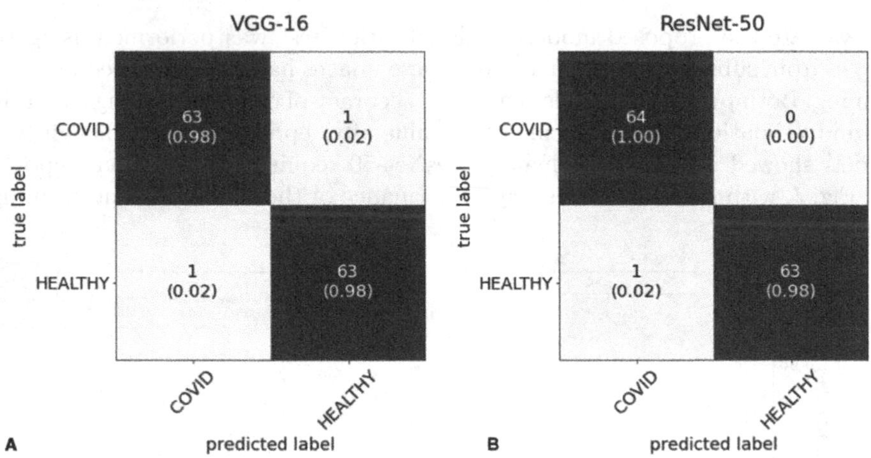

Fig. 9. VGG-16 and ResNet-50 confusion matrix obtained from the classification test.

The results of the classifications test are presented as a confusion matrix, where it can be visualised that both models correctly classified 98% of the images, see Fig. 9, which shows the confusion matrix for both models. VGG-16 mislabelling 2 images, one from each class, this generates the same metrics for both classes as it can be observed in Table 5. On the other hand, ResNet-50 correctly performed the classification of all images of **COVID** class, however, erroneous labelling of 1 image form **Healthy** class was obtained, achieving a sensitivity of 98% for that class. Metrics obtained can be visualised in Table 6.

Table 5. VGG-16 Performance metrics obtained from the confusion matrix (See Fig. 9A)

Class	Precision	Recall	Specificity	F1-Score
COVID	98.43%	98.43%	98.43%	98.43%
Healthy	98.43%	98.43%	98.43%	98.43%
Mean	98.43%	98.43%	98.43%	98.43%

Table 6. ResNet-50 Performance metrics obtained from the confusion matrix (See the Fig 9B)

Class	Precision	Recall	Specificity	F1-Score
COVID	98.46%	100%	98.43%	99.22%
Healthy	100%	98.43%	100%	99.21%
Mean	99.21%	99.21%	99.21%	99.21%

The two architectures were both over 98% accuracy for a binary classification using subset B. Considering the clinical approach, it is intended to prioritise recall to the **COVID** class, preventing sick patients from being classified as healthy; the ResNet-50 architecture demonstrated better performance under this criteria, obtaining a 1.57% higher accuracy than the VGG-16 architecture. See Fig. 10, which shows comparative graphs of each class.

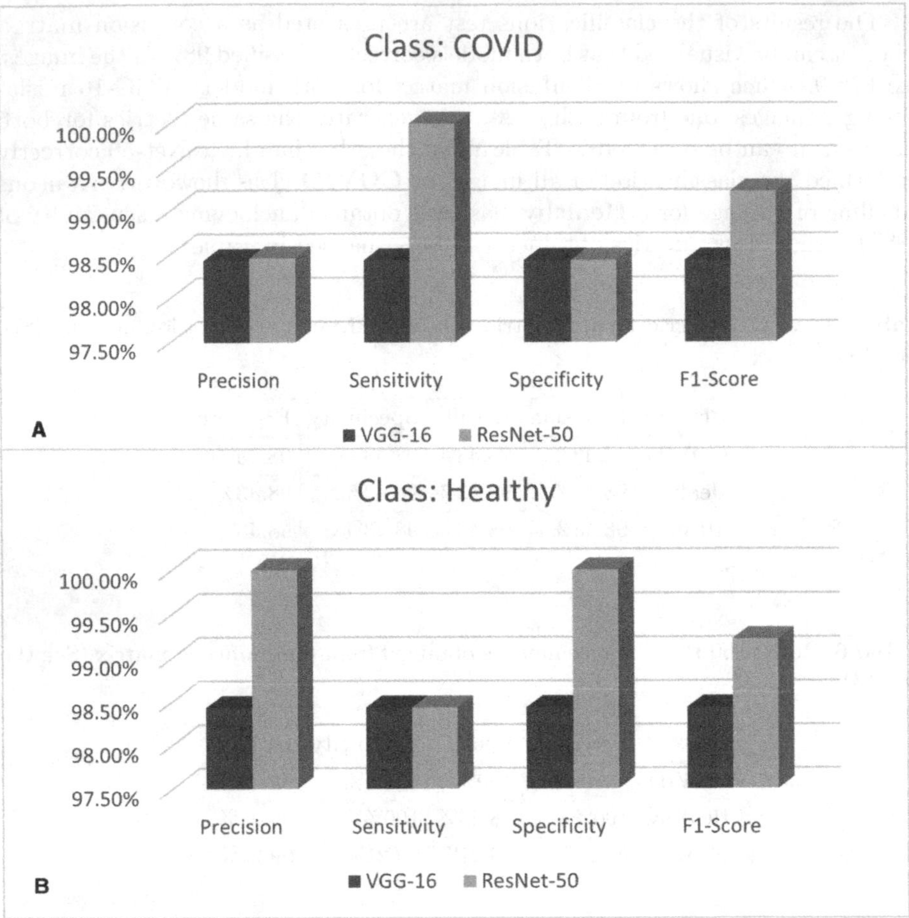

Fig. 10. Comparative graph of networks metrics, obtained from Tables 1 and 2.

5 Conclusions

In this work, two convolutional neural architectures have been presented in order to detect the presence of COVID-19 in chest X-ray images. The VGG-16 and ResNet-50 architectures were implemented using transfer learning techniques to perform this task, achieving an accuracy of 98.43% and 99.21% respectively, using the database generated for this study.

Based on the analysis of the behaviour of the training graphs, we could conclude that the networks perform the abstraction process of the images, allowing them to learn the characteristic patterns. The ResNet-50 model showed a performance of 0.78% higher than VGG-16, so the behaviour of this architecture under different scenarios will be explored in future works.

Due to the fact that we had a limited database with a reduce number of samples (<300), transfer learning was applied and contributed to the training of the models, allowing the learning from the model to be used for a different classification task by using the weights corresponding to the convolutional layers, which can already recognise patterns in images. This technique may help in the development of new diagnostic methods based on imaging studies, where lack of data to generate new models is a limitation.

Finally, two CNN models trained on a dataset of Mexican patients, which **COVID** label it is supported by the diagnosis of a radiologist and the positive RT-PCR test for SARS-CoV-2, are presented in this paper. As well as an automatic pre-processing stage to extract the area of interest from the radiographs in order to improve the performance of the models.

References

1. Gorbalenya, A.E., et al.: Severe acute respiratory syndrome-related coronavirus: the species and its viruses - a statement of the coronavirus study group. BioRxiv (2020). https://doi.org/10.1101/2020.02.07.937862
2. Hu, B., Guo, H., Zhou, P., Shi, Z.L.: Characteristics of SARS-CoV-2 and COVID-19. Nat. Rev. Microbiol. **19**, 141–154 (2021). https://doi.org/10.1038/s41579-020-00459-7
3. Torjesen, I.: Covid-19: many hospitals "are not declaring critical incidents" despite severe pressures. BMJ **376**, o60 (2022). https://doi.org/10.1136/bmj.o60
4. Filchakova, O., Dossym, D., Ilyas, A., Kuanysheva, T., Abdizhamil, A., Bukasov, R.: Review of COVID-19 testing and diagnostic methods. Talanta **244**, 123409 (2022). https://doi.org/10.1016/j.talanta.2022.123409
5. Steven D. Waldman MD JD, R.S.D.C.: Imaging of Pain Chapter 1 Radiography, pp. 3–5 (2011). https://doi.org/10.1016/B978-1-4377-0906-3.00001-8
6. Verma, H.K.: Radiological and clinical spectrum of COVID-19: a major concern for public health. World J. Radiol. **13**, 53–63 (2021). https://doi.org/10.4329/wjr.v13.i3.53
7. Sánchez-oro, R., Torres, J., Martínez-Sanz, G.: Radiological findings for diagnosis of SARS-CoV-2 pneumonia (COVID-19). Med. Clin. (Barc) **155**, 36–40 (2020). https://doi.org/10.1016/j.medcli.2020.03.004
8. Felipe Castillo, A., Diego Bazaes, N., Álvaro Huete, G.: Radiology in the COVID-19 pandemic: current role, recommendations for structuring the radiological report and our departments experience. Rev. Chil. Radiol. **26**, 88–99 (2020)
9. Sadiq, Z., Rana, S., Mahfoud, Z., Raoof, A.: Systematic review and meta-analysis of chest radiograph (CXR) findings in COVID-19. Clin. Imaging **80**, 229–238 (2021). https://doi.org/10.1016/j.clinimag.2021.06.039
10. Jangam, E., Barreto, A.A.D., Annavarapu, C.S.R.: Automatic detection of COVID-19 from chest CT scan and chest X-Rays images using deep learning, transfer learning and stacking. Appl. Intell. **52**, 2243–2259 (2022). https://doi.org/10.1007/s10489-021-02393-4
11. Liang, S., et al.: Fast automated detection of COVID-19 from medical images using convolutional neural networks. Commun. Biol. **4**, 35 (2021). https://doi.org/10.1038/s42003-020-01535-7

12. John, P.P.: Principios básicos en la interpratación de la radiografía del tórax. "Una guía práctica para el clínico"
13. Ana, B.B., Ingancio., S.H., Carlos, M.M.: Guía práctica de radiología de tórax para atención primaria (2005)
14. Chowdhury, M.E.H., et al.: Can AI help in screening viral and COVID-19 Pneumonia? IEEE Access **8**, 132665–132676 (2020). https://doi.org/10.1109/ACCESS.2020.3010287
15. Hussain, E., Hasan, M., Rahman, M.A., Lee, I., Tamanna, T., Parvez, M.Z.: CoroDet: a deep learning based classification for COVID-19 detection using chest X-ray images. Chaos, Solitons Fractals **142**, 110495 (2021). https://doi.org/10.1016/j.chaos.2020.110495
16. Zebin, T., Rezvy, S.: COVID-19 detection and disease progression visualization: deep learning on chest X-rays for classification and coarse localization. Appl. Intell. **51**, 1010–1021 (2021). https://doi.org/10.1007/s10489-020-01867-1
17. Tiwari, S., Jain, A.: Convolutional capsule network for COVID-19 detection using radiography images. Int. J. Imaging Syst. Technol. **31**(5), 1–15 (2021). https://doi.org/10.1002/ima.22566
18. Gianchandani, N., Jaiswal, A., Singh, D., Kumar, V., Kaur, M.: Rapid COVID-19 diagnosis using ensemble deep transfer learning models from chest radiographic images. J. Ambient Intell. Humaniz. Comput. (2020). https://doi.org/10.1007/s12652-020-02669-6
19. Wang, L., Lin, Z.Q., Wong, A.: COVID-Net: a tailored deep convolutional neural network design for detection of COVID-19 cases from chest X-ray images. Sci. Rep. **10**, 1–13 (2020). https://doi.org/10.1038/s41598-020-76550-z
20. Simonyan, K., Zisserman, A.: Very deep convolutional networks for large-scale image recognition. In: 3rd International Conference Learning Represent ICLR 2015 - Conference Track Proceedings, pp. 1–14 (2015)
21. Khandelwal, V.: The Architecture and Implementation of VGG-16. https://pub.towardsai.net/the-architecture-and-implementation-of-vgg-16-b050e5a5920b
22. Churruca, M., Martínez-besteiro, E., Couñago, F., Landete, P.: COVID-19 pneumonia?: a review of typical radiological characteristics. World J. Radiol. **13**, 327–343 (2021). https://doi.org/10.4329/wjr.v13.i10.327
23. Ranjan, S., Ranjan, D., Sinha, U., Arora, V.: Application of deep learning techniques for detection of COVID-19 cases using chest X-ray images: a comprehensive study (2020)
24. He, K., Zhang, X., Ren, S., Sun, J.: Deep residual learning for image recognition. In: Proceedings IEEE Computer Vision and Pattern Recognition, December 2016, pp. 770–778 (2016). https://doi.org/10.1109/CVPR.2016.90
25. Clarke, P.: ResNet-50 - a misleading machine learning inference benchmark for megapixel images. https://www.eenewseurope.com/en/resnet-50-a-misleading-machine-learning-inference-benchmark-for-megapixel-images/
26. Kim, H.E., Cosa-Linan, A., Santhanam, N., Jannesari, M., Maros, M.E., Ganslandt, T.: Transfer learning for medical image classification: a literature review. BMC Med. Imaging. **22**, 1–13 (2022). https://doi.org/10.1186/s12880-022-00793-7
27. Abhijeet, R.: Precision, Recall, Sensitivity and Specificity. www.iq.opengenus.org/precision-recall-sensitivity-specificity/
28. Pita Fernández, S., Pértegas Díaz, S.: Pruebas diagnósticas (2021)
29. Awad, M., Khanna, R.: Efficient Learning Machines. Apress, Berkeley (2015)
30. Skansi, S.: Introduction to Deep Learning. UTCS, Springer, Cham (2018). https://doi.org/10.1007/978-3-319-73004-2

Storytelling to Visualize Changes in Regions Based on Social Inclusion Indicators

Ernesto Emiliano Saucedo Pozos[1(✉)], Gilberto Lorenzo Martínez Luna[2], and Adolfo Guzmán Arenas[2]

[1] Unidad Profesional Interdisciplinaria en Ingeniería y Tecnologías Avanzadas del Instituto Politécnico Nacional, Av. Instituto Politécnico Nacional 2580, 07340 Ciudad de México, México
esaucedoop1601@alumno.ipn.mx

[2] Centro de Investigación en Computación del Instituto Politécnico Nacional, Avenida Juan de Dios Bátiz S/N, 07738 Ciudad de México, México
lluna@cic.ipn.mx

Abstract. This paper shows an application of data science in the healthcare system by using the Social Inclusion Indicators (ISS) of each entity in Mexico for 25 years to make a clustering based on the lack of primary healthcare. Multiple procedures were applied, like cleaning and transformation of open data published by the Mexican Health Department, the imputation of missing values. With the complete information, data was scaled, and then one of the most common clustering algorithms was applied, which is K-Means. This algorithm was initialized with previously defined centroids to make it more standardized and make it easier to notice changes amongst the classes through the years. Six clusters were defined using previous works. All the implementations were made in Python using the Scikit-Learn library to apply the algorithms and measure performance, like K-Means and Mean Squared Error respectively. Results obtained were displayed using Tableau to observe in a more interactive way, how the classes had changed over the years.

Keywords: Indicators · Imputation · Clustering & visualization

1 Introduction

Data science can be defined as the field that gathers data from multiple sources, informatics, and statistics tools to interrogate data and extract useful information [1], for these reasons. in recent years multiple procedures from data science have been applied to the healthcare system, because of their great utility and benefits they can give through the knowledge extraction from information [2]. With its help we can extract, clean, and process data to then visualize, analyze, and communicate useful information. This in turn opens new perspectives to describe, diagnose, predict, and prescribe events happening [3].

Nowadays some government agencies, like Mexican Health Department, are uploading free access data, which is called open data. Among that information we can find Social

M. F. Mata-Rivera et al. (Eds.): WITCOM 2022, CCIS 1659, pp. 173–188, 2022.
https://doi.org/10.1007/978-3-031-18082-8_11

Inclusion Indicators (SII) [4], which are health indicators and are going to be the main source of this paper.

Indicators can be defined in multiple forms depending on the author, one of their definitions is that they are quantitative observable expressions that allow us to describe some characteristics, behaviors, or specific phenomena [5], and show changes or progress in the observations [6].

Data published by the Mexican Health Department include two types of indicators:

- Percentage/Proportion: Compares a relation between the total amount of people that have a specific characteristic inside a category.
- Rate per Number of inhabitants: Defines a comparison between the total cases of a characteristic per Number of inhabitants.

1.1 Health Indicators Utility

Health indicators not only work to observe behaviors or characteristics, but they can help also to make better decision making in multiple fields. Some of its applications in the health care systems are [7]:

- To describe needs or diseases in certain population groups.
- To anticipate results with respect to the healthcare system in a population group.
- To explain why a group of people has a higher health level than others.

In a paper called "Mexico Regionalization based on primary health care indicators proposed by the WHO" [8], a clustering of federal entities in Mexico took place, searching for making groups considering the healthcare level, to explain every group deficiency. In other words, to show the entities with a hegemonic development and identify inequalities between different groups.

It has been proved that regionalization can help to improve healthcare systems and facilitates their administration, and the optimal way to work is with a decentralized administrative system and a resource rationalization based on each group's needs [9].

Nevertheless, there are complications dealing with inter-organizational complexity and balance between different command levels, and relationships between government and non-government institutions [10].

2 Procedures

The procedure that took place is the knowledge discovery from databases procedures proposed by Han, J.; et al. (2011) [11]. The first step is to extract information from an external source. Then, clean and integrate it in an owned database. Here, data can be mined to analyze it to find patterns of interest, to finally get knowledge.

2.1 Data Extraction

Raw data of the 24 indicators published was extracted to check the status of the information and if it was necessary to adequate them to the needs of the analysis, also we get the description of each indicator to know how they were obtained and calculated.

2.2 Data Cleaning

An exploration of data was made to check its composition and if it were any missing values to know if the information was useful for the analysis. In this step, two indicators were removed (percentage of homes with catastrophic expenditure per quintile and percentage of people with health insurance that use public medical care services), for having incomplete or irrelevant data. From the remaining indicators 3 parameters were extracted:

1. Year
2. Entity name
3. Indicator value

Other information in the tables was depurated because it was related to data used to calculate the indicator value, and this would make the table redundant.

In Table 1 data shown correspond to the first 6 rows of the indicator "Percentage of vaccination coverage". It can be noted that in the Entity parameter a name and a key is displayed in the columns, in some tables this key was different, and in other the key was absent.

Table 1. Head of vaccination coverage percentage table

Year	Entity	Proportion of 1 year old children with a complete basic vaccine schedule
1993	000-Nacional	69.2009
1993	001-Aguascalientes	89.8645
1993	002-Baja California	84.1691
1993	003-Baja California Sur	82.6226
1993	004-Campeche	85.6784
1993	005-Coahuila de Zaragoza	60.5825

Some names were with capital letters and others with only lowercase letters. Others were with a full name. Also, on some tables, there were names with accents and tables with names without them.

To clean all this data and make a standardized column, the following steps were taken:

1. Extract only the name
2. Change every character to lowercase
3. Remove accents
4. Extract the simplified name of the entities (Table 2)

Table 2. Relation between original and modified names

Original Name	Modified Name
Coahuila de Zaragoza	Coahuila
Michoacán de Ocampo	Michoacán
Querétaro de Arteaga	Querétaro
Veracruz de Ignacio de la Llave/Veracruz Llave	Veracruz

2.3 Data Verification

To find how many missing values were, the number of records for each indicator were obtained because the information was organized in different periods of years between 1990 and 2014, the indicators with the maximum number of records covered the whole range. As the main objective was to make a historical analysis, we decide to use only the indicators with at least 80% of the maximum amount of data. The full list of indicators is shown on Table 3, with a key number for an easier identification in further steps.

Table 3. Indicators and its keys

Number of indicator	Name of indicator
1	Mortality rate due to Motor Vehicle Traffic Accident (MVTA)
2	Proportion of live births assisted by qualified health workers
3	Proportion of live births with low birth weight
4	Mortality rate due to breast cancer
5	Mortality rate due to prostate cancer (45 + years)
6	Mortality rate due to cardiovascular diseases
7	Percentage of people with a lack health care services access
8	Percentage of live births by cesarean with respect of live births
9	Lethality rate due to dengue hemorrhagic fever
10	Mortality rate due to diabetes (type II)
11	Maternal mortality ratio
12	Mortality ratio in children under five years old
13	Neonatal mortality ratio
14	Mortality ratio due to neoplasms
15	Incidence ratio associated with malaria

(*continued*)

Table 3. (*continued*)

Number of indicator	Name of indicator
16	Percentage of premature births
17	Mortality rate due to Chronic Obstructive Pulmonary Disease (COPD)
18	HIV/AIDS mortality ratio
19	Mortality ratio due to youth suicide (10 to 29 years)
20	Incidence ratio associated to tuberculosis
21	Mortality ratio due to tuberculosis
22	Proportion of 1 year old children with a complete basic vaccine schedule

2.4 Data Imputation

The behavior of the indicators in relation to the time of some entities was graphed to check some of the missing data, visualize tendencies, and analyze possible solutions to fill missing values. It was found that decision trees were a good method to approximate values, according to Tsai, C.-F. (2022) [12]. Nevertheless, due to the non-linearity observed in graphs, other methods were considered. Ensemble methods were analyzed, these types of methods usually have a high accuracy by combining the result of base learners (weak estimators) [13]. Amongst multiple methods, Gradient Boosting Regressor was selected, which sequentially fits a gradient estimator to a loss function being minimized [14].

The algorithm first initializes the model with a constant value. Then it starts to iterate from 1 to the maximum number of base estimators (M).

In the iteration, it first calculates pseudo-residuals, with this information the base learners are fit to minimize the residuals to generate predictions. After this step, it is necessary to compute an optimization to find a local minimum. To finish the iteration the model is updated with the help of a learning rate. Then the process is finished. It is important to say, that the base learner used, was the decision tree.

3 Gradient Tree Boost Algorithm

$$F_0(x) = \underset{\gamma}{\text{argmin}} \sum_{i-1}^{N} \Psi(y_i, \gamma)$$

5. $Form = 1\, to\, M$:

i. $\tilde{y}_{im} = -\left[\frac{\partial \Psi(y_i, F(x_i))}{\partial F(x_i)}\right]_{F(x)=F_{m-1}(x)}, i = 1, N$

ii. $\{R_{lm}\}_1^L = L - terminal\ node\ tree\left(\{\tilde{y}_{im}, x_i\}_1^N\right)$

iii. $\gamma_{lm} = \arg\min_{\gamma} \sum_{x_i \in R_{lm}} \Psi(y_i, F_{m-1}(x) + \gamma)$

iv. $F_m(x) = F_{m-1}(x) + \nu \cdot \gamma_{lm} 1(x \in R_{lm})$

6. End of for

To find the best hyperparameters for the model, the Grid Search method was applied, this consists in iterating over a collection of hyperparameters shown in Table 4, a quarter of data was used as a test set, and to evaluate or model performance Mean Squared Error (MSE) was used as a metric.

Table 4. Hyperparameters for tunning.

Hyperparameter	Value
Learning rate	0.01 0.1
Number of estimators	100 500

This hyperparameter tunning was applied to every indicator with missing values for each entity.

To apply both, the Grid Search and the Gradient boost algorithm, Scikit-Learn methods were applied. For model performance comparison, Decision Tree Regressor (DTR) and AdaBoost Regressor (ABR) were also implemented with Scikit-Learn.

3.1 Clustering by K-Means

To perform the clustering, it was applied the K-Means algorithm, with a total number of 6 clusters. This number was taken from the prior work "Mexico Regionalization based on "Mexico Regionalization based on primary health care indicators proposed by the WHO" [8], they found this number by making a hierarchical clustering and analyzing the dendrogram created by the algorithm.

K-Means algorithm [16], splits data X of N samples into K disjoints clusters C, each one described by the average μ_j of the samples in the cluster. This average is normally called centroid.

This algorithm creates a cluster of the data by looking that each of the clusters has an equally variance, choosing the centroids that minimize the inertia.

$$\sum\nolimits_{i=0}^{N} \min_{\mu_j \in C}\left(\|x_i - \mu_j\|^2\right) \tag{1}$$

This algorithm consists of 3 basic steps:

1. Random points within the samples are selected as the initial centroids.
2. While the difference between the new centroid and the old one is greatest than a threshold, or the number of iterations reaches its limit:
   i. Assign every sample to the nearest centroid
   ii. Calculate a new centroid by averaging each value of the samples assigned to each of the centroids
3. End of loop

To calculate the nearest distance multiple criteria can be applied, in this case, Euclidean distance was applied.

$$d(X, Y) = \sqrt{\sum\nolimits_{i=1}^{N} (X_i - Y_i)^2} \tag{2}$$

For this case, 300 iterations were used, and a threshold of 1e–4.

First, the algorithm was run in the year 1990. To initialize the centroids a method where the random centroids are chosen to look for a large difference in the Euclidean distance between the samples. To secure the reproducibility of the algorithm, a seed was used to start the random number generator and make randomness deterministic.

The 1990 centroids were sorted by the average of the value of each of its features to define which ones had a higher SII level. To the next 24 years, the centroids were not selected randomly, the centroids obtained in the year 1990 were used this time to initialize the algorithm. With this action it was tried that the new centroids for the rest of the year would be similar and standardized, so labels could match.

To ensure that all the data had the same contribution to the algorithm a Min-Max Scaler method was applied, this method doesn't change the data distribution. The transformation of a sample x contained in a set X [16], is given by:

$$x_{scaled} = \frac{x - \min(X)}{\max(X) - \min(X)} \tag{3}$$

The scaler and the clustering were implemented using Scikit-Learn methods.

4 Results

As a final data depuration, indicators with a greater percentage than the threshold shown as a red line in the Fig. 1 were conserved. In the figure the indicators are numerated as in table 3. The total number of indicators in this step were 17.

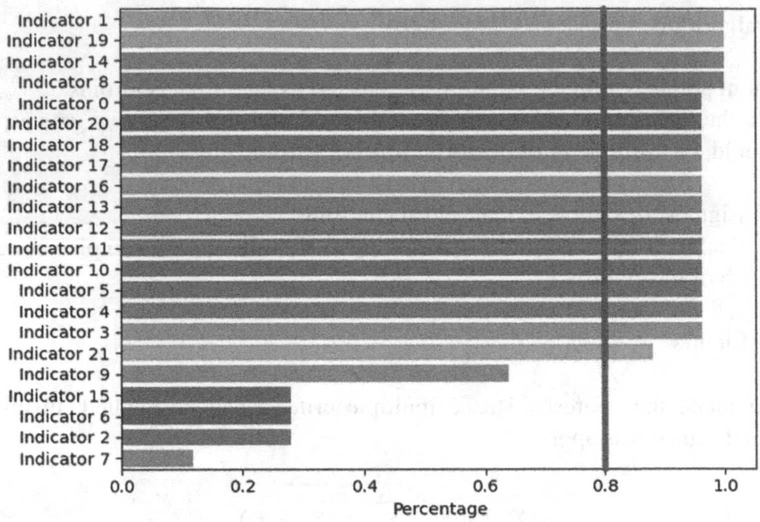

Fig. 1. Percentage of data for each indicator

After this selection, it was observed that two indicators (Lethality rate due to dengue hemorrhagic fever and Incidence ratio associated with malaria) had a large number of values equal to 0, making this behavior hard to adequate to a model and giving an erratic graph. Finally, only 15 indicators were used, which are a similar number to the 13 used by Valencia, et al. [9]. The final list is shown next.

- Mortality rate due to Motor Vehicle Traffic Accident (MVTA)
- Proportion of live births assisted by qualified health workers
- Mortality rate due to breast cancer
- Mortality rate due to prostate cancer (45 + years)
- Mortality rate due to cardiovascular diseases
- Maternal mortality ratio
- Mortality rate in children under five years old
- Neonatal mortality ratio
- Mortality ratio due to neoplasms
- Mortality rate due to Chronic Obstructive Pulmonary Disease (COPD)
- HIV/AIDS mortality ratio
- Mortality ratio due to youth suicide (10 to 29 years)
- Incidence ratio associated to tuberculosis
- Mortality ratio due to tuberculosis
- Proportion of 1 year old children with a complete basic vaccine schedule

Table 5 contains a resume of the final data used for imputation and clustering.

Table 5. Resume of final data

Year	Entity	Indicators (1 to 15)
Range of [1990, 2014]	All federal entities from Mexico	Scaled values of [0, 1]

4.1 Data Imputation

Indicators that needed data imputation are shown on Table 6.

Table 6. Indicators that require imputation

Indicator Name	Percentage of missing values
Mortality rate due to cardiovascular diseases	4
Maternal mortality ratio	4
Mortality ratio in children under five years old	4
Neonatal mortality ratio	4
Mortality ratio due to neoplasms	4
Mortality rate due to Chronic Obstructive Pulmonary Disease (COPD)	4
HIV/AIDS mortality ratio	4
Mortality ratio due to youth suicide (10 to 29 years)	4
Incidence ratio associated to tuberculosis	4
Mortality ratio due to tuberculosis	4
Proportion of 1 year old children with a complete basic vaccine schedule	12

For each graph, at first sight, the regressor shown congruent results, as can be seen in Fig. 2. Nevertheless, using the MSE criteria as a metric for validation, in some cases, there is a wide range between different estimations. For example, in Fig. 2 we have a MSE of 0.3 and in Fig. 3 the MSE is 52.21. Due to the number of times that this algorithm must run (480, one for each indicator with its respective entity), optimization of every case was not performed.

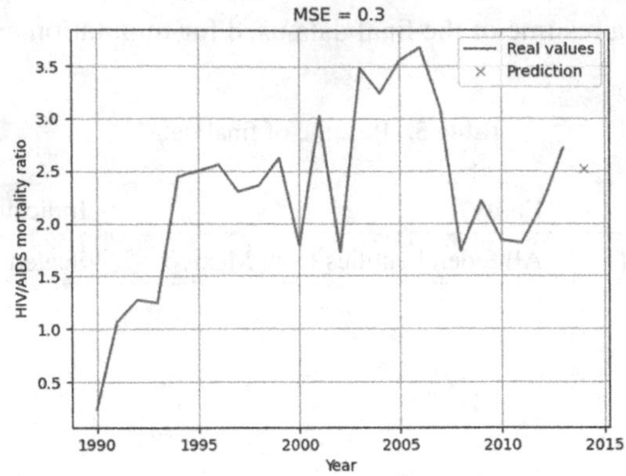

Fig. 2. HIV/AIDS mortality rate through the time and data estimation of Aguascalientes

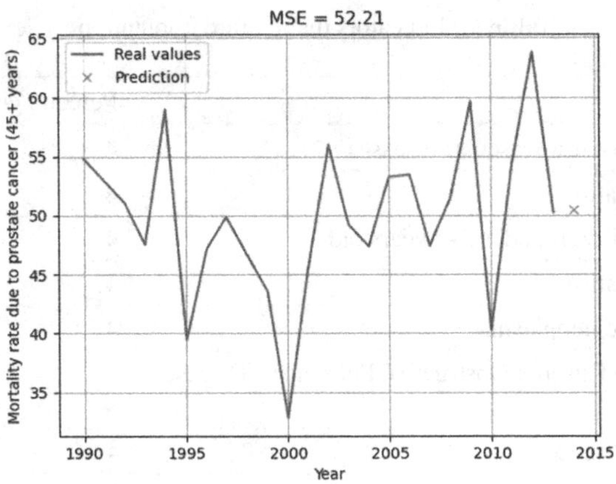

Fig. 3. Mortality rate due to prostate cancer through time and data estimation of Aguascalientes

Another two methods for imputation were tested to make a comparison between them, and show that the chosen method was the best, the average MSE obtained on the test set of all indicators for each entity, is displayed in Table 7. It is important to mention that every entity was assigned with a number corresponding to its alphabetic order, from 1 being Aguascalientes, and 32 Zacatecas.

Table 7. Average of MSE of each method for all indicators per entity.

Entity	Decision Tree MSE	Gradient Boosting Tree MSE	Adaboost MSE
1	55.20	44.21	53.88
2	27.39	25.54	27.02
3	98.54	86.57	97.76
4	58.28	48.30	57.24
5	15.46	17.90	15.31
6	185.23	160.22	183.01
7	17.89	14.51	17.44
8	45.51	29.05	43.96
9	26.19	28.20	25.97
10	59.86	61.13	58.83
11	22.94	20.94	22.73
12	38.58	43.54	38.39
13	33.97	32.62	33.76
14	29.09	27.58	28.98
15	20.61	12.59	20.42
16	28.96	19.32	27.51
17	41.24	38.45	40.29
18	103.42	105.67	101.95
19	19.58	15.88	19.39
20	25.58	22.24	25.49
21	38.33	37.75	37.76
22	54.95	58.96	54.31
23	63.65	67.70	63.34
24	38.94	38.89	38.88
25	24.58	23.92	24.01
26	23.62	21.52	23.23
27	37.52	29.22	36.47
28	29.70	24.52	29.40
29	55.49	38.48	54.58
30	15.57	12.53	15.43
31	42.98	31.91	41.80
32	56.70	51.62	54.35
Average	**44.86**	**40.36**	**44.15**

4.2 Clustering

On completion of the clustering, each entity had an assigned label corresponding to the group they belong, this information was stored, and it can be found also the corresponding year and state. Label 0 represents the entities with the lowest SII levels, while label 5 is the highest level. In Table 8 it can be seen the regions, and the entities inside for each year, where each entity is represented with a number, as before.

Table 8. Results of entities clustering every 5 years.

Year\ Region	0	1	2	3	4	5
1990	4, 12, 23, 27	5, 20, 21, 30	11, 13, 15, 22, 24, 29	1, 10, 16, 17, 31, 32	2, 3, 8, 18, 19, 25	6, 7, 9, 14, 26, 28
1995	4, 23, 27	5, 12, 20, 30	13, 15, 17, 21, 22, 24, 29	1, 10, 11, 16, 17, 31, 32	2, 3, 6, 7, 8, 18, 19, 25, 26, 28	9, 14
2000	4, 23, 27	5, 12, 20, 30	11, 13, 15, 21, 22, 29	1, 10, 16, 17, 24, 31	2, 3, 7, 8, 14, 18, 19, 25, 26, 28	6, 9, 32
2005	4, 23, 27	5, 12, 20	13, 15, 21, 29	1, 8, 10, 11, 16, 17, 22, 24, 31, 32	2, 3, 19, 25, 26, 28	6, 7, 9, 14, 18, 30
2010	4, 23, 27, 31	2, 5, 12, 20, 30	1, 6, 10, 11, 13, 15, 21, 22, 24, 29	9, 17	7, 19, 28	3, 8, 14, 16, 18, 25, 26, 32
2014	23, 27	2, 5, 12, 20	4, 10, 13, 15, 21, 29	1, 9, 11, 16, 17, 22, 24, 32	3, 18, 19, 25, 26	6, 7, 8, 14, 28, 30, 31
Most frequent Entities > 80%	**4, 23, 27**	**5, 12, 20**	**13, 15, 21, 29**	**1, 16, 17**	**3, 19, 25**	**14**

4.3 Storytelling

With the help of the region labels, each entity had a color assigned according to its SII level. In the visualization created the desired year can be selected, as well a single region. The color assigned to each region is shown and it has the relationship displayed on Table 9.

Table 9. Relationship between colors and regions

Region	Color
0	Red
1	Orange
2	Yellow
3	Green
4	Light blue
5	Dark blue

This color palette was selected to be easily identified as something to pay special attention on the regions with a low SII level.

In Fig. 4 it is shown the regionalization corresponding to 1990, in this year 4 Northern entities, Mexico City, and Jalisco have the highest SII level. Most of the entities in the center are in a mid-level. While most of the Southern entities are placed in the worst levels.

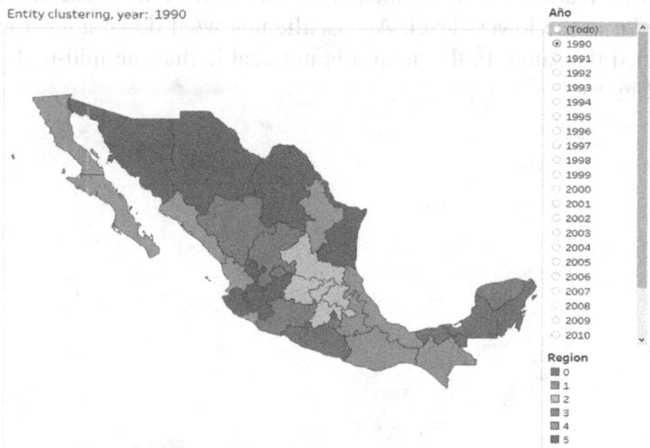

Fig. 4. Entity clustering, 1990

The result of clustering 10 years later can be seen in Fig. 5, in North Mexico only Coahuila remained in the highest level and Jalisco dropped a level. Another entity that dropped a level was San Luis Potosí. But there weren't only entities that dropped a level, Puebla, Guerrero, and Zacatecas move up at least one level. With the last one moving up to the top level.

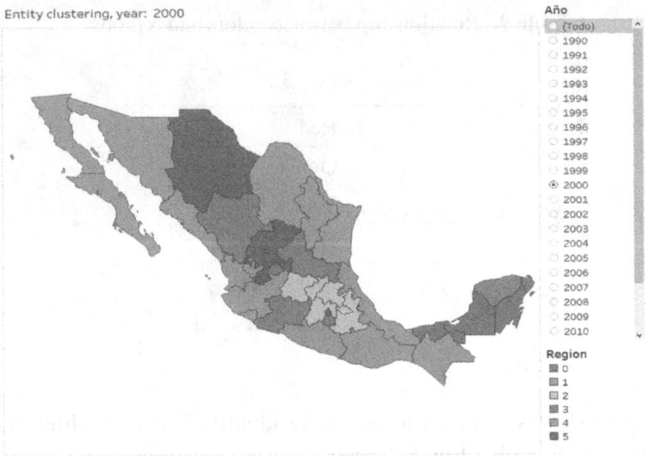

Fig. 5. Entity clustering, 2000

Moving another 10 years ahead, it can be noticed that multiple entities in West Mexico went-up to the highest SII level. San Luis got back to its first level, Baja California, Coahuila, Durango, and Yucatán went down more than one level, the last of these went down to the lowest level. Aguascalientes went down a level and the other entities remained the same. In this map it is noticeable that the mid-high level almost disappeared (Fig. 6).

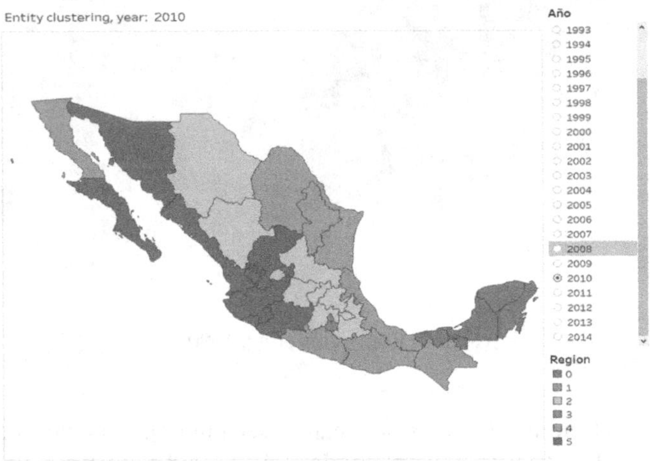

Fig. 6. Entity clustering, 2010

In the last reported year, it is shown that multiple entities change from levels, most of them to a higher one. This year has some interesting changes, because some states that weren't moving through levels, finally did it. The states that changed were Campeche, Veracruz, Querétaro, and Mexico City, the last one move to a lower level (Fig. 7).

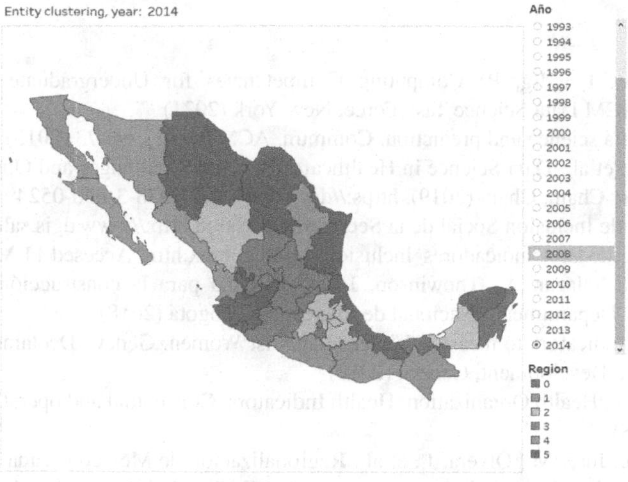

Fig. 7. Entity clustering, 2014

5 Conclusion

Gradient Boosting Regressor compared to other tested methods, like the ABR, and DTR, showed a better performance using MSE as a metric, other metrics weren't used for validation. Nevertheless, hyperparameter tunning of this method were computational expensive since Grid Search uses all combinations of the given values, so a Random Search, which looks for a maximum number of random combinations based on user preferences could have a faster training. This is something to take on consideration on which hyperparameter tunning method to apply and how to tune. In the future, to decide this will depend on how much time is required to finish the model training, and how high accuracy is wanted.

K-Means method made congruent clustering, since it could preserve a certain hegemony through each year classification, in addition it provides us to observe changes in the classifications. To this specific case, hierarchical clustering showed an erratic behavior, and multiple classes with just one state were generated.

The selected method for centroid initialization was the one that showed a good standardization to make sure that the classification was hegemonic. This was different with random centroid initialization where random label order was created with each algorithm run. Even so, with the way information is communicated, it is not possible to see how centroids has changed, for example, if they are like the 1990 centroids, or its values has move to a higher or lower level. So, this paper could be complemented with this information to see how far classes have changed.

This methodology can be followed by people interested in making a regionalization in other fields, cause information obtained can carry out the planning of better strategies to help regions to have better indicators values.

References

1. Danyluk, A., Leigdig, P.: Computing Competencies for Undergraduate Data Science Curricula. ACM Data Science Task Force, New York (2021)
2. Dhar, V.: Data science and prediction. Commun. ACM **56**(12), 64–73 (2013)
3. Abedjan, Z., et al.: Data Science in Healthcare: Benefits, Challenges and Opportunities. 1st edn. Springer Cham, Cham (2019). https://doi.org/10.1007/978-3-030-05249-2_1
4. Indicadores de Inclusión Social de la Secretaría de Salud http://www.dgis.salud.gob.mx/contenidos/basesdedatos/indicadores_inclusionsocial_gobmx.html Accesed 11 May 2022
5. Romero, O., Salazar, A., Thowinson, J., et al.: Guía para la construcción y análisis de indicadores. Departamento Nacional de Planeación, Bogotá (2018)
6. Jansen, H.: Indicators to measure Violence against Women. Geneva Declaration on Armed Violence and Development, Geneva (2010)
7. Pan American Health Organization: Health Indicators: Conceptual and operational considerations (2018)
8. Valencia, G., José, M., Olvera, J., et al.: Regionalización de México basada en indicadores de atención primaria a la salud propuestos por la OMS. Salud Pública México **33**(1), 29–37 (1991)
9. Ramos, M., Barreto, M., Shimizu, H., et al.: Regionalization for health improvement: a systematic review. PLoS ONE **15**(12), 1–20 (2020)
10. Tenbensel, T.: Health system regionalization - the New Zealand experience. Healthcarepapers **16**(1), 27–33 (2016)
11. Han, J., Pei, J., Kamber, M.: Data Mining: Concepts and Techniques, 3rd edn. Morgan Kaufmann Publishers, Burlington (2012)
12. Tsai, C.-F., Hu, Y.-H.: Empirical comparison of supervised learning techniques for missing value imputation. Knowledge Inf. Syst. **64**(4), 1047–1075 (2022)
13. Knoll, A., Nateking, A.: Gradient boosting machines, a tutorial. Front. Neurorobot. **7**(21), 1–21 (2013)
14. Friedman, J.: Stochastic gradient boosting. Comput. Stat. Data Anal. **38**(4), 367–378 (2002)
15. Friedman, J.: Greedy function approximation: a gradient boosting machine. Ann. Stat. **29**(5), 1189–1232 (2001)
16. Pedregosa, F., et al.: Scikit-learn: machine learning in python. J. Machine Learning Res. **12**, 2825–2830 (2011)

Open edX as a Learning Remote Platform for Mexico City-IPN

Vladimir Avalos-Bravo[1(✉)], Salvador Castro Gómez[2], Israel Jimenez Nogueda[2], and Julio Iván Ramírez Contreras[2]

[1] Instituto Politecnico Nacional, CIITEC-IPN, SEPI-ESIQIE, UPIEM, SARACS Research Group ESIME Zacatenco, Mexico City, Mexico
ravalos@ipn.mx

[2] Instituto Politécnico Nacional, DEV, Mexico City, Mexico
{scastrog,ijimenezn,jiramirez}@ipn.mx

Abstract. Covid-19, a respiratory illness, emerged in Wuhan province of China in December 2019. World Health Organization (WHO) has reported that the COVID-19 pandemic has spread to 213 countries and spread through Mexico two years ago, which had to choose to change education methodology to not affect the learning process of students. It generated that approximately 30 million students, of all educational levels, had to stop going to their schools because classes were suspended, Open edX and Moodle are platforms that enable e-learning for many learners through unique features and systems that were not available before. Mexico City-IPN must align and adapt to the national and international context, to become one of the advanced and strategic pillars of the growth and development model. This paper presents, a platform to support self-management courses like MOOCs, which were conceived as a means of support during a pandemic, due to its properties like asynchrony and flexibility, some results show the ease with which the platform and MOOCs were developed.

Keywords: Digital education; education 4.0; remote learning · Open edX · e-learning · Mexico City-IPN

1 Introduction

Pandemics all over the world come to modify the daily life of all citizens, the new coronavirus outbreak spread through different countries like Mexico had to choose to change education methodology to not affect the learning process of students [1]. Covid-19, a respiratory illness, emerged from the Wuhan province of China in December 2019 and it has since spread to the entire world. World Health Organization (WHO) has reported that the COVID-19 pandemic has spread to 213 countries with a fatality of 2,020,733 globally [2]. According to the National Institute for Education Evaluation (INEE), having adopted measures in the country to prevent the COVID-19 virus spread in Mexico, caused more than 30 million basic education, medium-high education, undergraduate and postgraduate education, had to stop attending school due to the measures taken by

M. F. Mata-Rivera et al. (Eds.): WITCOM 2022, CCIS 1659, pp. 189–200, 2022.
https://doi.org/10.1007/978-3-031-18082-8_12

the public education ministry [3]. It was not until March 2020 that the state of contingency was declared all over the country, like in other educational institutions in Mexico City-IPN, confinement measures and some actions recommended by health authorities took place, and decree the Academic Continuity Plan (ACP). In Mexico City-IPN, many resources are required to prepare students with new skills that allow them to adapt to changing environments; carrying out these tasks, such as developing the skills to team work remotely; generate solutions to the problems raised at an economic and environmental level, as well as reflect on proactivity and reflection. For example, in a technological ecosystem, the components that make it up are adaptable and flexible, due to this, an educational ecosystem is considered a set of learners, trainers, resources, principles, methods, systems, and processes [4]. A maxim dictates that basic innovation in all forms of education today must be guided by simple and forceful ideas [5].

One of the necessary perspectives to achieve this transformation in the educational sector and technological industry is digital education. To generate new social, economic, educational, and cultural contexts, the availability of technology and process automation is aimed at providing efficient, rapid, and consistent responses to user demand. Digital education from a cultural and technological context produces current social world reconstruction [6]. Implementing isolated computer systems that are oriented to specific situations solution, favors the underutilization of infrastructure used in the different offered services. This has led to the search for new models to relate to users, systems, services, and infrastructure, thus giving way to technological ecosystems [7]. We are immersed in an era called the knowledge age. This era focuses on technology as a benchmark, relying on the use of artificial intelligence, big data, data analysis, personalized services, and robotics. To meet these new needs, educational institutions must produce a qualified workforce capable of taking advantage of the available tools.

There is some evidence that the characteristics of traditional education altered in a short period, and it was no longer able to meet the educational system's criteria, accommodate vast numbers of learners at all stages, or allow for new kinds of learning [8]. Through the design of e-learning, there is a need to employ instructional design (ID) models as a kind of practice, development, and presentation of educational products and experiences, consistently and reliably, to provide knowledge efficiently and effectively through attractive and inspiring methods [9]. The awareness of the limitation teaching resources has is the result of the much concentration on the smooth supply of efficient instructions as in Massive Open Online Courses (MOOCs) [10]. Therefore, it is important to mention the literature review and examples on web pages, there is no evidence of these platforms used for remote learning, and it's well known that they can help to solve the knowledge demand through asynchronous devices. The main concepts addressed in this literature review are learning theories, instructional design, instructional design in digital education, and online learning during COVID-19 [11].

1.1 Education 4.0 Approach for New Careers at Mexico City-IPN

Since its origins, Mexico City-IPN has been characterized by supporting and promoting Mexican State policies development, related to the industrialization of the country and the permanent improvement of public, private, and social companies. Through preparation among engineers, masters, and doctors among other professions; executing scientific and technological research projects, with the necessary link to maintain its institutional actions relevance, and with knowledge dissemination that, in its classrooms or with its information technologies, is applied and innovated through the educational process. Mexico City-IPN must align and adapt to the national and international context, to become one of the advanced and strategic pillars of the growth and development model with which Mexico, within the 4IR framework, will face justice, sovereignty, independence, nationalism, and cosmopolitanism, the challenges and opportunities that arise, for successful and proactive insertion of the world governance and governability avant-garde modalities [12].

1.2 Open MOOCs Platform, Comparative Between Moodle and Open EdX

The constant changes in the technological landscape have led to developments in the education industry as well. Today, online education has become an integral part of the learning process. Not only educational institutions but also corporations worldwide are keen on developing e-learning programs. To develop these programs, numerous platforms have emerged over the years. Amongst these are Moodle and Open edX which are globally renowned for their services. Moodle is being used in 47 countries with 15.7 billion enrollments by over 278 million users. Open edX is being used in 196 countries with 118 million enrollments by over 38 million users [12], however, you can't choose an eLearning platform based on just this information. To make a sound decision, it is necessary to understand the difference between Open edX and Moodle. Open edX and Moodle are platforms that enable e-learning for many learners through unique features and systems that were not available before. Moodle is typically used as a Learning Management System for offering traditional e-learning while Open edX is typically used to support Massive Open Online Courses (MOOCs) [13].

Modern online courses are an extension of older forms of distance learning, going back to mail and correspondence courses of the 1700s. These courses were followed in the 1900s by radio, telephone, and television-based educational efforts. Computers were used to deliver educational programs as early as the 1970s, even though the technology was often a hindrance. However, with the rise of personal computers, better Internet connections, and digital video technology in the 1990s, many universities began offering more courses online. While this shift meant that online learning became more available to anyone with an Internet connection, these courses were often offered to select groups of learners. Starting in the 1970s and 1980s, various groups and universities began creating open learning or learning for all initiatives to take learning beyond the silos it was often contained within [14].

The term Massive Open Online Courses (MOOCs) came into existence in 2008 from an online course by George Siemens and Stephen Downes. MOOCs enabled digital ways of knowing and learning, and this concept became popular in 2013. Reputable universities started offering MOOCs because of their scalability and cost-effectiveness. MOOCs help educational institutions achieve their goals of extending reach and accessibility, building, and maintaining the brand, enhancing revenue, and bringing innovation to teaching and learning (Fig. 1).

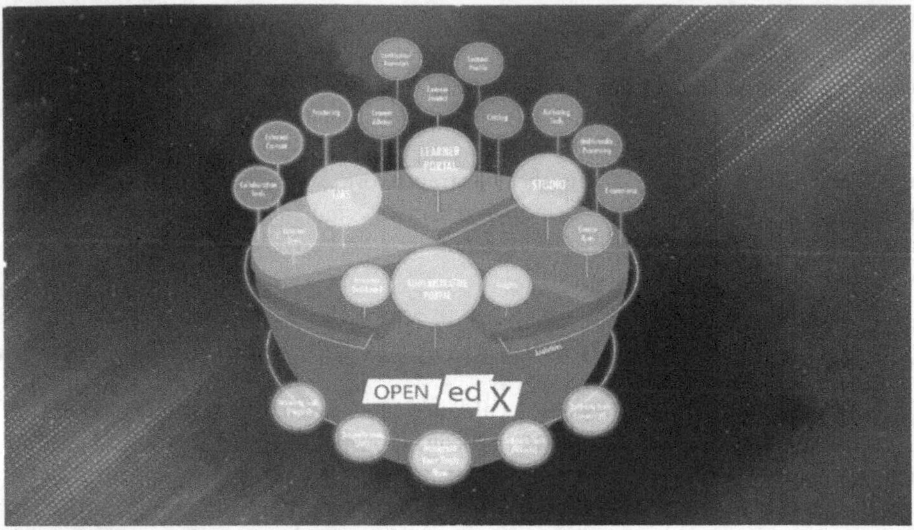

Fig. 1. Open edX platform modules

2 MOOCs Didactic Planning and Development

In the last decade, Language MOOCs have attracted a lot of interest for their potential to enhance language learning. However, how learners engage with MOOC environments and realize their benefits, remains unclear [15]. For Mexico City-IPN, a Digital Didactic Resource (DDR) is defined as all that educational content presented in digital format, which serves as sustenance and/or pedagogical support to promote learning in their different modalities [16], a MOOC has a didactic scope classified as Educational Treatment because it includes content that mediates access to information to ensure significant educational learning with an appropriate language according to the user to whom it is addressed; they have an implicit instructional or didactic design. At Mexico City-IPN, MOOC evaluation criteria must include in its structure an opening section where it is welcomed, explaining its objective, way of working, and evaluation. It must contain a content section, that is, that the content is developed by blocks, with short texts that connect one concept with another and the multimedia resources. It must contain a section of activities that are self-managed and in the case of integrating forums, this must-have feedback, and collaboration for the participants, credits, and references. The description of knowledge, skills, and attitudes that the participant must have, are the domain of arithmetic operations, management of calculation tools, know-how to propose algorithms for problem-solving, mastery of some diagramming techniques and discipline, creativity, and enthusiasm. The Objective of the MOOCs is that participants know and manage to acquire programming skills and know different functionalities to develop solutions to engineering problems based on Mathematical Thinking. The form of work and evaluation of MOOCs is self-managing and self-assessing, since the participant, as they advance in each of the different topics to be developed, will obtain an evaluation according to their achievements, in addition to being able to carry out each activity according to the time that you decide to dedicate to each of them.

At the end of each activity of the didactic planning, a score will be assigned according to established values, as well as a score for solving exercises at the end of each Unit and a score assigned according to the self-assessment carried out. at the end of them. MOOCs can be worked through screens that simulate environments, where examples and exercises will be presented, as well as the different autocomplete problems for mastering the exercises. Now that MOOCs are hitting the scene, everyone wants to jump on board, more providers are likely to spring up as we will only cover five potential options. As the entire MOOC industry evolves, expect to see more options at your disposal for this kind of thing [17].

2.1 MOOCs Development Software and Tools

To create a MOOC like the "Learn MATLAB" one, it is necessary to provide the guidelines, the workflow, and the concepts that are handled in the MATLAB software, which will allow the users (students, teachers, or community) to start practicing with the program or, if they have already used it, reaffirm their previous knowledge about its operation through practical examples. The MOOC is designed to be completed in a period of approximately 40 virtual hours; For they to take full advantage of this course, they must have the software installed on their computer or mobile device, otherwise, they will have to use the MATLAB grader application to perform the exercises that are shown as examples in the content. Advanced math proficiency is required but no prior knowledge of the software is required. Once the objective of the MOOC has been defined, the learning units are established:

I. Introduction to the use of MATLAB software
II. Charts
III. Mathematics and symbolic mathematics
IV. Control structures

Next, we choose the different software that will be used for the MOOC creation, First, the use of the Adobe CC Suite allows us to generate multimedia thanks to many applications for graphic modifications. Some others are Adobe Acrobat DC for creating and editing PDF Documents. Another one is Tumult Hype which allows us to develop interactive content and animations to give a more dynamic image to MOOCs. The software was also used Visual Studio Code for the development of Interactive content and web page development, we cannot fail to take advantage of the YouTube video repository that allows us to store or direct to some tutorials, and finally, the dynamic technology of H5P, when the MOOCs are developed in a programming code based on html5, we can make use of up to 52 dynamic and interactive resources for self-management such as word search, crossword puzzles, memory and some other activities that facilitate student learning.

2.2 Open edX Configuration

Open edX is an open-source learning management system and a course-authoring tool that empowers organizations worldwide to design customized and engaging online learning platforms and content. Open edX was created by Harvard University and the Massachusetts Institute of Technology (MIT) for the popular eLearning platform edX in 2012. It is a non-profit organization that provides the massively scalable, open-source learning software technology behind edX [12]. In November 2021, edX was acquired by 2U and a new nonprofit was established to manage the ongoing development of Open edX, and it is important to point out that the development of MOOCs witnessed rapidly growing between 2012 and 2017. The increased number of students counted in at least one course jumped to 58 million in 2016 [18].

Open edX has interesting features that cater to the needs of their respective target audiences, some features are:

- Interactive video lectures with subtitles
- Full out-of-the-box course authoring tools
- Online test assessments and examinations
- Virtual laboratory with simulations
- Multi-lingual support
- Discussion forums
- Unique types of grading systems
- Calendar-style course scheduling

Before the installation, it is necessary to make a review of the server properties where the Open edX platform will be installed (Table 1).

Table 1. Open edX server properties

Description	CERO B
Label	(0B) DarthMaul.31
Brand	DELL
Model	PowerEdge R930
Processor	Intel(R) Xeon(R) CPU E7–8855 v4 @ 2.10GHz, 56 cores
RAM	256GB
HDD	7.2TB 12@600GB (RAID 5 5.9TB)
Power Supplies	4@PWR SPLY,1100,RDNT,13G,DELTA,3

Once the server is selected, the following steps show the way the platform will be installed:

Operating System Installation Ubuntu Server 20.04 LTS
Version: “open edX Maple”

Installation Method:

Tutor, Native and Devstack

Tutor: (New for Lilac) A community-supported Docker-based environment suited for both production and development.

Native: (Deprecated in Lilac, to be removed in Maple) Provides a production-ready installation on an Ubuntu machine of your own, using an Ansible playbook.

Devstack: A development environment based on Docker; useful if you want to modify Open edX code locally.

Choose: Tutor (Único disponible en open-release "Maple")

Installation of < tutor >

…"

"A tutor is the official Docker-based Open edX distribution, both for production and local development. The goal of Tutor is to make it easy to deploy, customize, upgrade and scale Open edX. A tutor is reliable, fast, extensible, and it is already used to deploy hundreds of Open edX platforms around the world."

Features:

100% open source

Runs entirely on Docker

World-famous 1-click installation and upgrades

Comes with batteries included: theming, SCORM, HTTPS, web-based administration interface, mobile app, custom translations…

Extensible architecture with plugins

Works with Kubernetes

Amazing premium plugins are available in the Tutor Wizard Edition, including Cairn the next-generation analytics solution for Open edX.

No technical skill is required with the zero-click Tutor AWS image

"… (https://docs.tutor.overhang.io)"

" < tutor >" = open edX + docker

Requirements:

Supported OS: Tutor runs on any 64-bit, UNIX-based OS. It was also reported to work on Windows (with WSL 2).

Architecture: support for ARM64 is a work-in-progress. See this issue.

Required software:

Docker: v18.06.0+

Docker Compose: v1.22.0+

Ports 80 and 443 should be open. If other web services run on these ports, check the tutorial on how to set up a web proxy.

Hardware:

Minimum configuration: 4 GB RAM, 2 CPU, 8 GB disk space

Recommended configuration: 8 GB RAM, 4 CPU, 25 GB disk space

https://docs.tutor.overhang.io/install.html.

Docker Installation:

```
sudo apt-get install \
    ca-certificates \
    curl \
    gnupg \
    lsb-release
sudo apt install apt-transport-https ca-certificates curl software-properties-common -y
curl -fsSL https://download.docker.com/linux/ubuntu/gpg | sudo gpg --dearmor -o /usr/share/keyrings/docker-archive-keyring.gpg
echo \
  "deb [arch=$(dpkg --print-architecture) signed-by=/usr/share/keyrings/docker-archive-keyring.gpg] https://download.docker.com/linux/ubuntu \
  $(lsb_release -cs) stable" | sudo tee /etc/apt/sources.list.d/docker.list > /dev/null
sudo apt-get update
sudo apt-get install docker-ce docker-ce-cli containerd.io docker-compose-plugin

Installation docker-compose (standalone)
sudo curl -SL https://github.com/docker/compose/releases/download/v2.4.1/docker-compose-linux-x86_64 -o /usr/local/bin/docker-compose
sudo chmod +x /usr/local/bin/docker-compose
sudo ln -s /usr/local/bin/docker-compose /usr/bin/docker-compose
Installation <tutor>
sudo curl -L "https://github.com/overhangio/tutor/releases/download/v12.1.6/tutor-$(uname -s)_$(uname -m)" -o /usr/local/bin/tutor
sudo chmod 0755 /usr/local/bin/tutor
_TUTOR_COMPLETE=bash_source tutor >> ~/.bashrc
Run <tutor>
tutor local quickstart
```

…That's it?

Yes :) This is what happens when you run `tutor local quickstart`:

You answer a few questions about the Configuration of your Open edX platform.

Configuration files are generated from templates.

Docker images are downloaded.

Docker containers are provisioned.

A full, production-ready Open edX platform (Maple release) is run with docker-compose.

The whole procedure should require less than 10 min, on a server with good bandwidth. Note that your host environment will not be affected in any way, since everything runs inside docker containers. Root access is not even necessary.

There's a lot more to Tutor than that! To learn more about what you can do with Tutor and Open edX, check out the What next? section. If the QuickStart installation method above somehow didn't work for you, check out the Troubleshooting guide.

… https://docs.tutor.overhang.io/quickstart.html.

What next?:

You have gone through the QuickStart installation: at this point, you should have a running Open edX platform. If you don't, please follow the instructions from the Troubleshooting section.

Logging-in as administrator

Out of the box, Tutor does not create any user for you. You will want to create a user yourself with staff and administrator privileges to access the studio. There is a simple command for that.

Importing a demo coursehttps://docs.tutor.overhang.io/whatnext.html - importing-a-demo-course

To get a glimpse of the possibilities of Open edX, we recommend you import the official demo test course. A tutor provides a simple command for that.

Making Open edX look better

The tutor makes it easy to install and develop your themes. We also provide Indigo: a free, customizable theme that you can install today.

3 Discussion and Results

Open edX is adopted by a wide range of organizations like Google, among others for employee education, etc. some educational organizations all over the world use it to engage many students and provide them interactive content. In Mexico City-IPN the demand for LMS is too big, that's why the creation of an edX platform to support MOOCs was decided made it, so that students can fully exploit the use of the platform, two MOOCs were created, and one aimed at high school students was reused. So that they could enroll and start using the platform with these courses that will mark how the institution's dependencies can offer a new way of education, training, and innovation. Students are encouraged to interact with their classmates through online break-out discussion sessions, online group activities, and forums as a collaboration form and a sense of community among themselves. The model was developed to assess online feedback, interaction, online teaching effectiveness, online support, and continuous usage intention.

As remote online learning continues to develop during the Covid-19 pandemic, necessary adjustments need to be made in virtual education at Mexico City-IPN to improve e-learning, it is necessary to mention that Open edX is a well-established and advanced learning platform for multiple disciplines and is particularly used in STEM education, educators and students benefit from using Open edX platform and there is strong evidence of student's engagement, performance, and satisfaction. But is also necessary to compare open edX with other LMSs and elaborate on the many e-learning tools and associated plug-ins available. Learners participate in MOOCs with diverse motivational backgrounds ranging from academic to professionals, not only academic reasons for

MOOCs participation and completion are highly crucial, but also other important motivational types could considerably influence user decisions. A lot of students are looking for this new kind of solution and it is important to consider their opinion, they are experienced users of these trends, and the best way to motivate them is to use this new technology them (Fig. 2).

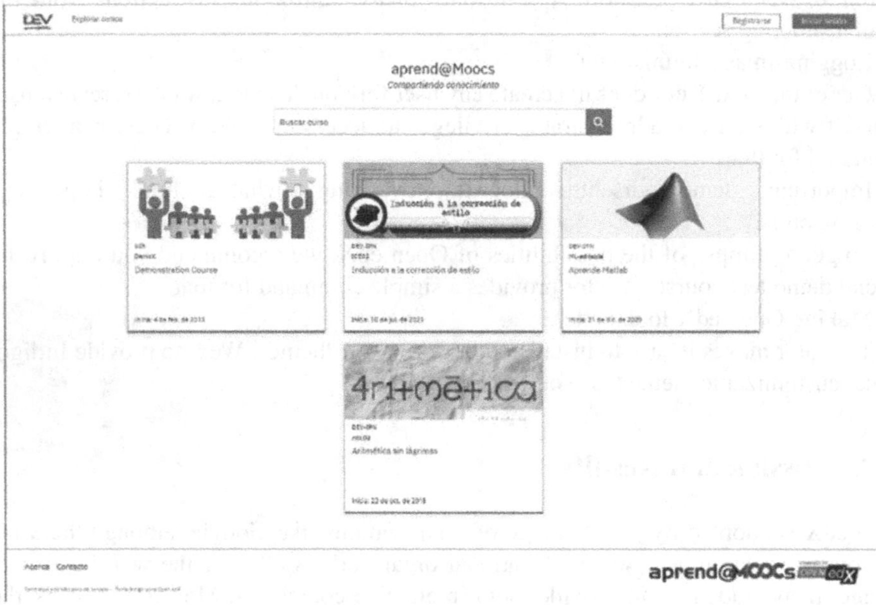

Fig. 2. Mexico City-IPN MOOCs platform based on Open edX.

4 Conclusions

A remote learning environment from students' perspective is important for higher education in the current pandemic situation.

Open edX and Moodle are excellent platforms that serve the same purpose for different target audiences and offer different features. Both have their benefits and drawbacks, so it is totally up to the LMS buyer's requirements and budget.

Open edX is suited for larger audiences for self-paced lessons. It has numerous features and a very friendly user interface.

Its key distinguishing feature is Open edX Studio, a full content authoring platform, and visual course editor. This, coupled with its immense scalability for thousands of users in a single course.

Open edX is an open-source learning platform created by Harvard and MIT for the online learning portal in the world. It was created to fulfill instructional design needs, pursuing goals with different learning scenarios.

Moodle is a much bigger platform suitable for the online classroom experience. It's ideal for organizations that need a low-cost solution.

It is easy to use user interface design as an essential part of the learning experience. The configuration of the software, especially the web server and database optimization, depends on the number of users that are going to carry out an activity simultaneously. An example of this is taking a timed exam at the same time. Fortunately, most users are generally uploading things that are not generating any demands on the server at all, unless they decide to move on to the next activity or page. Roughly speaking, a MOOC-based site can only handle 10–20 concurrent users per GB of memory.

It can influence a user's perception of the entire learning process because it has diverse purposes and community influence. Open edX has a clear and simple yet effective interface with everything that learners need.

More information about content and type of courses could be considered and led MOOCs' designers on what factors motivate MOOCs' users to complete them.

The importance of this kind of platform used during the COVID-19 outbreak should not be underestimated. Most universities rely on e-learning to ensure the students could continue their learning process through different issues they are experiencing.

Acknowledgments. This project was funded under the following grants: SIP-IPN: No-20220326, and the support of DEV-IPN Instituto Politecnico Nacional, Special thanks to Cris LaPierre for their comments, review, and help on one of the MOOCs developments.

References

1. Avalos-Bravo, V., Arellano, C.C., González, J.T.: Modular educational ecosystem as academic support during COVID-19 emergency at Mexico City-IPN in 2020. In: Mesquita, A., Abreu, A., Carvalho, J.V. (eds): Perspectives and Trends in Education and Technology. Smart Innovation, Systems and Technologies, vol 256. Springer, Singapore. (2022). https://doi.org/10.1007/978-981-16-5063-5_4
2. WHO Homepage, WHO News Timeline. https://www.who.int/news/item/27-04-2020-who-timeline---covid-19 Accessed 17 May 2022
3. The challenges of education in Mexico in the face of a pandemic. https://www.cetys.mx/trends/educacion/los-retos-de-la-educacion-en-mexico-ante-una-pandemia/ Accessed 15 Mar 2022
4. Martí, R., Gisbert, M., Larraz, V.: Technological learning and educational management ecosystems. Edutec. Revista Electrónica De Tecnología Educativa **64**(384), 1–17 (2018)
5. Luksha, P., et al.: Ecosistemas Educativos para la Transformación de la Sociedad, Global Education Futures 2018 (2018)
6. Martín-Barbero, J.: La educación desde la comunicación.: Gustavo Gili, México (2002)
7. Sergey, Y., et al.: Economics of digital ecosystems. J. Open Innovation. MDPI (2020)
8. Khtere, A.R., Yousef, A.M.F.: The professionalism of online teaching in Arab Universities. Educ. Technol. Soc. **24**, 1–12 (2021)
9. Gómez-García, G., Hinojo-Lucena, F.-J., Cáceres-Reche, M.-P., Navas-Parejo, M.R.: The contribution of the flipped classroom method to the development of information literacy: a systematic review. Sustainability **12**, 7273 (2020)

10. Al-Rahmi, W., Aldraiweesh, A., Yahaya, N., Kamin, Y.B.: Massive open online courses (MOOCS): systematic literature review in Malaysian higher education Waleed Kamin. Int. J. Eng. Technol. **7**(4), 2197-2202, (2018)
11. Aldosari, A.M., Eid, H.F., Chen, Y.-P.P.: A proposed strategy based on instructional design models through an LMS to develop online learning in higher education considering the lock-down period of the COVID-19 PANDEMIC. Sustainability **14**, 7843 (2022). https://doi.org/10.3390/su14137843
12. IPN Education 4.0 Homepage, definition https://e4-0.ipn.mx/educacion-4-0/ Accessed 27 Dec 21
13. Open edX versus Moodle: Understanding the Difference https://edly.io/blog/open-edx-versus-moodle-understanding-the-difference/ Accessed 27 Apr 22
14. Harting, K., Erthal, M.J.: History of distance learning. Inf. Technol. Learn. Perform. J. **23**(1), 35 (2005)
15. Jitpaisarnwattana, N., et al.: Understanding affordances, and limitations in a language MOOC from an activity theory perspective. In: Research and Practice in Technology Enhanced Learning. Springer (2022). https://doi.org/10.1186/s41039-022-00186-y
16. Didactic Digital Resources at DEV IPN. https://www.ipn.mx/assets/files/dev/docs/DII/Clasificacion-RDD.pdf/ Accessed 23 May 2022
17. MOOC building platforms. https://www.learndash.com/5-mooc-building-platforms/ Accessed 19 July 22
18. Shah: By The Numbers: MOOCS in 2016. MOOCs 2016, (December 25) (2016)

Implementation of Time-Frequency Moments for the Classification of Atrial Fibrillation Sequences Through a Bidirectional Long-Short Term Memory Network

Christian García-Aquino[1], Dante Mújica-Vargas[1](✉), Manuel Matuz-Cruz[2], Nimrod Gonzalez-Franco[1], and Gabriel González-Serna[1]

[1] Tecnológico Nacional de México, CENIDET, Cuernavaca, Mexico
{m21ce012,dante.mv}@cenidet.tecnm.mx
[2] Tecnológico Nacional de México, Campus Tapachula, Tapachula, Mexico

Abstract. This article proposes a method to classify atrial fibrillation signals using time-frequency characteristics through a BiLSTM network. The experiment was performed with the ECG signals, which are part of the PhysioNet CinC 2017 database. In addition to the BiLSTM network, machine learning algorithms such as k Nearest Neighbors, Linear SVM, RBF SVM, Decision Tree, Random Forest, Neural Net, AdaBoost, Naive Bayes and QDA were used for the classification experiments. To measure the efficiency and quality of the proposed method, the Accuracy, Precision, Recall, F1 Score metrics were used, as well as the Cohen Kappa score and the Mathews correlation coefficient. The results obtained show a better classification performance in the BiLSTM Network with 93.57%, 92.86%, 94.20%, 93.53%, 1.0 and 1.0 of the mentioned metrics.

Keywords: Atrial fibrillation · Feature extraction · BiLSTM · Time-frequency · ECG · PhysioNet

1 Introduction

Abnormalities of the circulatory system are the most common cardiac disorders addressed with Electrocardiography (ECG). The importance of these studies is motivated by the prevalence, which is relatively high considering that around 3% of the world population suffers from some anomaly. Such is the case that studies have been carried out focused on the classification of Atrial Fibrillation (AF), this being one of the most common types of arrhythmias [1].

In this sense, the use of deep learning has become popular for its classification, abstraction and, above all, learning capabilities that make it attractive in a wide range of approaches that can hardly be solved with conventional computing equipment [2,3]. Consequently, works are emerging that emphasize proposing

M. F. Mata-Rivera et al. (Eds.): WITCOM 2022, CCIS 1659, pp. 201–214, 2022.
https://doi.org/10.1007/978-3-031-18082-8_13

increasingly complex neural network models, so that the computational cost to train these models ends up increasing and ends up resulting in low performance. These limitations can be resolved by focusing on the field of digital signal processing, which would help improve the performance of deep models and would lead to the use of models with a relatively low computational cost for classification tasks.

In the literature, there are approaches to AF classification using LSTM convolutional neural networks (CNN-LSTM) [4], deep residual-jump convolutional neural networks [5], one-dimensional convolutional neural networks (1D-CNN) [6], Hierarchical Attention Networks (HAN) [7], Multiscale Fusion Neural Networks (DMSFNet) [8] and Deep Neural Networks with attention mechanisms [9]. As for classical learning algorithms, there are approaches using AdaBoost [10] and Support Vector Machines (SVM) [11].

Regarding the context of signal processing, there are works that focus on extracting RR peaks from ECGs [12,13], the characterization of heart rate shortage (HRV) [14], the use of the random process correlation function [15], ECG language processing [16], the decomposition of the signal in multiple scales [17], among other existing works in the literature just to mention those that are considered most relevant to the investigation.

As can be seen throughout this section, important approaches have been generated that contribute to the field of AF. However, the use of hybrid neural networks may give the impression of offering good classification performance, but by not employing significant or discriminating features, the models are unable to learn the dependencies of the ECG signals. In this sense, it would also entail an enormous computational cost generated by the model. On the other hand, a correct feature extraction method is not specified since the nature of ECG data is time dependent and such property cannot be exploited in depth.

There is a previous work where the classification of arrhythmias was carried out by extracting artisanal features using the wavelet packet transform and classifying them with classical machine learning algorithms [18]. Therefore, the purpose of this article is to propose a new method to classify AF this time using time-frequency characteristics. The main idea of this approach is to carry out a robust and efficient treatment of ECG signals by generating Spectrograms, which will allow us to obtain time-frequency moments to improve the performance of a Deep Hybrid Neural Network and reduce the computational cost.

The rest of this document is organized as follows. In Sect. 2, a brief introduction to the short-term fourier transform, as well as the classification algorithms used during the experimentation. The method of implementation for the classification of Atrial Fibrillation is indicated in Sect. 3. The results obtained from the experiments and a comparative analysis are presented in Sect. 4. Conclusions are mentioned in the final section and future work is described.

2 Background

2.1 Recurrent Neural Networks

Recurrent Neural Networks (RNN) are used to analyze data that changes over time. Commonly used for speech recognition, image subtitles or character prediction for source code generation [19]. To allow the network to store and access input histories, recursive connections are introduced to predict the current time step and transferring that prediction to the next step as an input. According to Fig. 1, an RNN model has the same structure as the classic ANN models, with an input layer, n hidden layers and an output layer, without forgetting the parameter t corresponding to time, being x_{t-1}, x_t and x_{t+1} are the inputs of the RNN model at different instants of time.

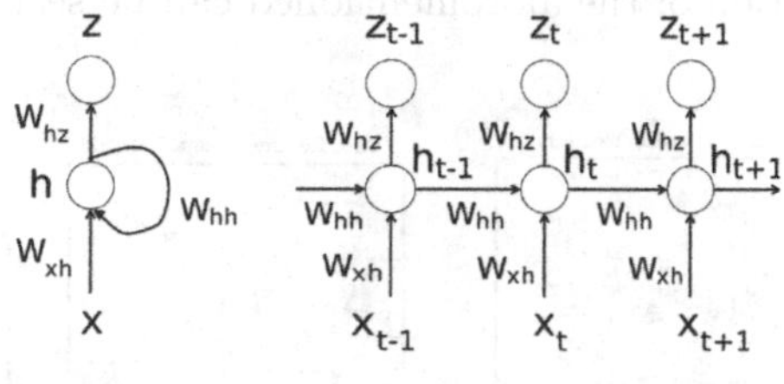

Fig. 1. Basic structure of an RNN [19].

In the most basic form of an RNN, its learning function is found in the Eq. 1 for the hidden layers and in the Eq. 2 for the output layer.

$$h[t] = f(W_x^h(x[t] + b_h) + W_h^h(h[t-1] + b_h)) \tag{1}$$

$$y[t] = g(W_h^o(h[t] + b_o)) \tag{2}$$

2.2 Short Time Fourier Transform

The Short Time Fourier Transform (STFT) is responsible for analyzing non-stationary signals through the Fourier Transform (TF). Where the STFT consists of dividing the signal into small time segments in such a way that it can be assumed that for each segment the signal is stationary, and thus calculate the TF in each portion of the signal, which is taken as a window that slides along the time axis, resulting in a two-dimensional representation of the signal [20]. Mathematically, it is written as:

$$STFTx(t) = X(\tau, \omega) = \int_{-\infty}^{\infty} x(t)w(t-\tau)\, e^{-j\omega t}dt \tag{3}$$

where $w(t)$ is the Hann or Gaussian hill window function initialized at 0 and $x(t)$ is the input signal to transform, $X(\tau, \omega)$ is essentially the TF of $x(t)$, $w(t-\tau)$ is a complex function that represents the phase and magnitude of the signal over time and frequency. Concurrently the instantaneous phase is used in conjunction with the time axis τ and the frequency axis ω to suppress any resulting phase jump discontinuities in the STFT. The time index τ is normally considered a "slow" time and is usually not expressed with as high a resolution as the time t.

3 Implementation

In order to classify arrhythmias, a methodology for classifying electrocardiographic signals is analyzed in this section, starting with their acquisition and the segmentation of the QRS complexes present. Likewise, the process of extraction of statistical characteristics is analyzed, which are subjected to a dimensionality reduction. Finally, the classification is performed with machine learning algorithms. A description of the aforementioned can be seen in Fig 2.

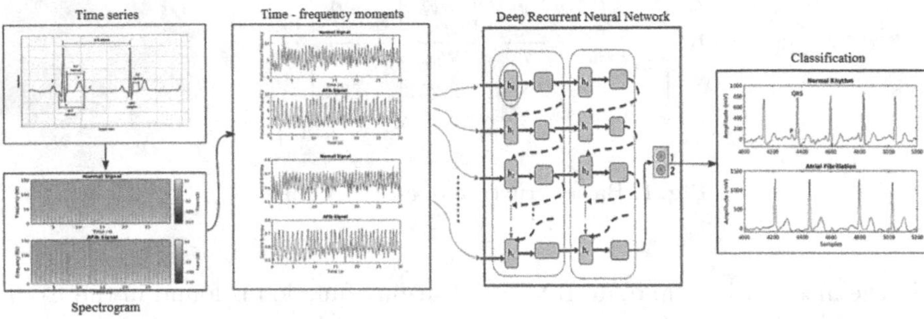

Fig. 2. Proposed classification method

3.1 Data Acquisition/Segmentation

For the experimentation of this research, the ECG data of the PhysioNet 2017 Challenge [21] were used, which consist of a set of ECG signals sampled 300 Hz and divided by a group of experts, which are classified as Normal (N), AFib (A), Noisy signal (~), and Other signal (O). The reason for using this data set is because it mainly contains the two classes that interest us for the classification tasks, these being: Normal (N), AFib (A), added to the fact that the characteristic of the ECG signals is that they are of a single derivation and the duration in seconds of an individual signal is mostly around 30 s. A graphic representation of the signals present in the ECG's can be seen in Fig. 3.

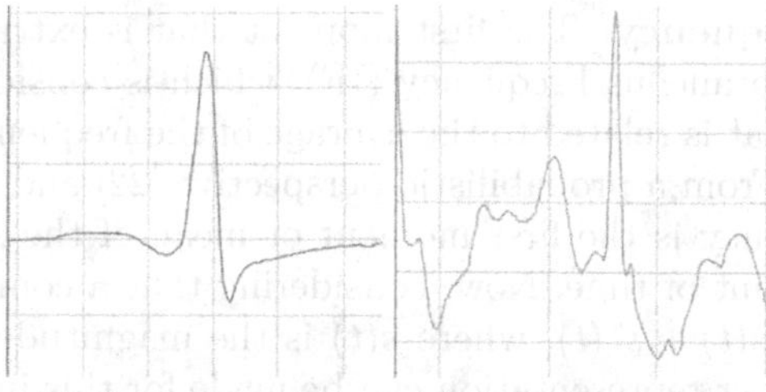

(a) Normal Signal (b) Signal with AF

Fig. 3. Signals from the selected database.

3.2 Feature Extraction

The next step after acquiring the signals and segmenting them is the generation of Spectrograms using the STFT, which will serve to extract specific characteristics such as the Time-Frequency moments, which for the work in question was considered the first moment as the Frequency Instantaneous and the second as Spectral Entropy.

Spectrograms. The spectrogram is a visual representation to identify variations in the frequency and intensity of a signal over a period of time. In this sense, to generate the spectrogram of an ECG signal, the STFT (Eq. 3) is used for continuous signals due to the nature of ECGs. To represent the series of spectra located in time by the STFT, the spectrogram is expressed as the squared series of the STFT of said spectra as $|X(k,l)|^2$.

Therefore, for the construction of the spectrogram, the power of each spectrum is shown segment by segment, representing the magnitudes side by side as an image with a magnitude-dependent color map, as illustrated in Fig. 4.

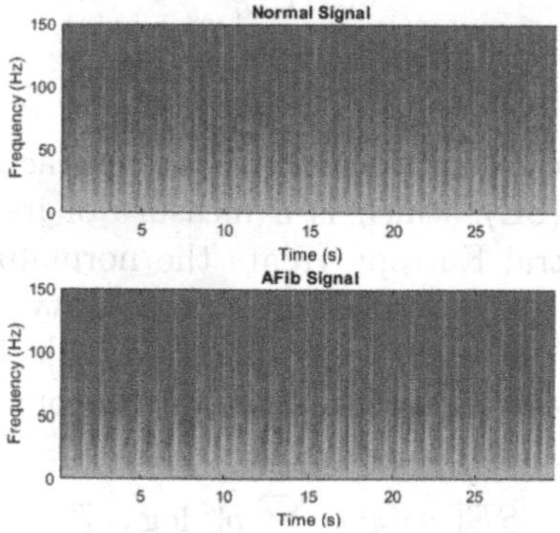

Fig. 4. Representation of a spectrogram of a normal signal and with FA.

Instantaneous Frequency. The first moment that is extracted from a spectrogram is the Instantaneous Frequency (IF), which is considered as a variable parameter in time that is related to the average of the frequencies present in the signal as it evolves. From a probabilistic perspective [22] and [23] show that the instantaneous frequency is the first moment or mean of the spectral density of the signal at an instant of time. Now, considering that a complex signal can be expressed as $\hat{s}(t) = s(t) + s^*(t)$, where $s(t)$ is the magnitude of the signal and $s^*(t)$ its phase, a better representation can be made for this investigation, so the complex signal representation is rewritten as:

$$\hat{s}(t) = A(t) + \exp^{\theta(t)} \tag{4}$$

Inferring that if the real terms of a complex signal are known or can be calculated, then the magnitude (time) $A(t)$ and instantaneous phase $\theta(t)$ of the signal can be found as:

$$A(t) = \sqrt{s^2(t) + s^{*2}(t)} = |S(t)| \quad and \tag{5}$$

$$\theta(t) = \arctan(\frac{s^*(t)}{s(t)}) \tag{6}$$

The phase variation with time is related to the angular frequency of the signal and is called the instantaneous angular frequency [24], Expressed another way, the instantaneous angular frequency is the derivative with respect to the phase time, expressed as:

$$\frac{d}{dt}\theta(t) = \omega(t) \tag{7}$$

In the case of this investigation, it is necessary to know the frequency, instead of the angular frequency, so the relationship between frequency and angular frequency $f = \omega/2\pi$ is used, with which the instantaneous frequency of a spectrogram using the expression [25]:

$$f(t) = \frac{1}{2\pi}\frac{d}{dt}\theta(t) \tag{8}$$

Spectral Entropy. The second moment that is extracted from a spectrogram is the spectral entropy (SE), which is a measure of its spectral power distribution. Therefore, Spectral Entropy treats the normalized power distribution of the signal in the frequency domain as a probability distribution and calculates the uncertainty or entropy of the spectrum [26]. Therefore, knowing the time-frequency power spectrogram, the Spectral Entropy in time is obtained by:

$$SE(m) = -\sum_{k=1}^{w} p_k^m \log_2 p_k^m \tag{9}$$

where again m is the window index, w is the duration of the windows and p_k^m is the Probability Mass Function (PMF) that corresponds to the m-th window, obtained from the power spectral density or also known as the spectrogram ($S^m(\omega_k)$)

$$p_k^m = \frac{S^m(\omega_k)}{\sum_{j=1}^{w} S^m(\omega_j)} \tag{10}$$

In this way, the function p_k^m is in charge of verifying the necessary condition of the FMPs: $\sum_k p_k^m = 1$. With the normalization carried out in (4.15), a measure is obtained that is independent of the total power of the signal, and therefore the SE is independent of the amplitude.

3.3 Training/Classification

The network with which we worked in this research is given by a Deep Learning Neural Network model, specifically, a Network with Bidirectional Short and Long Term Memory (BiLSTM). The architecture is initially formed with a sequence input layer, a bidirectional LSTM layer (BiLSTM) proposed by [27] formed by two LSTM hidden layers [28] to learn the bidirectional long-term dependencies between time steps, a third fully connected layer to obtain the probabilities of belonging to the different classes, a Softmax layer to represent the probabilities through a categorical distribution, and finally a classification layer. The architecture diagram can be seen in Fig. 5.

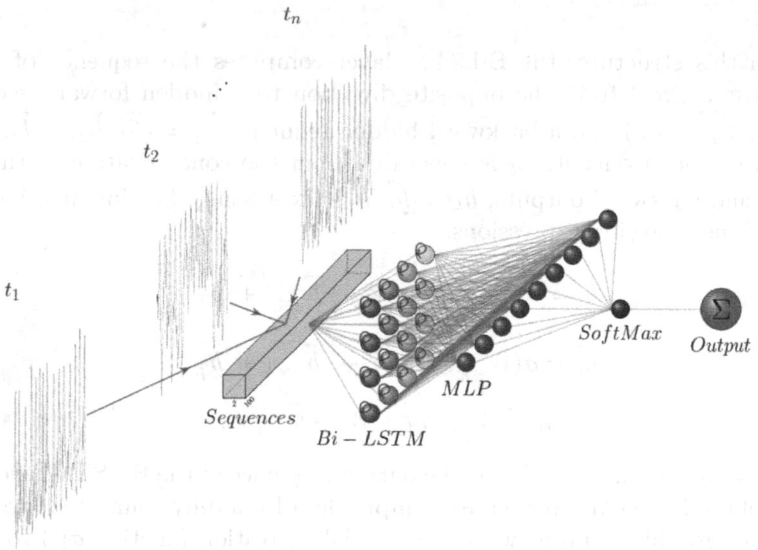

Fig. 5. Bidirectional LSTM hybrid neural network.

The model has two inputs $x = (x_1, x_2, ..., x_t)$ according to the two extracted features, where t is the length of the input signal to through time. These serve as input for the BiLSTM layer, which consists of 2 hidden LSTM layers with 100 neurons each. Since a single LSTM layer can only memorize past tenses which makes it impossible to memorize future tenses, to overcome this characteristic deficiency, in they proposed Bidirectional Recurrent Neural Networks (BiRNN) to be able to combine two hidden LSTM layers separated in directions opposite but always pointing to the same exit. The internal structure of a BiLSTM layer can be seen in Fig. 6.

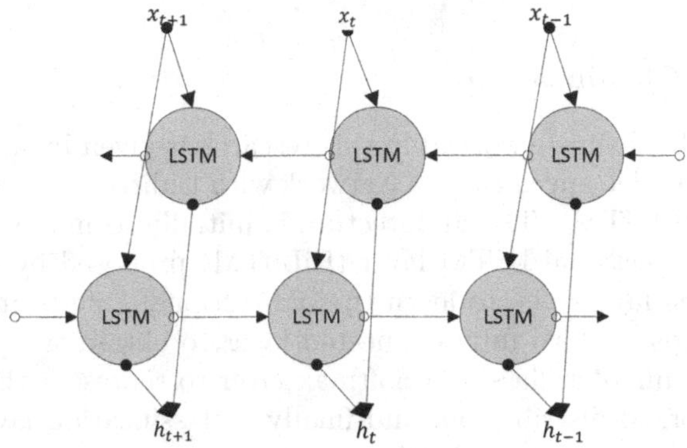

Fig. 6. Internal structure of a BiLSTM layer.

With this structure, the BiLSTM layer computes the sequence of inputs $x = (x_1, x_2, ..., x_n)$ from the opposite direction to a hidden forward sequence $\overrightarrow{h} = (\overrightarrow{h_1}, \overrightarrow{h_2}, ..., \overrightarrow{h_n})$ and a backward hidden sequence $\overleftarrow{h} = (\overleftarrow{h_1}, \overleftarrow{h_2}, ..., \overleftarrow{h_n})$. The encoded vector of outputs h_t is generated from the concatenation of the final forward and backward outputs, $h_t = [\overrightarrow{h_t}, \overleftarrow{h_t}]$. Expressing the aforementioned by means of the following expressions.

$$\overrightarrow{h_t} = \sigma(W_{x\overrightarrow{h}} x_t + W_{\overrightarrow{h}\overrightarrow{h}} \overrightarrow{h}_{t-1} + b_{\overrightarrow{h}}) \tag{11}$$

$$\overleftarrow{h_t} = \sigma(W_{x\overleftarrow{h}} x_t + W_{\overleftarrow{h}\overleftarrow{h}} \overleftarrow{h}_{t+1} + b_{\overleftarrow{h}}) \tag{12}$$

$$h_t = W_{y\overrightarrow{h}} \overrightarrow{h}_t + W_{y\overleftarrow{h}} \overleftarrow{h}_t + b_h \tag{13}$$

where $h = (h_1, h_2, ..., h_t, ..., h_n)$ is the output sequence of the BiLSTM layer. The output of the BiLSTM layer serves as input data for a fully connected layer with 100 perceptron-like neurons with a sigmoidal activation function $\sigma(\cdot)$ to generate outputs bounded at $[0, 1]$, this activation function is the one that is regularly used, however, other types of functions can be used depending on the criteria of each researcher. The output of the fully connected layer is passed through a softmax function to transform (normalize) these outputs to a probability distribution representation such that the sum of all probabilities of the outputs is 1

[31]. Defined in the following expression.

$$f(y_n) = \frac{\exp(y_n)}{\sum_{k=1}^{K} \exp(y_n)} \tag{14}$$

Finally, there is a classification layer to determine if the output obtained belongs to the class of signals with Atrial Fibrillation or signals with normal beats.

4 Experimentation and Results

Computational performance and cost for FA classification are quantified and compared using the CinC 2017 database obtained from PhysioNet. The experimentation was carried out in a computer equipment that consists of an Intel (R) Core (TM) i7-10870H CPU @ 2.20 GHz with 8 cores and 16 GB of RAM; as well as an NVIDIA RTX 3060 GPU, with 3840 CUDA cores and 6 GB of dedicated VRAM. The implementation was developed in MATLAB and other experimentations with classic machine learning algorithms were carried out in Python using the Scikit-learn library. To know the behavior of the proposed method in the proposed Hybrid Architecture compared to other machine learning approaches, algorithms such as Nearest Neighbors, Linear SVM, RBF SVM, Decision Tree, Random Forest, Neural Net, AdaBoost, Naïve Bayes and QDA.

4.1 Metrics

In order to carry out the objective evaluation of the proposed method for the classification of cardiac arrhythmias, 3 aspects were considered, which are mentioned below:

The confusion matrix was considered to evaluate the performance of a classification model, the weighting of correct and incorrect predictions are summarized with the count values and separated by class. This set of predictions are interpreted through metrics derived from the confusion matrix such as: Accuracy, Precision, Recall and F1-Score that are detailed in [32]. The Cohen's Kappa Score (KCS) is used to compare the observed agreement in a data set with respect to the expected agreement as mentioned in [33]. The Mathews Correlation Coefficient (MCC) is a contingency matrix method used to calculate Pearson's product-moment correlation coefficient between actual and predicted values, as discussed in [34].

4.2 Results

Taking into account the signals of the data set, the division was made in a data set for training, designating 90% and the rest in a test set. Both the training set and the test set were augmented in order to normalize the amount of data in both classes, and as can be seen in Table 4, 4438 training instances were obtained, as well as 490 test instances, which is summarized in Table 1.

Table 1. Split signals for training and testing.

Label	Data train	Data test
Normal	4438	490
Atrial fibrillation	4438	490

A first experimentation was carried out using the raw time series of the database in order to observe the classification behavior of the algorithms when using unprocessed signals.

Table 2. Performance results with raw data.

Algorithm/Arquitecture	Accuracy	Precision	Recall	F1-Score	CKS	MCC
Nearest Neighbors	0.5051	0.5149	0.5051	0.4079	0.0	0.0
Linear SVM	0.4949	0.4934	0.4949	0.4646	0.0	0.0
RBF SVM	0.5	0.25	0.5	0.3333	0.0	0.0
Decision Tree	0.5582	0.5734	0.5582	0.534	0.0	0.0
Random Forest	0.5214	0.5228	0.5214	0.5143	0.0	0.0
Neural Net	0.5204	0.5529	0.5204	0.4334	0.0	0.0
AdaBoost	0.5265	0.53	0.5265	0.5125	0.0	0.0
Naive Bayes	0.5102	0.5112	0.5102	0.4994	0.0	0.0
QDA	0.5	0.25	0.5	0.3333	0.0	0.0
Proposed	**0.5786**	**0.7000**	**0.5632**	**0.6242**	**0.0**	**0.0**

The average quantitative summary for each method and metric considered in the experimentation is presented in Table 2. From the results obtained, it is noteworthy to observe that the hybrid model used had the best classification performance despite being raw data, in contrast to classical machine learning algorithms where it can be seen that in some metrics I have a performance below 0.30, which shows that the algorithms did not reach a convergence in training and according to the literature, the value for an implementation to be acceptable it must be at least 0.80.

Now, for the second experimentation, the time-frequency characteristics proposed in this research work were used to observe the behavior and demonstrate an increase in the classification performance of the algorithms.

Table 3. Performance results of the proposed classification method.

Algorithm/Arquitecture	Accuracy	Precision	Recall	F1-Score	CKS	MCC
Nearest Neighbors	0.8199	0.8199	0.8199	0.8199	1.0	1.0
Linear SVM	0.574	0.5794	0.574	0.5665	0.0	0.0
RBF SVM	0.5	0.25	0.5	0.3333	0.0	0.0
Decision Tree	0.6357	0.636	0.6357	0.6355	0.0	0.0
Random Forest	0.6168	0.6236	0.6168	0.6115	0.0	0.0
Neural Net	0.6724	0.757	0.6724	0.6431	0.0	0.0
AdaBoost	0.6393	0.6425	0.6393	0.6372	0.0	0.0
Naive Bayes	0.6061	0.6093	0.6061	0.6033	0.0	0.0
QDA	0.5378	0.7067	0.5378	0.419	0.0	0.0
Proposed	**0.9357**	**0.9286**	**0.9420**	**0.9353**	**1.0**	**1.0**

The average quantitative summary for each method and metric considered in the experimentation is presented in Table 3. From the results obtained, it is noteworthy to observe that the hybrid model used once again had the best classification performance, surpassed even in all the metrics used the 0.90 in classification performance, in contrast to the classical machine learning algorithms where it can be seen that most of them had a performance below 0.80, due to the fact that the extracted features are in the time and frequency domain, are time dependent for which these classification algorithms were not designed. In addition to the above, it can also be verified that classical algorithms have a particular problem known as the performance plateau, which consists in that the greater the data load to train and evaluate said algorithms, the performance is truncated.

As a final part of the experimentations and another of the objectives of this research, the computational cost of each algorithm was calculated at the time of classifying the set of tests.

Table 4. Computational cost of classification.

Algorithm/Arquitecture	With raw data (in seconds)	With the proposed method (in seconds)
Nearest Neighbors	9.96	1.95
Linear SVM	13.99	5.27
RBF SVM	64.28	8.14
Decision Tree	**0.08**	**0.008**
Random Forest	0.08	0.009
Neural Net	0.39	0.02
AdaBoost	1.17	0.07
Naive Bayes	0.18	0.01
QDA	9.73	0.06
Proposed	**6.41**	**0.35**

As can be seen in Table 4, the computational cost of the algorithms and architectures considered was measured. The experimentation was performed by classifying the raw test dataset and the test dataset with the applied method. According to the results obtained, it was observed that the proposed architecture had a lower computational cost compared to classical machine learning algorithms. Although it is true that there were algorithms that seemed to have a lower computational cost, such as the case of the Decision Tree, however, according to the poor classification performance that can be seen in the previous table, the malfunction of said algorithm when classifying AF is evident.

5 Conclusions

In this research work, a method for the classification of Atrial Fibrillation and Normal Beats was proposed. The results obtained showed that the correct treatment of the signals, specifically, the use of time-frequency characteristics, improves the training process of the classification algorithms used during the investigation, also suggesting that the proposed Hybrid Neural Architecture obtained the best performance. For the classification of arrhythmias, since although algorithms such as k -Nearest Neighbors, the Decision Trees, despite being characterized as multiclass classification algorithms, do not manage to overcome the performance of the Hybrid Neural Architecture proposed when analyzing ECG signals, due to the aforementioned performance plateau that reduces their performance, which, apart from using other types of features, another of the objectives with respect to the previous work was to use deep learning algorithms. As future work, the implementation of the proposed method in low consumption embedded cards will be carried out in order to conceive a portable and remote system, in addition to improving processing times, in such a way that the system can work as close as possible to real time.

Acknowledgments. This work was supported by the Tecnológico Nacional de México/CENIDET trough the project entitled "Clasicador para detectar brilación auricular en señales electrocardiográcas utilizando una red recurrente profunda entrenada con momentos de tiempo-frecuencia", as well as by CONACYT.

References

1. Miyasaka, Y., Barnes, M.E., Gersh, B.J., Cha, S.S., Bailey, K.R., Abhayaratna, W.P., et al.: Secular trends in incidence of atrial fibrillation in Olmsted County, Minnesota, 1980 to 2000, and implications on the projections for future prevalence. Circulation **114**, 119–25 (2006)
2. Bartlett, P.L.: The sample complexity of pattern classification with neural networks: the size of the weights is more important than the size of the network. IEEE Trans. Inf. Theory **44**(2), 525–536 (1998)

3. Akesson, B.M., Toivonen, H.T.: A neural network model predictive controller. J. Process Control **16**(9), 937–946 (2006)
4. Wu, X., Sui, Z., Chu, C.-H., Huang, G.: Detection of atrial fibrillation from short ECG signals using a hybrid deep learning model. In: Chen, H., Zeng, D., Yan, X., Xing, C. (eds.) ICSH 2019. LNCS, vol. 11924, pp. 269–282. Springer, Cham (2019). https://doi.org/10.1007/978-3-030-34482-5_24
5. Sanjana, K., Sowmya, V., Gopalakrishnan, E.A., Soman, K.P.: Performance improvement of deep residual skip convolution neural network for atrial fibrillation classification. In: Bhateja, V., Peng, S.L., Satapathy, S.C., Zhang, Y.D. (eds.) Evolution in Computational Intelligence. AISC, vol. 1176, pp. 755–763. Springer, Singapore (2021). https://doi.org/10.1007/978-981-15-5788-0_71
6. Tutuko, B., Nurmaini, S., Tondas, A.E., et al.: AFibNet: an implementation of atrial fibrillation detection with convolutional neural network. BMC Med. Inform. Decis. Mak. **21**, 216 (2021). https://doi.org/10.1186/s12911-021-01571-1
7. Mousavi, S., Afghah, F., Acharya, U.R.: Han-ECG: an interpretable atrial fibrillation detection model using hierarchical attention networks. Comput. Biol. Med. **127**, 104057 (2020)
8. Wang, R., Fan, J., Li, Y.: Deep multi-scale fusion neural network for multi-class arrhythmia detection. IEEE J. Biomed. Health Inform. **24**(9), 2461–2472 (2020)
9. Kuvaev, A., Khudorozhkov, R.: An attention-based CNN for ECG classification. In: Arai, K., Kapoor, S. (eds.) CVC 2019. AISC, vol. 943, pp. 671–677. Springer, Cham (2020). https://doi.org/10.1007/978-3-030-17795-9_49
10. Wu, C., Hwang, M., Huang, T.H., et al.: Application of artificial intelligence ensemble learning model in early prediction of atrial fibrillation. BMC Bioinform. **22**, 93 (2021). https://doi.org/10.1186/s12859-021-04000-2
11. Kostka, P., Tkacz, E.: Support vector machine classifier with feature extraction stage as an efficient tool for atrial fibrillation detection improvement. In: Kurzynski, M., Puchala, E., Wozniak, M., Zolnierek, A. (eds.) Computer Recognition Systems 2. ASC, vol. 45, pp. 356–363. Springer, Heidelberg (2007). https://doi.org/10.1007/978-3-540-75175-5_45
12. Kisohara, M., Masuda, Y., Yuda, E., et al.: Optimal length of R-R interval segment window for Lorenz plot detection of paroxysmal atrial fibrillation by machine learning. Biomed. Eng. Online **19**, 49 (2020). https://doi.org/10.1186/s12938-020-00795-y
13. Hickey, B., Heneghan, C., De Chazal, P.: Non-episode-dependent assessment of paroxysmal atrial fibrillation through measurement of RR interval dynamics and atrial premature contractions. Ann. Biomed. Eng. **32**, 677–687 (2004). https://doi.org/10.1023/B:ABME.0000030233.39769.a4
14. Mandal, S., Sinha, N.: Prediction of atrial fibrillation based on nonlinear modeling of heart rate variability signal and SVM classifier. Res. Biomed. Eng. **37**, 725–736 (2021). https://doi.org/10.1007/s42600-021-00175-y
15. Wang, J., Wang, P., Wang, S.: Automated detection of atrial fibrillation in ECG signals based on wavelet packet transform and correlation function of random process. Biomed. Sig. Process. Control **55**, 101662 (2020)
16. Mousavi, S., Afghah, F., Khadem, F., Acharya, U.R.: ECG language processing (ELP): a new technique to analyze ECG signals. Comput. Methods Programs Biomed. **202**, 105959 (2021)
17. Cao, X.-C., Yao, B., Chen, B.-Q.: Atrial fibrillation detection using an improved multiscale decomposition enhanced residual convolutional neural network. IEEE Access **7**, 89152–89161 (2019)

18. García-Aquino, C., Mújica-Vargas, D., Matuz-Cruz, M.: Classification of cardiac arrhythmias using machine learning algorithms. In: Mata-Rivera, M.F., Zagal-Flores, R. (eds.) WITCOM 2021. CCIS, vol. 1430, pp. 174–185. Springer, Cham (2021). https://doi.org/10.1007/978-3-030-89586-0_14
19. Vogt, N.: CNNs, LSTMs, and attention networks for pathology detection in medical data (2019). arXiv preprint arXiv:1912.00852
20. Smith, J. O.: Mathematics of the Discrete Fourier Transform (DFT). W3K Publishing (2007). www.w3k.org/books/
21. Goldberger, A.L., et al.: PhysioBank, PhysioToolkit, and PhysioNet. Circulation **101**(23) (2000)
22. Flandrin, P.: Time-frequency/time-scale analysis (1998)
23. Barnes, A. E.: Instantaneous spectral bandwidth and dominant frequency with applications to seismic reflection data (1993)
24. Taner, M.T., Koehler, F., Sheriff, R.: Complex seismic trace analysis. Geophysics **44**(6), 1041–1063 (1979)
25. Boashash, B.: Estimating and interpreting the instantaneous frequency of a signal. i. fundamentals. Proc. IEEE **80**(4), 520–538 (1992)
26. Pan, Y.N., Chen, J., Li, X.L.: Spectral entropy: a complementary index for rolling element bearing performance degradation assessment. Proc. Inst. Mech. Eng. C J. Mech. Eng. Sci. **223**(5), 1223–1231 (2008)
27. Schuster, M., Paliwal, K.K.: Bidirectional recurrent neural networks. IEEE Trans. Sig. Process. **45**(11), 2673–2681 (1997)
28. Hochreiter, S., Schmidhuber, J.: Long short-term memory. Neural Comput. **9**(8), 1735–1780 (1997)
29. Elman, J.: Language as a dynamical system (2001)
30. Pattanayak, S.: Pro Deep Learning with TensorFlow. Apress, New York (2017)
31. Svensén, M., Bishop, C. M.: Pattern recognition and machine learning (2007)
32. Chen, H., et al.: GasHis-transformer: a multi-scale Visual Transformer approach for gastric histopathology image classification (2021). arXiv:2104.14528
33. Samiuc. www.samiuc.es/estadisticas-variables-binarias/medidas-de-concordancia/kappa-de-cohen/. Accessed 05 July 2021
34. Chicco, D., Jurman, G.: The advantages of the Matthews correlation coefficient (MCC) over F1 score and accuracy in binary classification evaluation. BMC Genom. **21**(1), 6 (2020)

Construction of a Technological Component to Support ISMS for the Detection of Obfuscation in Computer Worm Samples

Hernaldo Salazar(✉) and Cristian Barría

Centro de Investigación en Ciberseguridad CICS, Facultad de Ciencias, Universidad Mayor, Santiago, Providencia, Chile
hernaldo.salazar@mayor.cl, cristian.barria@umayor.cl

Abstract. In the world of malware, there is a category called computer worms, this type has a complex technological structure, but an ability to replicate itself automatically without the intervention of a human and can be distributed to other computers that are connected to the network, with a malicious code that can infect a computer that will later be used to infect others, spreading through the network. This malicious code used by computer worms could be found with ob- obfuscated code that allows it to hide part of its code when analyzed, not being able to classify it. In this framework, the research proposes the creation of a technological component (a piece of software) that allows a faster categorization of computer worms that have obfuscation in their code, proposing the development of a component that allows selecting a malicious file (computer worm) and that through the selection of a rule with the YARA (Yet Another Ridiculous Acronym) tool, verifies the obfuscation in it, having also a button that allows verifying the hash in the Virus Total platform. The purpose of this component is to help and support the Information Security Management Systems for the analysis of malware in investigations of threat intelligence units or cybersecurity teams that need to categorize this type of malware, automating the manual processes and validating the obfuscation in this type of malware.

Keywords: Malware · Computer worm · Obfuscation · Cybersecurity

1 Introduction

Computer worms are a type of malware that present a complex technological structure, having the ability to create replicas of themselves automatically without human interaction and distributing themselves to other computers connected to the network; they have a malicious code component that allows them to infect a computer and then use that computer to infect others, to spread using the network. This cycle repeats itself, increasing the number of infected computers rapidly if action is not taken in time.

M. F. Mata-Rivera et al. (Eds.): WITCOM 2022, CCIS 1659, pp. 215–224, 2022.
https://doi.org/10.1007/978-3-031-18082-8_14

This research is based on the classification of computer worms according to their obfuscation capacity, divided into four levels: species, type, class, and evasion [1]. This base allows devising a construction of a technological component (a piece of software) that allows a faster categorization of computer worms, which helps to understand that through development, manual processes can be automated, validating the obfuscation in this type of malware. That allows the categorization of computer worms more automatically, being more reliable for the user, being its main contribution, the support in the analysis and investigations of the threat intelligence units that need to perform the categorization of this type of malware.

2 Related Work

The main purpose of this section is to present a brief overview of the different classifications of computer worms. In the previous work done [1], it was noted that there are different types of classifications for computer worms. It addressed three taxonomies for the classification of worms, for example, the classification that is based on four main elements, classified as worm structure, worm attack, worm defense, and user defense. Allowing the user to understand how the computer worm acts and how to combat the computer worm [2] or another associated with the computer worm attack [3]. Considering these classifications that are used in different research, there is still no common vision to have a classification based on obfuscation [4].

Figure 1 presents a proposal for the classification of modern computer worms based on obfuscation on four levels, the first is the species, which is based on this type of malware, then there is the type, class, and evasion. With the research carried out through a systematic review, it was possible to arrive at a classification that provides information on the ability of computer worms to remain undetected.

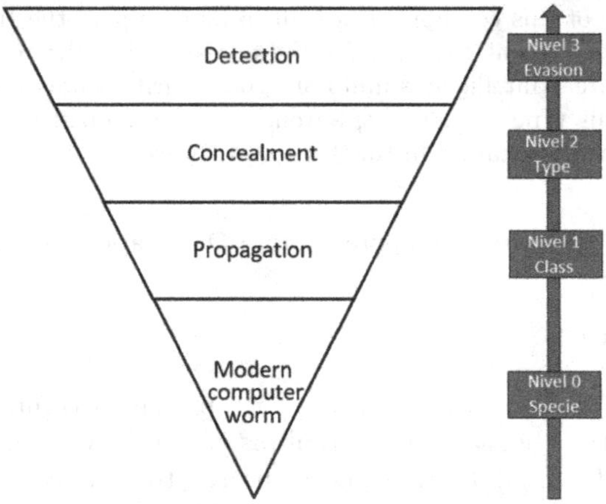

Fig. 1. Classification of computer worms into four categories [1].

3 Construction of a Technological Component

Taking into consideration the need for the development of a technological component, the C# programming language is chosen, with which we proceed to build a tool that allows us to classify computer worms by selecting a sample. The main idea of this is that it will allow us to classify the types of worms that have obfuscation and those that do not, with the main objective of having clarity of the number of computer worms that have their code obfuscated.

Through Visual Studio 2019 community version we built a program with the following features:

- Select any file type through a button.
- Select a rule through a combo box.
- Describe the selected rule in a text box.
- Button to search for the signature on the Virus Total website [7].
- Button to analyze the file.
- Display the result in a text box.

With the development of the application, the following design results were obtained (Fig. 2):

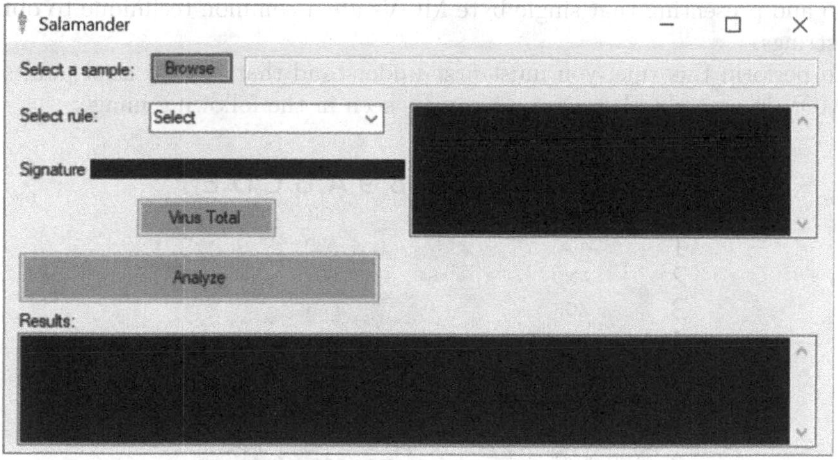

Fig. 2. Design of a program to analyze files.

3.1 Code Obfuscate

To understand what we mean by code obfuscation one could analyze the motive, as this one could understand how to hide data from a person who does not have permission to read or understand the data [5].

To obtain more details on how to obtain an identification of modern computer worms with obfuscation, we chose to work with YARA rules, since this tool was designed for the identification and classification of malware through the creation of rules, allowing the detection of different types of patterns within the analyzed files.

YARA was created by the company VirusTotal and in its official website there is a section describing the tool [6]:

YARA is an open-source tool designed to help malware researchers identify and classify malware samples. It makes it possible to create descriptions (or rules) for malware families based on textual and/or binary patterns. YARA is multi-platform, running on Linux, Windows, and Mac OS X. It can be used through its command-line interface or from Python scripts with the YARA-Python extension.

Already having a tool that allows us to identify Malware, for this research of computer worms, we need a rule that allows us to verify the obfuscation in the code allowing us to classify them.

So, through a search for rules created by companies and researchers, we came up with a rule that was developed by Andreas Schuster [7].

The rule created by this researcher allows to detection of obfuscated strings by single byte mov, with this you could already have an identification using YARA rules.

Andreas Schuster through a presentation made at the FIRST conference in 2014 in which he presents "YARA: An Introduction", in this presentation made by Andreas is a sample of obfuscation by Move Single Byte, in which he explains how to perform a YARA rule by searching the register and addressing mode for 0×45 and presenting that single byte MOVs are a common technique to obfuscate strings.

To perform this rule, you must first understand that the C6 used points to the MOV in assembly language, as can be seen in the following image:

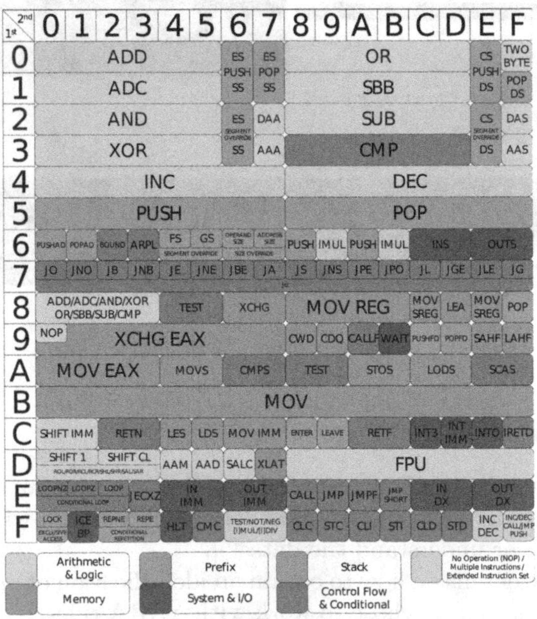

Fig. 3. x86 opcode structure and instruction overview [9].

In the Fig. 3, we can see that C6 is associated with MOV IMM, which indicates that the byte must be moved immediately.

Subsequently, the following is 45 which is defined as [EBP]+disp9 which means that the following value is added, for this reason, in the rule to search for obfuscation of a single byte movement, when it is fulfilled, the file is alerted with the YARA rule shown in Fig. 4.

When trying to explain the obfuscation the main reason why the code of a file, malware, or in this case for the present research "computer worm" is obfuscated is that it is difficult to read, but this might not be a problem for a reverse engineer.

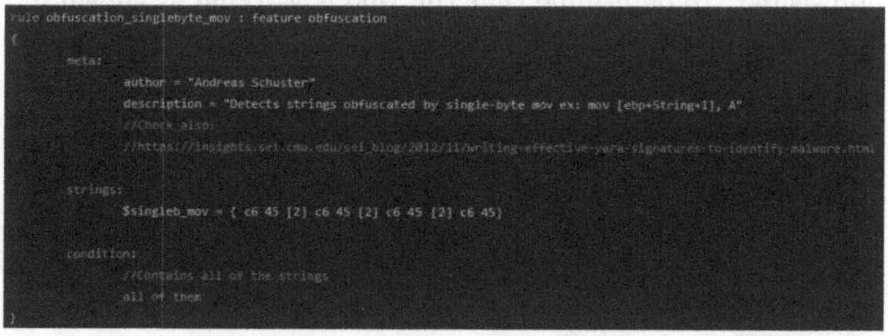

Fig. 4. YARA rule obfuscation single byte move.

Using YARA downloaded from their official website presented in Fig. 5.

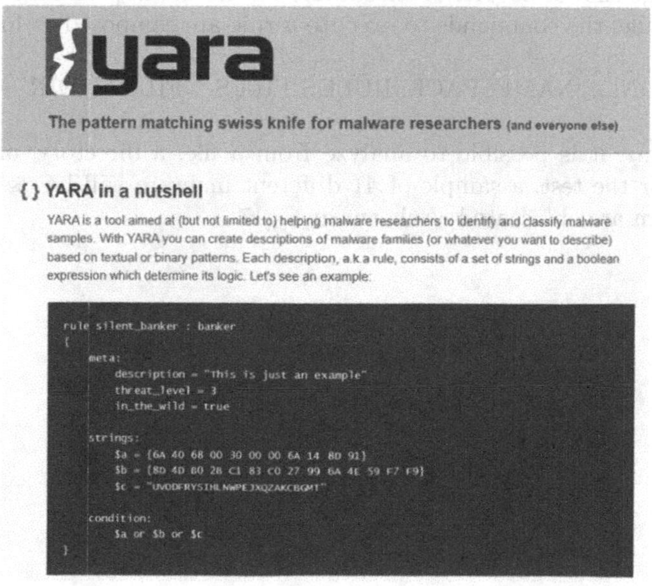

Fig. 5. Website YARA.

It is possible to obtain the tool that allows the manipulation of rules to detect different types of Malware characteristics, for this research we focus on obfuscation, for this reason, is that a test is performed using a virtual machine with the following characteristics:

- Windows 10
- RAM memory 8 GB
- Processor 2 of 4 cores
- 60 GB hard disk

In this virtual machine, we test the use of YARA and the rule to detect obfuscation. This exercise consists of taking malware samples and verifying if they are obfuscated. To determine that the rule is working as shown in Fig. 6.

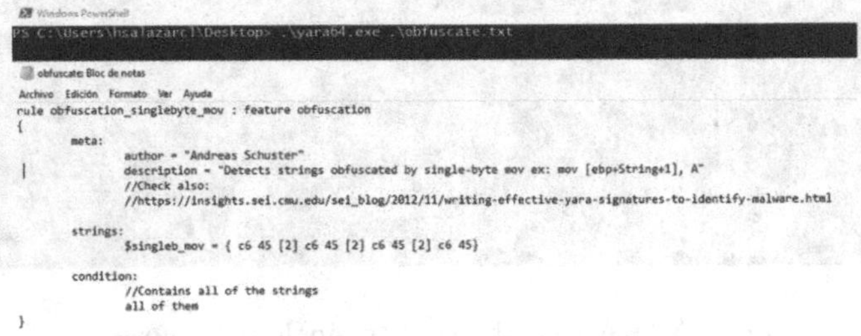
Windows PowerShell
PS C:\Users\hsalazarc1\Desktop> .\yara64.exe .\obfuscate.txt
obfuscate: Bloc de notas
Archivo Edición Formato Ver Ayuda
rule obfuscation_singlebyte_mov : feature obfuscation
{
meta:
author = "Andreas Schuster"
description = "Detects strings obfuscated by single-byte mov ex: mov [ebp+String+1], A"
//Check also:
//https://insights.sei.cmu.edu/sei_blog/2012/11/writing-effective-yara-signatures-to-identify-malware.html
strings:
$singleb_mov = { c6 45 [2] c6 45 [2] c6 45 [2] c6 45}
condition:
//Contains all of the strings
all of them
}

Fig. 6. Website YARA.

This image shows the YARA executable on the desktop and a text file containing the rule, the commands to execute a rule are composed as follows:

Yara [OPTION]... [NAMESPACE:]RULES_FILES... FILE — DIR — PID

In this way, it is possible to analyze from a file, a directory, or a process identifier. For the test, a sample of 41 different malware will be used to verify which of them are obfuscated as shown in Fig. 7.

000	11-07-2021 10:42	Aplicación	6.820 KB
Alerta	11-07-2021 10:42	Aplicación	111 KB
Ana	11-07-2021 10:42	Aplicación	2.123 KB
ArcticBomb	11-07-2021 10:42	Aplicación	126 KB
BlueScreen	11-07-2021 10:42	Aplicación	10 KB
Bolbi	11-07-2021 10:42	Archivo de secuen...	47 KB
BonziKill	11-07-2021 10:42	Documento de te...	1 KB
Carewmr	11-07-2021 10:42	Archivo de secuen...	4 KB
ClassicShell	11-07-2021 10:42	Aplicación	6.982 KB
ColorBug	11-07-2021 10:42	Aplicación	54 KB
DesktopPuzzle	11-07-2021 10:42	Aplicación	240 KB
DudleyTrojan	11-07-2021 10:42	Archivo por lotes ...	1 KB
elite.apk	11-07-2021 10:42	Archivo APK	534 KB
FlashKiller	11-07-2021 10:42	Aplicación	4 KB
Frankenstein.doc	11-07-2021 10:42	Archivo DOC	494 KB
FreeYoutubeDownloader	11-07-2021 10:42	Aplicación	397 KB
Gas	11-07-2021 10:42	Aplicación	18 KB
Grave.apk	11-07-2021 10:42	Archivo APK	561 KB
HMBlocker	11-07-2021 10:42	Aplicación	48 KB
IconDance	11-07-2021 10:42	Aplicación	301 KB
Ilerka.C	11-07-2021 10:42	Aplicación	379 KB
L0Lz	11-07-2021 10:42	Archivo por lotes ...	7 KB
LoveYou	11-07-2021 10:42	Aplicación	22 KB
Malum.apk	11-07-2021 10:42	Archivo APK	2.826 KB
MEMZ	11-07-2021 10:42	Aplicación	15 KB
mobelejen.apk	11-07-2021 10:42	Archivo APK	550 KB
Mobile_Legends_Adventure.apk	11-07-2021 10:42	Archivo APK	4.134 KB
Nostart	11-07-2021 10:42	Aplicación	233 KB
Offiz	11-07-2021 10:42	Archivo JavaScript	3 KB
PCToaster	11-07-2021 10:42	Aplicación	412 KB
Sevgi.a	11-07-2021 10:42	Aplicación	204 KB
TaskILL	11-07-2021 10:42	Aplicación	31 KB
VeryFun	11-07-2021 10:42	Aplicación	3.104 KB
vi4a.apk	11-07-2021 10:42	Archivo APK	38 KB
Whiter.a	11-07-2021 10:42	Aplicación	56 KB

Fig. 7. Sample of 41 different malwares.

When the YARA rule is executed, we will get a message of the file that complies with it and that will be the one that is obfuscated as shown in Fig. 8.

Fig. 8. YARA rule execution.

As this test was through a laboratory that was created to perform a rule testing exercise, this rule must work in an executable type of tool that allows any user to check the obfuscation of a computer worm and classify it.

3.2 Use of YARA Ruler in Worm Analysis Tool

The use of YARA with the rule to identify obfuscation of a single byte movement can be performed through a prompt if you work from Windows 10, but in this way, you should have an isolated virtual machine to perform the tests on samples. And for this research, we worked on the development of a tool that allows performing this task, but through a desktop executable in this way only performing the execution of this can detect code obfuscation in computer worms.

The tool was developed in the C# programming language and its operation is based on YARA to classify computer worms. This tool was named "Salamander" as shown in Fig. 9.

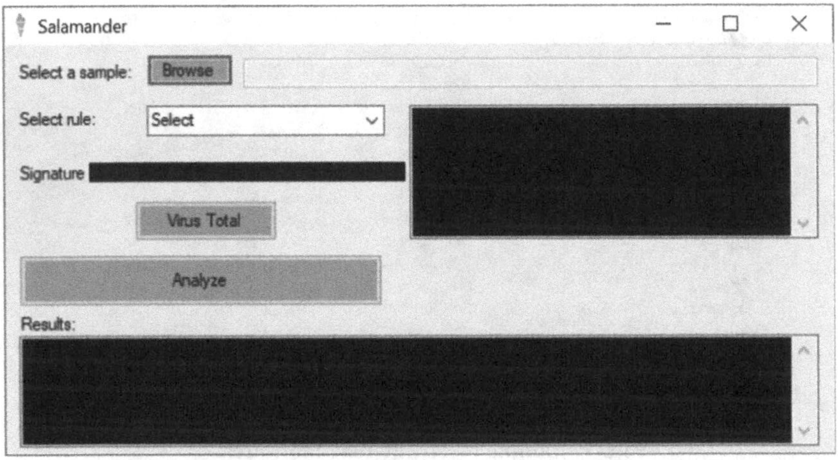

Fig. 9. Technological component, piece of software named Salamander.

Its main objective is to determine whether a computer worm has obfuscation, but it can also obtain its hash and perform a query to the Virus Total platform. This allows a broader analysis of the sample.

This tool works as follows, first select the sample to analyze, then choose the rule, in this case, the only one that is obfuscation and presents a description of the rule. The tool shows us the signature of this and a button to be able to consult the Virus Total website if the sample is cataloged as malicious by the antivirus brands. Finally, by clicking on the Analyze button we are presented with the result of whether the sample has obfuscated code, if it is negative, we get a message "No data" as shown in Fig. 10.

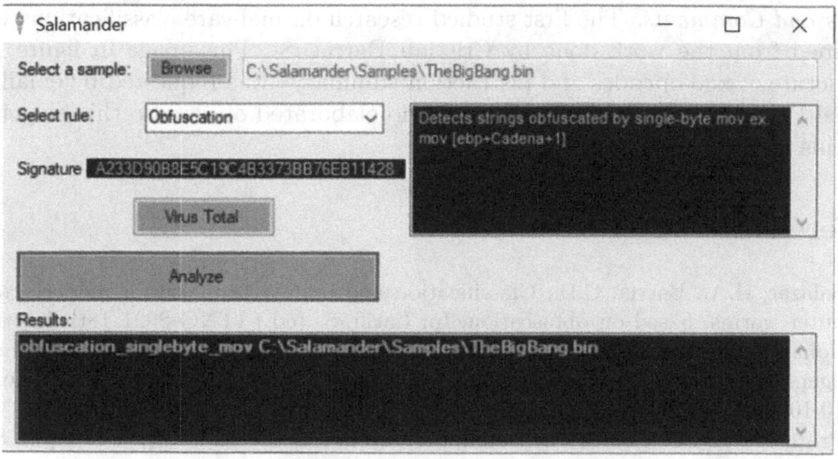

Fig. 10. Proof of concept salamander software.

4 Conclusion and Discussion

This research can be concluded with the development of a piece of software using the programming language C#, which through the use of YARA rules allows automated functionalities for the detection of obfuscation in the code using the analysis of samples of different specimens. Considering the above, the creation of a program that allows the detection of obfuscation in samples of computer worms was achieved.

The developed software improves the function of obtaining a result when analyzing a computer worm, increasing the effectiveness of the proposed classification model through the inverted pyramid.

The development of this technological component was taken as the research that worked on the development of a new proposal for the classification of modern computer worms based on obfuscation patterns [1].

5 Work Future

In future work, it is proposed to extend the development of the software piece so that it can store other types of rules, for example, to detect the type of packaging, not only for computer worms but also for other types of malware. Also, as a complement, a growth framework could be defined for people with different levels of knowledge in the area, who work in security teams, based on Mitre ATT&CK techniques used by APT type groups. This is expected to achieve a good balance between the software developed and the framework to be defined.

Notes and Comments. The first studied research on malware classifications was obtained from the work done by Cristian Barria [8]. The image in figure no. "Structure of x86 opcodes and instruction summary" was requested by email to Daniel Plohmann since he was the one who elaborated on it, also this one cites it in his research [9].

References

1. Salazar, H.A., Barría, C.D.: Classification and update proposal for modern computer worms, based on obfuscation. In: Latifi, S. (ed.) ITNG 2021 18th International Conference on Information Technology-New Generations. Advances in Intelligent Systems and Computing, vol. 1346. Springer, Cham (2021). https://doi.org/10.1007/978-3-030-70416-2_7
2. Pratama, A., Rafrastara, F.A.: Computer worm classification. Int. J. Comput. Sci. Inf. Secur. **10**, 21–24 (2012)
3. Khan, M.H., Khan, I.R.: Malware detection and analysis. Int. J. Adv. Res. Comput. Sci. 1147–1149 (2017). https://doi.org/10.26483/ijarcs.v8i5.3660
4. Barría, C., Cordero, D., Cubillos, C., Palma, M., Cabrera, D.: Obfuscation-based malware update, a comparison of manual and automated methods. Int. J. Comput. Commun. Control **12**(4), 461–474 (2017). https://doi.org/10.15837/ijccc.2017.4.2961
5. Yara rules: an Introduction. www.first.org/resources/papers/conference2014/first_2014_-_schuster-_andreas_-_yara_basic_and_advanced_20140619.pdf. Accessed 17 July 2022
6. Mohanta A., Saldanha A.: Malware packers. In: Malware Analysis and Detection Engineering. Apress, Berkeley, CA, pp. 189–191 (2020). https://doi.org/10.1007/978-1-4842-6193-4_7
7. VirusTotal. http://virustotal.github.io/yara/. Accessed 17 July 2022
8. Barría, C., Cordero, D., Cubillos, C., Palma, M.: Proposed classification of malware, based on obfuscation. In: 6th International Conference on Computers Communications and Control (ICCCC), pp. 37–44 (2016). https://doi.org/10.1109/ICCCC.2016.7496735
9. Plohmann, D., Bilstein, F.: YARA-Signator: automated generation of code-based YARA rules. J. Cybercrime Digital Invest. Botconf **5**, 9 (2019)
10. Sulieman, S.M.A., Fadlalla, Y.A.: Detecting zero-day polymorphic worm: a review. In: 21st Saudi Computer Society National Computer Conference (NCC), pp. 1–7 (2018). https://doi.org/10.1109/NCG.2018.8593085
11. Huidobro, C.B.: Nuevos espacios de seguridad nacional. cómo proteger la información en el ciberespacio, Ediciones UM (2020)
12. García, R.G.: Reversing Ingeniería Inversa. Ra-ma Editorial, Teoría y aplicación, Ediciones de la U (2017)

Design and Implementation of an Interactive Photoplethysmography and Galvanic Skin Response Based Gamepad

Alejandro Sánchez-Sánchez[1,2], Mauricio Gabriel Orozco-del-Castillo[1,2(✉)], and Alejandro Castillo-Atoche[3]

[1] Departamento de Sistemas y Computación, Tecnológico Nacional de México/IT de Mérida, Mérida, México
mauricio.orozco@itmerida.edu.mx

[2] Association for the Advancement of Artificial Intelligence, AAAI Student Chapter at Yucatán México (AAAIMX), Mérida, México

[3] Faculty of Engineering, Autonomous University of Yucatan, 97203 Mérida, Yucatan, Mexico

Abstract. Mental disorders in the young adult population are becoming more frequent, largely due to the COVID-19 pandemic. This has led to the need to find new ways to adapt to therapeutic methods, offering greater attractiveness for this age range, and in many studies, it has been reported that this can be achieved thanks to video games. In this work, a controller design for video games that allows to obtain some of the most relevant biological signals of the relationship between the physiological state and the mental state of the user is proposed. An accessible and non-invasive instrument was built, in the form of a video game controller, to make measurements of heart rate and the galvanic response of the skin, two physiological variables that play a vital role in determining a person's emotional state, that allows, in turn, to play video games that are designed to be able to perform actions based on the measurements of biosignals, such as modifying the difficulty, improving the user experience, etc. Making use of two biosignal sensors (photoplethysmography and galvanic skin response), the controller is developed to offer non-invasive biofeedback while playing computer video games, which provides an effective approach to developing interactive and customizable diagnostic and therapeutic psychological tools. This work, which involves the unification of various ideas and fields, could mean an advance in the field of the development of digital alternatives for therapies related to mental health, as well as a tool that allows a greater approach on the part of the community to which it is focused. This may mean that, in future developments, there is greater cohesion and a greater boom in treatments for people considered young adults.

Keywords: Biofeedback · Gamepad · Software · Video games

1 Introduction

Facing the increase in global cases of mental illnesses worldwide in the wake of the COVID-19 pandemic [1], a need for prevention has arisen in a wide range of ages.

M. F. Mata-Rivera et al. (Eds.): WITCOM 2022, CCIS 1659, pp. 225–236, 2022.
https://doi.org/10.1007/978-3-031-18082-8_15

As there is a wide spectrum of these conditions listed in the Diagnostic and Statistical Manual of Mental Disorders, Fifth Edition (DSM-V) [2], it has been shown that there is a relationship between the emotional state of an individual with the physical manifestation of the respective symptoms through nervous stimuli and electrical responses generated (also called biosignals) [3]. Thus, an analysis of the response of the psyche can be carried out through the biosignals present in the human body, such as heart rate (HR) and the galvanic skin response (GSR) as a measure of the conductance altered by the sweating of the skin [4].

Since a large part of the people affected by the different psychological disorders are young adults (people between 18 and 27 years old) [5], one of the biggest interests in this age range during the pandemic is the entertainment industry, specifically video games [6], which have been proven to have advantages and possibilities to treat mental conditions effectively [7]. Video games represent a great way of fixing the attention of such a population, precisely because of the capabilities they offer to provide short- or long-term entertainment, as well as the inherent elements of these (narrative, level design, mechanics, etc.). Therefore, in recent years, different scientific works have had their origin or purpose around video games as a tool for dissemination, training, treatments/procedures, etc. [8].

In this paper, we propose the design of a gamepad for video games that monitors two of the most relevant biological signals associated with the mental state of the user: HR and skin sweating [9] using photoplethysmography (PPG) and GSR approaches, respectively. Since video games are a great tool, because of how striking and the potential they have in the task of dissemination of information (through narrative, level design, etc.), it was chosen to build a video game controller that, without the player having difficulty using it, would allow the collection and analysis of the data of the most relevant biosignals to determine their emotional state. This non-invasive monitoring while playing computer video games is intended to provide an effective approach to develop, in future works, interactive and customizable diagnostic and therapeutic psychological tools.

In this section (Sect. 1), an introduction to the work, the fundamental ideas, and where it is directed is given; Sect. 2 establishes the theoretical precepts on which the work is based, as well as a summary of the state-of-the-art that allows the reader to obtain the preamble from which the work arises; Sect. 3 describes the methodology used and the development of the device in question.

2 Theoretical Background

2.1 Biosignals Detection Techniques

Emotions are manifestations of a person's mood, depending on the person's context. That is the reaction to various situations in which there may be an intervention (direct or indirect) of the person. These emotions are manifested, more commonly, by facial/body expressions, by direct verbalization (expressing feelings with words), or through actions carried out by the individual. However, in physiological terms, the body also manifests emotions in various ways. To capture this, various sensors are used that allow the detection/registration of the different physiological signals emitted by the human body, related to emotions. These signals can include electrodermal activity (EDA), HR, electrocardiography (ECG), electroencephalography (EEG), respiratory rate, etc. Among these, the most used variables (due to their greater correlation with mood changes) are HR (through PPG) and EDA [10].

PPG performs a measurement of light that is reflected in human tissues, where changes in blood volume denote the characteristic waveform of a PPG signal, also known as digital volume pulse (DVP) [11]. PPG is used for measurements of the level of oxygen saturation in the blood (SpO2) and HR (beats per minute or BPM) as indicators of vital signs in a patient. The operation of a PPG device uses a light emitting diode (LED) and a photodetector that allows the identification of changes in the intensity of the light emitted by the LED. During the systolic process (contraction) of the heart, the blood volume in the vessels increases, and during the diastolic process (relaxation), the volume decreases. This produces, respectively, an increase and decrease in the level of light absorption, resulting in the characteristic curve of the signal [12].

The GSR, also known as EDA, forms the unit of measurement of resistance on the surface of the skin or dermal conductivity, which can be determined through a pair of electrodes connected closely to each other, which allows to amplify and record the current variation caused by changes in skin resistance [13].

2.2 Video Games

Commercial video games represent a digital mimicry of an activity that allows human development since they allow to improve cognitive skills through the emotions they manage to evoke through design [14]. The action of playing (which is directly linked to the feeling of satisfaction/realization), can lead to a predominance of positive emotions that allow emotional improvement in psychological conditions [15]. During casual gaming sessions in cognitive stimulus games, cortisol and amylase are released, which is related to better cognitive performance [14]. Video games, in the field of health applications, have had a great boom in recent years, having uses ranging from physical rehabilitation to alternative methods of digital therapies for various mental disorders [7, 8, 16]. To this end, the potential presented by these software entertainment platforms in treatments on topics of relevance in the field of psychology, such as depression, anxiety, post-traumatic stress, etc., stands out in [16, 17].

2.3 State of the Art

As a different concept, video game controls have had applications and uses in topics related to the improvement of health. In physical rehabilitation terms, one of them is explained in [18], where a controller was designed for video games that would facilitate the rehabilitation of patients who have suffered strokes. This system consists of an adjustable control to the patient's arm, where he performs actions of the game through the pressure on a knob that allows him or her to quantify his strength at the limb and, based on this, perform various actions in the games customized for such control. Likewise, in [19] a similar concept is applied (oriented for physical rehabilitation for conditions of the central nervous system), with the combination of virtual reality to create a more immersive environment with the user experience and manage to promote a greater need for mobility that encourages therapy, even without a physical control that the user needs to sustain or place himself.

The use of biofeedback in video games has been widely approached. For example, in [20], the concept of serious video games [21] is explored to unify the idea of digital therapies in mental health with biofeedback, in order to highlight the relevance of rehabilitation applicable to various mental illnesses with the use of this interactive platform that is so striking. The combined use of physiological signals allows a more complete and integral analysis of the direct and indirect consequences of design in software and hardware. In a study oriented towards the design of video games whose concept revolves around biofeedback, it was determined that the users prefer to interact physiologically rather than "manually", using a combination of various applicable sensors that obtain the most important physiological signals for the determination of emotions [15]. Software design using biofeedback has allowed the development of applications to obtain a better understanding of various physical and mental disorders. In [22] the effectiveness of video games in dealing with the stress caused by military service in soldiers on duty was reported through the use of biofeedback. This kind of study allows the intervention in typical problems of the field, such as physical or psychological afflictions, search for social support, etc. Biofeedback applied to video games has also been used in virtual reality environments. In [23] these two concepts are combined to create a more immersive gaming experience that allows users to develop cognitive skills for the management and improvement of their emotions and mental state.

Given the wide range of possibilities involved in monitoring the physical response of the users during game sessions and how they relate to their emotional response (regardless of the origin, design, or objective of the video game itself), some devices have been designed to collect, through biofeedback, the various signals associated with different psychological conditions, e.g., stress, anxiety, depression.

PPG is a way to obtain the HR, as well as its variability. This is important because HR is one of the biosignals that is closely linked to the physiological manifestation of emotions in a person, which is why biofeedback applications consider PPG as one of the fundamental methods for such analysis [24]. For instance, in [25] a gamepad with a small sensor is implemented. The sensor is located at the bottom of the controller so that the player is always placing his finger on the sensor in a comfortable way, and through the data acquisition card, the collection and analysis of the sensor measurement can be carried out.

On the other hand, the GSR is an excellent indicator of emotional state. In [26], a study was carried out using virtual reality, in which, through the EDA, the 3D environment of the video game was adapted, ensuring that the player had a better response to the situation of the narrative of the video game. Since the video game was oriented to cognitive training (visual tasks, motor skills, etc.), due to these modifications because of the GSR sensor, the system allowed a better interaction with the user and, therefore, a higher rate of completion in the activities described above.

Similarly, other signals such as EEG, ECG, and electromyogram (EMG) have been implemented in video game controllers to serve users with different capabilities that allow them to replace computer peripherals such as the mouse or the keyboard to play [27]. Through the pattern of the different brain waves (captured by a headband with electrodes scattered throughout the head), the user can control the graphical user interface specially designed for that purpose, which, at the same time, allows the control of the game without requiring the action of the limbs.

3 Development/Methodology

3.1 Design of the Device

For the design of the gamepad, a programmable microcontroller Arduino Nano® [28] was employed. This device has an integrated interface that can process inputs/outputs of sensors and actuators through the programming of such devices. Three modules were connected to the analog ports of the Arduino Nano®: 1) in analog input ports 0 and 1, the *X* & *Y* axis values of a joystick, which serve for movement within the video game, 2) in analog port 2 the data pin of the GSR sensor, and 3) in analog port 3 the data pin of the PPG sensor. In digital I/O ports 2, 3, and 4, the pushbuttons are connected, which are used to perform actions within the video game. All components are powered through the 5V and GND outputs of the microcontroller. The result of this circuit is shown in Fig. 1.

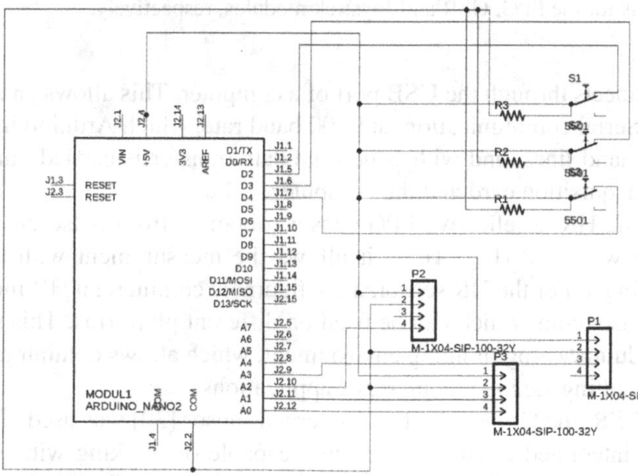

Fig. 1. Schematic diagram of the circuit, generated with Autodesk Eagle® CAD, where all the following elements are connected to the Arduino Nano® board: P1, P2, and P3 represent the connections of the PPG, GSR, and Joystick sensors, respectively; S1, S2, and S3 represent the pushbuttons, and R1, R2, and R3 are 10k Ω resistors.

Based on the above diagram, which was also simulated in Proteus® for functionality reference only, the printed circuit board (PCB) is made for the construction of the prototype, as shown in Fig. 2. The PCB shown below is the result of the compression of the schematic design in Fig. 1. This PCB was made by the method of ironing the printing on a phenolic plate, to which, subsequently, the components were added through welding manually. The final design of the PCB was carried out through Autodesk Eagle® CAD electronic design software.

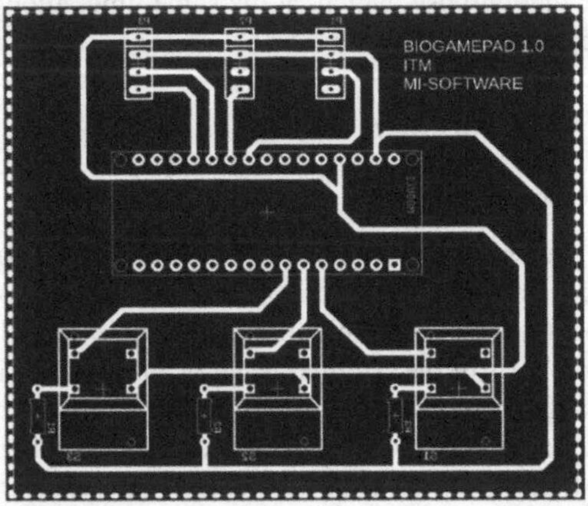

Fig. 2. Printed circuit board (PCB) of the gamepad, generated with Autodesk Eagle® CAD. Based on the previous schematic diagram in Fig. 1, the elements of the PCB are structured by the following: "Modul1" (according to the diagram) represents the Arduino Nano® board, S1, S2, and S3 are the gamepad buttons, R1, R2 and R3 stand for 10k Ω resistors, and P1, P2 and P3 represent connections for the PPG, GSR and Joystick modules, respectively.

The device connects through the USB port of a computer. This allows an immediate interface through Serial communication, at 9600 baud rate, which Arduino implements with its own command lines, and with which the data transfer is carried out, between the resulting data acquisition card and the computer.

To determine the HR, a reflective PPG sensor (obtained from pulsesensor® Heart Rate Sensor [29]) was used (Fig. 4), as it allows the measurement with the simple placement of the finger. For the HR sensor, a configurable commercial HR monitor was used from pulsesensor.com, which can be used on different platforms. This sensor has a library in the Arduino® programming environment, which allows obtaining the BPM, and plotting the resulting signal, among other applications.

To obtain the GSR, the Grove® GSR commercial sensor [30] was used. This sensor is made up of an integrated circuit in a module capable of working with Arduino®. Through its inputs (two electrodes that can be easily placed on the fingers through fabric thimbles), it allows the measurement of the EDA, as well as the impedance of the skin, in ohms. The sensor can be placed in the fingers of the right hand, as shown in Fig. 3.

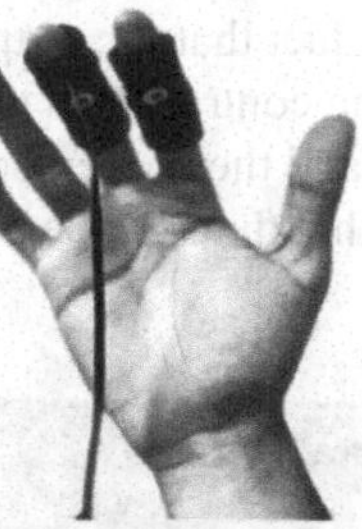

Fig. 3. Placement of the Grove® GSR sensor using electrodes on the index and middle finger. The electrodes are in the fabric thimbles and are directly connected to the integrated circuit module, which, in turn, is connected directly to the Arduino Nano® board.

3.2 Data Collection

The PPG and GSR sensors work in a single Arduino® Nano program, as follows: the PPG sensor allows, through its dedicated library, to obtain the numerical value of the BPM through the measurements. On the other hand, the GSR sensor makes it possible to obtain either the level of galvanic response of the skin (in micro-Siemens) through the electrical impulse detected in the epidermis (through changes in sweating in the region where the electrodes are applied) or the impedance of the skin in ohms. In both cases, the sensors give an output of numerical data, which is printed through serial communication. The data collected is stored in comma-separated value (CSV) files, where the following is reported: the exact time of measurement, pressed button, HR, and GSR. Since all the data is classified by collection time and timestamps, there are different gameplay possibilities according to the video game being used. The control allows to record multiple entries of the buttons/joystick, so it can replicate the game session accurately and have a comparison with the recorded values and nominal values of the biosignals. The data obtained from the gamepad input and the sensors could serve for further comparisons and analyses for detection of distress and other emotional states.

4 Results

4.1 Prototype

The video game controller was designed using a classic/retro style. Advantages of this gamepad includes: it was designed so that the user, at the time of playing, could move the joystick in a simple and comfortable way, and reach the action buttons with the other hand, in the same way. Also, the prototype, being a control assembled inside a small box, does not generate fatigue or discomfort at the time of attachment, as reported by the users. It is designed to be used in games that offer simple and uninterrupted gameplay, such as casual video games (sidescroll shooters, platform games, etc.) [17]. The PPG sensor was placed at the top left of the control. This was because, when held in the right way, the index finger rests naturally and not forced on it, allowing the user's HR to be measured without problems. As for the GSR sensor, it can be placed on the middle and ring fingers of the left hand or, preferably, on the index and middle fingers of the right hand. This is possible thanks to the fact that the output of the fabric thimbles is placed, like the PPG sensor, at the top of the control, thus preventing its placement from being uncomfortable. The action buttons and the movement joystick were placed on the front of the case, organized in such way that they can be comfortably accessed by the user, as shown in Fig. 4.

Fig. 4. Gamepad prototype. The joystick, as it is traditionally found in commercial controls of any kind, is placed on the left side, so that the player can make use of it with his left thumb while the action buttons were placed diagonally at the bottom right of the front face, to facilitate its reach with the right thumb.

The PPG sensor is located on the top face of the housing to ensure that the fingertip poses naturally and comfortably while holding the controller, without harming or affecting the gaming experience or comfort, if it is held in the appropriate way (Fig. 5).

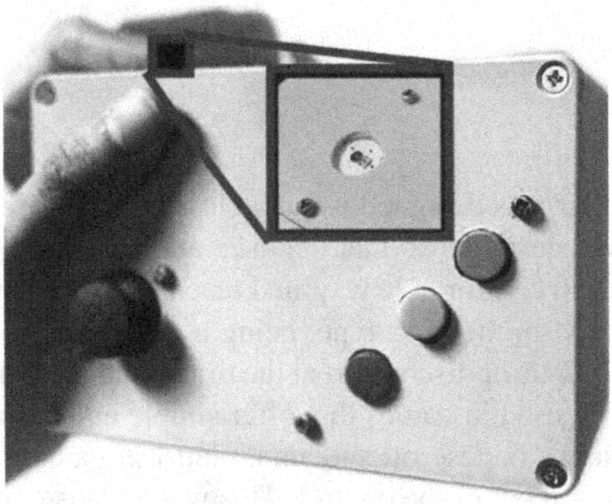

Fig. 5. PPG sensor placement. The PPG sensor is placed in the upper left region. This is because the position of the left hand requires that the joystick be operated, traditionally, with the left thumb (placed on the front), causing the index and middle fingers of that hand to rest on the upper face of the housing. Then, the user can place his finger naturally on top of the sensor without forcing the position of his hand.

At the top of the control, the USB connection cables and the terminals/electrodes of the GSR sensor are obtained, which are placed on two fingers of the right hand through fabric rings. By holding the controller correctly and naturally and having placed the electrodes of the GSR sensor on the fingers, measurements of HR and GSR are taken through the serial communication port between the Arduino Nano® and the computer, as shown in Fig. 6.

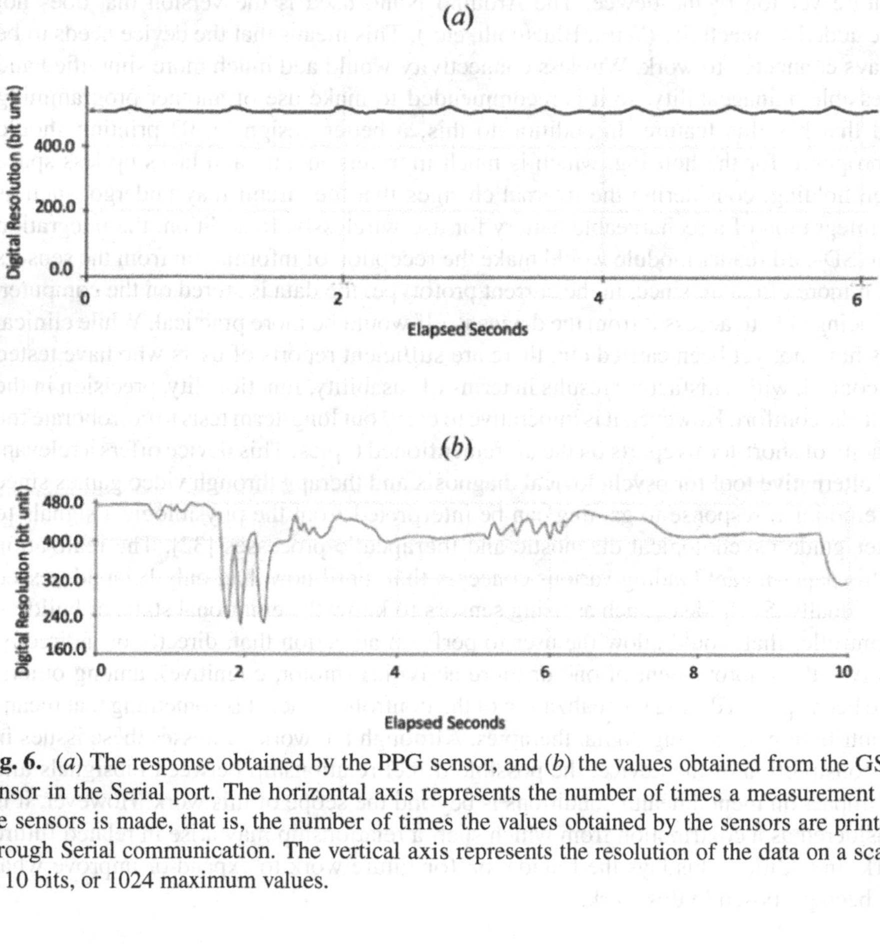

Fig. 6. (*a*) The response obtained by the PPG sensor, and (*b*) the values obtained from the GSR sensor in the Serial port. The horizontal axis represents the number of times a measurement of the sensors is made, that is, the number of times the values obtained by the sensors are printed through Serial communication. The vertical axis represents the resolution of the data on a scale of 10 bits, or 1024 maximum values.

5 Conclusions

A controller for customizable computer video games with a response to biofeedback is proposed. We designed a prototype that included the basic controls of movement and action of traditional control, adding two sensors of the main biosignals related to the physiological-emotional response: EDA and HR [31], in order to make the relevant measurements in the background, obtaining crucial data for a possible future analysis of therapeutic use through video games.

With the prototype properly assembled, it was possible to obtain a correct answer in the implementation of a video game, with which it was possible to check the operation of the motion and action controls. In a non-invasive design for the user, the remote control allowed GSR and HR measurements to be made by the sensors, and through the configuration of the interface between the computer and the data acquisition card made up of the Arduino Nano®, the measured data was stored in a log that allows further analysis in different applications. However, there are some considerations for a future version of the device. The Arduino Nano used is the version that does not have added connectivity (WiFi, Bluetooth, etc.). This means that the device needs to be always connected to work. Wireless connectivity would add much more simplified and accessible manageability, so it is recommended to make use of another programming card that has this feature. In addition to this, a better design in 3D printing should be proposed for the housing, which is much more ergonomic and takes up less space when holding, considering the internal changes that the circuit may undergo, such as the integration of a rechargeable battery for use wirelessly. In addition, the integration of an SD card reader module would make the reception of information from the sensors much more efficient, since, in the current prototype, the data is stored on the computer, and being able to access it from the device itself would be more practical. While clinical tests have not yet been carried out, there are sufficient reports of users who have tested the control, with satisfactory results in terms of: usability, functionality, precision in the controls, comfort. However, it is imperative to carry out long-term tests to corroborate the veracity of short-term reports on the aforementioned topics. This device offers a relevant and alternative tool for psychological diagnosis and therapy through video games since the emotional response to gaming can be interpreted from the physiological signals to better guide psychological diagnostic and therapeutic processes [32]. The realization of this paper meant landing various concepts that, until now, had only been addressed individually. Such ideas, such as using sensors to know the emotional state, or building a controller that would allow the user to perform an action that, directly or indirectly, involves the improvement of one or more activities (motor, cognitive), among others, have been applied during the realization of the controller since it is something that means a contribution to existing digital therapies. Although the work addresses these issues in the construction of the device, the possible direct relationship between biosignals and the impact on mental health conditions is beyond the scope of this work. However, it is considered as a contribution from which such a relationship may arise in related future work. In addition, this lays the foundation for future work to expand or improve what has been proposed in this work.

References

1. Santomauro, D.F., et al.: Global prevalence and burden of depressive and anxiety disorders in 204 countries and territories in 2020 due to the COVID-19 pandemic. Lancet **398**(10312), 1700–1712 (2021). https://doi.org/10.1016/S0140-6736(21)02143-7
2. American Psychiatric Association: Diagnostic and Statistical Manual of Mental Disorders, 5th Ed. (2013)
3. Awang, A., Nayan, N.A.: Early detection of mental disorder signs using photoplethysmogram : A review. https://doi.org/10.1080/09720529.2021.2009191 **24**(8), 2171–2180 (2021). https://doi.org/10.1080/09720529.2021.2009191

4. Apostolidis, H., Papantoniou, G., Tsiatsos, T.: Deployment and dynamics of a biofeedback system for anxiety awareness during online examination activities. Appl. Sci. **11**(2), 756 (2021). https://doi.org/10.3390/APP11020756
5. Creswell, C., Shum, A., Pearcey, S., Skripkauskaite, S., Patalay, P., Waite, P.: Young people's mental health during the COVID-19 pandemic. Lancet Child Adolesc. Heal. **5**(8), 535–537 (2021). https://doi.org/10.1016/S2352-4642(21)00177-2
6. Barr, M., Copeland-Stewart, A.: Playing Video Games During the COVID-19 Pandemic and Effects on Players' Well-Being. **17**(1), 122–139 (2021). https://doi.org/10.1177/15554120211017036
7. Dos Santos, I.K., et al.: Active video games for improving mental health and physical fitness—an alternative for children and adolescents during social isolation: an overview. Int. J. Environ. Res. Public Heal. **18**(4), 1641 (2021). https://doi.org/10.3390/IJERPH18041641
8. Thompson, D., et al.: Serious video games for health: how behavioral science guided the development of a serious video game. Simul. Gaming **41**(4), 587–606 (2010). https://doi.org/10.1177/1046878108328087
9. Katsis, C.D., Katertsidis, N.S., Fotiadis, D.I.: An integrated system based on physiological signals for the assessment of affective states in patients with anxiety disorders. Biomed. Signal Process. Control **6**(3), 261–268 (2011). https://doi.org/10.1016/J.BSPC.2010.12.001
10. Petrescu, L., et al.: Integrating biosignals measurement in virtual reality environments for anxiety detection. Sensors **20**(24), 7088 (2020). https://doi.org/10.3390/S20247088
11. Zhang, J., et al.: Diagnostic features and potential applications of ppg signal in healthcare: a systematic review. Healthc. **10**(3), 547 (2022). https://doi.org/10.3390/HEALTHCARE10030547
12. Kumar, A., Komaragiri, R., Kumar, M.: A review on computation methods used in photoplethysmography signal analysis for heart rate estimation. Arch. Comput. Methods Eng. **29**(2), 921–940 (2022). https://doi.org/10.1007/S11831-021-09597-4/TABLES/2
13. Sanchez-Comas, A., Synnes, K., Molina-Estren, D., Troncoso-Palacio, A., Comas-González, Z.: Correlation analysis of different measurement places of galvanic skin response in test groups facing pleasant and unpleasant stimuli. Sensors **21**(12), 4210 (2021). https://doi.org/10.3390/S21124210
14. Franceschini, S., Bertoni, S., Lulli, M., Pievani, T., Facoetti, A.: Short-term effects of video-games on cognitive enhancement: the role of positive emotions. J. Cogn. Enhanc. **6**(1), 29–46 (2021). https://doi.org/10.1007/S41465-021-00220-9
15. Kowal, M., Conroy, E., Ramsbottom, N., Smithies, T., Toth, A., Campbell, M.: Gaming your mental health: a narrative review on mitigating symptoms of depression and anxiety using commercial video games. JMIR Serious Games **9**(2), e26575 (2021). https://games.jmir.org/2021/2/e26575, https://doi.org/10.2196/26575
16. Carras, M.C., et al.: Commercial video games as therapy: A new research agenda to unlock the potential of a global pastime. Frontiers in Psychiatry **8**, no. JAN. Frontiers Media S.A., p. 300 (2018). https://doi.org/10.3389/fpsyt.2017.00300
17. Pine, R., Fleming, T., McCallum, S., Sutcliffe, K.: The effects of casual videogames on anxiety, depression, stress, and low mood: a systematic review. Games Health J. **9**(4), 255–264 (2020). https://doi.org/10.1089/g4h.2019.0132
18. Burdea, G.C., et al.: Feasibility of integrative games and novel therapeutic gamecontroller for telerehabilitation of individuals chronic post-stroke living inthe community. Top. Stroke Rehabil. **27**(5), 321 (2020). https://doi.org/10.1080/10749357.2019.1701178
19. Cortés-pérez, I., Zagalaz-anula, N., Montoro-cárdenas, D., Lomas-vega, R., Obrero-gaitán, E., Osuna-pérez, M.C.: Leap motion controller video game-based therapy for upper extremity motor recovery in patients with central nervous system diseases. a systematic review with meta-analysis. Sensors **21**(6), 2065 (2021). https://doi.org/10.3390/S21062065

20. Fleming, T.M., et al.: Serious games and gamification for mental health: current status and promising directions. Front. Psychiatry **7**, no. JAN (2017). https://doi.org/10.3389/fpsyt.2016.00215
21. Villani, D., Carissoli, C., Triberti, S., Marchetti, A., Gilli, G., Riva, G.: Videogames for emotion regulation: a systematic review. Games for Health J. **7**(2), 85–99 (2018). Mary Ann Liebert Inc. https://doi.org/10.1089/g4h.2017.0108
22. West Virginia University - Eberly College of Arts and Sciences, "Video games offer active military, veterans coping mechanism for stress. (2017) https://www.sciencedaily.com/releases/2017/06/170622122756.htm Accessed 27 May 2022
23. Maarsingh, B.M., Bos, J., Van Tuijn, C.F.J., Renard, S.B.: Changing stress mindset through stressjam: a virtual reality game using biofeedback. Games Health J. **8**(5), 326–331 (2019). https://doi.org/10.1089/G4H.2018.0145/ASSET/IMAGES/LARGE/FIGURE1.JPEG
24. Zhu, J., Ji, L., Liu, C.: Heart rate variability monitoring for emotion and disorders of emotion. Physiol. Meas. **40**(6), 064004 (2019). https://doi.org/10.1088/1361-6579/AB1887
25. Abe, E., Chigira, H., Fujiwarai, K., Yamakawa, T., Kano, M.: Heart rate monitoring by a pulse sensor embedded game controller. 2015 Asia-Pacific Signal Inf. Process. Assoc. Annu. Summit Conf. APSIPA ASC 2015, pp. 1266–1269 (2016). https://doi.org/10.1109/APSIPA.2015.7415478
26. Kosch, T., Chiossi, F., Welsch, R., Villa, S., Chuang, L., Mayer, S.: Virtual reality adaptation using electrodermal activity to support the user experience. Big Data Cogn. Comput. 6(2), 55 (2022). https://doi.org/10.3390/BDCC6020055
27. Kawala-Janik, A., Podpora, M., Gardecki, A., Czuczwara, W., Baranowski, J., Bauer, W.: Game controller based on biomedical signals. 20th Int Conf. Methods Model. Autom. Robot. MMAR **2015**, 934–939 (2015). https://doi.org/10.1109/MMAR.2015.7284003
28. Arduino, "Arduino Nano (V2.3) User Manual," Released under the Creative Commons Attribution Share-Alike 2.5 License. 2022, Accessed 16 Jul 2022. http://creativecommons.org/licenses/by-sa/2.5/
29. Digi-Key Electronics: Pulse Sensor Datasheet. https://www.digikey.pl/htmldatasheets/production/3024658/0/0/1/pulse-sensor-datasheet.html Accessed 16 Jul 2022
30. Seeed, Grove GSR Sensor Datasheet. http://www.seeedstudio.com/depot/Grove-GSR-p-1614.html Bazaar: http://www.seeedstudio.com/depot/Grove-GSR-p-1614.html Accessed 16 Jul 2022
31. Giannakakis, G., Grigoriadis, D., Giannakaki, K., Simantiraki, O., Roniotis, A., Tsiknakis, M.: Review on psychological stress detection using biosignals. IEEE Trans. Affect. Comput. **13**(1), 440–460 (2022). https://doi.org/10.1109/TAFFC.2019.2927337
32. Alneyadi, M., Drissi, N., Almeqbaali, M., Ouhbi, S.: Biofeedback-based connected mental health interventions for anxiety: systematic literature review. JMIR Mhealth Uhealth **9**(4) (2021). https://doi.org/10.2196/26038

Simulation and Implementation of an Environmental Monitoring System Based on LPWAN/IoT

F. Ramírez-López[1,5], G. A. Yáñez-Casas[2,3], G. E. Casillas-Aviña[1,5], J. J. Hernández-Gómez[2,3](✉), M. F. Mata-Rivera[4], and S. Ramírez-Espinosa[1]

[1] Centro de Estudios Científicos y Tecnológicos No. 9 "Juan de Dios Batiz", Instituto Politécnico Nacional, Mexico City, Mexico

[2] Centro de Desarrollo Aeroespacial, Instituto Politécnico Nacional, Mexico City, Mexico

jjhernandezgo@ipn.mx

[3] AAAI Student Chapter at Yucatán, México (AAAIMX), Association for the Advancement of Artificial Intelligence, Mexico City, Mexico

[4] Unidad Profesional Interdisciplinaria en Ingeniería y Tecnologías Avanzadas, Sección de Estudios de Posgrado e Investigación, Instituto Politécnico Nacional, Mexico City, Mexico

[5] Unidad Profesional Interdisciplinaria en Ingeniería y Tecnologías Avanzadas, Instituto Politécnico Nacional, Mexico City, Mexico

Abstract. Nowadays, the vertiginous development of wireless communications systems entails an exponential increase in the necessities of a digital society. Internet of Things (IoT) concept has played a key role in the delivery of remote control and monitoring of applications to the final user, which include but are not limited to industry, research, education, security, among many others. Within this context, IoT solutions based on Low Power Wide Area Networks (LPWANs) could be of fundamental aid to monitor environmental variables in both urban and countryside regions in order to face a global scientific problem beyond local climatic issues: climate change. In this work, we present the development of an environmental monitoring system, based on a web interface hosted in a cloud server as well as on the design and simulation of low power COTS-based acquisition nodes, aimed to sample environmental variables, previously defined from a strategic analysis of commercial sensing modules. IoT environmental sensing nodes are connected to the proprietary cloud server following principles of LPWANs. The outcome are low-power acquisition nodes for sensing environmental variables using COTS electronic components and transceptors along with a web interface that presents graphically the information as time series. The developed system for environmental monitoring shows to follow the LPWAN/IoT bases, showing a minimal power consumption. Moreover, it proves to be accessible, easily reproducible and to have a high compatibility with various web interfaces, posing this as a viable proposal for its mass implementation as an IoT application.

M. F. Mata-Rivera et al. (Eds.): WITCOM 2022, CCIS 1659, pp. 237–269, 2022.
https://doi.org/10.1007/978-3-031-18082-8_16

Keywords: IoT · LPWAN · Internet of Things · Low Power Wide Area Network · Monitoring · Sensing · Nodes · Environmental variables · Climate change · Web interface · Microcontroller · AVR architecture

1 Introduction

The current telecommunications context shows a notorious evolution towards a fully linked environment. An important example is that the Internet of Things (IoT) concept is evolving, allowing the arisal of the so called "smart world" [1]. As the applications of IoT grow exponentially, with more novel systems depending of real time transmission of information [2], the improvement in the efficiency of IoT devices and their inter-connectivity to the global networks is a fundamental goal.

Since the emerging of the IoT concept about 2012, applications of IoT have appeared covering as many fields of knowledge as it can be imagined. Some important examples are medical management systems [3], the development of meta-heuristic algorithms [4], cognitive computing [5], development of a novel physical layer (Li-Fi) [6], robotics [7], agriculture [8,9], big data [10], smart energy grids [11], sensor networks [12], among many others. In the field of sensor networks, one of the most pursued goals of IoT is the monitoring of diverse variables as water level and leakage [13], bio-metric parameters in patients [14,15], the preservation of architectural buildings [16], furnaces in foundry industry [17], flow in pipelines [18], micro-climate conditions [19], store shelves [20], agricultural parameters [21], early variables to identify typhoons [22], environmental chemical analysis [23], newborns' cradles within baby wards [24], etc.

One of the most promising monitoring applications of IoT-based systems is the study of variables that may unveil the regional and local effects of climate change [19,22,23,25]. The increasing tendency in temperature records around the world since the middle of the 20th century, along with paleo-climatic records, constitute a solid proof of global warming [26,27]. Global warming is defined as the increment in the global mean temperature over land and ocean [27], and it affects both urban and countryside regions. For instance, within urban areas, some of the impacts of climate change are interurban transportation [28], pollution [29,30], health problems [31,32], urban growth and land use [33,34], natural hazards in city environments [35,36], poverty and gender [37,38], adaptation of current urban infrastructure [39,40], feeding challenges [41,42], sustainability under population growth [43,44], forced migration/mobility [45,46], as well as pronounced temperature increments yielding to heat waves (heat islands) [47,48].

Although cities may have enough telecommunications infrastructure to deploy a large sensor network to monitor and analyse variables that could be used to predict and mitigate the effects of climate change locally, climate change is recognised to be a globally connected phenomenon [49,50]. Moreover, as in 2020, only about 44% of the world's population lived in non-urban areas [51], and it is expected to be reduced to 32% by 2050 [52], the monitoring of climate change related variables in both countryside and unpopulated regions could fail to effectively gather *in-situ* records that might be necessary to better understand, forecast and therefore, mitigate the effects of climate change in local, regional and global scales.

In this sense, IoT based systems able to take advantage of Low Power Wide Area Networks (LPWANs) benefits and capabilities may be an alternative to deploy large scale sensor networks in both urban and unpopulated areas, focused on the recording of large time scale meteorological variables that could be of aid in assessing *in situ* impacts of climate change. In this work, we develop very low cost, COTS-based, sensing nodes designed for ultra low power consumption and thus, a large lifetime, able to record the following meteorological variables: environmental temperature, atmospheric pressure, altitude, humidity, rain level, wind speed, intensity of ultraviolet light, concentration of hydrogen, methane, LPG gas, propane, butane, natural gas, ethyl alcohol, carbon monoxide and finally, the current consumption of the system. The sensing nodes herein developed, feature an LPWAN wireless connection that delivers data to an IoT server so to be able to record and visualise data in real time on a web interface. This work is organised as follows: in Sect. 2 we present in a deeper manner the principles of IoT and LPWAN systems as well as the materials and methods used along the paper, while in Sect. 3 we present the design and development of the whole proposed system. Then, Sect. 4 presents the results as well as a discussion on them, and finally, Sects. 5 and 6 pose some final remarks as well as some possible directions in which this work could be extended, respectively.

2 Materials and Methods

2.1 Low Power Wireless Communications Technologies

Wireless communications networks represent a very important portion of the total infrastructure within communications systems [53–55]. Nowadays, they constitute one of the most demanded data transmission systems, not only for common daily activities, but also for both research and industrial environments, due to their great implementation flexibility. In this sense, technological development has increased and diversified the capabilities of wireless networks, by providing novel concepts and standards that allow systems to be modified according to the rapidly evolving necessities of a very demanding sector [56].

Despite the benefits of wireless networks, they entail some drawbacks, mainly depending on the scale at which they are required to be designed and deployed. In the case of large-scale networks such as Wi-Fi, cellular networks or microwave systems, a complex infrastructure is required, their operation is based on strict industrial and government regulations, they are of high cost and they can only transmit within a limited bandwidth of the spectrum [57]. Thus, alternatives to typical wireless communications systems have emerged that are aimed to significantly mitigate the aforementioned drawbacks [58–60].

These alternatives lead to the emergence of the so called LPWANs [61], which consists of a standard whose objective is to present less expensive and more versatile options. The operation of LPWANs is based on increasing the efficiency of the energy consumption of their elements, leading to a decrease in their implementation cost [62]. The LPWAN standard has been developed and documented by the Internet Engineering Task Force (IETF) [63], which is an international standardisation organisation aimed to document standards and norms related to technologies whose operation is based on the use of the Internet as the main mean of publishing and using data, as it is the case of LPWANs and IoT applications.

LPWANs are usually designed to provide support to a large number of electronic devices of very low commercial cost, which can individually process and transmit limited data amounts. However, they carry it out with a very low energy consumption, thus increasing the scalability of the network, keeping a considerable number of devices in simultaneous operation, which in turn could also increase coverage. In this sense, solar cells and batteries are able to supply power to the network and can provide energy for time periods as long as of years. LPWAN systems tend to be limited in bandwidth and frequency of operation, which makes them less powerful compared to other wireless systems. However, it is possible to manage the operation bandwidth and frequencies through the use of time-operated duty cycles, to optimise the lifetime of the network [64].

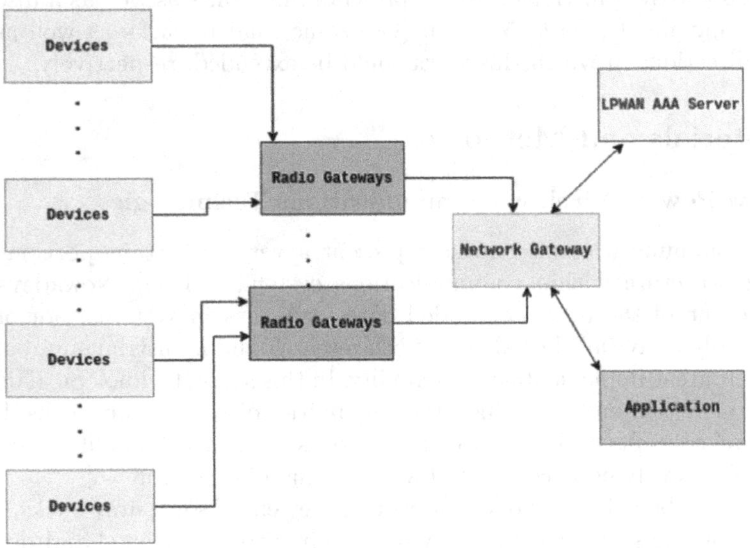

Fig. 1. LPWAN network Architecture [64].

In order to preserve the aforementioned attributes, the structure of LPWANs consists of specific entities that allow to use only the essential elements to carry out the operation of the network. In Fig. 1, the common topology of an LPWAN system can be observed. Such a basic structure consists of the following 5 elements [64]:

1. **Devices.** The acquisition devices, also called "things" in the context of IoT, allow obtaining the data to be used in the specific application of the network. Due to the scalable nature of LPWAN networks, there can be a large number of devices connected to the same Radio Gateway.
2. **Radio Gateway.** It is the wireless transmission element able to send the acquired data to the part of the network that manages and processes it.
3. **Network Gateway.** Interconnection point between the Radio Gateway and the internet. It can also be considered as a distribution point.
4. **Authentication, Authorisation and Accounting Server (LPWAN AAA Server).** Physical and logical infrastructure that allows connection to the cloud management service. Depending on the specific technology, it can be used to recognise and authorise access to users who require connection to the service.
5. **Application.** Also known as the user's final application, it allows the final use of the acquired data. It is usually a display and a control interface.

LPWAN communications systems have two phases: the first one is where the devices and radio gateways are located, which is where the designer have complete control since he can completely choose the components as well as the implementation technology. On the other hand, the second phase is typically an IP (Internet Protocol) connection, in which the LPWAN-sent data is recast through Internet up to the final application. In this second phase, that consists in the Network Gateway, the LPWAN AAA Server and the Application, there is usually less control of the implementation [65].

2.2 Internet of Things (IoT)

IoT fosters an environment where a large number of elements are interconnected through various techniques, allowing remote and effective transmission of the data acquired by such elements, relying in the infrastructure of IP networks. IoT focuses its efforts on presenting an open and very accessible environment, where the logical and physical components of the communications system have a high level of compatibility and interoperability, precisely due to the considerable variety of the available technologies and devices [66].

Deng et al. [67] use the "Edge Computing" concept to define the paradigm of extending isolated communications and information services regarded as independent systems, to an environment where they interact with each other as a whole, despite the complexity and size of each system. Such paradigm is applied by IoT to the connection of objects and users in an open environment.

The development of IoT applications implies three basic situations: extensive acquaintance of the devices of the dedicated network, complete mobility of the system, as well as adaptation of the network to the environment and users to which it should serve. Thus, the design of an IoT system requires general phases or layers for its implementation. Figure 2 shows the structure of layers or phases of an IoT system.

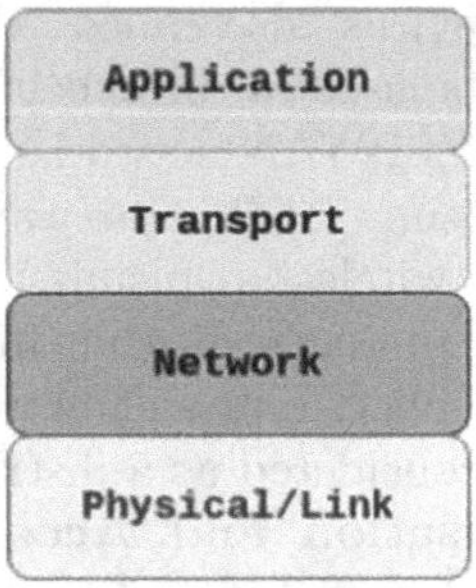

Fig. 2. IoT typical layers [68].

As the physical layer in Fig. 2 consists of small-scale devices, it is relatively common that the infrastructure of IoT applications to be mounted on LPWAN-type communications systems [69]. The network layer is formed by both the dedicated wireless link at the transmitter and the IP phase. The transport layer allows the correct addressing of large amounts of data coming from thousands or millions of devices. Finally, the application layer is where the final use of the acquired data is performed [66].

Since IoT presents a great opportunity for development, various public and private organisations focus in the design of techniques that allow the development of IoT applications, thus creating several standards that follow the structure of such applications. Examples of those standards are LoRa, Sigfox, LTE-M, NBIoT, ISA100.11A, among others [70].

Regardless of the creator of the standard, all IoT technologies have similar technical attributes, such as: operating frequencies within the 400–900 MHz band, communications protocols whose frames are based on User Datagram Protocol (UDP) structures, security algorithms based on device and/or user authentication, relatively low data transmission rates (Kbps), simple digital modulation techniques, restricted coverage and operation (typically dependent on geographic region) and star-shaped topologies [71–75].

Recent research trends have shown the importance of the interaction of LPWAN networks for IoT applications, as is the focus of this work. An extensive review of common IoT technologies based in LPWANs can be found in [69].

2.3 Serial Communication and Oriented Connection Protocols

Serial communication is one of the simplest data transmission methods. Various small-scale processing architectures, such as microcontrollers, microprocessors, etc., use this form of communication to exchange data between them and with other devices. The most common serial communication technique is based on the RS232 standard [76], in which a structure or frame of bits is sent from the transmitter to the receiver one bit at a time, specifying a certain symbol rate per unit of time (baudrate) [77].

The RS232 standard is an asynchronous type of communication consisting of a start bit, followed by a certain number of bits to represent payload data, and then ending with an optional parity bit and one or more stop bits. The common form of the protocol does not use the parity bit, where the least significant bit is sent first and the most significant bit at the end [78]. Figure 3 shows the structure of the serial communication frame based on the RS232 standard.

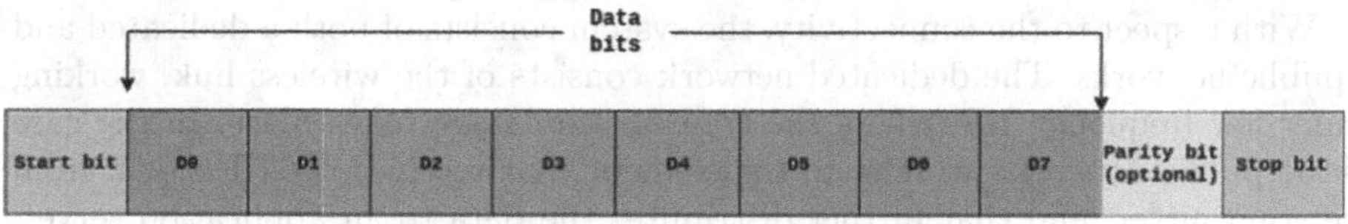

Fig. 3. RS232 serial communication frame format [76].

The simplicity of serial communication typically allows only three connection pins to be used on electronic devices, one assigned for transmission (Tx), another for reception (Rx), and the common pin (GND). Its simplicity poses the serial communication as a good option for exchanging data over relatively long distances, as it requires little implementation complexity, it has a minimal usage of resources, and it guarantees a high level of compatibility [78].

The serial communication protocol is considered as a basis for the constitution of different communications protocols in electronic devices. Some examples of protocols with slight variations to the base serial communication protocol (RS232) are I^2C (Inter-Integrated Circuit), UART (Universal Asynchronous Receiver Transmitter), USART (Universal Synchronous/Asynchronous Receiver/Transmitter), SPI (Serial Peripheral Interface), among others [79].

For data transport to the final application, an option is the usage of connection-oriented communications protocols. Connection-oriented services allow establishing an open and permanent line of communication between transmitters and receivers [80]. The principle of these services is based on the fact that before sending the corresponding data frame, a recognition and/or authentication is established between the devices that carry out the communication. Only then is when the data frame is transmitted. In this case, each frame contains an identifier that allows to keep the integrity and the correct sending sequence [80].

At first glance, it might seem that connection-oriented communications protocols could generate a greater load on the network. However, they provide security, efficiency, order and integrity to the link and to the transmitted data. In this sense, many technologies such as Ethernet [81], WiFi [82] or Bluetooth [83], allow their integration under the TCP/IP model, where TCP (Transfer Communication Protocol) is a completely connection-oriented protocol [66].

3 Development

3.1 Hardware

The monitoring system herein proposed is based on the design and implementation principles of the LPWAN communications standard, which implies that all the components of the system should be elements of low consumption and low cost, as well as being scalable and of implementation's relative easiness [64,84,85].

With respect to the connectivity, the system consists of both a dedicated and a public networks. The dedicated network consists of the wireless link, working under low frequency RF, where the transmission stage takes place. In the case of the public network, we refer to the element that receives the RF signal from the transmitter, and that further distributes the data to an application server. The Fig. 4 shows the block structure of the monitoring system.

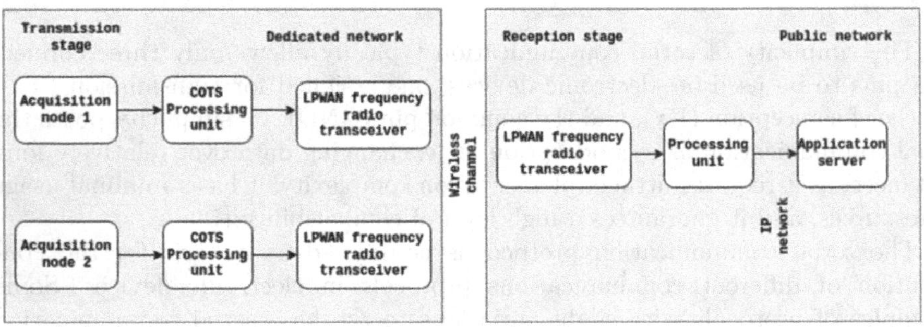

Fig. 4. Monitoring system design.

For the sake of redundancy and of modularity, the sensing platform consists of two acquisition nodes based in meteorological COTS sensors. Such sensors provide readings that pass to the processing unit and that are later sent to the RF transceiver to be transmitted wirelessly. Then, in the reception stage, a mirror circuit of the sending stage is used since the reception is carried out by means of a transceiver configured in reception mode, which sends the received data to a processing unit. Once data is received, it is then distributed through the public IP-based network so to mount such a data on the application server for their display and use. It is worth mentioning that a clear distinction is made in the design between the dedicated network stage and the public network stage to avoid ambiguities in operation. It is also possible to observe that we implement a star topology, typical of LPWAN systems. A summary of the main characteristics of the system components is shown in Table 1.

Table 1. Characteristics of the electronics components considered for the hardware of this system.

Type	Model	Variable(s)	Range	Unit	Voltage (V)	Current (mA)	Cost (USD)
Processing unit component							
Micro-controller	ATMEGA328P [86]	N/A	N/A	N/A	1.8–5.5	2.7	4.60
Conditioning and measure components							
Analogical multiplexer	CD4051 [87]	N/A	N/A	N/A	5.0 to 12.0	12.0	1.20
Analogical sensor	ACS712 [88]	Current consumption	0 to 60	A	5.0 to 8.0	10.0	3.10
Screen	LCD 1602A [89]	N/A	N/A	N/A	5.0 to 12.0	25.0	5.20
Communication components							
Radio transceiver	CC1101 [90]	Wireless transceiver	387 to 464	MHz	3.9	16.0	6.64
Acquisition node 1 sensors							
Digital sensor	BMP180 [91]	Atmospheric pressure, altitude, environmental temperature	300 to 1100 500 to 9000 −40 to +85	Pa, m, °C	1.8 to 3.6	5.0×10^{-3}	1.30
Digital sensor	DHT11 [92]	Humidity, environmental temperature	0 to 90 0 to 50	%, °C	3.0 to 5.5	0.5 to 2.5	2.15
Analogical sensor	YI-83 [93]	Rain level	0 to 100	%	5.0 to 15.0	15.0	2.20
Analogical sensor	ML8511 [94]	Intensity of ultraviolet light (UV)	100 to 700	mW/cm^2	3.3	0.3	6.20
Analogical sensor	PH0245S [95]	Wind speed	0 to 30	m/s	5.0 to 12.0	60.0	53.14
Acquisition node 2 sensors							
Analogical sensor	MQ-2 [96]	Propane, hydrogen, LPG gas	300 to 10,000	PPM	5.0	150.0	2.50
Analogical sensor	MQ-3 [97]	Ethyl alcohol	0 to 10	mg/L	5.0	150.0	2.50
Analogical sensor	MQ-4 [98]	Propane, methane (CH4), natural gas	300 to 10,000	PPM	5.0	150.0	2.50
Analogical sensor	MQ-5 [99]	Natural gas	200 to 10,000	PPM	5.0	150.0	2.50
Analogical sensor	MQ-6 [100]	Natural gas, butane, LPG gas	300 to 10,000	PPM	5.0	150.0	2.50
Analogical sensor	MQ-7 [101]	Carbon monoxide (CO)	10 to 10,000	PPM	5.0	150.0	2.50
Analogical sensor	MQ-8 [102]	Hydrogen, LPG gas, Methane (CH4)	100 to 10,000	PPM	5.0	150.0	2.50
Analogical sensor	MQ-9 [103]	LPG gas, Carbon monoxide (CO), methane (CH4)	100 to 10,000	PPM	5.0	150.0	2.50

For the main processing unit, a microcontroller of the AVR family is used [104]. The ATMEGA328P is a general purpose programmable element with 32 8-bit registers and Reduced Instruction Set Computing (RISC) architecture. Its operating frequency is 16 MHz, it has a 32 Kb flash memory and supports serial and I^2C communications protocols for connection with other devices [77,105]. This architecture supports programmation in C language, assembly language and in some versions of Python language [86].

In the dedicated network stage, we selected a RF transceiver whose operating range is within the Industrial, Scientific and Medical (ISM) bands [106], which coincide with the spectrum assigned to low-power transmission systems. The CC1101 transceiver from Texas Instruments, which operates in both the 300–400 MHz and the 800–900 MHz bands, has a range of up to 200 m in open field and its transmission power (dbm) can be modified for better performance [90].

For the physical conditioning and power consumption, three main elements have been used: a CD4051 series analogical multiplexer [107] is used in node 2 to increase the number of pins and to avoid direct contact of the microcontroller with the sensors; two ACS712 current sensor [88] are implemented to obtain the power consumption measurement of the whole circuit (one per sensing node). Finally, a LCD016 LCD screen [89] for visualisation and physical tests of readings is implemented.

Meteorological sensors with direct compatibility with Arduino® architecture are used for the acquisition nodes, due to their cheapness and wide availability. However, in order to achieve portability, low power consumption and low costs, the typical Arduino® [108] development card is completely substituted by a smaller-scale architecture able to manage this application's data, the previously mentioned ATMEGA328P micro-controller.

The first node features 5 meteorological sensors, two of digital readings and three of analogical ones. Such sensors can generally be powered with 5 V and consumes power in the order of mA (see Table 1). Thus, node 1 can acquire variables like atmospheric pressure, altitude, environmental temperature, humidity, rain level, intensity of ultraviolet light and wind speed. On the other hand, node 2 has analogical sensors for measuring the concentration of gas and particles in the environment, all from the MQ series whose materials are designed to make them sensitive to changes in the environment, inducing voltage variations. In this sense, node 2 can acquire readings of gases as propane, hydrogen, LPG, ethyl alcohol, methane (CH4), natural gas, butane and carbon monoxide (CO) [109].

Mathematical Modelling of Sensors. In order to address the readings of analogical sensors, as is the case of the YL-83, PH0245S and ML8511 sensors of node 1 [93–95] as well as of the MQ series gas sensors, their readings are performed through the Analogical-Digital Converter (ADC) integrated within the ATMEGA328P microcontroller, thus avoiding the integration of an external ADC. The rest of the sensors in Table 1 have integrated ADC in their structure that allows the direct acquisition of their digital reading.

The terminals of the ADC of the microcontroller are used, obtaining readings within a range from $x = 0$ to 1023, so the output voltage $Vout$ is calculated by means of the proportion

$$Vout = 5\frac{x}{1023} \qquad [\text{Volt}] . \tag{1}$$

MQ sensors have an internal voltage divider. The gas sensing circuit represents a variable resistor RS. The sensors' output voltage is measured at the fixed load resistor RL with a value of 1,000 Ω. Figure 5 shows the generic resistive array of any sensor of the MQ series.

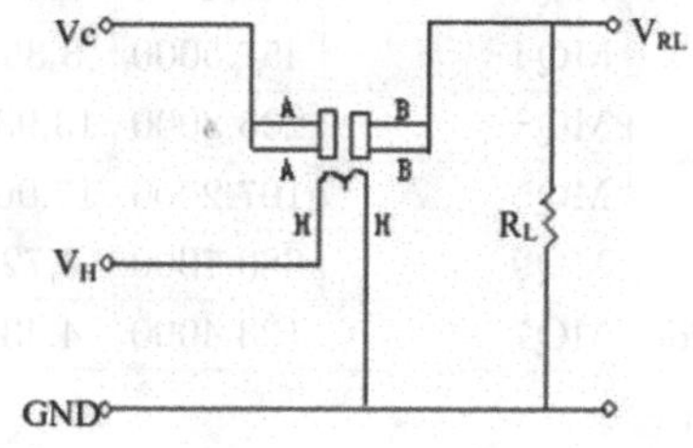

Fig. 5. Internal voltage divider for the sensors of the MQ series [97].

For the voltage divider, the output voltage $Vout$ is given by [110]

$$Vout = \frac{VC * RL}{RL + RS} \quad [\text{Volt}] \, , \tag{2}$$

where VC is the voltage with which the circuit is fed, the ratio RS/RO is a function of the gas concentration, RO is the value of the resistance, RS when it is exposed to an specific concentration of the sensed variable(s), according to their respective datasheets.

For the calculation of the concentration of any gas, C_{gas}, with its respective MQ sensor, the model of Eq. (3) is used,

$$C_{\text{gas}} = K \left(\frac{RS}{RO} \right)^{a} \quad [\text{mg/L}] \, , \tag{3}$$

where the values of K and a for an specific gas are obtained from an interpolation by a least squares fit with data provided by the manufacturer. Moreover, substituting Eq. (2) for RS in Eq. (3), it takes the form

$$C_{\text{gas}} = K \left(\frac{1,000(5 - Vout)}{RO(Vout)} \right)^{a} \quad [\text{mg/L}] \, , \tag{4}$$

which is the general model for the measurement of gas variables through the MQ sensors. Finally, in order to obtain the specific value of RO, the sensor is exposed to a saturated concentration $C_{\text{gas}_{\max}}$ of the sensed variable, obtaining a maximum voltage value of $Vout_{\max}$. Then, $C_{\text{gas}_{\max}}$ and $Vout_{\max}$ are substituted into Eq. 4 to obtain RO. Table 2 summarises the values of K, RO and a for all the gases obtained through the MQ sensors considered in Table 1.

On the other side, for the digital sensors, it is important to review the structure of the data provided by the sensors. The DHT11 module features a 1-terminal asynchronous serial communication protocol [92]. The portion of the

Table 2. Computed coefficients K, RO and a for the general gas concentration model of Eq. 4, for the distinct variables recorded by the MQ sensors.

Variable	Sensor model	K	RO	a
Hydrogen	MQ2	585.3000	2,500.70	−2.12
Alcohol	MQ3	0.4091	5,463.56	−1.49
Propane	MQ4	457.5000	3,353.09	−1.85
Methane	MQ8	235.3000	13,937.06	−1.23
Natural gas	MQ5	107.2000	17,966.86	−1.37
LPG	MQ9	689.7000	3,721.98	−1.54
Carbon monoxide	MQ7	123.4000	4,431.19	−2.32

DHT11 data frame that corresponds to the humidity and temperature values is divided into 4 bytes: the first 2 bytes contain units and decimals of the humidity percentage, while the last 2 bytes contain the units and decimals of the temperature measurement in Celsius degrees [92]. To correctly acquire the values, the decimal value of the bytes corresponding to the decimals are given by

$$LDecimal = \frac{VAcquired}{10} \,. \tag{5}$$

Finally, such a value is added to the decimal value of the integer bit reading and stored in a float type variable.

For the YL-83 digital module, the output voltage ranges from 0 to the reference voltage, which is inversely proportional to the amount of water accumulated on the surface of the capacitive sensor [93]. Equation 6 represents the percentage P_{rain} of the intensity of rain,

$$P_{rain} = 100\left(1 - \frac{Vout}{5}\right) \qquad [\%] \,. \tag{6}$$

Physical Conditioning of Sensors. In the case of the digital sensors, such as the DHT11, the module has the necessary pull up resistor for serial communication [92], so it is unnecessary to add external electronic elements for data acquisition. The physical implementation of the analogical sensors was based on a resistive voltage divider array to obtain the 3.3 V supply voltage that the rain and UV light sensors require [93,94].

For the acquisition node 2, the management of all the analogical sensors with a direct connection to the ATMEGA328P microcontroller would require large hardware resources such as a whole microcontroller port for the terminals of the ADC connected to each sensor, yielding also to the risk that such connection would expose the microcontroller to the variations of voltage presented by the sensors within their initial transitory states. In this sense, to manage the MQ sensors, the CD4051 analogical multiplexer/demultiplexer is implemented, which has 8 input/output terminals, a common terminal and a line selector bus [87].

3.2 Data Frame Structure

For data sending, it is necessary to use a suitable data structure. In the case of the present work, the frame structure of each sensor is used, as well as the native communication forms of both the sensors and the microcontroller. Table 3 shows the digital electronic components of the acquisition nodes, as well as the version of the serial communication protocol that they use.

Table 3. Specific serial communication protocols used by the digital components present in the acquisition nodes.

Components' model	ATMEGA328P [86]	CC1101 [90]	DHT11 [92]	BMP180 [91]
Serial communication protocol	SPI, I^2C, USART/UART	SPI	UART/USART	I^2C

The use of the native versions of serial communication available in each component allows a more direct communication between the devices. In what follows we describe the use of such native data frames for the digital sensors shown in Table 3.

The DHT11 sensor uses a communications protocol that works through a serial interface called Single-Wire Two-Way for data transmission and synchronisation. [92] The structure of the data frame for the payload data that the sensor transports to the microcontroller is represented in Fig. 6.

Field name	RH Integral Data	RH Decimal Data	T Integral Data	T Decimal Data
# bit	$1 \cdots 8$	$9 \cdots 16$	$17 \cdots 24$	$25 \cdots 32$

Fig. 6. DHT11 native frame structure [92].

For the structure of the native frame of the DHT11 sensor, the **RH Integral Data** field contains the integer part of the data for the relative humidity, the field **RH Decimal Data** has the decimal part of the relative humidity, the **T Integral Data** field holds the integer part of the temperature and finally the **T Decimal Data** field features the decimal part of the temperature. In total, the native frame of the DHT11 sensor consists of 32 bits.

The BMP180 sensor has a I^2C serial interface that requires a 4.7 KΩ pull up resistor connected to the sensor's SDA pin [91]. The native frame carrying the sensor's useful data is shown in Fig. 7.

Field name	Calibration data	MSB Temperature	LSB Temperature	MSB Pressure	LSB Pressure	XLSB Pressure
# bit	$1 \cdots 16$	$17 \cdots 24$	$25 \cdots 32$	$33 \cdots 40$	$41 \cdots 48$	$49 \cdots 56$

Fig. 7. BM180 data frame structure [91].

For the native frame structure of the BMP180 sensor, there is the **Calibration data** field that contains the calibration values for the sensor, the **MSB Temperature** field contains the Most Significant Bits for the temperature value, the **LSB Temperature** field contains the Least Significant Bits for the temperature value, the **MSB Pressure** field has the Most Significant Bits of the

Table 4. Analogical sensors' output voltage ranges.

Module	Voltage range (V)
MQ-2	0.00–3.02
MQ-3	0.00–3.02
MQ-4	0.00–3.04
MQ-5	0.00–3.02
MQ-6	0.00–3.02
MQ-7	0.00–3.05
MQ-8	0.00–3.06
MQ-9	0.00–3.01
YL-83	0.00–5.00
ML8511	0.00–5.00
PH0245S	0.00–5.00

atmospheric pressure value, the **LSB Pressure** field contains the Least Significant Bits for atmospheric pressure value, and the **XLSB Pressure** is an optional read register for high resolution mode. In total, the data frame sent by the BMP180 sensor consists of 56 bits.

On the other hand, analogical sensors only provides a voltage range, which is sent to the microcontroller. This voltage is used in the calculations of the Sect. 3.1 to determine the exact value of the reading for each analogical sensor. The voltage ranges for each analogical sensor are shown in Table 4.

3.3 IoT Final Application Development

In the reception stage (see Fig. 4), there is an application server where a graphical interface allows the final user to view and monitor the data coming from the dedicated network. Such interface graphically presents the data acquired in real time as graphs of the recorded variables. In order to better comply with the low-cost facet of an LPWAN/IoT based system [111], the presented interface is fully developed with open source software.

For the development of what is related to the visualisation of the sensor readings, JavaScript was selected as the main back-end and front-end language, which is based on prototypes, with dynamic typing and with support for object-oriented, imperative and declarative programming [112]. Node.js was used to compile the language, which is an asynchronous execution environment [113].

The communication implementation consists of two main stages, which are based on a client-server model, which is part of the transport layer according to the TCP/IP reference model [80]. In the server stage, the reception of data of each node from the dedicated network (transmitter) is constantly monitored, which is sent to the client stage. Such server is mounted using the Express library [114], available to be compiled through Node.js. Although the standard topology for LPWAN/IoT systems [64] requires the implementation of security and authentication techniques in the LPWAN AAA Server stage (see Sect. 2.1), they are not implemented in this work, because data for this particular application is not sensitive, as it is only data from meteorological sensors.

Once data is received and uploaded to the server, the new collected data is transmitted to all the connected clients so that the information can be displayed in real time through the socket.io library [115]. A TCP connection-oriented protocol was implemented because it is already included in the sockets due to its stability in the logical layer. For the rendering of the visual elements of the application, the React Front-End library is used because it allows to create applications with real-time execution in a practical and efficient way [116]. Since React allows to think of each library component as a function, it turns to be ideal for modular and scalable implementations [116], which is one of the cornerstones of the LPWAN/IoT systems.

According to the concept of IoT, open applications must be accessible anytime and on any devices, bearing in mind that data must be displayed correctly. Thus, a flexible and adaptable design philosophy is required. In this sense, media queries were used to allow the presentation of sensor measurements from any device (both personal computers and mobile devices), only requiring to know the web address of the application to access the interface. Additionally, the layout is carried out on a single screen in order to provide the user with the greatest ease of query and navigation [117].

The mockup for the implementation of media queries is based on the design through the use of CSS grid layout [118], which allows dividing the window by columns. Responsivity allows to decrease the number of columns according to the resolution of the window/device. Two designs are available, one with two columns when it comes to a resolution that takes at least 1,200 pixels width, and another with one column when dealing with resolutions between 500 pixels

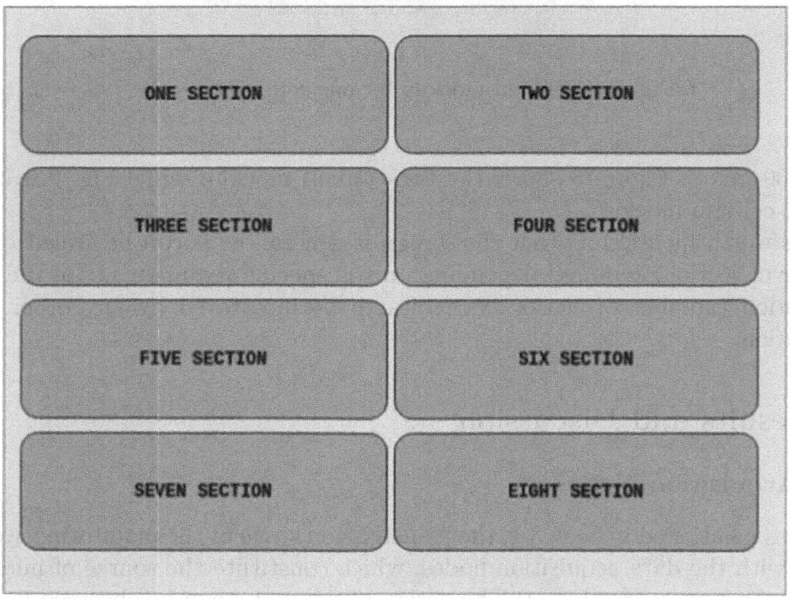

Fig. 8. CSS Grid mockup for two columns design.

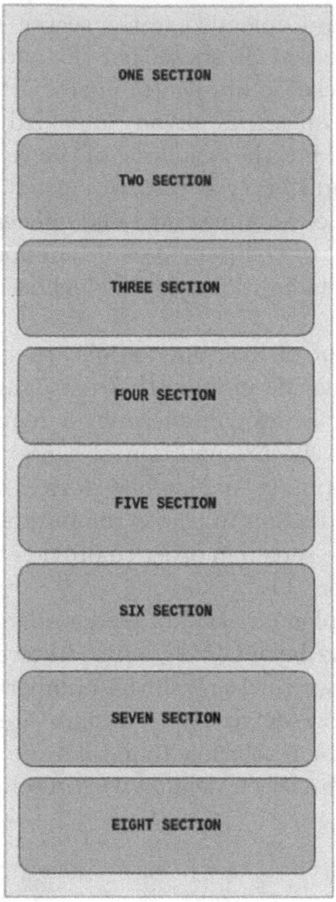

Fig. 9. CSS Grid mockup for one column design.

and 1200 pixels. Figure 8 shows the two-column mockup while Fig. 9 features the one-column mockup.

It is worth mentioning that the design is general, as it can be scaled to the number of sections required depending on the specific requirements of the final application (number of sensors/variables to be monitored by any other final application).

4 Results and Discussion

4.1 Acquisition Nodes

As it was mentioned in Sect. 3.1, the transmission stage of the monitoring system begins with the data acquisition nodes, which constitute the source of information for the system (see Fig. 4) The design of the nodes can be observed in their corresponding schematic circuits, where Fig. 10 corresponds to acquisition node 1 and Fig. 11 corresponds to node 2.

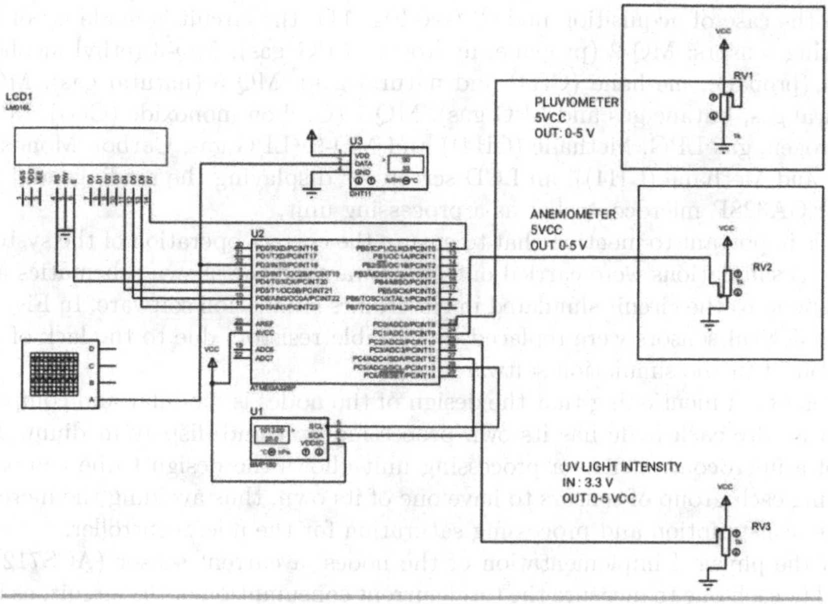

Fig. 10. Acquisition node 1 connection diagram.

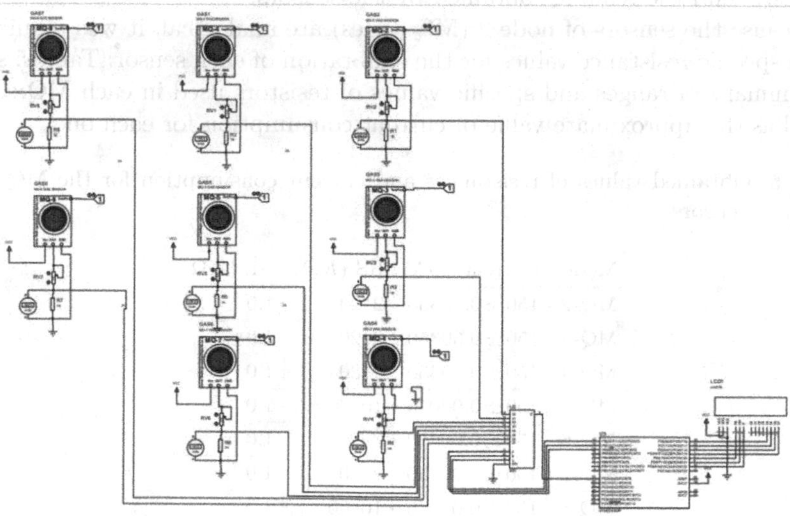

Fig. 11. Acquisition node 2 connection diagram.

As can be seen in Fig. 10, acquisition node 1 is made up of sensors BMP180 (temperature, atmospheric pressure and altitude), DHT11 (Humidity and temperature), ML8511 (ultraviolet light intensity (UV)), YL-83 (rain level), and PH0355S (wind speed), an LCD screen for physical display of the readings, and the ATMEGA328P microcontroller as the processing unit.

In the case of acquisition node 2 (see Fig. 11), the circuit is made up of the following sensors: MQ-2 (propane, hydrogen, LPG gas), MQ-3 (ethyl alcohol), MQ-4 (propane, methane (CH4) and natural gas), MQ-5 (natural gas), MQ-6 (natural gas, butane gas and LPG gas), MQ-7 (Carbon monoxide (CO)), MQ-8 (Hydrogen, gas LPG, Methane (CH4)) and MQ-9 (LPG gas, Carbon Monoxide (CO) and Methane (CH4)), an LCD screen for displaying the readings and the ATMEGA328P microcontroller as a processing unit.

It is important to mention that to ensure the correct operation of the system, previous simulations were carried out in software, so the shown schematics also correspond to the circuit simulated in electronics simulation software. In Fig. 10, the analogical sensors were replaced by variable resistors due to the lack of the component in the simulation software.

It is worth mentioning that the design of the nodes is modular and compact, which is why each node has its own processing unit and display medium. The use of a microcontroller as a processing unit allows the design to be compact, allowing each group of sensors to have one of its own, thus avoiding the increase in size, consumption and processing saturation for the microcontroller.

In the physical implementation of the nodes, a current sensor (ACS712) is added to each one to measure the total current consumption of the circuit, as it is important to obtain consumption metrics in the development phase, to guarantee a low-power design. Likewise, each node one contains a CC1101 transceiver to wirelessly send the readings obtained by the sensors.

Because the sensors of node 2 (MQ series) are analogical, it was required to obtain specific resistance values for the calibration of each sensor. Table 5 shows the summary of ranges and specific values of resistors used in each MQ sensor, as well as the approximate value of current consumption for each one.

Table 5. Obtained values of resistances and current consumption for the MQ series analogical sensors.

Model	Current (mA)	RS ($K\Omega$)	RL ($K\Omega$)
MQ-2	150 ± 0.00350	2–20	1.0
MQ-3	150 ± 0.00350	2–20	1.0
MQ-4	150 ± 0.00350	2–20	1.0
MQ-5	150 ± 0.00045	10–60	1.0
MQ-6	150 ± 0.00350	2–20	1.0
MQ-7	150 ± 0.00350	2–20	1.0
MQ-8	150 ± 0.00045	10–60	1.0
MQ-9	150 ± 0.00350	2–20	1.0

4.2 Final Structure of Data Frames

The data processed by the microcontroller, when received by the transceiver of each node, is sent in consecutive frames to the receiver. This allows more sensors to be added to the system, and independent data frames are assigned to them without affecting the sending and receiving structure of the other frames. Once the calculations specified in Sect. 3 are performed, the computed values are stored in floating-type variables with a 4-byte extension. To send the data frames, serial communication was used through an SPI interface between the ATMEGA328P microcontroller and the transceiver. The CC1101 transceiver works with a BIG ENDIAN data sending system [90]. For each data frame, the **ID** field was implemented as an 8-bit identifier to uniquely identify the sensor to which the information contained in each frame belongs. The payload data for the BMP180 sensor is placed in the **DATA BMP180** field and the DHT11 sensor payload data is placed in the **DATA DHT11** field. The length of such field varies depending on the type and number of variables for each sensor. Finally, the **CRC** field contains the sequence corresponding to the CRC (Cyclic Redundancy Check) error detection technique. Such integrity technique is native to the transceiver.

Figure 12 shows the final structure of the data frame used for the BMP180 sensor in which the values of atmospheric pressure, ambient temperature and height are sent.

Field name	ID	DATA BMP180	CRC
# bit	1 ··· 8	9 ··· 104	104 ··· 136

Fig. 12. Structure of the frame for sending the BMP180 data by the transceiver.

Figure 13 represents the final structure of the data frame used to send the DHT11 data.

Field name	ID	DATA DHT11	CRC
# bit	1 ··· 8	9 ··· 73	74 ··· 105

Fig. 13. Structure of the frame for sending the DHT11 data by the transceiver.

In the case of the analogical sensors present in the acquisition node 1, there is a general structure consisting of a sensor identifier field (**ID**) and a field that contains a floating point variable with the value calculated for each sensor reading. Finally, there is a **CRC** field containing the error detection method. The resulting data frames for YL-83 **DATA YL-83**, ML8511 **DATA ML8511** and PH02455S **DATA PH02455S** sensors are shown in Figs. 14, 15 and 16, respectively.

Field name	ID	DATA YL-83	CRC
# bit	1 ··· 8	9 ··· 40	41 ··· 72

Fig. 14. Structure of the frame for sending the YL-83 data by the transceiver.

Field name	ID	DATA ML8511	CRC
# bit	1 ⋯ 8	9 ⋯ 40	41 ⋯ 72

Fig. 15. Structure of the frame for sending the ML8511 data by the transceiver.

Field name	ID	DATA PH02455S	CRC
# bit	1 ⋯ 8	9 ⋯ 40	41 ⋯ 72

Fig. 16. Structure of the frame for sending the PH0245S data by the transceiver.

In the case of acquisition node 2, the same data frame structure is used for each MQ sensor. The structure consists of an **ID** field for assigning a unique 8-bit identifier for each sensor. For the payload data of each MQ sensor, the **DATA MQXX** field contains the binary sequence corresponding to the payload reading of the MQ-XX sensor; such a value is originally a floating point with 4 bytes extension. Finally, the **CRC** field is added for error detection. The data frame sent by the transceiver can be observed in Fig. 17.

Field name	ID	DATA MQ-XX	CRC
# bit	1 ⋯ 8	9 ⋯ 40	41 ⋯ 72

Fig. 17. General Structure of the MQ-series sensors data frame sent by the transceiver.

4.3 IoT Final Application Interface

The designed interface to show the data in real time can be observed in Fig. 18, where four screenshots that allow to display with detail the data in form of a graph as function of time are presented. To the right of each plot, the most actual record are displayed. As it can be observed, the default system shows the last 60 s of data, but such configuration can be changed to better fit the necessities of the users.

It should be also noted that, as the application layer was developed from zero, the colour palette can be fully customisable according to the profile of the end users that would access data.

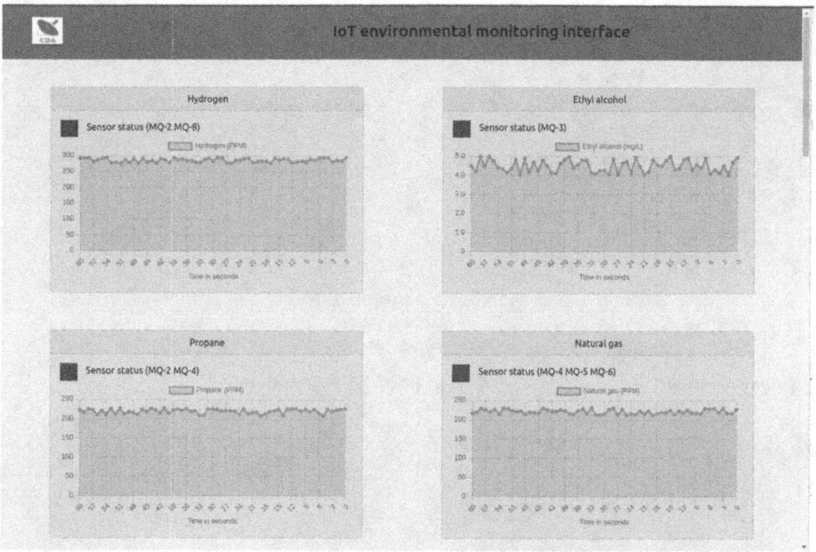

(a) Graphs for the hydrogen, alcohol, propane and natural gas variables.

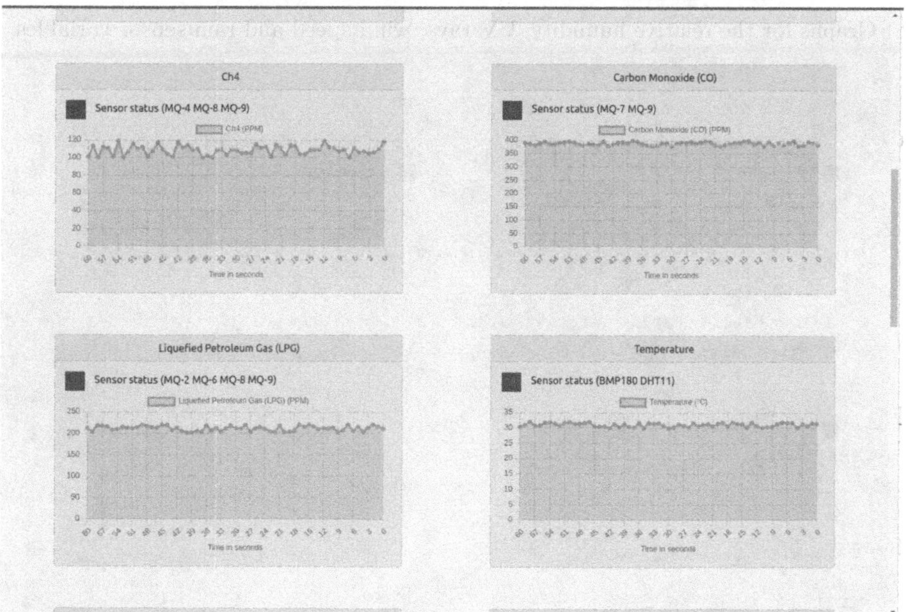

(b) Graphs for the methane, carbon monoxide, LPG and temperature variables.

Fig. 18. Screenshots of the general web data visualisation interface in a two-column browser, displaying all the variables shown in Table 1.

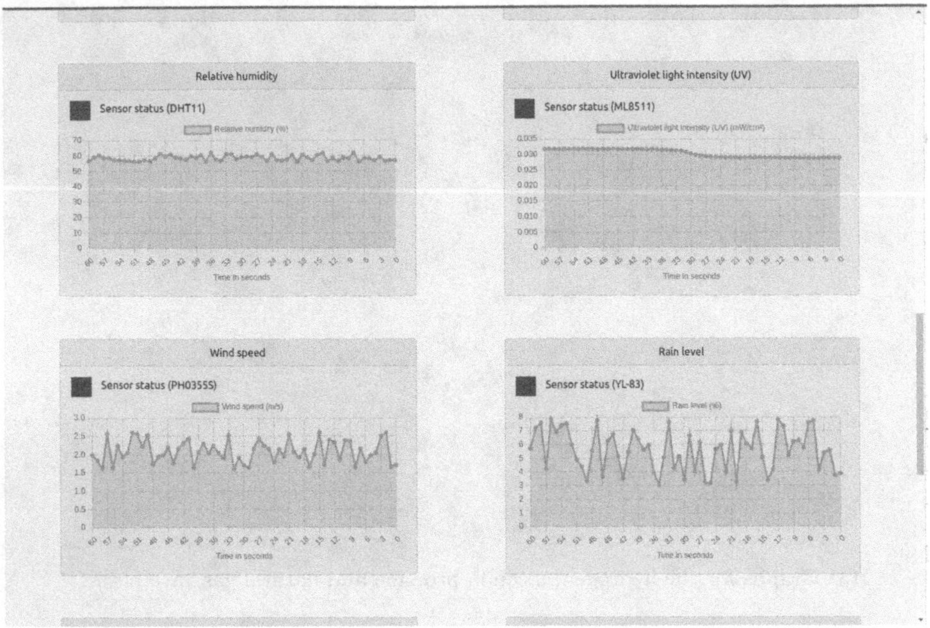

(c) Graphs for the relative humidity, UV rays, wind speed and rain sensor variables.

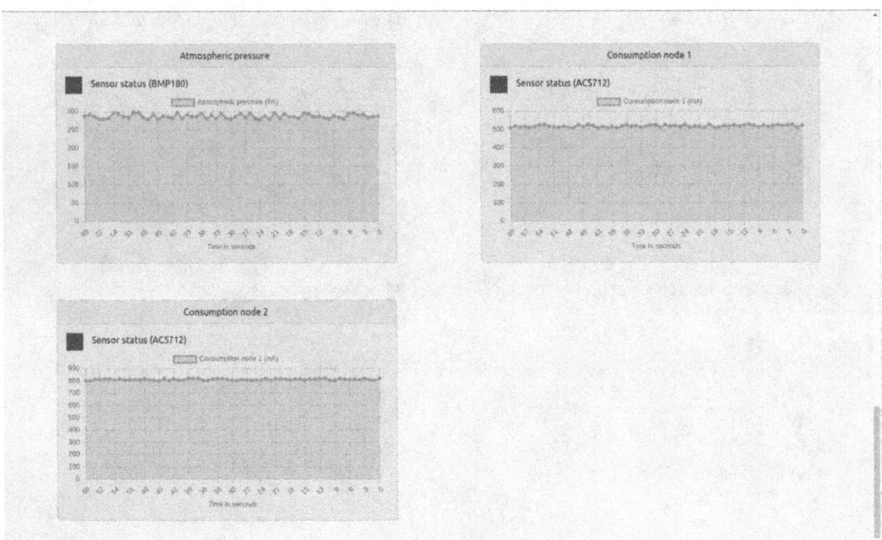

(d) Graph for the pressure variable and consumption of both nodes of the system.

Fig. 18. (*continued*)

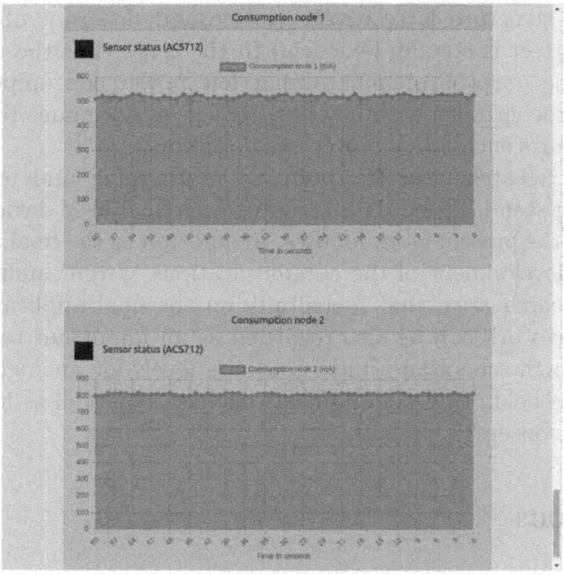

Fig. 19. General view of the interface to one column (for mobile devices).

Finally, as it was mentioned in Sect. 3.3, the interface was developed following responsiveness criteria, so the one column layout that follows from the one column mockup shown in Fig. 9 can be observed in Fig. 19.

It must be remarked that nowadays, most of the research based on LPWAN/IoT is based on the final user application as well as on the exploitation of the data gathered from an IoT system. In this sense, this research departs from such a main trend, by showing how to build and implement a system that follows the LPWAN/IoT development principles, with very low cost COTS components. The design of the communications system based on a personalized scheme has the purpose of controlling all the implementation aspects that are required to operate it, which is a remarkable aspect with respect to the use of out of the box solutions, prepared to only be connected and used [119–121]. Such turnkey products allow little (if any) participation of the final user in the design, yielding a lack of flexibility and scalability.

In this sense, despite the increased level of implementation complexity that an out of the box design may have, it is more beneficial in the long term to develop the system from zero, particularly when modifications or scaling are to be required. The same comparison can be made regarding the flexibility of operation provided by the construction of a graphical interface that works in an independent application server as proposed in this work, since cloud services such as those provided by [122,123] and [124], restrict the use and operation of the applications that are required. They also depend on the resources available to the system operator, since it is necessary to contract plans for their use, which increases the operation cost of the system.

The framing structure is relatively simple and does not obey a standard protocol. Such a fact is equally beneficial in the sense that the data modelling is adapted to the purpose of maintaining low power consumption. Likewise, the use of a microcontroller with low but enough performance to carry out the processing, supports such a low power consumption.

Finally, this research is at the point of prototyping and testing systems, not yet including standardised data structures or final user devices. It is worth mentioning that the present work focuses, in addition to the final application, on the design and development of the communications system, unlike most of the works in the research area, that focus only on the final application [125–127]. In this sense, this work can be also regarded as an important teaching tool for students in the high school and undergraduate levels for analogical and digital electronics, in the field of telecommunications basics, as well as for the teaching of IoT/LPWAN concepts.

5 Conclusions

In the present work, an environmental monitoring system was developed based on LPWAN/IoT networks' principles that uses low-cost COTS components and free software tools, which allows to acquire and display different meteorological variables.

Regarding the physical implementation of the system, the use of small-scale COTS processing architectures as the ATMEGA328 microcontroller, turns to be enough to acquire and process the required number of variables without any difficulties but the external conditioning implemented for the components. The ATMEGA328 microcontroller allows to maintain very low power consumption values, which makes it highly attractive and useful compared to microprocessors or programmable architectures already arranged on development cards.

External conditioning is especially important for the node featuring the MQ-series sensors, where a multiplexer circuit was required to expand the number of pins available on the microcontroller, reducing the necessity of two or more microcontrollers. Moreover, the multiplexer circuit also allows to avoid a direct interaction between the microcontroller and the sensors. This is an important feature, since voltage variations in the unstable initial transitory state could yield microcontroller malfunction.

Furthermore, the sensors' external conditioning is of low complexity, consisting in the usage of basic components such as resistors or simple integrated circuits, achieving the correct operation of the system in any way.

It is worth to mention that the selected sensors (see Table 1) are not directly compatible with the ATMEGA328 processing architecture, as they are designed to work flawlessly with the Ardunio® platform. However, the simplicity of serial communication, along with the mentioned external conditioning, allow to combine different architectures and components from different manufacturers without direct compatibility, expanding the design possibilities with a wider range of very low-cost COTS components.

On the other hand, the tools for the development of the graphical interface are completely based on free software, which allow more freedom and flexibility, clearly reducing the implementation costs when deployed. Although in this work we propose the use of a proprietary server to deploy the IoT final application, any cloud service could be used instead. Moreover, the used programming languages contain powerful utilities to develop rich and attractive display media.

Despite its simplicity, the use of serial communication as a transfer and construction protocol for the frame structure shows to be a useful method to provide simple and compatible communication between devices, since any of the used components allow communication through this protocol. Furthermore, serial communication also provided enough simplicity for the transfer and display of information in the graphical interface, since no other protocol or structure was required both for the reception of information as well as for its extraction and graphical presentation.

The transfer method used for the link between the dedicated network (transmitter) and the external network (receiver) is performed through a connection-oriented service. Despite representing an additional load for the system, it provides features such as security, integrity for the data and certain stability to the communication, which is desirable to guarantee an operation with the fewest possible interruptions.

The power supply and consumption parameters are kept within values of the order of 1.2 A. Although at first glance it may seem a high value, it represents a low power consumption if it is considered that several elements are placed in each acquisition node. In Table 6, a summary of such parameters can be observed.

Table 6. System consumption summary.

Node	No. node elements	No. acquired variables	Supply voltage (V)	Current consumption* (mA)
Node 1	14	9	3.3–5	509
Node 2	17	19	3.3–5	710
Total	**31**	**17**	**3.3–5**	**1,219**

* Current consumption presented in this Table is in the stationary state, after peaks of the initial transitory phase.

From Table 6, it should be noted that the consumed current is of about 43.53 mA per recorded variable, reaffirmating the low current consumption of the entire system, placing it within the parameters of IoT/LPWAN applications.

The system design proposal with more than one acquisition node allows to preserve the characteristics of modularity, scalability, portability and low energy consumption, also providing an attribute of security and stability to the physical structure since the number of elements within each circuit is kept limited.

It should also be remarked that the acquisition nodes were designed to be placed in a fixed location, known *a priori* by the user. However, the herein proposed methodology allows to implement a Global Positioning System (GPS) as well as an Inertial Measurement Unit (IMU) modules for location and monitoring of acceleration and orientation of the nodes, in case that they should be mobile, depending on the requirements of the developer.

As final remarks, the proposed methodology allows to design very low-cost COTS-based IoT monitoring solutions adapted to the specific requirements of any application, that can be mounted in any LPWAN system and server, through the use of open source software, providing the greatest flexibility in design and operation phases.

6 Future Work

This research can be extended in the following pathways:

- To assess the network performance with a large number of acquisition nodes.
- To implement a distributed embedded system based on the processing architecture herein used to increase the processing capacity.
- To implement different LPWAN standardised protocols to assess their performance with the data generated by these specific acquisition nodes.
- To improve the connection-oriented service proposal by implementing nearby transmission points to ensure permanent connection.
- To increase the number of variables acquired by the system.
- To improve the readability and options of the web monitoring interface.
- To assess cloud computing services in order to compare their performance with the proposal of this work.

Acknowledgements. The authors acknowledge partial economical support by projects 20220907, 20221182, 20222032 and 20220176, as well as EDI grant, provided by Secretaría de Investigación y Posgrado, Instituto Politécnico Nacional. Authors also acknowledge Prof. Irving Eleazar Pérez-Montes (CECyT 09 "Juan de Dios Batiz") for his support in the completion of this research.

References

1. Stankovic, J.A.: Research directions for the internet of things. IEEE Internet Things J. **1**(1), 3–9 (2014)
2. Pattnaik, S., et al.: Future wireless communication technology towards 6g IoT: an application-based analysis of IoT in real-time location monitoring of employees inside underground mines by using BLE. Sensors **22**(9), 3438 (2022)
3. Zhang, G., Navimipour, N.: A comprehensive and systematic review of the IoT-based medical management systems: applications, techniques, trends and open issues. Sustain. Cities Soc. **82**, 103914 (2022)
4. Sharma, V., Tripathi, A.: A systematic review of meta-heuristic algorithms in IoT based application. Array **14**, 100164 (2022)
5. Sreedevi, A., Harshitha, T.N., Sugumaran, V., Shankar, P.: Application of cognitive computing in healthcare, cybersecurity, big data and IoT: a literature review. Inf. Process. Manag. **59**(2), 102888 (2022)

6. Fazea, Y., Mohammed, F., Al-Nahari, A.: A review on 5g technology in IoT-application based on light fidelity (LI-FI) indoor communication. Lect. Notes Data Eng. Commun. Technol. **127**, 371–384 (2022)
7. Maranesi, E., Amabili, G., Cucchieri, G., Bolognini, S., Margaritini, A., Bevilacqua, R.: Understanding the acceptance of IoT and social assistive robotics for the healthcare sector: a review of the current user-centred applications for the older users. Stud. Comput. Intell. **1011**, 331–351 (2022)
8. de Abreu, C., van Deventer, J.: The application of artificial intelligence (AI) and internet of things (IoT) in agriculture: a systematic literature review. Commun. Comput. Inf. Sci. (CCIS) **1551**, 32–46 (2022)
9. Srivastava, A., Das, D.: A comprehensive review on the application of internet of thing (IoT) in smart agriculture. Wireless Pers. Commun. **122**(2), 1807–1837 (2022)
10. Mothe, R., Tharun Reddy, S., Vijay Kumar, B., Rajeshwar Rao, A., Chythanya, K.R.: A review on big data analytics in internet of things (IoT) and its roles, applications and challenges. In: Kumar, A., Senatore, S., Gunjan, V.K. (eds.) ICDSMLA 2020. LNEE, vol. 783, pp. 765–773. Springer, Singapore (2022). https://doi.org/10.1007/978-981-16-3690-5_70
11. Pal, R., et al.: A comprehensive review on IoT-based infrastructure for smart grid applications. IET Renew. Power Gener. **15**(16), 3761–3776 (2021)
12. Alawad, F., Kraemer, F.: Value of information in wireless sensor network applications and the IoT: a review. IEEE Sens. J. **22**(10), 9228–9245 (2022)
13. Jan, F., Min-Allah, N., Saeed, S., Iqbal, S., Ahmed, R.: IoT-based solutions to monitor water level, leakage, and motor control for smart water tanks. Water (Switzerland) **14**(3), 309 (2022)
14. Dankan Gowda, V., Swetha, K., Namitha, A., Manu, Y., Rashmi, G., Chinamuttevi, V.: IoT based smart health care system to monitor COVID-19 patients. Int. J. Electr. Electron. Res. **10**(1), 36–40 (2022)
15. Sharma, A., Nagajayanthi, B., Chaitanya Kumar, A., Dinakaran, S.: IoT-based COVID-19 patient monitor with alert system. Lecture Notes in Electrical Engineering, vol. 792, pp. 1019–1027 (2022)
16. Casillo, M., Colace, F., Lorusso, A., Marongiu, F., Santaniello, D.: An IoT-based system for expert user supporting to monitor, manage and protect cultural heritage buildings. Stud. Comput. Intell. **1030**, 143–154 (2022)
17. Dinesh, M., et al.: An energy efficient architecture for furnace monitor and control in foundry based on industry 4.0 using IoT. Scient. Programm. **2022**, 1–8 (2022). Article ID 1128717
18. Spang, C., Lavan, Y., Hartmann, M., Meisel, F., Koch, A.: DExIE - an IoT-class hardware monitor for real-time fine-grained control-flow integrity. J. Sign. Process. Syst. **94**(7), 739–752 (2022)
19. Gonzalez, C., Espinosa, A., Ponte, D., Gibeaux, S.: Smart-IoT platform to monitor microclimate conditions in tropical regions. In: IOP Conference Series: Earth and Environmental Science, vol. 835 (2021)
20. Fan, X., Yan, Y., Yang, P., Han, F.: CMSS: use low-power IoT cameras to monitor store shelves. In: Proceedings–2021 7th International Conference on Big Data Computing and Communications, BigCom 2021, pp. 309–315 (2021)
21. Sastrawan, I., Gunadi, I., Ernanda, K.: The use of IoT technology based on the forward chaining method to monitor the feasibility of rice field. J. Phys. Conference Series **1810**(1), 012006 (2021)
22. Wang, E., Wang, F., Kumari, S., Yeh, J.H., Chen, C.M.: Intelligent monitor for typhoon in IoT system of smart city. J. Supercomput. **77**(3), 3024–3043 (2021)

23. Hernandez-Alpizar, L., Carrasquilla-Batista, A., Sancho-Chavarria, L.: Monitoring adjustment based on current data of an IoT-cots monitor for environmental chemical analysis. In: 2021 IEEE 12th Latin American Symposium on Circuits and Systems, LASCAS 2021 (2021)
24. Chauhan, H., Gupta, D., Gupta, S., Haque, M.: A smart cradle system to monitor infants for healthcare baby wards based on IoT and blockchain. In: Proceedings - 2021 3rd International Conference on Advances in Computing, Communication Control and Networking, ICAC3N 2021, pp. 606–609 (2021)
25. Yuan, Z.L., Hua, Z.S., Chun, J.J.: Design of small automatic weather station monitoring system based on NB-IoT technology. Meteorol. Sci. Technol. **48**(06), 816–822 (2020)
26. Gallareta, E.S., Gómez, J.J.H., Balam, G.C., del Castillo, M.O., Sabido, M.M., Aguilera, R.A.S.: Sistema Híbrido Basado en Redes Neuronales Artificiales y Descomposición Modal Empírica para la Evaluación de la Interrelación entre la Irradiancia Solar Total y el Calentamiento Global. Res. Comput. Sci. **147**(5), 319–332 (2018)
27. Interngubernamental Panel on Climate Change: IPCC: Working Group I Contribution to the IPCC Fifth Assessment Report, Climate Change 2013: The Physical Science Basis. IPCC. AR5. Interngubernamental Panel on Climate Change (2014)
28. Landis, J., Hsu, D., Guerra, E.: Intersecting residential and transportation CO 2 emissions: metropolitan climate change programs in the age of trump. J. Plan. Educ. Res. **39**(2), 206–226 (2019)
29. Trájer, A., Nagy, G., Domokos, E.: Exploration of the heterogeneous effect of climate change on ozone concentration in an urban environment. Int. J. Environ. Health Res. **29**(3), 276–289 (2019)
30. Baldermann, C., Lorenz, S.: UV radiation in Germany: influences of ozone depletion and climate change and measures to protect the population. Bundesgesundheitsblatt - Gesundheitsforschung - Gesundheitsschutz **62**(5), 639–645 (2019)
31. Orimoloye, I., Mazinyo, S., Kalumba, A., Ekundayo, O., Nel, W.: Implications of climate variability and change on urban and human health: a review. Cities **91**, 213–223 (2019)
32. Woodward, A., Baumgartner, J., Ebi, K., Gao, J., Kinney, P., Liu, Q.: Population health impacts of China's climate change policies. Environ. Res. **175**, 178–185 (2019)
33. Doan, V., Kusaka, H., Nguyen, T.: Roles of past, present, and future land use and anthropogenic heat release changes on urban heat island effects in Hanoi, Vietnam: numerical experiments with a regional climate model. Sust. Cities Soc. **47**, 101479 (2019)
34. Chapman, S., Thatcher, M., Salazar, A., Watson, J., McAlpine, C.: The impact of climate change and urban growth on urban climate and heat stress in a subtropical city. Int. J. Climatol. **39**(6), 3013–3030 (2019)
35. Zhang, C., Li, S., Luo, F., Huang, Z.: The global warming hiatus has faded away: an analysis of 2014–2016 global surface air temperatures. Int. J. Climatol. **39**, 4853–4868 (2019)
36. Shastri, H., Ghosh, S., Paul, S., Shafizadeh-Moghadam, H., Helbich, M., Karmakar, S.: Future urban rainfall projections considering the impacts of climate change and urbanization with statistical-dynamical integrated approach. Clim. Dyn. **52**(9–10), 6033–6051 (2019)
37. Dodman, D., Archer, D., Satterthwaite, D.: Editorial: responding to climate change in contexts of urban poverty and informality. Environ. Urban. **31**(1), 3–12 (2019)

38. Castro, J.G., De Robles, S.R.: Climate change and flood risk: vulnerability assessment in an urban poor community in Mexico. Environ. Urban. **31**(1), 75–92 (2019)
39. Xiong, L., Yan, L., Du, T., Yan, P., Li, L., Xu, W.: Impacts of climate change on urban extreme rainfall and drainage infrastructure performance: a case study in Wuhan city. China. Irrigation Drainage **68**(2), 152–164 (2019)
40. De la Sota, C., Ruffato-Ferreira, V., Ruiz-García, L., Alvarez, S.: Urban green infrastructure as a strategy of climate change mitigation. A case study in northern Spain. Urban Forestry Urban Green. **40**, 145–151 (2019)
41. Lal, R.: Managing urban soils for food security and adaptation to climate change. In: Vasenev, V., Dovletyarova, E., Cheng, Z., Prokof'eva, T.V., Morel, J.L., Ananyeva, N.D. (eds.) SUITMA 2017. SG, pp. 302–319. Springer, Cham (2019). https://doi.org/10.1007/978-3-319-89602-1_35
42. Raimundo, I.: Food insecurity in the context of climate change in Maputo city. Challenges and coping strategies. ROUTLEDGE in association with GSE Research, Mozambique (2016)
43. Mahaut, V., Andrieu, H.: Relative influence of urban-development strategies and water management on mixed (separated and combined) sewer overflows in the context of climate change and population growth: a case study in Nantes. Sustain. Urban Areas **44**, 171–182 (2019)
44. Yang, D., Frangopol, D.: Societal risk assessment of transportation networks under uncertainties due to climate change and population growth. Struct. Saf. **78**, 33–47 (2019)
45. Januszkiewicz, K., Świtoń, M.: Climate change and population mobility - envisioning infrastructure to reduce disaster's impact on cities. In: International Multidisciplinary Scientific Geo Conference Surveying Geology and Mining Ecology Management, SGEM. 62, vol. 17, pp. 519–526 (2017)
46. Khavarian-Garmsir, A., Pourahmad, A., Hataminejad, H., Farhoodi, R.: Climate change and environmental degradation and the drivers of migration in the context of shrinking cities: a case study of Khuzestan province, Iran. Sustain. Cities Soc. **47**, 101480 (2019)
47. Trihamdani, A.R., Lee, H.S., Kubota, T., Iizuka, S., Phuong, T.T.T.: Urban climate challenges in Hanoi: urban heat islands and global warming. In: Kubota, T., Rijal, H.B., Takaguchi, H. (eds.) Sustainable Houses and Living in the Hot-Humid Climates of Asia, pp. 529–539. Springer, Singapore (2018). https://doi.org/10.1007/978-981-10-8465-2_48
48. Li, G., Zhang, X., Mirzaei, P., Zhang, J., Zhao, Z.: Urban heat island effect of a typical valley city in China: responds to the global warming and rapid urbanization. Sustain. Urban Areas **38**, 736–745 (2018)
49. Doose, K.: A global problem in a divided world: climate change research during the late cold war, 1972–1991. Cold War History **21**(4), 469–489 (2021)
50. Sahin, G., Ayyildiz, F.: Climate change and energy policies: European union-scale approach to a global problem. Lecture Notes in Energy, vol. 77, pp. 295–320 (2020)
51. World Bank: Urban population (% of total)—Data. https://data.worldbank.org/indicator/sp.urb.totl.in.zs (2020). united Nations Population Division. World Urbanization Prospects: 2018 Revision. Online. Accessed 9th May 2022
52. United Nations: World cities report 2020: The value of sustainable urbanization (2020), economics and Social Affairs series (2020)
53. Wang, C.X., et al.: Cellular architecture and key technologies for 5G wireless communication networks. IEEE Commun. Mag. **52**(2), 122–130 (2014)

54. Ahir, R.K., Chakraborty, B.: Pattern-based and context-aware electricity theft detection in smart grid. Sustain. Energy Grids Netw. **32**, 100833 (2022)
55. Junejo, A.K., Benkhelifa, F., Wong, B., Mccann, J.A.: LoRa-LiSK: a lightweight shared secret key generation scheme for LoRA networks. IEEE Internet Things J. **9**(6), 4110–4124 (2021)
56. Singh, N., Shukla, A.: A review on progress and future trends for wireless network for communication system. Lecture Notes in Electrical Engineering, vol. 776, pp. 445–453 (2022)
57. Jaruwatanadilok, S.: Underwater wireless optical communication channel modeling and performance evaluation using vector radiative transfer theory. IEEE J. Sel. Areas Commun. **26**(9), 1620–1627 (2008)
58. Haider, A., Chatterjee, A.: Low-cost alternate EVM test for wireless receiver systems. In: VTS, pp. 255–260 (2005)
59. Zhao, Y., Ye, Z.: A low-cost GSM/GPRS based wireless home security system. IEEE Trans. Consum. Electron. **54**(2), 567–572 (2008)
60. Kildal, P.S., Glazunov, A.A., Carlsson, J., Majidzadeh, A.: Cost-effective measurement setups for testing wireless communication to vehicles in reverberation chambers and anechoic chambers. In: 2014 IEEE Conference on Antenna Measurements & Applications (CAMA), pp. 1–4. IEEE (2014)
61. International Telecommunication Union: Technical and operational aspects of Low Power Wide Area Networks for machine-type communication and the Internet of Things in frequency ranges harmonised for SRD operation. Technical Report 1, International Telecommunication Union, Ginebra, Switzerland (2018)
62. Kim, D.Y., Jung, M.: Data transmission and network architecture in long range low power sensor networks for IoT. Wireless Pers. Commun. **93**(1), 119–129 (2017)
63. Internet Engineering Task Force: Mission and Principles. Online (2022). https://www.ietf.org/about/mission/. Accessed 15 May 2022
64. Internet Engineering Task Force (IETF): Low-Power Wide Area Network (LPWAN) Overview. Technical report, Internet Engineering Task Force (IETF), Dublin, Ireland (2018). https://datatracker.ietf.org/doc/html/rfc8376
65. Internet Engineering Task Force (IETF): Architectural Considerations in Smart Object Networking. Technical report, Internet Engineering Task Force (IETF), Dublin, Ireland (2015). https://datatracker.ietf.org/doc/html/rfc7452
66. Cirani, S., Ferrari, G., Picone, M., Veltri, L.: Internet of Things: Architectures, Protocols and Standards. Wiley (2018). https://books.google.com.mx/books?id=iERsDwAAQBAJ
67. Deng, S., et al.: Dependent function embedding for distributed serverless edge computing. IEEE Trans. Parall. Distrib. Syst. **33**, 2346–2357 (2021)
68. Kalatzis, N., et al.: Semantic interoperability for IoT platforms in support of decision making: an experiment on early wildfire detection. Sensors **19**(3) (2019). https://www.mdpi.com/1424-8220/19/3/528
69. Bahashwan, A., Anbar, M., Abdullah, N., Al-Hadhrami, T., Hanshi, S.: Review on common IoT communication technologies for both long-range network (LPWAN) and short-range network. Adv. Intell. Syst. Comput. **1188**, 341–353 (2021)
70. Celebi, H.B., Pitarokoilis, A., Skoglund, M.: Wireless communication for the industrial IoT. In: Butun, I. (ed.) Industrial IoT: Challenges, Design Principles, Applications, and Security, 1, vol. 1, chap. 1, pp. 57–63. Springer International Publishing, Gewerbestrasse, Switzerland, 1 edn. July 2020. https://doi.org/10.1007/978-3-030-42500-5_2
71. LoRa Alliance Corporate Bylaws: A technical overview of LoRa and LoRaWAN. Technical Report 1, LoRa Alliance, Fermont, California, United States (2015)

72. Sigfox: Sigfox Technical Overview. Technical Report 1, Sigfox, Labège, France (2021)
73. Global System for Mobile Association: LTE-M Deployment Guide to Basic Feature set Requirements. Technical Report 1, GSMA, London, UK (2019)
74. Global System for Mobile Association: NB-IoT Deployment Guide to Basic Feature set Requirements. Technical Report 1, GSMA, London, UK (2019)
75. ISA100 Wireless Compliance Institute: The Technology Behind the ISA100.11a Standard-An Exploration. Technical Report 1, ISA100, London, UK (2021)
76. Electronic Industries Alliance/Telecommunications Industry Association: EIA/TIA Recommended Standard (RS)-232C. Technical Report 1, EIA/TIA, Virginia, United States (2016)
77. Ibrahim, D.: PIC Microcontroller Projects in C: Basic to Advanced. Elsevier Science (2014). https://books.google.com.mx/books?id=xQajAgAAQBAJ
78. Bolton, W.: Programmable Logic Controllers. Engineering Pro collection, Elsevier Science (2011). https://books.google.com.mx/books?id=zsyTTGxCIdMC
79. Dawoud, D., Dawoud, P.: Serial Communication Protocols and Standards: RS232/485, UART/USART, SPI, USB, INSTEON, Wi-Fi and WiMAX. River Publishers Series in Communications Series, River Publishers (2020). https://books.google.com.mx/books?id=nj50zQEACAAJ
80. Tanenbaum, A.S.: Computer Networks. No. p. 3 in Computer Networks, Prentice Hall PTR (2003). https://books.google.com.mx/books?id=dRNLAQAAIAAJ
81. Institute of Electrical and Electronics Engineers: 802.3cg Standard - Ethernet. Tech. Rep. 802.3cg, Institute of Electrical and Electronics Engineers, New Jersey, United States (2019)
82. Institute of Electrical and Electronics Engineers: 802.11 Standard - Wireless LAN. Technical Report 802.11, Institute of Electrical and Electronics Engineers, New Jersey, United States (2016)
83. Institute of Electrical and Electronics Engineers: 802.15.4 Standard - Low Rate Wireless Network. Technical report 802.15.4, Institute of Electrical and Electronics Engineers, New Jersey, United States (2020)
84. International Telecommunication Union: Technical and operational aspects of low-power wide-area networks for machine-type communication and the Internet of Things in frequency ranges harmonised for SRD operation. Technical Report SM.2423-0, International Telecommunication Union, Ginebra, Switzerland, June 2018
85. Yuksel, M.E., Fidan, H.: Energy-aware system design for Battery-Less LPWAN devices in IoT applications. Ad Hoc Netw. **122**, 102625 (2021)
86. Atmel Corp.: ATmega328P 8-bit AVR Microcontroller with 32K Bytes In-System. Atmel Corp., California, United States, 1 edn. (2015)
87. National Semiconductor : CD4051BM/CD4051BC Single 8-Channel AnalogMultiplexer/Demultiplexer Module. National Semiconductor, Santa Clara, United States, 1 edn. (2013)
88. Allegro MicroSystems: Fully integrated, hall effect-based linear current sensor. Allegro MicroSystems, New Hampshire, United States, 60950-1-03 edn. (2003)
89. Hitachi: Dot Matrix Liquid Crystal Display Controller/Driver. Hitachi, Tokyo, Japan, hd44780u (lcd-ii) edn. (1998)
90. Chipcon Products.: Low-Cost Low-Power Sub-1GHz RF Transceiver. Texas Instrument., Texas, United States, 6 edn. (2015)
91. Bosch: BMP180 Digital Pressure Sensor. Bosch, Gerlingen, Germany, 2 edn. April 2013

92. Electronics, M.: DHT11 Humidity and Temperature Sensor, 1st edn. Mouser Electronics, Mansfield, Texas, United States (2019)
93. VAISALA: Yl-83 Rain Detector. VAISALA, Eindhoven, Netherlands, b01001en-b edn. (2015)
94. Keyestudio : GY-ML8511 Ultraviolet Sensor Module. Keyestudio, Ischia, Italy, 1 edn. (2013)
95. DFRobot: Wind speed sensor. Online (2022). https://wiki.dfrobot.com/Wind_Speed_Sensor_Voltage_Type_0-5V__SKU_SEN0170. Accessed 15 May 2022
96. Pololu: MQ-2 Semiconductor Sensor for Combustible Gas, Pololu, Las Vegas, United States, 1 edn. April 2013
97. Pololu: MQ-3 Semiconductor Sensor for Alcohol, Pololu, Las Vegas, United States, 1 edn. April 2013
98. Pololu: MQ-4 Semiconductor Sensor for Combustible Gas, Pololu, Las Vegas, United States, 1 edn. April 2013
99. Hanwei Electronics Co., LTD: MQ-5 Gas sensor. Hanwei Electronics Co., LTD, Beijing, China, 1 edn. January 2015
100. Pololu: MQ-6 Semiconductor Sensor for Combustible Gas, Pololu, Las Vegas, United States, 1 edn. April 2013
101. Pololu: MQ-7 Semiconductor Sensor for Combustible Gas, Pololu, Las Vegas, United States, 1 edn. April 2013
102. Hanwei Electronics Co., LTD: MQ-8 Gas sensor. Hanwei Electronics Co., LTD, Beijing, China, 1 edn. January 2015
103. Pololu: MQ-9 Semiconductor Sensor for Combustible Gas, Pololu, Las Vegas, United States, 1 edn. April 2013
104. Microchip Technology Inc.®: AVR MCUs®. https://www.microchip.com/en-us/products/microcontrollers-and-microprocessors/8-bit-mcus/avr-mcus# (2021). Accessed May 2022
105. Semiconductors, P.: AN10216-01 I2C Bus, an10216 edn. Phillips Semiconductors, Eindhoven, Netherlands (2003)
106. International Union of Telecommunications: short-range radio communication devices measurements. Technical report, International Union of Telecommunications, Ginebra, Switzerland (2010)
107. Instruments, T.: CMOS single 8-channel analog multiplexer, schs047g edn. Texas Instruments, Texas, United States (2003)
108. Arduino: Overview. Online (2022). https://www.arduino.cc/. Accessed 15 May 2022
109. Pololu Corporation: Pololu Robotics and Electronics. Online (2022). https://www.pololu.com/. Accessed 15 May 2022
110. Dorf, R., Svoboda, J.: Introduction to Electric Circuits. John Wiley & Sons (2010). https://books.google.com.mx/books?id=IwhxyuqsuZIC
111. Anass, D., Madi, A.A., Alihamidi, I., Charaf, L.A., Saber, M.: A novel autonomous remote system applied in agriculture using transmission control protocol. Int. J. Reconfigurable Embedded Syst. **11**(1), 1–12 (2022)
112. Mozilla: Javascript. https://developer.mozilla.org/es/docs/Web/JavaScript (2022). Accessed 12 June 2022
113. Joyent, N.D.: Node.js. https://nodejs.org/api/ (2022). Accessed 12 June 2022
114. Foundation, O.: Express 4.x. https://expressjs.com/en/4x/api.html (2017). Accessed 12 June 2022
115. Arrachequesne, D.: Socket.io. https://socket.io/docs/v4/ (2022). Accessed 12 June 2022

116. Platforms, M.: React. https://es.reactjs.org/docs/getting-started.html (2022). Accessed 12 June 2022
117. Massachusetts Institute of Technology: Breakpoints Bootstrap. Online (2022). https://getbootstrap.com/docs/5.0/layout/breakpoints/. Accessed 30 May 2022
118. Mozilla Foundation: CSS Grid Layout. Online (2022). https://developer.mozilla.org/es/docs/Web/CSS/CSS_Grid_Layout. Accessed 30 May 2022
119. Semtech: SX127x Development Kit. Semtech, California, United States, rev 1 edn. (2015)
120. DIGI: DIGI XBEE 3 cellular LTE-M development kit. DIGI, Minesota, United States, 91004244 a9/720 edn. (2020)
121. Sigfox: Sens'it Discovery 3.3. Sigfox, Labege, France, April 2020 edn. (2020)
122. Arduino: IoT cloud plans. Online (2022). https://www.arduino.cc/cloud/plans. Accessed 15 May 2022
123. Amazon Web Services: AWS Pricing Calculator. Online (2022). https://calculator.aws/#/?nc2=h_ql_pr_calc. Accessed 15 May 2022
124. LoRa: LoRa Geolocation Price Calculator. Online (2022). https://www.loracloud.com/#pricing. Accessed 15 May 2022
125. dos Santos Freitas, M.J., Moraes, A., Marques, J.C., Rodrigues, F.: A contribution to real-time space weather monitoring based on scintillation observations and IoT. Adv. Space Res. (2022)
126. Amiri-Zarandi, M., Fard, M.H., Yousefinaghani, S., Kaviani, M., Dara, R.: A platform approach to smart farm information processing. Agriculture **12**(6), 838 (2022)
127. Soheli, S.J., Jahan, N., Hossain, M., Adhikary, A., Khan, A.R., Wahiduzzaman, M., et al.: Smart greenhouse monitoring system using internet of things and artificial intelligence. Wireless Personal Commun. 1–32 (2022). https://doi.org/10.1007/s11277-022-09528-x

Blockchain Technology Applied to Health Care Supply Chain

Diego Alejandro Ochoa González[1(✉)] and Alejandra Guadalupe Silva Trujillo[2]

[1] Department of Computer Science, Université de Pau et des Pays de l'Adour, Anglet, France
d.ochoa@etud.univ-pau.fr

[2] Department of Computer Engineering,
Universidad Autónoma de San Luis Potosí, San Luis Potosí, S.L.P., México
asilva@uaslp.mx

Abstract. Supply Chain Management (SCM) has grown in the last years due to the changing and evolutionary environment. The SCM has become fundamental for gaining financial and social, among others, benefits. Currently, the traditional SCM mechanisms have some areas of improvement, such as the transparency and lack of information, long waiting times for information retrieval and data fidelity. The past months our daily lives have been changing in a drastic way due to COVID-19 and some industries were affected but with this change there has been some opportunities to improve. In this article we describe the main concepts about the blockchain technology, the smart contracts, and their main use. We talk about different areas that these technologies could help to improve in different ways of their internal and external processes. Our main discussion is the description and improvement in the performance inside a supply chain, how it could be possible to speed up the information sharing, how a smart contract could be applied to a consumer-supplier relationship in the healthcare supply chain and the benefits that it would bring to it due to the quick times that this area demands because of the nature of their transactions and operations that are critical to maintain the needs of the industry.

Keywords: Supply chain · Blockchain · Health care · Smart contract · Management systems

1 Introduction

Blockchain technology has become an important field of study and growth in the last years, this study aims to give an overview of the way we make transactions in our daily professional or personal life and the security of this transactions that becomes important for the use of this technology.

In the industry or in the business operation the transactions rely mostly on a centralized process or need the authorization from third parties, some of them are an extra step in the chain that they are used to follow. In the healthcare Supply Chain Management some actors are involved and take part in the decisions made to achieve a goal, in this case provide the needs to the final consumers. This process is important as we are involving

M. F. Mata-Rivera et al. (Eds.): WITCOM 2022, CCIS 1659, pp. 270–280, 2022.
https://doi.org/10.1007/978-3-031-18082-8_17

the people's health and life, thus, the processes that the supply chain follows must be accurate and efficient. The past years we have been involved in a global situation where the communications and transactions were affected due to COVID-19, the pandemic has brought to the industry many challenges such as lack of distribution in raw materials, consumables, times of delivery, etc.

The blockchain technology might bring new insights in the way transactions are made and how to redesign the model of operations with decentralized characteristics [2]. Moreover, the smart contracts are a helpful application of the blockchain technology capable of tackle most of the issues and challenges that the supply chain could face in the daily operations.

This technology presents some challenges such as law regulation, that in the future will help the present issues with the communication. This article is organized as follow; some preliminaries are provided in Sect. 2 where an overview of the blockchain technology and its main characteristics are described, usage of the smart contracts and the benefits provided. Potential uses of the smart contracts applied to different areas such as an overview are described in Sect. 3. A more detailed definition of the smart contracts applied to supply chain and how the BMPN could help in this application are described in Sect. 4. An overview of the challenges that healthcare Supply Chain Management is described with the comparison of different topics involved in some studies is shown in Sect. 5. Related works are presented in Sect. 6. Summary and conclusions are presented in Sect. 7.

2 Preliminaries

2.1 Blockchain

Blockchain is a decentralized chain of registers, agreed and distributed in several nodes of a network. Thanks to the nature of the blockchain it is not possible to modify an existing node, the structure of the blockchain data relies in timestamp, block version, a hash that will be used as a digital fingerprint of data [23]. Every block contains a hash to identify the previous block, and this provides a strict order to the blockchain [3, 21].

2.2 Main Characteristics of Blockchain

In a blockchain there are mainly the following characteristics.

- Decentralization. This characteristic allows the users of the blockchain to avoid the need to validate the transactions with a central user and reducing the cost that this process generates. Third parties are no longer needed in the blockchain. To maintain the data consistency in the network consensus algorithms are used.
- This improves data validity as the transaction stored in the blockchain cannot be deleted or modified. Invalid information in the transactions added to the blockchain could be discovered and deleted. [4]
- Anonymity. Users can interact with the blockchain without revealing their real identity.

However, there are some improvement points that we could find in the blockchain domain, such as:

- The lack of the regulation in this proposed technology.
- Technological immaturity
- Asset digitization, which will allow the users to integrate this type of system.
- There must be a collaboration between different agencies involved.

2.3 Smart Contracts

Since the 90's the smart contracts have been seen as an impossible way to operate things, but thanks to the blockchain technology this concept has become reality which aim is to automate contractual relationships between people or machines without the intervention of a trusted intermediary. The concept of smart contract was proposed by "Nick Szabo in 1994". In theory, the blockchain is a dual register share information between network nodes. [20]

The smart contracts are a technological innovation born after the creation of bitcoin in 2009 that aims to eliminate intermediaries, simplify processes, and save costs. Smart contracts are special code instructions stored in a blockchain that can self-execute actions based on a series of defined and programmed parameters, in an immutable, transparent, and secure way.

Smart contracts work in a similar way to a conventional contract, stating what can be done, how it can be done, and the consequences of an action not being executed, define the interaction that will take place between the interested parties but without the need for intermediaries, for example, removing lawyers or notaries. One of the most important qualities of smart contracts is that they are capable of being executed by themselves and do not need the review or interpretation of any of the parties involved. Smart contracts, being based on blockchain technology, are distributed in a high number of computers, thus avoiding centralization, censorship, and other aspects of conventional contracts.

2.4 Usage of Smart Contracts

To explain this subsection let us take an example where we could use this type of smart contracts and blockchain technology. Suppose that you want to sale a house, you can create a smart contract and publish it in an existing blockchain network. The community will be able to see the information about the property that will be stored in a cell of the blockchain. This is the way where you can find a buyer for your house without any third-party organization.

Smart contracts based on the blockchain technology offer the following benefits (Fig. 1):

- Speed and real-time updates.
- Verifiability.
- Observability.
- Consistency.
- Accuracy.

- Lower execution risk.
- Fewer intermediaries.
- Lower cost.
- New business models. [5, 21]

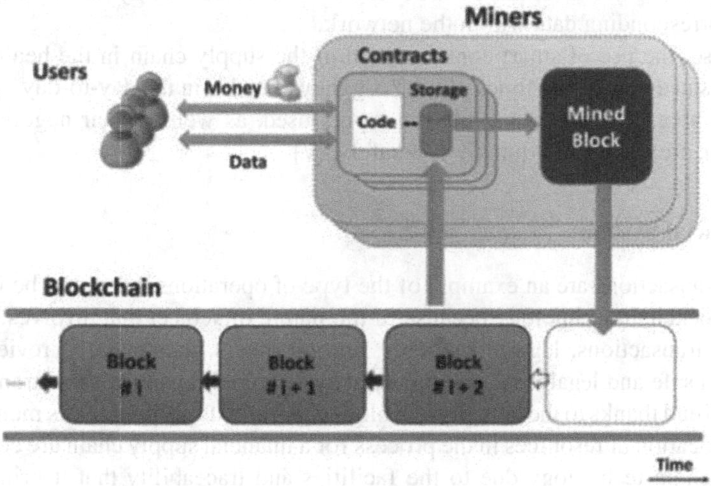

Fig. 1. Smart contract system [5]

3 Potential Uses

In this section we discussed about some potential application of the smart contracts. There are severe opportunity areas where this technology could be use and change the way to manage the transactions and eliminate the third-party organizations. We have identified different potential uses of the smart contracts and blockchain bases application. [19, 20]

3.1 Supply Chain

Supply chain management is the integration of key business processes, from the original suppliers to the end user. There are some challenges and limitations in this process, such as, demand forecasting and inventory management, risk management, unforeseen delays, search for greater transparency, lack of communication between services and consumers, among others [19].

With blockchain based smart contracts it is possible to manage these limitations, when a smart contract is placed into the blockchain the number of advantages in the supply chain increase because the system become autonomous as well as secure, the actors will be participating between them without any third party, the transactions will be now verified for the blockchain nodes, the transaction gain trust and transparency, thus, the trades and processes related to this application become more trusted.

3.2 Healthcare System

Within the health area, personal data is usually shared, as well as bank accounts, transactions between insurance, patients and the hospital, medical records, etc. For all the data involved in the processes of the health system, it is important to work on the issue of their security, being able to process data safely is of great importance. The use of blockchain technology allows this information to be treated in a secure way by introducing a block with the corresponding data within the network.

Likewise, the use of smart contracts within the supply chain in the health area is important, since not only in times of high urgency, but also in the day-to-day operations within this area, it is important that the inputs used, as well as their negotiation and distribution, are carried out quickly and safely. [7]

3.3 Financial System

Financial transactions are an example of the type of operations that could be improved with the blockchain technology because of the nature of subject that involves, personal data, bank transactions, legal documents, among others, that must be reviewed and execute in a safe and legal way. The financial system could gain trust and transparency from end to end thanks to the benefits of a blockchain and its properties. As mentioned in [14] the allocation of resources in the process for a financial supply chain are compatible with blockchain technology due to the facilities and traceability that it brings to the information flow and helps to construct a more reliable and safe information stream.

As shown in this section, it is possible to remark several fields of action where an improvement could be done by the application and usage of the smart contracts thanks to the fast sharing inbound and outbound information different areas and how this utilization can be applied to the relationship between actors from the healthcare supply chain flow.

4 Smart Contract in Supply Chain

In the supply chain management area, we can find different types of information flows as the inbound or outbound ones that includes different actors in the process. To obtain the goal of deliver a product to a final customer it is essential to follow some steps that will help the industry to accomplish the expected results. The supply chain process integrates two different types of data flows, internal and external. The internal flow is the one in charge of communicate inside the operations of the industry what needs to be taken in count to create the external requirements and handle the information to get the flows as clean as possible in terms of the information.

For the internal processes and operations, it is essential to have a fast and agile communication and avoid every lack of information that could exists. The literature is showing that some fundamental characteristics that are involved in the supply chain that must be considered to achieve a result in the most secure possible way. The information that is treated and shared in a working flow becomes the principal source along with the properties involved with it. As shown in table one we have compared different sources to identify and summarize these elements to have a clear image of what is happening inside and outside the functioning of this solution. There is a lack of study in the performance and traceability as described in [13]. Traceability could be improved with the solution proposed but there the performance remaining that is a priority to create a good channel of communication. Therefore, the use of smart contracts inside a company, could help to improve these parameters with the security of themselves.

4.1 Business Process Model and Notation

BPMN is an important diagram notation that is being used in the industry to provide a notation, as mentioned in [8], for specifying business processes in a business process model that helps to represent the different actions that happen in the full flow of operations and that is understandable for all the users involved in the processes, such as, the business analysts, the technical developers, and the business actors. One of the usages of BPMN goals is to create simple mechanism for creating business process models and at the same time handle their complexity.

With the purpose of study of this investigation we will be using a BPMN diagram to understand the flows of information that occurs in a supply chain process.

5 Healthcare Supply Chain Management

In this section we will discuss about a proposed flow that aligns with some of the needs of a healthcare supply chain process and the different aspects and data exchanges that may occur during this cycle. As described in the previous section we are going to focus the possible introduction of a smart contract and blockchain technologies with a diagram example in the Fig. 2, that will allow us to follow in an easier way the benefits of these changes and improvements.

In this example process we can identify four different actors that are communicating between them, it is not mandatory that they interact with every of the other actors because in a real scenario it is not how it works. We can find in this schema the healthcare professional, the hospital pharmacy, pharmaceutical manufacturer, and the raw material

Table 1. Systematic review: Challenges in smart contracts.

Challenges	[9]	[10]	[11]	[12]	[13]
Supply chain operations	✓	✓	✓	✓	✓
Human interaction	✓	✓	✗	✗	✗
Transparency	✓	✗	✓	✓	✓
Price	✗	✓	✓	✓	✗
Inventory management	✓	✗	✗	✓	✗
Use of smart contract	✗	✗	✓	✗	✓
Security	✗	✗	✓	✗	✗
Performance	✗	✗	✓	✗	✓
Traceability	✗	✗	✗	✗	✓

manufacturer as the main actors in the process. These four actors will share information, transactions, personal data, among others and that is why a blockchain implementation could help to keep the safety, transparency, and traceability of the data.

In this workflow we have many parameters described in the Table 1 as challenges that are the ones that we will be focused on for the study to better understand where in the process could be possible to allocate the smart contracts and blockchain technologies. Having a smart contract could be a complex addition but a very beneficial one too because it will allow the flow to automate some conditional parts of it such as the email notifications the in a real-life situation involves the human interaction and this can cause a lack of time and in the information because the human job could be done in a bad way or with some errors because of the human nature.

In the case that will be described, many critical processes need to be saved and shared with the actors involved in order to achieve the main purpose of the healthcare supply chain management, this is why an important part of the challenges mentioned in the Table 1 is the traceability as discussed in [13] because this allows us to keep track of the important exchanges that take part in the actions at an operational level.

5.1 BPMN Model Description

As discussed, we will focus on the diagram that shows how the flow of a healthcare supply chain works. As described in the Fig. 2, it is possible to observe in the process that two types of communication occur, inbound and outbound exchanges of information. The

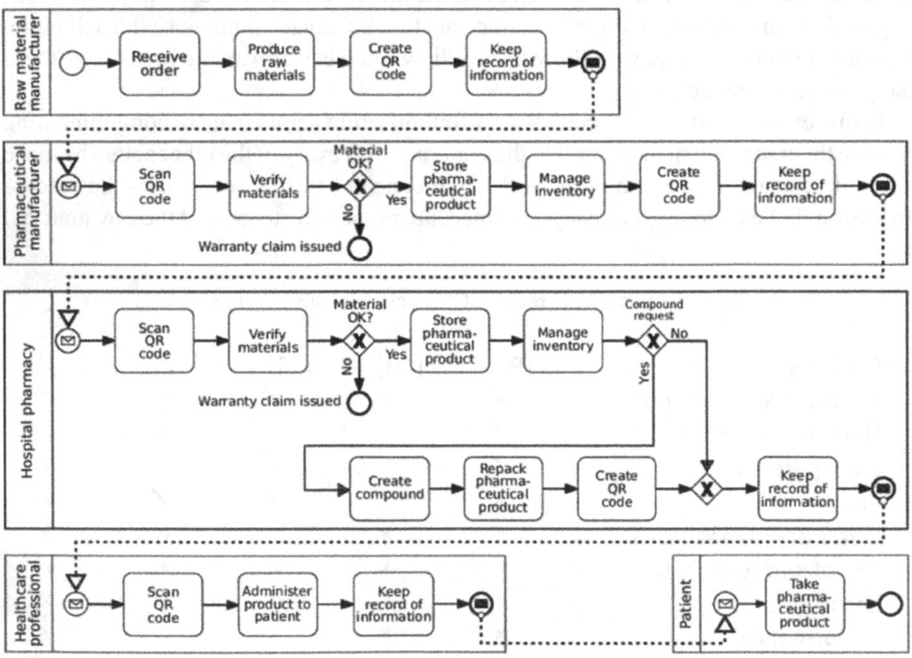

Fig. 2. BPMN diagram for healthcare supply chain [13]

inbound communication is the one that will internally describe the actions that need to be accomplished for a single actor and the outbound communication will represent the exchanges between different actors. In the literature there are few actions taken in count for these types of communication and it is at this point where the flow of a transaction can be disrupted by any kind of interruption such as human interaction, failures in the network, bad requests between actors among others. This kind of ruptures in the process are the ones that a smart contract based on the blockchain technology can improve thanks to their nature, if a smart contract is placed once an action finished will trigger the next one that has been defined in the sequence of actions. To better understand the full activity, we propose a description for the actors involved.

The first actor that will be described is the raw material manufacturer. This pipeline in the Fig. 2 describes the external communication and how it starts since the manufacturer receive and order request, after this request the actor will process this information until the end of internal actions that will launch an email to the next actor, that normally in a real-life situation it is a human in charge of the execution. This kind of interactions are the ones that a smart contract could supersede in a more efficient way because the action will be launched once another action finish, thus, the performance in terms of communication and data sharing are being benefited.

As described before, we can find internal communication as well. The hospital pharmacy pipeline is a clear example of how the information interacts with the different steps of the flow. Inside the transactions we can find conditions that will decide the course of the operation. Normally in a real-life situation an operator will be in charge of taking decisions that will affect the next steps to be triggered, thus, mistakes can be added and disrupt the course. Once again, we could spot a lack of fidelity in the process and consequently an area of improvement where the technology discussed in this article could contribute to enhance.

6 Related Works

Even though smarts contracts are mostly implemented for targets that involve legal transactions, the technology emerging is being used in applications that need to keep a trail of the different actions involved in an exchange of information. In Table 2 we aim to present different works that have been done in the health care field. As said in [16] smart contracts present a beneficial solution to rely on the information that is being shared when a smart contract is executed, security, accuracy and efficiency are three important characteristics that are defended to trust in a block chain-based contract. A basic smart contract implementation for an application such as mentioned in [16] could be a good approach for the results expected in this paper thanks to the facility that it provides to keep track of the related transactions.

As mentioned in [18], block chain technology can be adapted to other technologies to get a better approach to the implementation to obtain the results expected. Using a semantic web approach combined with the block chain technology allows the flow to be connected and to keep trail of the transactions that occur in the process thanks to the nature of the relationships that it offers. With this approach smart contracts are more organized and linked and it offers a better traceability of the components that are being used and shared in the chain. As discussed in [17], with a smart contract, the information that is being generated could be preserved in a secure way thanks to the main characteristics of the technology that allow the information to be shared also in a secure way. This approach allows to reduce the time execution of the operations that involves a transaction that is going to be added to the chain and shared to be authorized depending on the user that is being sharing the information.

As shown in Table 2, there are different characteristics involved in the application of a smart contract that will be helpful to achieve the final objective depending on the nature of the problem, in the case of this paper we find that these characteristic are necessary to implement a smart contract for it to can be used in a supply chain and more specific in the health care area because of the information sensitivity and the time of execution that can be improved thanks to this applications.

Table 2. Smart contracts implementation in health care.

Characteristics	[15]	[16]	[17]	[18]
Accuracy	✓	✓	✗	✗
Efficiency	✓	✓	✗	✗
Security	✓	✓	✓	✓
Integrity	✗	✓	✓	✓
Privacy	✗	✓	✓	✓
Performance	✗	✓	✗	✗
Traceability	✗	✓	✓	✓

As described in Fig. 2 there is a complete flow to determine the operations and activities that could be included in a supply chain process. To identify the use case for a smart contract and the way it could improve in a better way in Fig. 3 we describe a simple flow between two entities that are interacting inside the full flow. As we described

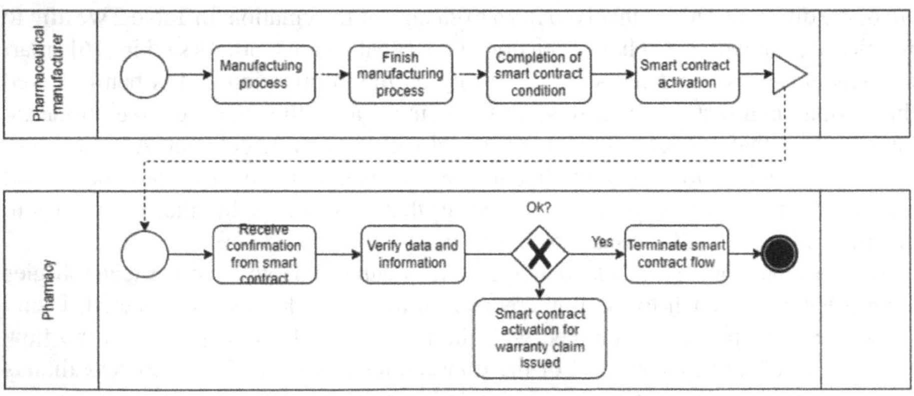

Fig. 3. Smart contracts use case for a simple flow

in Fig. 3, the smart contract can be included when an actor finishes his operations inside the flow that must share with another actor of the process, then the smart contract will be executed to share the end or the fulfilment of his actions to then start to execute the actions for another actor of the deal.

7 Conclusions

This article analyzes the possible implementation of the smart contracts inside a healthcare supply chain operation. The study case that is described in this article is a possible flow of transactions in a healthcare example. We found that inside the real-life operations there is a lack of performance in the information sharing and in the communication actions due to different actors that manipulate the course of execution of the flow. Time execution is an important characteristic to be improved because of the nature of the operations involved in the health care area. Whit this work we were able to remark different flows and operations that could be directly enhanced and impacted with the block chain and smart contracts technology. Our future work to continue improving the process is the investigation and implementation of a smart contract based in a test blockchain technology such as Ethereum, taking in count the main actors that are involved in the process and the characteristics that must be taken in count to achieve an optimal result. Finally, we aim to present results based in the solution to be implemented.

References

1. Vadapalli, R.: Fundamentals of Blockchain. vol. 1 (2020)
2. Michailidis, M., Valavanis, K., Rutherford, M.: Literature review. In: Nonlinear Control of Fixed-Wing UAVs with Time-Varying and Unstructured Uncertainties. STAS, vol. 1, pp. 9–28. Springer, Cham (2020). https://doi.org/10.1007/978-3-030-40716-2_2
3. Moulouki, R., Dominique Bernard, K., Taif, F., Mohamed, A.: Blockchain in Health Supply Chain Managment: State of Art Challenges and Opportunities **1**, 1-4 (2020)
4. Zibin, Z., Shaoan, X., Hongning, D., Xiangping, C., Huaimin, W.: An overview of blockchain technology: Architechture, consencus and future trends. Ieee 6th Internatioanl Congress on Big Data 1, 1–9 (2017)
5. Alharby, M., van Moorse, A.: Blockchain-based Smart Contracts: A Systematic Mapping Study. School of Computing Science, Newcastle University, Newcastle, UK
6. Tama, B.A., et al.: A critical review of blockchain and its current applications. Electrical Engineering and Computer Science (ICECOS), 2017 International Conference on. IEEE (2017)
7. Ilhaam, A.O.,, Raja, J., Mazin, S.D., Khaled, S., Ibrar, Y., Mohamed, O.: Automating Procurement Contracts in the Healthcare Supply Chain Using Blockchain Smart Contracts. 10 March 2021
8. Stephen, A.W.: Introduction to BPMN (2004)
9. Srikanta, R., Anuj, D., Sunil, K.D.: A systematic literature review of healthcare supply chain and implications of future research. 27 June 2019
10. Kim, S.-H., Kwon, I.-W.G.: The Study of Healthcare Supply Chain Management in United States: Literature Review. 26 Dec 2015
11. Rouhani, S., Deters, R.: Security, Performance, and Applications of Smart Contracts: A Systematic Survey. 26 April 2019

12. Clauson, K.A., Breeden, E.A., Davidson, C., Mackey, T.K.: Leveraging Blockchain Technology to Enhance Supply Chain Management in Healthcare: An Exploration of Challenges and Opportunities in the Health Supply Chain. 23 March 2018
13. Di Ciccio, C., et al.: Blockchain-Based Traceability of Inter-organisational Business Processes (2018)
14. Zhang, T., Li, J., Jiang, X.: Analysis of supply chain finance based on blockchain. Procedia Computer Sci. **187**, 1–6 (2021). https://doi.org/10.1016/j.procs.2021.04.025
15. Sookhak, M., Jabbarpour, M.R., Safa, N.S., Yu, F.R.: Blockchain and smart contract for access control in healthcare: A survey, issues and challenges, and open issues. J. Network Computer Appl. **178**, 102950 (2021) https://doi.org/10.1016/j.jnca.2020.102950
16. Hilal, A.A., Badra, M., Tubaishat, A.: Building Smart Contracts for COVID19 Pandemic Over the Blockchain Emerging Technologies. Procedia Computer Sci. **198**, 323–328 (2022) https://doi.org/10.1016/j.procs.2021.12.248
17. Lee, J.S., Chew, C.-J., Liu, J.-Y., Chen, Y.-C., Tsai, K.-Y.: Medical blockchain: Data sharing and privacy preserving of EHR based on smart contract. J. Information Security Appl. **65**, 103117 (2022) https://doi.org/10.1016/j.jisa.2022.103117
18. Chondrogiannis, E., Andronikou, V., Karanastasis, E., Litke, A., Varvarigou. T.: Using blockchain and semantic web technologies for the implementation of smart contracts between individuals and health insurance organizations. Blockchain: Research and Appl. **3**(2), 100049 (2022) https://doi.org/10.1016/j.bcra.2021.100049
19. Professor, CSE Department, Easwari Engineering College, Chennai, Tamil Nadu. et al.: «Food Supply Chain Traceability using Block Chain», IJRTE **9**(1), 437–443 (2020) https://doi.org/10.35940/ijrte.A1226.059120
20. Kumar, K., Davim, J.P. (eds.): Supply Chain Intelligence. MIE, Springer, Cham (2020). https://doi.org/10.1007/978-3-030-46425-7
21. Larruceam, X., Pautasso, C.: Blockchain and Smart Contract Engineering. IEEE Software **37**(5), 23–29 (2020) https://doi.org/10.1109/MS.2020.3000354
22. Hu, K., Zhu, J., Ding, Y., Bai, X., Huang, J.: Smart Contract Engineering. Electronics **9**(12), 12 (2020) https://doi.org/10.3390/electronics9122042
23. Pranto, T.H., Noman, A.A., Mahmud, A., Haquem, A.B.: Blockchain and smart contract for IoT enabled smart agriculture. PeerJ Comput. Sci. **7**, e407 (2021) https://doi.org/10.7717/peerj-cs.407

Analysis of Music Provenanced of Intelligence Artificial and its Possible Advantages in Therapeutic Non-pharmacologic

Orozco Pacheco Moisés(✉)

Facultad de Estudios Superiores Acatlán, Universidad Nacional Autónoma de México, Mexico City, Mexico
moisesorozco.mac@comunidad.unam.mx

Abstract. The conception of the music created by Intelligence artificial was born close to the '80s, ever since, its applications are deeply used in the industry. In this article, we analyze the spectral structures of two samples of music provenanced and non-provenanced of AI, searching significative differences between them, whole abovementioned with the objective of exploring the possible features from the music created by software in the cognitive throughput of a population between 15 and 29 years old, belonging to one school music from "Estado de México". Finally, we define a posture about the employment of music provenanced of AI in a therapeutic non-pharmacologic environment, like could be music therapy.

Keywords: Spectral analysis · Time series · Sound · Music provenanced of AI

1 Introduction

In 1981, began the creation of Experiments in Musical Intelligence by the American compositor and scientist David Cope, with the objective of programming the first software capable of composing music algorithmically. After 7 years, was released its first CD called "Bach by design: Computer Compose Music-Experiments in Musical Intelligence", was released, followed by "Classical Music Composed by Computer: Experiments in Musical Intelligence" in 1997, and "Virtual Mozart (Experiments in Musical Intelligence)" in 1999.

Perhaps, the immediate question could be if the mentioned works, which come from Artificial Intelligence, are really considered music in the whole sense of the word.

To answer this dilemma, we will deduce its possible features and consequences in the context of its advantages and disadvantages, more specifically, in a therapeutic non-pharmacologic environment. where we will look at potential uses of

M. F. Mata-Rivera et al. (Eds.): WITCOM 2022, CCIS 1659, pp. 281–296, 2022.
https://doi.org/10.1007/978-3-031-18082-8_18

the music to lead cognitive stimulus capable of propitiating the learning, mobilization, expression, organization, and communication between others attitudes and behaviors.

Existing several works above realized by the community, we identify 2 main, that help to prove the plurality of music therapy:

- **Music Therapy and Under-Priviledged Children** [2]: Article written by the School of Performing and Visual Arts of New Delhi, which proves the importance of the creation of the right environment based on tools like music therapy, to increase the stimulation of attitudes that help the development of intelligence, within a group of 36 underprivileged children.
- **Music Therapy on Parkinson's Disease** [3]: Master thesis done by Irini Ionannon in the University of Jyväskylä, proved the importance of the creation of right environments based on tools like music therapy, to the stimulation of behaviors that help a rhythmic mobilization and relaxation of patients with Parkinson disease, controlling the main symptoms

Therefore, we want to analyze the curve of this investigation toward if the music that comes from AI can achieve these universal features that belong to the music that does not come from AI, and in the case this takes place, if there is a significant difference.

2 Experimental Design

The experiment contains two phases, which are:

2.1 Structural Phase

Proofs if exists a significant difference in the spectral composition of music that comes from AI and the one that doesn't come from AI.

We take a set of 38 music pieces in format .wav, divided in two samples of the same size, those coming from AI and others not coming from AI.

- Music created by AI: Clustered of the following CD's.
  1. Classical Music Composed by Computer: Experiments in Musical Intelligence.
  2. Emily Howell: Breathless.
  3. Individual pieces clustered: Into the moment, was not identified in any album above publication. However, we recognize EMI like the author, given its divulgation by David Cope:
     (a) Chopin style Nocturne Emmy.
     (b) David Cope Emmy Vivaldi.
     (c) David Cope Messiaen Emmy.
     (d) David Cope Mahler.
     (e) Bach style chorale Emmy David Cope.
     (f) David Cope Emmy Beethoven 2 beg.

- Music no created by AI: Being mostly recognized the classic music like the music genre of the above sample, to achieve a better and punctual estimation, we decided to contain within the classic music the second sample, obtained by a Telegram's bot called "Classic Music".

Data Set: To the construction of the Data Set, we will collect the following spectral features per song, were used specialized libraries of python Librosa and Pandas:

1. Spectral Centroid (SC): It Is a measurement used in the processing of digital signals to characterize a spectral. It indicates where the center of the mass of the spectral is, it is mainly used as a good predictor of the brightness from the sound. It is defined by the following formula:

$$Centroid = \frac{\sum_{n=0}^{N-1} f(n)x(n)}{\sum_{n=0}^{N-1x}(n)}$$

2. Spectral Rollof (SF): is the frequency below which a specified percentage of the total spectral energy. Define for the following formula:

$$\sum_{n=1}^{R_t} M_t[n] = 0.85 * \sum_{n=1}^{N} M_t[n]$$

3. Time Domain Zero Crossings: Describe the domain of the signal per frame t. Provides a measure to the signal noise. This is defined by the following formula:

$$Z_t = \frac{1}{2} \sum_{n=1}^{N} |sign(x_n]) - sign(x[n-1])|$$

4. Mel-frequency Cepstral Coefficient: These are coefficients for the representation of the speech-based in the perception of human hearing. These are widely used for the automatic recognition of discourse. Define for the following formula:

$$C(x(t)) = F^{-1}[log(F[x(t)])]$$

Data Analysis. Accomplished in totality the clustering of the data, then, we will realize two procedures else per studied feature (SC, SF, ZCR, and MFCC) (Fig. 1):

- Correlation Coefficients: Establishing both samples within the concept of temporal series, then, we will realize a matrix of correlation to find patterns that would relate the two kinds of structural forms.

– Wilcoxon test: Later, we will realize a non-parametric proof to know if the measures of each sample are not significantly different. The analysis about the selected proof will be discussed later.

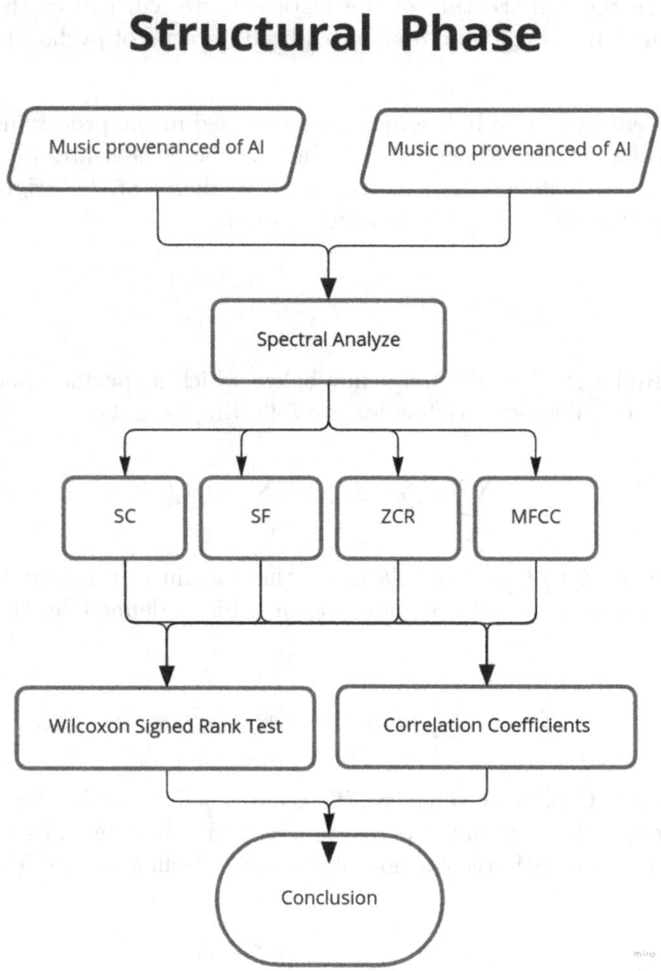

Fig. 1. Mind map of structural phase

2.2 Cognitive Phase

Objective: To prove if there are significant differences in the indexes of concentration and perception in a group of 60 students, to find advantages or disadvantages in the music coming from AI in possible sessions of therapy and study.

To this section was applied a psychometric test from Toulouse-Piéron in two populations of people range of 15 to 30 years old, belonging to the first two grades from the "técnico en Ejecución Musical" from "Escuela de Bellas Artes de Naucalpan".

The experimental design was developed in 2 layers, which are explained in the following points:

- **First Layer:**
  1. It will give them the first test in paper form.
  2. It will verify that the population had obtained the proof and one pencil.
  3. It will request their age, sex, and school year in course.
  4. It will reproduce the song come of AI source, "Symphony(after Mozart): I, Allegro", and then, begin the test with time to 10 min.
- Second Layer: One time, finished the first test, then, will realize a second test, establishing a different template, where the music won't create of AI. which is: "Mozart Sonata for Two Pianos in D Major, K.448: I.Allegro with Spirito".

Both pieces are represented by Mozart, in a literal and inspirational sense. With the goal of obtaining similar results based on the article "Music Therapy and Under-Privileged Children". 60 tests were applied, from which 7 were cancelled due to bad execution (Fig. 2)

2.3 Background

The Toulouse-Piéron test is a psychometric test of concentration and resistence to monotony. The main task of the studied subject is to select the figures that are coincidental with the figures displayed at the beginning of the page.

One main characteristic, that allows the Toulouse Test to be the best option for this study, is the wide field of application, since it doesn't discriminate population, being of any kind of economic level or culture. This has the capability to evaluate the resistance to fatigue, perceptive speed, and concentration.

2.4 Materials

The template contains 1600 figures (of 40 rows times 40 items), which, in average, a fourth part (10 per row) will be equal to the figures displayed at the beginning of the page. (A example of realized test, can be viewed in Fig. 8)

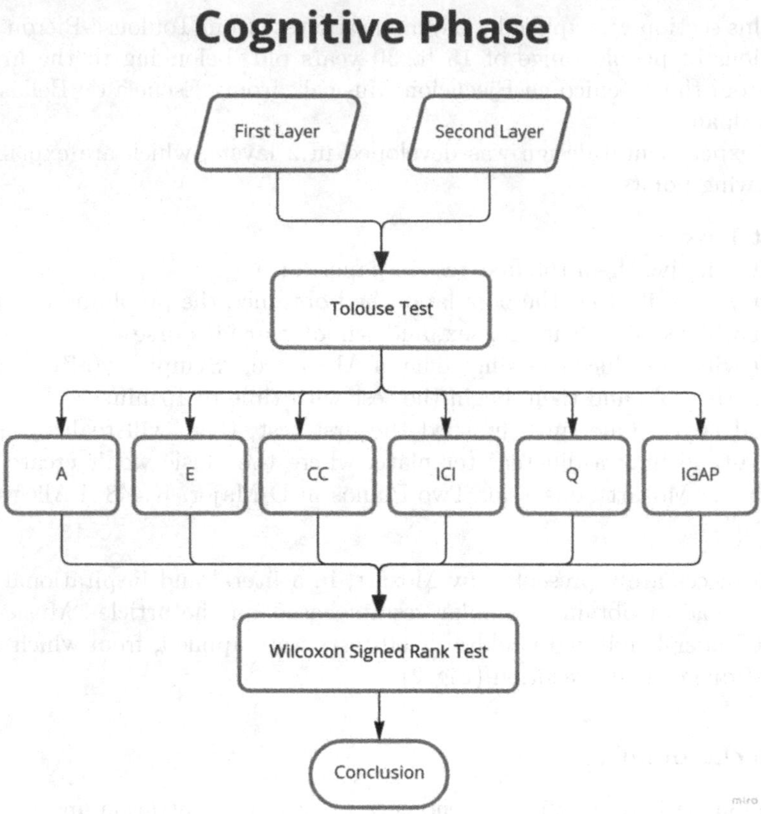

Fig. 2. Mind map of cognitive phase

2.5 Selected Data

The Toulouse test has two types of evaluation, within the quantitative evaluation, where the following data will be obtained:

- Hits (A): Number of selected figures by the evaluated subject that are coincidental with the given model.
- Omissions (O): Hits that were not selected.
- Mistakes (E): Number of selected figures by the evaluated subject that aren't coincidental with the given model.
- Index of Attention and Perception (IGAP): Represent the perceptive capability and attention of the studied subject. It is evaluated by the following formula

$$IGAP = A - (E + O)$$

- Concentration Quotient (CC): It is calculated by the following formula:

$$CC = \frac{A - E}{A + O}$$

- Impulsivity Control Index (ICI): This allows determining if the answers were led by an impulsive pattern and determines the percentage of hits. Is calculated for the following formula:

$$ICI = (\frac{A - E}{R})100$$

3 Results

All files mentioned in this article are contained in the following repository: https://github.com/MoisesOrozcoPacheco/MusicIntelligence

In Structural Phase was employed the script ScriptValores.py to get data on the musical spectrum. In Cognitive Phase were employed the scripts Script1.R and Script2.R were to clean the data and make their histograms.

3.1 Structural Phase

A carpet for each sample was created. These can be consulted in the following link: https://drive.google.com/drive/folders/1Xyxn6uBG8aT2FGvU8kAs7A6EoRKFQkmD?usp=sharing (Tables 1, 2, 3 and 4)

Table 1. Sample of the firsts three items of S_C_Final.csv

	2760_Don_Giovanni_K_527_-_Overture.wav	J.S Bach-La passion Selon Saint Matthieu-1st Partie-1.wav	J.S Bach-La passion Selon Saint Matthieu-2ndPartie-2.wav
0	1870.701518	0	3728.782467
1	2100.210273	0	3867.284668
2	2412.044177	0	3859.701134
...	...	...	...
2583	1425.610504	1293.962423	788.1829774

3.2 Data Set

Data Set After of had employed the script ScriptValores.py the following .csv files were generated:

1. S_C_Final.csv: The summary of the Spectral Centroids of both samples.
2. S_F_Final.csv: The summary of the Spectral Rollof of both samples.

Table 2. Sample of the firsts three items of S_F_Final.csv

	2760_Don_Giovanni_K_527_-_Overture.wav	J.S Bach-La passion Selon Saint Matthieu-1st Partie -1.wav	J.S Bach-La passion Selon Saint Matthieu-2ndPartie-2.wav
0	32.29980469	10.76660156	129.1992188
1	1496.557617	10.76660156	172.265625
2	2659.350586	10.76660156	172.265625
...	...	...	...
2583	3229.980469	2680.883789	3789.84375

Table 3. Sample of the firsts three items of Z_R_Final.csv

	2760_Don_Giovanni_K_527_-_Overture.wav	J.S Bach-La passion Selon Saint Matthieu-1stPartie -1.wav	J.S Bach- La passion Selon Saint Matthieu-2ndPartie-2.wav
0	32.29980469	10.76660156	129.1992188
1	1496.557617	10.76660156	172.265625
2	2659.350586	10.76660156	172.265625
...	...	...	...
2583	3229.980469	2680.883789	3789.84375

3. Z_C_R_Final.csv: The summary of the Zero Crossings Rate of both samples.
4. MFCC_Final.csv: The summary of the Mel-Frequency Cepstral Coefficients of both samples.

3.3 Histograms

Script2.R was used to plot the following histograms. The next steps were employed:

1. Create an array for each .csv file, for example: S_F.csv and S_F_AI.csv are use to create mean_SF and mean_SF_AI.

Table 4. Sample of the firsts three items of MFCC_Final.csv

	2760_Don_Giovanni_K_527_-_Overture.wav	J.S Bach-La passion Selon Saint Matthieu-1st Partie-1.wav	J.S Bach- La passion Selon Saint Matthieu-2nd Partie-2.wav
0	−590.8096924	−540.2865601	−570.0366211
1	−546.5894775	−541.9003906	−570.0366211
2	−520.7844849	−543.0895996	−569.8865356
...	...	...	...
2583	−307.0622864	−186.3615417	−199.1676483

2. On a cycle for, obtain the mean for each item on S_F.csv and S_F_AI.csv and store as array on mean_SF and mean_SF_AI.
3. Make the histogram of mean_SF and mean_SF_AI (Figs. 3 and 4).

As can be observed, the distributions are not normal.

3.4 Matrix of Correlation

Next, was processed a matrix of correlation realizad by the estatistic software Gretl. The matrixes are repsented with a heat map, where the color blue represents an inverse correlation and vice-versa (Figs. 5, 6 and 7).

We have to focus on the 1st and 3rd quadrants of all the plane. Although the files S_C_Final.csv, S_F_Final.csv, and Z_C_R_Final.csv represent a null relation, the file MFCC_Final.csv is unique, which represents a clear positive correlation between both samples.

3.5 Wilcoxon

3.5.1. Discussion The reason for which was used this non-parametric proof is based on the following indicators:

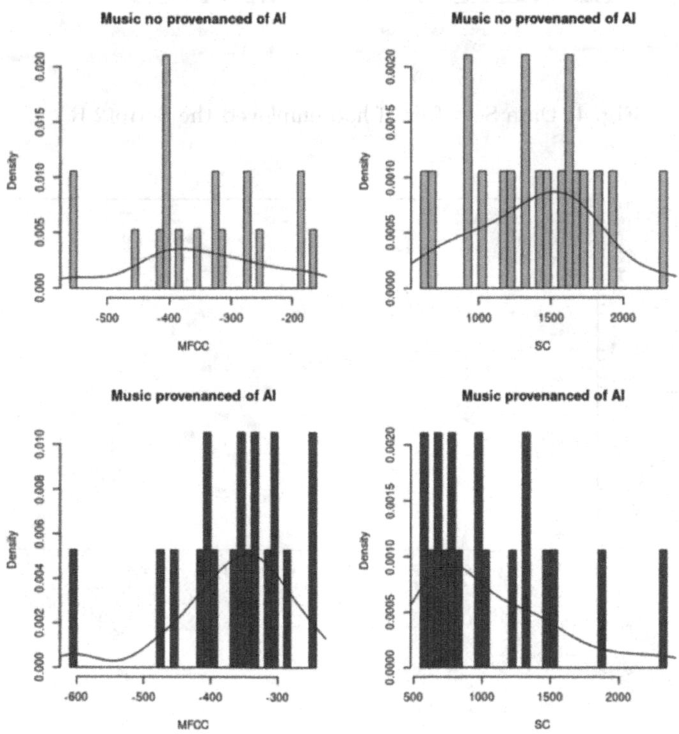

Fig. 3. Data Set after of had employed the Script2.R

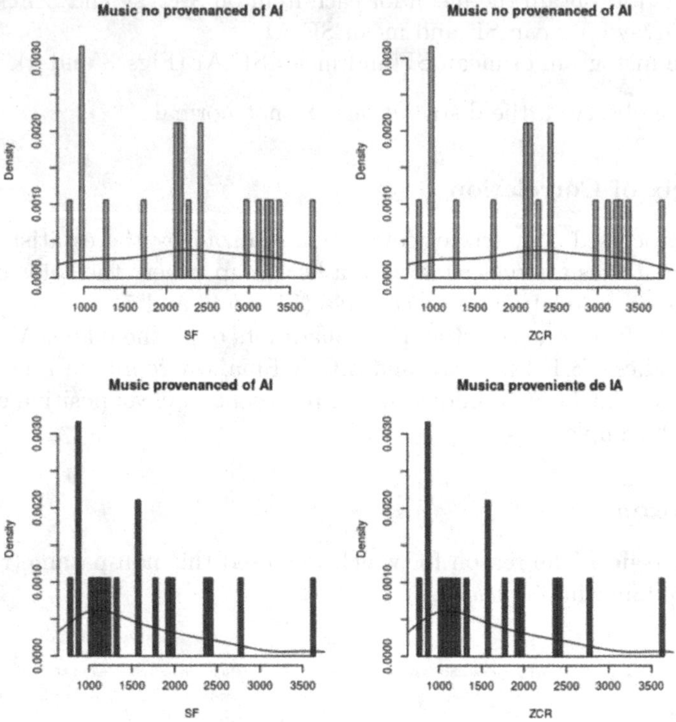

Fig. 4. Data Set after of had employed the Script2.R

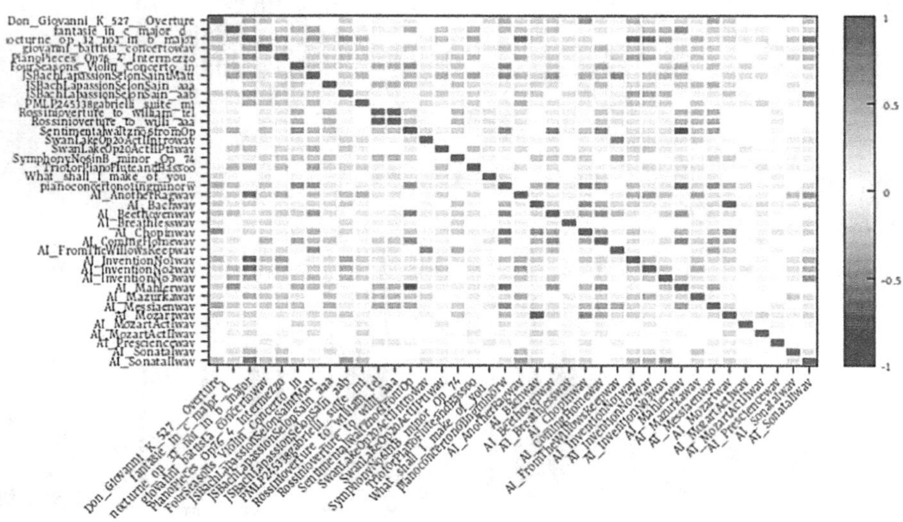

Fig. 5. Matrix of correlation from file *S_C_Final.csv*

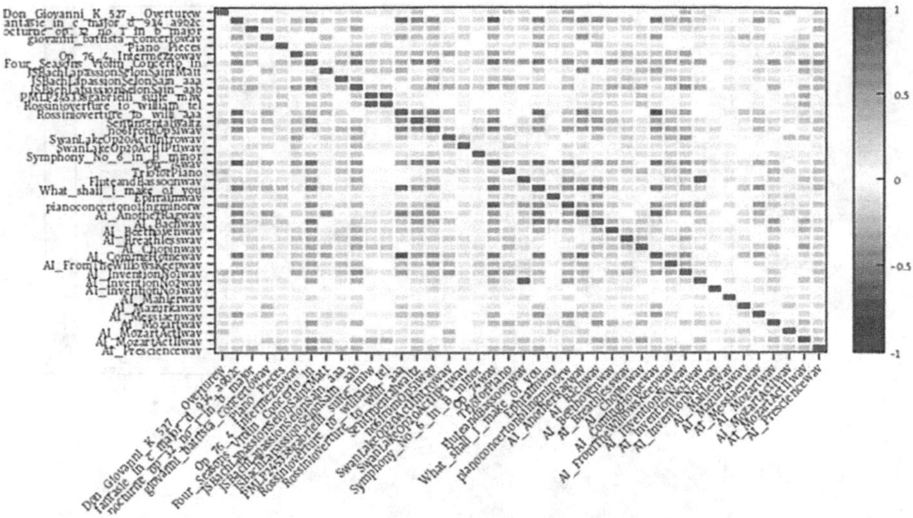

Fig. 6. Matrix of correlation from file *S_F_Final.csv*

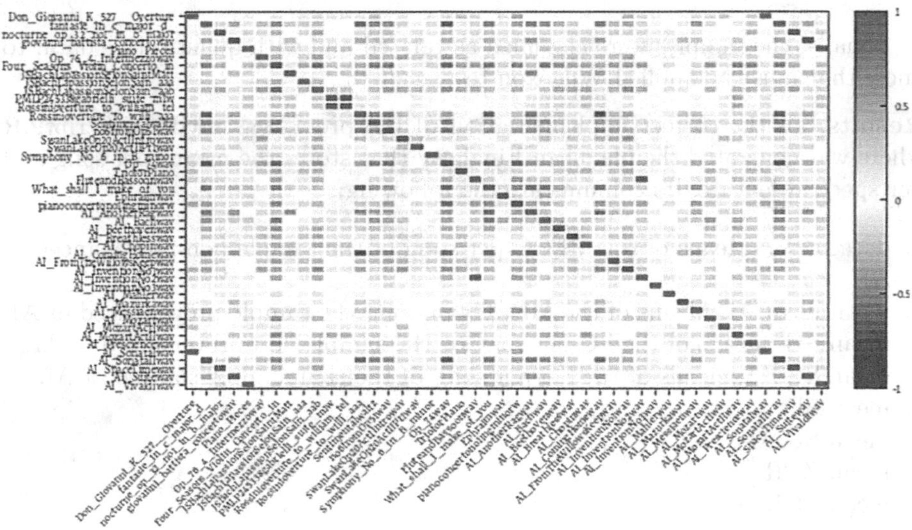

Fig. 7. Matrix of correlation from file *Z_C_R_.csv*

1. The samples displayed atypical data that cannot be ignored.
2. The samples displayed a distribution not normal.

However, the discussion begin, regard to other indicators, like the size of the sample (such that is upper than 2000 records) and its representation of the median.

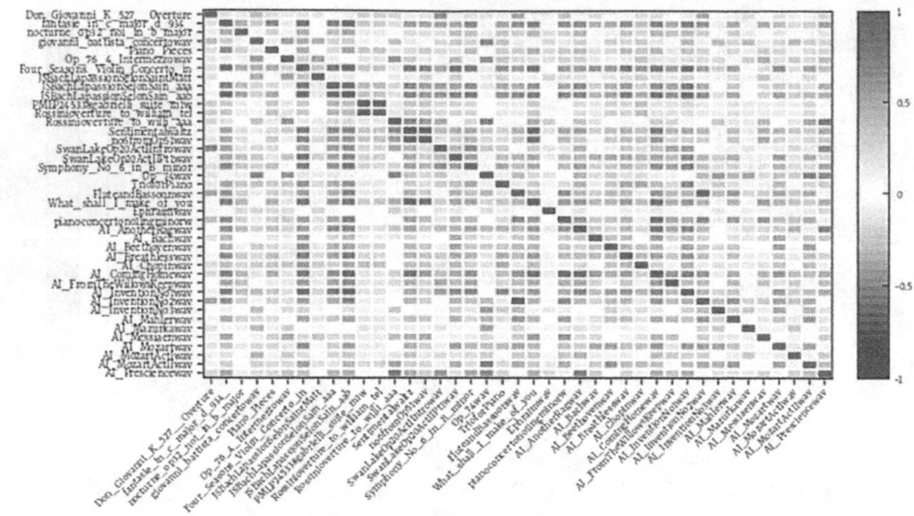

Fig. 8. Matrix of correlation from file *MFFC_Final.csv*

Finally, the samples were classified as related and with quantitative data, to know that must be applied Wilcoxon test.

Results. To the correct implementation of the proof, was used the Script2.R where was generated the file mean_Final.csv that stores the means per song and per spectral feature. Its columns are the following;

1. data_mean: Means of the MFCC per song of the sample non-provenanced of AI.
2. *d*ata_mean_AI: Means of the MFCC per song the sample provenanced of AI.
3. mean_SC: means of the SC per song of the sample non-provenanced of AI.
4. mean_SC_AI: means of the SC per song of the sample provenanced of AI.
5. mean_SF
6. mean_SF_AI
7. mean_ZCR
8. mean_ZCR_AI

Based on the calculated results of the statistical software Gretl, we get to the following table where each column represents the proof realized between both samples per spectral feature, the value p was taken to 2 tails (Table 5).

Table 5. xxx

	MFCC	SC	SF	ZCR
Z	0.33574	2.32098	2.08742	2.08742
p	0.737067	0.0202878	0.0368498	0.0368498

3.6 Interpretation of Results

In both statistical contexts was looked at that the unique feature spectral where was a clear positive correlation and non-significant difference, were the Mel-Frequency Cepstral Coefficients, but, what means this?

One of the main applications of the MFCC is the identification of the sound pitch, varying since of the speech thus like any other musical genre or instrument. The word Cepstral, referenced in colloquial words, to the spectrum of the spectrum, means, the clarification of the changes of the sound in a punctual way to the human ear.

Therefore can be deduced that both samples belonging to the classic musical genre cannot be distinguished between them.

3.7 Conclusions About Structural Phase

I conclude that structurally the samples are significantly different, with the characteristic of being listened to of similar form to the human ear.

3.8 Cognitive Phase

Was applied the Toulouse test to one population of 60 students belonging to the first and second year of the "Técnico en Ejecución Musical " of "Escuela de Bellas Artes de Naucalpan", with 18 female subjects and 42 male subjects. The next table shows the distribution of frequencies per age.

Edad	Freq. Relativa	Freq
< 16	6.67%	4
16–18	13.33%	8
18–20	18.33%	11
20–22	18.33%	11
22–24	23.33%	14
24–26	6.67%	4
26–28	6.67%	4
>=28	6.67%	4

3.9 Data Set

We obtain as result the file ToulouseTest.csv, where was employed the Script1.R to eliminate all NA records and divide for samples: provenanced and non-provenanced AI. The data frames, finish of the following way:

- ***ToulouseTest.csv***:

1. No. of test
2. Test type: reference if is the first second layer
3. Age.
4. Sex.
5. n responded files.
6. Answers.
7. Hits.
8. Mistakes.
9. Omissions.
10. IGAP.
11. CC.
12. ICI.

- dataIA.csv: Records exclusively not nulls belonging to the first layer.
- dataNoIA.csv: Records exclusively not nulls belonging to the second layer.

3.10 Histograms

It resulted in the following histograms (Fig. 9).

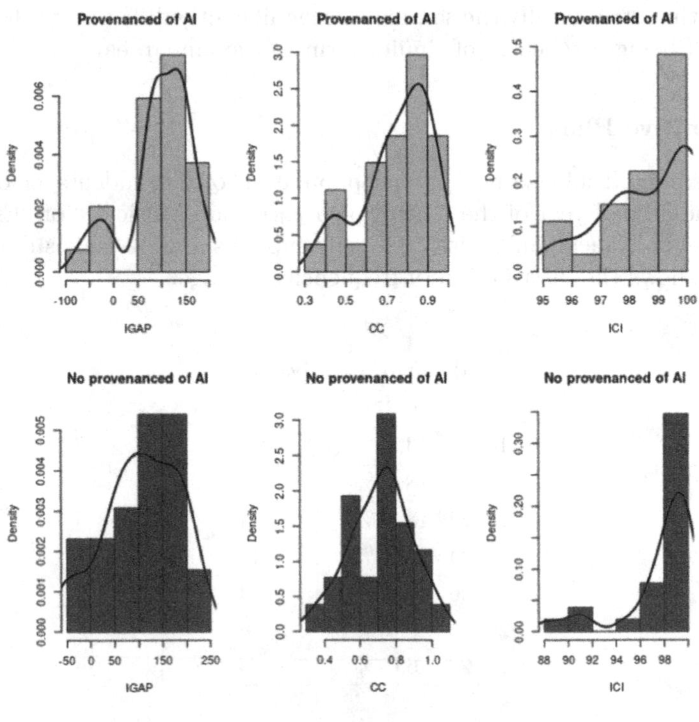

Fig. 9. histograms of the evaluated rubrics

3.11 Wilcoxon

Discussion. The decision of applied a proof non-parametric was taken based on the following indicators.

1. The distribution isn't normal, also has discontinue data that cannot be ignored.
2. The population one time, divides into the two samples, isn't upper than 30 records.
3. The rubrics are quantitative in nature.

Results. The following table shows the results of the proof.

	IGAP	CC	ICI
valor Z	0.355572	−0.914327	−0.0803608
valor p a dos colas	0.722161	0.360545	0.421623

We can look at that no value of Z goes beyond of range of (1.96, −1.96) and no value of p is upper than 0.95 or lower than 0.05, therefore I conclude of this phase, that not exist a significant difference in the cognitive throughput from the studied subject at the moment of listening to music provenanced of AI.

4 Conclusions

4.1 Discussion

To me, art is defined as the intersection point between two or more subjectivities, a set of transcendental methods of expression, rebellion, and devotion capable of giving voice to the intangible, and invisible; the black box that converts us into rational beings to the image of the creator, with the capability of creating, of loving and be loved.

Art can be defined between several things, minus in the conception of Intelligence Artificial. In community words, making this mix could be considered a humiliating precariousness of human beings.

In part, I would liked to explore some beneficial features that could be establishes by the music produced by AI within a progressive society that requires collective wellness, however, the argumentative void was the enough punctual, about the almost null differences between both samples. This does not mean, an answer but a succession of new asks, mainly when we give context about the confusion that can cause to distinguish on the human ear if the music is created by AI.

Perhaps, beyond the scope of this controversy, if a machine has the capability to create art, in the deep, the music that sounds in our malls or media, wasn't composed by a human.

4.2 Final Posture

I conclude in a neutral state about if the music provenanced of AI, could be employed in a therapeutic non-pharmacologic environment. Given the non-existent proof of a significant advantage or disadvantage in the cognitive throughput of the listener

4.3 Future Work

The genre isn't complete still, for this, I think that the study must be retaken in 10 years when the society is more open to accept the influence of Artificial Intelligence in its daily life, with the hope that the trajectory wis more defined and expanded to other musical genres from the side of the creators and developers.

About the methodology, establish an higher plurality in the population sample to do the study, and data set of the pieces .wav to compare, varying in the time, genres and artist. Also the spectral rubrics can be reconsidered, adding more items to give a more punctual estimation about the relation of both samples.

The study could be expanded to find correlations, regarding age, occupation, and sex of the studied subjects with music provenanced of AI, and the social reaction about their feelings.

References

1. World Federation of Music Therapy Information. https://wfmt.info/2011/05/01/announcing-wfmts-new-definition-of-music-therapy/
2. Priyanka & School of Performing & Visual Art: Music Therapy and Under-Privileged Children. Noad-Nartan Journal of Dance and Music **2**(1), 150–152 (2015). ISNN:2349–4654
3. Ioannou, I.: Music Therapy in Parkinson's Disease, Master's Thesis, University of Jyväskylä (2014)
4. Alvarez Munárriz, L.: Música e inteligencia artificial. Perspectiva antropólogica. Música Oral Del Sur **4**, 123–130 (1999)
5. Gale, E., Matthews, O., de Lacy Costello, B., Adamatzky, A.: Beyond Markov Chains, Towards Adaptiva Memristor Network-based Music Generation. The University of the West of England. Published (2003)
6. Meenu, and Vashisht, S.: Categorization of music b extracting features from affective audio through data mining. Trans Stellar **3**(2) (2013). ISNN: 2249–6831
7. Wieczorkowska, A., Synak, P., Lewis, R., Ras, Z.: Extracting Emotions from Music Data. University of North Carolina (2010)
8. Weihs, C., Ligges, U., Sommer, K. (n.d.): Analysis of Music Time Series. Compstat 2006 - Proceedings in Computational Statistics, 147–159. https://doi.org/10.1007/978-3-7908-1709-6_12
9. Silva, P.: David Cope and Experiments in Musical Intelligence (2003)
10. Nierhaus, G.: Algorithmic Composition: Paradigm of Automated Music Generation. SpringerWienNewYork (2009). ISBN: 978-3-211-77539-6
11. Fletcher, N.H., Rossing, T.D.: The Physics of Musical Instruments. Springer (1995). https://doi.org/10.1007/978-1-4612-2980-3

Methodology for the Acquisition and Forensic Analysis of a Remote Piloted Aircraft System (RPAS)

Julio Olivos Jaiba(✉)

Mayor University, Manuel Montt 367, Providencia, Santiago, Chile

Julio.olivos@mayor.cl

Abstract. This research proposes a "Methodology for the Acquisition and Forensic Analysis of a Remotely Piloted Aerial System (RPAS)", commonly known as Drone, which allows contributing to those forensic investigations that are carried out on this type of aircraft in different areas.

For the fulfillment of this research and according to the proposed objective, we will proceed to identify, study, analyze and evaluate the main regulations and standards on digital and electronic evidence, in addition to the architecture of hardware, electronics, and software of this type of aircraft, where the "DJI Drone range Phantom 4" stands out as a case study, due to its technical characteristics and worldwide recognition for being one of the most used professional drones in the world, thus allowing to propose a methodology of acquisition and forensic analysis specific to this type of technology, based on real background, which can be very useful for future investigations required in the area of computer forensics and that is associated with Drones, considering that this type of evidence can be fundamental in an investigation process.

Keywords: Remotely Piloted Aircraft System (RPAS) · Forensic analysis · Digital and electronic evidence · Methodology and forensic informatics · Drones

1 Introduction

A Remotely Piloted Aircraft System (RPAS), commonly known as a Drone, is an electronic device with robotic and aeronautical technology that has a unique architecture of hardware, electronics, and software, which allows them to perform multiple functions, flying at high altitudes, over different terrains and traveling long distances. The most common uses of these aircraft are focused on the scientific, civil, military, and even aerospace fields, highlighting "the flight of the Drone Ingenio", carried out during the year 2021 over the planet Mars, as a NASA project.

There are different types of Drones, such as fixed wing and rotary wing or multirotor, the latter being the most common in the market, specifically in the semi-professional and professional field, where the models of Drones of the Mavic and Phantom range belonging to the Chinese company of sciences and technologies "DJI" stand out, which has become the manufacturer and world leader in remotely piloted aircraft systems for

M. F. Mata-Rivera et al. (Eds.): WITCOM 2022, CCIS 1659, pp. 297–321, 2022.
https://doi.org/10.1007/978-3-031-18082-8_19

aerial photography and videography, due to this is that the Phantom 4 model is chosen as the Drone of study.

Additionally, we must consider that these technologies can be misused, even to commit illegal acts that could be very harmful, costly, and damaging to our society and emerging technologies in these areas of science. Given the above, forensic sciences take relevance in terms of research on the use of these aircraft, especially when it comes to next-generation technologies, little studied and where there are no specific methodologies of acquisition and forensic analysis to contribute to the investigations that require it.

It is here, where the need to study the current regulations and the functional architecture of a Drone to propose a "Methodology for the Acquisition and Forensic Analysis of a Remotely Piloted Aircraft System" is born.

The present investigation contemplates three phases, addressed in points 4 and 5 of this document, which constitute the main subjects of this investigation, according to the following detail:

Phase N° 1: Identify the regulations, standards, and methodologies related to the treatment of digital and electronic evidence.

Phase N° 2: Analyze the hardware, electronics, and software architecture of a rotary wing drone - multirotor, model DJI Phantom 4, classified as professional and "proposed as a case study".

Phase N° 3: Develop a methodology for the acquisition and forensic analysis of a Drone, based on the regulations, standards, and methodologies studied, through the result of the analysis of the hardware, electronics, and software architecture of the Drone proposed as a case study.

The above allows to support this research and its results, generating an added value in research aspects of specific methodologies associated with the field of computer forensics in Drones, in addition to providing background for the development of expertise regarding the investigations that require it, forensic science, technology and especially contribute to society.

Finally, we can establish that the scope of this research does not consider those Drones for military, aerospace, and fantasy use (toys), leaving only the range of those Drones used in the civil-commercial field of semi-professional and professional character, of the rotary wing, where the DJI Phantom 4 Drone used as a case study stands out.

2 Research Problem

2.1 Description of the Problem

As a first problem, we must mention the growing and rapid development of hardware, electronics and software technologies applied to Drones, added to the wide variety of models, prices, and applications, causing these aircraft to become increasingly used, ranging from military to private, a situation that has even facilitated the commission of illegal acts with the help of these aircraft, such as the transport and delivery of drugs, theft of information, and infringement of people's privacy, among others. By 2025, the global market for commercial and private drones is expected to generate more than 42.8

billion dollars, with an annual growth rate of 13.8% [1]; it should be noted that this statistic does not take into account the military sphere.

Another relevant aspect to mention as a problem is the lack of knowledge about these technologies when it comes to carrying out a major assessment or evaluation by those conducting forensic investigations in this field to shed light on an illegal act or other matter of interest. In this regard, we must consider that drones can contain very valuable information associated with images, videos, geopositioning, dates, time, or other data that may be of a sensitive or strategic nature that can be extracted and analyzed, even after this data has been erased from the device that stores it.

Additionally, we must consider the lack of methodologies regarding the forensic analysis of Drones, as there are only regulations and standards for the treatment of digital evidence dating back to 2002, mainly oriented to those typical storage devices, such as hard drives, USB drives or mobile phones, generating as the main problem the lack of a specific methodology for the acquisition and forensic analysis of Drones. Given the above, the availability of an applicable methodology for the forensic analysis of Drones would greatly facilitate the work of the experts in charge of their analysis.

2.2 Research Justification

The misuse that is often being given to this type of aircraft, in addition to the illegal acts that can be committed using the technological capabilities of Drones, can be detrimental to society and even to a country. The above, due to the increased production of different brands and models of Drones, in addition to their availability in the market, highlights illicit acts such as: "drug smuggling, invasion of personal privacy, hacks, terrorist operations and even destruction of critical infrastructures" [2]. Additionally, taking into account that remotely piloted aircraft can store a large amount of information, which can be of vital importance when clarifying an illegal act, or any relevant fact, regardless of the geographical area in which it is performed, that the need arises to investigate this type of technology and its forensic treatment as digital or electronic evidence to provide a "specific methodological tool that allows the Acquisition and Forensic Analysis for this type of aircraft", taking into account the lack of specific methodologies in these matters.

2.3 Research Contribution

This research proposes a new methodology, specifically and exclusively oriented to the acquisition and forensic analysis of remotely piloted aircraft (Drones), highlighting that unlike the methodological proposals expressed in the various regulations and standards studied on the treatment of digital or electronic evidence, based on common storage devices such as external and internal memories, and cellular devices, this methodology presents 7 stages that are the collection, acquisition, preservation, documentation, analysis, presentation and transversely the knowledge of the evidence, as a primary differentiating factor at the moment of surveying information with Drones, complemented in addition with 29 phases, duly diagrammed that allow to systematically carry out this type of surveys.

The topics covered in this document can be very useful for forensic science experts dealing with digital evidence after an incident or investigation associated with Drones in any area that requires it, as well as those professionals interested in learning more about these topics.

2.4 Hypothesis

Considering the hypothesis is defined as that which "indicates what is sought or intended to be proven and can be defined as tentative explanations of the phenomenon under investigation, formulated as propositions" [3]. We can point out, concerning the present research, that, according to the technological architecture of Drones, they generate, collect and store different types of data, which can be acquired and analyzed using a forensic acquisition and analysis methodology suitable for Drones. In addition, consider the knowledge that must be had about this type of technology at the time of its analysis.

3 Theoretical Framework

The background information presented below is relevant to the development of this research and its objective.

3.1 Existing Mythologies Regarding Forensic Analysis of Digital and Electronic Evidence

Regarding forensic methodologies, first of all, we must point out that: forensic methodologies seek the way to evaluate, obtain and analyze evidence in a safe, reliable, and effective way through methods and professionals that safeguard the integrity of the evidence, as well as the chain of custody and allow to establish an impartial diagnosis of the evidence found, which can even be a Drone. The conclusions of these professionals called experts will be reflected in a forensic report and will serve as a complement and support when taking legal action on an incident.

In this sense, among the norms, standards, and methodologies most commonly used by experts for the treatment of digital evidence are the following: the ISO/IEC 27037:2015 standard, the RFC (Request for Comments) 3227:2002 Guide, the UNE: 71506:2013 standard, and the NIST 800–86:2006 Guide.

3.2 Fundamental Operating Components of a Remotely Piloted Aircraft System

The functional architecture of a Remotely Piloted Aircraft System is composed of three components: the aircraft (Drone), the communications link, and the command-and-control station, which will be explained below (see Fig. 1).

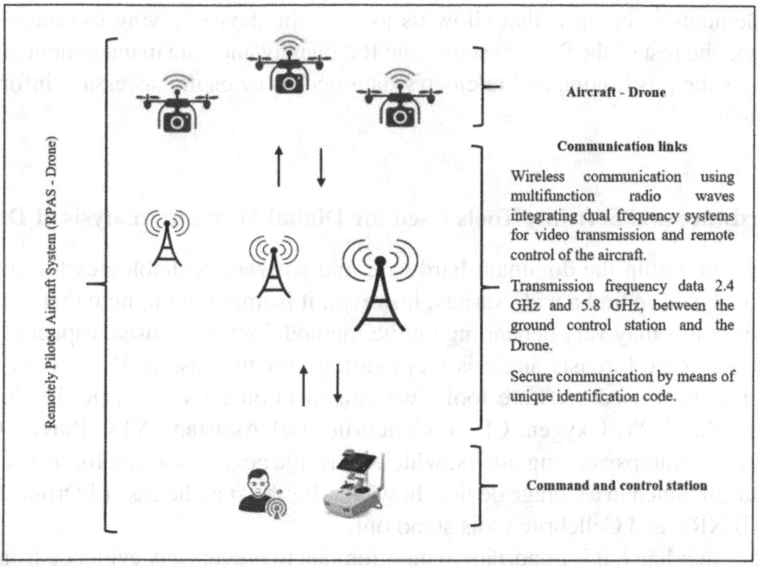

Fig. 1. Functional architecture of a Remotely Piloted Aircraft System. Source: Own elaboration.

Aircraft - Drone. A vehicle capable of moving through the air using a propulsion system composed of a series of high-tech hardware, electronics, and software elements, such as the frame or fuselage, propulsion unit (engines and propellers), sensors, flight controller board (gyroscope, altitude sensors, altitude variation, speed and position regulators and compass), batteries, gimbal, camera, landing gear, and information storage devices. There are two types; fixed-wing and rotary-wing or multi-rotors. Fixed-wing aircraft are mainly used for military operations and rotary-wing aircraft for other types of operations, such as surveillance, transport, rescue, agriculture, meteorology, field, and aerospace, among others.

Data Link. Means of connection between the aircraft and the command-control station (pilot). It is in charge of transferring the information acquired by the platform in flight, guaranteeing communication between the aircraft and the command-and-control station, based on wireless communication using multifunction radio waves that integrate the aircraft's dual frequency video transmission and remote-control systems. The data transmission frequency range is 2.4 GHz and 5.8 GHz, between the ground control station and the Drone. To achieve remote control of a Drone the transmitter (Tx) and receiver (Rx) must be tuned to the same frequency; otherwise, they will not be able to connect and send directional information.

Command and Control Station or Base Station. Essentially it allows the supervision and piloting of the aircraft through a communications link, which consists of three parts, which are the signal transmitter/receiver that sends information to the Drone for flight control and receives data from the sensors via radio signals through an antenna, the control elements or controls that allow us to pilot the device, giving us control of the engines and the rest of the flight systems and the display and data management elements that process the positioning and telemetry data and show us the necessary information for the flight.

3.3 Hardware and Software Tools Used for Digital Forensic Analysis of Drones

Currently and within the dominant hardware and software technologies for computer forensic analysis we find a wide variety, however, it is important to note that the proper use of these tools may vary depending on the methodology to be used, especially when there is no specific forensic analysis methodology for the case of Drones. Regarding some of the most used software tools, we can mention FTK Forensic Toolkit, FTK Imager, MSAB XRY, Oxygen, CFID, Cellebrite, DJI Assistant, VLC Player, Google Earth Pro, and Autopsy among others, which allow the acquisition and forensic analysis of the data contained in a storage device, however, for the specific case of Drone analysis the MSAB XRY and Cellebrite tools stand out.

On the other hand, it is important to mention that to prevent any evidence from being modified in terms of its data content and therefore being doubted, generating doubt about its authenticity, origin, or authorship, several write blocking tools allow only the reading of the storage devices and not the writing of these, thus preventing any modification of the evidence. Some of the most widely used write blockers are those of the Tableau line. We should mention that many of the software tools already mentioned also allow data blocking, but by software.

3.4 Legislation in Force Regarding the Operation and Use of Drones

The existing regulation regarding the operation and use of Drones varies from one country to another, however, worldwide, work is being done to create legal homogeneity, for example: in Europe through the European Aviation Safety Agency (EASA), in the United States through the Federal Aviation Administration (FAA). It is important to highlight the International Civil Aviation Organization (ICAO) which is an agency of the United Nations Organization created in 1944 by the Convention on International Civil Aviation, formed by 193 member countries and founded to study the problems of international civil aviation and promote unique regulations and standards in global aeronautics, within which it considers the issue of Drones.

On the other hand, we should point out that a study conducted by Condé Nast Traveler Magazine, from Spain to 200 countries around the world on regulatory matters on the use of Drones, points out that [4]:

-"The Middle East and Central Asia are where the strictest regulations are collected. Twenty-one percent of its countries maintain an absolute ban. The rest of the countries are torn between effective bans, which make up 15% of the countries, but also more relaxed rules, as in Japan, which aspires to be able to fly drones out of the field of vision. This requirement in the rules of the East and Asia contrasts, however, with the fact that China is the largest manufacturer of drones. Or countries like Iran, where their public use is forbidden. Meanwhile, the rest of Asia and Oceania, hardly have legislation that welcomes the use of Drones (56% of the countries). Despite this, places like New Zealand have made Drone tourism fashionable. In this case, it is especially the aesthetic aspect, considering that it is one of the countries with the most beautiful landscapes in the world.

In Africa, more than half of its countries do not have specific regulations either. However, while in the previous area there are no places with absolute or effective bans, in Africa, 21% have a total ban and 13% have an effective one.

Here they also advocate good use, in countries such as Ghana or Rwanda, where they use drones to deliver medical supplies to small villages. In fact, in Ghana, flying one of these devices without a license can cost up to 30 years in prison.

What this text is intended to highlight is that even though owning a Drone is becoming increasingly common, the laws are still very disparate. It is striking how they can differ in such a way from one country to another. One thing must be clear, as the good of technology advances, we must know how to curb the evil it can cause"-.

4 Methodological Framework

The methodological framework aims to present the different guidelines to be followed during the development of this research project, to contribute to the achievement of the objectives and the problem posed, which consists mainly of the lack of a specific methodology for the acquisition and forensic analysis of a Drone. The above, considering the following aspects:

4.1 Phase 1 - Identification and Analysis of the Regulations, Standards, and Methodologies Associated with the Treatment of Digital and Electronic Evidence

In this phase, the regulations, standards, and methodologies related to digital and electronic evidence, applicable to the execution of a computer forensic analysis, are investigated.

4.2 Phase 2 - Analysis of the Hardware, Electronics, and Software Architecture of a Drone

In this phase, the analysis of the hardware, electronic, and software architecture of the DJI Phantom 4 Drone, proposed as a case study, is carried out.

4.3 Phase 3 - Experimental Method

In this phase, a methodology for the acquisition and forensic analysis of a Drone is developed, based on the analysis of the regulations, standards, and methodologies associated with digital and electronic evidence, considering the hardware, electronic and software architecture of the Drone understudied.

5 Development

Digital forensic analysis or computer forensics is the application of a series of scientific, professional, and specialized techniques on those technologies that present an investigative interest often associated with corporate aspects, internal investigations, civil litigation, criminal investigations, intelligence investigations, and even national security issues. It should be noted that the digital forensic analysis according to the National Institute of Cybersecurity of Spain (INCIBE), considers within its fundamental methodological aspects, five phases that are: "preservation, acquisition, analysis, documentation and presentation" [5], considered as part of the analysis within this research.

In this sense, and to develop a "Methodology for the Acquisition and Forensic Analysis of a Remotely Piloted Aircraft System", the research is carried out in three phases, according to the following detail:

5.1 Phase 1: Identification and Analysis of Regulations, Standards, and Methodologies Associated with the Treatment of Digital and Electronic Evidence

Currently, there are several regulations, standards, procedures, and methodologies that can contribute to the execution of the forensic analysis of a Drone. These methods are mainly oriented to the proper handling of the digital evidence, the preparation of a copy of the evidence for later forensic analysis, and finally the generation of the forensic report. Regarding digital or electronic evidence, we must point out that there are several differences and aspects to consider, it is not the same to analyze a Drone as a personal computer, a server, a mobile device, or an external storage medium, such as a hard drive, a Pendrive, a MicroSD memory or other component.

On the other hand, and as far as Drones are concerned, it must be taken into account that some of the most relevant aspects are the following: type, brand, model, size, purpose and use, ease of transport, data storage, whether in volatile and non-volatile memories, ease of access to the storage device or devices, in addition to the hardware and software of each Drone technology. These factors highlight the need to investigate or formulate new proposals or methodological tools for forensic analysis specific to these devices.

In this sense, and considering the above, four of the main normative and methodological documents that can be applied for the forensic analysis of digital and electronic evidence are identified, which are analyzed in terms of their description, type of evidence, advantages, disadvantages, legal aspects, methods observed based on the phases of forensic analysis, and four principles, which are: auditable, reproducible, defensible and admissible. This allows identifying the most common and used methodological factors, to obtain the best of each one of them, and through the study of the hardware, electronic and software architecture of the DJI - Phantom 4 Drone, to develop a specific methodology that is exclusively adapted to the forensic analysis of Drones (the methodological proposal is developed in Phase 3 of this chapter). Given the above, the documents analyzed are:

ISO/IEC 27037:2015 Standard. SO/IEC 27037:2015 Standard. On Information technology - Security techniques - Guidelines for the identification, collection, acquisition, and preservation of digital evidence, was published in 2012 by the "International Organization for Standardization (ISO)", composed of 164 countries.

The methodology proposed by this standard is mainly based on the treatment of digital evidence through four stages: identification, collection, acquisition, and preservation of evidence, without making specific distinctions for the electronic devices under analysis, but attempts to present a methodology of general application for electronic devices [6]. See Table 1, for an analysis of this regulation.

Table 1. Analysis of regulations and standards on methodologies for forensic analysis of digital and electronic evidence (ISO 27.037).

Standards	Orientation	Advantages	Disadvantages	Legal Aspects
ISO 27.037 year 2015 (latest revision 2018) Information technology - Security techniques - Guidelines for the identification, collection, acquisition and preservation of digital evidence.	Evidence digital	It provides comprehensive guidelines for the identification, collection, acquisition and preservation of digital evidence. It covers a wide range of devices and situations, it is applicable to computer equipment, storage media (sata, ide, usb and ssd drives among others) and peripheral devices, as well as critical systems, databases, networked devices, endpoint and mobile devices. It can be adaptable and applicable to different storage media for analysis. Digital evidence is governed by three fundamental principles; relevance, reliability and sufficiency. These elements define the quality of any investigation based on digital evidence.	It does not present specifications on the forensic analysis of Drones. It presents a general treatment of digital evidence without further specifications.	It does not distinguish between the laws of each country, establishing a methodological framework adaptable to each country's reality. It allows evidence, due to its proper treatment, to be presented in a valid manner, in order to facilitate its credibility in trials and legal processes. On the other hand, it presents the concept and treatment of the chain of custody.

Methods observed on the basis of the stages of forensic analysis.	Principles observed			
	Auditable	Reproducible	Defendable	Admissible
1. Identification: system and application logs should be established, including e-mail logs, web logs, access logs, password files, system configuration files, host IP information, device functionality and dependency, ability to understand the impact on volatile and non-volatile evidence. 2. Collection: formulation and execution of the evidence collection process, generation of evidence documents, evidence chain of custody, quality control of the evidence collection process and interviews. 3. Acquisition: determining storage requirements, performing the image acquisition procedure (e.g., acquisition of partial and full digital storage media), acquisition performed on an on or off system, and generation of the hash value. 4. Preservation: knowledge about the generation of evidence audit documents, definition of parameters for documents, information security assurance, threats, vulnerabilities and controls for digital evidence.	The ISO 27.037:2015 standard allows the procedures performed and the documentation generated regarding digital evidence to be validated and contrasted by good professional practices. It presents traces and evidences of what has been performed, together with their respective results.	The methods and procedures applied can be reproducible, verifiable and arguable to the level of understanding of those knowledgeable in the field, who can provide validity and support for the actions carried out.	The tools used may be mentioned in the forensic reports and these must have been validated and contrasted in their use for the purpose for which they are used. In general, it allows and guides the use of specialized tools for data blocking by means of hardware or software, as well as for the analysis of digital evidence. Therefore, it is defensible in a judicial or private process.	Presents recognized forensic methods and techniques that are admissible to the investigator. Adequate treatment of evidence.

RFC Guide 3227:2002. RFCs (Request for Comments) are documents published by the Internet Engineering Task Force (IETF) where a series of expert proposals are presented on a specific subject, to establish, for example, a series of guidelines for carrying out a process, the creation of standards or the implementation of a protocol.

The methodology proposed by this guide published in 2002 by Dominique Brezinski and Tom Killalea in the United States, is based on the treatment of digital evidence through two stages: the collection of evidence and its storage, being able to serve as a standard without having been agreed or legitimized by a standardization body, for the collection of information in security incidents [7]. See Table 2, for an analysis of this guide.

Table 2. Analysis of regulations and standards on methodologies for forensic analysis of digital and electronic evidence (RFC Guide 3227).

Analysis of regulations and standards on methodologies for forensic analysis of digital and electronic evidence				
Standards	**Orientation**	**Advantages**	**Disadvantages**	**Legal Aspects**
RFC 3227:2002 Guidelines for evidence collection and archiving.	Evidence digital	Provides guidelines for collecting and storing digital evidence without putting it at risk. Shows best practices for determining data volatility (establishes an order of data volatility). Applicable to computer equipment, archival media, peripheral devices, networked devices and mobile devices. Takes chain of custody into account.	It does not present specifications on the forensic analysis of Drones. It only presents two aspects associated with the treatment of digital evidence, which only refer to the collection and storage of evidence. In general, it is very incomplete and depends on other complementary documents. It presents a marked orientation to security incidents and their treatment.	It has not been agreed upon or endorsed by a standardization body. The guidelines that make up this document may not be appropriate in all jurisdictions. Presents privacy considerations. It specifically sets out the following legal considerations with respect to computer evidence, which should be: - Admissible: it must conform to certain legal standards before it can be brought before a court. - Authentic: it must be possible to positively link the evidence associated with the incident. - Complete: it must tell the whole story and not just a particular perspective. - Reliable: there must be nothing about how the evidence was collected and manipulated that raises doubts about authenticity and veracity. - Credible: it must be easily believed and understood by a court of law.

Methods observed on the basis of the stages of forensic analysis.	Principles observed			
	Auditable	**Reproducible**	**Defendable**	**Admissible**
1. Collection: this procedure should be as detailed as possible. It should be unambiguous, and should minimize the amount of decision making. It considers the type of evidence and its treatment for data extraction. 2. Storage: the chain of custody of the evidence should be properly documented and treated.	It is not compatible in auditing aspects, since it is incomplete in the detail of the treatment of digital evidence, which can be tested and questioned by experts in the field and by independent auditors.	The methods for collecting and storing evidence are transparent, but difficult to reproduce, as they are prone to security incidents and not specifically to the treatment that should be given to evidence through a chain of custody.	It is incomplete in terms of analysis of digital evidence, so the principle of defense is not fully complied with.	It presents forensic methods and techniques recognized by an organization or other standardizing body, however, it does not fully cover the handling and treatment of digital or electronic evidence (it requires complements), making it impractical for the forensic analysis process, so its admissibility could be questioned.

Standard UNE 71506:2013. This standard published by the Spanish Association for Standardization and Certification in 2013, presents a series of steps to perform the forensic analysis of electronic evidence [8].

The methodology proposed by this standard is based on the treatment of electronic evidence through five stages: preservation, acquisition, documentation, analysis, and presentation of digital evidence, and can be applied in any organization regardless of its activity or size, as well as for any professional competent in this field. See Table 3, for an analysis of this standard.

Table 3. Analysis of regulations and standards on methodologies for forensic analysis of digital and electronic evidence (Standard UNE 71506).

Standards	Orientation	Advantages	Disadvantages	Legal Aspects
UNE: 71506:2013 Methodologies for the forensic analysis of electronic evidences.	Electronic evidence	It does not specify storage devices, however, it refers to the physical space where the data is stored in digital format. It presents a model of expert report. It presents guidelines regarding the equipment for the forensic analysis of electronic evidence. It is very complete in terms of definitions and concepts. It presents a very interesting aspect, regarding the recognition and treatment of evidence in virtualized environments.	It does not present specifications on the forensic analysis of Drones. It does not consider the preservation and storage of evidence prior to acquisition (these are considered in UNE 71505) so it generates dependence on other documents.	It is applicable to any organization regardless of its activity or size, as well as for any professional competent in this field, a situation that may be possible due to the rise of new technologies, such as drones. Its scope of action is oriented in first instance for Spain.

Methods observed on the basis of the stages of forensic analysis.	Principles observed			
	Auditable	Reproducible	Defendable	Admissible
1. Preservation: process that guarantees the inalterability and reproducibility of the studies to be carried out on the electronic evidence, ensuring its legal validity. This preservation entails the storage of the original electronic evidence in isolated supports or places that avoid external interferences that may modify it. 2. Acquisition: which distinguishes the processing of information obtained in systems that are switched on and off. That is to say, the electronic evidences on which the pertinent forensic analysis will be carried out may have their origin in static data from switched-off systems, data in transit from systems in operation, volatile data, data from embedded systems, as well as data from large systems, mobile devices and networks, with all the information to be analyzed being located in a single place or in several physical repositories. 3. Documentation: this is done in order to guarantee the chain of custody and traceability of the evidence under forensic analysis, through the implementation of a forensic document management system, which records all the processes carried out on the evidence, whether they are originals, copies or clones of it. 4. Analysis: to be performed on the information of interest of the different electronic evidences under study. 5. Presentation: associated with the results obtained to the judicial authority or entity requesting the respective expert report.	This standard presents a series of steps to be followed with respect to the treatment and analysis of electronic evidence, which facilitates and allows the procedures performed and the documentation generated with respect to the evidence to be validated and contrasted by good professional practices. It is a model that can be audited in terms of the handling, analysis and results obtained with respect to the evidence.	Due to the orderly scheme and the step-by-step approach proposed in each of the phases of electronic evidence processing, it can be highly reproducible in a suitable forensic environment.	It is observed that the principle of defense is fulfilled, considering the step by step presented by this regulation regarding the treatment of electronic evidence, in addition to the legal aspects that it contemplates, it is very complete.	Presents recognized forensic methods and techniques that are admissible to the investigator. Adequate treatment of evidence.

NIST Guide 800–86:2006. This guide for the integration of forensic techniques in incident response was published by the National Institute of Standards and Technology of the United States in 2006 [9].

The methodology proposed by this standard is based mainly on the treatment of digital evidence through four stages: collection, examination, analysis, and reporting, and can be applied in any organization at the international level, as well as by any professional competent in this field. See Table 4, for an analysis of this guide.

5.2 Phase 2: Analysis of the Hardware, Electronics, and Software Architecture of a Drone

In this phase, the hardware, electronics, and software architecture of the DJI Phantom 4 Drone are presented as a case study [10]. In this regard, we must point out that depending on the type, model, and manufacturer of the aircraft to be analyzed, through a methodology of acquisition and forensic analysis, these will always present differences in their capabilities and performance, however, they will maintain patterns that are common and relevant to take into account when performing forensic analysis to these technologies, these patterns are the means made available by the manufacturer of the aircraft to perform

Table 4. Analysis of regulations and standards on methodologies for forensic analysis of digital and electronic evidence (NIST Guide 800–86).

Analysis of regulations and standards on methodologies for forensic analysis of digital and electronic evidence				
Standards	Orientation	Advantages	Disadvantages	Legal Aspects
NIST 800-86:2006 Guidance for the integration of forensic techniques in Incident Response.	Digital evidence	It provides four main data sources, these are: Files, operating systems, network traffic and applications. It presents an important reference regarding the extraction of volatile and non-volatile data. It is very complete in terms of definitions. It indicates a series of storage devices for digital evidence and how they should be treated.	It does not present specifications on the forensic analysis of Drones, however, it presents a wide range of actions regarding the proper handling of digital evidence.	The guide presents forensic analysis from an IT perspective, not from a law enforcement standpoint.

Methods observed on the basis of the stages of forensic analysis.	Principles observed			
	Auditable	Reproducible	Defendable	Admissible
1. Collection: describes it as the first forensic process of identifying potential data sources and how to acquire data from those sources. It corresponds to the identification, labeling, recording and acquisition of data from the possible relevant data sources, following procedures that preserve the integrity of the data. 2. Examination: is the evaluation and extraction of relevant information from the collected data, preserving the integrity of the data. 3. Analysis: once the relevant information has been extracted, the analyst must study and analyze the data to generate conclusions from it, using legally justifiable methods and techniques for the treatment of information that are useful for the investigation. 4. Report: process of preparation and presentation of the resulting information where the results of the analysis are reported, which may include the description of the actions used, explaining how the tools and procedures were selected, and determining what further actions can be taken.	It describes each of the phases in detail, making it possible to audit each of them independently; the collection, examination, analysis and the respective expert report.	Each phase of the presented computer forensic analysis can be reproduced independently by a specialist.	Due to the level of detail presented in this guide in each phase of forensic analysis, and with the appropriate use of hardware and software forensic tools, it meets the criteria of defensible, based primarily on the technological perspective and methodology presented.	Presents recognized forensic methods and techniques, so they are admissible to the investigator. It presents an adequate treatment of the evidence.

data capture (high-resolution cameras), data storage media and software that allows the correct synchronism between the various components of the Drone.

This professional multi-rotor rotary wing drone was selected as a case study due to its high performance, use, application, and technological components.

5.3 Phase 3: Experimental Method

To develop a methodology for the Acquisition and Forensic Analysis of a Remotely Piloted Aircraft System (RPAS - Drone), the analysis of the regulations and standards on the treatment of digital and electronic evidence (detailed in Phase 1, point 5.1 of this document) is considered, extracting a first methodological common factor based on the stages of forensic analysis of the regulations and standards studied, and a second methodological common factor based on the first common factor obtained vs. the methodological standard of traditional forensic analysis (referenced by INCIBE). This allows obtaining a single factor, which is composed of 6 stages: Collection, Acquisition, Preservation, Documentation, Analysis, and Presentation. It should be noted that the following was done to obtain each common factor:

The First Common Factor - Comparative Analysis Between the Norms and Standards Studied Versus the Methods Observed Based on the Stages of Forensic Analysis

The first step is the execution of the "first comparative analysis" between the norms and standards studied versus the methods observed based on the stages of forensic analysis that each of them present, being able to establish as the "first common factor" the following stages: "Collection, Acquisition, Preservation, and Analysis". See Table 5, for an analysis of common factors.

Table 5. Comparative analysis between the standards studied versus the methods observed based on the stages of the forensic analysis of the standards studied.

	Methods observed on the basis of the stages of forensic analysis of the regulations studied									
Normative / Standard	Identification	Collection	Acquisition	Preservation	Storage	Documentation	Analysis	Presentation	Examination	Report
ISO 27.037 (2015)	√	√	√	√						
RFC 3227 (2002)		√			√					
UNE: 71506 (2013)			√	√		√	√	√		
NIST 800-86 (2006)		√					√		√	√
Common factor 1		√	√	√			√			

The Second Common Factor - Comparative Analysis Between the Norms and Standards Studied - the Methods Observed Based on the Stages of Forensic Analysis Versus the Traditional Forensic Analysis Standard

In this second instance, a "second comparative analysis" is performed based on the regulations and standards studied, and the methods observed based on the stages of forensic analysis of each of them versus the methodological standard of traditional forensic analysis (referenced by INCIBE), where the following stages are established as a "second common factor": "Collection, Acquisition, Preservation, Documentation, Analysis and Presentation", allowing to consider the best of each of them, aligned with the Drone technology. See Table 6, for an analysis of common factors.

Table 6. Comparative analysis between the standards studied and the methods observed based on the stages of forensic analysis vs. the traditional forensic analysis standard.

	Methods observed based on the stages of forensic analysis of the standards studied and the methodological standard of traditional forensic analysis									
Normative / Standard	Identification	Collection	Acquisition	Preservation	Storage	Documentation	Analysis	Presentation	Examination	Report
ISO 27.037 (2015)	√	√	√	√						
RFC 3227 (2002)		√			√					
UNE: 71506 (2013)			√	√		√	√	√		
NIST 800-86 (2006)		√					√		√	√
Estandar metodológico del Análisis Forense Tradicional (Fuente Incibe)			√	√		√	√	√		
Common factor 2		√	√	√		√	√	√		

Given the above, and based mainly on the experience obtained from the study of the architecture of these aircraft, their high technology, and their spectrum of use, a seventh stage is added transversally, corresponding to the "Knowledge of the evidence", which as a whole allows forming a methodology that is undoubtedly super positioned concerning those methodologies and regulatory standards in force dating from 2002, and that let us glimpse their lack of updating to this type of Drones technologies. Therefore, and based on the above, the new methodology called METAF-RPAS consists of seven stages, and 29 phases detailed in Sect. 6 - Result of this document (see Fig. 2. With the METAF-RPAS methodology designed, and Fig. 3. With the scheme of the experimental method developed).

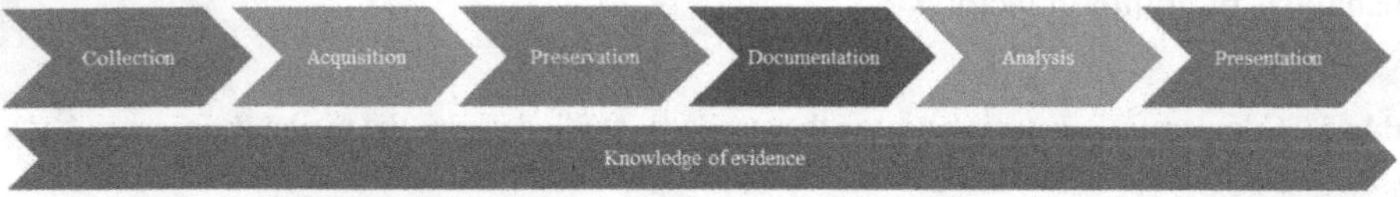

Fig. 2. With the METAF-RPAS methodology designed. Source: Own elaboration.

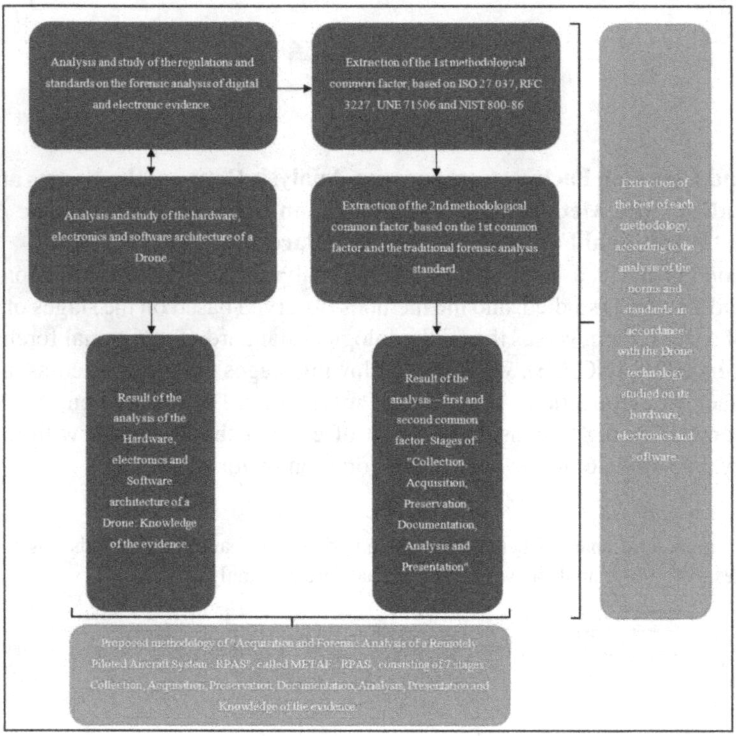

Fig. 3. Scheme of the experimental method developed. Source: Own elaboration.

6 Results

As a result of the study conducted regarding the regulations associated with the forensic analysis of digital and electronic evidence, issued mainly by American and European countries, under normative and methodological standards such as ISO, UNE, NIST, and RFC-IEFT; in addition to the study of the hardware, electronic and software architecture of a Drone (case study Drone Phantom 4); it is proposed as a methodology, with a specific orientation, for the "Acquisition and Forensic Analysis of a Remotely Piloted Aircraft System – RPAS" the methodology called "METAF-RPAS", which consists of 7 stages: collection, acquisition, preservation, documentation, analysis, presentation, and transversely the stage of knowledge of the evidence (see Fig. 4), and a total of 29 phases.

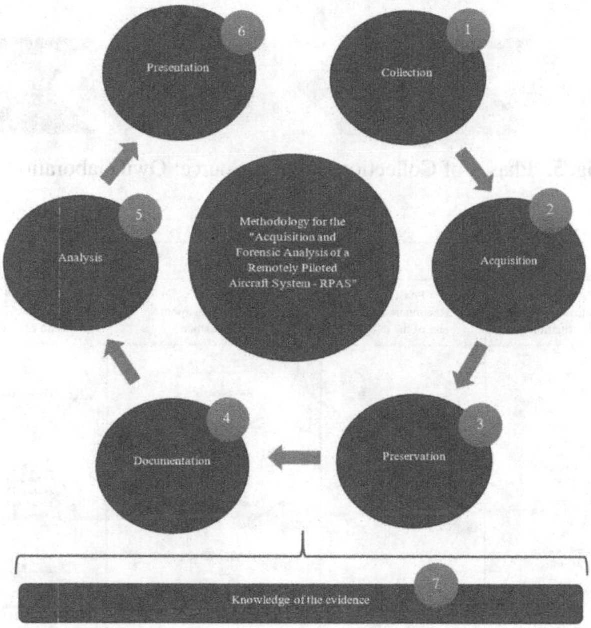

Fig. 4. Methodology for the acquisition and forensic analysis of a remotely piloted aircraft system - RPAS, called METAF-RPAS. Source: Own elaboration.

The 7 stages of the proposed methodology are described below, together with its 29 phases.

6.1 Stage 1 - Collection

It corresponds to the first stage of approach and formalization with the investigation to be developed and the evidence to be analyzed, for which all the necessary information regarding the investigation must be collected, recognize, identify, analyze and describe the site of the event, perform the recognition of the evidence, where aspects such as type of Drone, brand, model, series, storage media of the Drone or other complementary as cellular devices, remote control or cloud (which could be used), the location of the device, the origin of the evidence, general characteristics (descriptive) and state of operation must be considered. In general, Drones need other devices for their control or content visualization, such as remote control, cell phones, FPV goggles (remote vision piloting), and tablet, which are also part of this reconnaissance.

Subsequently, the evidence must be photographed and the chain of custody must be established, which is recognized as a document that generally indicates the details of the evidence, those responsible, origin, destination, date, and time (the legal aspects of its formality depend on the type of investigation to be carried out and the legislation in force in each country). See Fig. 5. Phases of Collection Stage 1, and Fig. 6. Flowchart - execution of the Collection Stage 1.

Fig. 5. Phases of Collection Stage 1. Source: Own elaboration.

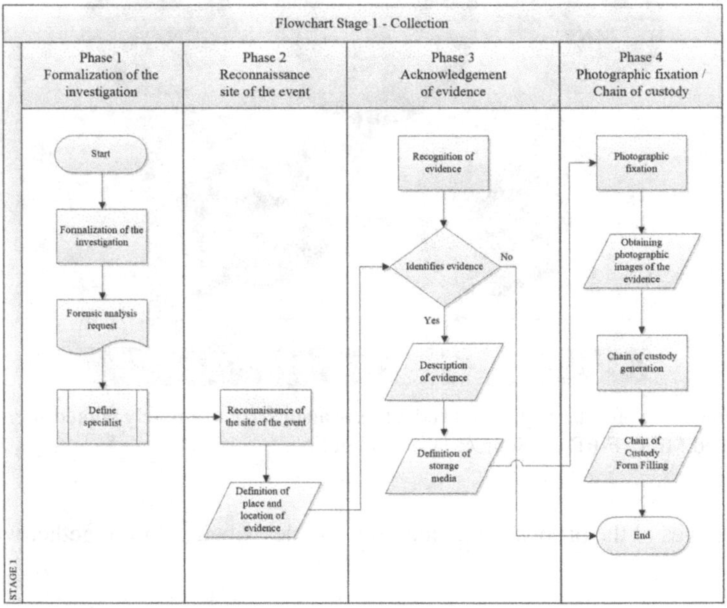

Fig. 6. Flowchart - execution of the Collection Stage 1. Source: Own elaboration.

6.2 Stage 2 - Acquisition

At this stage a forensic copy (image or cloning) of the identified digital evidence is created, that is, of the Drone and its storage media, whether internal (chip type) or removable such as MicroSD cards, additionally we must keep in mind that complementary to the aircraft there are other data storage devices, such as; the remote control, cell phone, Tablet, cloud or another laptop, which will later be used in the stage of analysis of the evidence. We must remember that this stage is mainly oriented toward preserving the integrity of the digital evidence, since, depending on the type of data extraction to be performed, an identical copy of the data must be obtained without altering in any way the content of the evidence.

For the specific case of Drones, there are 4 ways to extract the data, according to the following detail:

Physical Extraction. It allows the acquisition of raw data from the storage media, processed mainly with specific forensic tools, such as UFED and XRY, being able to access live and deleted data.

Logical Extraction. It involves receiving information from the Drone and allows the device to present the data for analysis. If the data is on removable media it must be analyzed separately.

File System Dump. It is a hybrid between both methods of data extraction, allowing to recover of the device's file system and interpret the data, however, it does not allow to recover of all the deleted data, as it is only feasible with physical extraction.

Chip-off. In deteriorated drones or those with only internal memory, it is generally possible to recover information by extracting the chip and then reading it, which is very complex since it requires very specialized tools and techniques.

Additionally, and depending on the type of extraction performed, it is recommended to create two copies of the source of information, where one copy will be kept as a master file and the other can be used for the execution of the respective forensic analysis.

Once the image file has been created, the hash value of the source and that of the image file (which must be the same) must be recorded. The hash values are used to prove that the image file is identical to the content of the sample, it is generally recommended to generate a double or triple hash (for example the Sha-256 hash function, which ensures the security of the information). On the other hand, it is essential to use hardware and forensic software tools that allow data blocking, only reading the data and not writing it to the storage device under acquisition and forensic analysis (a situation that would modify the evidence). See Fig. 7. Phases of Acquisition Stage 2, and Fig. 8. Flowchart - execution of the Collection Stage 2.

Fig. 7. Phases of Acquisition Stage 2. Source: Own elaboration.

6.3 Stage 3 - Preservation

At this stage it is essential to label, consider any method of transfer, and keep the evidence in appropriate storage media that allow its protection, preventing it from being altered or modified, ensuring its legal validity and its reproducibility for any required

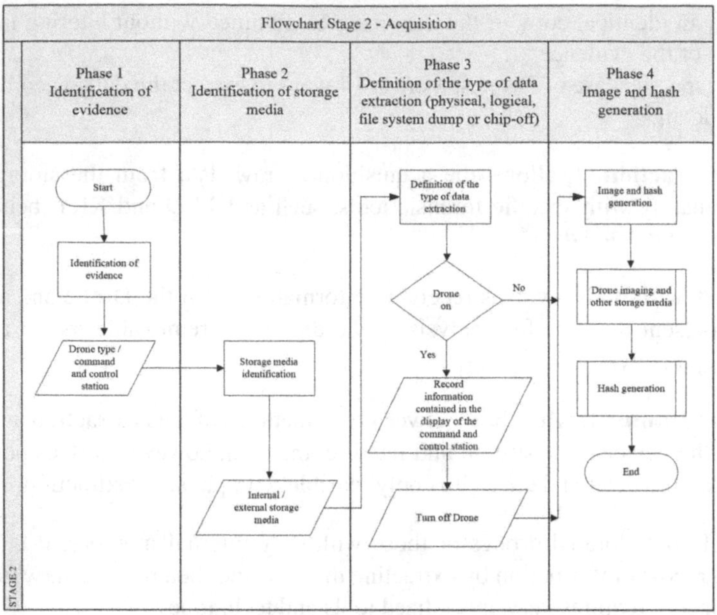

Fig. 8. Flowchart - execution of the Acquisition Stage 2. Source: Own elaboration.

analysis through proper monitoring of the chain of custody of both the aircraft and the remote control and the various complementary devices such as a Tablet or Smartphone. The storage of the evidence foresees its transportation and storage, which is generally associated with isolated places that avoid external interventions or manipulations by unauthorized personnel. Evidence storage containers will vary according to the size of the evidence, they can be antistatic bags, sponges, or polyurethane-lined containers. In the case of drones, a shock-proof container is required to prevent damage to the aircraft and its decalibration. Each piece of evidence can be stored separately, as long as it is properly identified and linked to its respective chain of custody.

On the other hand, and concerning the Drone battery, which is generally of the highly dangerous LiPo (Lithium Polymer) type, they must be stored in bags designed to stop the fire that could be produced by the combustion of the LiPo batteries during their inadequate charging and storage. See Fig. 9. Phases of Preservation Stage 3, and Fig. 10. Flowchart - execution of the Preservation Stage 3.

Fig. 9. Phases of Preservation Stage 3. Source: Own elaboration.

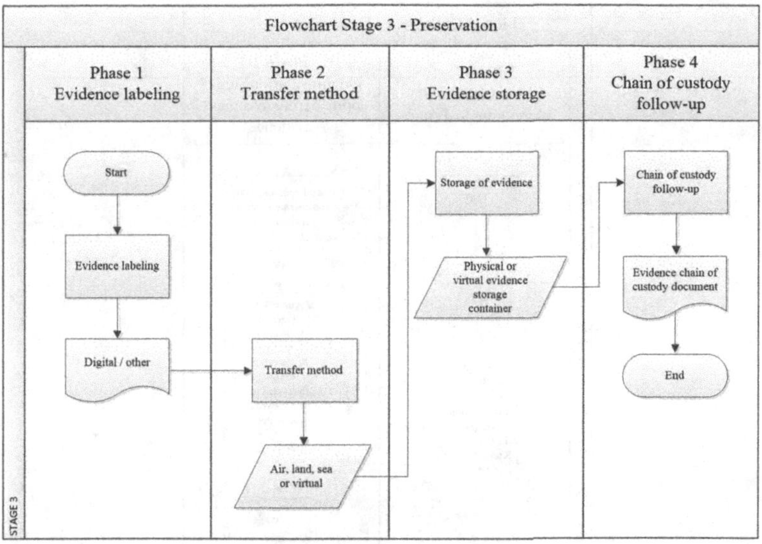

Fig. 10. Flowchart - execution of the Preservation Stage 3. Source: Own elaboration.

6.4 Step 4 - Documentation

The documentation stage consists mainly of writing down, recording, and evidencing all the actions carried out from the beginning of the investigation until it ends, going through each of the stages proposed in this forensic acquisition and analysis methodology. The most relevant aspects to consider are the treatment and analysis of the evidence, the presentation of the results, the backups, and the records obtained. See Fig. 11. Phases of Documentation Stage 4, and Fig. 12. Flowchart - execution Documentation Stage 4.

Fig. 11. Phases of Documentation Stage 4. Source: Own elaboration.

6.5 Stage 5 - Analysis

At this stage, four fundamental aspects must be considered: the preparation of the evidence, the definition of hardware and software tools to be used, in addition to the recovery and analysis of the data. The above is to be able to determine and establish the means of proof required in the forensic investigation to be able to establish conclusions according to the analysis of the information obtained. In this regard, we must consider that during the forensic analysis process it is essential not to modify the evidence, safeguarding its integrity at all times.

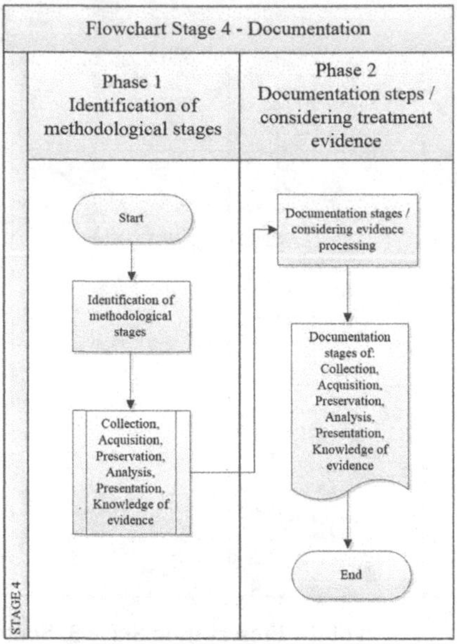

Fig. 12. Flowchart - execution Documentation Stage 4. Source: Own elaboration.

The data that can be extracted from a Drone, the remote control, and the Tablet or Smartphone are images and video, flight records, such as; GPS positions, dates and times, specific parameters (rotor speed, altitude, and direction), telematics data, diagnostic fault codes and associated media records, applications or software, user activity, such as; Drone on and off times, configuration settings, device usage, user IDs and accounts, connections to wireless networks and other devices, as well as telematics logs and any configuration information associated with remote data storage in the cloud, such as emails and users. See Fig. 13. Phases of Analysis Stage 5, and Fig. 14. Flowchart - execution Analysis Stage 5.

Fig. 13. Phases of Analysis Stage 5. Source: Own elaboration.

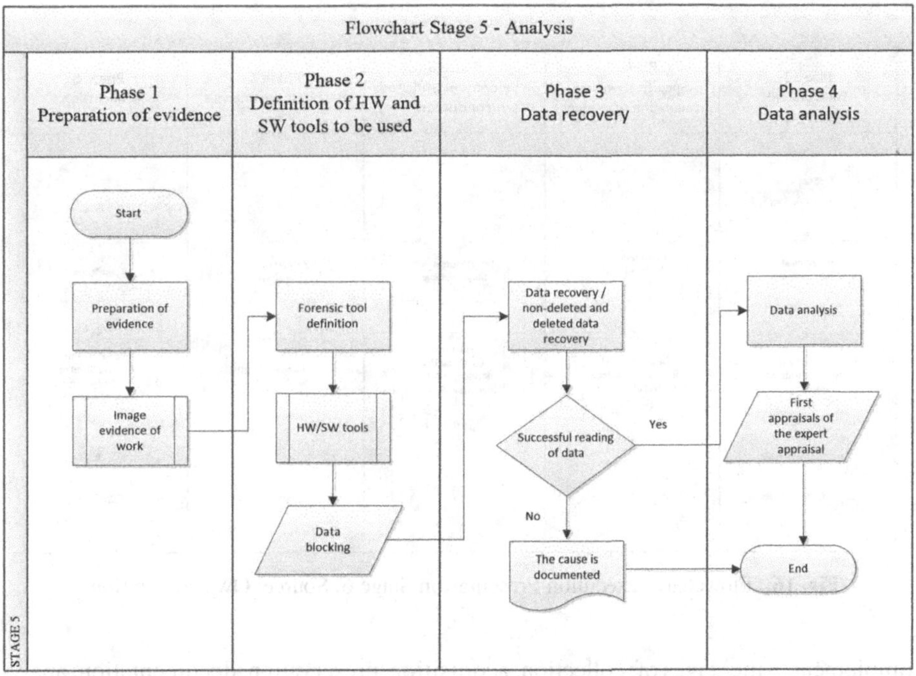

Fig. 14. Flowchart - execution Analysis Stage 5. Source: Own elaboration.

6.6 Stage 6 - Presentation

At this stage the expert report must be generated, which must consider all the background or issues associated with the investigation and expertise in progress, in addition to the specification of the evidence under analysis (aircraft, remote control, Tablet, Smartphone, etc.), the development and study carried out on the evidence (s), the results obtained, and finally, the conclusions of the expertise carried out. See Fig. 15. Phases of Presentation Stage 6, and Fig. 16. Flowchart - execution Presentation Stage 6.

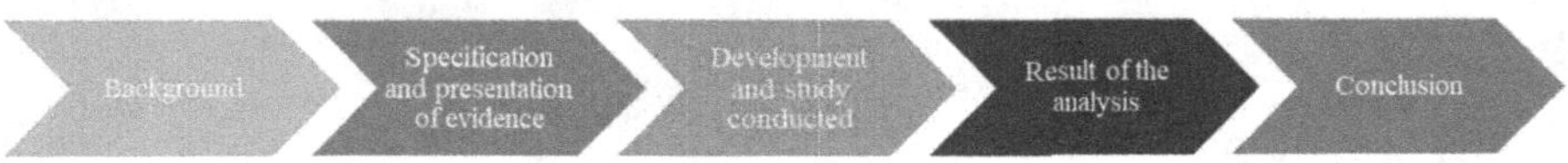

Fig. 15. Phases of Presentation Stage 6. Source: Own elaboration.

6.7 Stage 7 - Knowledge of the Evidence

Considering the speed at which Drone technologies and their different applications are advancing, it is essential to have full knowledge of this type of evidence when applying and executing the different stages of an acquisition methodology and forensic analysis of a remotely piloted aircraft system. Therefore, this stage is considered a cross-cutting

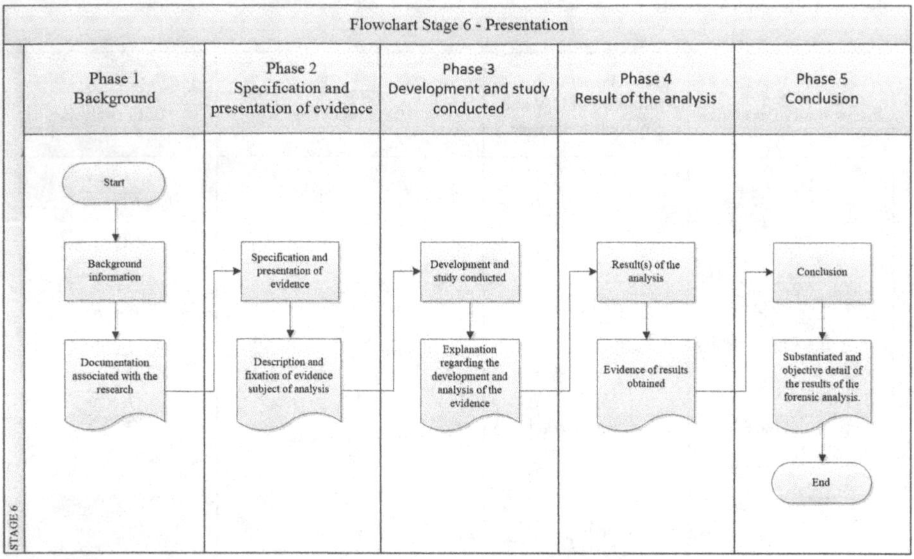

Fig. 16. Flowchart - execution Presentation Stage 6. Source: Own elaboration.

complement to the stages of: collection, acquisition, preservation, documentation, analysis, and presentation, which mainly consists of observing, identifying, and understanding the hardware, electronic and software architecture of a Drone, in addition to the general operation of each of its components. See Fig. 17. Phases of the knowledge of evidence Stage 7, and Fig. 18. Flowchart - execution Knowledge of evidence Stage 7.

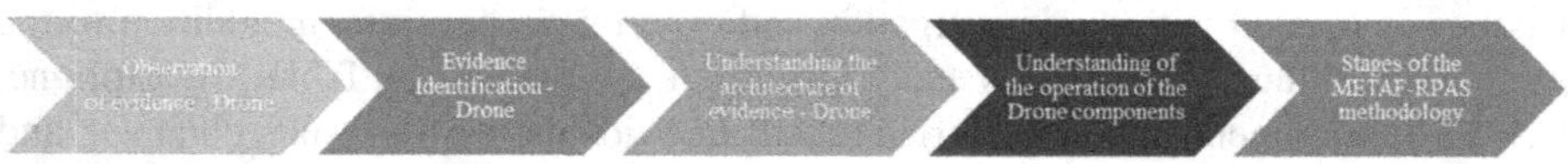

Fig. 17. Phases of Knowledge of the evidence Stage 7. Source: Own elaboration.

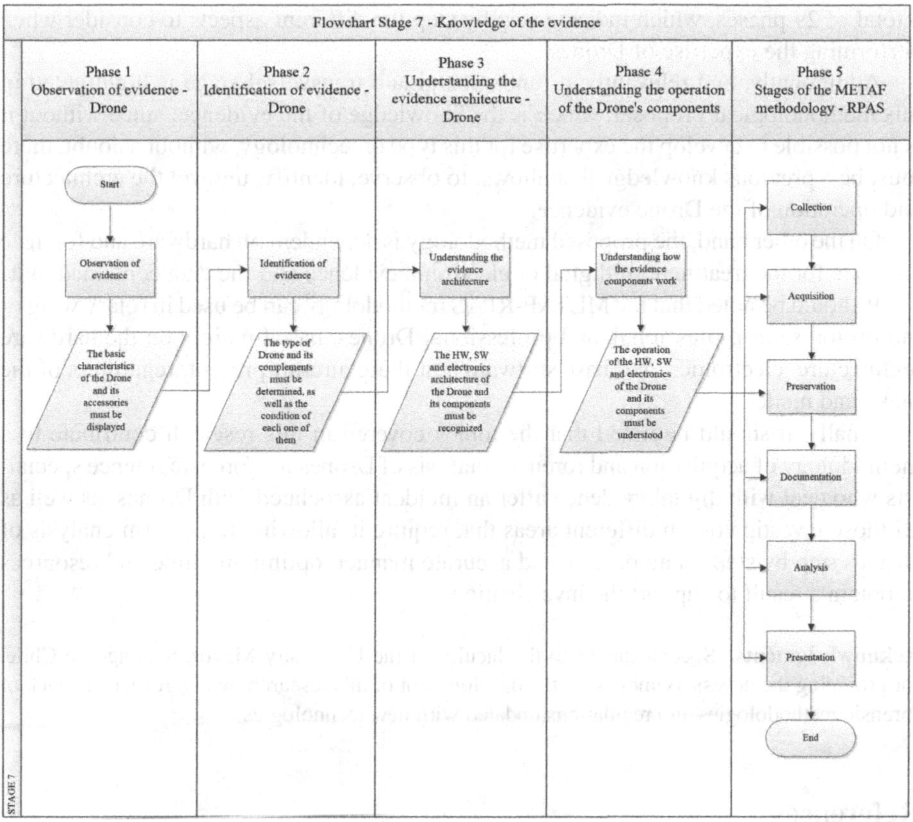

Fig. 18. Flowchart - execution Knowledge of the evidence Stage 7. Source: Own elaboration.

7 Conclusions

Currently, there are several standards and regulations such as ISO 27037, RFC 3227, UNE 71506, and NIST 800–86, which were studied in this document, and which establish methodologies oriented to the forensic analysis of digital or electronic evidence, however, these standards and regulations date from 2002, This situation is relevant because it does not contemplate new technological advances, such as the "Remotely Piloted Aircraft System - RPAS, known as Drone", which due to their use and applicability, could be the object of investigations or studies that require the performance of a computer forensic analysis.

Undoubtedly, new technologies advance faster than regulations and methodological standards. Given the above, a specific methodology of Acquisition and Forensic Analysis is proposed for a "Remotely Piloted Aircraft System", called "METAF-RPAS" which allows performing the "Acquisition and Forensic Analysis" of this type of aircraft in an efficient and detailed way, through 7 stages which are: collection, acquisition, preservation, documentation, analysis, presentation, and transversely the knowledge stage, with a total of 29 phases, which indicate step by step the different aspects to consider when performing the expertise of Drones.

Additionally, and relevantly, a fundamental and transversal stage is highlighted in this methodological proposal, which is the knowledge of the evidence, since without it is not possible to develop the expertise for this type of technology, without a doubt, there must be a previous knowledge that allows: to observe, identify, unravel the architecture and operation of the Drone evidence.

On the other hand, the proposed methodology is dependent on hardware and forensic software for the treatment of digital or electronic evidence and the data contained in it.

It should be noted that the METAF-RPAS methodology can be used in rotary wing or multirotor, semi-professional, and professional Drones, based mainly on the hardware architecture, electronics, and base software that these aircraft present, regardless of the make and model.

Finally, it should be noted that the topics covered in this research contribute to a methodology of acquisition and forensic analysis of Drones for forensic science specialists who deal with digital evidence after an incident associated with Drones, as well as all those investigators in different areas that require it, allowing to perform analysis of Drones step by step, in an orderly and accurate manner, optimizing time and resources to obtain a result to support the investigation.

Acknowledgments. Special thanks to the faculty of the University Mayor, Santiago de Chile, for providing the necessary means for the development of this research, which reveals the lack of forensic methodologies and regulations updated with new technologies.

References

1. Lukas Schroth, F.: Statistics 2020–2025 Drone Industry Insights. LNCS Homepage. https://droneii.com/the-drone-market-size-2020-2025-5-key-takeaways 22 June 2020
2. Notinerd, Crimes are committed with the help of Drones. Retrieved from Notinerd.com. LNCS Homepage. https://notinerd.com/9-delitos-que-se-cometieron-con-la-ayuda-de-drones/. March 2018
3. Hernández, R.: Research Methodology MTE 2nd Edition - Hypothesis. LNCS Homepage. https://sites.google.com/site/metodololgdelainvestig/modulo-5 23 Feb 2011
4. Cano, M.: Conde Nast Traveler Magazine - A look at global drone regulations. LNCS Homepage. https://www.traveler.es/viajeros/articulos/mapa-legislacion-uso-de-drones-en-cada-pais/19717 1 Dec 2020
5. INCIBE Spain National Institute of Cybersecurity Spain- Fundamental forensic methodological aspects. LNCS Homepage. https://www.incibe-cert.es/blog/rfc3227 6 June 2014
6. INN Chile. National Standards Institute ISO 27037:2015 on "Information technology - Security techniques - Guidelines for the identification, collection, acquisition, and preservation of digital evidence". NCh-ISO27037:2015. LNCS Homepage. https://ecommerce.inn.cl/nch-iso27037201552523 30 Sep 2015
7. Brezinski & Killalea. RFC 3227 Treatment of digital evidence. LNCS Homepage. https://datatracker.ietf.org/doc/html/rfc3227 February 2002
8. AENOR Spain. UNE 71506 - Methodology for the forensic analysis of electronic evidence - Spanish Association for Standardization and Certification. LNCS Homepage. https://docer.com.ar/doc/sn0ev1v. July 2013

9. NIST U.S. National Institute of Standards and Technology - Guide to forensic science integration. LNCS Homepage. https://nvlpubs.nist.gov/nistpubs/legacy/sp/nistspecialpublication800-86.pdf August 2006
10. DJI China. Drone Phantom4 maintenance and startup guide. LNCS Homepage. https://dl.djicdn.com/downloads/phantom_4/es/ES-Phantom%204%20Quick%20Start%20Guide%20v1.2.pdf

Multiobjective Model for Resource Allocation Optimization: A Case Study

Edgar Jardón, Marcelo Romero(✉), and J. Raymundo Marcial-Romero

Autonomous University of State of Mexico, Toluca, Mexico
mromeroh@uaemex.mx
https://www.scholar.google.com.mx/citations?user=0OR6O9wAAAAJ%26hl=en

Abstract. Multiobjective allocation models are useful tools for the distribution of clients to public services or facilities. The correct distribution of clients considers various variables that increase the complexity of the study problem, but at the same time help to obtain results that are closer to reality. In this paper, a two-target allocation model for the distribution of clients to public facilities is presented. The two objective functions considered are: 1. Minimize the cost of transfer and 2. Maximize the service coverage of the facilities. The case study contemplates the 88,107 inhabitants between 17 and 18 years of age at the Metropolitan Zone of the Valley of Toluca (ZMVT) who, for the first time, process their voting cards in some of the 10 service modules of the Instituto Naional Electoral (INE), located in the same geographical area. The problem is solved using a Genetic Algorithm, considering 9 days to serve the total population of the ZMVT. The results obtained are encouraging because they respect the term spatial justice within the area of urban planning.

Keywords: Multiobjective model · Optimization problem · Genetic algorithm

1 Introduction

The diversity of services offered in recent years reflects the dynamic development of society, as well as the needs that affect the population. Among the services offered are the traditional public services, which seek to meet basic needs. In most of the studies carried out, it has been concluded that planning the logistics of this type of service is a difficult task since there must be a balance between the available offer, concerning the demand requested by the population [11].

The planning of public services has various dimensions and associated problems. Two of the problems that stand out involve the distribution of districts (or zoning) and the location-assignment of facilities in a strategic way. When dividing an area into smaller parts, experts or decision-makers must specify the criteria for the distribution of districts and facilities used to cover the operational requirements [12]. It is essential to create strategies for the benefit of public or private organizations, since in the event of wrongly establishing the number of

M. F. Mata-Rivera et al. (Eds.): WITCOM 2022, CCIS 1659, pp. 322–334, 2022.
https://doi.org/10.1007/978-3-031-18082-8_20

facilities or their location. They would cause adverse effects on operating costs, thus harming the quality of the services offered [1].

Currently, within the field of location, there are two study needs according to the facilities: find the optimal location and allocate a certain demand considering its capacity. From the two needs mentioned, the so-called location-assignment models arise. These models evaluate the quality of the current locations and produce alternatives that improve the spatial distribution, considering the term of *justice or equity* by optimally allocating a certain demand to the facilities [13].

Based on the foregoing, it should be considered that the location theory has been of greater interest within the field of operations research since it is a transcendental optimization issue for the strategic planning of public services [1]. Therefore, Jardón-Torres [8] mentions that one of the most important challenges is to achieve the design of a policy that can adapt to the development of demands over time, considering the evolution and growth of the population to be served.

Finally, this research work is constituted into five sections. 1. Study problem: explains the study scenario, as well as its features. 2. Related work: summarizes works that have addressed similar problems. 3. Mathematical model: formally presents the mathematical postulates of the problem. 4. Experimentation and results: presents the main findings found in this research. 5. Conclusions: establishes the areas of opportunity and future work.

2 Study Problem

As the demand for goods and services increases, a series of problems are produced that impact the quality of life of the population. Among all these problems, the ones that stand out the most according to [5] are:

- Know the best location and assign the population to service.
- The impact on the demand for goods and services with respect to population growth.
- Control of land use before the urbanization of growing areas.
- The correct assignment of police forces, which guarantees the safety of the population.

This is how, in this research work, the first problem of the aforementioned is addressed, considering as a case study the strategic allocation of the population of the Valley of Toluca (ZMVT) to certain modules of the Instituto Nacional Electoral (INE).

Every year the young population between 17 and 18 years of age goes to register at INE, this reduces the attention capacity of the population in certain modules. In addition, other sectors of the population are affected, since the waiting time increases when carrying out any other procedure, whether it is a change of address or modification of personal data, an example of the affected population is elderly, because in addition to the time of waiting face health conditions that make it impossible for them to stand for long. Although there is a preference for care for this sector of the population, the number of people who attend the modules is so high that it hurts the efficiency of the services offered [7].

To solve this location-assignment problem, INE has implemented various strategies, the most recent of which allows anyone to carry out a certain procedure in any module in the country, which provides citizens with greater freedom. However, there are certain modules that have a higher level of preference, which causes an overload that affects vehicular traffic around such facilities and therefore increases the level of pollution in the cities where these modules are located.

From the area of urban planning, when trying to solve a location-allocation problem, exact solution methods that use gradients are initially used to solve non-linear problems, however, they are inadequate to solve large-scale optimization problems, since the mathematical formulas proposed as part of an exact solution are computationally complex to solve, with high execution times, even implementing advanced programming techniques [15]. That is why alternate solution methods are used to determine semi-optimal solutions called heuristics. Although the solution generated by a heuristic is not optimal, it helps to reduce the search space and therefore the execution time [16].

It is necessary to consider that the generation of optimal solutions for the aforementioned problem requires the development of models that simultaneously evaluate the most representative variables of the study problem, in order to obtain results close to reality. That is why in this paper a multi-objective location-allocation mathematical-computational model is proposed for the allocation of the municipal population to certain INE modules. This model is solved using the heuristics of genetic algorithms.

Genetic algorithms are based on Darwin's theory of evolution and are widely used to solve complex problems. The basic principles of these algorithms are self-adaptation and self-optimization. To solve a problem, the study variables are abstracted through a binary coding called their chromosomal elements, which are crossed, mutated and selected during a certain number of iterations, until the value of an objective function improves. Genetic algorithms select the best elements of each generation, this avoids reaching local optima. Being considered the final element as the optimal solution [4].

Genetic algorithms are used to solve problems within various stochastic scenarios, where parameter optimization is sought regardless of whether the problems are linear, discrete, or continuous. Genetic algorithms have the advantage that they are not limited to a single objective, but simultaneously evaluate multiple objectives with few computational resources, since current technology contributes to obtaining better solutions in less time.

3 Related Work

Due to the nature of today's various location-allocation problems, different solution techniques exist in both the public and private sectors. The solutions produced by such techniques are efficient to the extent that the parameters involved in the study problem are configured correctly. That is why in this section some of the most used solution techniques in the state of the art are addressed.

In the area of public security, [14] proposes a model for locating surveillance cameras in a mass public transport network based on graph theory. The objective is to determine the best location of surveillance cameras in the stations that are part of a transport network, considering economic and technical factors. The model seeks to maximize the number of crimes captured by the cameras, as well as the quality of the installed cameras. In addition, they recommend the use of heuristic methods to find optimal solutions faster. Finally, they recommend that the model parameters should be stochastic and not static since with this models closer to reality are generated.

For its part, [5] carried out a spatial analysis of the buildings damaged by the 19S-2017 earthquake in Mexico City. They seek to identify the properties affected in the 19S-2017 earthquake, in addition to assigning Mobile Attention Units (UMAS) that cover the greatest possible demand. Also, compare the patterns of buildings damaged in the 1985 earthquake concerning the 2017 earthquake, showing clusters of areas damaged by the 19S-2017 earthquake to position UMAS at a radius of no more than 500 m in the first scenario and 1,000 m in the second scenario.

Within the area of home health care, [2] employs the clustering model to establish a semi-optimal district plan in Cote-Des-Neiges, Canada. In their study, they use criteria such as workload equity, connectivity, and mobility. The mobility criterion represents the dynamics of personnel who use public transportation and/or walk, which can be used to determine the time spent providing home health care. In addition, the tabu search heuristic is used to find [12] semi-optimal service clusters. The model used represents the study problem, which is given by two objective functions. First minimizes the level of mobility, second maximize workload balance.

Thus, the aforementioned implementations show the existing areas of opportunity that service location-assignment models provide for the benefit of proper urban planning. The challenge of providing services that consider spatial justice, since it implies elements of uncertainty and stochastic parameters such as visit times and travel times. Therefore, future research directions may include the investigation of stochastic optimization models, which are robust in the context of public services [12].

4 Mathematical Model

In recent decades, the number of operations research proposals for continuous or discrete optimization of facility location-allocation (LA) problems has increased. Such proposals have been extended to the modeling and design of algorithms with applications in public and private organizations [5].

In addition, due to the diversity of applications for facility location-allocation problems, it is necessary to establish specific objective functions or decision variables, for example: minimizing time to market for locating warehouses along a supply chain, maximizing distance to residential areas to locate unwanted facilities, minimize delivery time by locating train stations, maximize accessibility for people by locating ATMs, among others [6].

Usually, facility location-allocation problems employ an objective function that tries to minimize the costs of locating a set of facilities according to the amount of demand requested by customers under a set of constraints [5]. However, when working with more complex problems like the one presented in this work, more than one objective function is required. Therefore, the two implemented objective functions are presented below, as well as the definition of their variables and the restrictions of said functions.

4.1 Objective Functions to Model

In this work, two objective functions were chosen because they are relevant to the study problem: 1. Minimize the cost of transfer from clients to facilities, 2. Maximize coverage of facilities, subject to capacity restrictions.

Minimize Transportation Cost from Customers to Facilities

$$Min\ (f_1) = \sum_{i}^{n} \sum_{j}^{m} d_{ij} \alpha X_{ij} \tag{1}$$

Subject to:

$$X_{ij} = \begin{cases} 1 \ \textit{Demand of client}\,(\mathrm{i})\,\textit{is assigned to facility}\,(\mathrm{j}) \\ 0 \qquad\qquad\qquad\quad \textit{Other case} \end{cases} \tag{2}$$

Equation 2, allows knowing which clients j are assigned to a certain installation i.

Maximize Facility Coverage, Subject to Capacity Constraints

$$Max\ (f_2) = \sum_{i}^{n} \sum_{j}^{m} r_{ij} D_{mij} Y_{ij} \tag{3}$$

Subject to:

$$D_{mij} = \begin{cases} 1 \ \ d_{ij} \leq d_{mij} \\ 0 \ \textit{Other case} \end{cases} \tag{4}$$

$$Y_{ij} = \begin{cases} 1 \quad c_{ij} \geq r_{ij} \\ 0 \ \textit{Other case} \end{cases} \tag{5}$$

Equations 4 and 5 validate that a client j is assigned to a facility i as long as the maximum allowed distance is not exceeded and the maximum capacity of a service.

4.2 Additional Restrictions

$$\sum_{i}^{n} = X_{ij} \tag{6}$$

$$X_{ij} \epsilon \{0,1\} \tag{7}$$

$$Y_{ij} \epsilon \{0,1\} \tag{8}$$

Equation 6 validates that each client is assigned to only one facility. While Eqs. 7 and 8 guarantee that the variables X_{ij} and Y_{ij} are binary.

4.3 Variable Definition

This section presents the description of the variables used in Eq. 1 and in Eq. 3, as well as the restrictions:

- I : Set of clients (i)
- J : Set of facilities (j)
- n : Number of clients
- m : Number of installations
- d_{ij} : Distance between client (i) and facility (j)
- d_{mij} : Maximum acceptable distance between clients and facilities (can be variable or constant)
- D_{mij} : Validation of maximum acceptable distance between customers and facilities
- α : Constant transportation cost per km traveled by each customer
- X_{ij} : Load allocation from customer (i) to facility (j)
- Y_{ij} :Validation of the capacity assigned to the installation (j) by the client (i)
- r_{ij} : Amount of demand requested by the customer (i) to the facility (j)

From the presented model, it is necessary to determine solution proposals. The literature reports different types of solution techniques, among which two stand out: exact equations and heuristic methods. However, as the problem to be solved is NP-Hard, its solution is complex, so the location assignment problem does not support an exact algorithm in polynomial time with a fixed performance ratio. Thus, heuristic algorithms are used to solve the problem [10].

5 Experimentation and Results

As mentioned in the previous sections, the complexity of a location-allocation problem depends on the number of variables considered in the modeling, as well as the number of facilities and clients involved in the study scenario. That is why, for this research work, the population of the Metropolitan Zone of the Valley of Toluca with an age between 17 and 18 years who processed their voting card for the first time was chosen as the object of study. The decision to elect this sector of the population is because they are part of an annual event that impacts the attention capacity of the modules of the Instituto Nacional Electoral (INE). While the study area was chosen due to population dynamics and because it has certain characteristics that allow mobility between the different municipalities of the ZMVT. Figure 1 shows the geographical characteristics of the ZMVT.

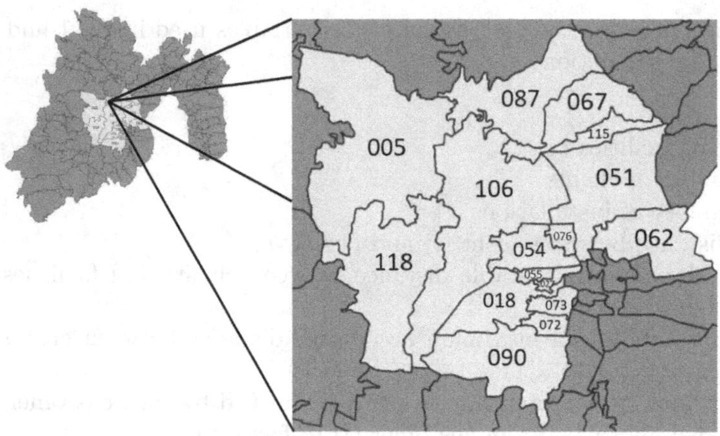

Fig. 1. Geographic location of the 16 municipalities of the ZMVT, those in blue do not have any service module.

The ZMVT is made up of 16 municipalities (see Table 1), which together have a population of 88,107 inhabitants (according to the last census of the National Institute of Statistics and Geography), with an age between 17 and 18 years. Therefore, the aim is to establish the configuration that assigns a certain population from the ZMVT to the 10 service modules available to process their voting credentials for the first time.

Table 1. Inhabitants from the valley of Toluca between 17 and 18 years old.

INEGI ID	Municipality	Inhabitants
005	Almoloya de Juárez	6,748
018	Calimaya	2,645
027	Chapultepec	498
051	Lerma	6,521
054	Metepec	8,248
055	Mexicaltzingo	543
062	Ocoyoacac	2,752
067	Otzolotepec	3,684
072	Rayón	625
073	San Antonio la Isla	1,285
076	San Mateo Atenco	3,803
087	Temoaya	4,269
090	Tenango del valle	3,444
106	Toluca	32,815
115	Xonacatlán	2,122
118	Zinacantepec	8,105
	Total	**88,107**

The 10 ZMVT care modules have a care capacity of 117,792 inhabitants in 9 days. The service capacity of each module depends on the number of tables and available staff, so Table 2 summarizes the service capacity for each module, in addition, the municipal IDs referred to in Fig. 1 are shown.

Table 2. Attention capacity for each municipal module in a period of nine days.

INEGI ID	Module	Working hours	Service desks	Attendees
005	Almoloya de Juárez	8:00 - 15:00	Basic +1 Basic +1	5,544
051	Lerma	8:00 - 20:00	Basic +2 Basic +2	13,068
054	Metepec	8:00 - 15:00	Basic +3 Basic +3	11,088
076	San Mateo Atenco	8:00 - 15:00	Basic +2 Basic +1	8,316
087	Temoaya	8:00 - 20:00	Basic +2	6,534
090	Tenango del valle	8:00 - 15:00	Basic +2	4,158
106	Toluca 1	8:00 - 20:00	Basic +7 Basic +7	34,848
106	Toluca 2	8:00 - 15:00	Basic +7 Basic +7	21,168
115	Xonacatlán	8:00 - 20:00	Basic +1	4,356
118	Zinacantepec	8:00 - 20:00	Basic +3	8,712

Thus, in this section the solution to the proposed model is presented, which allows assigning population from different locations to certain care modules, considering two objective functions: 1. Minimize the cost of transportation and 2. Maximize care coverage of the facilities.

Currently, there are more than 190 natural metaphors listed on the Evolutionary Computing Bestiary website, which is maintained by [3], with topics ranging from "American Buffalo" to "Zombies". This shows a clear problem since most algorithms maintain a set of traditional solutions, also known as population-based heuristics, derived from natural metaphors, so the full set is often confused with its subset [9]. In addition, since the proposed model cannot be solved using exact methods, it is decided to use the Genetic Algorithms (GA) heuristic, implemented through the following pseudocode:

Algorithm 1. Pseudocode Genetic Algorithms.

```
function GA(iter,n,f1,f2);
t = 0
Initialize a population P(t)
fitness = Evaluate P(t) based on f1 and f2
While(t < iter):
        Select n parents of P(t)
        Apply crosses to the n parents of P(t)
        Mutates new individuals with probability Pr
        Introduce the new individuals to the population P(t + 1)
        fitness2 = Evaluate P(t) based on f1 and f2
        if(fitness2 is better than fitness):
                fitness = fitness2
        t = t +1
End while
```

To implement the GA, the population of each municipality is divided into 4 parts, since this allows any of the divisions to be assigned even to the service module with the least capacity. The parameters used to configure the GA are listed below:

- $iter$: a value of 300 iterations is set.
- n : ree elements are selected as parents for the next generation.
- f_1: minimizes the cost of transportation from customers to facilities.
- f_2: maximizes facility coverage, subject to capacity constraints.
- $fitness$: to simultaneously evaluate the objective functions f_1 and f_2, the values of the Eq. 9 are considered.
- Length of individuals: the dimension of each arrangement has a value equal to 64 (16 municipalities divided into 4 parts).
- Population: 10 individuals are considered as part of the initial population, which are used to make combinations and thus create new generations.

$$fitness = 1 - Max\left(\frac{Min(f_{t1} - f_{t2})}{(f_1 - max) - (f_2 - min)}\right) \tag{9}$$

where *min* and *max* are the minimum and maximum values of the objective functions reached. Equation 9 normalizes the parameters of the functions f_1 and f_3 while calculating a single value from both functions. This makes it possible to give the same level of importance to both minimizing the cost of transportation and maximizing the service coverage of the facilities.

Based on the execution of the previously explained GA, the results obtained are presented. Table 3 shows the amount of population assigned to each care module, as well as the municipalities to which said population belongs. The results obtained by the GA were produced in a total time of 7 min and 32 s on a computer with 8 GB of RAM, 1 TB of hard disk, and an Intel Core–i7 processor at 3.2 GHz. This demonstrates the complexity of the study problem since the GA performs multiple executions until finding a fitness value that improves or maintains the configuration.

Table 3. Municipalities allocated to each module.

Module: Toluca 1								
Toluca 8204 Xonacatlán 531	Toluca 8204 Chapultepec 124	Lerma 1630 Chapultepec 124	Lerma 1630 Rayón 156	San Mateo Atenco 951 Rayón 156	Otzolotepec 921 San Antonio la Isla 321	Ocoyoacac 688 San Antonio la Isla 321	Ocoyoacac 688 San Antonio la Isla 322	Xonacatlán 531
Module: Toluca 2								
Toluca 8204 Mexicaltzingo 136	Metepec 2062 Mexicaltzingo 136	Almoloya de Juárez 1687 Chapultepec 125	Ocoyoacac 688 Chapultepec 125	Ocoyoacac 688	Calimaya 661	Calimaya 661	Xonacatlán 531	Xonacatlán 529
Module: Lerma								
Toluca 8203	Almoloya de Juárez 1687	Calimaya 661						
Module: Metepec								
Metepec 2062	Zinacantepec 2026	Lerma 1630	Lerma 1631	Tenango del Valle 861	Rayón 156	Mexicaltzingo 136		
Module: Zinacantepec								
Temoaya 1067	Temoaya 1067	Otzolotepec 921	Otzolotepec 921	Calimaya 662	Almoloya de Juárez 1687	Mexicaltzingo 135		
Module: San Mateo Atenco								
Metepec 2062	Zinacantepec 2026	San Mateo Atenco 951	Tenango del Valle 861	Tenango del Valle 861				
Module: Temoaya								
Zinacantepec 2026	Temoaya 1067	Otzolotepec 921	San Mateo Atenco 951					
Module: Almoloya de Juárez								
Almoloya de Juárez 1687	Rayón 157	Temoaya 1068	San Antonio la Isla 321					
Module: Xonacatlán								
Zinacantepec 2027	San Mateo Atenco 950							
Module: Tenango del Valle								
Metepec 2062	Tenango del Valle 861							

From the results reported in Table 3 and through Fig. 1 it is observed that the population is assigned to the modules considering both the minimization of the cost of transportation and the maximization of the coverage of the modules, which supports the term *spatial justice*. This allows to configure the strategic supply of services in dynamic cities and therefore improves the quality of life of the population.

Regarding the logic of assigning the population of the GA, it can be said that the GA grants attention priority by the module to the municipal population, however, it does not attend to said population in its entirety, since the proposed model seeks to expand the coverage of service, so it allows other municipalities that do not have a module to be served by any other module considered to be nearby.

The equitable distribution of the population allows for 9,093 free service spaces in the municipalities of the ZMVT. Table 4, shows the relationship between the capacity of each module and the amount of assigned population, which reflects the places available for each municipal module to serve other sectors of the population.

Table 4. Total load assigned to each module

Municipal module	Toluca 1	Toluca 2	Lerma	Metepec	Zinacantepec	San Mateo Atenco	Temoaya	Almoloya	Xonacatlán	Tenango del Valle
Total assigned population	28512	18144	10692	9072	7128	6804	5346	4536	3564	3402
Available space	25500	16236	10552	8500	6460	6761	4966	3232	2977	2923

The modules with the largest population served are Toluca 1 and Toluca 2, this is due to the fact that being in the center of the ZMVT they are accessible by the surrounding municipalities, which causes these municipalities to compete with each other to take their population to the modules central and in turn central modules seek to expand their coverage and meet a greater amount of demand.

The solution proposal presented can be implemented in any other type of location-allocation problems in which certain clients access a service under certain restrictions, since the genetic algorithm allows to reach feasible solutions only by changing the objective functions to be evaluated. By using a standard genetic algorithm, its replication is simple and allows other researchers to reproduce the experimentation within the area of study of their interest.

6 Conclusions

From the development of this research work, the following conclusions are reported:

- The proposed solution assigns the population of the ZMVT to certain modules, leaving spaces available to serve other sectors of the population (see Table 4). This allows unprotected sectors such as older adults to have a greater probability of being served in any of the modules.
- The results obtained show that the implementation of the two objective functions proposed in this work contribute to the generation of real and spatially *fair* solutions.

- Despite being a model focused on the allocation of public services, it can be used within the private sector. However, the inclusion of additional parameters that fit the reality of the problem to be solved should be considered.
- The use of the proposed model, together with the GA, allows optimal decisions to be made in less time since the experts focus more of their time on the analysis of results and less on the calculation of solutions.
- Although the case study addresses the population of the ZMVT, the model can be implemented in any part of Mexico, which allows a solution to a national problem.
- The implementation of multi-objective models contributes to obtaining results close to reality, so the complexity of the models must consider more sophisticated solution techniques such as those used in this research.

In future work, the development of a GA that implements a catalog of objective functions for general problems of localization-allocation of public services is suggested, since this allows solving specific purpose problems by changing key parameters of the objective functions. In addition, it is suggested to reproduce the proposal presented in this work through the computational parallelism approach (one thread for each proposed objective function), since this helps to reduce the execution time of the GA.

References

1. Ahmadi-Javid, A., Jalali, Z., Klassen, J.: Outpatient appointment systems in healthcare: a review of optimization studies. Eur. J. Oper. Res. **258**(1), 3–34 (2017)
2. Blais, M., Lapierre, S.D., Laporte, G.: Solving a home-care districting problem in an urban setting. J. Oper. Res. Soc. **54**(11), 1141–1147 (2003)
3. Campelo, P., Neves-Moreira, F., Amorim, P., Almada-Lobo, B.: Consistent vehicle routing problem with service level agreements: a case study in the pharmaceutical distribution sector. Eur. J. Oper. Res. **273**(1), 131–145 (2019)
4. Deng, W., et al.: An enhanced fast non-dominated solution sorting genetic algorithm for multi-objective problems. Inf. Sci. **585**(1), 441–453 (2022)
5. Garrocho, C., Chávez, T., Lobato, J.A.Á.: La dimensión espacial de la competencia comercial, 1st edn. El Colegio Mexiquense, México (2002)
6. Hale, T.S., Moberg, C.R.: Location science research: a review. Ann. Oper. Res. **123**(1), 21–35 (2003). https://doi.org/10.1023/A:1026110926707
7. INE preguntas frecuentes. https://www.ine.mx/preguntas-frecuentes-credencial-para-votar/. Accessed 09 June 2022
8. Jardón, E., Jiménez, E., Romero, M.: Spatial Markov chains implemented in GIS. In: Guerrero, J.E., (ed.) 2018 International Conference on Computational Science and Computational Intelligence, CSCI, USA, vol. 1, pp. 361–367. IEEE (2018)
9. Khaparde, A., et al.: Differential evolution algorithm with hierarchical fair competition model. Intell. Autom. Soft Comput. **33**(2), 1045 (2022)
10. Lin, M., Chin, K.-S., Fu, C., Tsui, K.L.: An effective greedy method for the Mealson-wheels service districting problem. Comput. Indust. Eng. **2**(106), 1–19 (2017)
11. Rebolledo, E.A.S., Chiaravalloti Neto, F., Giatti, L.L.: Experiencias, beneficios y desafios del uso de geoprocesamiento para el desarrollo de la atención primaria de salud. Rev. Panam. Salud Publica **2**(153), 42–45 (2018)

12. Ríos-Mercado, R.Z.: Optimal Districting And Territory Design, 1st edn. Springer, Cham (2020). https://doi.org/10.1007/978-3-030-34312-5
13. Sánchez, Y.R., Figueroa, O.G., Matellan, E.D., Rosales, L.D.L., González, L.R.: Localización-asignación de los servicios de atención primaria en un área de salud. Revista Médica Electrónica **38**(6), 837–885 (2016)
14. Solano-Pinzón, N., Kuzuya, M., Izawa, A., Enoki, H.: Modelos de localización de cámaras de vigilancia en una red de transporte público masivo. Ingeniería y Ciencia **13**, 71–93 (2017)
15. Soroudi, A.: Power System Optimization Modeling in GAMS, 1st edn. Springer, Cham (2017). https://doi.org/10.1007/978-3-319-62350-4
16. Yarmand, H., Ivy, J.S., Denton, B., Lloyd, A.L.: Optimal two-phase vaccine allocation to geographically different regions under uncertainty. Eur. J. Oper. Res. **233**(1), 208–219 (2014)

Reinforcement Learning Applied to Position Control of a Robotic Leg: An Overview

Cervantes-Marquez Aldo(✉), Gorrostieta-Hurtado Efrén, Ramos-Arreguín Juan-Manuel, and Takács András

Universidad Autónoma de Querétaro, Querétaro, Mexico
aldocema04@gmail.com

Abstract. The use of learning algorithms (based on artificial intelligence) have been widely used to solve multi-purpose problems, generating a gap in their development and improvement. One of its applications is that of the control area since the algorithm is adapted to its use for decision-making in complex systems that are: nonlinear, non-deterministic, and that require stability in continuous spaces over a long time. On the other hand, robotics has been an area of study of great interest within the field of its applications, so its study has intensified, creating new models, designs, and challenges to be able to control increasingly complex designs. This has allowed intelligent algorithms to serve as controllers. Among the one that stands out is the reinforcement learning algorithm, which has many configurations and combinations depending on the type of problem to be solved. Therefore, it will be addressed by generating a proposal, discussion, and overview of the system that can control a leg with 3 degrees of freedom in a hexapod in appropriate positions, presenting some variants of the algorithm in solving control problems. This article, is presented an Overview that shows a description of the implications of working with these systems, based on a compilation of related works recently made and followed by key points that will be discussed.

Keywords: Reinforcement learning in control systems · Hexapod Robotic Leg with 3 degrees of freedom · Policy search in reinforcement learning

1 Introduction

Over time, control systems have been a point of interest within robotics, which has allowed the development of new techniques and control strategies to obtain the expected results, applied to increasingly complex mechanisms, since they have more degrees of freedom and more elaborate movement patterns [1]. This allows us to observe the technological and infrastructure barriers to its use in the control of walking robots, search robots, and hexapods, mainly [2].

M. F. Mata-Rivera et al. (Eds.): WITCOM 2022, CCIS 1659, pp. 335–351, 2022.
https://doi.org/10.1007/978-3-031-18082-8_21

The implementation of algorithms has been widespread, from classical control through linear controllers, nonlinear controllers, and controllers based on artificial intelligence are currently trending. In the last years, they have been used to develop several hybrid controllers based on fundamental principles of artificial intelligence such as neural networks and heuristic algorithms [3].

1.1 Reinforcement Learning

Reinforcement learning (abbreviated as RL) has its conceptual bases from elemental fields of study, among which are: computational sciences, statistics, algorithmic analysis, machine learning, psychology, and mathematics, principally. Having as the main objective is to obtain a way in which it can behave in a suitable path for the application that is required, which is called policy.

The reinforcement learning algorithm is a machine learning technique based on behavioral psychology, which consists of the action of an actor in an environment, and based on its results, it can be rewarded or penalized, for its actions, improving over time, through experience and feedback received. It takes the characteristics of supervised and unsupervised learning (shown in Fig. 1).

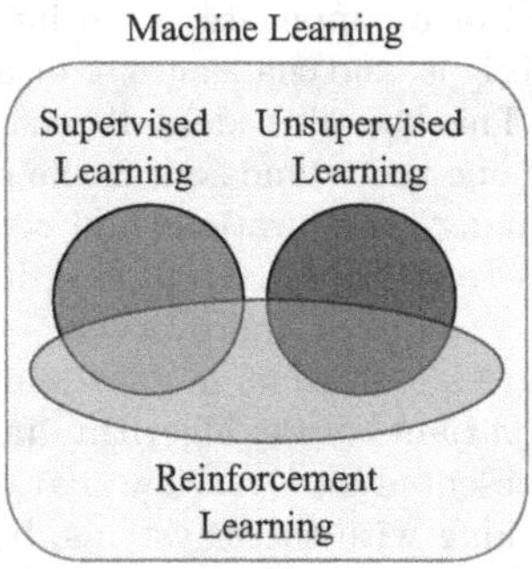

Fig. 1. Reinforcement learning diagram.

Its use in the control area has been applied and has as reference the problem of controlling an inverted pendulum mounted on a cart (cart pole) as shown in Fig. 2.

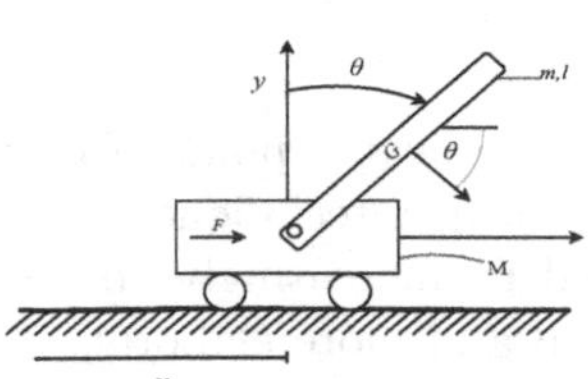

Fig. 2. Cart pole system problem.

Its precedents dating back to 1972 with the work entitled Brain Function and Adaptive Systems: A Heterostatic Theory, where an investigation was carried out, containing several essential ideas for the use of adaptive systems based on intelligence artificial through the use of hedonistic learning systems [4].

However, its creation and most formal works of this algorithm were not carried out until 1989 and 1998 after many years passed, because the computing capabilities and algorithmic complexities implied a large amount of effort for the computers of that time. The first consists of the learning algorithm based on Q-Learning, through the use of stochastic programming, a method was obtained to solve a calculation problem to optimize animal behavior problems according to the environment in which they operate [5,6].

On the other hand, the second shows a complete algorithm that integrates reinforcement learning, focusing on fields of artificial intelligence and engineering [7]. Being a solid base on the definition and conceptualization of the structure of the algorithm to date, it continues to be one of the most important references of the works related to this algorithm.

1.2 Robotic Leg with 3 Freedoms of Liberty

The robotic leg is based on the natural mechanics of a hexapod, which consists of 3 degrees of freedom, which allow it to take appropriate positions for its locomotion [8,9]. From a control point of view, this system has a high nonlinearity due to its positional control based on tilt angles and the obtaining of its models from nonlinear functions.

he proposed a system that consists of 3 angles denoted as θ_1, θ_2 and θ_3, which can move a certain amount of inclination according to their physical properties among them the actuators which will be electric motors and their bars that are joined as links to form the structure (shown in Fig. 3) [10]. This allows getting parabolic trajectories to obtain the best movements and synchronization for the leg in its steps, avoiding crashes in the locomotion control.

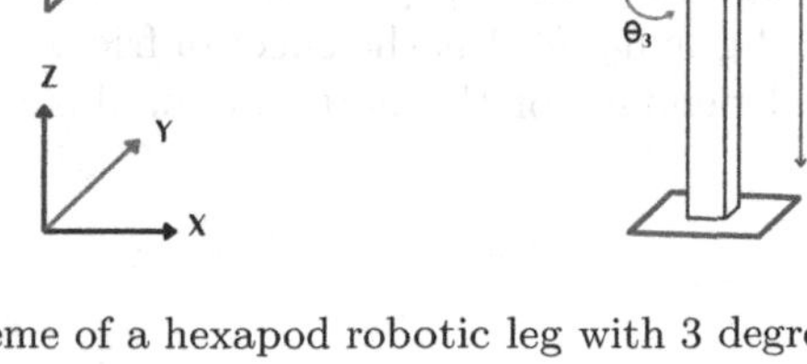

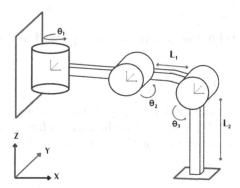

Fig. 3. Scheme of a hexapod robotic leg with 3 degrees of freedom.

The model that describes the parabolic trajectory of the angles to obtain their angular position is [11]:

$$\theta_1 = d\phi - A\phi(cos(\xi) - 1) \tag{1}$$

$$\theta_2 = d\beta - A\beta(cos(\xi) - 1)e^{k1\xi} \tag{2}$$

$$\theta_3 = d\chi - A\chi(cos(\xi) - 1)e^{k1\xi} \tag{3}$$

where $d\phi, d\beta, d\chi$ are constant values given by the angles θ_1, θ_2 and θ_3 that represent the initial angle state of the system in degrees. The variable $A\phi$ defines the step length of the leg, and $A\beta$, $A\chi$ define the step height and ξ is an angle mobility factor (independent variable in radians), finally $k1$ is the slope variable at the end of the step (see Fig. 4) [11,12].

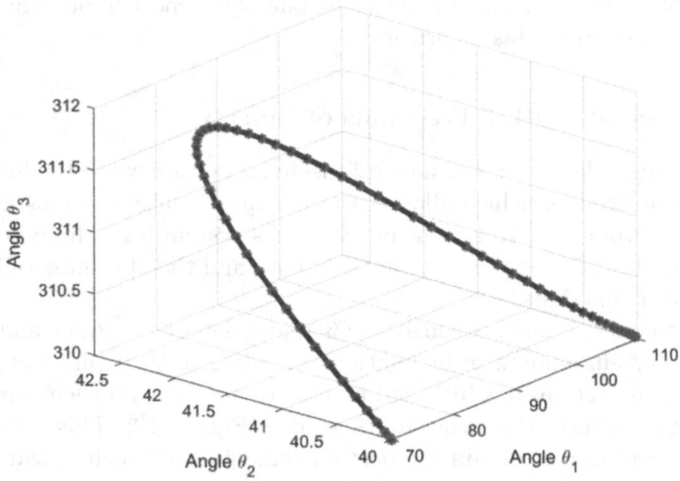

Fig. 4. Parabolic trajectory of the leg for one step.

The dynamic model of the system can be expressed in a generalized form as follows:

$$D(q)\ddot{q} + c(q, \dot{q}) + g(q) + b(\dot{q}) = \tau \tag{4}$$

where $D(q)$ is the inertial function, $c(q, \dot{q})$ is the Coriolis and centrifugal force terms, $g(q)$ is the effect of gravity, $b(\dot{q})$ is the effect of friction and τ is the torque generated. This one is dependant of the actuator, in this case it is an electric motor (DC motor).

The general Eq. (4) can be extended to a matrix function with coefficients dependant of the physics of the model, but with the same structure as the general equation [13]:

$$\begin{bmatrix} a_{11} & 0 & 0 \\ 0 & a_{22} & a_{23} \\ 0 & a_{32} & a_{33} \end{bmatrix} \begin{bmatrix} \ddot{\theta}_1 \\ \ddot{\theta}_2 \\ \ddot{\theta}_3 \end{bmatrix} + \begin{bmatrix} 0 & 0 & 0 \\ b_{21} & 0 & b_{23} \\ b_{31} & b_{32} & 0 \end{bmatrix} \begin{bmatrix} \dot{\theta}_1^2 \\ \dot{\theta}_2^2 \\ \dot{\theta}_3^2 \end{bmatrix} + \dots$$
$$+ \begin{bmatrix} c_{11} & c_{12} & 0 \\ c_{21} & 0 & c_{23} \\ 0 & 0 & c_{33} \end{bmatrix} \begin{bmatrix} \dot{\theta}_1 \dot{\theta}_2 \\ \dot{\theta}_1 \dot{\theta}_3 \\ \dot{\theta}_2 \dot{\theta}_3 \end{bmatrix} + \begin{bmatrix} 0 & 0 & 0 \\ 0 & f_{22} & f_{23} \\ 0 & 0 & f_{33} \end{bmatrix} \begin{bmatrix} m_1 g \\ m_2 g \\ m_3 g \end{bmatrix} = \begin{bmatrix} \tau_1 \\ \tau_2 \\ \tau_3 \end{bmatrix} \quad (5)$$

The coefficients of the 3×3 matrixes are defined by the architecture of the leg and τ is defined by the transfer function of the actuator because it provides the torque for the movement of the system. Its calculus implies hard to research and knowledge of the entire system to apply formal mathematics and physic laws. For that reason, the system is considered a nonlinear second-order (includes trigonometric functions).

2 Reinforcement Learning for Control Systems

2.1 Problem Context

The use of reinforcement learning can be seen from the point of formulating the problem of controlling a stochastic agent in a Markov decision process (MDP) [14], which expresses the property:

$$P_{k+1} = (S_{k+1} | S, a) \quad (6)$$

Showing its ability to obtain a probability of an event happening based on previous events and actions (transition function). Allowing to have an exit action defined as [15]:

$$a = \pi_\theta(S_t) \quad (7)$$

showing that the action will depend on the policy according to the parameter vector θ it has.

The reinforcement learning algorithm consists of two main elements, which are minimal and indispensable: the agent and the environment (see Fig. 5) [16].

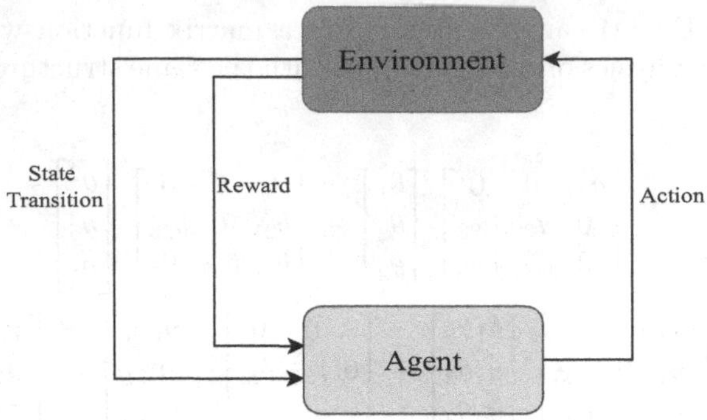

Fig. 5. Reinforcement Learning block model.

Within reinforcement learning, the following elements embedded within the block model are considered:

- **Agent:** Is the subject of the experiment. In this case, it is the reinforcement learning algorithm that allows decisions to be made, according to its interaction with the environment, and is represented as a.
- **Environment:** It is the one that interacts with the agent and provides the information to the agent. In this case, it refers to the system to be controlled.
- **State:** Refers to the moment in which the agent is, based on the conditions variants of the environment (somewhat analogous to iterations of an algorithm). Usually represented with the letter S and it is the element that at its output can obtain a collection of the variables of interest that are required.
- **Policy:** This is how the agent can act on a certain problem. In this case, it can be a control rule that the agent can act on the system. In a general way, can be seen as a function of the form $\pi(S, a)$ that associates the state (S) and the agent's action (a).
- **Reward:** It is how the agent obtains feedback on his actions, this allows him to know if his actions were good or bad. The reward can be modeled or modified, for future actions and agent policy. To improve the learning of the algorithm.
- **Value or utility function:** It is a parameter that allows complementing the reward, defining if the reward, in a long state space, is adequate for the behavior of the system. It is somewhat analogous to a reward governor. However, it is not necessarily required by the algorithm.
- **Model:** It is a representation of the environment that the agent inhabits, performing a simulation of the complete system and allowing optimization of the previous parameters. It should be noted that this element is optional.
- **Episode:** is a series of steps to reach a final moment or to go to the next state, restarting the episode, the sequence to reach that moment is called an episode.

Therefore, in a more specific way integrated with the control systems, which have the characteristic of being able to be feedback systems, that is, they can be measured and controlled from their output [17]. This interaction is shown in Fig. 6.

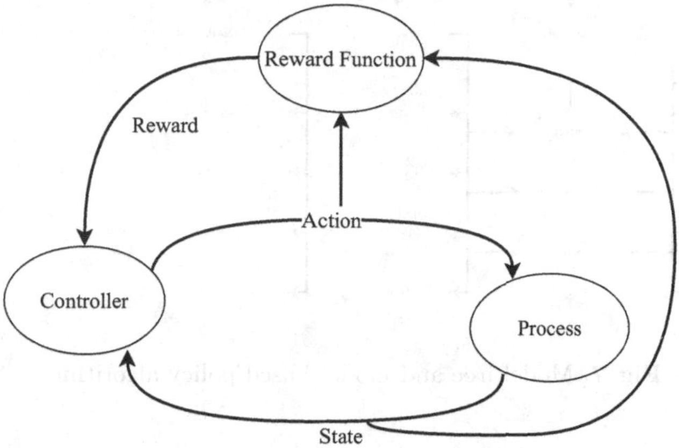

Fig. 6. Interaction of control system components with reinforcement learning.

However, this implies that the states tend to be infinite, as consequence reinforcement learning algorithms for discrete and finite systems are not a viable option for solving the problem, as a result, the following methods are proposed for updating the policy (this being the most important component of the algorithm so that it can learn to control the system) to obtain the desired system response for the required position of the leg employing the free model techniques [18], since that it is allowed to solve the problem without having a detailed knowledge of the system to be controlled, there are 3 ways to control the system without knowing its parameters or its dynamic model based on the updating of the policy, which are: Optimization Policy, Actor-Critic and Q-Learning [19]. These have three properties that allow characterizing the behavior of learning algorithms for policy search to obtain the expected result: policy evaluation strategies, policy update strategies, and exploration strategies [20]. In this case, it will focus more on Policy Optimization and Q-Learning because they are the most varied and modifiable mechanisms depending on the application.

Policy Search and Model-Free Policies. The policy is the most important element of the reinforcement learning algorithm because it describes the behavior and updates itself. It is divided into model-free and model-based, based on machine learning techniques, where it can be applied supervised, unsupervised and deep learning (see Fig. 7) [17].

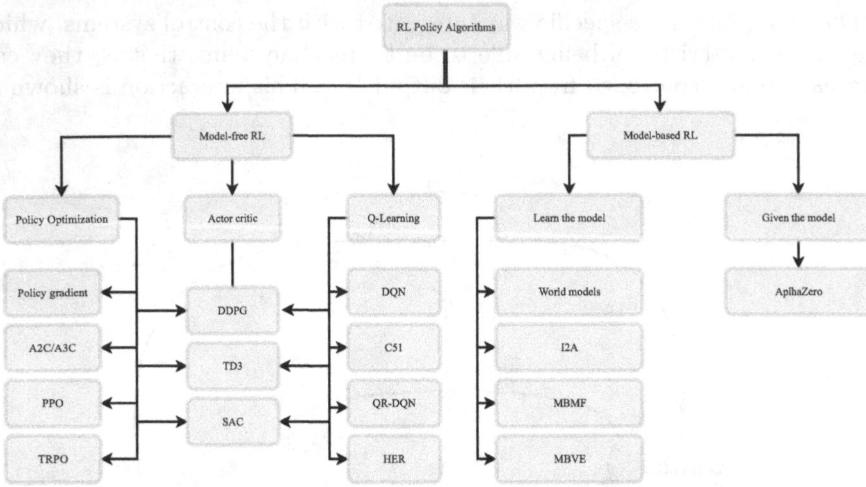

Fig. 7. Model-free and model-based policy algorithms.

The most common policies in control systems are the policy gradient optimization and the Q-learning methods.

The policy optimization method consists of the addition of exploration noise and the variation of search trajectories to have an exploration strategy, considered as low-level policies [17,21]. There are also high-level policies, which consist of exploring the states of interest in the parameter vector θ. The purpose of all this is to update the policy model by evaluating it according to the optimization method.

Here is the gradient policy expression, a method of optimizing search and updating policy, being high level algorithm:

$$\pi_{w,t+1} = \pi_{w,t} + \alpha \nabla_w J_w \tag{8}$$

where α is a learning rate, w is the high-level parameters, J is the expected rate of return, and R is the reward function.

$$\nabla_w J_w = \int_\theta \nabla_w \pi_w(\theta) R(\theta) d\theta \tag{9}$$

On the other hand, Q-Learning is a learning technique that allows updating the policy. This method is the most popular due to the simplicity of implementation.

$$Q(S, a) = R_t + Jmax_a Q(S_{t+1}, a) \tag{10}$$

It divides the policy and adds an updater policy to the first one. The agent is modified and displayed as follows in Fig. 8.

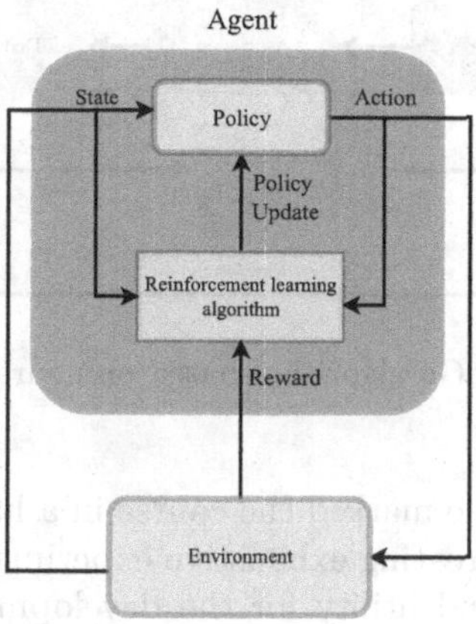

Fig. 8. Q-learning agent in model-free policy.

In computing and algorithmic terms, it can be described as a equation of update (11) [5,20].

$$Q(S_t, a_t) \leftarrow Q(S_t, a_t) + \alpha[r_{t+1} + \gamma max_a Q(s_{t+1}, a_{t+1}) - Q(s_t, a_t)] \tag{11}$$

Reward Function it allows facilitating the learning while maintaining an optimal policy. The reward function is a big problem in reinforcement learning since there is usually no correct way to use it because it depends on the application. However, it has been found that it must be added to obtain the maximum reward in an infinite horizon, that is, we will not know when the algorithm will finish working. This is very useful for model-free and in control systems [5,22,23].

$$R_t = \sum_{k=0}^{\infty} = \gamma^k r_{k+t} = r_0 + \gamma r_{1+t} + \gamma^2 r_{2+t} + ... + \gamma^n r_{n+t} \tag{12}$$

3 Related Work

Although reinforcement learning has been proposed for more than 30 years, it was not until 2016 that its potential could be observed due to the computing capabilities of that time. In that year, a virtual player called AlphaGo was developed, which could play an ancient board game called Go. This game requires high creativity and an awareness of the moves that the opponent could make, so it must anticipate the moves. As a result, the Go world champion could be beaten 4 out of 5 times, being the first computer program to win [24] in this game. Its operating mechanism was quite simple and sequential, from an algorithmic point of view and without taking into account computing capabilities based on neural networks (see Fig. 9) [14,25].

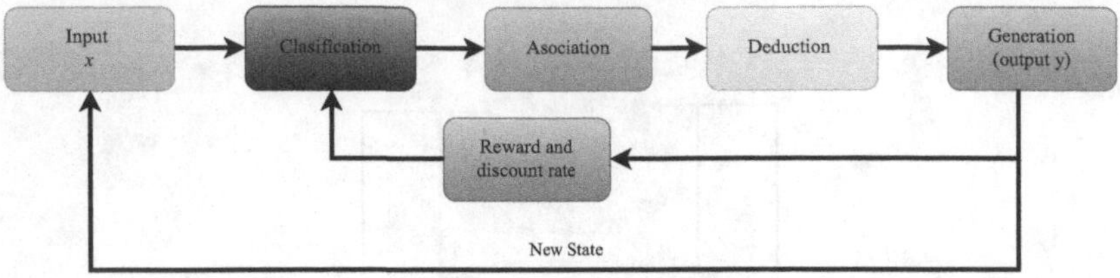

Fig. 9. AlphaGo algorithm based on neural networks.

Therefore, this milestone marked the course in a harder and more consistent way on these algorithms, creating exhaustive experimentation, addressing applications of great interest and utility for the development and versatility of the algorithm.

3.1 Reinforcement Learning Applied to Multi-purpose Situations

Below are a couple of articles that had an important contribution to this article.

In 2020, the article entitled *"A multi-objective deep reinforcement learning framework"* was published, showing a multi-objective DRL Algorithm (MODRL) [26], which consists of an algorithm that combines the RL's single-policy and multi-policy strategies for multi-purpose problem solving based on Q-Networks. It was possible to propose a high-performance scalable MODRL, implemented in Python, marking a future in the implementation and development of these algorithms based on deep neural networks.

In 2019, the article entitled *"Model-free Adaptive Optimal Control of Episodic Fixedhorizon Manufacturing Processes Using Reinforcement Learning"* was published, where an RL algorithm applied to manufacturing processes in repetitive processes such as hydraulic presses was developed. Which they press specific figures on molds. Having an optimal control agent to know the appropriate position through a prediction model. They proposed a free model with the implementation of Q-Learning, allowing the adaptability of the processes by continuously varying the conditions through learning [27].

3.2 Reinforcement Learning Applied to Control Systems

Below in Table 1 a comparison of the works carried out with the reinforcement learning algorithm is made, taking into account its contribution in control systems, control strategy, as well as motion control, and position of the hexapods in the most recent years. Additionally, a disadvantage or problem that was had in the realization, implementation, or execution of the controller is included. All this is to observe a contrast and areas of opportunity on which the problem can be addressed and therefore offer a value proposition as a contribution for future work.

Table 1. Latests RL works applied to control systems.

Ref	Year	Authors	Aportation	Disadvantage
[22]	2013	Shahriar and Khayyat	Use of fuzzy logic to obtain a reward	Use of more than 150000 episodes (despite a lot of exploration there is not enough exploitation)
[28]	2015	Polydoros et al.	Use of self-organized neurons in networks	Performance variation of the proposed model
[20]	2016	Pastor et al.	Appropriate Policy Analysis	Inadequate training
[18]	2018	Bruin et al.	They Selection of some applications where the algorithm can perform better	Many control limitations possibly mishandled (sampling rates, sensor noise, computational limitations)
[29]	2019	Puriel-Gil et al.	Stability of a complex system	Low effectiveness of isolated Q-Learning
[30]	2020	Puriel-Gil et al.	Hybrid use of PD control with reinforcement learning	High difficulty finding suitable reward
[31]	2020	Mullapudi et al.	Deep reinforcement learning (DRL) applied to a dam control system with multisensory networks can take action according to the duration and amount of rain at the time of year it is	Difficult to obtain adjustments to the reward and architecture of the system, it is usually done by trial and error to make adjustments
[27]	2020	Dornheim et al.	Integration of adaptive control with reinforcement learning. Assumption of the control system. Prepared for parameter changes	Large number of iterations. Use of auxiliary neurons
[32]	2021	Fu et al.	Using deep reinforcement learning in variable environments	A lot of training time
[33]	2021	Sierra-García et al.	Variety of proposals based on reinforcement learning	Limitations in choosing the right policy
[23]	2021	Vassiliadis et al.	Obtention of a suitable reward	Limitations on the policy choice
[34]	2021	Klink et al.	Use of optimization algorithms and training curricula	High computational capacity due to training complexity
[35]	2022	Tzuu-hseng et al.	Using a double Q deep neural network and fuzzy control	High system complexity

The use of reinforcement learning in control systems is widely used for nonlinear systems as it was seen in Table 1. As consequence, most of the articles have reached their goals. They have developed an RL strategy to solve a problem. In the advantages it can be pointed out that they have adopted the strategy by adding complements such as Q-learning, neural networks, linear and nonlinear controllers (PID), and other hybrid strategies to solve the problem, elaborating combinations of artificial intelligence techniques and complicating the computing and response way. However, their disadvantages are focused on the basics of RL components, such as the reward, transition function, and the policy search in the use of RL, having problems with reward search because of the nature of the problem, every application will have its reward. The transition function is related to the reward and MDP because it is hard to obtain an adequate probability to shift to the best next-state due to the bad selection of the reward and the insufficient exploration of possibilities (exploration vs exploitation dilemma) [36]. Finally, the policy search is complicated for most of the authors because of the multiple options that can be used at first (see Fig. 7), therefore, the choice of their policy can be misleading in the way that the algorithm will not fit with the combination of the other components chosen (reward, MDP, hybrid techniques, etc.).

4 Proposed Methodology

The work that will be developed in the future time will be centered on the use of simulations for the model and embedded in software by using high-level programming languages (such as MATLAB and Python). It is divided into two sections, the data acquisition section and the proofs and results section. It is shown in the Fig. 10.

The data acquisition section is based on the model building and data acquisition of the model, filtering and clustering the data under criteria of which data can be best for the training and learning of the RL algorithm.

The proofs and results section is where the RL algorithm will be developed and trained to enhance its behavior in multiple situations such as perturbances and unexplored cases for the RL algorithm. The basic metrics for the evaluation will be stablished in the trajectory tracking, the time response, the overstep. Also it will be checked if it can reach the movement of an hexapod (an ant for example) in their locomotion and response [32].

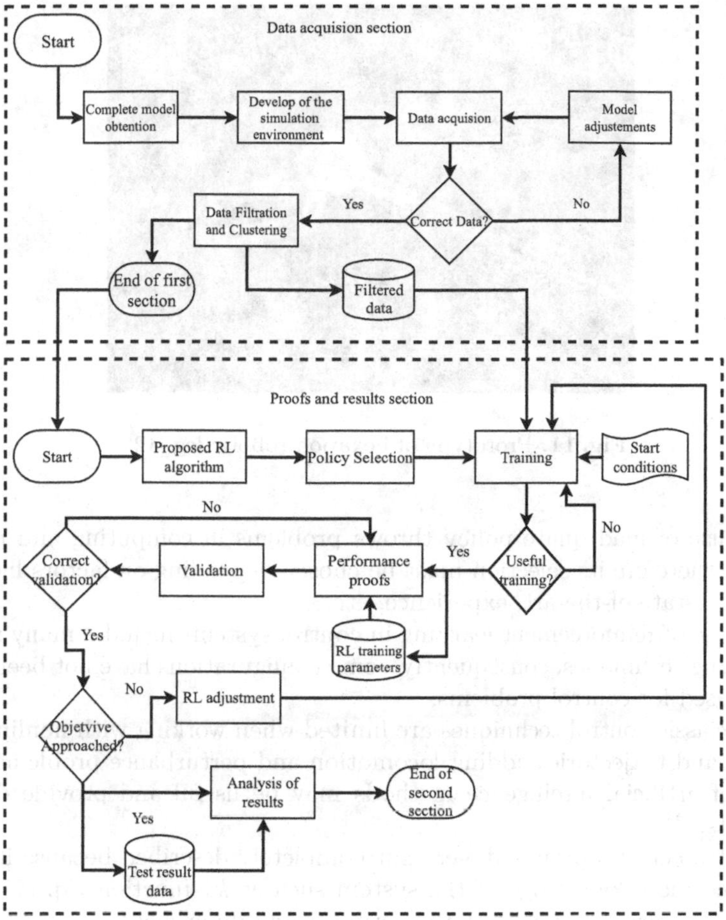

Fig. 10. Proposed methodology.

5 Discussion

The Table 1 and the related work show that reinforcement learning has been used for multiple applications, in the control area also it has been successfully implemented for most of the systems, as a result, it can be stated some points from them.

1. There is not a reinforcement learning algorithm applicated to the model proposed [12] (see Figs. 3 and 11).
2. Despite the use of reinforcement learning in hexapod robot locomotion, they do not contemplate the individual dynamic system (which aggregates the kinematic model) Eq. (5).

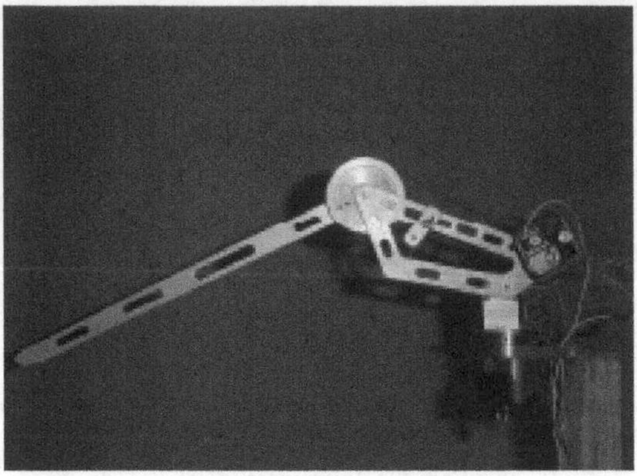

Fig. 11. Prototype of hexapod robotic leg [12].

3. The use of inadequate policy throws problems in computing and response time, therefore its selection must be chosen depending on factors like application, state-of-the-art, experience, etc.
4. The use of reinforcement learning in control systems includes many machine learning techniques, consequently, some configurations have not been proved and used for control problems.
5. The classic control techniques are limited when working with nonlinear systems and trajectories adding locomotion and perturbance problems, so the use of artificial intelligence methods may be useful and provide desirable results.
6. The trajectories proposed were not completely described because it will be needed more knowledge of the system such as $k1$ function Eq. (2),(3) and they can vary depending on the actuator and dimensions.
7. The use of an adequate reward function can improve policy learning and accelerate the training time.
8. The trajectories may change due to the algorithm learning or can be proposed by another algorithm that manages the trajectories.
9. The transition function also has to be stated by the MDP or another method of prediction [37].
10. The use of multi-policy can be used for the resolution of the problem [38].
11. The use of model-free RL is more used because of the complexity of the mathematical system, but model-based RL also can be used if it is known the model and after being implemented on the physical system [18].

6 Conclusions and Future Work

Reinforcement learning is an elaborated algorithm that has many elements to make it up. It has supervised learning features such as the reward function, the discount rate, and the value function, which allows the algorithm to have prior knowledge of the system. It also has features of unsupervised learning, by updating policy that can learn autonomously through its experience with the model to work with.

Based on what is reported in Table 1, it was observed that many configurations and implementations allow the algorithm to solve the problem satisfactorily, since the elements, when working together, generate a system in its most robust and dependable.

The most important parts of the algorithm for the control of the robotic leg are the policy update, which is based on machine learning for its use and continuous improvement, and the reward because it allows maximizing profit and allowing the exploration of solutions to avoid stagnation in policies that are not entirely adequate or that partially meet the problem (exploration vs. exploitation paradigm).

When developing and evaluating the algorithm, it has to be contemplated the metrics for validation and evaluation. First, once it has been developed the algorithm and the dynamic model, it has to make a proof design that allows to train the system and evaluate if the training is appropriate. Then when testing the algorithm in some situations, there will be examined if the response of the robotic leg has done a good performance compared to the setpoint trajectory (see Fig. 4) and measure the error in each step evaluated, and it will be satisfactory if it is calculated an average error lower than 0.1 ($\bar{e} < 0.1$).

For future work, it is proposed to conduct an analysis of the forces on the leg and the current in the actuators that control the mechanism. In such a way to be able to adjust the policy so that it can be contemplated these factors during its training/test to avoid stress within it. All this so that in the future there is a database of the same and it is not required to measure these variables at the time of future tests. Also from a computational point of view, it is proposed, in the future, a computational analysis of the complexity and cost of the system for the computer or controller that is used, consequently, an analysis of the optimal policies (π^*) that allow knowing and concluding the best learning strategies for updating the policy and therefore obtaining a fine control with the desired characteristics.

References

1. Tedeschi, F., Carbone, G.: Design issues for hexapod walking robots. Robotics **3**(2), 181–206 (2014)
2. Flechsig, C., Anslinger, F., Lasch, R.: Robotic process automation in purchasing and supply management: a multiple case study on potentials, barriers, and implementation. Journal of Purchasing and Supply Management (2022)
3. Kuhnle, A., Kaiser, J.P., Theiß, F., Stricker, N., Lanza, G.: Designing an adaptive production control system using reinforcement learning. **32**, 855–876 (2021)
4. Klopf, A.H.: Brain Function and Adaptive Systems: A Heterostatic Theory (1972)
5. Watkins, C.: Learning from Delayed Rewards. Kings College (1989)
6. Watkins, C., Dayan, P.: Technical Note: Q-Learning. Kluwer Academic Publishers **9**, 279–292 (1992)

7. Sutton, R.S., Barto, A.G.: Reinforcement Learning: An Introduction. Volume 3. The MIT Press (1998)
8. Tseng, K.Y., Lin, P.C.: A model-based strategy for quadruped running with differentiated fore- and hind-leg morphologies. Bioinspiration Biomimet. **17**(2), 026008 (2022)
9. Holmes, P., Full, R.J., Koditschek, D., Guckenheimer, J.: The dynamics of legged locomotion: models, analyses, and challenges. SIAM Rev. **48**(2), 207–304 (2006)
10. Cero, I.: DISEñO DE TRAYECTORIAS DE DESPLAZAMIENTO PARA UN ROBOT HEXAPODO BASADO EN LA DINAMICA DE UN ROBOT 3GDL, November 2019
11. García-López, M.C., Gorrostieta-Hurtado, E., Emilio Vargas Soto, J.R.A., Sotomayor-Olmedo, A., Moya-Morales, J.C.: Kinematic analysis for trajectory generation in one leg of a hexapod robot. In: Iberoamerican Conference on Electronics Engineering and Computer Science 3, pp. 342–350 (2012)
12. Gorrostieta-Hurtado, E., Vargas-Soto, E.: Diseño de un Controlador Aplicado a la Generación de Pasos en un Robot Caminante. 6
13. Gorrostieta, E., Vargas, E., Aguado, A.: A neuro pd control applied for free gait on a six legged robot. WSEAS Trans. Comput. **3**(4), 1–7 (2004)
14. Li, Y.: DEEP REINFORCEMENT LEARNING: AN OVERVIEW. Cornell University (2018)
15. Torres, J.: Introducción al aprendizaje por refuerzo profundo. Kindle Direct Publishing, Teoría y práctica en Python (2021)
16. Arranz, R., Echeverría, L.C., Caño, J.R.D., Ponce, F., Romero, J.L.: Aprendizaje por refuerzo profundo aplicado a juegos sencillos. Universidad Complutense de Madrid (2019)
17. Buşoniu, L., Babuška, R., Schutter, B.D., Ernst, D.: Reinforcement learning and dynamic programming using function approximators, vol. 2. CRC Press (2010)
18. Bruin, T.d., Kober, J., Tuyls, K., Babuška, R.: Experience selection in deep reinforcement learning for control. J. Mach. Learn. Res. **19**, 1–56 (2018)
19. He, J., Zhou, D., Gu, Q.: Logarithmic regret for reinforcement learning with linear function approximation. In Meila, M., Zhang, T., eds.: Proceedings of the 38th International Conference on Machine Learning. Proceedings of Machine Learning Research, vol. 139, PMLR, pp. 4171–4180, July 2021
20. José-Manuel Pastor, Henry Díaz, L.A.A.S.: Aprendizaje por Refuerzo con Búsqueda de Políticas: Simulación y Aplicación a un Sistema Electromecánico. Actas de las XXXVII Jornadas de Automática, 710–717 (2016)
21. Puterman, M.: Markov decision processes: discrete stochastic dynamic programming. John Wiley & Sons (2014)
22. Shahriari, M., Khayyat, A.A.: Gait Analysis of a Six-Legged Walking Robot using Fuzzy Reward Reinforcement Learning. Iranian Conference on Fuzzy Systems (IFSC) (2013)
23. Vassiliadis, P., et al.: Reward boosts reinforcement-based motor learning. iScience 24(102821) (2021)
24. Wang, F.Y., et al.: Where does AlphaGo Go: from church-turing thesis to AlphaGo thesis and beyond. IEEE/CAA J. Automatica Sinica **3**(2), 113–120 (2016)
25. Laparm, M.: Deep Reinforcement Learning Hands-On. Packt (2018)
26. Nguyen, T.T., Nguyen, N.D., Vamplew, P., Nahavandi, S., Dazeley, R., Lim, C.P.: A multi-objective deep reinforcement learning framework. Int. J. Intell. Real-Time Autom. **96**(103915) (2020)

27. Dornheim, J., Link, N., Gumbsch, P.: Model-free adaptive optimal control of episodic fixed-horizon manufacturing processes using reinforcement learning. Int. J. Control Autom. Syst. **18**, 1–12 (2019)
28. Polydoros, A.S., Nalpantidis, L., Krüger, V.: Advantages and Limitations of Reservoir Computing on Model Learning for Robot Control. Sustainable and Reliable Robotics for Part Handling in Manufacturing Automation (STAMINA) (2015)
29. Puriel-Gil, G., Yu, W., Sossa, H.: Reinforcement Learning Compensation based PD Control for a Double Inverted Pendulum. IEEE Lat. Am. Trans. **17**(2), 323–329 (2019)
30. Puriel-Gil, G.: Control PD / PID de Robots Manipuladores y Sistemas Electromecánicos usando como Compensación de Términos Dinámicos el Aprendizaje por Reforzamiento. Instituto Politécnico Nacional (2020)
31. Mullapudi, A., Lewis, M.J., Gruden, C.L., Kerkez, B.: Deep reinforcement learning for the real time control of stormwater systems. Adv. Water Resourc. **140**(103600) (2020)
32. Fu, H., Tang, K., Li, P., Zhang, W., Wang, X., Deng, G., Wang, T., Chen, C.: Deep reinforcement learning for multi-contact motion planning of hexapod robots. In: International Joint Conference on Artificial Intelligence (IJCAI-21), pp. 2381–2388, August 2021
33. Sierra-García, J.E., Santos, M.: Redes neuronales y aprendizaje por refuerzo en el control de turbinas eólicas. Revista Iberoamericana de Automática e Informática Industrial **18**, 327–335 (2021)
34. Klink, P., Abdulsamad, H., Belousov, B., D'Eramo, C., Peters, J., Pajarinen, J.: A probabilistic interpretation of self-paced learning with applications to reinforcement learning. J. Mach. Learn. Res. **22**, 1–52 (2021)
35. Li, T.H.S., Kuo, P.H., Chen, L.H., Hung, C.C., Luan, P.C., Hsu, H.P., Chang, C.H., Hsieh, Y.T., Lin, W.H.: Fuzzy double deep Q-network-based gait pattern controller for humanoid robots. IEEE Trans. Fuzzy Syst. **30**(1), 147–161 (2022)
36. Govers, F.X.: Articial Intelligence for Robotics. Volume 1. Packt Birmingham-Mumbai (2018)
37. Afshar, R.-R., Zhang, Y., Vanschoren, J., Kaymak, U.: Automated Reinforcement Learning: An Overview. Cornell University, pp. 1–47, January 2022
38. Raman, J., Sriram, D., Tsai, E.: Evolutionary Language Development in Multi-Agent Cooperative Learning Games. UC Berkeley (2018)

Digital Transformation of Higher Education: Mexico City-IPN as a Practical Case

Vladimir Avalos-Bravo[1](✉), Jorge Toro González[2], and Alma Delia Torres-Rivera[3]

[1] Instituto Politécnico Nacional, CIITEC-IPN, SEPI-ESIQIE, UPIEM, SARACS Research Group ESIME Zacatenco, Mexico City, Mexico
ravalos@ipn.mx

[2] Instituto Politécnico Nacional, ESFM, Mexico City, Mexico
jtoro@ipn.mx

[3] Instituto Politécnico Nacional, UPIEM, Mexico City, Mexico
atorresri@ipn.mx

Abstract. In the knowledge society, the goal of providing education for all as a universal right is a priority with digital technology integration. Therefore, it is relevant to establish learning trends in higher education institutions and the possible strategic actions to be implemented in them for their digital transformation. This paper aims to systematize various debates, approaches, arguments, priorities, and conclusions for the digital transformation of higher education institutions in the fourth industrial revolution scenario from a teaching point of view. The results highlight teacher as the main protagonist of digital transformation by integrating emerging technologies of the fourth industrial revolution into teaching through educational innovation processes despite the obstacles of infrastructure and technological inequalities typical of the academic context. The study's novelty focuses on using prospective planning tools with SmartDraw software help, to promote digital transformation from the teaching role to make lifelong learning more flexible, encourage greater student mobility, and relocate educational spaces. Educational environments displace physical barriers with interconnection so that the classroom is multimodal, thus accounting for the new scope and purposes of higher education in the knowledge society.

Keywords: Digital transformation · Education 4.0 · Teaching · Higher education · Perspective planning · Mexico city-IPN

1 Introduction

The analysis of higher education has been treated in different international forums since the late '90s as anticipation, debate, and construction of a global vision, which recognizes that the academic changes of the late twentieth and early twenty-first century are more extensive for being global and by the set of institutions and people who drive a change [2]. It is also recognized that there is a need to implement actions in HEIs to offer

M. F. Mata-Rivera et al. (Eds.): WITCOM 2022, CCIS 1659, pp. 352–363, 2022.
https://doi.org/10.1007/978-3-031-18082-8_22

access to higher education in an equitable way that meets the characteristics, conditions, context, and needs of all.

From this edge because the main difficulty lies in the complexity of academic institutions to meet the needs of the society of knowledge, in the face of the technological advances of the fourth industrial revolution such as artificial intelligence (AI), advanced robotics, neurotechnology, nanotechnology, blockchain, data analysis, biotechnology, cloud technology, 3D printing and the internet of things (IoT), actively participate in the preparation and transformation of educational systems.

The recommendation for higher education to remain relevant is to recalibrate its cascade alignment strategies toward research, technological innovation, and scientific development that generate substantial changes in society, specifically in the way students get involved in the process of learning, and how the information is appropriate and processed.

In higher education, the reflective nature of digital practices or, the development of its competencies out. In this context, several approaches are intended to develop a more experimental learning process using open educational resources, game-based learning, and project-based in the context of the 4IR. By systematizing various debates, approaches, arguments, priorities, and conclusions for the future of higher education, derived from the literature review, the experiences and actions that have been implemented in higher education institutions are summarized. Therefore, this article not only focuses on the instrumental role of digital technologies in higher education but also on the dynamics of the digital transformation process to establish feasible trends and the behavior of different actors trying to reveal possible futures. Scenarios as a methodological tool for decision-making help the construction of possible futures with the actions of the present [6].

The article, in addition to including an introduction, offers a brief description of the tendencies of higher education through the prism of social and economic changes and the future of learning of the fourth industrial revolution 4.0, to continue with the method of study He designed, based on the principles of perspective planning, in three phases: i) delineation of possible future education; ii) intervention to use the future to change the present; and iii) Presentation of the report of the results of the digital transformation of higher education as a window of opportunity to rethink the role of the teacher in this changing environment. Finally, the conclusions and references are presented.

1.1 Higher Education in Future Society

The future of higher education is closely linked to the development of digital technologies that are located as the main change catalyst in the way we live, work, produce, and learn [7]. The Fourth Industrial Revolution 4.0 is governed by interoperability, information transparency, technical support, real-time acquisition and data processing, modularity, and distributed decision, through the Internet (Internet of Things), production moves to physical cyber systems, which means that the entire process from production to consumption is in communication with each other [4]. The assumption here is that digital skills influence the digital transformation of the Knowledge Society [11].

Drucker 1999 pointed out that the Society of Knowledge arises with the decrease in physical work as the main wealth generation factor, which establishes knowledge as a central value and as a production factor [5]. A central change, which places knowledge and learning throughout life as conductors of economic development and social progress. People around the world are acquiring, developing, and improving their cognitive skills from greater interconnectivity between people, networks, and sensory machines, and, consequently, with the evolution of work, it is not yet possible to answer what kind of skills will be needed to live in Future societies, therefore in knowledge societies education advances towards inclusion, equity, and quality to guarantee to learn throughout life as a universal right of humanity.

In recent years, they have reflected deeply on the future of education when it is related to learning beyond the physical classroom in educational institutions given the integration of digital technologies [1]. So, the Internet becomes a pillar of educational multimodality, since not only through electronic books you learn, but also using articles (scientists), digital resources, discussion lines, databases, texts, images, images, Sounds, games, simulations, and documentaries and digital artistic videos. Additionally, Internet access interacts in various collaboration networks with everyone [16].

In 2020, UNESCO published "Cooking the futures of education: contradictions between the emerging future and the walled past" [14] that Sohail Inayatullah performed. This exercise of prospective reflection with the participation of teachers, students, professionals, experts, and managers from different countries about their expectations and visions about the future of education. The final report emphasizes the need to link education with markets and in essence in any scenario is a learning tool on oneself, the world, and the future" [9].

Learning at home and work is a reality. Digital technologies are easily integrated into everyday life and the ways of learning people by their rhythms, needs, and preferences. It begins, then the use of the potential of digital technologies to promote collaboration and promotes the use of infrastructure and tools to align pedagogy and technology for the benefit of students. Technology is a vehicle to arrive at a global knowledge-based society.

Under this scheme, it is justified that many future skills are completely related to the use and understanding of digital technologies as one of the pillars to improve problem-solving capacity in the next knowledge society. In addition to this, the Internet together with the growing number of applications (from the cloud) allows students and teachers (CO) to create new content in different formats that are available in interconnected databases that make up: new ways of learning and new skills for future jobs.

In HEIs with the use of the Internet [14], Technological Platforms, Open Resources, Use of Social Networks, and Mobile Devices that support the interaction and collaboration tools between teachers and students create new learning spaces. For example, the growing ubiquity of social networks such as Facebook, Twitter, and YouTube promotes that students stop being consumers of content to become creators with the use of the latest technological tools. In the case of teaching staff, it has the inverted classroom, learning analysis, 3D printing, games and gamification, and virtual assistants among others.

Kurzweil prognosis that educational institutions would move to a decentralized educational system in which each person will have access to knowledge and quality teaching making use of the extensive knowledge available on the web and effective computer-assisted teaching. The new generations of educational software will facilitate the task of the teacher to develop personalized teaching strategies " [10]. The relationship of digital technologies with higher education from the instrumental perspective translates educational changes to improve learning processes and in the restructuring of the cost and from a substantive perspective translates into the social as the democratization of the fluid and highly qualified use of digital technologies as a learning objective in the curriculum.

Digital technologies will allow higher education teachers to improve their practice with the integration of teaching methods and training professionals, either as entrepreneurs, researchers, or professionals, and always as citizens with the capacity to "learn to learn" from the Internet. Digital technologies have developed their potential with enormous speed and are connecting people worldwide. The consequences of this are, on the one hand, a huge increase in productivity in almost all aspects of life and, on the other hand, a huge variety of applications and activities for learning in the knowledge society.

1.2 Higher Education Institutions Digital Transformation

Since the mid-nineteenth century, knowledge is the cornerstone of industrial development and the prosperity of nations, which opened the way for the transfer of the knowledge generated by HEIs. The replacement of the value-work binomial with the value-saber binomial raises the knowledge to a distributable social good mean for economic development, cultural and social progress the incorporation of the social good as a distinctive component of the knowledge society. That is, digital transformation (DT) arises with the knowledge society that together with the digital connectivity tools is forcing HEIs to change their structures so that they adapt better to 21st century needs and requirements [17].

DT is a complex phenomenon. It is defined at the micro level as the possible forms of interaction between digital technologies and individuals, while at the macro level refers to a set of changes with the use of digital technologies both in institutions and in society [15]. At the institutional level, innovation processes are promoted with these technologies through the development of adaptation mechanisms based on the implications of digital transformation and promoting a better performance through combinations of information, computing, communication, and connectivity technologies [8].

The DT is the engine of the fourth industrial revolution [13] that frames a series of deep changes in all aspects of human life [7]. In this sense, the OECD [12] defines digital transformation as the product of the digitalization of economies and societies in an ecosystem that involves 5G, artificial intelligence, big data, and blockchain with three different elements of the Processes: (1) technological, (2) organizational and (3) social. This combines an opportunity to create networks, share and create knowledge, and form and certify knowledge and skills. Therefore, HEIs are obliged to accelerate the transformation required by the digital revolution, which significantly impacts educational, academic, and pedagogical models.

HEIs have always been committed to the progress of humanity, during its evolution throughout history, it has been assuming functions and missions induced by changes, sometimes disruptive, experienced by society. Consequently, the DT not only implies the development of infrastructure for the use of digital media and technologies in the teaching, learning, research, administration, and communication services process but also the development of a digital culture within the academic communities.

In the analysis of the 19 HEIs, the DT process made between 2016 and 2019 by Castro et al. Three sequenced central trends are identified: technological architecture, organizational structure, and social configuration. The dimensions most influenced by the integration of digital technologies are teaching, infrastructure, curriculum, and administration, highlighted as the main actors of the transformation of teachers and students derived from the benefits of DT are directly related to learning the learning of Students [3].

Higher education institutions need a strategic vision to join efforts in the implementation of digital initiatives. A clear vision involves the entire community and interest groups and invests more in the digital transformation process. This process involves the acquisition of digital infrastructure, the improvement of the teaching skills of academic staff to use active methods and digital resources in their teaching, and changes in educational, academic, pedagogical, and curricular models to achieve knowledge leadership.

Therefore, HEIs must induce, and promote their transformation, which will allow, on the one hand, to take advantage of the enormous potential offered by the field of educational technology and, on the other, to offer new professional training opportunities, as well as provide new alternatives of learning and accreditation for anyone interested in any sector.

2 Research Design

Prospective studies are intended to follow and the actions to be implemented that attend to the priorities to achieve the deep changes that are required in the transformation of the National Polytechnic Institute, so it was emphasized that because of a reflexive participatory the environment is understood, and the environment is dimensioned to the development of the country.

The present investigation was carried out in two stages. In stage one a documentary investigation of the Prospective of Higher Education was developed through the consultation of the web databases of Science, Eric, and Scopus. There was a literature review of 30 articles in the English and Spanish language on DT; After information discrimination, this article bases its bibliography on 26 works. The synthesis is presented in the section called Higher Education in the society of the future.

In the second stage, the workshop "Prospective Strategic Planning was held: Towards Education 4.0 Mexico City-IPN", on December 4th, 5th, and 6th, 2019, at Mexico City-IPN training and innovation management facilities, with the Use of Prospective Strategic Planning Tools. A reflective exercise to weaving roads and routes to transform education and implement in the best way education 4.0, the central axis of Mexico City-IPN transformation agenda (Fig. 1).

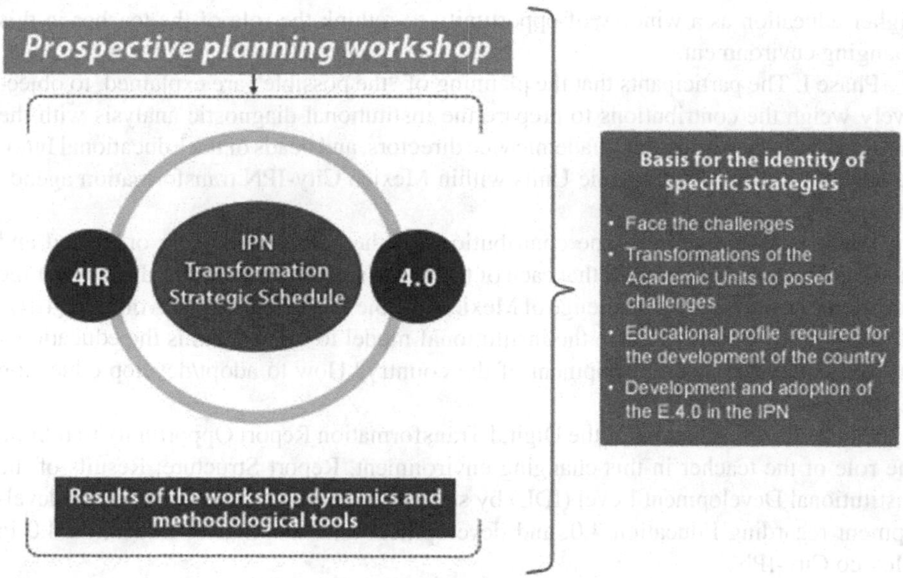

Fig. 1. Prospective strategic planning.

Under this logic, the workshop began with an initial diagnostic worktable: institutional challenges and opportunities in the context of national educational policy, through a group dynamic they were addressed as main topics:

For country's conditions, as well as the technological development that accompanies the fourth industrial revolution requires reinventing, critical thinking development, and human beings formation.

The fourth industrial revolution transformed the reality of second and higher education students. Complex, uncertain, ubiquitous, and radical changes determine the new condition of learning. In Mexico, the global environment affects its economic growth and employment. The national challenge is, to rethink education, and teacher improvement and link all substantive functions of Mexico City-IPN in the face of the changes in the environment.

For quality and relevant professional training of the Mexico City-IPN consider both, the needs of the professional practice of graduates and the socio-economic situation of the students of the labor market in correspondence with the social needs of the country.

2.1 Prospective Software Tools

The prospective reflection exercise was developed to project a digital transformation plan based on three reference objects: education 4.0 (E4.0), the fourth industrial revolution (4IR), and the educational policy context of the current government of Mexico. For this purpose, a prospective planning workshop divided into three phases was held: i) delineation of possible future education; ii) intervention to use the future to change the present; and iii) Presentation of the report on the results of the digital transformation of higher education as a window of opportunity to rethink the role of the teacher in this changing environment.

Phase I: The participants that the planning of "the possible" are explained, to objectively weigh the contributions to prepare the institutional diagnostic analysis with the participation of the directors, academic vice directors, and heads of the Educational Innovation Department of Academic Units within Mexico City-IPN transformation agenda framework.

Phase II Intervention. - The contributions of the participants were organized and tabulated with the information that each of the discussion instruments used to answer the questions: how to face the challenge of Mexico and the fourth industrial revolution (4IR)? How to transform to articulate the institutional model to 4IR? What is the educational profile required for the development of the country? How to adopt/develop education 4.0 at the Mexico City-IPN?

Phase III.- Presentation of the Digital Transformation Report Opportunity to rethink the role of the teacher in this changing environment. Report Structure: Results of the Institutional Development Level (IDL) by strategic priority, level of institutional development regarding Education 4.0, and development and adoption of Education 4.0 in Mexico City-IPN.

To develop these three previously mentioned phases, it was necessary to use free software that allows us to make use of administrative tools for continuous improvements, such as SWOT matrices, balanced score cards, PEST analyses, and OKR adjustments. SmartDraw is a great tool to help to organize concepts and represent them visually. It sets itself apart from similar programs with a vast number of high-quality industry-specific templates. Unlike its competitors Mindmanager and Mindview, this one can help to build organizational trees, mind maps, and many different types of charts. The interface is not as advanced as the others but is free.

SWOT analysis saved time and produced better-looking results than other strategic planning programs. The information captured allowed the software does the rest, aligning the text and applying professional design themes for great results. Then the SWOT analysis was inserted into the Microsoft Office® word app for easy documentation and presentations. As for the PEST diagrams the professors' teams worked on the same diagrams by saving them to a shared Smartdraw folder or by using sharing apps like google drive. The balanced scorecard models developed by professors' teams help them to take stock of Mexico City-IPN performance against four different perspectives or components: Budget, Learning, Internal Academic Processes, and Perspective.

The major products of the strategic planning process were a set of strategic goals and objectives. In this regard, the Goals Grid was a useful and flexible strategic planning tool. Below are listed some of its many uses:

- prompt and facilitate discussion aimed at setting goals and objectives.
- document the results of such discussions.
- provide a visual array and means of organizing goals and objectives.
- classify, clarify, and analyze an existing set of goals and objectives

As the structure of the Goals Grid suggests, there are four basic categories of goals and objectives: Achieve, Preserve, Avoid and Eliminate. This structure was used as a framework for generating goals and objectives.

3 Discussion and Results

Mexico City-IPN congruent with its avant-garde spirit is transformed to maintain its excellence and relevance, coupled with its strong conviction to strengthen the social commitment that distinguishes it by forming the talent of the leaders demanded by the country. That is why, in 2018 Institutional Development Program (IDP), which is incorporated into the "Strategic Transformation Agenda" (STA) whose governing axis is Education 4.0 (E4.0).

Mexico City-IPN's strategic transformation agenda is the action plan with a vision of the future to strengthen its leadership in scientific and technological education, as established by its Organic Law, and contribute to social progress and impact the development of Mexico. The workshop establishes that Mexico City-IPN is rapidly located in convergence with the 4IR where they are expected to assume an avant-garde role in the development of the country from knowledge. In summary:

- Mexico City-IPN is acting as a hinge and strategic in the use of knowledge by replicating it throughout the country.
- Mexico City-IPN for its history and social recognition is an academic authority that participates in decision-making from a perspective of sustainability and widespread well-being. The industry is in favor and of course, substantially improves the quality of life of social groups. Therefore, in the educational project of Mexico City-IPN, the strategies to design free, open, accessible, and flexible learning modalities that attend not only young people, but the entire population attending to people's living conditions (the Learning throughout life and life) and to diversity in forms of learning (designing personalized teaching-learning routes and accompanying the movement of people) that contribute to overcoming the social exclusion of population sectors, through fulfilling its right to an education of high humanistic, scientific, technological and ethical level (Table 1).

The education of the 21st century from their spheres has in their nature an effective means of social mobility of the families of the urban, rural, and indigenous popular sectors; and form highly qualified human capital to perform in the productive sector in the full transformation to raise its productivity and, therefore, its competitiveness, within the framework of a new economic model that integrates sustainability.

The teaching staff of the 45 participating academic units perceives that the strategic agenda of the Mexico City-IPN is in development and has not yet been fully internalized. Only the one that refers to the new Polytechnic student and professor, Priority 3, was considered in the embryonic phase and has been internalized by the group that supports the project. They also recognize the need for an institutional reconversion of the great draft and refer that E4.0 is an embryonic phase. In addition, everyone agrees that internalization processes have not been fully rooted in polytechnic culture.

Table 1. Institutional development level by strategic priority.

Priority	Strategy	IDL
P1 Education 4.0	Develop the new Polytechnic talent through education 4.0 at the three educational levels	
P2 Relevance and social commitment	Create entrepreneurial culture in the Polytechnic Community to innovate and influence the transformation of the country	
P3 The new Polytechnic Student and Professor	The new Polytechnic Student and Professor redesign the personnel contracting and stimuli programs, within a new institutional regulatory framework, for the implementation of education 4.0	
P4 Commitment to equity, coverage, and quality	Expand access to educational, social, sports and cultural programs of IPN, with equality and inclusion criteria, strengthening integral and excellence training	
P5 Polytechnic governance	Generate internal cohesion mechanisms and external communication for governance based on collaborative participation oriented to great institutional objectives	
P6 Infrastructure and equipment	Generate a strategic plan for equipment, infrastructure and institutional services and specific plans by polytechnic dependence that are articulated to education 4.0	

The governing priority that guides the strategic Mexico City-IPN transformation agenda is education 4.0. It integrates the other five priorities. The strategic action of this is to develop the new polytechnic talent through education 4.0 at the three educational levels. Some elements for this strategic action are (Table 2):

- Design a system for the Institute for the certification of personnel about E4.0.
- Academic units must prepare a work plan for E4.0 incorporation.
- Define awareness document and socialize it by sectors.

In the perception of teaching staff that participated in the workshop, there is a strong institutional self-perception to face and face the challenges of political, social, and economic changes that refer to complex problems derived from scientific-technological revolutions. It is convenient to discuss how Mexico City-IPN will align with new public policies in the field of higher education, science, and technology; For example: in the extension of educational coverage (inclusive and quality), in the coverage of needs of the productive and social sectors, and the creation/adaptation of productive technologies to the service of poor and vulnerable communities.

Table 2. Institutional development level according to education 4.0.

Number	4.0 Components	IDL
1	Management staff, academic and research qualified in the technologies that detonate 4IR.	
2	Adequate infrastructure to carry out education 4.0 (connectivity, distance education platforms, equipment).	
3	New study plans and programs aligned at 4IR.	
4	Linking education with industry.	
5	Regulations for education 4.0.	
6	Expansion of education in virtual spaces for academic and labor purposes according to the needs of the community.	
7	Integrate the educational process new methodologies and technologies: Problem solution, e-learning, m-learning, blended-learning, Maker Spaces, Lab-Spaces.	
8	Modify and boost learning evaluation.	

The fourth industrial revolution can be used to the extent that the country prepares to create human capital and companies that participate with products and services based on the knowledge and technologies from which the new economy derived from it is based. The Mexico City-IPN has the ability and responsibility of being a fundamental actor in the integration of Mexico to 4IR.

In a hyper-connected world that changes rapidly and faces increasingly global, complex, and dynamic problems, such as poverty, income disparities, environmental crises, organized crime, and health quality problems. In this context, higher education institutions (HEIs) as knowledge supplies, assume a leading role in associativity as a dynamic of development and innovation, considered the pillars of the knowledge economy. It contributes to the adoption of new ideas, expansion of knowledge, and learning throughout life.

The results show that digital transformation improves the skills demanded by the knowledge society: it also has an important role in reducing education related to education but also implies infrastructure investments.

4 Conclusions

Digital transformation can be the last step to achieving specific social objectives, such as opening higher education and training professionals capable of dealing with a dynamic and complex environment. From the perception of teachers and students, they live the transformation without infrastructure into digital technologies, since they are on construction, added to the low technical support and intermittent connectivity. So, they must adapt the learning processes so that all students, regardless of their condition, are favored and better prepared to face the global challenges of the digital era to meet the social needs demanded by the 4IR. It is important to mention that when talking about the TD of education, the use of software should be considered in the preparation of the objectives according to the new trends, in this case, we are talking about using the software. In this article, the Smartdraw was used to be able to represent the diagrams that were built to represent the ideas and objectives planted in the Mexico City-IPN that seek to make manifest the proposal to guide the current educational model in the HEIs towards that of education. 4.0 marks us that learning must be self-managed, flexible, personalized, asynchronous, and adaptive.

Acknowledgments. This project was funded under the following grants: SIP-IPN: No-20220326, and the support of DEV-IPN Instituto Politecnico Nacional.

References

1. Aceto, S., Borotis, S., Devine, J., Fischer, T.: Mapping and analyzing prospective technologies for learning. In: Kampylis, P., Punie, Y. (eds) Results from a Consultation with European Stakeholders and Roadmaps for Policy Action. JRC Scientific and Policy Reports. European Commission-Joint Research Centre, IPTS, Seville (2013)
2. Altbach, P.G., Reisberg, L., Rumbley, L.E.: Trends in global higher education: tracking an academic revolution. A Report Prepared for the UNESCO 2009 World Conference on Higher Education. UNESCO (2009)
3. Brooks, C., McCormack, M.: Driving digital transformation in higher education. ECAR research report. ECAR (2020)
4. HoseiniMoghadam, M.: Global trends in science and technology and the futures studies of higher education in Iran: priorities and strategies. J. Iran Futures Stud. **6**(2), 1–28 (2022). https://doi.org/10.30479/jfs.2022.16183.1332
5. Castro, L.M., Tamayo, J.A., Arango, M.D., Branch, J.W., Burgos, D.: Digital transformation in higher education institutions: a systematic literature review. Sensors **20**(3291), 1–22 (2020)
6. Fell, M.: Roadmap for the Emerging Internet of Things - Its Impact, Architecture and Future Governance (2014)
7. Godet, M., Durance, P.: La prospectiva estratégica para las empresas y los territorios (2011)
8. Grosseck, G., Malita, L., Bunoiu, M.: Higher education institutions towards the digital transformation-the WUT case. In: Curaj, A., Deca, L., Pricopie, R. (eds.) European higher education area: Challenges for a new decade, pp. 565–581. Springer (2020)https://doi.org/10.1007/978-3-030-56316-5_35
9. Hess, T., Matt, C., Benlian, A., Wiesboeck, F.: Options for formulating a digital transformation strategy. MIS Q. Exec. **15**(2), 123–139 (2016)
10. Institute for the Future. The Future Exploring the Future of Youth Employment: Four Scenarios Exploring the Future of Youth Employment (2014)
11. Kurzweil, R.: The Singularity is Near: When Humans Transcend Biology. Viking Press, ISBN: 0670033847 (2005)
12. OECD. Going digital: Shaping policies, improving lives. OECD Publishing (2019). 9789264312012-en.pdf. Accessed 5 Feb 2021
13. OECD. Digital transformation and capabilities. In: Supporting Entrepreneurship and Innovation in Higher Education in Italy. OECD Publishing (2019)
14. UNESCO. Shaping the Future, We Want. UN decade of Education for Sustainable Development (2005–2014). Final report (2014)
15. UNESCO IITE. Technologies in Higher Education: Mapping the Terrain. Compiled by Neil Butcher (2015)

16. Vial, G.: Understanding digital transformation: a review and a research agenda. J. Strat. Inf. Syst. **28**, 118–144 (2019)
17. Wheeler, S.: Learning with 'e's: Educational Theory and Practice Digital Technologies in the Digital Age. ISBN 978-1-84590-939-0 (2015)

An Approach to Simulate Malware Propagation in the Internet of Drones

E. E. Maurin Saldaña[1(✉)], A. Martín del Rey[2], and A. B. Gil González[3]

[1] Escuela de Ingeniería en Computación e Informática, Universidad Mayor, Santiago, Chile
emaurin@usal.es

[2] Department of Applied Mathematics, IUFFyM, Universidad de Salamanca, 37008 Salamanca, Spain

[3] BISITE Research Group, University of Salamanca, Edificio Multiusos I+D+i, 37007 Salamanca, Spain

Abstract. This research addresses the problem of malicious code propagation in a swarm of drones. Its main objective is to establish the conceptual basis and its setting for the modelling framework of malware propagation using mathematical epidemiology as a core. Specifically, this work identifies the disadvantages associated with the traditional mathematical models employed to simulate malware spreading, revealing the most relevant factors to be considered in order to achieve an ad-hoc modeling that better represents the behavior of the propagation of such malicious code in the drone configuration under study. The relevance of this work is both to contribute to a better understanding of how vulnerabilities in these devices could be exploited and to guide the formulation of cybersecurity measures in line with these problems.

Keywords: Malware propagation · Drone swarm · Mathematical epidemiology · Complex networks · Individual-based models

1 Introduction

Currently, the use of Unmanned Aerial Vehicles (UAV) or Remotely Piloted Aircraft (RPA), both for civil and military uses is expanding, and along with it the diversification in their areas of application, such as agriculture, mining, environmental, civil works, aerial surveillance, last mile delivery of retail products, fire control, disaster support, recreational uses, etc.

In turn, in [1], the authors have described the role of these devices in the control of the COVID-19 pandemic for surveillance actions, announcements to the population, sanitizing of public places, among others.

On the other hand, they have also been used for illicit activities such as entry into prisons, smuggling and entry of prohibited items [2]. In [3], the authors presented several case studies related to the transport of drugs and prohibited substances.

Moreover, in [4] the author referred to the so-called narco-drones and their crossing between the U.S. Mexico border.

M. F. Mata-Rivera et al. (Eds.): WITCOM 2022, CCIS 1659, pp. 364–373, 2022.
https://doi.org/10.1007/978-3-031-18082-8_23

In [5], the authors conducted a study analyzing 19 types of unmanned aerial vehicles and their various applications, concluding the fact that "drone's technology will be advancing with the current rate of development of technology and it will be more applicable to our daily life in the future".

In military domain, this technology is gaining relevance, not only in its classic use in "Air Intelligence and Reconnaissance" tasks, but also as potential weapons in a configuration known as "Swarm", being able to direct an armed attack on one or several specific targets or objectives, as well as suicide-type actions, by directly impacting these strategic objectives. The use of this type of swarm configuration and its various applications has aroused the interest of several researchers in the area, even giving rise to the term "Internet of Drones (IoD)" [6] in an effort to standardize vocabulary and propose a universal architecture for this type of technology.

This paper focuses on the design of mathematical models to study and analysis of the propagation of malicious code in a swarm of drones. Specifically, the purpose of this work is establishing the conceptual basis on which a framework for modeling this phenomenon could be based, taking mathematical epidemiology as a basis, and thus improve the understanding of the problem and serve as a guide for efficient simulations. The rest of the paper is organized as follows: In Sect. 2 a summary of the works related to the scope of the research is presented, focusing on the basic components of a drone system and the categorization of its type of communications. Section 3 is oriented to the basic aspects of cybersecurity, including the most common types of attack in this type of architecture. Section 4 is divided to explain conceptually what is meant by Internet of Drones Networks (IoD), proximity malware, several strategies to deploy swarm drones configuration, and finally, present some attacks examples scenarios. Section 5 is devoted to introduce the conceptual bases behind the mathematical models that can be associated with the spread of malware in a swarm of drones.

Finally, the conclusions are shown in Sect. 6 as well as the challenges and future work that could complement this topic.

2 Basic Components of a Drone/UAV System and Communications for Swarm Configuration

The most common components for the configuration of a UAV-based architecture are:

- The unmanned aircraft (drone/UAV/RPA).
- The Ground Control Station (GCS).
- Communications link (Data Link-CDL).
- Other: the operator, launch/recovery systems, or other additional aspects within the system can be considered.

In [7], a categorization for the type of drone communications can be found in four main types: "Drone to Drone (D2D)", "Drone to Ground Station (D2GS)", "Drone to Network (D2N)", "Drone to Satellite (D2S)".

The next figure shows a brief of the several communications topologies in the IoD architecture (Fig. 1):

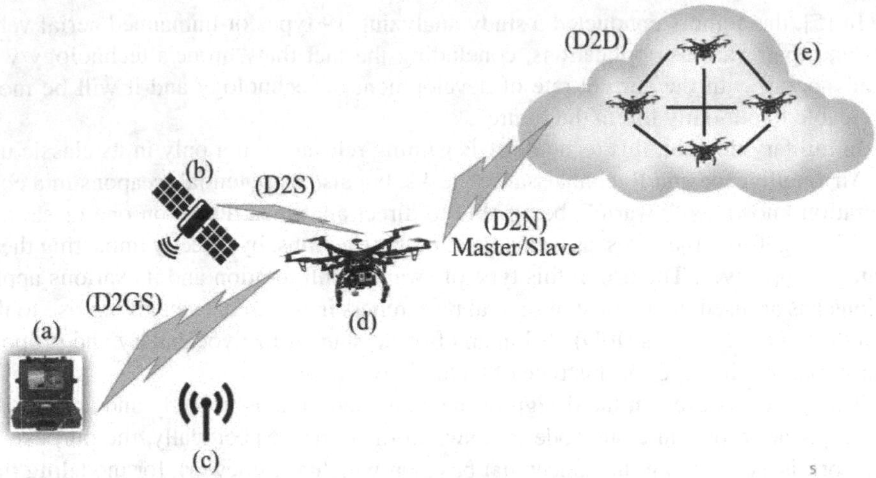

Fig. 1. Example of IoD communication topology.

At the figure, we can describe the following elements:

(a): Ground Control Station. Could be as simple as Remote Control used by the drone operator, or other complex system like a Mission Control Room.
(b): Satellite.
(c): Radiofreq. (3G,4G,Wi-Fi, or other protocol)
(d): Drone /RPA. Could be master configuration
(e): Swarm drone configuration. Could be at slave configuration or autonomous one.
(D2GS): Drone to Ground Station link. (Could by radriofreq, 3G,4G,WiFi, or other protocol).
(D2S): Drone to Satellite communication (Due to GPS, or telecommands, or other)
(D2N): Drone to Network. In this case to communicate between the master and slave's devices.
(D2D): Drone to Drone communication, could be Bluetooth, Zigbee, or other protocol.

These technologies involve the use of various protocols, such as Bluetooth, ZigBee, Wi-Fi 802.11, and potentially the use of 4G, 5G cellular communication, always in search of more reliable and low latency communications URLLC (Ultra Reliable and Low Latency Communications), aimed at optimizing the range of distances from line of sight (VLOS: Visual Line Of Sight) to BVLOS (Beyond Line Of Sight) distances, by incorporating the use of communication through satellites.

Given the above context, regardless of the communication protocol or the architecture component target, the malicious code could spread through drones at swarm configuration, affecting the whole system or part of it.

According to that, in [8], the authors point out that, for a swarm drone configuration, the use of Ad-Hoc communications is frequently used, in addition to what is described in [9, 10], presenting the various existing communications protocols, along with the various options for control of swarm formations and the disadvantages for each of them, respectively.

3 Cybersecurity Aspects

The analysis of drone security was reviewed in [11] and [12], as well as the cybersecurity methods applicable when assembling AVNs (Aerial Vehicle Networks). In [9], the authors also presented the most common techniques of attacks on this type of technology, with various objectives, such as: degrading, denying, interrupting and/or modifying the information processed through the components of the drone network. This kind of attacks could be done through the following techniques:

- Denial of Service
- Spoofing
- Hijacking
- Jamming
- Others.

Among the latter are those of interest for this research, since they deal with attacks by means of Trojans (malware), reverse engineering and deauthentication.

Focused now on the state of the art of malware propagation in drone networks, there was some evidence showing successful infection cases, as in 2014, during the cybersecurity conference CODEBLUE, in which the CTO of the company SEWORKS Dongcheol Hong presented the result of the malware infection of an AR.Drone 2.0 device, with the malicious code "HSDRONE", incorporating in one of its conclusions that such malware could spread from a smart type device or by infecting between drones [13].

On the other hand, there is also evidence of the development of malicious code affecting an UAV, individually and outlining the possibility that such compromise could affect other vehicles within the same network.

Specifically, in 2015 was published in the media, the development of the malware called "maldrone" by Rahul Sasi [14], which was of the persistent type (tolerant to equipment reboots) and which took remote control of the victim drone, even blocking the use of the autopilot. In particular, this type of attack exploited a vulnerability in the Parrot AR quadcopter model, allowing the execution of the malicious code as a backdoor, in an ARM Linux operating system, disabling the platform's security and selfcontrol options and allowing a reverse TCP connection to finally take control and allow the attacker to modify the device's actions.

Finally, according to [15], one of the threats described is the possibility of the existence of "malicious drones" or "compromised drones" in an IoD environment, which would affect the integrity of the network or system, giving an example of how a drone can provide false routing information or collude with other drones.

4 Malicious Code Propagation Aspects

4.1 Internet of Drones Networks

According to [16] "An attacker may target the vehicle's on-board systems, the GCS computer, the vehicle's sensors, or the communication between the vehicle and GCS".

Indeed in [17] the authors highlight that the Internet of Drones (IoD), is vulnerable to malicious attacks over radio waves frequency space due to the increasing number of attacks and threats to a wide range of security measures for IoD networks.

In [18] the author expresses that "UAVs are mainly used on a wireless network, and data traveling over these wireless channels provides an opportunity for cyber attackers to capture sensitive, highly confidential military information. Attackers can plant viruses, Trojans, and other manifestations of malware into the interconnected communication network".

4.2 Proximity Malware

Due to this scenario, and considering a swarm drone network as a type of Wireless Sensor Network (WSN), appears the concept "Proximity Malware". This kind of malware "spreads from one device to another using short-range communication interfaces like Bluetooth and WiFi" [19].

The epidemic dynamics, the associated network model, and the main assumptions were described also. Recent publications [20] consider the drone swarms as "Networked Control Systems (NCS) where the control of the overall system is done enclosed within a wireless communication network". This publication also explains that "drone systems are mission-oriented" in most cases, encompassing the several network topologies and their different approaches, leading the deployment based on two strategies, as mentioned in [21] where the authors explain several communication architectures of UAV swarms, centralized and decentralized ones, including in the last approach different configurations, for example, the "single-group swarms ad hoc network", "multi-group swarm ad hoc network", and "multi-layer swarms ad hoc network", within the different advantages and disadvantages.

4.3 Attacks Examples Scenarios

A suitable attack example for the mentioned scenario could be feasible by using the Mirai botnet, where the malicious code could be injected into a hijacked UAV.

A based case study was shown in [22], where a mobile attacker drone breaks into UAV communication, creating a bot-network, infecting several devices. In that case "the botmaster can issue a command to a peer bot, and the command will propagate through the network".

Another infection vector could be done "infiltrating the design, implementation and production phases to create backdoors in the control software and communications protocols of the drone". In this case, the Mirai source code [23] could be injected to propagate to another neighbor UAVs, then as mentioned in [24], this malware could "exploited default account passwords and hidden backdoors for IoT devices to gain control and carry out a DDoS attack", using device firmware modification as a vector attack, gaining full remote access. Several proposed techniques to detect this kind of attack are discussed in that publication, too.

Focusing now on the Mirai botnet, it has spawned many variants following the same infection strategy that could be adapted to reach the desired goals.

For example, in [25] there is a detailed explanation about this botnet structure and propagation through different stages, including a scanning phase, then passthrough brute-force login stage and wait the first successful login to send the victim IP and credentials to a hardcoded report server, while a separate loader program infected these vulnerable devices, downloading and executing specific malware (stage 4).

Finally, the attacker could send attack commands from the command-and-control server, while simultaneously scanning for new victims, according to the publication. Mirai, commonly performs scanning phase looking Telnet service, under ports 23 and 2323, and could be modified to look other ports or services into the victim device, also include HTTPS, FTP, SSH, and others.

Adding to that, in [26] the authors made a security analysis of the DJI Phantom 3 Standard, and mentioned the previous work related to the insecurities exposed by models like Phantom 2 and Parrot AR 2.0, through unprotected WiFi communications, or exploit vulnerabilities using software like skyjack/aircrack or maldrone used as a backdoor and then was able to connect to the WiFi of another drone and insert a file (in our case modified Mirai source code could be loaded).

Even more, in the same publication, Telnet and FTP vulnerability in Parrot AR 2.0 was discussed mentioning that it is not applicable in Phantom 3 cases, concluding that this standard is more secure than its predecessors.

5 Conceptual Foundations of the Propagation Model

The proposed framework is based on the possibility of malware infection of drones in swarm configuration, which could affect the aircraft itself (considered as a node), its control station, its communication links, among others, and could spread to other devices in the same network, or other susceptible devices, causing risk to the entire formation.

Our contribution will be oriented to the study of propagation of malicious software (malware) instead of biological agents spreading, and could be based on the work done by Kermack and McKendrick, within the so-called mathematical epidemiology, being its first approach the use of ordinary differential equations to simulate such behaviors, between years 1927 and 1933, and nowadays applicable to various types of simulations and models.

One of these models is the MSEIR type (M: immune class, S: susceptible class, E: exposed class, I: infectious class, R: recovered class) and their derivations according to [27].

A way to describe the basic model by Kermack and McKendrick is show in the following figure (Fig. 2):

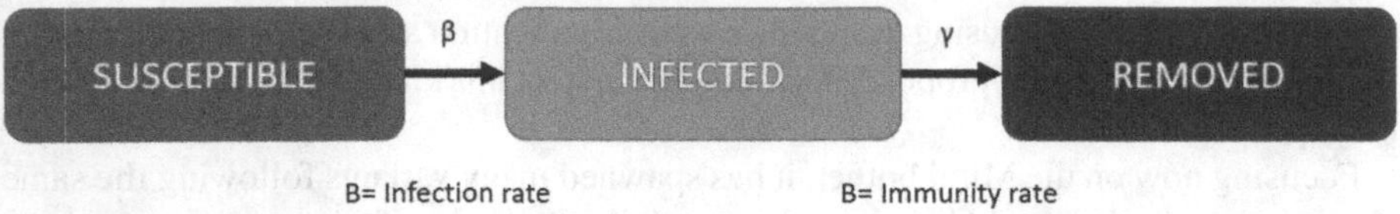

Fig. 2. Kermack and McKendrick mathematical basic model applied to epidemiology.

The model is represented by the following equations:

$$dS/dt = -\beta I(t)\, S(t) \tag{1}$$

$$dI/dt = \beta I(t)\, S(t) - \gamma\, \mathrm{I(t)} \tag{2}$$

$$dR/dt = \gamma\, \mathrm{I(t)} \tag{3}$$

In our case:
S = Susceptible drones into a swarm configuration.
I = Infected drones into a swarm configuration.
R = Removed malicious code into a drone in swarm configuration.

Notice that R, could be understanding in the way that the malicious code was running into a drone impacting his behavior causing damage or critical lost (as like when a human is dead cause the infection), or the malware was removed by the device due to different cybersecurity mechanism (like software updates, intrusion detection techniques, or others).

In general, these models are mostly global and deterministic type, which do not consider the particular characteristics of each agent, node, or infected equipment (drone, in our case), nor the particular way in which they interact. To solve the disadvantages of such models, there are publications that have referred to the use of cellular automata, agent-based models, being a more realistic approach and covering global, particular issues, in a discrete and stochastic manner, without departing from the advantages of the basic differential equations.

In [28], the authors proposed a mathematical model to simulate the propagation of malware in Wireless Sensor Networks, based on cellular automata and also considered real factors such as the use of intrusion detection devices (IDS), antivirus solutions, autonomy and heterogeneity properties of the agents (nodes), mechanisms used by viruses to propagate, among others, reaching different conclusions for each type of test scenario performed, including its application in complex networks. This led to the conclusion that it is possible to better simulate the epidemiological state of a certain agent, equipment or device, whether exposed, infected, susceptible, recovered, etc., at a given time, and to predict its behavior both individually and globally, in the case of being isolated or forming part of a network.

The following figure shows the SEIRS-D model representation done by the authors in the paper mentioned in [28] (Fig. 3):

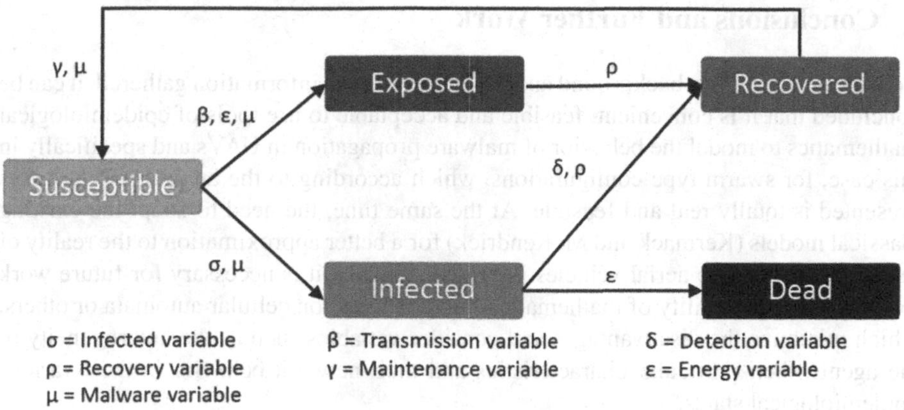

Fig. 3. Scheme with SEIRS-D Model proposed by the authors in [28] (Batista et.al, 2020, p.5).

In that case a WSN was study, with similarities with our investigation about swarm drones, finding and individual, discrete and stochastic model. In our case the sensor is equivalent to an internal component of our drone that could be susceptible to a malicious code infection (operative system, communication links, onboard memory, payload as a camera, or other).

For our research, the dead phase was determined by the D2GS communication lost for example, or drone's damage by malware action, causing his lost, running out of control, or crash into the terrain, or other alternatives.

At the malware propagation modeling point of view, the models can be classified according to different characteristics: basically, we have deterministics or stochastics models, continuous or discrete models, and (this is the most important for us) global or individual-based models. Obviously, this classification is not only typical of malware modeling but also of biological disease modeling, and so on.

Finally, they are compartmental models where the population of devices can be divided into several classes depending of the role or the state of the device with respect to malware: susceptible, infectious, exposed, recovered, damaged, etc. We propose some possibilities to study:

- One of them is to reformulate global models dividing the original compartments into subclasses that depend on the number of connections.

Thus, continuous models on complex networks are obtained and some characteristics of the network (degree of each node) are considered.

- The other possibility is to consider individual-based models where each agent represents a device and all local interactions are represented by means of a complex network. In this case, we will refer to those models whose dynamics is defined by means of cellular automata.

6 Conclusions and Further Work

Considering the above background and the analysis of the information gathered, it can be concluded that it is convenient, feasible and acceptable to use tools of epidemiological mathematics to model the behavior of malware propagation in UAVs and specifically in this case, for swarm type configurations, which according to the analysis of the cases presented is totally real and feasible. At the same time, the need to adapt the existing classical models (Kermack and McKendrick) for a better approximation to the reality of the behavior of these aerial vehicles is evident. Finally, it is necessary for future work to study the applicability of mathematical models based on cellular automata or others, which minimize the disadvantages and consider variables such as the heterogeneity of the agents, their particular characteristics and their network behavior in their various epidemiological states.

Acknowledgments. This research has been supported by the project "Intelligent and sustainable mobility supported by multi-agent systems and edge computing (InEDGEMobility): Towards Sustainable Intelligent Mobility: Blockchain-based framework for IoT Security", Reference: RTI2018–095390-B-C32, financed by the Spanish Ministry of Science, Innovation and Universities (MCIU), the State Research Agency (AEI) and the European Regional Development Fund (FEDER).

References

1. Chamola, V., Hassija, V., Gupta, V., Guizani, M.: A comprehensive review of the covid-19 pandemic and the role of IOT, drones, AI, blockchain, and 5G in managing its impact. IEEE Access **8**, 90225–90265 (2020). https://doi.org/10.1109/ACCESS.2020.2992341
2. Post, T.W.: Prisons try to stop drones from delivering drugs, porn and cellphones to inmates, webpage (2016). https://www.washingtonpost.com/local/prisons-try-to-stop-drones-from-delivering-drugs-porn-and-cellphones-to-inmates/2016/10/12/645fb102-800c-11e6-8d0c-fb6c00c90481story.html
3. Turkmen, Z.: A new era for drug trafficking: drones. Forensic Sci. Addict. Res. **2**, 2–3 (2018). https://doi.org/10.31031/fsar.2018.02.000539
4. Schmersahl, A.R.: Fifty feet above the wall: Cartel drones in the U.S.–Mexico border zone airspace, and what to do about them, Naval Postgraduate School Thesis (2018)
5. Chan, K.W., Nirmal, U., Cheaw, W.G.: Progress on drone technology and their applica tions: a comprehensive review. In: Proceedings of the American Institute of Physics Inc., vol. 2030, p. 020308 (2018). https://doi.org/10.1063/1.5066949
6. Yahuza, M., et al.: Internet of drones security and privacy issues: taxonomy and open challenges. IEEE Access **9**, 57243–57270 (2021)
7. Yaacoub, J.-P., Noura, H., Salman, O., Chehab, A.: Security analysis of drones systems: attacks, limitations, and recommendations. Internet of Things **11**, 100218 (2020). https://doi.org/10.1016/j.iot.2020.100218
8. Zhou, Y., et al.: Secure communications for uav-enabled mobile edge computing systems. IEEE Trans. Commun. **68**, 376–388 (2020). https://doi.org/10.1109/TCOMM.2019.2947921
9. Kotesh, P.: A comprehensive review of unmanned aerial vehicle attacks and neutralization techniques. Ad Hoc Networks (2020). https://doi.org/10.1016/j.adhoc.2020.102324

10. Alfeo, A.L., Cimino, M.G.C.A., De Francesco, N., Lega, M., Vaglini, G.: Design and simulation of the emergent behavior of small drones swarming for distributed target localization. J. Comput. Sci. **29**, 19–33 (2018). https://doi.org/10.1016/j.jocs.2018.09.014
11. Lv, Z.: The security of internet of drones. Comput. Commun. **148**, 208–214 (2019). https://doi.org/10.1016/j.comcom.2019.09.018
12. Sedjelmaci, H.: Cyber security methods for aerial vehicle networks: taxonomy, challenges and solution. J. Supercomputing **74**, 4928–4944 (2018). https://doi.org/10.1007/s11227-018-2287-8
13. Hong, D.: Codeblue cybersecurity conference. CODEBLUE (2014). https://codeblue.jp/2014/en/contents/speakers.html
14. News, T.H.: Maldrone — first ever backdoor malware for drones. THN (2015). https://thehackernews.com/2015/01/MalDrone-backdoor-drone-malware.html
15. Almulhem, A.: Threat modeling of a multi-uav system. Transp. Res. Part A **142**, 290–295 (2020). https://doi.org/10.1016/j.tra.2020.11.004
16. Jares, G., Valasek, J.: Investigating malware-in-the-loop autopilot attack using falsification of sensor data. Int. Conf. Unmanned Aircr. Syst. (ICUAS) **2021**, 1268–1276 (2021). https://doi.org/10.1109/ICUAS51884.2021.9476717
17. Gorrepati, R.R., Guntur, S.R.: DroneMap: an IoT network security in internet of drones. In: Krishnamurthi, R., Nayyar, A., Hassanien, A.E. (eds.) Development and Future of Internet of Drones (IoD): Insights, Trends and Road Ahead. SSDC, vol. 332, pp. 251–268. Springer, Cham (2021). https://doi.org/10.1007/978-3-030-63339-4_10
18. DeLaOsa: The promising yet vulnerable reality of unmanned aerial vehicles. ECN Electronic Component News **61**(2), 11–13 (2017)
19. Zema, N.R., Natalizio, E., Ruggeri, G., Poss, M., Molinaro, A.:Medrone: on the use of a medical drone to heal a sensor network infected by a malicious epidemic. Ad Hoc Networks **50**, 115–127 (2016). https://doi.org/10.1016/j.adhoc.2016.06.008. https://www.sciencedirect.com/science/article/pii/S1570870516301561
20. Asaamoning, G., Mendes, P., Rosario, D., Cerqueira, E.: Drone swarms as networked control systems by integration of networking and computing. Sensors **21**(8), 2642 (2021). https://doi.org/10.3390/s21082642. https://www.mdpi.com/1424-8220/21/8/2642
21. Chen, X., Tang, J., Lao, S.: Review of unmanned aerial vehicle swarm communication architectures and routing protocols. Applied Sciences **10**(10), 3661 (2020). https://doi.org/10.3390/app10103661. https://www.mdpi.com/2076-3417/10/10/3661
22. Reed, T., Geis, J., Dietrich, S.: Skynet: A 3g-enabled mobile attack drone and stealth botmaster. In: Proceedings of the 5th USENIX Conference on Offensive Technologies, WOOT 2011, USENIX Association, USA, p. 4 (2011). https://doi.org/10.5555/2028052.2028056
23. jgamblin: Leaked mirai source code for research/ioc development purposes (2016). https://github.com/jgamblin/Mirai-Source-Code
24. Tien, C.-W., Tsai, T.-T., Chen, I.-Y., Kuo, S.-Y.: UFO - hidden backdoor discovery and security verification in iot device firmware. In: 2018 IEEE International Symposium on Software Reliability Engineering Workshops (ISSREW), pp. 18–23 (2018). https://doi.org/10.1109/ISSREW.2018.00-37
25. Antonakakis, M., et al.: Understanding the mirai botnet. In: 26th USENIX Security Symposium (USENIX Security 17), USENIX Association, Vancouver, BC, pp. 1093–1110 (2017)
26. Trujano, F., Chan, B.Y.Q., May, R.R.: Security analysis of dji phantom 3 standard (2016)
27. Hethcote, H.W.: The mathematics of infectious diseases. SIAM Rev. **42**, 599–653 (2000). https://doi.org/10.1137/S0036144500371907
28. Batista, F.K., del Rey, A.M., Queiruga-Dios, A.: A new individual-based model to simulate malware propagation in wireless sensor networks. Mathematics **8**, 410 (2020). https://doi.org/10.3390/math8030410

Gamification and Usability in Educational Contexts: A Systematic Review

Cristian Valencia Aguilar[1](✉) and Cristian Barría Huidobro[2]

[1] San Buenaventura University, Santiago de Cali, Colombia
cdvalenciaa1@correo.usbcali.edu.co
[2] Major University, Santiago de Chile, Chile
cristian.barria@umayor.cl

Abstract. The introduction of gamification in educational environments in recent decades has gained relevance thanks to the flexibility it presents to adapt to the wide variety of platforms and applications that have resulted in the integration of technology, entertainment, and education [1]; however, the implementation of gamification in classrooms presents challenges, which are mainly associated with low playability [2], often due to lack of motivation of users. Requires that these platforms are designed under the application of usability metrics in pedagogical terms that make it possible to identify and manage the limitations or deficiencies in achieving learning objectives. Therefore, this paper aims to explore the scientific literature on usability heuristics from a pedagogical point of view used in gamification in teaching-learning processes. We worked under the method of three main activities: planning, review, and publication [3]. The reviewed productions provide empirical and theoretical data in the field of pedagogical aspects to be considered to evaluate the pedagogical usability as the user interface for a conducive interaction, ability to entertain, and a learning experience. In addition, it was found that the methods and/or techniques used are associated with external assessments focused on user-centered design because they identify the degree of user satisfaction.

Keywords: Gamification · Usability · Education

1 Introduction

Currently, information technologies have been transfigured into pedagogical tools, producing new ways of learning in which technology and education are articulated to assist the learning and teaching processes as an alternative to making knowledge a possibility of transforming the environment [4]. ICTs have helped to narrow the space-time gap, which has led to the search for new pedagogical tools that strengthen the teaching-learning processes [5]. Virtual learning environments, especially gamification, are contributing to the transformation of pedagogical processes in general; this has encouraged other international research that has allowed to know the potential of these tools in different areas of

M. F. Mata-Rivera et al. (Eds.): WITCOM 2022, CCIS 1659, pp. 374–384, 2022.
https://doi.org/10.1007/978-3-031-18082-8_24

knowledge, highlighting the role of immersion and motivation of learners in the implementation of these tools, in addition to the challenges involved in adapting these tools to school environments.

In Colombia, the implementation of gamification has been gaining relevance in recent years. Although it is still incipient, it is worth highlighting the efforts made by the Ministry of Education promoting virtual learning environments seeking to promote new learning routes in the educational process, framed in the quality of the same, promoting by some research centers a vision of the subject of usability in these platforms [6].

In this sense, Gómez [7] defines gamification as the art of using fun and captivating elements, usually games, and applying them to real and productive environments in a conscious and studied way. While Carreras [8] conceptualizes it as the use of game elements and mechanics in non-game contexts, to guide people's behavior and achieve certain goals, such as stimulating interest, encouraging a behavior change, or conveying a message or content.

Currently, different technological tools have been developed to address education, acquiring great relevance to the use of gamification as a didactic instrument, seeking the union of technological resources and education [9]; to which, Perosi & Lion [10] state that these initiatives need to develop intellectual activities that challenge thinking about game design in cognitive and learning terms, demanding the implementation of usability heuristics in terms of learning in gamification initiatives used in pedagogical processes, only currently, there are limited methods and/or techniques built to quantify usability in these educational platforms [11].

Usability is conceptualized as a set of evaluation techniques that offer a series of results that allow conclusions to be drawn about the use of software in an environment [12]. While González and Farnós [13] define it as the assessment of the degree of ease of use of a digital program and the type of satisfaction that this use generates in the user, which refers to the fact that software, especially educational software, should induce the user's interest in the contents offered by its ease of access and understanding, as well as the degree to which it satisfies the user's needs.

Viñals, Blanco & Cuenca Amigo [1] state that gamification of learning has become scientific didactic par excellence, producing its acceptance, especially in young people who skillfully handle these technologies, particularly those of entertainment; however, this does not guarantee that they manipulated for the development of personal learning. This leads to the fact that young people do not use information technologies for educational purposes, making necessary the search for the integration of technological and educational resources, being this the case of video games in educational processes, which present difficulties in adapting these tools to school environments, while ensuring that these are attractive, developed to entertain and must provide a learning experience related to educational objectives [2]; This is one of the challenges of the digital era where the teacher must influence the construction of the competent digital being.

The introduction of gamification in classrooms presents significant challenges, which are mainly associated with low playability to such an extent that, in many cases, they look like a textbook or a test-type exam, causing students to lose motivation [14]; by leaving out different aspects related to the characteristics present in the game [15]. In addition, Rubio-Méndez [14] exposes that the selection/design of the type of video games must be adjusted to the knowledge, practices, skills, or competencies that are to be transmitted, making it necessary to identify those that will be appropriate in each case to offer students a good and effective tool for their learning. Therefore, it is required, as exposed by Massa [15], to work to understand how to design, manage and evaluate gamification in different contexts that allow the fulfillment of the proposed learning achievements.

Gamification has had a great reception, especially by young people, as a method of entertainment; however, its potential in educational environments has been wasted, but these initiatives must be designed under the integration of technologies, entertainment, and education. Requires that these platforms are designed under the application of methods and/or techniques that allow value the usability in terms of learning, achieving when implementing these initiatives contributing to the development and selection in school environments. This is the challenge of contemporary society in the immersion of gamification in the teaching-learning processes to establish indicators to assess the usability and usefulness of these platforms that enable the identification and management of limitations or deficiencies in its implementation in school environments used in pedagogical processes; Therefore, the purpose of this paper is to explore the scientific literature on usability heuristics from a pedagogical point of view used in these gamification platforms in educational processes, which can serve as a basis for the construction of a usability heuristic from a learning perspective in these platforms in the teaching-learning processes that contribute to the design and/or selection of these programs.

State of the Art. In the educational context, gamification of learning has been implemented in various disciplines of science, technology, engineering, mathematics, and medicine [16]; focusing largely at the university level, with various approaches and pedagogical results but, to a lesser extent at the high school level, therefore, it is required to reduce the gap present in the implementation of gamification at different levels of education [17]; which are associated with the difficulties in adapting these tools to pedagogical processes, while ensuring the game's characteristic features such as being attractive, developed to entertain, in addition to providing a learning experience related to educational goals [2].

Promoting the generation of tools to evaluate gamification in educational contexts, highlighting usability by allowing to determine the impacts of gamification implementation [17]. Usability metrics in learning processes have been oriented in ISO standards, inducing assessments focused on technical aspects of a design accessible to the user, while the assessment aimed at knowing about the pedagogical usefulness of gamification as a tool for teaching and learning has been highlighted [18].

2 Methodology

For the development of the present research, a systematic review was carried out, this being a process that concentrates the results of multiple original investigations based on different strategies to reduce bias. For the execution of the present study, we worked under the proposed method, which consists of three main activities: planning, review, and publication [3]. As stated by Gomes, Cruz, and Horta [19], it is necessary to focus on five relevant aspects for the review: (i) Formulation of the Research Question, (ii) Search Strategy, (iii) Selection of Studies, (iv) Extraction of Information, and (v) Summary of Results.

2.1 Formulation of the Research Question

The present exploratory systematic review had the purpose of knowing the usability heuristics from the point of view of learning in gamification platforms based on the following research questions:

- What pedagogical aspects should be taken into account to evaluate the usability of a gamification platform used in the teaching-learning process of environmental education in middle school students?
- Usability heuristics has used what methods and/or techniques from the learning perspective to evaluate gamification platforms?
- Do usability heuristics from a learning perspective contribute to the design and/or selection of gamification platforms in the teaching-learning process for middle school students?

2.2 Search Strategy

The research was conducted using the advanced search option in the electronic databases Scopus, Dialnet, and Redalyc. Likewise, the search string was defined based on the following keywords of the research questions, both in Spanish and English, which are presented in Table 1.

The search strategy employed was similar in all four databases, using the title sections, abstracts and keywords using AND and OR complements to select specific datasets. An example of the search strategy used is presented below TITLE-ABS-KEY (usability AND gamification AND education).

Table 1. Search strategy and results by descriptors.

Fuente	Estrategia de búsqueda	Número de resultado
Scopus		13
	TITLE-ABS-KEY (usability AND gamification AND education) AND (LIMIT-TO (EXACTKEYWORD, "Gamification") OR LIMIT-TO (EXACTKEYWORD, "Education"))	121
		9
Dialnet	usabilidad AND gamificación AND educación	5
Redalyc	"usabilidad AND gamificación AND educación"	175
	TITLE-ABS-KEY (usability AND gamification AND education)	173
	usabilidade AND gamificação AND educação	153

2.3 Selection of Studies

For the present study, the following selection criteria lived selected: to include all publications between the years 2015 to 2022, published in English, Spanish and Portuguese; as a type of document, articles from indexed journals refereed academic publications and graduate theses were considered. Also, the content of the documents had to deal with usability heuristics from a pedagogical point of view used in gamification platforms in educational processes.

The exclusion criteria included articles in languages other than English, Spanish, and Portuguese. In addition to publications whose title, keywords, abstract and content were not directly related to the research question and were not related to the review's objective. Likewise, the publications were subjected to filtering of duplicate articles. The results obtained are shown in Figure or Table 1.

3 Results

The results of the research are presented below, following the proposed methodology, 24 articles were selected for the synthesis and review based on the reading of the articles that allow the extraction of information, which contributes to the resolution of the research questions and thus, compare them qualitatively.

3.1 Pedagogical Aspects to be Taken into Account to Evaluate the Usability of Gamification Platforms Used in the Teaching-Learning Process

Gamification is conceptualized by Carreras [8] as the use of game elements and mechanics in non-game contexts; to guide people's behavior and achieve certain goals. While Kenwright [20] defines it as the application of game principles to something that is not necessarily a game that has among its objectives to help people motivate themselves, placing it within the boundaries of serious games. The authors Ishaq, Rosdi, Mat, & Abid [21] propose four recommendations that should be taken into account in the development of gamified platforms in the educational context associated with: a) goal orientation, b) achievement, c) reinforcement, and d) a fun orientation.

In the ISO 25000 Standard of 2015 and ISO 25010 Software Quality Requirement Evaluation (SQUARE), a common framework was created for the evaluation of the quality of software products, where it is expressed, that usability is the "ability of the software product to be understood, learned, used and be attractive to the user when used under certain conditions". Too, it is made up of the following sub-characteristics that help in its assessment: Ability to recognize its suitability, Ability to learn, Ability to be used, protection against user errors, and Aesthetics of the user interface, Accessibility [22].

The measurement of usability in learning processes has been based on ISO standards fundamentally on three postulates evaluated by users: the first is the ease of learning that refers to predictability; the second is flexibility, inherent to the possibilities of information exchange between the user and the system; and the third is robustness that responds to the perceived level of support for the achievement of objectives [23].

Cocunubo-Suárez, Parra-Valencia, & Otálora-Luna [24] express that there have been some difficulties in evaluating usability in educational platforms from the international software quality standards associated with the characteristics or pedagogical aspects that must be assessed for educational software to be usable in educational environments. This has contributed to the fact that in educational contexts, the evaluation of usability is mainly oriented to technical aspects of a design accessible to the user, while to a lesser extent, assessments aimed at knowing about the pedagogical usefulness of the resources that can be used as tools for teaching and learning are used [18].

Therefore, proposals have been designed based on the ISO 25000 standards of the aspects to be taken into account in usability evaluations in virtual learning environments, such as Pedagogical ease, Support, help, and documentation, Content, User interface, Error handling, Tools, Flexibility, Standards, in addition, they are complemented with eight sub-characteristics [24].

Turpo [23] proposes pedagogical usability based on three aspects to be taken into account in the assessment of virtual educational environments: the first is the user interface for a conducive interaction, the second is the design of training activities relevant to learning and the third is the verification of the scope of learning: In addition, it accompanies them with three fundamental sub-characteristics associated with the organization of teaching, the process, and achievement of learning and the development of learning skills.

Also, the perceived usability of the application of gamified platforms has been parameterized from the evaluation of aspects such as attractiveness, clarity, manageability, stimulation, and innovation of the application [25]. While the assessment of usability in game-based learning platforms is divided into three aspects: the first is the enrichment and transfer of knowledge, and the second is the usability of the platform and overall experience of the game session compared to other modes of learning [26].

3.2 Techniques and/or Methods Used in Usability Heuristics from a Learning Perspective to Evaluate Gamification Platforms

Usability can be measured in two different contexts; the first is an internal method from the application of heuristics performed by a panel of experts, which is usually implemented in the development stage; the second is an external method that allows assessment used by end-users, i.e., when the platform is finished [24]. It is worth mentioning that these evaluation methods complement each other in practice.

Different techniques have been used to evaluate usability in educational environments, among which are:

- Fun Experience Design (FED), has been used to know the degree of usability of gamified platforms by knowing the degree of satisfaction of students by evaluating the user experience [27].
- User Experience Questionnaire (UEQ), implemented to identify the level of usability satisfaction by allowing the evaluation of specific aspects of the application of gamification through scales ranging from positive to negative assessment [25].

- System Usability Scale (SUS), allows us to analyze usability variables and learnability through a 10-item questionnaire with five response options, ranging from strongly disagree to strongly agree [28].
- User Experience (UMUX), is used to evaluate the perceived usability of an application after a short period of interaction; from a Likert scale, a questionnaire alternating positive and negative statements with which respondents rate their satisfaction [29].
- Goal-Question-Metric (GQM), has been applied to evaluate usability characteristics by taking international software quality standards as a guide, assessing goals, through quantifiable questions, and using quantitative as well as qualitative metrics [30].

The techniques used to evaluate the pedagogical usability have been designed mostly from the Likert scale, which is a psychometric instrument that allows obtaining quality data from a series of questionnaires where the respondent must indicate their agreement or disagreement on a statement [31].

3.3 Contribution of Usability Heuristics from a Learning Perspective to the Design and/or Selection of Gamification Platforms in the Teaching-Learning Process

For the development of gamified platforms, it is necessary to follow usability guidelines from the learning perspective to achieve the construction and consolidation of a tool for the development of user learning [21]. Because the application of this type of heuristics allows achieving a balance between technology, pedagogy, and the learning objectives sought, in addition to knowing the satisfaction propitiated from the interactions with the gamified platform [23].

Aspects related to usability and pedagogy are fundamental for gamification to be successful and meet the objectives proposed in the teaching-learning process [24], because, as expressed by Turpo [23] usability in pedagogical processes, goes beyond the aesthetics of the interface, attractive or ergonomic design, it implies satisfaction with the service and/or training product, through the achievement of content and activities proposed when developing certain competencies.

By applying usability heuristics associated with pedagogy, we seek to achieve full harmony of using technology in conjunction with pedagogy, because the important thing is not only to focus on technological artifacts but, it is essential to focus attention on didactics and human cognition, [18]. This is a criterion that influences the quality of the design of the e-learning platform in the overall satisfaction of the learning experience [26].

Therefore, the use of usability heuristics in gamified platforms used in teaching-learning processes is considered a main issue when evaluating any application [32]; because it allows having enough assessment criteria to work on the correct application of gamification in educational environments [27].

4 Discussion

The evaluation of usability in gamified platforms used in teaching-learning processes is mainly oriented to technical aspects of a design accessible to the user, while to a lesser extent assessments aimed at knowing about the pedagogical usefulness of the resources that can be used as tools for teaching and learning are used learning [18]; thus, it is necessary a broader look that integrates technological features such as interfaces, the characteristics of gamification and pedagogical characteristics allowing to achieve a balance between technology, entertainment, and educational processes.

Therefore, the design of usability assessment metrics is required, as proposed by Turpo [23] and Chan, Chan, & Agnes [26], an assessment based on three main aspects related to the enrichment and transfer of knowledge, the design of training activities relevant to learning and the overall user experience when using the platform. This will allow us to know relevant aspects that lead to the successful introduction of gamification in educational contexts. This makes it necessary to incorporate usability metrics focused on user-centered design (UCD) [33]; which makes it possible to know the degree of satisfaction of end consumers, this is an important criterion to work on the maximize application of gamification in educational environments.

The above may be an explanation for the perceived trend in the techniques used in usability metrics applied to educational platforms that are mostly applied in external contexts that allow the end-user to evaluate gamification from a questionnaire designed using the Likert scale methodology (Peters, Oleari, & Sardu, 2019). Resulting in knowing the usability problems presented by gamification from real users of the system leading to its solution [33].

This implies exploring the relationships between the perceived usability of a gamified educational application and the impact on student motivation, allowing not only to help design better interfaces, but also to obtain an impact on the learning processes of users (Andrade, Law, Farah, & Gillet, 2020). Therefore, this research should serve as a basis for the construction of usability heuristics from a pedagogical point of view in gamified platforms in the teaching-learning processes that contribute to the design, selection, and assessment of the effects of these programs on students. Techniques and/or methods used in usability heuristics from a learning perspective to evaluate gamification platforms.

5 Conclusions

Gamification has great potential to become a pedagogical tool, thanks to the nature of the human being to want to play more than to work, experience, and enjoy more than to possess [34]. In addition, it increases the motivation to learn but, for this to happen, the user's educational needs must be met [28]; it is here where the use of usability heuristics in gamified platforms becomes relevant to achieve harmony between technology, entertainment, and pedagogy; so that the gamification strategy is successful and meets the objectives proposed in the teaching-learning process.

The findings of this review show the interest in analyzing the possibilities offered by gamification in the teaching-learning processes, recognizing the importance of maintaining the characteristics of the game such as its ability to entertain, in addition to providing a learning experience according to the proposed objectives. Thus, it has been emphasized the need to design and deliver pedagogical usability heuristics that allow its measurement from three main aspects related to the enrichment and transfer of knowledge, the design of training activities relevant to learning, and the overall user experience when using the platform [23].

Among the methods and/or techniques used, external evaluations focused on user-centered design stand out, since these metrics allow identifying the degree of user satisfaction, which is an important criterion to work on the application of gamification in educational environments [33]; by allowing adapting these to the contexts and needs of students; likewise, designing accessible and usable platforms. Usability metrics based on user evaluation are constructed from a questionnaire using the Likert scale methodology [29].

6 Future Investigations

After conducting the research, it is considered that there is still much work to be done to obtain usability metrics from the point of view of pedagogy used in gamified platforms to assess the user interface for a conducive interaction and ability to entertain, in addition to a learning experience according to the proposed objectives.

References

1. Cuenca, J., Viñals, A.: El rol del docente en la era digital. JCR of Revista Interuniversitaria de Formación del Profesorado **30**(2), 103–114 (2016)
2. Silveira, A.C., Martins, R.X., Vieira, E.A.O.: E-Guess: usability evaluation for educational games. RIED JCR of Revista Iberoamericana de Educación a Distancia **24**(1), 245 (2020). https://doi.org/10.5944/ried.24.1.27690
3. Pedreira, O., Piattini, M., Luaces, M., Brisaboa, N.: Una revisión sistemática de la adaptación del proceso software. J. REICIS Revista Española de Innovación, Calidad e Ingeniería del Software **3**(2), 21–39 (2007)
4. Gutiérrez, L.: Problemática de la educación ambiental en las instituciones educativas. JCR of Revista científica **23**(3), 57–76 (2015)
5. Romero, M., López, M.: Luces, sombras y retos del profesorado entorno a la gamificación apoyada en TIC: un estudio con maestros en formación. JCR of Revista electrónica interuniversitaria de formación del profesorado **24**(2), (2021)
6. Ceballos, O., Mejía, L., Botero, J.: Importancia de la medición y evaluación de la usabilidad de un objeto virtual de aprendizaje. JCR Panorama **13**(25), 23–37 (2019)
7. Gómez, A.: Gamificación y los Juegos Serios. Curso practico, RA-MA (2021)
8. Planas, C.C.: Del homo ludens a la gamificación. JCR of Quaderns de filosofía **4**(1), 107–118 (2017)
9. Aguilar, L., Adell, F.: Instrumento de evaluación de un videojuego educativo facilitador del aprendizaje de habilidades prosódicas y comunicativas. JCR of Revista de Educación a Distancia (RED) **18**(58), (2018)
10. Lion, C., Perosi, V.: Los videojuegos serios como escenarios para la construcción de experiencias. e-ducadores del mundo. Journal of Revista telecolaborativa internacional, 4–8 (2018)
11. Ramírez, C., Otálora, J.: Medición de la usabilidad en el desarrollo de aplicaciones educativas móviles. JCR of Revista Virtual Universidad Católica del Norte **47**, 128–140 (2016)
12. Tramullas, J.: Documentos y servicios digitales: de la usabilidad al diseño centrado en el usuario. Jounal of El profesional de la información **12**(2), 107–110 (2003)
13. González, A., Farnós, J.: Usabilidad y accesibilidad para un e-learning inclusivo. Journal of Revista de educación inclusive **2**(1) (2016)

14. Méndez, M.: Retos y posibilidades de la introducción de videojuegos en el aula. Journal of Revista de estudios de juventud **98**, 118–134 (2012)
15. Massa, S.: Videojuegos en el aprendizaje: oportunidades y desafíos. JCR of Prometeica revista de Filosofía y Ciencias **15**, 50–58 (2017)
16. Sandrone, S., Carlson, C.: Gamification and game-based education in neurology and neuroscience: applications, challenges, and opportunities. J. Brain Dis. **1**, 100008 (2021)
17. Andrade, P., Law, E., Farah, J., Gillet, D.: Evaluating the effects of introducing three gamification elements in STEM educational software for secondary schools. In: Proceedings of the 32nd Australian Conference on Human-Computer Interaction, New York (2020)
18. Colorado, B., Escobar, A., Solano, E.: La usabilidad pedagógica en los entornos virtuales de aprendizaje. In: Hernanz, J., Watty, M. (eds.) IX Congreso Internacional de Innovación Educativa Tendencias y Desafíos, pp. 1369–1383. Fundación para la Educación Superior Internacional, A.C., Boca del Río (2015)
19. Biolchini, J., et al.: Systematic review in software engineering. System engineering and computer science department COPPE/UFRJ. Technical Report ES **679**(05), 45 (2005)
20. Kenwright, B.: Brief review of video games in learning & education how far we have come. In: Proceedings of the SIGGRAPH Asia 2017 Symposium on Education (SA 2017), pp. 1–10. Association for Computing Machinery (ACM), Bangkok (2017)
21. Ishaq, K., Rosdi, F., Zin, N.A.M., Abid, A.: Serious game design model for language learning in the cultural context. Educ. Inform. Technol., 1–39 2022.https://doi.org/10.1007/s10639-022-10999-5
22. ISO/IEC 25000 Homepage. https://iso25000.com/index.php/normas-iso-25000/iso-25010. Accessed 30 May 2022
23. Turpo, O.: La usabilidad pedagógica en la formación del profesorado: un estudio de caso. Journal of Revista Espacios **39**(15), (2018)
24. Cocunubo-Suárez, J.I., Parra-Valencia, J.A., Otálora-Luna, J.E.: Propuesta para la evaluación de entornos virtuales de enseñanza aprendizaje con base en estándares de usabilidad. TecnoLógicas **21**(41), 135–147 (2018). https://doi.org/10.22430/22565337.732
25. Lerma, L., Rivas, D., Adame, J., Ledezma, F., López, H., Ortiz, C.: Realidad virtual como técnica de enseñanza en educación superior: perspectiva del usuario. Journal of Enseñanza & Teaching: Revista interuniversitaria de didáctica **38**(1), 111–123 (2020)
26. Chan, C.S., Chan, Y.H., Fong, T.H.: Game-based e-learning for urban tourism education through an online scenario game. Int. Res. Geogr. Environ. Educ. **29**(4), 283–300 (2020)
27. Labrador, E., Villegas, E.: Unir gamificación y experiencia de usuario para mejorar la experiencia docente. JCR of RIED: revista iberoamericana de educación a distancia **19**(2), 125–142 (2016)
28. Yanfi, Y., Udjaja, Y., Sari, A.: User's demographic characteristic on the evaluation of gamification interactive typing for primary school visually impaired with system usability scale. JCR Adv. Sci. Technol. Eng. Syst. J. **5**(5), 876–881 (2020)
29. Paiva, J., Queirós, R., Leal, J., Swacha, J., Miernik, F.: Managing gamified programming courses with the FGPE platform. JCR of Information **13**(2), 45 (2022)
30. Peters, R., Oleari, E., Sardu, F., Neerincx, M.A.: Usability of the PAL objectives dashboard for children's diabetes self-management education. In: Proceedings of the 2019 the 5th International Conference on e-Society, e-Learning, and e-Technologies, New York (2019)
31. Matas, A.: Diseño del formato de escalas tipo likert: un estado de la cuestión. JCR of Revista electrónica de investigación educativa **20**(1), 38–47 (2018)
32. Lana, I., Jusoh, S.: Usability evaluation on gamified e-learning platforms. In: Proceedings of the Second International Conference on Data Science, E-Learning and Information Systems, pp. 1–6. Association for Computing Machinery (ACM), Dubai (2019)

33. Najjar, A., Alhussayen, A., Jafri, R.: Usability engineering of a tangible user interface application for visually impaired children. JCR Hum.-Centric Comput. Inf. Sci. **11**(14), 891–921 (2021)
34. Han, B.-C.: No-cosas. Quiebras del mundo de hoy, 1nd edn. Taurus, Barcelona (2021)

Groups in the Educational Institutions, a Glance from the Administration Perspective

Carlos Alberto Ruiz Maldonado(✉) and Miguel Ranferi Silva Millán(✉)

Instituto Politécnico Nacional, México City, México
carlosalbertoruiz@outlook.com, m.ranferi.silva@gmail.com

Abstract. This paper presents a review regarding to the groups formation and presence in the educational institutions, as well as a reflection towards its formation. Likewise, a classification proposal is reviewed in order to develop an information source which provides a perspective that allow the scholar executives fuel their vision, expand their lines of thought and, especially invite them to analyze their management and understanding of their own organizations with the particularities implied.

Keywords: Educational institutions · Groups in organizations and types of groups

1 The Educational Organizations

Accepting that an organization seeks to achieve particular objectives (Hall, 1996), it's natural results is to identify the existence of different objectives to fulfill, as well as the singular origins that caused the intention and formation of an organization to reach them. Such condition follows certain distinction and diversity of organizations, which lead some authors [1, 7] to take the task to propose certain typologies and classifications.

In this respect, we approached [1] a position referring that the educational organizations are categorized under the service sector, which groups together those organizations that offer services to the community and whether or not they are not-for-profit or for-profit organizations. In this aspect, the consolidation of this concept, are refer to the description in [13], who defines the educational organizations as any institution in which a formal teaching-learning process takes place.

Complementing the preceding position that considers that the educational organizations provide teaching services, Rossana del Valle [6] incorporates the elements associated to this organization modality, capturing that the educational institutions represent a human organization formed by individuals that assume different roles: students, teachers, executives, employees, whose basic purpose is to guarantee the transmission, acquisition and production of knowledge. In such way, the educational organizations operation is fundamentally based on the teachers, students, executives, and employee's roles which people therein get integrated. Accordingly, on the effect of this study, these concepts are identified as follows:

M. F. Mata-Rivera et al. (Eds.): WITCOM 2022, CCIS 1659, pp. 385–393, 2022.
https://doi.org/10.1007/978-3-031-18082-8_25

Teacher:

In accordance to the basic conception that the Royal Spanish Academy (known in Spanish as RAE) provides, the teacher is the one who teaches an art or science.

In accordance to the basic conception that the Merriam-Webster Dictionary [8] provides, a teacher is the one that causes to know something, guides the studies and/or imparts the knowledge in certain subject.

Therefore, it is a key element within the educational organizations whose main purpose is to offer educational services.

1.1 Student

The Royal Spanish Academy [10] notes that the student is the person that attends its studies in a teaching establishment, in other words, the student represents the direct beneficiary of the main service that the educational organizations offer.

The Merriam-Webster Dictionary [8] notes that the student is a person who attends a school or studies under a teacher; it also refers to a person who has gained knowledge or understanding of skills by studying, instruction, or experience. In other words, the student represents the direct beneficiary of the main service that the educational organizations offer.

It is in this line distinguished that the student interacts in a total way with the organization, since besides receiving the educational service, it keeps an interaction with the different areas which involves a daily coexistence. For this reason, the student represents a core part of the educational organizations.

1.2 Executive

As it is currently the case in other organizations, the executive or executives of the educational organizations represent the head and guide of the institution, and it's in charge of the operation, planning and strategies.

1.3 Employee

They are individuals who perform an activity or position related to the activities of administration, maintenance, security, medical services or education service inside the educational organization.

This perspective delivers the possibility to distinguish the different actors that participate in the educational organizations, which leads to a natural lecture on the internal groups recognition, in this case are groups among the teachers, students, executives and employees. However, the groups formed inside the organizations are not only differentiated by the affinity of the roles they play at the organization or by their hierarchical position, groups could be constituted either as a result of formal conditions or the coincidences and particular identifications that arise apart from the organizational structure.

1.4 Groups in the Organizations

After observing that organizations sets its bases, mainly, in the individual engagement and their social relationships, by a hierarchical structure, achieves its objectives, it results unavoidably to identify in this context certain establishment of groups inside of the organization. In the same way, this condition is observed in the groups that arise inside an educational institution: teachers, students, executives and employees.

Those grouping are usually a result of the specific characteristics of the task performed by several individual, or a consequence of personal or social affiliations that arise spontaneously among the members of the organization.

Within this framework, a group is defined as a set of people that interact between themselves in a way that the behavior or the performance of one of its members is influenced by the behavior or performance of the rest of the group's members [4]. Naturally, all the groups that interact inside an organization develop their basic structure in both a formal and informal environment. In this way, the group's labor and development represent a key element for the organizational functionality.

The different groups held inside an organization are governed by their plurality, variety and complexity of the activities they perform, the objectives they must achieve, and the tasks they need to fulfill. A significant amount of the influence that an organization exerts on its members is caused by the groups [5]. To this effect, groups work like social systems within another system, which is the organization.

1.5 Why are Groups Formed Inside an Organization?

The establishment of groups inside an organization meets different factors since its formation can be a result of the circumstances and personal affinities or, in the other hand, it can be a consequence of the conditions focused in achieve common goals for their members. Therefore, authors in [3] and [4] concur on presenting a series of reasons related with the group formation, which they recognized might occur as a result of the needs' satisfaction, closeness and attraction, goals or economy.

According to this approach, first of all, it's identified that the formation can be related to the needs' satisfaction because this might represent an incentive that promotes the groups' construction. Particularly, the social needs, the needs of confidence and appreciation, can be covered to some extent for the individuals through their group belonging. In this regard, the members of a group can give each other confidence and feel that they can face together the administrative conditions and the organization system. Otherwise, groups can also cover a certain social need as a logical consequence of the individual's condition that requires interaction, recognition and belonging [14].

Therefore, within the different groups that could exist inside an organization, there would be some of them that will be perceived with a high reputation level and, therefore, their members will have certain level of recognition among the rest of the organizational members. A group of this nature can satisfy their members' needs of appreciation through their participation [4].

In this same way, the closeness and attraction are also adopted as a one of the reasons that can promote the groups formation. In the case of the closeness, the physical distance that could exist among the members of an organization that meet their activities will open, proportionally to the closeness, opportunities to form connections and this could result as a group formation. On the other hand, the attraction that exist between people either by the similarities in their thoughts, tastes, attitudes, perception and even their personal aspirations, can condition a group's formation [2, 14].

Likewise, the goals represent a circumstance that can result in a group because if these are understood clearly, they can be the detonator of empathy that calls new members. This characteristic is related in certain way with the economy aspect of group formation since, in this context, the individuals believe that establishing groups they could access greater monetary benefits [4].

Against this background, the incorporation of such factors and their relationship with the basis of the organization and its individuals reflects a prevailing scenery in any type of organization, in other words, an organism where different groups coexist. Turning back to the specific case of the institutions of educational nature, we observe that teachers as well as executives, employees and students can find in their colleagues the possibility to satisfy those particular concerns which we had talked about previously or distinguish affinities that result in friendship. Of course, it also exists the condition and role that each of them plays inside the institution which can integrate them as a part of a specific group. However, whichever the circumstance is, each group will respond to a certain filiation and traits that distinguish it.

1.6 Characteristic Traits of Groups

As a group emerges and develops, it will inevitably acquire characteristic traits that will be defined from their structure, hierarchy, duties, rules, leadership, cohesion and conflict [3]. Below we review the properties of each one of these particularities.

1.7 Group's Structure

Along its operation, any group will display a structure that will be constituted from the different factors that their members show, eg, experience, aggressiveness, power and status [3]. Each member of the group will take a position within it, being the framework of relation between the different positions of the resultant structure.

An example of this element can be the case of a group of students that share a classroom during certain time at school. The way they treat each other, or the daily circumstances will generate an interaction in which each of them will take a particular role: "overachiever", "nerd", "natural leader", "bully", "daydreamer", "class clown", among others.

1.8 Hierarchy

The hierarchical status sets an individual in a particular position and it is commonly a result of the characteristics that distinguish one position from another. Conditions like seniority, age, or capacities are the general parameters of status assignment of each individual within the group [3].

An example of this quality inside an educational institution can be distinguished in the discernment of the teachers based on their maximum study degree, in other words, distinguishing the teachers that have only a bachelor's degree from those who have master's degree or PhD.

1.9 Duties

Within the structure of the group, each person has assignments to fulfill, which defines the conduct and procedures desired to accomplish by the position occupier. In addition to these expected duties, there are also included the perceived duties and the executed duties [3]. The perceived duties are the set of behaviors that the person that occupies a position must perform; this may sometimes match with the expected duties. Conversely, the executed duties represent the real conduct of the individual. Naturally, the groups will often encourage the consistency between the expected and perceived duties, however the conflicts can cause disparities among the different duties.

This confusion that usually shows up to the individuals in a group or an organization, can be illustrated with a particular case of the security guards of an educational institution. Within this framework, the institution expects that the guard monitor can maintain the safety conditions in its facilities. However, it is common to notice that there are cases in which the security guards forget their authentic duty and focus on keeping the students' discipline or their compliance against the scholar regulations.

1.10 Rules

They represent the standards shared by the members of a group that consists in a referral developed from the interaction and lifetime of the group [3]. Those rules are constructed based on the meaningful things for a group. They can be established on paper although they are often established and communicated orally; likewise, they can be presented informally as long as all the members of the group are aware of them. Certainly, those rules are accepted in different level by the individuals and they can even be applied differently among them.

The case of the rules within the groups can be grounded using as an example the common treatment that usually occurs on informal environments among the teachers group. When the conditions and infrastructure allow it, it is common that the teachers have a room or hall inside the facilities of the institution where they can frequently spend their leisure time. Among other things, this place works as a spot where teachers can take some snacks and, consequently, there is usually certain distribution between them that results in rules that may establish an order or responsibility assignment for each, in order to provide common use items (e.g. coffee, tea, cookies, etc.) in an equitable way.

1.11 Leadership

This is distinguished as the action of causing influence over people for them to exert greater strength in certain task or to transform their conduct. The leader is the embodied symbol of the principles, motives, and aspirations of a group; also acting as a mediator and representative of the group [15].

The leadership trait can be detected easily inside an educational institution and any person who had been a student in any stage of their life can confirm it. It is difficult to identify a group of students that doesn't have a leader: the individual that expresses its personal or group position to executives and teachers, serves as a voice, guide, and influence whether it is positive or not; and, under certain conditions, conducts the group's actions.

Cohesion: It expresses a force that causes, in the members of a group, the intention of remain together. The increase of cohesion will occur proportionally to the observance of the group's rules. Therefore, a cohesive group will provide a higher sense of affiliation to its members and, altogether, it will result more attractive for other individuals [4].

Within the conditions of an educational institution, we can find an example of cohesion in a group of rebel and naughty students because their intention is to denote certain strength or even hierarchy through their actions, which locates them in a singular position among the rest of their schoolmates and professors.

1.12 Types of Groups

Within an organization, considering that several people participate in order to achieve established goals and recognizing that those goals are a natural detonator for groups, formation (even without considering the attraction and closeness that arise among people), we can tell that inevitably an organization will likewise be constituted by different groups with diverse origin and objectives, hierarchies, duties and structures. This creates a diversification that is worth categorizing.

Several authors have established that classification based mainly in a division judgment that designates groups as formal and informal (Goldhaber, 1984; Wexley and Yukl, 1990; Hall, 1996; Robbins, 1996;). Nevertheless, other authors have agreed and developed a more ambitious categorization that grants the possibility of a higher scope. This classification defines five main criteria from which they set their categories: Temporal dimension, Formality level, Purpose and Hierarchical level (Gil and García, 1998; Palomo, 2003; Rodríguez et. al. 2004).

2 Temporal Dimension: It Mainly Refers to the Relationships' Stability, Including Two Types of Groups: Permanent and Temporal

- Permanent: They are groups in charge of customary activities at the organization, like distribution and maintenance, that are in certain level promote the daily activities of the organization [12]. This characteristic inside the educational institutions is observed, for example, the person that gives maintenance to the facilities whose labor is steady and even cyclical.
- Temporal: They are limited duration groups formed to develop a particular task or face a specific circumstance that dissolve once their work is concluded. Due to their characteristics and especially due to the changing situations the organizations must address. The groups that are also named ad hoc are increasingly common inside and outside an organization [9]. This temporality condition of groups can be illustrated in the field of educational institutions, particularly in the case of the science fairs, conference cycles and accreditation activities, where the organization requires that

its members perform specific tasks for those events. These activities are frequently assigned under work groups structured exclusively for these aims and that will remain alive only while that event is taking place.

3 Formality Level: Groups with Their Timeliness are Recognized as Formal and Informal

- Formal: They are established by the organization in a legitimate way and their creation is focused on goals' achievement [12]. Regarding to this category, it is worth to refer to the case that often occurs in the educational institutions in which, under certain circumstances, a group of professors is designated by the executives in order to develop a specific project. Even though this is related to their duty within the institution, it surpasses their daily activities inside the lecture halls. Some examples that may result in this type of group are art fairs and workshops.
- Informal: They arise spontaneously, and they develop according to their personal common interests needs and satisfaction [9]. In this aspect, we should recognize the groups that are established within any organization, including educational institution, as a consequence of particular common filiations that result in friendship bonds and that have nothing to do with the groups or structures established by the organization.

4 Purpose: It Points Towards the Groups that are Established to Fulfill a Specific Purpose. It Includes the Following Types

- Production: It considers the groups formed by members that perform specific tasks which constitute departments and organizational units [9]. This type is distinguished within the educational organizations in the departments that integrate the student services, whose duties take into account students enrollment management or the grade report.
- Problem solution: They are groups focused on solving problems that are inherent in the organization [5]. For example, in the educational institutions, considering specifically the high school ones, there are several problems that should be faced day-to-day, however, one of the most recurrent problems is related to the student's behavior. In this context, it is observed that this type of organizations usually has a task force formed by prefects and psycho-pedagogical advisers, whose main duties are to solve these issues.
- Conflict solution: This considers those groups who are dedicated to negotiate [12]. To exemplify this within an educational organization, it is worth to bring up again the case of prefects and psycho-pedagogical advisers because, as it was previously mentioned, in their daily activities that are closely linked to the students. Therefore, it is common to observe how they solve and even negotiate some situations with the students, acting as a communication channel between students and executives.
- Change and development: It incorporates the groups of awareness and motivation; those who are in training or developing teams [5]. This group trait is common to be found within educational institutions in the cases where professors receive capacity development or when they take a workshop together related with their duties and whose purpose is that they perform their work in a better way.

5 Hierarchical Level: Contingent upon the Category and Subordination, There are Identified in Two Dimensions

- Vertical differentiation: These groups are formed by the different command groups that are hierarchized according to their decision making and grouped in directors of planning, executives, middle managers, and groups of employees, and non-managerial workers, operational personnel or subordinates [12]. Within the educational institutions' framework, this trait is observed among the structure defined in their organization chart in which it usually appears in a general management or rector area at the upper part. This principal area is followed downwards by secretariats and departments that include the professors and employees. Hence, under these characteristics and graphic layout, the different groups of the organization can be observed.
- Horizontal definitions: This considers groups that provides specialized services, related to research or particular skills [5, 9]. To demonstrate this characteristic in a more detailed way on the educational organizations' context, the medical unit of an institution can be highlighted. This area stands outside the academic issues because its duty is to provide medical care in case any member of the organization has certain health issue or has suffered an accident inside the facilities.

By noticing the scenery described previously regarding to the groups classification, it is recognized that a single group can be located among more than one category, just as an individual within an organization can be part of different groups. Certainly, this complies on one hand, the different reasons that allow and provide the groups formation (needs, satisfaction, closeness and attraction, goals or economy) and, on the other hand, that a group can have different particular traits that based on its position in an organization that can be categorized in more than one type. This can be the case of prefects, who can be represented both in a group conflict solution or in a group of problem solution.

6 Conclusions

As we have observed throughout this document, it results interestingly that within the roles considered to be performed inside an educational institution it is found to be the "student role". Even though this seems to be obvious at glance, as we reviewed at the definition of this concept, the student represents the principal beneficiary of the services that organizations offer. From the administration's perspective, this characteristic distinguishes these institutions because, unlike the other organizations, in the educational area, the final user (speaking in terms of the traditional presential programs) interacts in the organization totally and permanently, with the degree of relation that it involves. In fact, as it was detailed previously, the students become part of the formal and informal groups within the educational institutions, which causes a context that is different from the one that takes place in other kinds of organizations where the beneficiary doesn't take action in its practices. Naturally, this reality opens a wide range of possibilities to study such as the recognition of the influence degree of the final user in the organization's environment, a particularity that would be worth to approach in future studies, focusing on the educational organization's administration.

References

1. Camus, G.: Administración integral en la empresa. Trillas, México (2001)
2. Fonseca, S.: Comunicación oral Fundamentos y práctica estratégica. Prentice Hall, México (2000)
3. Gámez, R.: Comunicación y cultura organizacional en empresas chinas y japonesas. Edición electrónica gratuita (2007)
4. Gibson, J., Ivancevich, J., Donnelly, J., Konopaske, R.: Organizaciones: Comportamiento, estructura, y procesos. McGraw Hill, México (2003)
5. Gil, F., García, M.: Grupos en las organizaciones. Pirámide, Madrid (1998)
6. Guzmán, E.: Propuesta de un modelo de desarrollo organizacional en una escuela de nivel medio superior de educación pública. Tesis de maestría. Escuela Superior de Ingeniería Mecánica y Eléctrica. México (2007)
7. Hall, R.: Organizaciones, Estructuras, procesos y resultados. Prentice Hall, México (1996)
8. Merriam-Webster: Online Dictionary (2019). https://www.merriam-webster.com/
9. Palomo, M.: Liderazgo y motivación en equipos de trabajo. ESIC, Madrid (2003)
10. Real Academia Española. Diccionario de la lengua española (22.aed.) (2019). http://www.rae.es/rae.html
11. Robbins, S.: Comportamiento organizacional. Teoría y práctica. Prentice Hall, México (1996)
12. Rodríguez, A.: Psicología de las organizaciones. Editorial UOC, Barcelona (2004)
13. Santos, M.: La lis del prisma. Para comprender las organizaciones educativas. Ediciones Alebrije, México (2000)
14. Verderber, R.: ¡Comunícate! International Thomson Editores, México (1999)
15. Wexley, K., Yukl, G.: Conducta organizacional y psicología del personal. CECSA, México (1990)

Senior Citizens' Training Experience in Secure Electronic Payment Methods

Clara Lucía Burbano González[1,2](✉), Miguel Ángel Castillo Leiva[2](✉), Alex Torres[3](✉), and Sandra Rodríguez[3](✉)

[1] Military Aviation School (EMAVI), Santiago de Cali, Colombia
clara.burbano@emavi.edu.co, clara.burbano@umayor.cl
[2] Mayor University, Santiago, Chile
miguel.castillo@mayor.cl
[3] University Corporation Comfacauca - Unicomfacauca, Popayán, Colombia
{atorres,srodriguez}@unicomfacauca.edu.co

Abstract. Virtual training is a mechanism that enables contemporary society to be literate, allowing up-to-date information on the technological environment, improving cognitive abilities as well as soft skills required in the workplace where individuals can develop their maximum performance; The following article presents results obtained in the literacy of older adults of Santiago de Chile, belonging to the Los Andes Compensation Fund in the area of Information Security in Electronic Payment Means, through the application of the Alternative Action Research Method under an Apprehensive Level Methodology of the Comparative Analytical type of quantitative data, oriented in the development of a Virtual Object that allows to reduce the knowledge gap and lose the fear of the use of technology through the integration of Media Literacy and Informational (MIL) focused on the transmission of updated knowledge and training in technological resources.

Keywords: Learning and knowledge technologies (TAC) · Media and information literacy (AMI) · Computer security · Andragogy · Electronic payment methods

1 Introduction

Technology has transformed our environment from face-to-face to virtuality, inverting the interaction with individuals, allowing active communication between the community through technology, due to the massive sending of information considered a slow, imprecise and above all complex process. However, with the technological evolution, the speed at which information is accessed has increased, increasing accuracy as an essential characteristic, which encompasses resources such as databases, micro processors and servers, to provide immediate response to user requests. Decreasing the complexity of technology allows it to be accessible to all types of people in society to be appropriated effectively [1]. The above perspective evidences the need to train society in technological

M. F. Mata-Rivera et al. (Eds.): WITCOM 2022, CCIS 1659, pp. 394–409, 2022.
https://doi.org/10.1007/978-3-031-18082-8_26

aspects related to the use of secure tools, allowing end users to access with peace of mind [2]; in this sense, efforts to transform learning have migrated towards the search for tools that contribute to improve knowledge, keeping it accessible and available to the whole society. In this sense, it was proposed from the Magister in Cybersecurity of the Universidad Mayor de Chile, the use of a technological tool in which Andragogy (Training of the elderly) is applied from the Appropriation of Technology (Virtual Learning Object (OVA)) based on Media and Information Literacy (AMI) as a structure to finally bring knowledge to older adults enrolled in the Caja de Compensación los Andes-Chile in the safe use of electronic means of payment; through the development of the article it will be possible to observe the results obtained in the experience of training older adults in electronic means of payment and the process carried out to reach an appropriate solution in the intervention of society and especially to train in impact topics according to the Technological Evolution of the 21st century defined as the Networked Society [3].

2 Methodology of Experience

The development of the training experience of the older adult is a process that integrates contents that are not very complex, understandable and extensive; this means that knowledge is transformed from a block of information to a component that can be molded to the experience and knowledge management of the individual. An older adult does not learn at the same pace as a child, young person or adult, in the first instance it must be guaranteed to capture the interest, breaking the barrier and allowing the training experience to be enjoyable; secondly, relevant contents must be captured where the older adult can put into practice his experience and it is necessary to extract problems related to the environment, in order to simplify the processes of use and appropriation of the information and technological environment; thirdly, the training structure from the perspective of Meaningful Learning promotes the decentralization of knowledge by uniting the aforementioned aspects in a final product that intervenes for a defined period of time with the chosen population and finally generates an "Update" of knowledge from experience and work based on cases extracted from the environment [4]. This can be seen in the following figure (Fig. 1):

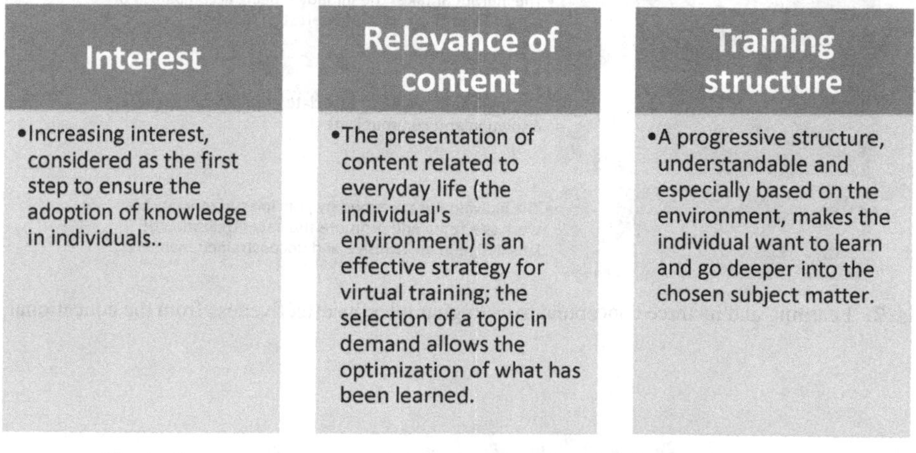

Interest
•Increasing interest, considered as the first step to ensure the adoption of knowledge in individuals..
Relevance of content
•The presentation of content related to everyday life (the individual's environment) is an effective strategy for virtual training; the selection of a topic in demand allows the optimization of what has been learned.
Training structure
•A progressive structure, understandable and especially based on the environment, makes the individual want to learn and go deeper into the chosen subject matter.

Fig. 1. Interest, relevance and structure for virtual training in older adults.

From the figure above it is possible to evidence three important aspects which help to configure an effective knowledge structure, related to the individual's environment, from this moment on he/she will be called an older adult; the individual must be guided through a series of steps where propo-sitive, reflexive and especially communicative strategies are integrated, what is learned will be expressed with continuity and appropriation of knowledge.

In order to reach this result, a literature review was conducted with the following conceptual categories: a. Use of TAC in Media and Information Literacy (AMI), as a strategy for the transmission of knowledge and the formation of skills in accordance with the needs of contemporary individuals; b. Technological Mediations from Virtual Learning Objects (VLO), as a tool to convert face-to-face learning focused only on content, to a decentralized strategy where the teacher ceases to fulfill the role of knower/trainer and becomes a companion/mediator, giving his previous role to the learner to make his own decisions about the learning modality to which he best fits; c. Cybersecurity in secure electronic means of payment, represents the specific knowledge, relates strategies to make secure payments and reduce the technological gap, by transforming the resilience to change that sustains the study population (older adults recognized by the Caja de Compensación Los Andes-Chile), in evolution and adoption of knowledge through digital channels, promoting the advancement of cyberculture as well as training in older adults.

2.1 Training of the Elderly

Among the fundamental elements constituted in the Theory of Education, mainly the social context, which segments the main objective of education [5], proposing three conceptual axes that will guarantee efficiency and the successful completion of the proposed strategy as shown below:

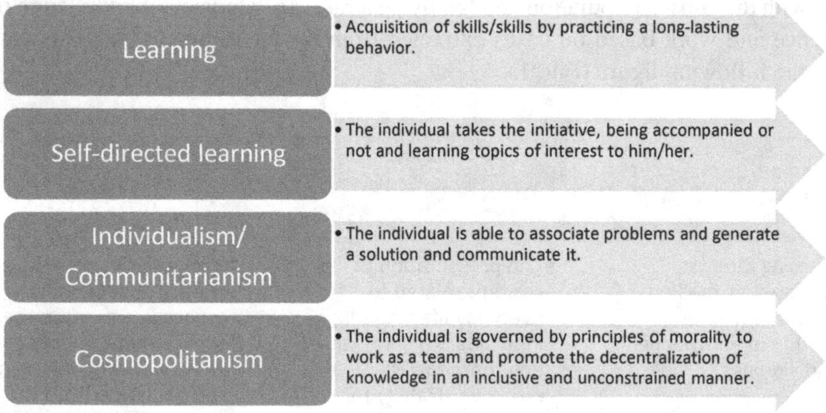

Fig. 2. Learning and its three conceptual axes to guarantee its effectiveness from the educational
|

Figure 2 presents the use of three fundamental axes to reach the creation of Meaningful Learning that directly impacts the needs of the individuals to be trained, guaranteeing the vanguard of knowledge and technical management, regardless of the strategy and tools for the transmission of information used. Additionally, it is understood that one of the main behavioral objectives of education has been presented since the society of the 20th century, understood as the era of "Self-Directed Lifelong Learning", where the term "Self-Directed" comes from the psychological need of the adult being to feel the master of his life and his directly proportional relationship between the progress of his studies and the increase of the independence demanded on his learning experience; The term "Lifelong" is generated thanks to the acceleration of human obsolescence (the passing of the years), where the human being's capacity for attention, concentration, retention and disposition to understand and face the technological world of contemporaneity decreases, forcing change and continuing the training process in a continuous manner, developing the skills and abilities necessary to evolve with the world [6]. In the case of training for the elderly, the central objective is to promote lifelong learning; within companies and governmental institutions, it does not seem that the intention is to prevent the inability to learn and participate in today's globalized world or to ensure the right to self-realization and the maximum development of potentialities that comes from hu-manism; On the contrary, the aim is to make the "labor force" hard-working and productive, otherwise, to promote "active aging", which, in simple terms, means remaining attached to one's job until the investment in training is completed and one obtains one's pension as late as possible.

2.2 Learning and Knowledge Technologies (LKT) in Media and Information Literacy (MLI)

Education is a right for everyone, regardless of race, sex or even age, where the latter aspect has revolutionized the way we think when building a technological tool that contributes to the acquisition of knowledge in any area. In the case of older adults, it is important to highlight that they do not have the same capabilities as children or young people, who will be alert to any change in their learning environment; on the contrary, older adults will only accept learning if it is something they do on a daily basis and in a repetitive manner, classifying new information into three types: "It is useful for my life"; "Maybe I will use it later"; "It is definitely not useful for me". The three aspects mentioned above are linked to the real needs of those who really need the knowledge, therefore it is important at all stages of Cognitive Development to emphasize motivation, decentralization of knowledge, familiarity with the subject matter and the pedagogical usability obtained, ensuring that the proposed tool contributes to the development of skills, abilities and competencies necessary for the development of technology in today's society.

> "The transmission of knowledge is one of the main duties of the educational programs implemented by governments worldwide, as stated in the Universal Declaration of Human Rights of 1948, where education was established as a Universal Human Right". [7].

In this context, Learning and Knowledge Technologies (LKT) have gained popularity thanks to the advances obtained in real environments, making it easier to take information and knowledge to different places without being limited by the type of technological device used; some types of LKT are: Blogs, podcast, the web (internet), e-book, LMS (Moodle), YouTube, Facebook, Prezzi. The above techno-logies permeate our daily context, whether sharing information on social networks, watching videos on YouTube or making presentations on Prezzi; this brings to the table a wide variety of tools and possibilities that can be used by experts in pedagogy and learning to transform the way in which knowledge is acquired and dynamize the learning process from experimentation; in this sense, adult education should be constituted under the following pillars, shown in Fig. 3 below:

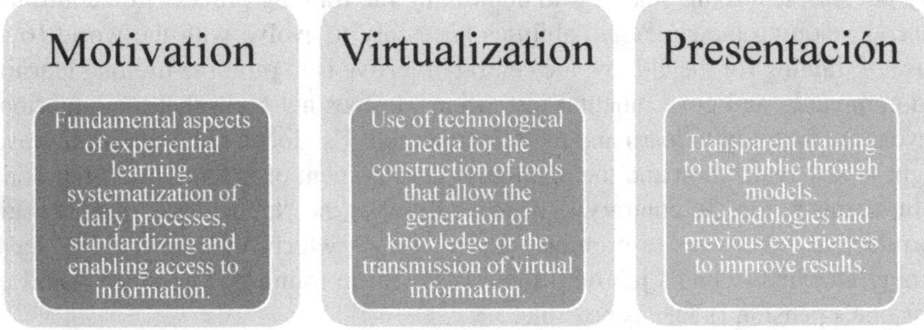

Fig. 3. Triangulation of knowledge towards the formation and transmission of knowledge in the older adult.

Figure 3, contemplates three fundamental pillars that allow to generate in the individual/learner, an optimal experience from a Virtual Learning Object (VLO), however, there is still a doubt about what is a VLO, in this sense and in a simplified way it can be segmented into two parts: "Virtual Object" and "Learning". A "Virtual Object" is a set of digital resources that can be reusable and easily accessible in order to ensure that the individual develops skills and competencies visually, at their own pace and didactically; the "Learning" is focused on the acquisition of knowledge through a medium where study, exercise and experience are used to learn. From the above, it is possible to observe the instrument (Virtual Object) and the technique (Learning) with leads to identify that a Virtual Learning Object is the composition between the instrument and the technique to be dynamic and interactive towards the acquisition of knowledge mediated by technological tools [8]. In support of the correct development of a techno-logical product that projects individuals to the improvement of their technological skills and knowledge, it is possible to start from the creation of an effective user experience, which does not apply only to the construction of ICT tools, on the contrary, it can also be hybridized and applied to the TAC, so as to improve the processes of "Educommunication" and "Media and Information Literacy"; Accordingly, "it is important that in addition to the disciplinary competencies, professionals should acquire soft and analytical skills that facilitate better professional performance" [9], therefore digital transformation through technological tools becomes a constant and steady process from the concept of "Andragogy", where four factors are explained that will allow the adoption of knowledge or the abandonment of the training process from the perspective of the older adult and the instructor [10], which are presented below in Fig. 4:

Senior citizens	Being Successful
	Having Control of Learning
	Learning Something Relevant (Worthy)
	Experiencing Learning
Instructors	Effective communication
	Enthusiasm
	Commitment to Learning
	Empathy

Fig. 4. Main factors to ensure acceptance of a meaningful training process [10].

The importance of the notions of Gamification as a factor of didactic innovation in the qualification of professionals and adults, allow the improvement of their experience as users through ICT, ensuring the strengthening of cognitive and soft skills of the individual as is the case of: Analysis-Interpretation and Collaboration/Communication respectively [9].

2.3 Elderly Education, Technological Mediation and Information Security

Within the functioning of payment systems, it is necessary to ensure that transactions carried out by this means are safe and fast; through these features, central banks have the ability to monitor and regulate the payment system satisfactorily [11], exposed by the increasing level of acceptance of the use of digital means of payment in Chile (América Economía, indicates that the pandemic has triggered the increase of 64% of digital payments in Chile in 2020). A background of this aspect shows that at least 38% of those interviewed tried to use a new type of payment (digital or contactless) during the pandemic months; 37% acknowledged having changed their payment behavior due to the crisis and therefore, we will describe the standards and models that govern digital payment methods in Chile, in a context of technologies that have been contributed by other more developed countries and that are applied in Chile, supervised by the Super Intendencia de Bancos y Servicios Financieros [12]; The Payment Card Industry Data Security Standard (PCI DSS) was developed by a committee formed by the most important card companies (debit and credit), named PCI SSC (Payment Card Industry Security Standards Council), The PCI SSC (Payment Card Industry Security Standards

Council) was developed as a guide to support organizations that process, store and transmit card (or cardholder) data in order to secure data and prevent fraud involving debit and/or credit payment cards, allowing them to focus their efforts on improved and comprehensive mechanisms for end users. Companies that process, store or transmit card data ensure compliance with the standard and non-compliance leads to the loss of their permission to process credit and debit cards (loss of franchises), facing rigorous audits or fines; Merchants and credit and debit card service providers must periodically validate their compliance with the standard by authorized Qualified Security Assessors (QSAs) and only companies that process less than 80,000 transactions per year are allowed to perform a self-assessment using a questionnaire provided by the PCI Consortium called PCI SSC; the current version of the PCI-DSS regulation, referred to as 3. 2, specifies twelve compliance requirements, organized into six logically related sections called "control objectives", as shown below (Table 1):

Table 1. Control objectives and their requirements of the PCI-DSS for IT security in electronic means of payment.

Control objective	#	Requirement
Develop and Maintain a Secure Network	1	Install and maintain a firewall configuration to protect cardholder data
	2	Do not use system passwords and other default security settings provided by vendors
Protect Cardholder Data	3	Protect stored cardholder data
	4	Encrypt cardholder data and confidential information transmitted over open public networks
Maintain a Vulnerability Management Program	5	Use and regularly update anti-virus software
	6	Use and regularly update anti-virus software.
Implement strong access control measures	7	Restrict access to data on a need-to-know basis
	8	Assign a unique ID to each person who has access to a computer
	9	Restrict physical access to cardholder data
Regularly monitor and test networks	10	Track and monitor all access to network resources and card-owner data
	11	Regularly test security systems and processes
Maintain a Security Policy	12	Maintain a policy that addresses information security

The massive disclosure of frauds in Chile is a major factor for older adults to distrust electronic means of payment, being vulnerable to this type of fraud due to the lack of support from the "Financial System", having as an alternative offered to contract anti-fraud insurance; for most Chileans, it is seen as a "double fraud or as taking advantage of a situation" that financial entities must assume, however, it generates an attached business and a solution to the directly associated problem, sending fraud costs to the user of the system and forcing them to contract additional anti-fraud insurance, simply because they are unaware of the ways to avoid being victims of the process and make good use of their cards; reasons for training older adults in secure electronic payment methods are presented, which allows to reduce the levels of electronic fraud, creating a safe culture in this population vulnerable to attacks by cybercriminals due to lack of knowledge and prevention of security risks.

3 Methodological Design

The study carried out through the degree thesis entitled "Training of the elderly in secure electronic means of payment" used as a basis, focused on the projective research methodology, which consisted of finding the solution to practical problems and was concerned with establishing how it should work to achieve the ends and function properly [13]. In this sense, the development of a model was proposed to solve the problem/need related to the training of older adults regarding the use of electronic means of payment in a secure manner. The quantitative action research method proposed makes it possible to analyze the data of a population of 40 older adults recognized in the compensation fund of Chile and from which a sample of 12 individuals was extracted to whom a pre- and post-test was performed to determine the level of adoption of knowledge regarding electronic means of payment before and after implementing the training process mediated by the OVA SIMPA-APP, which is conformed by the quantitative research approach. The strategy for implementing quantitative research is presented below (Fig. 5):

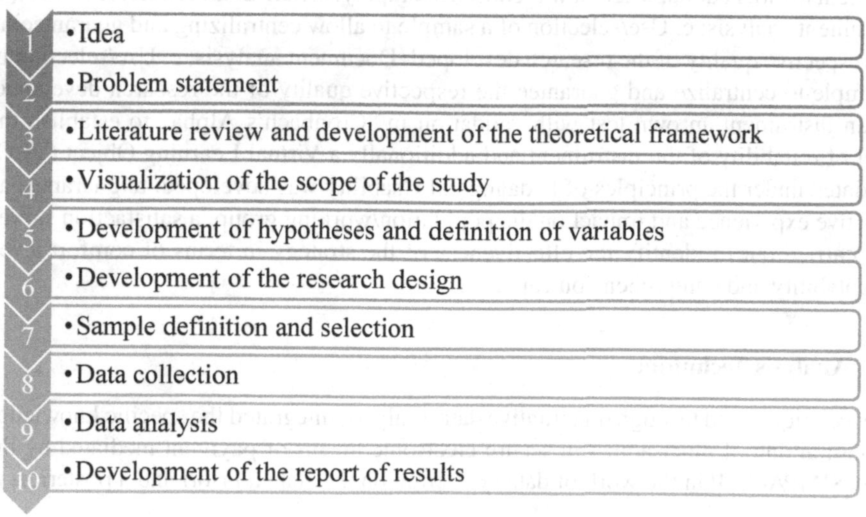

1
• Idea
2
• Problem statement
3
• Literature review and development of the theoretical framework
4
• Visualization of the scope of the study
5
• Development of hypotheses and definition of variables
6
• Development of the research design
7
• Sample definition and selection
8
• Data collection
9
• Data analysis
10
• Development of the report of results

Fig. 5. Sequence for the methodological development of the research [14].

The project was oriented towards alternative action research [15] as a study method for social problems that require a solution/improvement where three stages are proposed to achieve the application of the research process, based on the methodological proposal of M. Sampieri [14] and adapted to the specific research need for the case of training mediated by an OVA in secure electronic payment methods (Fig. 6):

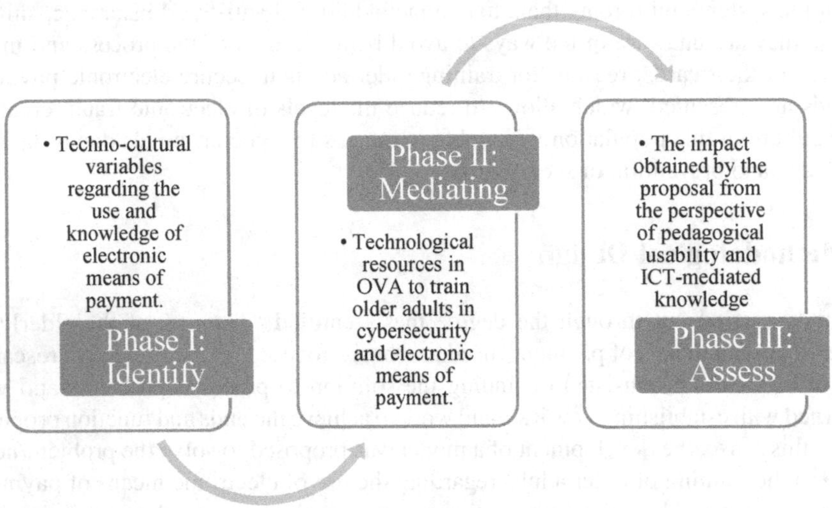

Fig. 6. Phases of the methodological design

3.1 Techniques and Instruments

Evaluated the state of knowledge and satisfaction on the training in electronic means of payment in older adults, where it was chosen to employ: a. Self-authored test (Pre/Pos); b. Document analysis; c. Use/selection of a sample to allow centralizing and guaranteeing the respective quality of the research developed. Document analysis; c. Use/selection of a sample to centralize and guarantee the respective quality of the research developed. As an instrument an own test with validation in "Cronbach's Alpha" to establish the level of reliability of the instrument and additionally a Virtual Learning Object (VLO) validated under the principles of Pedagogical Usability was developed, to guarantee an effective experience and impact on the population/working group, a satisfaction survey was carried out to identify the effectiveness of the strategy in terms of comfort level, acceptability and comprehension capacity.

3.2 Analysis Technique

The technique used through quantitative data analysis, integrated the specific knowledge of the training of older adults in secure electronic means of payment mediated by the OVA SIMPA-APP in the work of data collection on the state a priori and a posteriori to the implementation of mediation, allowing to analyze the state of knowledge of the focus group, the pedagogical usability and satisfaction through the statistical tool "SPSS" for data analysis.

4 Results

4.1 CRONBAch's Alpha Consistency Test and Intervention Results

Determining the method of internal consistency by finding Cronbach's alpha, allows determining the reliability of a measurement instrument, therefore in order to carry out the process of constructing a test that is effective, the evaluation of reliability becomes an indispensable process commonly used in the measurement of attributes of interest; In short, the reliability of a test to determine the state of knowledge before and after the interaction with the OVA SIMPA-APP, allows to study the properties of the measurement scales; in this order of ideas, the reliability analysis procedure is integrated to calculate a number of reliability measures (scale) and also provides information on the existing relationship between individual items of the scale as shown in the following table (Table 2):

Table 2. Scale for reliability measurement

Test	Value	Consistency
Cronbach's alpha coefficient	> 0,9	Excellent
	> 0,8	Good
	> 0,7	Acceptable
	> 0,6	Questionable
	> 0,5	Poor
	< 0,5	Unacceptable

The scale above measures the same highly correlated characteristic [16]; the closer the value of Cronbach's Alpha test is to one (1), the higher the internal consistency of the items analyzed for the measurement of the state of knowledge in secure electronic means of payment in older adults. The result can be seen below when calculating Cronbach's Alpha coefficient to determine the state of knowledge of secure electronic means of payment in older adults:

Table 3. Reliability coefficient calculation result

Tool	Cronbach's alpha	Decision
Pre test	0.81	Good
Pos test	0.96	Excellent

By means of Table 3 it is possible to determine that the result obtained in the application of Cronbach's Alpha test, the reliability of the test in each of its applications, presents a good level of confidence (Cronbach's Alpha > 0.8) in the Likert measurement scale. Another important aspect in the data analysis stage is the descriptive analysis that accompanies the results obtained in the two-time measurement (Pre/Post Test). This with the objective of establishing the level of appropriation of knowledge in the specific knowledge of electronic means of payment in a secure manner in older adults, selecting a focal group of twelve (12) older adults as unit of analysis belonging to the Andes-Chile compensation fund with estimated ages between 45 to 58 years old, residents in the city of Santiago de Chile-Chile (Analysis Variable) and to whom a test with two intervention times was structured and developed: a. Pre test (Before); b. Post test (After), applied to the aforementioned group. In this sense, through Table 4, the results were consolidated according to the scores obtained by each older adult, in sum, the Variation Percentage Value is presented, which described the relationship between the a priori test value and the post-test value.

Table 4. Percentage variation analysis pre/post test

Subject	% Variation	Average % variation
A1	250	**218.1**
A2	0	
A3	33.3	
A4	50	
A5	600	
A6	250	
A7	33.3	
A8	0	
A9	400	
A10	350	
A11	300	
A12	350	

Table 4 shows the transformation and impact of technological mediation, which contributed to achieve an optimal development of knowledge with a 218.1% improvement; in principle, it is consolidated that the strategy fulfilled its established purpose of training older adults through an OVA on secure electronic means of payment. Figure 7 shows the results obtained from the calculation of the mean in relation to the pre/post-test interventions, where a positive impact of technological mediation on knowledge formation can be seen:

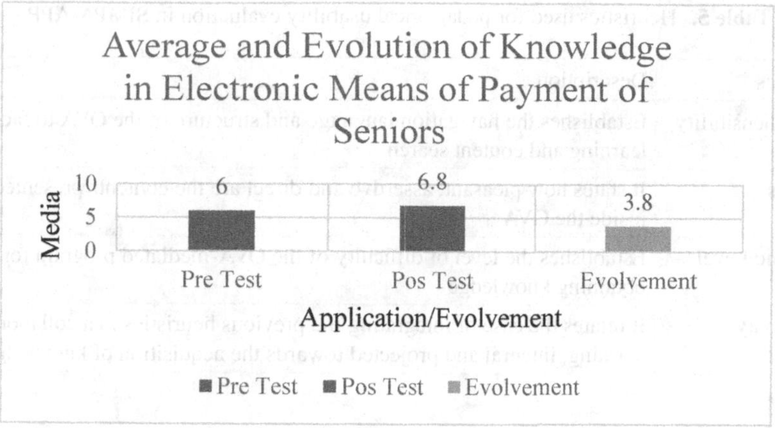

Fig. 7. Average and evolution of knowledge in electronic means of payment of older adults

From the previous figure it is possible to quantitatively determine that the evolution of knowledge regarding electronic payment methods in a secure manner and mediated by the OVA SIMPA-APP, was 3.8 on average, which shows that ICT-mediated learning is possible and effective as long as strict guidelines are followed to improve the final product.

4.2 Pedagogical Usability

The information society poses an ecosystem where Information and Communication Technologies (ICT) play a leading role in economics, politics and especially education [17]. This implies the use of various techno-pedagogical mechanisms aimed at the design of educational materials using digital formats and the modeling of applications [18]. In this sense, higher education institutions have been forced to adopt digital strategies that allow them to respond correctly to the needs of the New Information and Communication Technologies (NICT) to compete with greater advantage among their peers through alternatives for access to knowledge called disruptive trends; this type of trend in short is to offer to the society of impact, learning alternatives and playful adaptation, within innovative technology compared to traditional ways of learning and obtaining knowledge [19]. Now, most higher education institutions are aware of the importance of adopting technological strategies created in response to new trends in the educational field, supported by the incorporation and implementation of Information and Communication Technology (ICT) [19]. This generates new alternatives of educational interaction in a ubiquitous way in formal education and higher education through the following proposed heuristics (Table 5):

Table 5. Heuristics used for pedagogical usability evaluation in SIMPA-APP

Heuristics	Description
Comprehensibility	Establishes the navigation language and structure of the OVA to facilitate learning and content search
Contents	It states how pleasant, assertive and direct are the contents presented inside the OVA
Academic Level	Establishes the level of difficulty of the OVA-mediated program for obtaining knowledge
Interactivity	It relates the ease of integrating the previous heuristics in a collaborative learning, integral and projected towards the acquisition of knowledge

The table above describes the characteristics of the pedagogical usability which was evaluated by experts in pedagogy, ICT in education and information security to ensure that both the content, the platform used and the training path is effective and can obtain the greatest possible impact on older adults who serve as a study group in the training on secure means of payment; In this sense, the usability evaluation has 15 questions which were rated on a Likert scale established from 1 to 5, where 1 is the lowest rating and 5 is the highest, additionally, in order to obtain a good level of Pedagogical Usability, a minimum viable point was established where the product can be accepted, which corresponds to a score greater than or equal to four, obtaining the following results (Fig. 8):

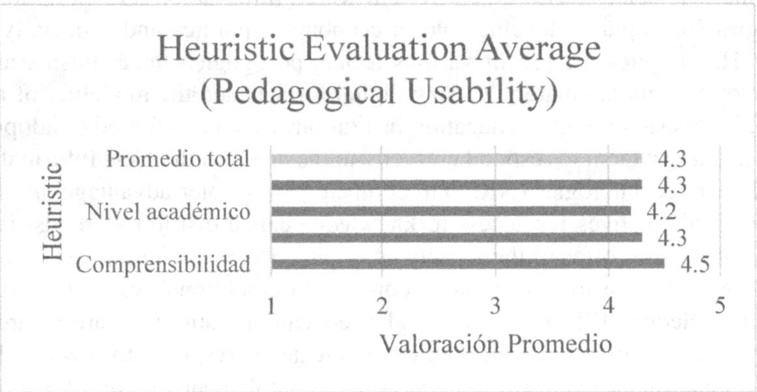

Fig. 8. Average of heuristic evaluation (Pedagogical Usability)

From the previous figure it is possible to determine that the final percentage obtained by the heuristic evaluation is 86% of compliance with the requirements established in the expert evaluation, therefore, it is possible to conclude that the SIMPA-APP Tool is interactive, understandable, of impact and with a good academic level to carry out the training process of older adults in the specific knowledge of secure electronic means of payment. Below are some screenshots of the SIMPA-APP Virtual Learning Object (VLO) (Fig. 9):

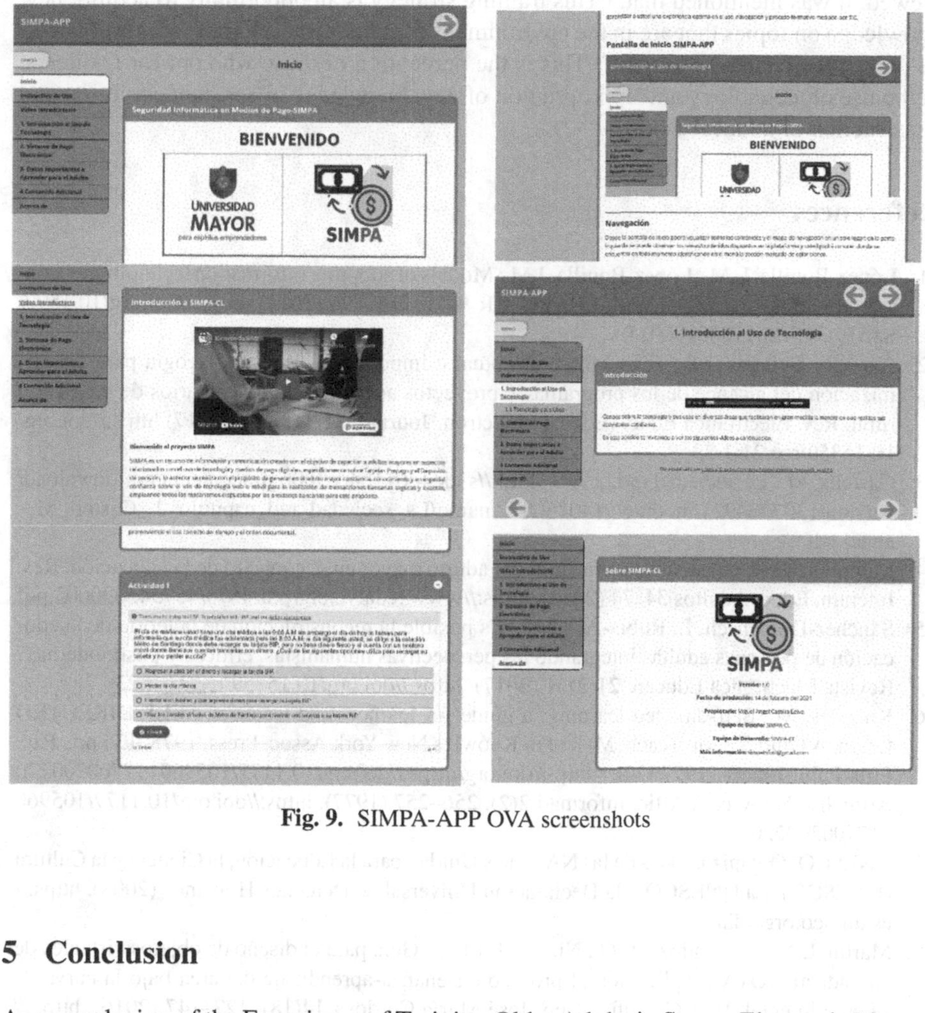

Fig. 9. SIMPA-APP OVA screenshots

5 Conclusion

As a conclusion of the Experience of Training Older Adults in Secure Electronic Means of Payment, it was possible to demonstrate that techno-technology is taking a leading role in the transmission of knowledge, especially by integrating knowledge nomads (Knowmads) in learning and self-training processes mediated by Information and Communication Technologies (ICT) [20]; thanks to studies conducted by authors, references were found that contributed to improve and systematize training processes in older adults with respect to specific knowledge of computer security, obtaining results on the improvement of knowledge in secure electronic payment methods. From this study it was possible to identify, analyze, design, develop and implement an impact training strategy under the guidelines of Andragogy, allowing to train older adults in secure payment methods in the use of technology in everyday life, making them understand the operation, uses and applications of new trends. The results obtained in the development of this research showed that older adults had an improvement in the appropriation of knowledge in secure electronic means of payment. In the words of the individuals interviewed, it was mentioned that: "This training strategy is an opportunity to acquire new knowledge on topics that are in the environment every day, therefore, I feel fortunate to be part of the changing society". This is the perception of those who opt for resilience in the use of technology and appropriation of new knowledge in constant evolution and construction of an ideal world.

References

1. López-Bonilla, L.M., López-Bonilla, J.M.: Models of adopting information technologies from the attitudinal paradigm. Cad. EBAPE. BR **9**(1), 176–196 (2011). https://doi.org/10.1590/S1679-39512011000100011
2. Azofeifa Bolaños, J.B.: Evolución conceptual e importancia de la andragogía para la optimización del alcance de los programas y proyectos académicos universitarios de desarrollo rural. Rev. Electrónica Educ. (Educare Electron. Journal) **21**(1), 1–16 (2017) https://doi.org/10.15359/ree.21-1.23
3. Castells, M.: La sociedad red (1996). http://s3de4d611b4ec3006.jimcontent.com/download/version/1393284927/module/9140750878/name/La_sociedad_red_capitulo_2._Castell_Manuel.pdf
4. Mogollón, E.: Una perspectiva integral del adulto mayor en el contexto de la educación. Rev. Interam. Educ. Adultos **34**, 74 (2012). https://www.redalyc.org/pdf/4575/457545090005.pdf
5. Sánchez-Domenech, I., Rubia-Avi, M.: ¿Es posible la reconstrucción de la teoría de la educación de personas adultas integrando las perspectivas humanistas, críticas y postmodernas? Revista Electrónica Educare **21**(2), 1 (2017). https://doi.org/10.15359/ree.21-2.23
6. Knowles, M.: Self-directed learning: a guide for learners and teachers. SELF-DIRECTED Learn. A Guid. Learn. Teach. Malcol m Knowles New York Assoc. Press. 1975. 135 pp., Pap. First Publ. June 1, 1977 Other https//doi.org/https://doi.org/10.1177/105960117700200220 Artic. Inf. No Access Artic. Informati 2(2), 256–257 (1977). https://doi.org/10.1177/105960117700200220
7. UNESCO: Organizaciones de las NAciones Unidad para la Educación, la Ciencia y la Cultura (UNESCO). La UNESCO y la Declaración Universal de Derechos Humanos (2008). https://es.unesco.org/udhr
8. Martín, L.Y.M., Mendoza, L.G., Nieves, L.M.A.: Guía para el diseño de objetos virtuales de aprendizaje (OVA). Aplicación al proceso enseñanza-aprendizaje del área bajo la curva de cálculo integral. Rev. Científica Gen. José María Córdova **14**(18), 127–147 (2016). https://doi.org/10.21830/19006586.46
9. Plaza Arias, J.L., Constain Moreno, G.: Experiencia de diseño de aplicaciones móviles basada en estrategias de gamificación para el fortalecimiento de habilidades cognitivas Mobile application design experience based on gamification strategies to. Rev. Digit. AIPO **2**(1), 17–24 (2021). https://revista.aipo.es/index.php/INTERACCION/article/view/31/43
10. Morales Pacavita, O.S., Leguizamón González, M.C.: Teoría andragógica: aciertos y desaciertos en la formación docente en tic. Rev. Investig. y Pedagog. Maest. en Educ. Uptc **9**, 161–181 (2018). https://doi.org/10.19053/22160159.v9.n19.2018.7926
11. Figueroa, J.G., Martínez, F.V.: Impacto de los medios electrónicos de pago sobre la demanda de dinero. Investigación Económica **75**(295), 93–124 (2016). https://doi.org/10.1016/j.inveco.2016.03.003

12. Alves, P.: MasterCard. Encuesta Mastercard: 63% de los chilenos quisiera poder realizar pagos en tiempo real (2020). https://www.mastercard.com/news/latin-america/es/sala-de-prensa/comunicados-de-prensa/pr-es/2020/junio/encuesta-mastercard-63-de-los-chilenos-quisiera-poder-realizar-pagos-en-tiempo-real/
13. Córdoba, M.N., Monsalve, C.: Tipos de investigación, predictiva, interactiva, confirmatoria y evaluativa. Fund. Sypal., 139–140 (2008). http://2633518-0.web-hosting.es/blog/didact_mate/9.TiposdeInvestigación.Predictiva%2CProyectiva%2CInteractiva%2C ConfirmatoriayEvaluativa.pdf
14. Hernández Sampieri, R., Fernández Collado, C., Baptista Lucio, M. del P.: Metodología de la Investigación. Mexico: McGRAW-HILL / INTERAMERICANA EDITORES, S.A. DE C.V (2005)
15. Páramo Bernal, P.: La Investigación en Ciencias Sociales: estrategias de investigación. Univ. Pilot. Colomb., 1–8 (2013). https://books.google.com/books?hl=es&lr=&id=2uk0DwAAQBAJ&oi=fnd&pg=PT75&dq=La+investigación+en+Ciencias+Sociales:+Estrategias+de+investigación.+&ots=SWIu17_QHM&sig=J87Vg2M_FApbK_l7ltLwGRgjR68
16. Welch, S., Comer, J.: Quantitative methods for public administration: techniques and applications, 2nd edn. Ill Dorsey Press, Chicago (1988)
17. Galvis Panqueva, A.H., del Pedraza Vega, L.C.: Desafíos del eLearning y del bLearning en educación superior: análisis de buenas prácticas en instituciones líderes. Cent. Innovación en Tecnol. y Educ. – Univ. los Andes., p. 48 (2013). https://conectate.uniandes.edu.co/images/pdf/desafios_conectate.pdf
18. Paur, A.B., Rosanigo, Z.B.: Objetos de Aprendizaje: factores que potencian su reusabilidad. XIV Congr. Argentino Ciencias la Comput. (02965), 1–12 (2008). http://sedici.unlp.edu.ar/handle/10915/22004
19. Plaza Arias, J.L.: Ambiente Virtual de Aprendizaje para la Formación en Seguridad Informática. Corporación Universitaria Comfacauca-Unicomfacauca (2021)
20. Futures, E.: Knowmad Society. Educ. Futur., 1–273 (2013). http://www.knowmadsociety.com

Study of Energy Consumption of UAVs to Temporarily Assist Wireless Communication Systems

Luis Ibarra[1(✉)], Mario E. Rivero-Angeles[2], and Izlian Y. Orea-Flores[3]

[1] Mechanical Engineering Department, Massachusetts Institute of Technology, Cambridge, USA
lcibarra@mit.edu

[2] Network and Data Scienece Laboratory, CIC-Instituto Politécnico Nacional, CDMX, Mexico
mriveroa@ipn.mx

[3] Telematics Academy, UPIITA-Intituto Politécncio Nacional, CDMX, Mexico
iorea@ipn.mx

Abstract. Cellular systems are typically designed to provide high coverage in a certain region with low blocking probability (0.02 or lower) in order to provide an adequate Quality of Service (QoS). However, when traffic peaks occur, this blocking probability increases beyond this acceptable value and the system offers an unacceptable QoS. In order to avoid the installation of additional channels in the base station, that would be active all the time, even when the traffic load is low, the use of Unmanned Aerial Vehicles (UAVs) can reduce energy consumption and alleviate traffic from the base station temporarily. We believe that this alternative is aligned with Green Communication Networks while efficiently solving the problem of higher traffic loads due to abnormal user concentrations. UAVs can also be used to assist WSNs by gathering information directly from the nodes, avoiding expensive transmissions to a fix far away sink. To this end, we develop a simulation model to calculate the hovering times of different commercial UAVs to evaluate the possibility of using these mobile base stations and sinks in future applications in wireless communications systems.

Keywords: Cellular systems · Wireless Sensor Networks · UAVs · Energy consumption · Hovering times

1 Introduction

Green communication systems are developed to reduce energy consumption in modern networks, where the main objective is no longer to offer an adequate Quality of Service (QoS) for the users but rather, having the less possible impact on the planet even at the cost of slightly degrading the experience of the clients. In this sense, cellular systems consume high amounts of energy since base stations usually operate at full capacity all the time and every day, even in low traffic conditions. Indeed, cellular systems are designed to provide sufficient channels to attain a lower blocking probability than 0.02

M. F. Mata-Rivera et al. (Eds.): WITCOM 2022, CCIS 1659, pp. 410–421, 2022.
https://doi.org/10.1007/978-3-031-18082-8_27

in peak traffic hours (the highest traffic in the day). Hence, when traffic is low, there are many channels being unused, effectively wasting energy.

In view of this, we consider that increasing the capacity temporarily may be a better option in terms of energy consumption than permanent channels in base stations. One alternative is the use of UAVs (Unmanned Aerial Vehicles) to fly over the zone where traffic is higher than the base station's capacity to handle and return when the traffic peak decreases. Also, UAVs can be used for many other applications, such as providing coverage in remote areas where it is not economically viable or in case of emergencies where the cellular infrastructure has been damaged.

UAVs are becoming increasingly more popular as electronic components become cheaper and more readily available for hobby and commercial use. On top of the required components necessary to generate lift (motors, propellers, body frame, battery), next generation GPS, cameras, and sensors are paving the way for drones to disrupt various industries (such as, agriculture, emergency response, telecommunications, shipping, insurance, construction). This paper will focus primarily on UAVs in the context of green communication systems to offset total energy consumption with next generation IoT (Internet of Things) technologies being developed at a rapid scale. There are several ways UAVs can be applied to existing WSNs via aerial base stations, relaying, data gathering, mobile-edge computing, and energy harvesting [3]. In [4], the authors expose how to improve the spectrum efficiency, with integration of multiple drones that can conform cellular clusters to share the spectrum to the base station directly. This article exposes an alternative to solve the demand that it has the traditional networks Ground-To-Ground, especially to up-links used between the mobile devices and base stations. In [5], field measurements and system-level simulations are used to assess interference mitigation solutions that can improve aerial-link reliability. Also, drones can be used in emergency cases, for example in [6], the work proposes the use of drones in cellular networks to coverage extend connectivity, with improved energy efficiency in terms of the propagation gain after natural disasters. The results in this work demonstrate the efficiency of UAV system capacity with different path loss exponents for reliable connectivity to ground user devices. In [7], the authors consider the same applications as we do, i.e., they cover two main scenarios of drone applications as follows. The first type of applications can be referred to as drones Assisted Cellular Communications. Second type of application is to exploit drones for sensing purposes, such as smart agriculture, security monitoring, and traffic surveillance. In [8], the authors expose the research and experimental aerial for advanced technologies focused to design architectures to allow the research over controlled environments. In [9], a novel method is proposed based on cooperative game theory to select the best drone during handover process and optimize handover among drones by decreasing the end-to-end delay, handover latency, and signaling overheads. In [10], a novel approach is proposed that enables efficient coverage using a set of drones. Two scenarios are considered, the first allows selecting a minimum number of appropriate drones for deployment as Low-Altitude-Platforms. The second is a coverage optimization that enables controlling drones hover locations. Both scenarios are focused on a surveillance system.

The projected growth of connected IoT devices is anticipated to be as many as 100 billion by 2025, ranging from smart devices in our pockets to industrial sensors strategically relaying information to each other in densely populated areas [2]. In order to account for the higher demand of traffic on telecommunications networks, UAV swarms could be utilized to extend coverage of existing networks and improve the QoS in hot-spot areas [3]. It is well known that the introduction of new cellular base station in an urban environment is no easy task, especially when the new base station is aimed at offering connectivity to users in temporary events, such as music concerts, cultural and sporting events, political rallies, etc., where traffic load can be greatly increased. Indeed, in such events, many users may suffer from high blocking probability. Also, in emergency events, such as forest fires, earthquakes, floods, etc., normal channels in neighbor base stations may not be sufficient to attend the high demand of people trying to communicate in these areas. Hence, implementing a new base station in these regions, where already base stations can handle the normal traffic, but not exceptional high traffic, may not be the best option.

In this paper, we focus primarily on evaluating practical hovering times of UAVs to be used in different applications, such as cellular systems and Wireless Sensor Networks (WSNs) to reduce overall energy consumption by temporarily using the UAV. Before a commercial implementation of this proposal, we need to know real and practical flying times that highly depend on weather conditions, flying patterns and commercial models of UAVs. As such, we first focus on evaluating hovering times of three widely available UAV models that can be used for these purposes. Note that the hovering time of UAVs is the most important parameter for the use of these devices in extending the coverage and capacity of ground wireless system like cellular systems and WSNs. Indeed, these hovering times represent the time that additional users will be served in case of high traffic loads or the distance that the data can be stored to be retrieved in a WSN scenario. As such, we only focus on this parameter to study the possibility of using UAVs as an alternative to reduce energy consumption.

However, the use of UAVs is not straightforward to reduce energy in wireless systems. For instance, the type of UAV, the flying pattern, the weather conditions, and the coverage area are some major factors that will impact the performance of the UAV. One important drone statistic used to classify performance, which unfortunately is often not reported consistently, is average flight time. This value is often reported at its optimal cruise speed in steady flight and optimal weather conditions, ultimately disregarding the other stages of flight (Takeoff, Hover, Landing) and the induced drag from atmospheric conditions. This paper will aim to report the average flight time of a "cheap", 'mid cost', and 'expensive' drone flying in 'bad', 'average', and 'good' conditions.

Based on these results we can assess if using commercial drones would enhance the wireless system, either increasing the capacity of the base station of a cellular system or reducing transmissions of nodes in a WSNs. To evaluate the flight time, we mathematically model the takeoff, landing and horizontal flying patterns of the drones. In order to validate the viability/profitability of going through the trouble of developing and maintaining UAVs, there have been various energy consumption models proposed, such as [12]. However, even when the key performance metrics were kept constant/consistent, these models produced different results ranging from 16–400 J/m (Joules per meter). The reason for this is that many papers consider simulation results or the use of very complex models that involve flying patterns that are very hard to replicate. Conversely, in our work we provide average flying times that clearly show the utility of these devices for different applications instead of focusing on the specific mechanical details of the UAV. Also, by showing the average flight time, the system administrator can calculate the number of UAVs needed to attend the cellular system with additional channels or the monitored area of the WSNs where the UAV can recollect data form the nodes.

The rest of the paper is organized as follows: In Sect. 2 we present the main parameters involved in the average flight times of the different commercial UAVs, then in Section we describe the simulation used to calculate such average times. Following this, in Sect. 4 we present the most relevant results, and we end the paper with our Conclusions.

2 System Model

In this section we explain in detail the system variables and main assumptions. In Table 1 we present the main parameters and variables of the UAV that are related to energy consumption, in other words, related to the flying operation of the device. All of these parameters should be considered for the theoretical models or simulations. However, this can lead to unattractable analytical models that may be too difficult to solve and in many cases are not feasible to know in advance, such as the parameters related to the weather.

Building on this, we opt for a simple model to introduce in our simulations with the aim of obtaining approximated hovering times of the UAV which represent the time that the UAV would enhance the capacity of the different systems.

Table 1. UAV main parameters related to energy consumption

Symbol	Description	Units
ρ	Air density (e.g., 1.225 kg/m^3 at 15 °C at sea level)	kg/m^3
g	Acceleration of gravity	m/s^2
v_i	Induced speed (the change in the speed of the air after it flows through an object)	m/s
v_a	Air speed (speed of drone relative to the air)	m/s
φ	Ratio of headwind to airspeed	*unitless*
v	Drone ground speed, so $v = (1 - \varphi)v_a$	m/s
d	Drone one-way travel distance for a single delivery trip	m
r	Lift-to-drag ratio	*unitless*
η	Battery and motor power transfer efficiency (from battery to propeller)	*unitless*
η_c	Battery charging efficiency	*unitless*
k	Index of the drone components: drone body = 1; drone battery = 2; payload (package) = 3	

(continued)

Table 1. *(continued)*

Symbol	Description	Units
C_{D_k}	Drag coefficient of drone component k	*unitless*
A_k	Projected area of drone component k	m^2
m_k	Mass of drone component k	*kg*
γ	Maximum depth of discharge of the battery	*unitless*
s_{batt}	Specific energy of the battery (energy capacity per kg)	J/kg
f	Safety factor to reserve energy en the battery for unusual conditions	*unitless*
R	Maximum one-way distance of drone travel per battery charge	m
P	Power required to maintain a steady drone flight	$Watt = J/s$
P_{avio}	Power required for all avionics on the drone (independent of drone motion)	$Watt = J/s$
n	Number of rotors for a rotocopter drone	*rotors*
N	Number of blades in one rotor for a rotocopter drone	*blades*
c	Blade chord length	m
c_d	Blade drag coefficient	*unitless*
ς	Area of the spinning blade disc of one rotor	m^2
α	Drone angle of attack	*radians*
Epm	Energy required for steady drone flight per unit distance	J/m

Although more complete models provide accurate results, our main goal in this work is to provide approximate average flight results that can be easily produced by simple numerical system simulations. As such, there is no need to consider many complex variables that may not be easy to find or use such as the angle of each individual rotor of the UAV or many different variables for the disturbances in the environment during the take-off and landing procedures, and so on and so forth.

In this regard, we believe that not considering these specific aspects would not change the conclusions of our work because we simply want to compare the performance of different drone models, by considering a simplified environment, i.e., by ignoring certain variables in all the different simulations would still give a valid comparison. Additionally, this has the great advantage of performing much faster simulations that also require less computational resources and would give preliminary performance metrics. For more detailed results, a completer and more accurate simulator that considers many more parameters can be used.

In Table 2 we show the mathematical expressions used to calculate the energy consumption of the UAV for different environmental conditions. These expressions are used by the simulator develop for this project.

Table 2. UAV main parameters related to energy consumption

Reference	Travel components	Thrust assumptions	Weather	Epm
D'Andrea (2014)	Horizontal	T = W/r	Wind	T = $\frac{(\frac{1}{1-\sigma})(\sum m*g)}{r*\eta}$ E = T × D
Hasini et al. (2007)	Hovering only (dorling)	T = W	Air density	P = $\frac{(\Sigma m*g)^{3/2}}{\sqrt{2*\pi*\rho*r^2}}$ E = P × t
Stolaroff et al. (2018) & Liu et al. (2017)	Horizontal, hover, vertical	T = W + D + L (angle)	Wind, air density	$\frac{T(V_a*\sin(\alpha)+V_i)}{V_a*\eta}$ where T = (our model)

Based on these expressions and parameters, we developed our own Monte Carlo simulator, where at each time increment, we follow the position of the drone, based on its trajectory and velocity to account for energy consumption. To this end, we consider that the drone must leave the monitored area to return to the base station with enough energy to reach the charging base and avoid malfunction due to lack of energy. In the following section, we provide more details regarding these issues.

3 Monte Carlo Simulation

Monte Carlo simulations are widely used to study the main dynamics of different systems. The main idea is to consider all possible variations in the state of the system at each time increment. In this case, the state of the system is given by the position of the drone which is affected by the thrust of it respective motors.

Also, since the objective of the drone is to visit the cellular system or WSN, we have to consider the position and coverage radius of the base station. Indeed, the drone will fly from the base station to the coverage radius around this base station.

For the simulator developed in this work, we consider different classes to select the different parameters of the system. For one part we have the base station class and for the other hand we have the drone and weather classes to select the parameters of the drones and parameters that affect the drone flight respectively. These classes are now explained in detail.

- **Wireless Sensor Network Class**

For this class the parameters that we consider for the simplified simulation are the following:

Parameters

- width: int = x boundary
- length: int = y boundary
- radius: int/float = cell radius
- nodes: list = waypoints
- BS: tuple = Base Station loc (x, y)
- C: tuple = WSN center loc (x, y)
- emergency = imp. Route to consider during emergency (i.e. natural disaster, public event, etc.)

With these variables we can calculate the boundaries of the cell in such a way that the drone will remain inside this area, leaving before the battery energy gets completely depleted.

The different activities that this class performs during the simulations are as follows.

Methods

- get_random_position()
- is_pos_in_boundary()
- is_pos_in_cell()

Our results will be based on a Simple Network, i.e., a single cell. However, we consider in a future work additional characteristics as detailed in Table 3.

Table 3. Characteristics of the cells.

	Characteristics	
Simple network	2D	1 cell
Standard network	2D + emergency routes	1–5 cells
Complex network	2D + emergency routes + obstacles	5–20 cells

Drone Class

The variables considered for the drones are the following:

Parameters

- name: str = for GUI reference
- position: obj = Position Object (x, y) that must be within WSN boundaries
- direction: int = Angle in Degrees (0 = North, 90 = East)
- network: obj = WSN Object
- battery: float = Capacity in mAh
- speed: int = Drone's speed relative to the ground in m/s

- weight: float = payload weight in kilograms
- L_D: float = Lift to Drag ratio of drone propellers (unitless)
- c: float = Drag coefficient of frame build
- A: float = Frontal surface area of frame design (m^2)

And the operations performed in this class are:
Methods

- get_drone_name()
- get_drone_direction()
- get_drone_position()
- get_drone_speed()
- set_drone_direction()
- set_drone_position()
- set_drone_speed()
- check_position() #WSN boundaries and radius
- update_position_and_clean()
- travel_to_loc()
- hover_at_loc()

3.1 Weather Class

Finally, for the weather class, the variables considered that can directly affect the flying operation of the drones are:
Parameters

- temp: int = Temperature in degrees Celsius.
- p: float = Air Density (at sea level is roughly range of 99–102 kPa or 25.6 kg/m^3)
- wind_S: float = wind speed in m/s
- wind_D: int = wind direction (N, S, W, E, NW, NE, etc. which corresponds to an angle in Degrees)
- Rain/Humidity = #Rain %, assuming x area is covered for x duration

And the operations performed in this class are:
Methods

- set_weather ()
- set_wind()
- random_wind() #Gusts that impact relative velocity of drone, Drag force calc not included

Some of these operations are not used for the results obtained in this paper for the sake of simplicity and to maintain the model in the more basic operations as possible but we mention it here to illustrate the capabilities of the proposed simulator.

4 Numerical Results

In this section. We show some of the most relevant results obtained from the Monte Carlo simulations for three commercial drones that could be used to recollect data in a WSN or to carry additional channels to increase the capacity in a cellular network. Specifically, we considered the characteristics of wight and propulsion of the DJJ Mini 2, DJJ MavicAir 2 and EVO II Pro drone models with the idea of considering a range of low end to high end commercial drones.

The parameters used to perform the different simulations are presented in the following Table, where the weigh and drag of the different nodes are specified. Also, we consider a simple network model, where no obstacles are present, and the drones follow a simple straight line trajectory. Although this may be a simple drone movement, it may be an accurate in many practical situations such as a WSN in a remote area, where the drone leaves the base station directly to recollect data form the sensors placed on site. Even if many trees can be in the way of the base station and the sensors, the drones can be capable of flying above the tree line, since they do not have to land near the sensors, instead, they can remain hovering over the nodes to retrieve the data. In the case of cellular networks, this may also be an accurate approximation since the additional capacity may be required in cases where many people have gathered for a specific event, such as a sportif match, a music concert or a cultural or political event. In all these cases, the drone does not have to follow many complex trajectories, since it just has to hover the crowd and not travel throughout the cellular cell. For example, the base station of the drone can be placed on the stadium where the event is taking place. In this case, it leaves, hovers over a certain section of the stadium, where no obstacles are present and then returns to the base station. Then, a simple straight line trajectory is more than enough to provide additional channels (Table 4).

Table 4. Simulation parameters

Drone 1	StandardDrone	DJJ_Mini_2	SimpleNetwork	2250	15	.250	.75	.82	.016
Drone 2	StandardDrone	DJJ_MavicAir_2	SimpleNetwork	3500	15	.570	.75	.82	.0195
Drone 3	StandardDrone	EVO II Pro	SimpleNetwork	7100	15	1.174	.75	.82	.195

In Fig. 1, we present the average flight time of the three commercial models of the drones. These results were obtained through exhaustive simulations of the previously described simulator. We can see that, as expected, as the wight of the drones increases, the flying times decreases. However, we now have an approximation of this average flying times, which in turns is related to the time that the drone will serve the wireless system. Hence, these results will give a clear idea of the times that users will experience higher capacity or the times that data form the sensors can be retrieved. Then, the system administrator can consider these specific times in the design.

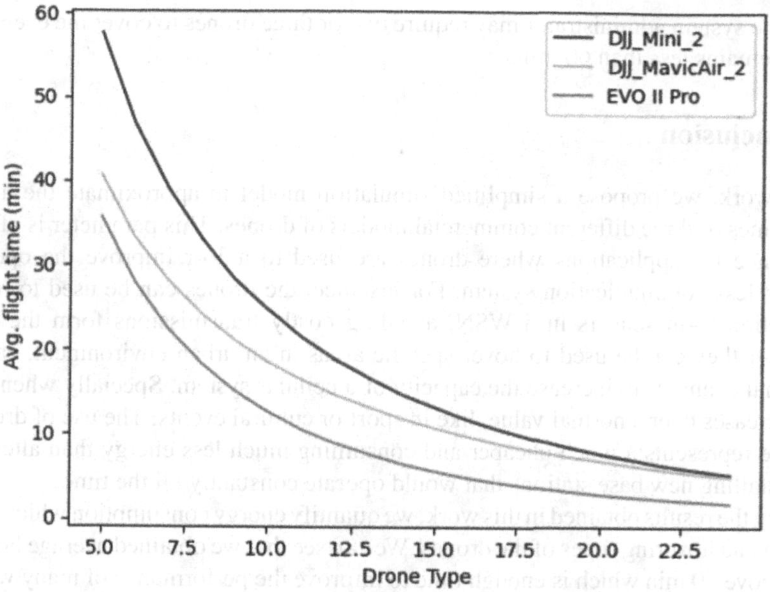

Fig. 1. Minimum flight time for different wight of the drones (min)

In Fig. 2, we show the average hovering times, which clearly consumes different amounts of energy than a horizontal flying motion. Since drones will serve the users in a cellular system or retrieve data form sensor nodes in a WSN, the drone will spend most of the time hovering a certain zone. For instance, we can see that the DJJ_Mini_2 drone can remain hovering for over 160 min, which is enough time to serve different events when traffic load in the cellular system is expected to increase. For the case of the EVO

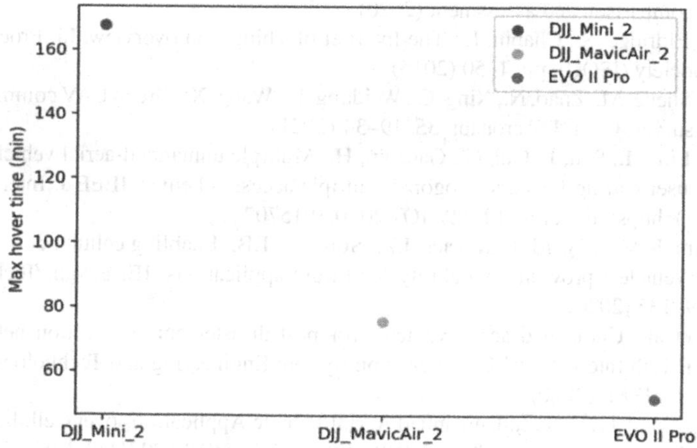

Fig. 2. Maximum hovering time for different drone models (min).

II Pro, the system administrator may require two or three drones to cover the event since it only remains less than 60 min.

5 Conclusion

In this work, we propose a simplified simulation model to approximate the average flying times of three different commercial models of drones. This parameter is of major importance for applications where drones are used to aid or improve the operation of a wireless communication system. For instance, the drones can be used to retrieve information form sensors in a WSN, avoiding costly transmissions form the sensor nodes. Or they can be used to hover specific areas in an urban environment, carrying additional channels to increase the capacity of a cellular system. Specially when traffic load increases over a normal value, like in sport or cultural events. The use of drones in this case represents a much cheaper and consuming much less energy than alternative than installing new base stations that would operate constantly all the time.

From the results obtained in this work, we quantify energy consumption which results in flying and hovering times of the drones. We can see that we obtained average hovering times above 60 min which is enough time to improve the performance of many wireless systems. As such, these results can be considered in the design of future communication systems, using a more detailed simulation for more accurate results.

In a future work, we will consider different drone trajectories, more weather related aspects such as wind and rain, and also commercial drones specifically conceived for cellular systems and not just for the general public. These simulations will certainly render more accurate results, although the complexity and running times will be increased.

References.

1. Zhang, J., Campbell, J., Sweeney, D., Hupman, A.: energy consumption models for delivery drones: a comparison and assessment (2020)
2. Rose, K., Eldridge, S., Chapin, L.: The Internet of Things: an overview. In: Proceedings of Internet Society (ISOC), pp. 1–50 (2015)
3. Jiang, X., Sheng, M., Zhao, N., Xing, C., Weidang, L., Wang, X.: Green UAV communications for 6G: a survey. Chin. J. Aeronaut. **35**, 19–34 (2021)
4. Wang, J., Liu, M., Sun, J., Gui, G., Gacanin, H.: Multiple unmanned-aerial vehicles deployment and user pairing for nonorthogonal multiple access schemes. IEEE J. Internet Things **8**(3) (2021). https://doi.org/10.1109/JIOT.2020.3015702
5. de Amorim, R.M., Wigard, J., Kovacs, I.Z., Sorense, T.B.: Enabling cellular communication for aerial vehicles: providing reliability for future applications. IEEE Veh. Technol. Mag. **15**(2), 129–135 (2020)
6. Saif, A., et al.: Unmanned aerial vehicles for post-disaster communication networks. In: 2020 IEEE 10th International Conference on System Engineering and Technology (ICSET), pp. 273–277. IEEE (2020)
7. Zhang, H., Song, L., Han, Z.: Unmanned Aerial Vehicle Applications over Cellular Networks for 5G and Beyond. Springer, Cham (2020). https://doi.org/10.1007/978-3-030-33039-2
8. Marojevic, V., et al.: Advanced wireless for unmanned aerial systems: 5G standardization, research challenges, and AERPAW architecture. IEEE Veh. Technol. Mag. **15**(2), 22–30 (2020)

9. Goudarzi, S., et al.: Employing unmanned aerial vehicles for improving handoff using cooperative game theory. IEEE Trans. Aerosp. Electron. Syst. **57**(2), 776–794 (2020)
10. Mohamadi, H., Kara, N., Lagha, M.: Efficient algorithms for decision making and coverage deployment of connected multi-low-altitude platforms. Expert Syst. Appl. **184**, 115529 (2021)
11. Stolaroff, J.K., Samaras, C., O'Neill, E.R., Lubers, A., Mitchell, A.S., Ceperley, D.: Energy use and life cycle greenhouse gas emissions of drones for commercial package delivery. Nat. Commun. **9**(1), 409 (2018)
12. D'Andrea, R.: Guest editorial can drones deliver? IEEE Trans. Autom. Sci. Eng. **11**(3), 647–648 (2014)

Validation of Security Variables for Audits in Wireless Wi-Fi Networks

Lorena Galeazzi[1,2](✉), Camilo Garrido[1], and Cristian Barría[1]

[1] Universidad Mayor, Manuel Montt 367, Santiago, Chile
{lorena.galeazzi,Cristian.barria}@umayor.cl,
lorenagaleazzi@unicauca.edu.co, Camilo.garrido@mayor.cl
[2] Universidad del Cauca, Calle 5#4-70, Popayán, Colombia

Abstract. Wi-Fi wireless networks are an integral part of everyday life and as such security, the protection of these networks according to their evolution over time has been a constant challenge due to their use and the information that is transmitted through it and changes in the purpose of their use and the current needs of electronic devices [1].

Currently, there are several sources of documentation that aim to guide both designers of Wi-Fi wireless networks and security managers who must perform audits to networks, and consequently with the need to incorporate the principle of defense in depth. This study presents an experimental review [2] to validate established security variables to measure their effects and obtain results on how these multivariables [3] relate to each other and affect the gap in the results of an information security audit.

Keywords: Security · Wireless networks · Variables validation

1 Introduction

The security of wireless networks has had a substantial advance caused by the magnitude of its use and its different purposes, with this arises the need to increase the protection and management to counteract threats [1].

Nowadays, there are different and varied sources of information to be able to perform a security audit in wireless Wi-Fi networks [4–7], therefore, a security auditor needs to acquire information from the associated literature, current regulations, experience, and expertise in the different areas related to information security [8].

The evolution of wireless networks because of their successful use has also marked a trend in the number of associated attacks, hence several studies have focused on analyzing types of attacks, types of encryptions and their corresponding processes and vulnerabilities. This study aims to validate the variables established in the research "Conceptual model of security variables in Wi-Fi wireless networks: Review" [9], adding other obtained variables in this review, to fill the gap in studies that delve into the effects that occur in a real scenario to measure different parameters at the moment of a malicious attack.

The methodology used to carry out the research is a Meta-Analysis type review [2], allowing to measure the effects and analyze the variables applied in the experiment.

M. F. Mata-Rivera et al. (Eds.): WITCOM 2022, CCIS 1659, pp. 422–433, 2022.
https://doi.org/10.1007/978-3-031-18082-8_28

2 Problem Statement

Currently, there is a lack of studies that consolidate and validate the different security variables in Wi-Fi wireless networks, generating a gap in the audits for this technology. Similarly, understanding how these multivariables [3] are related and integrated would allow to identify which effects associated with an attack influence the results of the attack.

3 Research Contribution

The contribution of the research lies in the validation and integration of variables that were established in the "Conceptual model of security variables in Wi-Fi wireless networks: Review" [9] and the new ones identified in this study.

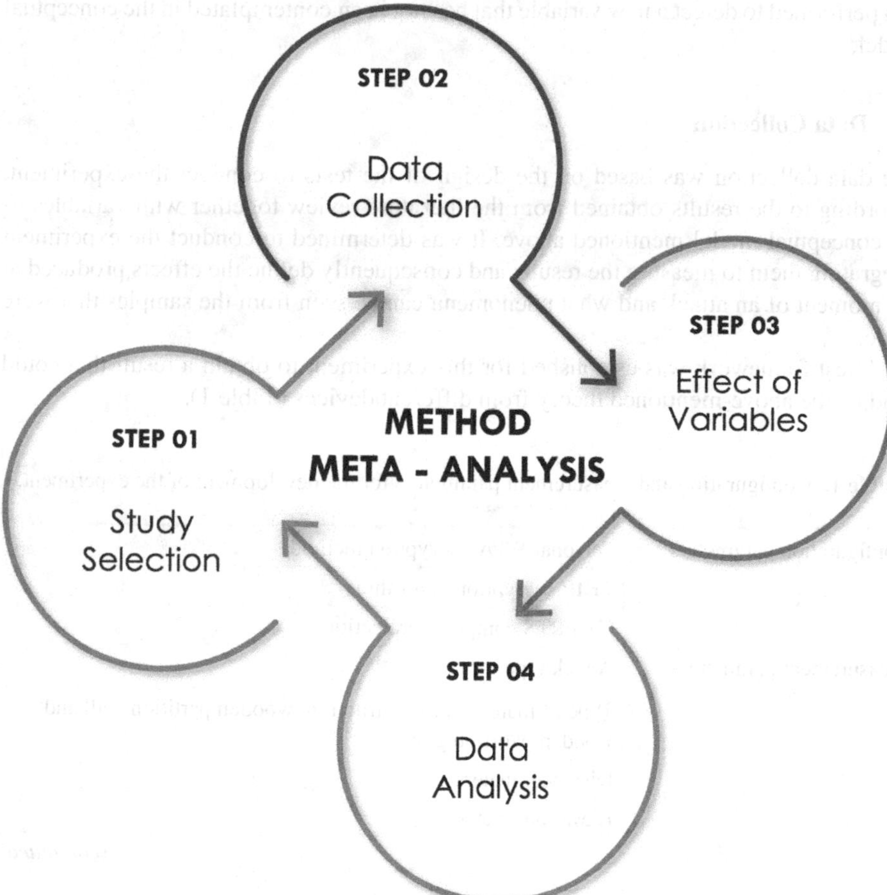

Fig. 1. A figure caption shows the steps of the methodology used. (Own source)

4 Method

The research method used in this study is a Meta-Analyses type review [2]. It includes specific techniques to measure its standard effects, considering that the nature of the primary sources is empirical, quantitative, therefore it is possible to calculate more accurate estimates on effects and phenomena derived from studies allowing to draw significant inferences, which are divided into four phases as shown in the below Fig. 1.

4.1 Studies Selection

The first stage addresses a review aimed to determine whether there are studies related to security in wireless Wi-Fi networks, seeking to establish a concrete scenario of variables to integrate them and obtain results that can help in a network audit. So, the variables established in the "Conceptual model of security variables in Wi-Fi wireless networks" [5] were considered and besides, literature review of sources updated from 2018 to 2022 was performed to detect a new variable that has not been contemplated in the conceptual model.

4.2 Data Collection

The data collection was based on the design of the tests to conduct the experiment, according to the results obtained from the literature review together with variables of the conceptual model mentioned above. It was determined to conduct the experiment integrating them to measure the results and consequently define the effects produced at the moment of an attack and what phenomena can be seen from the samples that were made.

A test framework was established for this experiment to obtain a result that could validate the above-mentioned theory from different devices (Table 1).

Table 1. Configuration and measurement parameters for the development of the experiment.

Configuration parameters	Personal WPA encryption method
	TKIP encryption algorithm
	CTS/RTS computer protection
Measurement parameters	Attack type
	Type of material of construction: wooden partition wall and wooden partition glass
	Distance: meters
	Elevation: meters

(*continued*)

Table 1. (*continued*)

	Time: seconds
Handshake capture tool	PineApple Wifite tool – Kali Linux
Access point	TP-Link - TL-WR802N Linksys - WRT610N Ruckus - R550 - unleashed (autonomous) Aruba - AP-303 - IAP (autonomous)

The measurement parameters were established to perform the tests in the same scenario.

To carry out the experiment, it was determined to use the "Handshake capture" as the measurement parameter "attack type", since this is a main phase for most of the existing attack types for Wi-Fi wireless networks, according to the following Fig. 2.

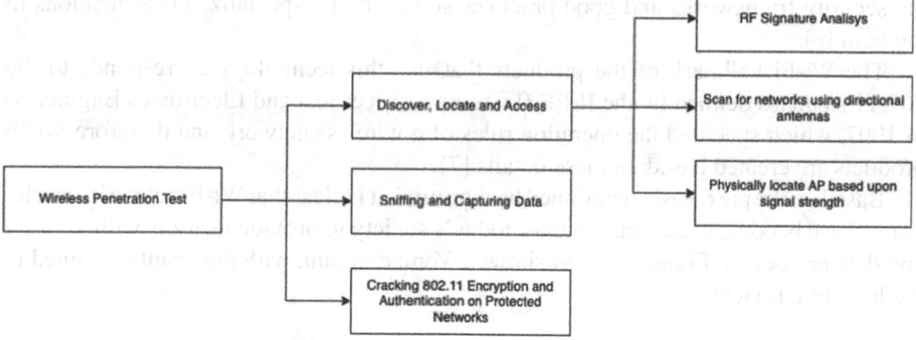

Fig. 2. A figure caption shows the steps for the measurement parameters. (Own source)

4.3 Variable Effects

According to what was established in the data collection, the variable integration experiment was carried out within a test framework to compare the results obtained for the following analysis.

4.4 Data Analysis

To perform the analysis of the data obtained, the results of the experiment were taken and compared in their totality under the same parameters according to the test framework, it is worth mentioning that they were correlated with the intention of detecting all the phenomena that were produced by the integration of the measured variables.

5 Results

The results obtained were divided in two parts, the first one includes variables established after the review and the second, the results obtained in the experiment.

5.1 Literature Review Results

In today's digital world it is complex to interact if it is not through wireless technologies in different areas, such as Wi-Fi, Bluetooth, radio, among others. An example of this are smartphones devices that are not prepared for wired connection, all their functions are based on wireless communication. Other devices that follow the same trend are wearable devices (watches, GPS, headphones, etc.), which have had a great boom due to their practicality [10].

In addition, the growing need to share on social networks and not to be absent from work has contributed to increase the usage of this type of technology. All this generates an overexposure of data producing security breaches, which are necessary to consider. For this reason, it is necessary to have a multi-standard guide of security variables, selected, analyzed, and validated. These variables will be obtained considering the security frameworks and good practices suggested by specialized organizations in the field [6].

The Wi-Fi hallmark of the products that use this technology corresponds to the 802.11 standard defined by the IEEE (Institute of Electrical and Electronics Engineers) in 1997, which specified the operation rules of a wireless network and therefore Wi-Fi products are created based on these details [7].

Based on the previously mentioned background, it is clear that Wi-Fi network security issues have become a relevant topic for today's society to provide its users with security and data protection. Figure 3 below shows a Venn diagram, with the results obtained in the literature review.

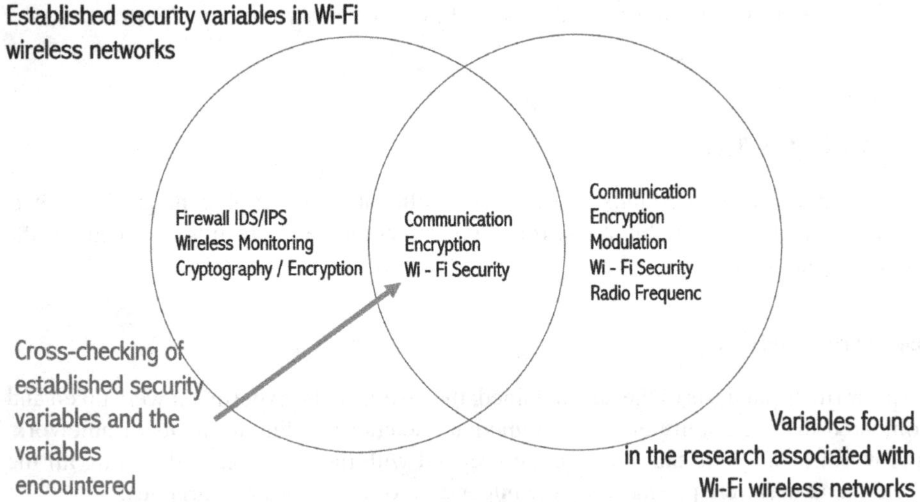

Fig. 3. A figure caption shows Venn diagram with variables established for the empirical tests. (Own source)

5.2 Experiment Results

The variables obtained from the literature in the global review are validated through the Wireless equipment of the home type and Enterprise mode. As a result of the review, it is possible to visualize four families of variables that are deployed by all these devices and based on this, the tests for the experiment are constructed (Fig. 4).

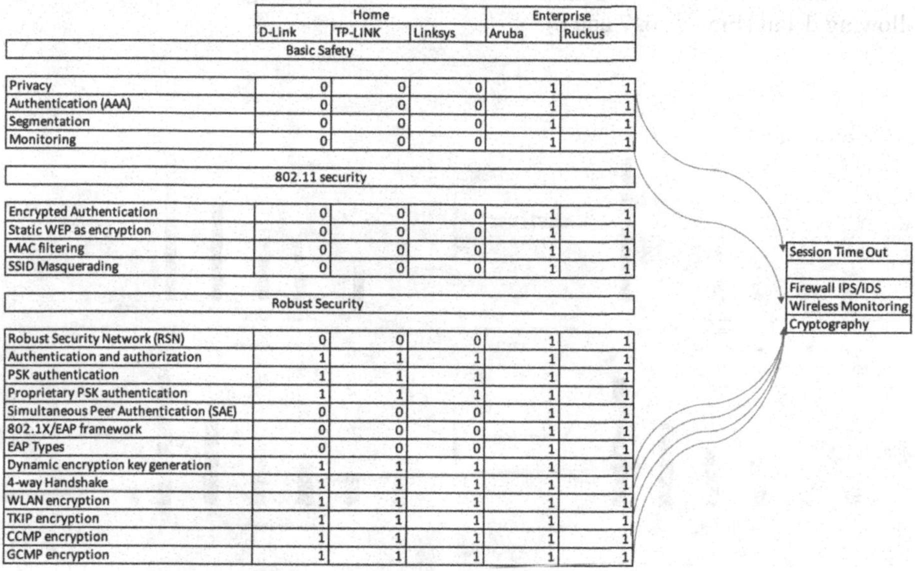

	Home			Enterprise	
	D-Link	TP-LINK	Linksys	Aruba	Ruckus
Basic Safety					
Privacy	0	0	0	1	1
Authentication (AAA)	0	0	0	1	1
Segmentation	0	0	0	1	1
Monitoring	0	0	0	1	1
802.11 security					
Encrypted Authentication	0	0	0	1	1
Static WEP as encryption	0	0	0	1	1
MAC filtering	0	0	0	1	1
SSID Masquerading	0	0	0	1	1
Robust Security					
Robust Security Network (RSN)	0	0	0	1	1
Authentication and authorization	1	1	1	1	1
PSK authentication	1	1	1	1	1
Proprietary PSK authentication	1	1	1	1	1
Simultaneous Peer Authentication (SAE)	0	0	0	1	1
802.1X/EAP framework	0	0	0	1	1
EAP Types	0	0	0	1	1
Dynamic encryption key generation	1	1	1	1	1
4-way Handshake	1	1	1	1	1
WLAN encryption	1	1	1	1	1
TKIP encryption	1	1	1	1	1
CCMP encryption	1	1	1	1	1
GCMP encryption	1	1	1	1	1

Fig. 4. A figure caption shows description of variables based on home and enterprise type equipment. (Own source)

5.2.1 Test Results with PineApple

For the results of automatic type device for the development of pentesting attacks, the PineApple Mark VII device from Hak5 [8] was used to obtain the behavior of Wi-Fi wireless technology devices, such as Linksys, TP-Link, Ruckus Wireless and Aruba Network. Consequently, two types of tests were determined based on their configurations, as detailed below.

Test No. 1

- WPA Personal Encryption Method
- TKIP Encryption Algorithm
- Communication Protection CTS/RTS off

Test No. 2

- WPA2 Personal Encryption Method
- AES Encryption Algorithm
- Communication Protection CTS/RTS on

The results of tests 1 and 2 are shown in the following diagrams, according to the following detail (Figs. 5, 6, 7 and 8):

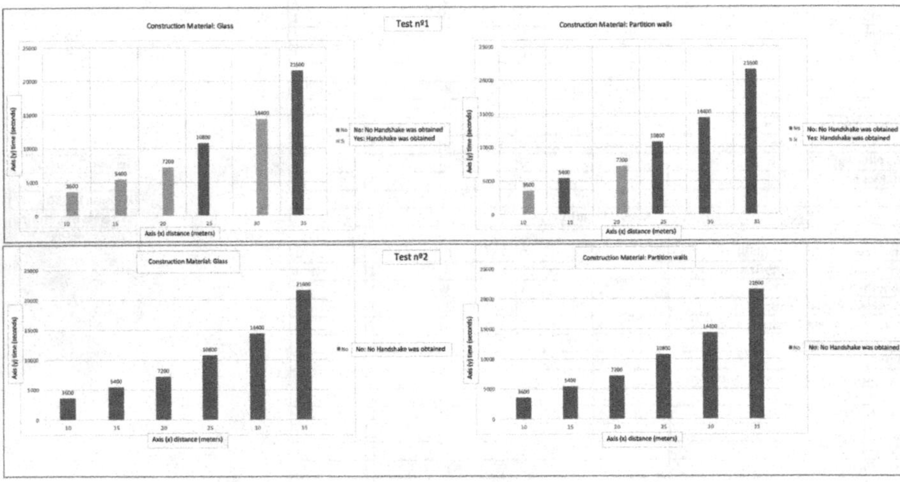

Fig. 5. The graphs show the results obtained from the test performed on the Linksys Wi-fi wireless device with PineApple. (Own source)

5.2.2 Test Results with Kali Linux – WiFite Tool

For the results of a manual device for the development of pentesting attacks, the attack tool available in the Kali Linux operating system [9] was used to audit wireless networks as a result to obtain the behavior of Wi-Fi wireless technology devices, such as Linksys, TP-Link, Ruckus Wireless and Aruba Network. Consequently, same as with PineApple, two types of tests were determined, based on their configurations, as detailed below.

Test No. 1

- WPA Personal Encryption Method
- TKIP Encryption Algorithm
- Communication Protection CTS/RTS off

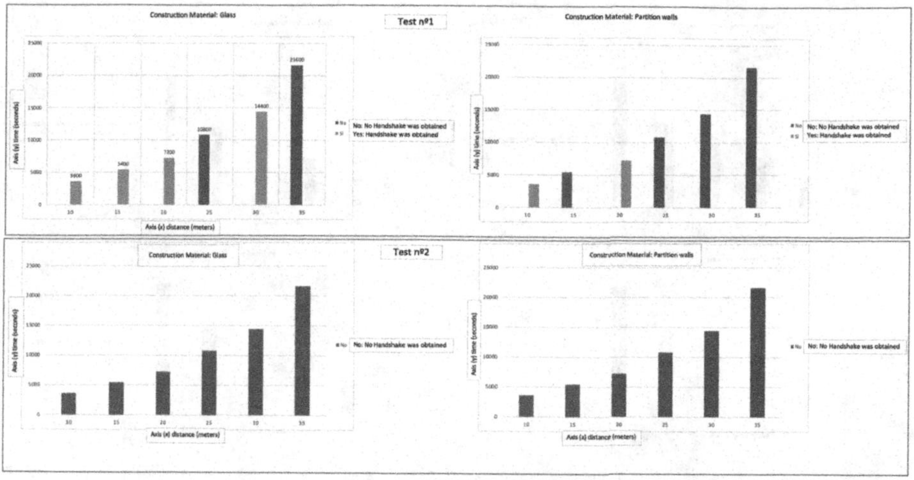

Fig. 6. The graphs show the results obtained from the test performed on the TP-Link Wi-fi wireless device with PineApple. (Own source)

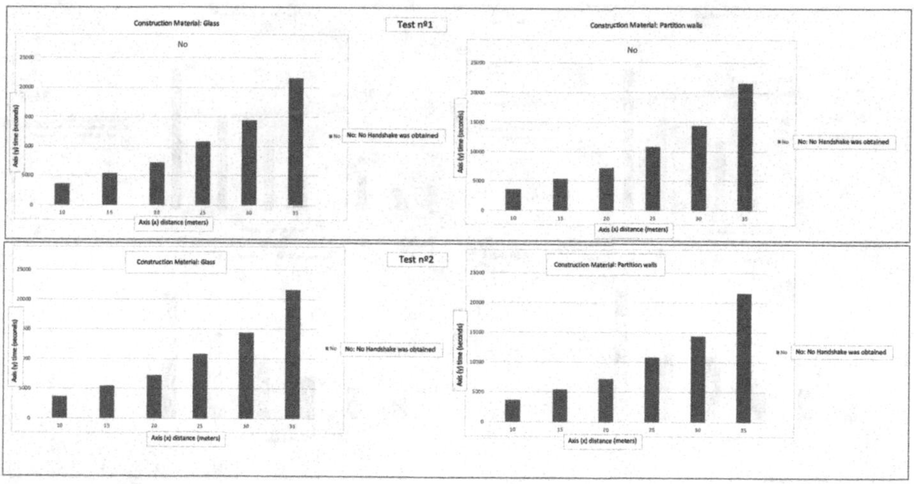

Fig. 7. The graphs show the results obtained from the test performed on the Ruckus wireless device with PineApple. (Own source)

Test No. 2

- WPA2 Personal Encryption Method
- AES Encryption Algorithm
- Communication Protection CTS/RTS on (Figs. 9, 10, 11 and 12)

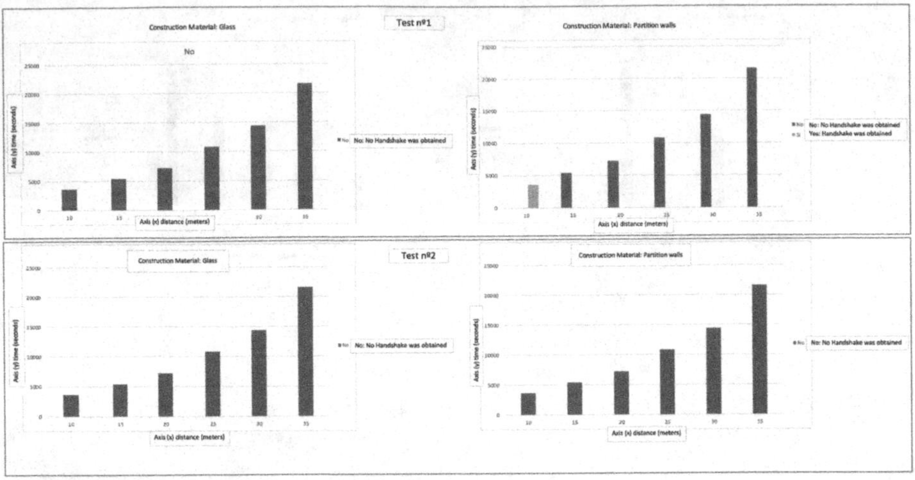

Fig. 8. The graphs show the results obtained from the test performed on the Aruba Networks Wireless device with PineApple. (Own source)

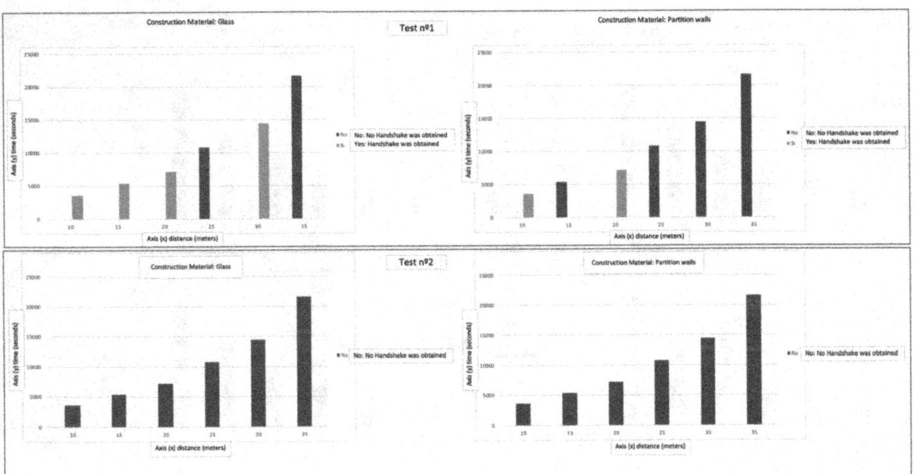

Fig. 9. The graphs show the results obtained from the test performed on the Linksys Wi-fi wireless device Wifite tool. (Own source)

5.2.3 Analysis of Results

In the tests with the PineApple device in contrast to the Wifite tools software, it has been shown that there are differences according to the following detail:

The amount of security features that a device has can determine a security breach, consequently, the home type devices are more exposed to threats than one Enterprise, identifying the difference according to successful results in relation to the "handshake" capture obtained.

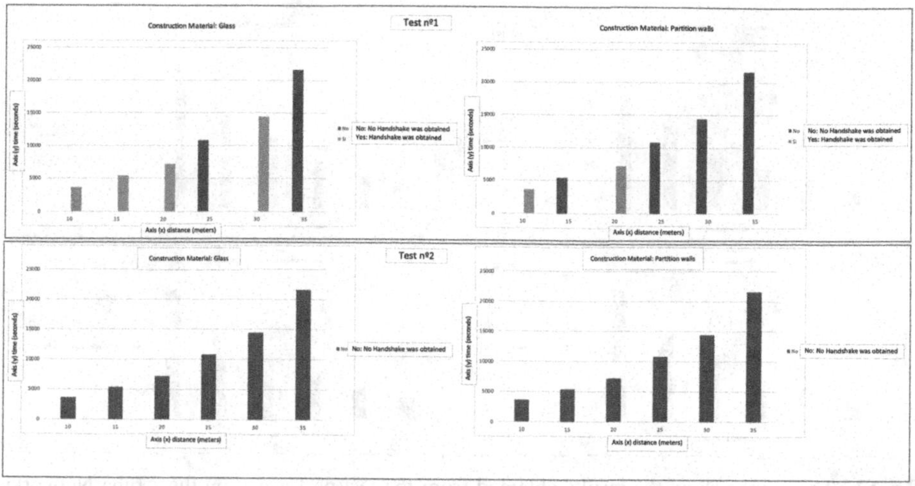

Fig. 10. The graphs show the results obtained from the test performed on the TP-Link Wi-fi wireless device Wifite tool. (Own source)

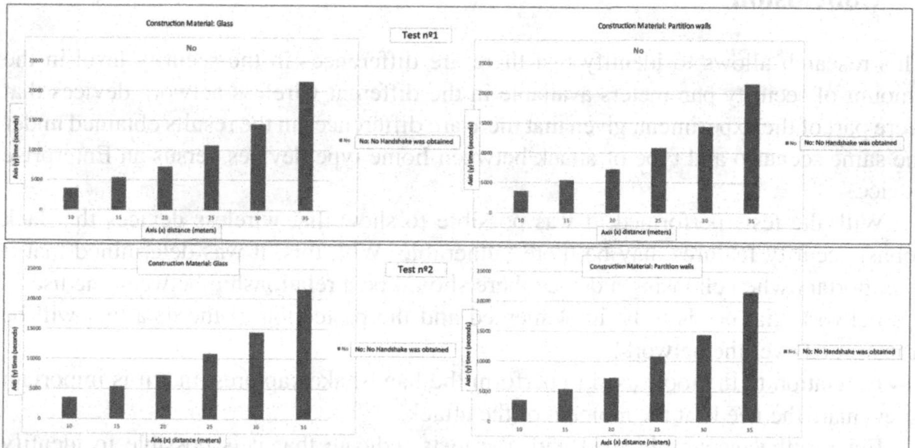

Fig. 11. The graphs show the results obtained from the test performed on the Ruckus wireless device Wifite tool. (Own source)

The graphs show the results obtained with the two tests performed in the same scenario, measurement parameters and configuration, where it is possible to show that there is a direct relationship between time (y-axis) and distance (x-axis), identifying that the greater the distance, the longer it takes to obtain a handshake capture.

According to the different tests carried out on the equipment with different attack tools, it could be seen that the handshake captures were more successful with PineApple.

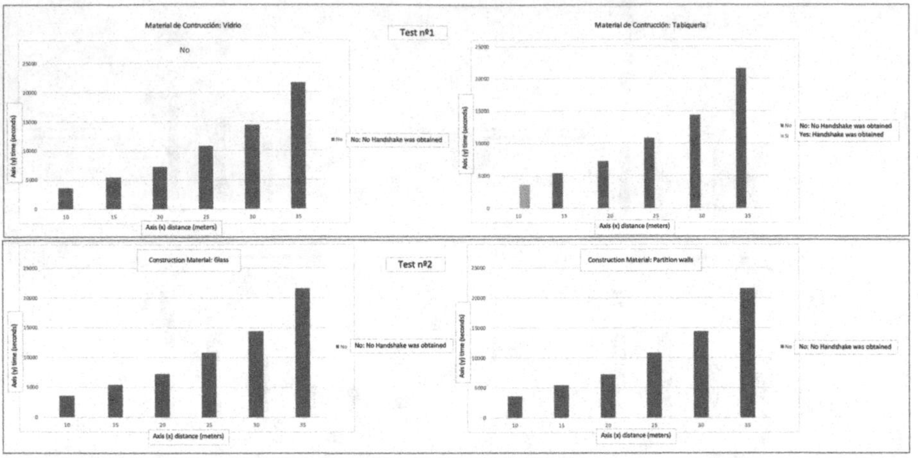

Fig. 12. The graphs show the results obtained from the test performed on the Aruba Networks Wireless device with Wifite tool. (Own source)

6 Conclusion

This research allows to identify that there are differences in the security level in the amount of security parameters available in the different wireless network devices that were part of the experiment, given that there are differences in the results obtained under the same scenario and type of attack between home type devices versus an Enterprise device.

With the tests performed, it was possible to show that wireless devices that lack robust security features may be more vulnerable. With this, it was determined that it is important when choosing a device there should be a relationship between the use of the network that needs to be implemented and the protection of the data that will be transmitted over the network.

In relation to the tools used to perform the handshake captures, that it is important to evaluate the needs at the moment of the attack.

Finally, the results obtained with the tests indicate that it is possible to identify security gaps with the variables that were identified in the literature review in contrast to the experiment, therefore, the importance of each of them and their integration affect the results of an audit of wireless Wi-Fi networks, consequently, it was possible to validate the security variables for an audit of wireless Wi-Fi networks.

7 Future Work

For future work, it is recommended to extend the tests with more context variables to identify other effects related to the behavior in the integration of a greater number of variables, which are part of the connectivity in Wi-Fi wireless technology.

References

1. WiFi Alliance. https://www.wi-fi.org/who-we-are. Accessed 01 June 2022
2. Paré, G., Trudel, M., Jaana, M., Kitsiou, S.: Synthesizing information systems knowledge: a typology of literature reviews. Inf. Manag. **52**(2), 183–199 (2014)
3. Barría, C., David, C., Galeazzi, L., Acuña, A.: Proposal of a multi-standard model for measuring maturity business levels with reference to information security standards and controls. In: 8th International Conference on computers Communications and Control, ICCCC 2020, Romanian, Oradea (2020)
4. IEEE. https://standards.ieee.org/. Accessed 02 June 2022
5. ISO. https://www.iso.org/about-us.html. Accessed 02 June 2022
6. NIST. https://www.nist.gov/800-53. Accessed 02 June 2022
7. CIS. https://www.cisecurity.org/about-us/. Accessed 02 June 2022
8. Ávalos, L.G., Huidobro, C.B., Hurtado, J.A.: A review of the security information controls in wireless networks Wi-Fi. In: Mata-Rivera, M.F., Zagal-Flores, R., Barria-Huidobro, C. (eds.) WITCOM 2020. CCIS, vol. 1280, pp. 420–427. Springer, Cham (2020). https://doi.org/10.1007/978-3-030-62554-2_30
9. Galeazzi, L., Barría, C., Hurtado, J.: Conceptual model of security variables in Wi-Fi wireless networks: review. In: Latifi, S. (ed.) ITNG 2021 18th International Conference on Information Technology-New Generations. AISC, vol. 1346, pp. 59–67. Springer, Cham (2021). https://doi.org/10.1007/978-3-030-70416-2_8
10. INCIBE, 14 May 2019. http://www.incibe.es/sites/default/files/contenidos/guias/doc/guia-de-seguridad-en-redes-wifi.pdf
11. IEEE. https://ieeexplore.ieee.org/browse/standards/get-program/page/series?id=68. Accessed 21 June 2022
12. HAK5. https://shop.hak5.org/products/wifi-pineapple. Accessed 10 June 2022
13. KALI. https://www.kali.org/tools/wifite. Accessed 01 June 2022
14. DATATRACKER. https://datatracker.ietf.org/doc/html/rfc8110. Accessed 01 June 2022

Integration of a Virtual Object on Formative Object Oriented Programming for the Emavi Military Aviation School Cadets

Clara Lucia Burbano González[1(✉)], Alex Torres[2(✉)], Carlos Andrés Parra Guzmán[1(✉)], and Natalia Hernández Moreno[1(✉)]

[1] Escuela Militar de Aviación EMAVI, Santiago de Cali, Colombia
{clara.burbano,caparrag,nhernandezm}@emavi.edu.co
[2] Corporación Universitaria Comfacauca – Unicomfacauca, Popayán, Colombia
atorres@unicomfacauca.edu.co

Abstract. Learning and acquiring a knowledge base on object-oriented programming (OOP), is an undertaking that future computer engineers must embrace due to the increasing complexity of the apposition of Information and Communication Resources (ICR) as per the quotidian activities of contemporary societies, thus begetting the need to construct knowledge in a more effective and direct way that guarantees the tutelage of the future Colombian Air Force officers in the computer science field. Throughout the elaboration of the article, the outcome of said formation was observed by means of an experimental research under a coed (qualitative-quantitative) method wherein the lore of Objectoriented Programming (OOP) was gauged by the development of the Virtual Object (VO) which complied with the knowledge accessibility mission, fostering decentralized learning aimed towards the formation of competencies of the teaching staff, athwart the implementation of Smart Learning as a primordial factor in the creation of an oriented Virtual Object.

Keywords: Object-oriented programming · Pedagogical usability · Virtual object · Components · Cadets · Military

1 Introduction

The current article exhibits the results obtained in the intervention of the cadets at the EMAVI with aims to develop technological knowledge competencies that promote a Smart Learning approach in the programming foundations II subject with a view to actuate such knowledge in today's society, allowing for technology-based feedback and enactment of technological resources that enable the implementation of the flagship model that characterizes the backbone of the educational futurity of the Colombian Air Force officers. Stemming from this perspective, it is purported that the contribution to the learning process and betterment of computer science skills and Computational Thought in the precinct of Object-oriented Programming (OOP) is established. In this manner, it is therefore necessary to erect an Information and Communication Technology resource

M. F. Mata-Rivera et al. (Eds.): WITCOM 2022, CCIS 1659, pp. 434–450, 2022.
https://doi.org/10.1007/978-3-031-18082-8_29

(ICT) such as the Virtual Object (VO), whose intent is to furnish the development of a technological tool for the assessment of academic themes, such as: methods, attributes, categories, abstraction, encapsulation, modularity, legacy and polymorphisms, giving rise to the need for the creation of instructive material that enhances the existing pedagogical experience in the virtual classroom, with regards to the COVID-19 contingency, as well as the structure of an on-site learning model.

In light of the sanitary crisis spawned by the COVID-19 and its financial backlash, Colombia finds itself in the face of multiple unprecedented challenges in the modern history of the country in terms of magnitude and complexity. On one hand, the pandemic has evidenced the high exposure and vulnerability of the country with respect to both domestic and foreign shocks. Conversely, a new opportunity looms in the consolidation of the country by means of economic, social and institutional changes that confer a solid medium-term growth, that proves inclusive and sustainable amidst climate alterations. The aforementioned challenges brought about by the COVID-19 are duly analyzed in the fiscal, foreign, corporate and social forefronts, wherein the country's vulnerabilities are depicted. By the same token, a slew of political proposals to tackle the crisis in order to retrieve a resilient financial stability in post-COVID-19 stances are observed. These proposals tend to instill political dialogues, both proactively and constructively [1].

For the purpose of developing Virtual Learning Objects (VLO), it was crucial to consider the following requirements: 1 Pedagogical usability, 2. Flexibility, 3. Portability and 4. Facility of reuse and interoperability. The foregoing practice allowed the students of computer engineering to have access to a virtual tool that would aid them in the burgeoning of their competencies and the unlocking of their achievements as regards the programming foundations II subject, emphasizing on basic concepts of Object- oriented Programming (OOP) in the way of reviewing its algorithmic structures, cycles and arrangements. Though it was indeed arduous to draw on measurements aimed at the processes of theme units, it was feasible to elaborate a user-friendly and comprehensive interface capable of appraising the subjects in question supported by the suggested activities.

2 Virtual Object in the Formation of the Programming Foundations Subject as Applied to the Military Aviation School Cadets

The upbringing of skills represented from a cognitive, communicative and technological viewpoint, is a strategy being adopted by the EMAVI to educate the second lieutenants (senior cadets) and cadets, bearing in reference the technological evolution which permeates the minds of the students in an adaptive and collaborative manner while evincing that in the construction of knowledge, there exist didactic schemes that contribute to the improvement of its quality and its transfer rather effectively, thus highlighting the Colombian Air Force's (FAC) institutional outlook in terms of bolstering the military capabilities of its personnel when it comes to the execution of their offices depending on the specialties acquired therein. During the delivery of lessons by the teachers of this subject, namely, those who belong to the academic group as well as to the computer engineering program, it becomes possible to bridge the gaps existing in the learning process of the students while maintaining a robust base to seize the concepts pertaining to the topics posed by the OOP subject, so as to be applied to reality through factual mechanisms and tools based on quotidian simulations unique to the Force without the need for memorization. The foregoing posture conceives the purposefulness of the endeavor in question in terms of the development of a Virtual Object (VO) that serves as a contraption for a greater facility in the acquisition of knowledge, enabling the refinement of the quality in the education of the cadet by dint of using smart tools in a systematic perusal of literature whilst identifying the breaches in conceptual categories, such as: a. computational thought; b. knowledge and learning technologies and c. development of a virtual object.

2.1 Development of Competences in the Cadets of the EMAVI Military Aviation School

The establishment of knowledge as currently proposed in a formative school centered in the endowment of competencies and abilities of the second lieutenants (senior cadets) and cadets for life, integrates knowledge and learning experiences required to complete their military and academic training, made easy by using didactic learning tools in such a way that the set of goals of the OOP subject is achieved. Similarly, a VO is devised specifically for the education and formation of second-year cadets in the computer engineering program. The Escuela Militar de Aviación "Marco Fidel Suárez" is located in Santiago de Cali, Valle del Cauca. It is a university which reckons on a "Peak" model-based internal regime constituted by five components, namely, **military, sports, aviation, professional development, and service.** Accordingly, the model allows the students to anchor solid values and moral tenets, as well as to optimize **skills and dexterities** targeting studies, innovation, design, and control of airships. The pursuance and projection of this model revolves around the interaction of the aforementioned five components. The second lieutenants (senior cadets) and cadets of the EMAVI military aviation school abide by a code of honor and integrity which is consequently reinforced by their daily activity, for the purpose of upholding these two aspects in their everyday endeavors. Thus are the leaders of air and space power in the Colombian Air Force bred [3].

> *In compliance with the institution's perspective, the efforts aimed thereof are directed towards the adoption of digital competencies which are deemed a strategy turned into tendency within this century's education framework supported by Technological Mediations. These are defined as "the existence of complex competencies founded in the development of a technological culture, isolated from technophilia, and conceived as the ability to seize and harness reality - changing opportunities"* [4].

The foregoing aspect is reflected under the concept of assimilation in which the modern student displays different needs from those of students in centuries past; they would be more concerned about memorizing information inputs, whereas today the focus relies mostly on developing lifelong competencies that enable the relationship between knowledge and learning experiences, which in turn, transform the classroom into an interactive and correlative space of information streams.

"Many critics of today have moved away from the premise dictating that a masterpiece can very well be unpopular, to the premise which decrees that if said masterpiece is not popular, it cannot be considered as such." [5]

The contemporary student must be aware that knowledge is directly acquired from the instructor of the OOP subject, who, in turn, must be prepared for any setback brought about by the brisk arrival of virtuality as ushered in by the onset of the pandemic. It became imperative to train cadets in the usage of technology in its broad sense, particularly in the implementation of academic platforms which, during the global lockdown, allowed for the continuity of educational processes by substituting an on-site classroom for a virtual one, in order to draw upon teacher-student interactions. The military aviation school incorporated different alternate forms of instruction to confect the students' knowledge while supplying its acquisition more specifically in the computer engineering program, thereby evincing the need to bring on a virtual object that would replace the whiteboard, notebooks and pencils, for a multiplicity of didactic, dynamic and formative activities, as well as synchronous and asynchronous tutoring to the academic process, thus instilling both students and teachers alike, to foster a technological approach to it. By the same token, the teachers devised a more effective tool to reach out to the students, motivating them to learn and consequently, to prepare for the future by employing state-of-the-art contraptions that facilitate the interaction in between and increase the acceptance of resources. This resulted in more comprehensible themes which would otherwise negatively impact the learning process, to the extent that it became considerably easier to recall knowledge based on context alone; "The teachers who work in collaborative cultures, foster and nourish a more positive attitude towards the acquisition of knowledge" [6]. Collaboration as a method in the propagation of lore, gains its power thanks to a series of transformations put forward by the utilization of an ecosystem wherein the students interact with one another whilst the instructor acts as a virtual promoter of knowledge, thus exercising Computational Thought so as to observe the different behaviors shown by the cadets in the face of software, as illustrated in Fig. 1. Computational Thought stages.

It is possible to evince the wide spectrum that encompasses the development of technological, cognitive and communicative competencies which are to be exerted by second-year cadets, for the mediated implementation of Computational Thought. The VO was used as a means to correlate the cognitive approach in this regard upon coming across an aspect that binds the search for a feasible solution in the different stages that comprise it. This competence suffuses in the student the need for a clear and concise output according to the object of analysis and its theme enclosed in a given moment, in such a way that representative aspects may be garnered. Even though the constitution of the competencies of a cadet may very well be rather complex provided the merger of his or her own academic and military experiences as subjected to an internal regime, this can be ultimately achieved thanks to the implementation of a strict structure designed to serve that precise purpose. This conviction is set out to establish a series of practices which optimize the students' perception of the enclosure of which he or she is a part, while promoting Mediated Learning rigged with didactic strategies which must abide by the "Peak" model-based education, through the boosting of these undertakings. This results in a more conducive military aviation school in the pursuit of becoming a cultural ecosystem by excellence which sets the stage for knowledge transition in an opportune and up-to-date manner in conformity with the needs of the institution.

"Education is the most powerful weapon you can excogitate to change the world".[7]

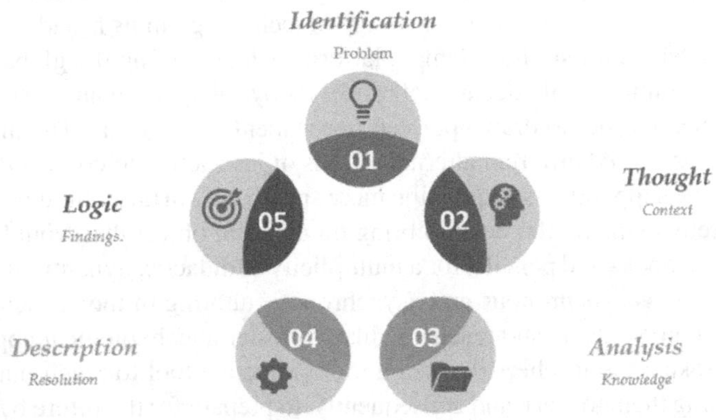

Fig. 1. Computational thought stages.

2.2 Smart Learning and the Relationship Among Competencies in the Up Bringing of the Cadets at the Marco Fidel Suárez Military Aviation School

The Smart Learning concept is thus far incomplete in terms of a clear and unified definition, which is also the case for similar concepts. Notwithstanding, we may still draw forth some interesting intakes:

Hwang (2014) and Scott and Benlamri (2010) deem smart learning to be an omnipresent, context-based concept. Gwak (2010) brought forward a similar approach to it as follows: first and foremost, it shall be centered around the students and the subject's content rather than around the arrangements. Secondly, it is out to be an effective type of learning adapted to the advanced IT infrastructure.

Technology plays a crucial role in the support of Smart Learning, but its scope should not be limited to the usage of smart devices.

Kim et al. (2013) esteems that a smart learning system that combines the advantages of an omnipresent social learning approach, is but a paradigm revolving around the student and the purpose it serves, instead of merely focusing on the utilization of smart devices.

Middleton (2015) also stipulates on the aspects directed towards the student and how the latter benefits from smart technology usage. Personal and smart technologies vie for allowing the students to partake in their learning process while bolstering their sense of independence in a more open and connective fashion, augmented by richer contexts. Moreover, others zero in on the traits of this smart learning system. MEST (2011) presented the smart learning characteristics defined as self-directed, motivated, adaptable, resourceful and technology-incorporated. Lee et al. (2014) propounded the smart learning characteristics to comprise both formal and informal learning, as well as social and collaborative knowledge input. This practice should also include tailored learning, focused and situated on content [8].

From the aforementioned vantage points as adopted at the EMAVI military aviation school, in the capacity of an institution for higher education, it projects itself to showcase leadership in learning and exchange practices, wherein experts of the air and space industry come together to bring forth the world's technological and scientific advancements. The learning environments are improved through the implementation of new scenarios, which pose technical and pedagogical challenges in their own right. As such, the roles played by teachers and students alike must be aligned with these scenarios while maintaining a steady focus on the attainment of the primary objectives as per the new, mediated, artificial intelligence-based technologies [9]. As it is the case for Latin America and the Caribbean, there are approximately 25 million tertiary education students affected by the pandemic; an average of 45% of the households count on a stable connection, whereas in rural areas, this coverage is significantly lower. Keeping into consideration that 40% of indigenous communities across the region are currently set on rural zones, there is a large quota of potentially excluded population bereft of access to any sort of education process. There are currently over 800 indigenous peoples which make up an estimate of 58 million members and citizens [10].

As a consequence, virtuality played a vital role in the education process of the cadets, seeing as how the institution adopted new virtual platform-based strategies such as Blackboard, Teams and Zoom alternatively to quell the negative impact that the pandemic had on the education of the future Colombian Air Force officers as a whole. Said strategies correlate to learning and awareness of technological tools usage, dubbed Smart Learning by many authors, defining it as that which can be carried out indistinctly from the conventional education model be it adaptive or contextualized in the transmission of knowledge and training of individuals [11]; thus, this formation can reach far more people, given the fact that it transcends the space-time barriers.

Thusly, people that have otherwise shown signs of struggle when engaging in constant contact with formative processes, because of commute problems, lack of time, a physical impairment, or living in the outskirts of their cities isolated from the outside world, are now able to have access to a wide variety of possibilities at their disposal to guarantee a continuous formation of knowledge.[11] Such formation is brought about by a VO, which facilitated the conveyance of content to the cadets belonging to the computer engineering program, offering theoretical and practical tools in search for the optimization of newly acquired knowledge in a traditional yet dynamic way. (Virtuality, Technology and Collaboration).

Smart learning boasts a number of instructive advantages in comparison to the Adaptive, Contextualized Learning approach, to model a homogeneous structure wherein individuals can be educated on high impact, up-to-date topics that are especially appealing to the student. A set of outreaches based on the learning models is exposed hereunder (Table 1):

Table 1. Comparison between Smart Learning and contextualized-adaptive learning

COMPARATIVE

ASPECT	INTELLIGENT	CONTEXTUALIZED	ADAPTIVE
Context-based experience	YES	YES	**YES**
Real-scenario positioning	YES	YES	**NO**
Individual content adoption	YES	NO	**NO**
Improved user's experience	YES	YES	**YES**
Feedback sourcing	YES	YES	**YES**
Interactive support offering	**YES**	**YES**	**YES**

The table above evinces the fact that Smart Learning is regarded as the complement of its contextualized-adaptive learning counterpart. This is so due to its integrating of the upturns that contribute to the processing of large-scale information, diminishing its complexity upon sharing said contents. In like manner, it optimizes design and implementation times within educational institutions; Smart Learning lends itself for seamless implementation on academic processes by making use of virtual education principles and the accommodation of knowledge towards new cognitive trends of development in today's society. Another important component of Smart Learning in its right setting, is that of Digital Competencies. These allow for the effective usage of technology, erecting virtual content such as classrooms, videos, podcasts, as well as activities and evaluations that pervade the knowledge of end users, ameliorating the learning quality and collaterally, sewing a netting of experiences aimed at the implementation of modern technologies and virtual training.

> *"Digital competencies rely on the utilization of computer terminals in order to retrieve, assess, store, produce, present and exchange information and partake in web-based collaborative networks."* [12]

At present, the progression of Digital Competencies allows students to improve on their quality of life by empowering them to fully and rapidly adapt to ever-growing digital environments, hence generating a continuous learning process wherein information can be tapped into and abstracted (conceptualization) upon the desired topic. Lastly, Technological Evolution is ushered in by interacting with a myriad of devices that channel the communication streamlines with the transmission of newly acquired knowledge as derived from different networks. The utilization and fostering of these competencies is a factor of utmost importance due to its capability to promote the decentralization of knowledge. In times past, this knowledge was imparted by the headmaster, who, in turn, was interpreted to be the most experienced and seasoned entity, whereas the student, was merely an attendee to the lectures delivered therein, and who would also take everything that came his way for granted in this regard; creating gaps and breaches in comprehension of the subject being discussed; lack of motivation or the use of highly advanced teaching method for knowledge transitioning, being the main culprit. The foregoing picture equates to modern education in the sense that it is seeking to fall back on technology in order to generate a proper environment for the transition of actualized information, wherein the browsing method is undoubtedly one that facilitates the acquisition, adoption and creation of new knowledge. It should be stressed therefore, that the expansion of competencies on behalf of the society is an innate trait of human beings, the unchanging wish to learn more and more about our surroundings. This is where the military aviation school fits in; bringing forth an auspicious environment for information transfer, striving for the connection of knowledge and experiences as lived out by the cadets in general, to motivate in them the urge to become better and better in terms of learning processes during their sojourn in the school, redirecting their studies towards the creation of new strategies seeking to optimize design and implementation times within the institution. References to universities and education benchmarks are presented in the following table (Table 2).

Table 2. Contributions to the 21st century University

Author	Contribution
[13]	Lab practices conceived of as didactic strategies, are set out to allow students to take in the manner in which knowledge is constructed within a scientific community
[14]	On this, asset education does not seek to form experts in a given field, but rather to trigger curiosity and a sense of belonging to a given group or place, drawing from the knowledge of its nearest counterparts, so as to make use of them in a sustainable guise
[15]	Two of the hurdles that hinder current higher education is the growing level of attrition and poor performance on behalf of the students. These are thought to be "difficulties that may be experienced by the apprentices throughout their formation process."
[16]	The "Peak" model-based approach permits the cadets in general to strengthen their knowledge base on moral values and tenets as the process unfolds. In addition, they are forged to leverage skills and dexterities as applied to the study, innovation, design and control of aircrafts. The application and projection of this model consists of and relies on the interaction of the five components
[17]	The cadets' formation process is guided by military instruction, founded in the moral values and principles of the Colombian Air Force, wherein both women and men have boosted and reinforced their poised character to impart knowledge

(*continued*)

Table 2. (*continued*)

Author	Contribution
[18]	The Academic Group reports directly to the school's Management Board, which is held accountable for the professional upbringing of second lieutenants (senior cadets) and cadets alike, internally organized by a series of subordinate divisions led by the Group. Command that lend support in the optimization in the functioning of the Academic Programs as well as the development of substantial research, teaching, international scope and welfare practices, as established in the Institutional Education Project

> "The members of the public force are bred inside a rigorous, ethical and moral framework, upholding the law and the observance of human rights and international humanitarian law." [19]

In accordance with the constitutional writ, the public force in Colombia is instituted to protect the life, honor and freedom of each and every citizen dwelling within our national territory. In order to see this pact through, the women and men that constitute our military and police forces have submitted to a priceless sacrifice to stand as a bulwark around Colombia, and by reason, the National Defense Ministry vows to look after their well-being and formation [20]. In compliance with the foregoing statements, the Colombian Air Force purports to mold future airspace leaders, this is why it infuses such traits of character in their formation as put forward by the extant Proyecto Génesis (Genesis Project) normativity, recently conflated to the EMAVI.

2.3 Computational Thought as a Key Component in the Formation, Usability, and Adoption of Knowledge

"Man discovers himself when faced with an obstacle" [21]. Recently, desktop computers b came an essential asset for the industry in general and for the daily activities and ventures of each individual. In the 90s, the might of personal computers skyrocketed exponentially. Only those with a vision towards the future, conceited the influence that computers would have on society. Technology development has made way for mobile devices to match the capacities of regular computers, being able to communicate with one another via the Internet. Consequently, we live in an era of ubiquitous computing, since these devices are accessible to just about anyone. In our daily lives and professional undertakings, we rely on both software and hardware for their completion. On one hand, we vastly ignore the internal workings of these gadgets and how they came to be. Onthe other hand, if we did have the knowledge in this regard, the possibilities for innovation or implementation of a new idea would be rather limited. Particularly, if one possesses basic grounds of knowledge in programming, then an idea may be devised and developed in one of the many programming languages out there. Finally, said idea can and will be posted for worldwide observation and disposal [22].

> "Technology is but a tool. When it comes to motivating children and having them work collectively, the tutor remains the most important resource." [23]

3 Output

3.1 Methodological Design and Analysis Technique

The conducted study stems from experimental-type research wherein the following hypothesis may be validated: "Competencies in cadets can be accomplished by means of OOP learning" [20]. It is proposed that the design, development and implementation of a Virtual Object (VO) be acted on in such a way that it contributes to the intake of knowledge thereof through a carefully customized strategy to bond with the know-how of the cadets at the EMAVI military aviation school, ensuring the elaboration of competencies as suggested in the Object-oriented Programming subject. The selected method for this purpose, namely, Alternative action research [21] studies a specific social issue that requires a resolution/improvement by using a mixed- type analysis (quantitative/qualitative) on a group of 20 cadets of the computer engineering program, from which a sample of 11 students was extracted and tested to determine the initial and final state obtained ex post to the utilization of a Virtual Object on the formation process and the determination of its evolution as derived from the pertaining competencies. This technique was executed through the collection and examination of both quantitative and qualitative data, integrating the specific knowledge on OOP directed towards the formation of cadets mediated by the Virtual Object dubbed "Harddisk", allowing for a status and development analysis of competencies in the sample study, established as: a. Cognitive: Topic proficiency; b. Communicative: Reflexive dialogue; c. Cultural: Collaborative work; d. Social: Empathy; e. Technological: Use of technology. Additionally, the Harddisk Pedagogical Usability was evaluated by dint of the 25th version of the SPSS tool for data analysis.

3.2 Categorization of Population and Use of Technology

The characterization of population was made possible thanks to the realization of a survey which found that 60% of the sample is composed of cadets aged between 16 and 20, and 40% of said sample makes reference to those aged between 21 and 25. The foregoing findings contemplate the formation process being implemented through dynamic and critical-computational thinking strategies, which allow for the appropriation of a reading,

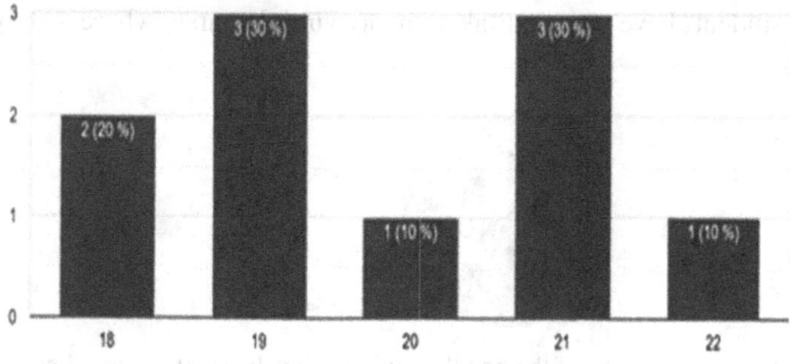

Fig. 2. Categorization of the population by age

interpretation and interaction inside the Harddisk Virtual Object. Figure 2 unveils the answer to the question subtracted from the questionnaire “Informed Consent”.

In observing Figure 3, it was validated that the cadets do not show sign of previously acquired knowledge in the matter of OOP before signing up for the program. It is, hence, that the need to implement an education strategy that commissions the obtainment of computational logic skills is born, which is also directed towards the growth of knowledge and communication, wherein 90% of the cadets yielded a negative answer to the OOP question as opposed to the positive, remaining 10%.

¿Do you have any previously acquired knowledge in the way of Object-oriented Programming?

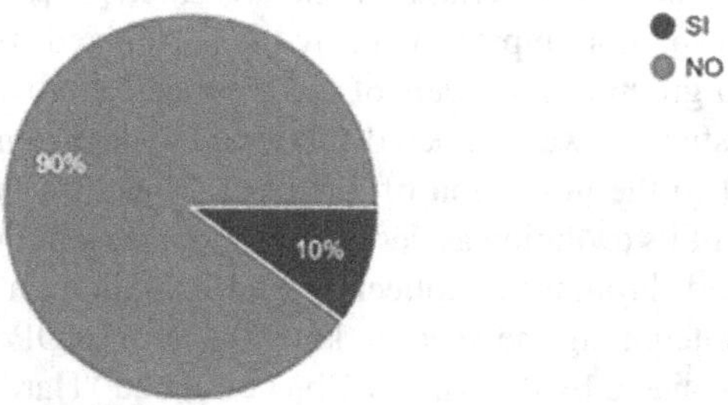

Fig. 3. Categorization of the population for previously acquired concepts of Object-oriented Programming

It was then necessary to know the cadets’ perspective first-hand regarding the use of technology, particularly in the field of Programming logics, whereupon a new query arises in terms of characterization of the population, evincing that the cadets are well aware of the technology outreach in the way of knowledge transmission. Figure 4 showcases the work overview aiming towards the implementation of first-stance mediation strategies, conscious use of Information and Communication Resources (ICR), knowledge acquisition and its relationship with reality and the cadets’ experiences, while simultaneously and indirectly enhancing the required competencies for knowledge transmission in and out of the classroom. Another equally important aspect to consider, and which, by the way, enticed the breeding of this research project, was the poor participation on behalf of the cadets in the use of tools for virtual education, in which 70% of the surveyed students have never partaken in any virtual course, whereas only 30% said

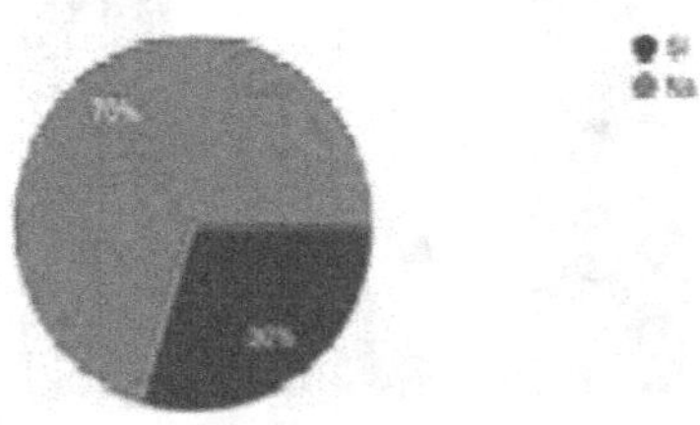

Fig. 4. Categorization of the population in the involvement in virtual courses

yes. Under this light, the Harddisk Virtual Object Virtual proves to be an innovative factor at the EMAVI military aviation school as a promising proposal devised to reinforce the adoption of knowledge, seeing as how this sort of implementation was otherwise unknown.

¿Have you ever partaken in any virtual education course?

3.3 Evolution of Knowledge and Development of Competencies

It is a cunning strategy to determine whether the communicative resource, which in this case is the virtual object, complied with the purpose it was set out to achieve. Virtual education offers the necessary companionship and conveyance of tools so that the students may engage in the digital transformation of their environment and the way the obtain knowledge. Through this section, the results observed during the intervention pre and post testing and its relationship with the expansion of Competencies in Object-oriented Programming-related matters will be shared.

For continued observation, the competencies developed in Harddisk Virtual Object-mediated interventions are exposed as follows (Fig. 5):

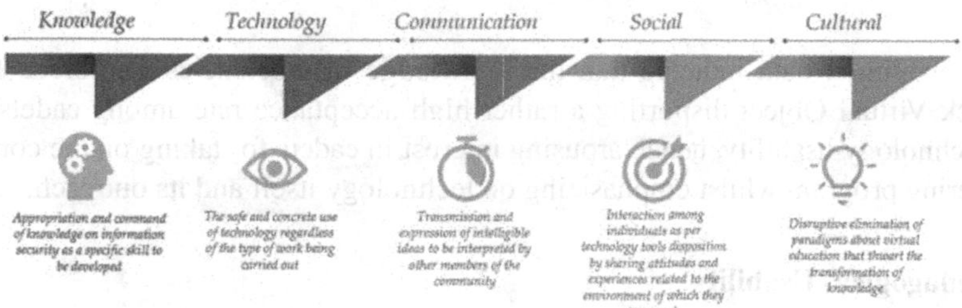

Fig. 5. Competencies developed by the Harddisk Virtual Object

It became necessary to fully grasp how these competencies were identified in the cadets during their formation period. However, thanks to the development of a mixed-formation strategy wherein academic content in addition to particular aspects extracted from the individual's context were included, it was then feasible to glean a topical comprehension thereof in a more practical manner. In order to identify the evolution of knowledge via the Harddisk Virtual Object, two tests were carried out in first instance; the initial state of knowledge was determined so as to adjust the formation structure as per the group's previously acquired knowledge and subsequently the resource is implemented by effecting a post test, whose purpose is to assess the cadets' knowledge progression, thus validating the extant changes within the group. The foregoing practice yielded a 5.2% variation margin both pre and post testing on the 11 surveyed students, allowing for knowledge appropriation identification on OOP at EMAVI, bearing a transformation in Technology Medialization Learning, which, in turn, guarantees the adoption of different technologies and tools by the computer engineering program so that the knowledge and learning aspects contained therein may be retrofitted while promoting virtuality in this regard. Consequently, during the first pre-testing intervention, the exercise delivered a median score of 69.5% effectiveness on topic conduct. During the second intervention, which relied on a rural Harddisk-Virtual-Object mediated training session which bore a median score of 79%, wherein it would be safe to surmise that the overall evolution as regards the teachers was 1.9 points, which coequals a 9.5% against the acquisition and command of the topics being taught, demonstrating that the knowledge in this field was indeed consolidated and internalized (Fig. 6).

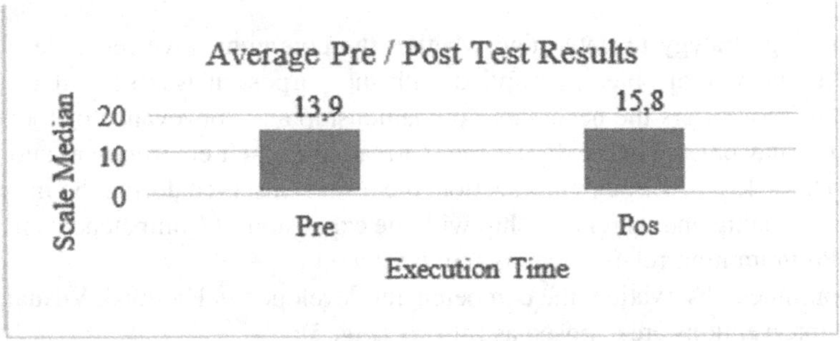

Fig. 6. Results median in pre/post-testing on cadets at EMAVI

The exhibited data indicate that the knowledge Competencies reinforced by the Harddisk Virtual Object disporting a rather high acceptance rate among cadets, optimize technology usability, hence arousing interest in cadets for taking on the computer engineering program whilst emphasizing on technology itself and its outreach.

3.4 Pedagogical Usability

It is understood as a strategy commonly used to measure the level of usage corresponding to technology platforms and/or tools in teaching. The constant insertion of Communication and Information Technology (CIT) into education, commissions an embracement of Technology, Knowledge and Learning (TKL), arranging an educational innovation particularly relevant in institutions for higher education. The employment of TKL, permeates Digital Literacy (DL) in a cross-sectional and innovative fashion, centering its efforts unto the elaboration of fundamental competencies for life (Soft and hard skills).

> "For the management of information, immediate interactivity and the search for information" [22]

The foregoing approach permitted the resolution on the main requirements of the Digital Society, upon the creation of highly accepted usable media and virtual education design which boasts a myriad of positions among its participants; the efficacy of the formative model is closely related to pedagogical designs, rendering the evaluation of usability and its acceptance rate necessary for the sake of harnessing the maximum benefit of the suggested resource.

> "Measurements that are revealed through the confidence in fulfilling the goal at hand, brought about by the actions carried out in the interest of achieving concrete

results and which succinctly contribute to the continuity of tasks and activities and the persistence of effort" [24]

"Perceived efficacy: results evinced in a significant relationship between utility and satisfaction of academic resources" [25]

It was adjudged hat the usability viewed from the knowledge transmission and adoption of technological tools standpoint, refers to a necessary process in the pursuit of securing the content/knowledge shared with the user, due to the demand for a balanced design that facilitates its implementation in the educational segment [26] (Fig. 7).

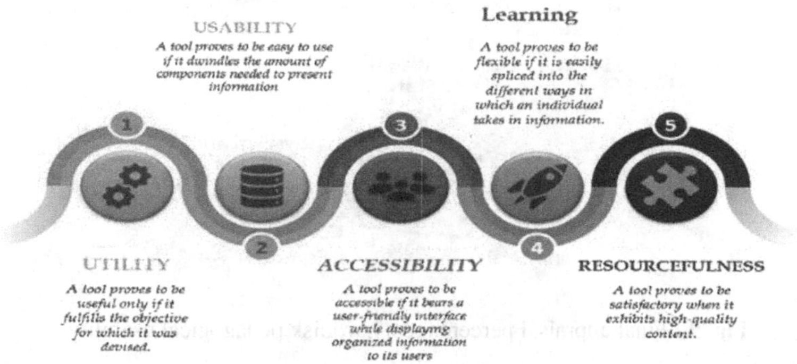
USABILITY
A tool proves to be easy to use if it dwindles the amount of components needed to present information
Learning
A tool proves to be flexible if it is easily spliced into the different ways in which an individual takes in information.
1
2
3
4
5
UTILITY
A tool proves to be useful only if it fulfills the objective for which it was devised.
ACCESSIBILITY
A tool proves to be accessible if it bears a user-friendly interface while displaying organized information to its users
RESOURCEFULNESS
A tool proves to be satisfactory when it exhibits high-quality content.

Fig. 7. Keys to consider in the assessment of usability

Pedagogical usability relies on a sequence wherein the generated end resources allow for an easy and dynamic grasp of the usability, and for the purpose and decentralization of securing the content/knowledge shared with the user, due to the demand for a balanced design that facilitates its implementation in the educational segment [26].

The following considerations must be observed upon creating a virtual education tool, in which Pedagogical Usability is regularly focused on the functionality and adaptability to the environment.

Upon seeking to add value to the Rural Harddisk Virtual Object Pedagogical Usability, the foregoing perspective carried out an evaluation composed of 20 questions as per the Likert scale by a group of 3 specialists in the field of Pedagogical Usability and Educational Communication and Information Technologies. For this purpose, 4 heuristic assumptions were determined, namely, Visibility and system status; System and reality; Control and user freedom; Aesthetics and design. The aforementioned heuristic assumptions allowed for the establishment of the level of usability as obtained prior to the implementation of the virtual object in the study group. Consecutively, the yielded results are shown down below (Figs. 8 and 9):

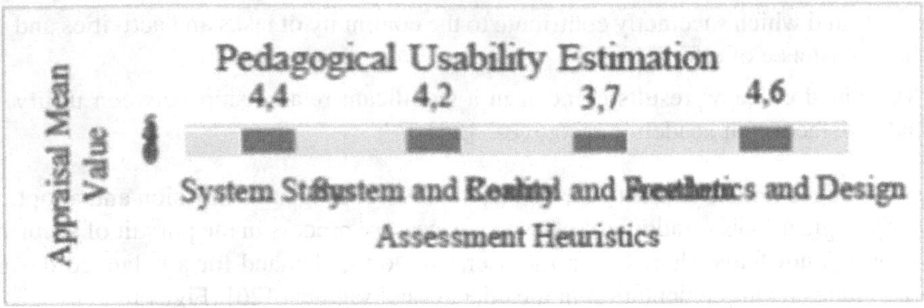

Fig. 8. Harddisk virtual object pedagogical usability forecast

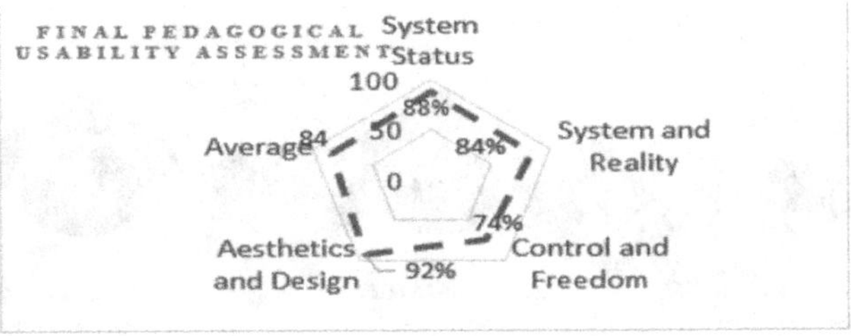

Fig. 9. Final appraisal percentages, harddisk pedagogical usability

It was possible to evince that the proposed heuristic assumptions for the assessment in question, achieved global acceptance; Aesthetics and Design scoring the highest, and conversely, Control and Freedom scoring the lowest. The results interpretation gives rise to technology improvement in terms of usability, providing the users with an upgraded, high-quality proposal. In conclusion, the total usability value as yielded by the Harddisk Virtual Object was 4.2 points, which equals to a 84% against content, aesthetics, relationship with the environment technological means and the management of the group integrated in the platform.

4 Conclusions

Competencies can be regarded as a process to be developed in each and every individual, given the need for knowledge and usage of New Communication and Information Technologies (NCIT) so as to make the knowledge transmission on Smart Learning possible according to Object-oriented Programming (OOP). In this sense, it is discerned to be the new horizon towards which all the efforts for human quality betterment are directed, along with the interaction and management of technology in educational institutions, particularly in the EMAVI military aviation school.

By the use of this article, the main ideas for the conception of Smart Learning were portrayed on Technological Mediations on cross-sectional Competencies development for the knowledge on object-oriented programming in order to study the initial and final statuses regulated by the usage of Communication and Information Resources (CIR), such as the development of a Harddisk. This prowess was custom-made by the cadets

Carlos Andrés Parra Guzmán, and Leidy Natalia Hernández Moreno, of the computer engineering program at the EMAVI military aviation school, appointed to the Colombian Air Force (FAC). The results obtained thereby, proved effective in terms of the adoption of knowledge and technology usability, by diagnosing the intervention and improvement margin as viewed from the virtual education experience and knowledge thereof.

A powerful inclusive setting was accomplished in reference to the way in which technology is integrated in the classroom from a didactic outlook which incorporates the pedagogical practice and the Communication and Information Technology resources, such as the Harddisk Virtual Object. This was achieved sensibly, relevantly and pertaining to the collective and individual stances in the second-year cadets, allowing for the retrieval of a response to their need for knowledge on the development of Critical Thinking skills, as well as of Computational Thought as per the Object-oriented Programming subject.

References

1. IADB ORG (2019). https://publications.iadb.org/es/colombia-desafios-del-desarrollo-en-tiempos-de-covid19
2. Arteaga, J., Álvarez Rodríguez, F., Chan Núñez, M.: Tecnología de objetos de aprendizaje. Cavano y McCall, p. 133 (1978)
3. Escuela Milital de Aviación (2022). https://www.emavi.edu.co/academica/modelo-de-formacion
4. Avogadro Thomé, M.E., Quiroga Macleimon, S.R.: La mediación tecnológica y las TIC: fenómenos y objetos técnicos (2015)
5. RAZÓN Y PALABRA Prim. Rev. Electrónica en Iberoamérica Espec. en Comun., vol. 92, pp. 1–18 (2015). https://www.redalyc.org/pdf/1995/199543036052.pdf
6. Flores, M.A., Day, C.: Contexts which shape and reshape new teachers' identities: a multi-perspective study. Teach. Teach. Educ. **22**(2), 219–232 (2006). https://doi.org/10.1016/j.tate.2005.09.002
7. SMART Learning. https://eserviciosеducativos.com/blog/que-es-el-smart-learning/
8. Sánchez, M.: Sistema de Aprendizaje Inteligente con Objetos de Aprendizaje "ProgEst". http://kali.azc.uam.mx/clc/02_publicaciones/tesis_dirigidas/tesis_final_lsgnov09.pdf
9. UNESCO. https://www.iesalc.unesco.org/2021/06/01/covid-19-su-impacto-en-la-educacion-superior-y-en-los-ods/
10. Hwang, G.-J.: Definition, framework and research issues of smart learning environments - a context-aware ubiquitous learning perspective. Smart Learn. Environ. **1**(1), 1–14 (2014). https://doi.org/10.1186/s40561-014-0004-5
11. Vuorikari, R., Punie, Y., Carretero, S., Van Den Brande, L.: DigComp 2.0: The Digital Competence Framework for Citizens, June 2016
12. García, D., Guerra, Y., Leyva, J.: Método para la solución de tareas experimentales cualitativas de biología. Prax. Saber **11**(27), e10985 (2020). https://doi.org/10.19053/22160159.v11.n27.2020.10985
13. Barth, M., Godemann, J., Rieckmann, M., Stoltenberg, U.: Developing key competencies for sustainable development in higher education. Int. J. Sustain. High. Educ. **8**(4), 416–430 (2007). https://doi.org/10.1108/14676370710823582
14. Glenda, C., Ríos, B., Alonso, C., Azema, J., Andrés, R., Cáceres, C.: Aprendizaje y formación valórica en la enseñanza mediante tutorías entre pares

15. Ríos, C.B., Azema, C.J., Cáceres, R.C.: Aprendizaje y formación valórica en la enseñanza mediante tutorías entre pares. Prax. Saber 10(22 SE- Artículos) (2019). https://doi.org/10.19053/22160159.v10.n22.2019.8796
16. EMAVI. https://www.emavi.edu.co/es/academica/modelo-de-formacion
17. EMAVI. https://www.emavi.edu.co/es/academica/formacion-profesional

Spatio-Temporal Analysis in Open Dataset from Respiratory Diseases

José Ángel Macías Méndez[1,2,3], José Guillermo Sandoval Huerta[1,2,3], Yesenia Eleonor González Navarro[1,2,3], Roberto Zagal Flores[1,2,3](✉), Edgar Armando Catalán Salgado[1,2,3], Giovanni Guzman Lugo[1,2,3], and Miguel Félix Mata Rivera[1,2,3]

[1] Unidad Profesional Interdisciplinaria en Tecnologías Avanzadas, Instituto Politécnico Nacional, Cd. de México, Mexico
{jmaciasm1400,jsandovalh1500}@alumno.ipn.mx, {ygonzalezn, rzagalf,ecatalans,mmatar}@ipn.mx, jguzmanl@cic.ipn.mx

[2] Escuela Superior de Cómputo, Instituto Politécnico Nacional, Cd. de México, Mexico

[3] Centro de Investigación en Computación, Instituto Politécnico Nacional, Cd. de México, Mexico

Abstract. An approach is presented to analyze a dataset of respiratory diseases in the space-time domain from Mexico City. The focus of paper is centered in to know how the relation between (high or low air quality) in certain season of the year and the registration of respiratory diseases in people from Mexico City is. Datasets available in open platforms were used mainly of respiratory diseases and air quality. Data Mining, Machine Learning and geographic data analysis techniques were applied to analyze and understand the behavior of respiratory diseases in several mayoralties from Mexico Cit. Results from the analysis are displayed in Dashboards to visualize the trace of the diseases and their historical series. Exploratory analysis was applied into datasets available at the National Institute of Statistics and Geography (INEGI) and the Atmospheric Monitoring System (SIMAT), some patterns associated to the air quality and respiratory diseases registration in specific location are shown. The future work considers including social data to have a broad understanding of the phenomena.

Keywords: Respiratory diseases dataset · Data mining · Machine learning · Spatial analysis

1 Introduction

Applying techniques to large volumes of data that are derived from medical practice can generate many applications that help both doctors in a particular way in the exercise of their praxis and to be able to see the impact of the diseases that exist in a certain population, managing to innovate how that information is used. Therefore, the development of this project seeks to contribute to technological innovation in the health sector in Mexico, where its purpose is to provide an understanding of a large volume of data

M. F. Mata-Rivera et al. (Eds.): WITCOM 2022, CCIS 1659, pp. 451–465, 2022.
https://doi.org/10.1007/978-3-031-18082-8_30

collected by different sources of public and private domain, which at the time of their unification and through the use of data science techniques can provide indications of the incidences of respiratory diseases presented for the areas of Mexico City, which can serve as consultation and support for people related to this field.

Through various statistics, it has been observed that respiratory diseases are one of the main causes in demand for care in health centers [1]. In the case of Mexico City, according to environmental pollution indices, for every 10 people, 6 suffer from some respiratory disease, with a higher number of incidences in children under 5 years of age and prevalence in adults of 25 to 45 years [2, 3].

Respiratory diseases cause significant morbidity and mortality, especially in countries such as Mexico City.

For this reason, a strategy is sought for the understanding of health data, and that these include considering space-time attributes for certain diseases of the inhabitants of Mexico City, particularly respiratory ones. However, being able to describe and understand the problems that exist in disease registry data is an enormous challenge, since many of the dimensions (attributes) associated with the diseases of those who suffer from them (place of residence, socioeconomic aspect, etc..) are produced by various institutions, with different storage schemes and without prior agreement for their integration, that is, there is a problem of isolated and heterogeneous data.

Given this context, it was proposed to develop an integrating system capable of analyzing respiratory diseases with time-space criteria, applying Data Mining and Machine Learning techniques, as well as Geographic Information Systems (GIS), for the time-space analysis of CDMX.

Currently, one of the problems that affects the health of the inhabitants of Mexico City is air pollution, but what is the impact by specific area where there are high rates of pollution where there are also certain diseases, and recognize the behavior of the diseases registered in the city and, of course, characterize the diseases and offer mechanisms to mitigate them or attend them in a better way, which would contribute to the national health strategy [6]. In this work, the challenge was to analyze the health data in Mexico City, by integrating data from heterogeneous sources available in open data, which are isolated and that offer their data on open platforms and process?

In addition to considering large volumes immersed and required for the study of the behavior of diseases.

The rest of the paper is organized as follows, Sect. 2 details the related work, Sect. 3 background, Sect. 4 shows the data description, Sect. 5 the methodology, Sect. 6 the exploratory analysis is detailed, Sect. 7 the spatio temporal analysis and finally the results in Sect. 8 and conclusions are described.

2 State of Art

A similar approach to our work is presented in [5] but focused on temperature, the work Data on respiratory disease mortality, meteorological elements and air pollutants during 2014–2017 were collected from Yancheng in China. We applied the distributed lag non-linear model (DLNM) and performed a quasi-Poisson distribution fitting to evaluate the baseline relationship between the mean temperature and total respiratory diseases mortality. For another hand, remote sensing is used to analysis respiratory disease in the research of [6] they use Remote Sensing and environmental variables to estimate the prevalence of respiratory disease, based on the hypothesis of a possible relationship between environmental variables and respiratory health parameters.

In the work of [1] the outcomes of public health measures on containing other respiratory infections among the Thai population were investigated. Hospitalization data spanning from 2016 to 2021 of six respiratory infectious diseases, namely influenza, measles, pertussis, pneumonia, scarlet fever, and tuberculosis (TB), were examined. First, the expected respiratory infectious cases where no public health measures are in place are estimated using the seasonal autoregressive integrated moving average (SARIMA) model. Other work is [2]are focused on Show how Multi-modal information is useful for diagnosing. Including Diagnosis-assistant system can work without changing the diagnostic process. In particular a pediatric fine-grained diagnosis-assistant system is proposed to provide prompt and precise diagnosis using solely clinical notes upon admission, which would assist clinicians without changing the diagnostic process.

The work of [9] collected for the 52 provincial capital cities in Spain, between 1990 and 2014. The association with temperature in each city was investigated by means of distributed lag non-linear models using quasi-Poisson regression. In the results Heat and cold exposure were identified to be associated with increased risk of cardiovascular and respiratory mortality. Heat was not found to have an impact on hospital admissions.

While in [3] provide an overview, evaluation, and challenges of already available surveillance systems or datasets in the Netherlands, which might be used for near real-time surveillance of severe respiratory infections, following suggestions of WHO to establish a national severe acute respiratory infections (SARI) surveillance system for preparedness and emergency response.

The work in [7] studied the impact of fire incidence on respiratory diseases in Brazilian Amazon, they compare remote sensing data, meteorological variables and health indicators, they conclude Drought-fire compounded effect boosts respiratory illness in elderly and children. In addition, the research in [5] presents The non-linear temperature-related mortality relationship between total respiratory disease and mean temperature. In [8] a discussion is presented using the question: Do chronic respiratory diseases or their treatment affect the risk of SARS-CoV-2 infection? they use the hypothesis of One might anticipate that patients with chronic respiratory diseases, particularly chronic obstructive pulmonary disease (COPD) and asthma, would be at increased risk of SARS-CoV-2 infection and more severe presentations of COVID-19.

Other field like veterinary are studied respiratory diseases but of course in animals, the work of [10] develop immediately applicable decision trees for pathogen identification in outbreaks of bovine respiratory disease based on circumstantial factors. Data from a cross sectional study, involving 201 outbreaks of bovine respiratory disease in dairy and beef farms between 2016 and 2019 was used. Nevertheless in [4] studies using from small data sets are success where data collected from a questionnaire based survey that aimed to evaluate patients' expectations, perceived quality, satisfaction with hospital care and financial ability of hospitalized patients suffering from acute or chronic respiratory diseases.

3 Background

Respiratory diseases are identified as those affect the respiratory system, such as nasal passages, pharynx, larynx, trachea, bronchi and lungs among others.

The International Code of Diseases (ICD 10), prepared by the World Health Organization, is intended to allow the systematic recording, analysis, interpretation, and comparison of mortality and morbidity data collected in different countries or areas, and in different times. It is used to convert diagnostic terms and other health problems from words to alphanumeric codes that allow easy storage and subsequent retrieval for information analysis [24]. The ICD is one of the universal systems that allows the production of statistics on mortality and morbidity that are comparable over time between units or regions of the same country and between different countries. Being our case of interest the diseases of the respiratory system, Chapter X refers to said diseases. As a sample. The classification in ICD-10 and ICD-9 is presented in Table 1.

Table 1. Respiratory diseases and CIE10 and CIE 9 codes.

Name	CIE-10	CIE-9
Influenza (gripe)	J10, J11	487
Neumonía	J12–J18	480–486
Enfermedades crónicas de las vías respiratorias inferiores (excepto asma)	J40-J44, J47	490–492, 494–496
Asma	J45, J46	493
Insuficiencia respiratoria 4	J96	786.0
Otras enfermedades del sistema respiratorio	Resto J00–J99	Resto 460–519

4 Open Data Sources Description

The data sources used in this research are divided into: Health Data (respiratory diseases and deaths), Geographic Data, and Air Quality Data.

From these datasets, it will be processed to observe the relationship between the air pollution indices in the different years in relation to the different mayor-days of CDMX and the registered reports of respiratory illnesses. The data and where they were obtained from are described as follows:

4.1 Health

The General Directorate of Health Information (DGIS) is responsible for coordinating and standardizing the processes to produce, capture, integrate, process, and disseminate health information of the National Health System, contained in the general laws on health and statistical and geographic information of Mexico. Through its digital platform, different databases with information related to health issues were obtained. Some have a data catalog, data dictionary and an entity relationship model. The collection made was 20 data sets, each one covering a year starting from 2001 and ending in 2020.

Health Database The database with emphasis on hospital admissions for men and women, indicating the types of respiratory disease with the highest incidence for both sexes in CDMX during the period from 2000 to 2015.

From the processing of this database with geographical data is obtained a relationship between respiratory diseases according to the geographical area where each individual resides. It is planned to obtain this information after the cleaning stage and data screening. Through the platform of the Federal Government of Mexico, it makes available to the general public more than 40,727 data from 280 institutions, being a very useful tool for a project such as the one proposed. Where 7 databases will be used from this platform, with data related to respiratory diseases for CDMX, from 3 public institutions listed below, and summarized in Table 2.

- General Directorate of Epidemiology (DGE).
- Mexican Social Security Institute (IMSS).
- National Institute of Public Health (INSP).

Table 2. Datasets from open data platforms.

Source	Name	Year	Format
DGE	Morbidity Yearbooks	2017	XLSX
	Morbidity Yearbooks	2016	XLSX
	Morbidity Yearbooks	2015	XLSX
IMSS	Medical Services, hospitalization by mayoraltiy	2000–2020	CSV
	Medical Services, hospitalization by mayoraltiy	2000–2020	CSV
	Medical services, diagnostic assistants, mayoralty	2000–2020	CSV
INSP	National Health Survey 2000 ENSA2000	2000	CSV/XLS

These databases are integrated as a single data volume. To understand the meaning and type of data of each field, it is necessary to consult the "Guide and formats for the exchange of health information regarding the report of hospital discharge information" provided by the DGIS, where the complete set represents a period of 16 years from 2000 to 2015. Total records 1546596. In Table 3. The most relevant fields in the database are shown, where there is a total of 49.

Table 3. Attributes in health data

Attribute name	Description
ID_EGRESOS	Code that identifies the registration number
CLUES	Key that identifies the CLUE that provides the information
AGE	Patient's age
GENDER	0 = Male 1 = Female
WEIGHT	Patient weight
SIZE	Patient height
ENTITY	Code that identifies the federal entity
DIAG_INI	Code that identifies the patient's diagnosis
AFECPRIN	Code that identifies the detected affectation of the patient
INFEC	0 = do not have an infection 1 = have an infection
ID_CIE10	Code that identifies the type of disease by ICD10

4.2 Geographic Data

The National Institute of Statistics and Geography (INEGI) is the main body of the country, in charge of capturing and disseminating information on Mexico regarding the territory, resources, population and economy, allowing the characteristics of our country to be known and help to decision making [69].

The collection made was 20 data sets, each one covering a year starting from 2001 and ending in 2020. INEGI databases are displayed in a CSV format with dictionaries, entity-relationship model, metadata and catalogues. General Deaths were selected: Detailed causes CIE from the year 2001, 2002 to 2020 with record numbers 7856, 8097, 8244 respectively.

The attributes that they contain are: year (in which the registration was taken), age, sex, mayor, cie code.

In addition to INEGI, different databases were obtained with information on deaths at the municipal level in different periods of time, where the cause of death is related to some respiratory disease. They all have a data catalog, data dictionary and an entity relationship model.

From the SIMAT data, an index was taken (2000–2020) with 8760 records per year, which includes the area where the recorder was made, station, parameters and units.

From the DGE, the morbidity yearbooks for 2016 and 2017 were kept with 4,576 and 4,672 records, respectively. Which have the following attributes. A Summary is listed in Table 4.

Table 4. Some Attributes in health data

Domain name	Description
CVE_ESTADO	Code that identifies the federal entity
DES_ESTADO	Name of the federal entity
CVE_DIAGNO	Code that identifies the disease diagnosis
DES_DIAGNO	Name of the disease diagnosis
CVE_CIE10	Code that identifies the disease by ICD10

4.3 Air Quality

In Mexico City, the Atmospheric Monitoring System (SIMAT) is responsible for the permanent measurement of the main air pollutants.

SIMAT has more than 40 monitoring sites distributed in the metropolitan area, including demarcations of CDMX and the metropolitan area of the State of Mexico. In addition to being made up of subsystems such as the Automatic Atmospheric Monitoring Network (RAMA), the Manual Atmospheric Monitoring Network (REDMA), the Meteorology and Solar Radiation Network (REDMET), a laboratory for the physicochemical analysis of samples (LAA) and a data processing and dissemination center (CICA) [70].

Through its portal, different databases related to air quality were obtained in different periods of time for each of the CDMX city halls. The collection made was 40 data sets, 20 being related to quality indices and 20 to air pollution, from 2001 to 2020 in CSV format.

5 Methodology

The methodology used is based on a phase of data collection and processing, description of the data and the exploration of said data, to apply exploratory analysis with a space-time approach. For this, an architecture divided into four modules was developed.

5.1 Data Exploration and Analysis Module

This module is in charge of selecting the data provided by the different sources, allowing to identify the dirty data (Dirty Data) that refer to all the possible inconsistencies that the records present, such as those incomplete, incorrect or inaccurate data [7], later They will be cleaned in such a way that they can be modified or deleted, trying to achieve compatibility between the different records from one source to another. The objective is to find that the data is suitable, to treat them in the following modules.

5.2 Data Integration Module

This module is in charge of implementing data integration mechanisms, so that it seeks to adapt them in a single standardization scheme, modifying their attribute type and combining the different annual records of each source, obtaining a single unified record.

5.3 Mining and Machine Learning Module

This module is responsible for classifying the previously processed data, seeking to form temporal trends in the growth of the incidence and prevalence of respiratory diseases, which through the implementation of Machine Learning algorithms such as classification algorithms or association methods.

5.4 Spatial-Temporal Analysis Module

Through geographic information techniques, this module is responsible for classifying the data obtained from the previous module, under a geographic and temporal scheme, providing a record of the areas where there is a greater number of cases of some disease and identify the trend of a disease at a given time in relation to the area.

6 Exploratory Data Analysis

This section is dedicated to the exploratory process of the data towards the final volume of unified data, these fall into two main categories of study, data on incidences of respiratory diseases in Mexico and data on mortality due to respiratory diseases in Mexico provided within the catalogs of de-general functions of the INEGI, both sets in a period of 15 years from 2000 to 2015. The CLUES dictionary was used to identify the locality of the health centers, to have 221056 localities in the dataset.

The following domains were used:

Age, Sex, Weight, Height, Illness. These were taken since, within all the information of the datasets, it is the only "constant" information, however there was inconsistent information having the following cases: Consistent weight, but Age and Height were not consistent, for example, 56 kg, 2.10 m and 999 years old. Consistent Age and Height, but inconsistent Weight, for example, 44 years old, 1.64 m and 0 kg.

Both in the case of the HEALTH and INEGI datasets, they lack a geographic component that helps to discern between the different localities of the CDMX, Use of dictionaries.

Given the problems observed in the datasets lacking a geographic identifier, the use of the CLUE key was resorted to, through the Single Key of Health Establishments (CLUE), the locality or region from which the record of each was extracted. fact. From the page of the DGIS, in its section of information and dynamic cubes, From the page of INEGI, in its section of catalogs, the dictionary referring to the type of diseases was taken, and through the International Statistical Classification of Diseases and Problems Related to Health (ICD.10), the name of each disease related to its statistical code was provided. The number of incidences was counted by the type of disease presented in the patients. Mainly to order the diseases by the number of total cases and not by delegation (Fig. 1).

	CODIGO	NOMBRE_AFEC	CASOS
2	J010	SINUSITIS MAXILAR AGUDA	73
3	J011	SINUSITIS FRONTAL AGUDA	17
4	J012	SINUSITIS ETMOIDAL AGUDA	21
5	J013	SINUSITIS ESFENOIDAL AGUDA	6
6	J014	PANSINUSITIS AGUDA	18

Fig. 1. Total number of cases by diseases

7 Spatial Temporal Analysis

By means of a mapping, the name of the mayor's office corresponding to the record was added to the dataset, this by means of the relationship of the CLUES code provided by the dictionary of the same name, the total number of records per mayor's office was counted, The total number of most frequent illnesses was grouped by municipality using the following fragment. For the total number of records, a statistic was made of the values related to the characteristics of people with respiratory diseases, such as weight, height, sex, etc., as can be seen in the following code fragments. Therefore, the total size of data used was 223,081 records.

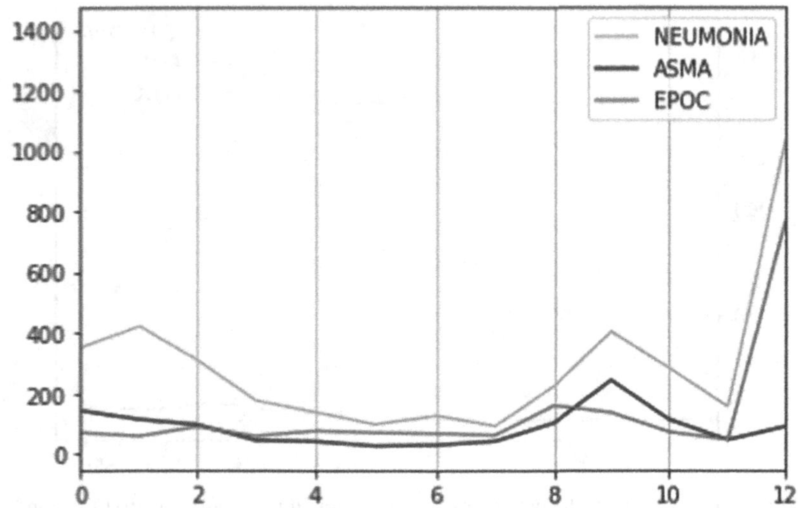

Fig. 2. Traceability of the behavior of diseases in the year 2000

To understand the behavior of the data, some analyzes were carried out, the first of which was to understand its traceability during the different time intervals. This traceability was carried out by counting the total number of cases for each month in an interval of one year. See Fig. 2.

Finally in Fig. 3 the traceability behaviour is shown for the year 2015, for three diseases (the system is in Spanish) and it is possible to observe the differences in behavior.

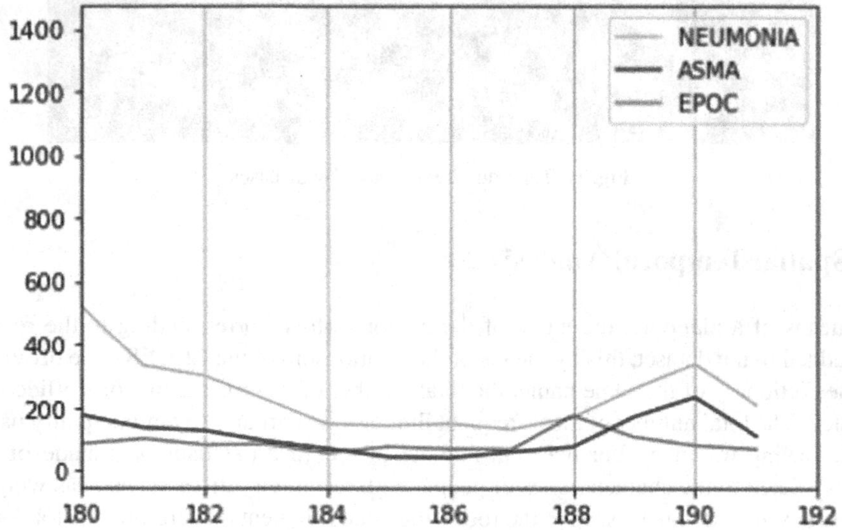

Fig. 3. Traceability of diseases in 2015.

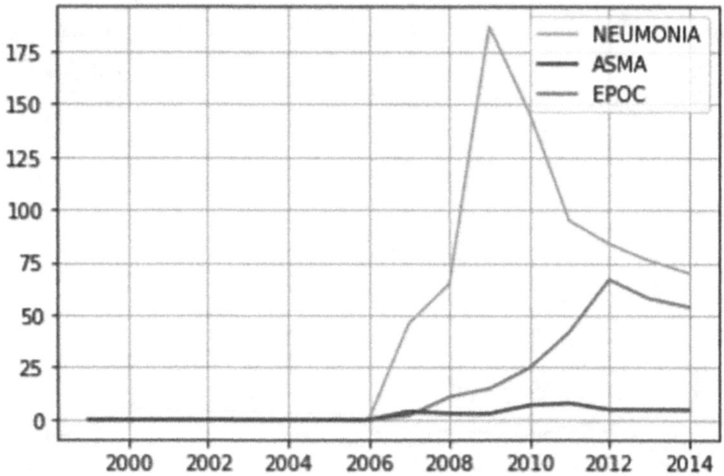

Fig. 4. Traceability of the behavior of the diseases in mayoralty Álvaro Obregón.

The highest number of incidents occurs in the winter season within the months of December and January, and the lowest number of incidents in the summer season within the months of June and July, so the behavior of the data presents a curve characteristic where the maxima appear at the beginning and end of each year. Another of the analyzes carried out was the traceability of the total number of incidents presented in each year for each mayoralty. The results to visualize its behavior are shown in Figs. 4 and 5.

To contrast with traceability of the total number of incidents presented in each year for other mayoralties are shown in Figs. 5 and 6.

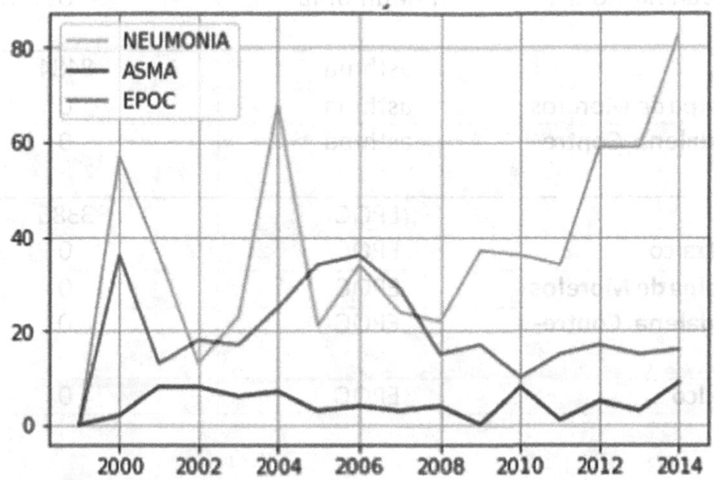

Fig. 5. Traceability of the diseases behavior in mayoralty Benito Juárez.

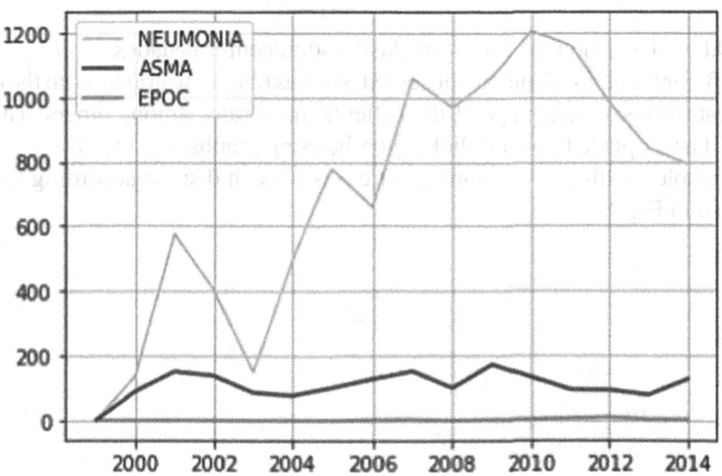

Fig. 6. Traceability of the behavior of the diseases in Mayoralty *Coyoacán*.

Now, to identify the mayoralties with the highest and lowest number of registered cases of illness, The table indicates in green those municipalities with the highest number of registered cases (Table 5).

Table 5. Maximum and minimum number of incidents registered in mayoralties.

Mayoralty name	Disease	Total
Tlalpan	Pneumonia	13373
La Magdalena Contreras	Pneumonia	0
Tlalpan	asthma	8484
Cuajimalpa de Morelos	asthma	0
La Magdalena Contreras	asthma	0
Tlalpan	EPOC	3386
Azcapotzalco	EPOC	0
Cuajimalpa de Morelos	EPOC	0
La Magdalena Contreras	EPOC	0
Xochimilco	EPOC	0

8 Results

In the dashboard available in: http://ml.clasificadordeenfermedades.com/

The different functionalities are observed, such as obtaining graphs with the data classified by categories: disease, age of the patients, mayoralty, among others. The disease indices will be displayed now of clicking on it, using graphs, see Fig. 7.

For example, to display the number of cases of each disease according to age, this is illustrated in Fig. 8.

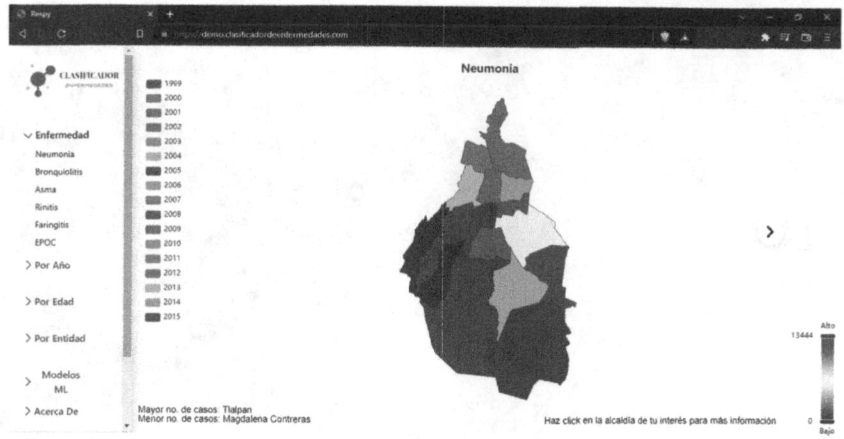

Fig. 7. Spatio temporal Dashboard

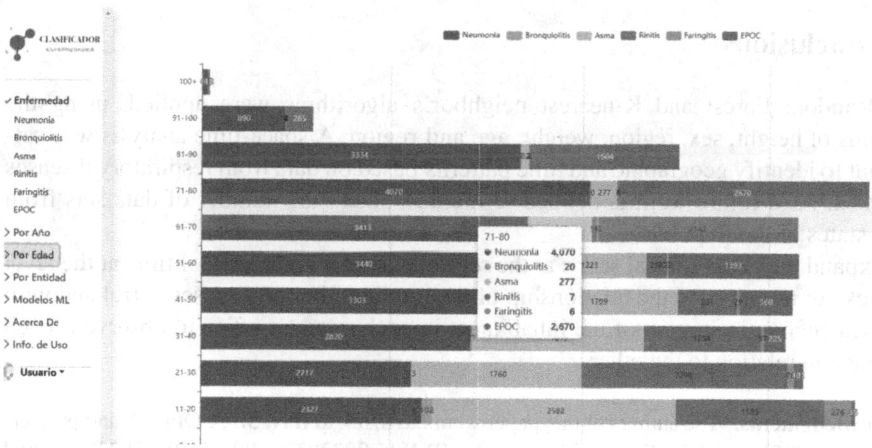

Fig. 8. Respiratory diseases by age

Finally, it is possible to display the incidence of diseases by each mayoralty and show a forecast according to one model of machine learning. It is shown in Fig. 9.

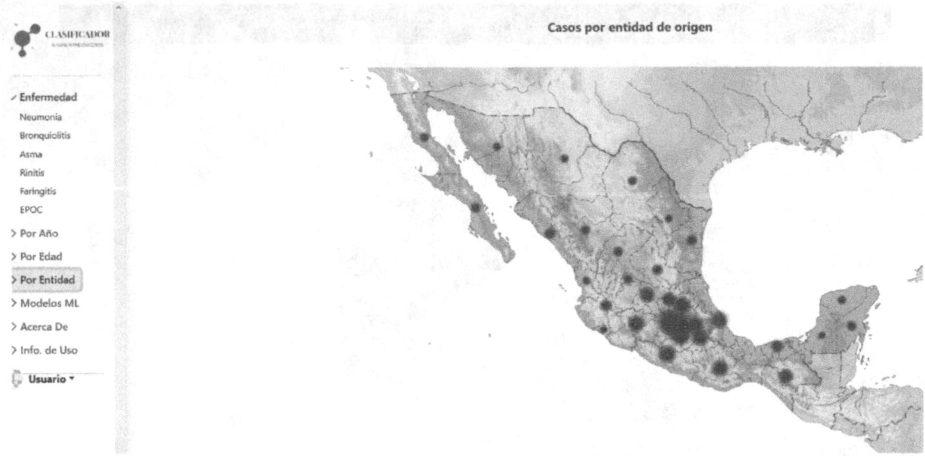

Fig. 9. Incidences of diseases by mayoralties

9 Conclusions

The Random Forest and K-nearest neighbor's algorithms were applied, using the domains of height, sex, region, weight, age and region. A space-time analysis was carried out to identify geographic and time patterns based on data from respiratory diseases analyzed. As a future work is defined to include others the number of data sets from other states of the Republic.

Expand the geographical scope at the regional level. Granularity of time at the level of weeks or months and the relationship of the total number of diseases correlated with the socioeconomic stratum of the inhabitants in each mayor's office to observe if each influence in relation to the other.

Acknowledgments. The authors of this paper wants to thank to IPN, SIP, COFFAA and projects CONACyT 7051 and 2016/2110 and projects SIP-IPN 20220378, 20220835, 20220065 and 20220557.

References

1. Ndeh, N.T., Tesfaldet, Y.T., Budnard, J., Chuaicharoen, P.: The secondary outcome of public health measures amidst the COVID-19 pandemic in the spread of other respiratory infectious diseases in Thailand. Travel Med. Infect. Dis. **48**, 102348 (2022)
2. Yu, G., et al.: Identification of pediatric respiratory diseases using a fine-grained diagnosis system. J. Biomed. Inform. **117**, 103754 (2021)
3. Marbus, S.D., van der Hoek, W., van Dissel, J.T., van Gageldonk-Lafeber, A.B.: Experience of establishing severe acute respiratory surveillance in the Netherlands: evaluation and challenges. Public Health Pract. **1**, 100014 (2020)
4. Koutsimpou, P., Gourgoulianis, K.I., Economou, A., Raftopoulos, V.: Data on expectations, perceived quality, satisfaction with hospital care and financial ability of patients who suffer from acute and chronic respiratory diseases, in Central Greece. Data Brief **30**, 105564 (2020)

5. Dong, S., Wang, C., Han, Z., Wang, Q.: Projecting impacts of temperature and population changes on respiratory disease mortality in Yancheng. Phys. Chem. Earth Parts A/B/C **117**, 102867 (2020)
6. Alvarez-Mendoza, C.I., Teodoro, A., Freitas, A., Fonseca, J.: Spatial estimation of chronic respiratory diseases based on machine learning procedures—an approach using remote sensing data and environmental variables in Quito, Ecuador. Appl. Geogr. **123**, 102273 (2020)
7. Machado-Silva, F., et al.: Drought and fires influence the respiratory diseases hospitalizations in the Amazon. Ecol. Ind. **109**, 105817 (2020)
8. Halpin, D.M., Faner, R., Sibila, O., Badia, J.R., Agusti, A.: Do chronic respiratory diseases or their treatment affect the risk of SARS-CoV-2 infection? Lancet Respir. Med. **8**(5), 436–438 (2020)
9. Iñiguez, C., Royé, D., Tobías, A.: Contrasting patterns of temperature related mortality and hospitalization by cardiovascular and respiratory diseases in 52 Spanish cities. Environ. Res. **192**, 110191 (2021)
10. Lowie, T., Callens, J., Maris, J., Ribbens, S., Pardon, B.: Decision tree analysis for pathogen identification based on circumstantial factors in outbreaks of bovine respiratory disease in calves. Prev. Vet. Med. **196**, 105469 (2021)

Author Index

Printed in the United States
by Baker & Taylor Publisher Services